TOEFL® CBT
SUCCESS

SUPER PREP TEST

PETERSON'S
THOMSON LEARNING ™

Australia • Canada • Mexico • Singapore • Spain • United Kingdom • United States

PETERSON'S

THOMSON LEARNING

About Peterson's

Founded in 1966, Peterson's, a division of Thomson Learning, is the nation's largest and most respected provider of lifelong learning online resources, software, reference guides, and books. The Education Supersite^{SM} at petersons.com—the Web's most heavily traveled education resource—has searchable databases and interactive tools for contacting U.S.-accredited institutions and programs. CollegeQuest® (CollegeQuest.com) offers a complete solution for every step of the college decision-making process. GradAdvantage^{TM} (GradAdvantage.org), developed with Educational Testing Service, is the only electronic admissions service capable of sending official graduate test score reports with a candidate's online application. Peterson's serves more than 55 million education consumers annually.

Thomson Learning is among the world's leading providers of lifelong learning, serving the needs of individuals, learning institutions, and corporations with products and services for both traditional classrooms and for online learning. For more information about the products and services offered by Thomson Learning, please visit www.thomsonlearning.com. Headquartered in Stamford, Connecticut, with offices worldwide, Thomson Learning is part of The Thomson Corporation (www.thomson.com), a leading e-information and solutions company in the business, professional, and education marketplaces. The Corporation's common shares are listed on the Toronto and London stock exchanges.

About the Author

Bruce Rogers has taught English as a second language and test-preparation courses at the Economics Institute in Boulder, Colorado, since 1979. He has also taught in special programs at Bank Indonesia and Bank Negara Indonesia in Jakarta, Indonesia; at the National Economics University in Hanoi, Vietnam; at Yonsei University in Seoul, South Korea; and at the Samsung Human Resources Development Center in Yong-in, South Korea. He is also the author of *The Complete Guide to TOEIC* and *The Complete Guide to TOEFL: Practice Tests*.

TOEFL Success is adapted from *The Complete Guide to TOEFL*, second edition, by Bruce Rogers and published by Heinle & Heinle/ITP.

For more information, contact Peterson's, 2000 Lenox Drive, Lawrenceville, NJ 08648; 800-338-3282; or find us on the World Wide Web at: www.petersons.com/about

ISBN 0-7689-0764-0 (text and audiocassettes)
ISBN 0-7689-0682-4 (text with CD)
ISBN 0-7689-0682-2 (text only)

Printed in the United States of America

10 9 8 7 6 5 4 3 2 1   03 02 01

CONTENTS

CONTENTS

Peterson's TOEFL CBT Success

CONTENTS

THREE COMPLETE PRACTICE TESTS

PRACTICE TESTS: TAPESCRIPTS AND ANSWER KEYS

ANSWER KEYS AND TAPESCRIPTS

Peterson's TOEFL CBT Success

PREFACE

ABOUT THIS BOOK

If you are preparing for TOEFL, you are not alone. More than three quarters of a million people all over the world took the test last year. A high score on this test is an essential step in being admitted to graduate or undergraduate programs at almost all colleges and universities in North America. But preparing for this test can be a difficult, frustrating experience. Perhaps you haven't taken many standardized, multiple-choice tests such as TOEFL. Perhaps you are not familiar with the format of the computer-based TOEFL. Maybe you've taken TOEFL once but were not satisfied with your score, or maybe you've taken the test several times but can't seem to improve your score beyond a certain point.

In any of these cases, you need a guide. That's why this book was written—to help students preparing for this important exam to maximize their scores.

This is the most complete, accurate, and up-to-date TOEFL preparation book now available. It is based on twelve years of classroom experience teaching TOEFL preparation classes in the United States and abroad and on several years of research on the test. *TOEFL CBT Success* is simply written and clearly organized and is suitable for any intermediate or advanced student of English as a second or foreign language.

TOEFL CBT Success offers a step-by-step program that teaches you critical test-taking techniques, helps you polish the language skills needed for the exam, and generally makes you a smarter test-taker. And the guide is an efficient way to prepare for TOEFL; by concentrating only on the points that are actually tested in TOEFL, it lets you make the most of your preparation period and never wastes your time. If you have purchased the CD version of this book, you can access three online CBT practice tests.

Good luck on the TOEFL CBT!

Getting Started The first section of the book serves as an introduction to the exam. The opening portion of this section, **Questions and Answers About the TOEFL CBT**, provides you with information about the format of the test, guides you through the process of registering for the exam, and helps you understand your scores. The next portion of this section, **Keys to High Scores**, presents the "secrets" of being a good test-taker—picking the right test date, arranging your preparation time, using the process of elimination, coping with test anxiety, pacing yourself during the test, and other important techniques.

The main body of the book is divided into three sections, reflecting the three main sections of the test: Listening comprehension, structure and written expression, and reading comprehension. Each of these sections consists of the following components:

- An introduction containing basic strategies for that section of the test.
- A full-length sample test to give you a feel for each part of the test and to provide a basis for understanding the lessons.
- An introduction to each subsection of the test, with specific tactics for attacking the items in each portion of the test.
- Lessons that break down the knowledge and skills needed for each part of the test into comprehensible "bites" of information. Each of the forty-eight lessons in the book contains sample items that illustrate exactly how the point brought up in that lesson is tested in TOEFL. Furthermore, each lesson contains one or more exercises for practicing the relevant points. Some of these items follow TOEFL format, others follow formats appropriate for the particular point being taught, but all of them have the same "feel" as actual

TOEFL items. There are 48 of these exercises in this book.

- Mini-tests that review the points brought up in the previous lessons. These tests put together the points practiced in isolation in the lessons and allow you to chart your progress. All the items on the mini-tests are identical in form to items on actual tests.
- Mini-lessons covering important testing points that require more time to master than points brought up in the lessons. You should begin studying and working the exercises in the mini-lessons as soon as you begin each section of this book.

Section 1: Listening Comprehension This section is subdivided into three parts, each one designed to familiarize you with the problems commonly encountered on the three parts of the revised Section 1: Dialogues, Extended Conversations, and Mini-Talks. The exercises and tests in this part of the book are intended to be used with the tapes that accompany this book. The mini-lessons for this section teach common idioms and figurative expressions that are often heard in Part A.

Section 2: Structure and Written Expression The first part of this section categorizes common grammatical points tested in structure problems and suggests ways to solve these problems. The second part lists the usual errors that must be identified in written expression problems and offers ways to identify these mistakes. The mini-lessons for this section cover preposition usage.

Section 3: Reading Comprehension This section of the book prepares you for the revised third section of TOEFL. The Reading Comprehension portion of the book suggests reading attack skills, lists the various types of questions asked about the passages, and offers suggestions for answering each type of question. There are in-depth reading exercises to practice these techniques. The mini-lessons for this section permit further practice with vocabulary building.

The Test of Written English This part of the book introduces the TWE and presents the best methods for planning, writing, and checking the essay you must write if you take this portion of the exam. There are two models of strong TWE essays, and there are two practice TWE exams.

Three Complete Practice Tests

Practice tests provide one of the best ways to get ready for TOEFL because they draw together all the points you have studied. These tests duplicate the format, content, and level of difficulty of actual tests. You may want to take one of these tests as a diagnostic when you begin your studies. To get the most out of these exams, follow the recommendations in **Taking the Practice Tests**. Scoring information is also included here.

SUGGESTIONS FOR USING THIS BOOK

TOEFL CBT Success is designed to be used either as a textbook for TOEFL preparation classes or as a tool for individuals preparing for the exam by themselves. If you are working alone, you will need the tapes to accompany the textbook as well as the answer keys and tapescripts.

Whether working alone or in a group, you should begin your preparation for TOEFL by reading the introductory chapters entitled *Getting Started*. You can then work through the book in the order in which it is written or begin with the section in which you are weakest (or in which the majority of the students in a class are weakest). Generally, you can make the fastest progress by working in your weakest area. You can

determine which area is your weakest by looking at the scores from a previous test or by using one of the practice tests as a diagnostic test.

The amounts of time required to cover each segment of this book are given below. Keep in mind that these times are approximate and do not include review sessions.

Getting Started. . . . . 1–3 hours
Listening Comprehension. . . . . 12–16 hours
Structure and
   Written Expression . . . . 20–25 hours
Vocabulary and
   Reading Comprehension. . . . 15–20 hours
The Test of Written English. . . . . 3–5 hours
Three Complete Practice Tests. . . 6–8 hours

ACKNOWLEDGMENTS

I would like to thank the following professionals for their comments and suggestions during the development of this text:

Steven A. Stupak, Korea International Human Resources Development Center; Virginia Hamori, American Language Institute, American University of Paris; Jim Price, International Language Center, Bangkok; Stephen Thewlis, San Francisco State University; Connie Monroe, Queens College; Steven Horowitz, Central Washington University; Dan Douglas, Iowa State University; Frederick O'Connor, Washington State University, and Claire Bradin, Michigan State University.

I would like to thank Donald Pharr for his expert proofreading.

Thanks to Maggie Barbieri at Maxwell Macmillian and to David Lee and Ken Mattsson at Heinle & Heinle for their editorial help.

Special thanks to all of the students in my TOEFL Preparation Classes at the Economics Institute.

ACKNOWLEDGMENTS FOR THE SECOND EDITION

First, I would like to thank the many subscribers to the Material Writers branch of TESOL-L (an electronic bulletin board for teachers of English as a Second Language) who responded when I asked for suggestions on revising this text.

I would also like to thank the following for their reviews of an early draft of the manuscript:

Thanks also to the following for their painstaking reviews and proofreading of the "final" draft of the manuscript:

Ian Palmer, Seth Sycroft, University of California at Davis.

Domo arigato to Kayoko Otani, translator of the Japanese edition of *The Complete Guide to TOEFL*, for suggesting some of the vocabulary-in-context items in Section 3.

Thanks to my editors at Heinle & Heinle, David Lee and Eric Gunderson, and of course to Associate Editor Ken Mattsson for keeping the project on track.

And again, special thanks to the students in my TOEFL preparation courses at the Economics Institute.

At the time of this writing (spring 1998), the TOEFL was available throughout the world as a paper-and-pencil test. Starting in July 1998, however, Educational Testing Service (ETS) introduced the computer-based TOEFL test in the United States, Canada, Latin America, Europe, the Middle East, Africa, and selected Asian countries. According to ETS, the computer-based test will eventually completely replace the paper test. Some parts of the TOEFL will be a linear computerized test, which is scored the same way as a paper test. Other parts of the TOEFL will be a computer-adaptive test (CAT).

WHAT IS A COMPUTER-ADAPTIVE TEST?

A computer-adaptive test (CAT) is—as the title says—adaptive. That means that each time you answer a question the computer adjusts to your responses when determining which question to present next. For example, the first question will be of moderate difficulty. If you answer it correctly, the next question will be more difficult. If you answer it incorrectly, the next question will be easier. The computer will continue presenting questions based on your responses, with the goal of determining your ability level.

It is very important to understand that questions at the beginning of a section affect your score more than those at the end. That's because the early questions are used to determine your general ability level. Once the computer determines your general ability level, it presents questions to identify your specific ability level. As you progress farther into a section, it will be difficult to raise your score very much, even if you answer most items correctly. That's because the later questions affect your score less, as they are used to pinpoint your exact score once the computer has identified your general ability level. Therefore, take as much time as you can afford to answer the early questions correctly. Your score on each section is based on the number of questions you answer correctly, as well as the difficulty level of those questions.

You need only minimal computer skills to take the computer-based TOEFL. You will have plenty of time at the test center to work through a tutorial that allows you to practice such activities as answering questions, using the mouse, using the word processor (which you will need for your essay responses), and accessing the help function.

The computer-based tests will be given at designated universities, bi-national institutes, ETS field offices, and Sylvan Technology Centers all over the world. Once the computer-based test has been phased in, you will no longer have the option of taking the paper-based test. Keep in mind that the computer-based test will be more expensive than the paper-based test. In North America, it will initially cost US$80 and outside of North America, it will cost US$100.

WHAT KINDS OF QUESTIONS WILL BE ON THE COMPUTER-BASED TOEFL?

Like the paper test, the computer-based TOEFL will have three sections:

1. Listening Comprehension (40–60 minutes, 30–50 questions, CAT)

2. Structure and Written Expression (15–20 minutes, 20–25 questions, CAT)

3. Reading Comprehension (70–90 minutes, 44–60 questions, linear)

Some questions will be similar to those on the paper test while others will be very different. The Listening and Reading Comprehension questions will include new question types that are designed specifically for the computer. An essay will also be included that can be handwritten or typed on the computer.

How are the computer-based TOEFL scores calculated?

The computer-based TOEFL will report separate scores for each of the three test sections. The Listening Comprehension will be scored as a CAT. The Structure and Written Expression section will be scored as a CAT and on the basis of the essay. The Reading Comprehension section will be scored as a linear test. The scores for all three sections will be factored into a scaled total score, just like on the current test.

The range of possible scores on each of the three multiple choice sections is from 0–30. The range for the entire test will be from 0–300. (The range on the paper version is from 200–667).

Test-Taking Tips for the CAT Sections of the Computer-Based TOEFL

- The purpose of TOEFL CBT Success is to help you prepare for all forms of the test. You will increase your chances of scoring high on the TOEFL by being completely familiar with the content and format you will encounter on test day. The strategies and review sections of this book, as well as the practice tests, provide lots of opportunity to review relevant content. Keep in mind the following test-taking tips, most of which are unique to the CAT format.
- Understand the directions for each question type. Learn the directions for each type of question. The directions in this book are very similar to those on the actual test. Understanding the directions for each question type will save you valuable time on the day of the test.
- Focus on answering the questions at the beginning of sections 1 and 2 correctly. Remember that questions at the beginning of a section affect your score more than questions at the end. Be especially careful in choosing answers to questions in the first half of both the quantitative and verbal sections. Once the computer determines your general ability level with these initial questions, you will be unable to dramatically improve your score, even if you answer most of the questions toward the end correctly.

- In sections 1 and 2 be completely sure of each answer before proceeding. With a CAT, you must answer each question as it is presented. You cannot skip a difficult question and return to it later as you can with a paper test. Nor can you review responses to questions that you have already answered. Therefore, you must be confident about your answer before you confirm it and proceed to the next question. If you are completely stumped by a question, eliminate as many answer choices as you can, select the best answer from the remaining choices, and move on.
- Pace yourself. To finish all sections, you will need to work both quickly and accurately to complete each section within the time constraints. You will still receive a score, even if you do not complete all of the questions in a section.

QUESTIONS AND ANSWERS ABOUT TOEFL

Q: What is TOEFL?

A: TOEFL stands for *Test of English as a Foreign Language*. It is a test designed to measure the English language ability of people who do not speak English as their first language and who plan to study at colleges and universities in North America.

Educational Testing Service (ETS) of Princeton, New Jersey, prepares and administers TOEFL. This organization produces many other standardized tests, such as the Test of English for International Communication (TOEIC), the Scholastic Assessment Test (SAT), the Graduate Management Admission Test (GMAT), and the Graduate Record Examinations (GRE).

Although there are other standardized tests of English, TOEFL is by far the most important in North America. ETS has offered this exam since 1965. Each year, almost 850,000 people take TOEFL at more than 1,250 testing centers all over the world. Around 2,500 colleges and universities in the United States and Canada require students from non-English-speaking countries to supply TOEFL scores as part of their application process.

Q: What format does TOEFL follow? How long does it take to complete?

A: All the questions on the TOEFL paper-based test (PBT) are multiple-choice questions with four answer choices. The test is divided into three sections, each with its own time limit. These sections are always given in the same order.

TOEFL Format

	Standard Form	Long Form
Listening Comprehension	50 items 30 minutes (approx.)	80 items 45 minutes (approx.)
Structure and Written Expression	40 items 25 minutes	60 items 40 minutes
Reading Comprehension	50 items 55 minutes	75 items 80 minutes
Totals	140 items 1 hour 50 minutes	215 items 2 hours 45 minutes

The long form of TOEFL is sometimes given in the U.S. and Canada. The exact number of items and time limits vary somewhat from test to test on the long form. Only 150 out of the total number of items are scored. (The rest will appear on future TOEFL tests.) Unfortunately, there is no way to know which items are scored.

Because of the time it takes to check identification, show people to their seats, give directions, and pass out and collect exams, you will actually be in the testing room for about 2½ hours for the standard form of the test and around 3 hours for the long form.

Q: How has TOEFL changed?

A: In July 1995, ETS began giving a slightly different form of TOEFL. In the Listening Comprehension Section, the old Part A, called Single Statements, was eliminated. This part was replaced by a greater number of the old Part B Dialogs (short conversations). This became the new Part A. The old Part C, Extended Conversations and Mini-Talks, was divided into two parts. The new Part B consists of Extended Conversations; the new Part C consists of Mini-Talks (short lectures). The new Listening Comprehension section lasts about as long as the old one did (30 minutes). There are no new types of items.

There were no changes in Section 2, Structure and Written Expression.

Section 3, Vocabulary and Reading Comprehension, became Reading Comprehension. The thirty separate vocabulary items that formerly began this section were eliminated. Twenty more reading comprehension questions were added, including many more vocabulary-in-context items that ask about words in the reading passages. There are five or six passages, and the passages tend to be slightly longer than before. The new Section 3 takes 10 minutes longer to complete than the old version. There are no new item types.

There are no changes in the means of calculating scores.

The overall changes are summarized in the following chart:

More information is given about specific changes in the TOEFL in the introductions to the Listening Comprehension and Reading Comprehension parts of this book

Q: What is an Institutional TOEFL?

A: Institutional TOEFL tests are given by English language schools and other institutions. Sometimes they are used for placement in a school's English program or for testing a student's progress. Institutional tests are made up of items that previously appeared on tests administered by ETS.

Because ETS does not supervise these tests, some universities won't accept the results. However, many other universities will. You should check with the admissions offices of universities to see what their policy is. You must arrange for the institute where you took the exam to send the scores to the university.

Old TOEFL PBT Format

Section 1: Listening Comprehension
    Part A: Statements
        20 items
    Part B: Dialogs
        15 items
    Part C: Extended Conversations and
        Mini-Talks
        4 conversations/talks
        15 items
            ±30 minutes

Section 2: Structure and Written Expression
    Structure (Sentence Completion)
        15 items
    Written Expression (Error Identification)
        25 items
            25 minutes

Section 3: Vocabulary and Reading Comprehension
    Vocabulary
        30 items
    Reading Comprehension
        5 passages
        30 items
            45 minutes

New TOEFL PBT Format

Section 1: Listening Comprehension
    Part A: Dialogs
        30 items
    Part B: Extended Conversations
        2 conversations
        7–8 items
    Part C: Mini-Talks
        3 talks
        12–13 items
            ±30 minutes

Section 2: Structure and Written Expression
    Structure (Sentence Completion)
        15 items
    Written Expression (Error Identification)
        25 items
            25 minutes
        (No changes in Section 2)

Section 3: Reading Comprehension
    5–6 passages
    50 items (including an increased
            number of vocabulary-in-context
            questions)
            55 minutes

Q: Has the format of the Institutional TOEFL also changed?

A: According to ETS, Institutional TOEFL tests will continue to follow the old format until January 1997. At that time, they will begin to follow the new format as well.

Q: What is TWE?

A: TWE (*Test of Written English*) tests your ability to communicate in written English by requiring you to write a short essay on a specified topic. You have 25 minutes to complete your essay. TWE is given before the main part of TOEFL five times a year. There is no additional fee for taking TWE.

The format for TWE has not changed.

Some universities require both TOEFL and TWE scores, but many universities do not require TWE.

Q: What is TSE?

A: TSE (*Test of Spoken English*) tests your ability to communicate in spoken English. All of your responses are recorded on audiotape so that they can be evaluated later. The test takes about 20 minutes to complete and is given twelve times a year at various test centers. On TSE, you must answer questions about pictures or graphs, complete sentences, express your opinions on various topics, give short presentations, and so on. TSE is administered separately from TOEFL and must be paid for separately.

TSE is generally required only for students who are applying for positions as teaching assistants or for special programs or certificates.

Q: How do I register for TOEFL?

A: The first step is to obtain a current copy of the ETS publication, *Information Bulletin for Computer Based Testing*. In North America, these are usually available at English language centers and at the international student offices or admission offices of universities. You may also request one directly from ETS.

Address: TOEFL/TSE Services
P.O. Box 6151
Princeton, NJ 08541-6151
U.S.A.
Telephone: 609/771-7100
Fax Number: 609/771-7500
E-mail: toefl@ets.org

If you are going to take TOEFL outside North America, you will probably need to obtain a *Bulletin* prepared specifically for your country or region. These are available from many U.S. cultural or educational facilities, English language programs, bi-national centers and libraries, U.S. information service offices, and many other locations.

The *Bulletin* contains a schedule of tests, a registration form, and an envelope for sending it to ETS. Follow the directions in the *Bulletin* for completing the registration form. Payment for taking TOEFL in the United States must be in the form of a money order (in U.S. dollars) or a check from a U.S. bank.

Q: When should I register for TOEFL?

A: The deadline for applying for TOEFL is approximately one month before the testing date in the U.S. and Canada and six weeks before in other countries. To get the location and testing date that you want, apply as early as possible. You might be assigned to an alternate site if your first choice of locations is full.

Q: After I've registered for the test, when will I receive my admission ticket?

A: You should receive it about two weeks before the exam. The admission ticket will tell you exactly when and where to take the test. It's not possible to change the date and location. If you haven't received this form five days before the test date, call ETS at 609-771-7100 and inform them.

When you receive your admission ticket, fill it out according to the directions. Be sure you correctly copy the codes for the institutes that will receive your score. (These codes are listed in the *Bulletin*.)

Keep your admission ticket in a safe place. You'll need it to be admitted to the test center and later, if you correspond with ETS about the test, you'll need the registration number that appears on the ticket.

Q: What should I bring with me to the exam site?

A: You should bring the following:

- Your passport or other appropriate identification document (the *Bulletin* explains what forms of identification are acceptable)
- Your admission ticket
- A watch
- Several pencils
- Your photo file record, with a recent 2¼ inch by 2½ inch photograph attached (see the *Bulletin*)

If you take a disclosed test admission and want to receive a copy of the test, you will also need to bring a self-addressed, stamped envelope (see Key #4, page 8 for more information).

Don't bring any reference books, such as dictionaries. You are not permitted to smoke, eat, or drink in the test center.

Q: When will I receive the results of the test?

A: ETS sends scores to you and to the institutions that you request about four weeks after you have taken the test. ETS will not send your scores early or give out scores over the telephone.

Results for the TOEFL CBT tests are available immediately after taking the exam.

Q: How does ETS calculate my TOEFL score?

A: There is a total score and three sub-scores, one for each section of the test. Each section counts equally toward the total score. To obtain these scores, ETS's computers count the number of correct answers in each section. The results are called raw scores. The raw scores are then converted into scaled scores. By means of a statistical process called test equating, a score from one TOEFL test is equivalent to the same score on another TOEFL, even if one of the tests is slightly simpler or more difficult than the other.

The scaled scores from each section are added together, multiplied by 10, and divided by 3 to arrive at a total score, as shown:

	Part 1	Part 2	Part 3	
Scaled Scores	49 +	58 +	55 =	162

Total Score

(162 × 10) = 1620 ÷ 3 = 540

Total scores range from a high of 670 to a low of 200, although scores of below 320 are rare. (Even if you don't open the test book and fill in the blanks on your answer sheet at random, your score should be around 320.) You must answer at least 25 percent of the questions in all three sections to receive a test score.

Q: Is every item on the test scored?

A: No, there is usually at least one unscored item in each part of the test. This is generally the last item in each part. For example, in Section 2, item 15 (the last item in Structure) and item 40 (the last item in Written Expression) are usually not scored. However, it's not recommended that you skip these items—ETS could always change its system!

Q: What is a passing score on TOEFL?

A: There isn't any. Each university has its own standards for admission, so you should check the catalog of universities you are interested in, or contact their admissions offices. Most undergraduate programs require scores between 500 and 550, and most graduate programs ask for scores between 525 and 600. In recent years, there has been a tendency for universities to raise their minimum TOEFL requirements. Of course, the higher you score, the better your chance of admission.

A chart in the *Bulletin* allows you to compare your TOEFL scores with those of other people who have taken the test in the last year. For example, the chart tells you that, if your total score was 540, 60 percent of all test-takers had lower scores than you did.

Q: How are universities informed of my scores?

A: ETS reports your score to three institutions for free. For a charge, ETS will send your scores to additional institutions. There is a form for requesting this service in the *Bulletin*. Some universities will also accept photocopies of the test results that were mailed directly to you.

Q: If I feel I haven't done well on TOEFL, can I have my scores canceled?

A: Yes, but only for a certain period of time. At the end of the test, you can fill in the Score Cancellation section of the answer sheet. You may also fax ETS at 609-771-7500 within a week of taking a test; write "Attention, TOEFL Score Cancellation" at the top of your fax message. Include your name, test date, number of your testing center, and registration number (from your admission ticket), and sign the fax.

You can't cancel your scores after you have seen the results, and you can't cancel TOEFL and TWE scores separately.

It is generally NOT a good idea to cancel scores. You may have done better on the test than you think you did.

Q: Is it possible to improve one's score by cheating?

A: Don't try. Test-takers are seated carefully; it is very difficult for them to see anyone else's answer sheet. Even if a test-taker can see someone else's answers, there are different forms of the same exam. In other words, the items in one person's test book do not appear in the same order as they do in another person's. ETS also runs computer checks to detect patterns of cheating.

It is also very difficult to have someone else take the exam for you. You must bring an official identification document with your picture on it. You are also required to bring a photo file record with a recent photo of yourself. ETS copies this photo and sends it with your scores to universities. If the person in the photo is not the same person who enrolls, that person may not be admitted.

The following are also considered cheating:

- Taking notes during the Listening section
- Talking to or signaling any other test-takers
- Copying any test material
- Working on one section during the time allotted for another section
- Continuing to work on a section after time is called

Persons who are believed to be cheating will receive a warning for minor acts of cheating. For more serious matters, a person's scores will be canceled.

Q: How many times may I take TOEFL?

A: As often as you want; there is no limit. ETS will only send your most recent scores to institutions. It is not uncommon for people to take the test three, four, or more times before they obtain satisfactory scores.

Q: How can I get more information about TOEFL?

A: You can now contact ETS via the Internet or get up-dated information about the test from its home page on the World Wide Web:
E-Mail: toefl@ets.org
Web Site: http://www.toefl.org

TWELVE KEYS TO HIGH SCORES ON TOEFL

Key #1:

Increase your general knowledge of English.

There are two types of knowledge that will lead to high TOEFL scores:

- A knowledge of the tactics used by good test-takers and of the ''tricks'' of the test (which you will learn by using *TOEFL CBT Success*)
- A general command of English (which must be built up over a long period)

Following a step-by-step TOEFL preparation program, such as that presented in *TOEFL CBT Success*, will familiarize you with the tactics you need to raise your scores. The practice tests in this book will help you polish these techniques.

The best way to increase your general knowledge of English is simply to use English as much as possible. Classes in English will be useful, and so will opportunities to speak, read, write, or listen to English.

Some people who are preparing for TOEFL think that conversation classes and practice are a waste of time because speaking skills are not tested on the exam. In fact, one of the best ways to get ready for the exam is to converse in English whenever you can. Not only will you improve your ability to listen to everyday English, but you'll also learn to think in English. If you are living in an English-speaking country, don't spend all your time with people from your own country. If you are living in your home country, try to arrange opportunities for conversations in English.

You can improve your listening comprehension skills by going to English language lectures and movies. Listening to news and informational broadcasts on the radio is especially useful. Reading books, magazines, and newspapers in English can help you prepare for the Reading Comprehension part of the test.

One of your most important jobs is to systematically improve your vocabulary. Vocabulary building will help you, not just in that part of the exam, but throughout the exam. You may want to keep a personal vocabulary list. When you come across an unfamiliar word, look it up in a dictionary and write the word and its definition in your personal vocabulary list. Keep this list with you and study it when riding buses, eating lunch, taking coffee breaks, or whenever else you have a free moment.

Key #2:

Make the most of your preparation time.

You need to train for TOEFL just as you would train for any important competitive event. Obviously, the sooner you can start training, the better, but no matter when you begin, you need to get the most out of your preparation time.

Make a time-management chart. Draw up an hour-by-hour schedule of your week's activities. Block out those hours when you are busy with classes, work, social activities, and other responsibilities. Then pencil in times for TOEFL preparation. You will remember more of what you study if you schedule a few hours every day or several times weekly instead of scheduling all your study time in large blocks on weekends. After following this schedule for a week, make whatever adjustments are necessary. After that, try to keep to this schedule until the week before the testing date. During that last week, reduce your study time and begin to relax. If possible, reserve a special place where you do nothing but work on TOEFL preparation, separate from where you do your regular homework or other work. This place should be as free of distractions as possible.

A good method of studying for TOEFL is the ''30-5-5'' method:

- Study for 30 minutes.
- Take a 5-minute break—leave your desk and do something completely different.
- When you return, take 5 minutes to review what you studied before the break and preview what you are going to study next.

Incidentally, it's an excellent idea to meet regularly with a small group of people who are also preparing for TOEFL. Research has shown that this study-group approach to test preparation is very effective.

Key #3:

Be in good physical condition when you take the exam.

When you make out your time-management schedule, don't forget to leave time for physical activities—sports, aerobics, jogging, bicycling, or whatever else you prefer.

The most important physical concern is that you not become exhausted during your preparation time. If you aren't getting enough sleep, you'll need to reduce your study time or another activity. This is especially important in the last few days before the exam.

Key #4:

Choose your test date carefully.

If you need test scores quickly, you should sign up for the earliest test date available. But if it's possible, sign up to take TOEFL on one of the Disclosed Test Administration dates. These dates are marked with an asterisk (*) on the ETS schedule of exams on the cover of the *Bulletin*. They are generally given on Fridays in July and September and on Saturdays in May, August, and October.

There are two advantages to taking tests on these dates:

- You can keep the test book, which can be a valuable tool for study if you take the exam again.
- The tests given on these dates are always standard (150-item) forms. Taking the shorter form of the test is less tiring and stressful than taking the long form.

To receive a copy of the test, you must bring a 6 inch by 9 inch (15.3 centimeters by 22.8 centimeters) envelope that you have addressed to yourself. You'll need enough postage on the envelope for a package weighing 1.5 ounces (43 grams). If your mailing address is in the United States, two first-class U.S. stamps will be sufficient.

Key #5:

Be familiar with the format and directions.

You should have a clear "map" of the TOEFL test in your mind. Then, as you're taking the exam, you'll know exactly where you are and what's coming next. You can familiarize yourself with the basic TOEFL format by looking over the chart on page 2.

The directions for each part of the TOEFL test are always the same; even the same examples are used. If you're familiar with the directions, you won't have to waste time reading them during the test. You can become familiar with these directions by studying the directions for the practice tests in this book.

Key #6:

Organize your pre-exam time.

You shouldn't try to "cram" (study intensively) during the last few days before the exam. Last-minute studying can leave you exhausted, and you need to be alert for the test. The night before the exam, don't study at all. Get together the materials you'll need in the morning, then go to a movie, take a long walk, or do something else to take your mind off the test. Go to bed when you usually do.

If the exam is in the morning, have breakfast before you leave. Wear comfortable clothes because you'll be sitting in the same position for a long time. Give yourself plenty of time to get to the test site, keeping in mind traffic, weather, and parking problems. If you have to rush, that will only add to your stress.

Key #7:

Use time wisely during the test.

TOEFL would be a far easier test if you could spend an unlimited amount of time working on it. However, there are strict time limits. Doing well on TOEFL means that you must find a balance between speed and accuracy. You don't want to rush through any section, but you do want to finish each section before time is called. The ideal is to finish Sections 2 and 3 with a few minutes remaining so that you can go back to questions that you found difficult. (The timing on Section 1 is controlled by the tape and you can't go back and check your answers after completing this section.)

The questions on TOEFL are not equally difficult. Items can be classified as easy, medium, and difficult.

Approximate Distribution of Items on a Typical TOEFL Test

Easy	30%
Medium	40%
Difficult	30%

Easy items are usually found at the beginning of each part of the test, medium items are usually found in the middle of each part, and difficult items are usually found at the end of each part. You may be tempted to rush through the easy items to save time for the difficult ones at the end of each part. This is not a good strategy. Your goal is to get as many right answers as possible. Therefore, you want to concentrate on the items that give you the best chance of a correct answer—in other words, the easiest ones.

> **Hint:** Remember, you don't get any extra points for answering difficult questions.

Work steadily. Never spend too much time on any one problem. If you are unable to decide on an answer, guess and go on. Answer each question as you come to it, even if you are not sure of the answer. You can mark difficult items on your answer sheet with check marks (as shown in Key #8). Then, if you have time at the end of the section, you can return to these problems. Sometimes when you come back to an item, you will find it easier. (Be sure to erase all of these check marks before you hand in your answer sheet.)

The most important tool for timing yourself is a watch, preferably one with a "count down" feature that you can set at the beginning of Sections 2 and 3. (Watches with alarms are not permitted.)

Key #8:

Know how to mark your answer sheet on the PBT.

One of the worst surprises you can have during a test is to suddenly discover that the number of the item that you are working on doesn't correspond to the number of the answer you are marking for that item. You have to go back to find where you first got off track, then change all the answers after that number. You can avoid this problem by using the test book itself as a marker. Cover all the unanswered items in each column on your answer sheet. Then uncover one item at a time as you advance. Every five items or so, quickly glance at the number of the question that you are working on and the number of the answer to make sure they are the same.

Mark answers by filling in the oval so that the letter cannot be seen. Don't mark answers any other way.

Correct

1. Ⓐ Ⓑ ● Ⓓ

Incorrect

1. Ⓐ Ⓑ Ⓒ✓ Ⓓ

1. Ⓐ Ⓑ Ⓒ✗ Ⓓ

1. Ⓐ Ⓑ Ⓒ◉ Ⓓ

Bring several #2 black lead pencils. Make sure each has a functioning eraser. Do not use a pen, a liquid lead pencil, or any other kind of marker.

By the way, you may see either of two types of answer sheets. On one the answer choices are displayed horizontally, while on the other they are displayed vertically.

Horizontal

1. Ⓐ Ⓑ Ⓒ ●
2. Ⓐ ● Ⓒ Ⓓ
3. Ⓐ Ⓑ ● Ⓓ
4. Ⓐ Ⓑ ● Ⓓ ✓
5. ● Ⓑ Ⓒ Ⓓ
6. Ⓐ Ⓑ Ⓒ ● ✓

Vertical

Always be sure you have filled in a circle completely and have filled in only one answer per item. If you have to erase an answer, erase it completely.

Notice the check marks by numbers 4 and 6. The test-taker found these items difficult. He or she guessed at the answers, and then used the marks as a reminder to come back to these items if time allowed. These marks should be erased before the end of the test.

Incidentally, if you mark the same answer four times in a row, you'll know one of those four answers is wrong. The same correct answer will occur at most three times in a row on TOEFL.

Hint: Don't sharpen your pencils too much before the exam. You can fill in circles more quickly if your pencil is not too sharp.

Key #9:

Improve your concentration.

The ability to focus your attention on each item is an important factor in scoring high. Two and a half hours or more, after all, is a long time to spend in deep concentration. However, if your concentration is broken, it could cost you points. When an outside concern comes into your mind, just say to yourself, "I'll think about this after the test."

Like any skill, the ability to concentrate can be improved with practice. Work on it while you are taking the practice tests in this book.

Key #10:

Use the process of elimination to make the best guess.

Unlike some standardized exams, TOEFL has no penalty for guessing. In other words, incorrect answers aren't subtracted from your total score. Even if you are not sure which answer is correct, you should always, always, always guess. But you want to make an educated guess, not a blind guess. To do so, use the process of elimination.

To understand the process of elimination, it may be helpful to look at the basic structure of a multiple-choice item. On TOEFL, multiple-choice items consist of a stem and four answer choices. (The stem in the Listening section is spoken; in the other two sections, it is written.) One answer choice, called the key, is correct. The three incorrect choices are called distractors because their function is to distract (take away) your attention from the right answer.

STEM..........................

(A) distractor
(B) distractor
(C) key
(D) distractor

The three distractors, however, are usually not equally attractive. One is usually "almost correct." This choice is called the main **distractor**. Most people who answer an item incorrectly will choose this answer.

STEM......................

(A) main distractor
(B) distractor
(C) key
(D) distractor

To see how this works in practice, look at this simple Structure item:

Winter wheat _____ planted in the fall.

(A) because
(B) is
(C) which
(D) has

If you are sure of the answer, you should mark your choice immediately and go on. If not, you should use the process of elimination. In this item, choices (A) and (C) are fairly easy to eliminate. Because this sentence consists of a single clause, connecting words such as *because* and *which* are not needed. It may be a little more difficult to choose between choices (B) and (D) because both form correct verb phrases. Even if you are unable to decide between these two choices, you have a 50 percent chance of guessing correctly. That's twice as good as the 25 percent chance you would have if you had guessed blindly. (Choice (B) is the key, of course; a passive verb, not a present perfect verb, is required to complete the sentence correctly.)

What if you eliminate one or two answers but can't decide which of the remaining choices is correct? If you have a "hunch" (an intuitive feeling) that one choice is better that the others, choose it. If not, just pick any remaining answer and go on.

If you have no idea which of the four answers is correct, it's better to use a standard "guess letter" than to guess at random.

You should NEVER leave any items unanswered. Even if you don't have time to read an item, you have a 25 percent chance of guessing the key. If you are unable to finish a section, fill in all the unanswered ovals on your answer sheet with your guess letter in the last few seconds before time is called. Remember: Use the same guess letter all the time so that you can fill in the ovals quickly.

Key #11:
Learn to control test anxiety.

A little nervousness before an important test is normal. After all, these tests can have an important effect on your plans for your education and career. If you were going to participate in a big athletic contest or give an important business presentation, you would feel the same way. There is an expression in English that describes this feeling quite well: "butterflies in the stomach." These "butterflies" will mostly disappear once the test starts. And a little nervousness can actually help by making you more alert and focused. However, too much nervousness can slow you down and cause you to make mistakes.

You may become anxious during the test because it seems very hard, and it seems that you are making many mistakes. Try not to panic. The test seems hard because it *is* hard. You can miss quite a few items and still get a high score.

One way to avoid stress on the day of the test is to give yourself plenty of time to get to the test center. If you have to rush, you'll be even more nervous during the exam.

If you begin to feel extremely anxious during the test, try taking a short break—a "10-second vacation." Close your eyes and put down your pencil. Take a few deep breaths, shake out your hands, roll your head on your neck, relax—then go back to work.

Of course, you can't take a break during the Listening Comprehension section when the items are being read. However, if you're familiar with the directions, you can relax during the times when the directions are being read.

A positive, confident attitude toward the exam can help you overcome anxiety. Think of TOEFL not as a test of your knowledge or of you as a person but as an intellectual challenge, a series of puzzles to be solved.

Key #12:
Learn from taking practice tests and official TOEFL exams.

One of the most important steps in preparing for TOEFL is taking realistic, complete practice tests. There are three tests in this book.

In addition, you may take the official TOEFL test several times. Each time you take a test, either a practice test or a real one, you should learn from it. Immediately after the exam, write down your reactions: Which section seemed difficult? Did you have problems finishing any sections? When you look at your results, is the score for one section significantly lower or higher than the scores for the other two sections? You can use this information to focus your studies for the next time you take the test.

Hint: Whenever you take a practice test, pretend that you are taking an actual TOEFL exam. Whenever you take an actual exam, pretend you are taking a practice test.

Section 1:

LISTENING
COMPREHENSION

RED ALERT

The Listening Comprehension section of TOEFL is always given first. The purpose of this section is to test your understanding of spoken English.

The directions for this section are given on the tape as well as printed in your test book. There are four speakers, two men and two women. The speakers read the items at a normal speed. All four have standard North American accents. The tone of the items is conversational, much less formal than the items in the two other test sections.

Section 1 is divided into three parts, each with a different format and different directions. Since July 1995, it has followed this format:

Listening Comprehension Format

	Standard Form	Long Form
Part A: Dialogs	30 items	45 items
Part B:	2 conversations	3 conversations
Extended Conversations	7–8 items	10–12 items
Part C:	3 talks	5 talks
Mini-Talks	12–13 items	13–15 items
Totals:	49–51 items	68–72 items
	±30 minutes	±45 minutes

Listening Comprehension actually tests both your listening ability and your reading skills since you must understand both the material on the tape and the answer choices written in your test book.

Many test-takers find the Listening Comprehension section the most difficult. Because it is given first, you may be more nervous during this part of the test. Furthermore, it is difficult to understand voices on tape (just as it is on the telephone or radio) because you can't see the speakers' gestures, facial expressions, or lip movements as you can during "live" listening. Finally, the test-writers at ETS employ a number of "tricks" that make choosing the correct answer more difficult.

The exercises and tests in the Listening Comprehension part of this text are designed to help you overcome these difficulties. You will become more comfortable listening to taped materials in general and to TOEFL items in particular. You'll also become alert to many of the test-writers' tricks.

Strategies for Section 1

- Familiarize yourself with the directions for each part before the exam. But remember, you are not permitted to turn the page to look over answer choices while the directions are being read. (No answer choices appear on the same page as the directions.

- If you have any difficulties hearing the tape, inform one of the proctors during the introductory section. Once the test has begun, the proctors cannot stop the tape.

- Never skip any items. If you're not sure of an answer, guess.

- Answer each item as quickly as you can, then preview the answer choices for the next item. Try to guess what the next item will be by the form of the answer choices.

- Concentration is very important in this part of the test. Once you choose an answer, don't think about the last item—start thinking about the next one. Don't daydream. Focus your attention on the tape and on the choices in your test book.

Begin your preparation for Section 1 by taking the Sample Listening Comprehension Test on the following pages. This will familiarize you with the first section of the exam.

This section tests your ability to comprehend spoken English. It is divided into three parts, each with its own directions. You are *not* permitted to turn the page during the reading of the directions or to take notes at any time.

PART A

Directions: Each item in this part consists of a brief conversation involving two speakers. Following each conversation, a third voice will ask a question. You will hear the conversations and questions only once, and they will *not* be written out.

When you have heard each conversation and question, read the four answer choices and select the one—(A), (B), (C), or (D)—that best answers the question based on what is directly stated or on what can be inferred. Then fill in the space on your answer sheet (on page 16) that matches the letter of the answer that you have selected.

Here is an example.

You will hear:*

M1: Do you think I should leave this chair against the wall or put it somewhere else?

F1: Over by the window, I'd say.

M2: What does the woman think the man should do?

You will read:

(A) Open the window.
(B) Move the chair.
(C) Leave the room.
(D) Take a seat.

Sample Answer

Ⓐ ● Ⓒ Ⓓ

From the conversation you find out that the woman thinks the man should put the chair over by the window. The best answer to the question "What does the woman think the man should do?" is (B), "Move the chair." You should fill in (B) on your answer sheet.

(WAIT)

---

* Note: M1 = first male voice   M2 = second male voice   F1 = first female voice   F2 = second female voice

Answer Sheet

Sample Listening Comprehension Test

1.	Ⓐ	Ⓑ	Ⓒ	Ⓓ	21.	Ⓐ	Ⓑ	Ⓒ	Ⓓ	41.	Ⓐ	Ⓑ	Ⓒ	Ⓓ
2.	Ⓐ	Ⓑ	Ⓒ	Ⓓ	22.	Ⓐ	Ⓑ	Ⓒ	Ⓓ	42.	Ⓐ	Ⓑ	Ⓒ	Ⓓ
3.	Ⓐ	Ⓑ	Ⓒ	Ⓓ	23.	Ⓐ	Ⓑ	Ⓒ	Ⓓ	43.	Ⓐ	Ⓑ	Ⓒ	Ⓓ
4.	Ⓐ	Ⓑ	Ⓒ	Ⓓ	24.	Ⓐ	Ⓑ	Ⓒ	Ⓓ	44.	Ⓐ	Ⓑ	Ⓒ	Ⓓ
5.	Ⓐ	Ⓑ	Ⓒ	Ⓓ	25.	Ⓐ	Ⓑ	Ⓒ	Ⓓ	45.	Ⓐ	Ⓑ	Ⓒ	Ⓓ
6.	Ⓐ	Ⓑ	Ⓒ	Ⓓ	26.	Ⓐ	Ⓑ	Ⓒ	Ⓓ	46.	Ⓐ	Ⓑ	Ⓒ	Ⓓ
7.	Ⓐ	Ⓑ	Ⓒ	Ⓓ	27.	Ⓐ	Ⓑ	Ⓒ	Ⓓ	47.	Ⓐ	Ⓑ	Ⓒ	Ⓓ
8.	Ⓐ	Ⓑ	Ⓒ	Ⓓ	28.	Ⓐ	Ⓑ	Ⓒ	Ⓓ	48.	Ⓐ	Ⓑ	Ⓒ	Ⓓ
9.	Ⓐ	Ⓑ	Ⓒ	Ⓓ	29.	Ⓐ	Ⓑ	Ⓒ	Ⓓ	49.	Ⓐ	Ⓑ	Ⓒ	Ⓓ
10.	Ⓐ	Ⓑ	Ⓒ	Ⓓ	30.	Ⓐ	Ⓑ	Ⓒ	Ⓓ	50.	Ⓐ	Ⓑ	Ⓒ	Ⓓ
11.	Ⓐ	Ⓑ	Ⓒ	Ⓓ	31.	Ⓐ	Ⓑ	Ⓒ	Ⓓ					
12.	Ⓐ	Ⓑ	Ⓒ	Ⓓ	32.	Ⓐ	Ⓑ	Ⓒ	Ⓓ					
13.	Ⓐ	Ⓑ	Ⓒ	Ⓓ	33.	Ⓐ	Ⓑ	Ⓒ	Ⓓ					
14.	Ⓐ	Ⓑ	Ⓒ	Ⓓ	34.	Ⓐ	Ⓑ	Ⓒ	Ⓓ					
15.	Ⓐ	Ⓑ	Ⓒ	Ⓓ	35.	Ⓐ	Ⓑ	Ⓒ	Ⓓ					
16.	Ⓐ	Ⓑ	Ⓒ	Ⓓ	36.	Ⓐ	Ⓑ	Ⓒ	Ⓓ					
17.	Ⓐ	Ⓑ	Ⓒ	Ⓓ	37.	Ⓐ	Ⓑ	Ⓒ	Ⓓ					
18.	Ⓐ	Ⓑ	Ⓒ	Ⓓ	38.	Ⓐ	Ⓑ	Ⓒ	Ⓓ					
19.	Ⓐ	Ⓑ	Ⓒ	Ⓓ	39.	Ⓐ	Ⓑ	Ⓒ	Ⓓ					
20.	Ⓐ	Ⓑ	Ⓒ	Ⓓ	40.	Ⓐ	Ⓑ	Ⓒ	Ⓓ					

1. (A) It's brand new.
   (B) She just repaired it.
   (C) Someone painted it.
   (D) It's just been sold.

2. (A) Give the woman cash.
   (B) Go to his car.
   (C) Return some merchandise.
   (D) Use his credit card.

3. (A) He shouldn't have thrown away the list.
   (B) He doesn't have to read all the books.
   (C) All of the books on the list are required.
   (D) Some of the books are available now.

4. (A) She enjoyed it very much.
   (B) She thought it was too long.
   (C) She thought it was boring.
   (D) She only liked the ending.

5. (A) Either a pen or pencil can be used.
   (B) It's not necessary to fill out the form.
   (C) She doesn't have either a pen or a pencil.
   (D) A pen is better than a pencil.

6. (A) The software isn't convenient to use.
   (B) He's not familiar with the software.
   (C) Using the software is simple.
   (D) He wishes he'd bought that software.

7. (A) The man ordered it, but it hasn't arrived yet.
   (B) It isn't working.
   (C) Someone else is using it.
   (D) The man doesn't know how to operate it.

8. (A) What time his brother called.
   (B) Where to meet his brother.
   (C) Why his brother called.
   (D) When to meet his brother.

9. (A) He left on a long trip yesterday.
   (B) His letter arrived unexpectedly.
   (C) He seemed to be sad yesterday.
   (D) The letter he sent was very funny.

10. (A) It's on the wrong floor.
    (B) There are too many bedrooms.
    (C) It's too small.
    (D) The rent is too high.

11. (A) He'll probably give the man another grade.
    (B) He doesn't teach chemistry anymore.
    (C) He rarely changes his grades.
    (D) He'll probably retire soon.

12. (A) She mailed the grades to her students.
    (B) She left the students' tests in her office.
    (C) She can't get into her office.
    (D) She put a list of grades on the door.

13. (A) He should get something for his friends to eat.
    (B) There isn't time for him to go out now.
    (C) The game won't be played today.
    (D) He should have invited his friends to the game.

14. (A) His class has been canceled.
    (B) He shouldn't drop the class.
    (C) An earlier class would be better for him.
    (D) He doesn't need to study political science.

15. (A) Sitting in other seats.
    (B) Going home.
    (C) Turning up the music.
    (D) Asking the usher for a refund.

16. (A) He has a good excuse for being late.
    (B) He's been feeling very weak recently.
    (C) He's still waiting to be contacted.
    (D) He doesn't take responsibility for errors.

17. (A) She doesn't have her camera.
    (B) The sun hasn't set yet.
    (C) There isn't any film in the camera.
    (D) Her camera is broken.

18. (A) He got on the wrong bus.
    (B) He's afraid he'll be late for his flight.
    (C) He's sorry he took a bus instead of flying.
    (D) He had to wait for the bus.

19. (A) The meeting will have to be rescheduled.
    (B) She doesn't care whom the board picks as dean.
    (C) She's not sure where the meeting will be.
    (D) The board will not choose a dean this month.

20. (A) He's upset about the card game.
    (B) He's getting ready for the game.
    (C) He knocked over the card table.
    (D) He sat down to have dinner.

21. (A) They wish they hadn't paid attention to Harvey.
    (B) They asked for some information about Harvey.
    (C) Harvey told them not to ignore him.
    (D) Only Harvey could give them any assistance.

22. (A) Most of the audience joined in the performance.
    (B) Some people don't enjoy performing.
    (C) Not many people were in the audience.
    (D) A few people didn't like the performance.

23. (A) A hotel room.
    (B) The man's family.
    (C) A reasonable offer.
    (D) The man's schedule.

24. (A) He must change his syllabus.
    (B) The woman cannot take his class.
    (C) He has extra copies of the syllabus.
    (D) Some students are not on his list.

25. (A) It's inconvenient for him to go to Mount Pleasant Street.
    (B) Those antique stores aren't very nice.
    (C) There are many inexpensive shops on Mount Pleasant Street.
    (D) The antiques in those stores are a little expensive.

26. (A) He's gone to San Diego many times.
    (B) He's attended a lot of conferences.
    (C) He has already gotten enough information.
    (D) He's living in San Diego now.

27. (A) He once drove in a race.
    (B) He's going to the races soon.
    (C) He drives quite fast.
    (D) He's thinking about a new car.

28. (A) The bowls are stacked on the shelves.
(B) This soup is no worse than the other brands.
(C) The new bowls are very attractive.
(D) He plans to stock up on this soup.

29. (A) Peter wouldn't be favored in the match.
(B) The match had already been played.
(C) The match wouldn't be played.
(D) Peter would win the match.

30. (A) He hasn't finished working on the bookshelves.
(B) The tools have been misplaced.
(C) He's not very good with tools.
(D) The tools have already been returned.

PART B

Directions: This part of the test consists of extended conversations between two speakers. After each of these conversations, there are a number of questions. You will hear each conversation and question only once, and the questions are *not* written out.

When you have heard the questions, read the four answer choices and select the *one*—(A), (B), (C), or (D)—that best answers the question based on what is directly stated or on what can be inferred. Then fill in the space on your answer sheet that matches the letter of the answer that you have selected.

Don't forget: During actual exams, taking notes or writing in your test book is *not* permitted.

Peterson's TOEFL CBT Success

31. (A) Student and adviser.
    (B) Museum curator and visitor.
    (C) Manager and job applicant.
    (D) Professor and teaching assistant.

32. (A) In a few weeks.
    (B) Next year.
    (C) In three years.
    (D) In four years.

33. (A) Change her major.
    (B) Make a quick decision.
    (C) Take elective courses in art history.
    (D) Work full-time at a museum.

34. (A) She couldn't get airline reservations.
    (B) She can't find an important book.
    (C) She's been studying too much.
    (D) She doesn't have a car.

35. (A) Amounts of money.
    (B) Names of riders.
    (C) Types of cars.
    (D) Regions of the United States.

36. (A) Information about places to visit.
    (B) Help with expenses and driving.
    (C) Plane reservations.
    (D) A used car.

37. (A) In the campus cinema.
    (B) Next door to the Student Union building.
    (C) In a travel agent's office.
    (D) On the second floor of the Student Union building.

PART C

Directions: This part of the test consists of several talks, each given by a single speaker. After each of these talks, there are a number of questions. You will hear each talk and question only once, and the questions are *not* written out.

When you have heard each question, read the four answer choices and select the *one*—(A), (B), (C), or (D)—that best answers the question based on what is directly stated or on what can be inferred. Then fill in the space on your answer sheet corresponding to the letter of the answer that you have selected.

Here is an example.

You will hear:*

M1: Students, this evening we'll have a chance to observe a phenomenon that we've discussed several times in class. Tonight there will be a lunar eclipse. As we've said, when an eclipse of the Moon occurs, the Earth passes between the Sun and the Moon. Therefore, the shadow of the Earth moves across the surface of the Moon and obscures it. Because you won't be looking at the Sun, it is not necessary to use the special lenses and filters that you need when observing a solar eclipse. You can observe a lunar eclipse with your unaided eye or with a telescope and photograph it with an ordinary camera. So if the weather's not cloudy tonight, go out and take a look at this eclipse of the Moon. I'm sure you'll find it interesting.

M2: Now here is a sample question . . .

You will hear:

In what course is this lecture probably being given?

You will read:
(A) Philosophy.
(B) Meteorology.
(C) Astronomy.
(D) Photography.

Sample Answer

The lecture concerns a lunar eclipse, a topic that would typically be discussed in an astronomy class. The choice that best answers the question "In what course is this lecture probably being given?" is (C), "Astronomy." You should fill in (C) on your answer sheet.

* Note: M1 = first male voice   M2 = second male voice   F1 = first female voice   F2 = second female voice

Here is another sample question.

You will hear:

According to the speaker, which of the following occurs during a lunar eclipse?

You will read:

(A) The Earth's shadow moves across the Moon.
(B) Clouds block the view of the Moon.
(C) The Moon moves between the Earth and the Sun.
(D) The Sun can be observed without special equipment.

Sample Answer

From the lecture you learn that a lunar eclipse occurs when the Earth moves between the Sun and the Moon and the shadow of the Earth passes across the Moon. The choice that best answers the question "According to the speaker, which of the following occurs during a lunar eclipse?" is (A), "The Earth's shadow moves across the Moon."

Don't forget: During actual exams, taking notes or writing in your test book is *not* permitted.

38. (A) An airplane.
    (B) A satellite.
    (C) A fireworks display.
    (D) A flying saucer.

39. (A) To change tires.
    (B) To get some gasoline.
    (C) To get a hotel room.
    (D) To change drivers.

40. (A) From the news on the radio.
    (B) From a newspaper.
    (C) From his mother.
    (D) From the news on television.

41. (A) It burned up in the upper atmosphere.
    (B) It injured a woman as she was sleeping.
    (C) It caused damage to a parked car.
    (D) It broke into pieces before striking the ground.

42. (A) Frightened.
    (B) Upset.
    (C) Fortunate.
    (D) Relieved.

43. (A) At the top of the Washington Monument.
    (B) On board a bus.
    (C) On an elevator.
    (D) At the Lincoln Memorial.

44. (A) Four years.
    (B) Thirty-six years.
    (C) Forty years.
    (D) Forty-eight years.

45. (A) Walk up 898 steps.
    (B) Take the elevator to the top.
    (C) Come down on the elevator.
    (D) Walk down the stairs.

46. (A) They jumped over it.
    (B) They took pictures of it.
    (C) They wrote their names on it.
    (D) They touched it.

47. (A) Music appreciation.
    (B) American history.
    (C) Dance.
    (D) Geography.

48. (A) They were an important part of the daily lives of the people of the frontier.
(B) They were all extremely old.
(C) They were all written as theme songs for political campaigns.
(D) They were primarily written as dance music.

49. (A) They weren't as enduring.
(B) They were harder to sing and play.
(C) They were livelier.
(D) They weren't concerned with politics.

50. (A) Sing songs.
(B) Look at some sheet music.
(C) Go to a dance.
(D) Listen to a recording.

THIS IS THE END OF THE SAMPLE LISTENING COMPREHENSION TEST. STOP WORK ON THIS TEST.

Part A

ABOUT DIALOGS

The first part of the Listening Comprehension section consists of spoken dialogs (conversations) between two speakers. A third speaker asks a question about what was said or implied in the conversation. You must decide which of the four answer choices printed in your test book is the best answer for the question you hear and then mark that choice on your answer sheet. Between each of the dialogs is a 12 second pause. There are thirty dialogs on the standard form, forty-five on the long form.

Sample Item

You will hear:*

M1: Do you think I should leave this chair against the wall or put it somewhere else?

 F1: Over by the window, I'd say.

M2: What does the woman think the man should do?

You will read:

(A) Open the window.
(B) Move the chair.
(C) Leave the room.
(D) Take a seat.

Sample Answer

The woman indicates that she thinks the man should put the chair over by the window rather than leave it where it is. In other words, he should move it. The best answer is therefore (B).

---

* Note: M1 = first male voice   M2 = second male voice   F1 = first female voice   F2 = second female voice

THE DIALOGS

Most of the dialogs in Part A involve a man and a woman. A few involve two men or two women. Each speaker usually speaks one or two sentences. Many dialogs (about 25 percent) are about facets of life at American universities: attending classes, talking to professors, writing research papers, and taking tests. Other dialogs are about more general activities: shopping in grocery stores, looking for housing, taking vacations, and going to meetings and parties. The tone of the dialogs is informal. Idioms, first names, contractions (*I'm, doesn't, can't*) are often heard. Some of the items test your ability to understand various language functions. For example, you must be able to determine if a speaker is agreeing or disagreeing with the other speaker, or if one speaker is accepting or rejecting the other speaker's offer.

THE QUESTIONS

Most of the questions about the dialogs focus on what the second speaker says. However, it is usually necessary to understand the entire dialog in order to choose the correct answer. For example, in the Sample Item, it is not clear what the woman means when she says "Over by the window" unless you understand what the man says first. One or two questions in each test may focus instead on what the first speaker says.

Common Part A Question Types	Examples
1. **Meaning questions** These are the most common questions (about 50 percent). They ask for a restatement of what the second speaker or both speakers say. They may be general questions or ask what the speakers say about some specific topic. They often follow dialogs that contain idioms.	"What does the man/woman mean?" "What do the speakers say about _____?"
2. **Inference questions** These are the second most common Part A questions (about 20 percent). The answers for these questions are not directly stated in the dialog, but they can be inferred (concluded) from what the speakers say.	"What does the man/woman imply?" "What can be inferred from the conversation about _____?" "What can be concluded from the conversation about _____?"
3. **Questions about suggestions** Generally the first speaker talks about a problem or asks for advice. The second speaker makes a suggestion for solving the problem.	"What does the woman suggest the man do?" "What does the man suggest they do?" "What does the woman suggest?" "What does the woman think the man should do?"
4. **Questions about future actions** These ask what one or both of the speakers will do next or in the near future, or what one or both are planning to do.	"What will the man do?" "What will they probably do next?" "What are the speakers planning to do?"
5. **Topic questions** These ask about the subject of the dialog.	"What are they talking about?" "What are they discussing?"
6. **Questions about opinions** These ask how one or both of the speakers feel about some topic.	"How does the man/woman feel about _____?" "What is their opinion of _____?"

7. **Questions about assumptions** These ask what the second speaker thought (assumed) before he or she spoke to the first speaker.

"What had the man assumed about _____?"
"What had the woman previously assumed?"

8. **Questions about questions** The first speaker makes a statement; the second speaker asks a question to get more information.

"What does the man want to know?"

9. **Questions about time** These ask when a conversation is taking place or when an event the speakers mention in the conversation will take place.

"When is this conversation taking place?"
"When will the _____ take place?"

10. **Questions about reasons** These ask why one or both of the speakers did something.

"Why did the man/woman _____?"
"Why did they _____?"

11. **Questions about problems** These ask about some trouble one or both of the speakers are having.

"What problem is the man having?"
"What is the problem?"

12. **Questions about activities** These ask what one or both of the speakers are doing.

"What are the speakers probably doing?"

Note: Two types of questions that were commonly asked about dialogs in the past are seldom or never asked about in the new-format test. These are location questions ("Where does this conversation probably take place?") and occupation questions ("What is the man's occupation?" or "Who is the man?").

THE ANSWER CHOICES

All four of the answer choices are logical answers for the question, but only one—the key—is correct according to the dialog. However, as in all parts of TOEFL, not all of the answer choices are equally attractive. You can often eliminate one or two choices easily even if you are not sure which answer is correct and so make a better guess.

Correct answers are seldom stated word for word by either of the speakers. Correct answers often contain synonyms (words with the same meaning) for words in the dialogs and use different sentence structures.

Grammatically, there are three types of answer choices:

1. Complete sentences (about 75 percent)

2. Incomplete sentences, usually beginning with verb forms—most often the simple form of the verb (about 20 percent)

3. Short noun or prepositional phrases (about 5 percent)

The form of the answer choice can sometimes help you guess what the question will be, and you can therefore focus your listening.

Question types and examples	**Usual form of answer choice and examples**
Meaning questions: "What does the man mean?"	Complete sentences: (A) He prefers coffee to tea. (B) He'd like some lemon in his tea.
Questions about inferences: "What does the woman imply about the article?"	Complete sentences: (A) She will probably read it today. (B) She wasn't able to find it in the library.

Peterson's TOEFL CBT Success

Questions about suggestions:

"What does the woman suggest John do?"

"What does the man suggest?"

Questions about future actions:

"What will the speakers probably do next?"

Topic questions:
"What are the speakers discussing?"

Questions about opinions:
"What was their opinion of the play?"

"How does the man feel about the announce-ment he heard?"

Questions about assumptions:

"What had the man assumed about Kathy?"

Questions about questions:

"What does the woman ask about Professor Tolbert?"

"What does the man ask about the department store?"

Questions about time:
"When will the man play the piano?"

Questions about reasons:

"Why did Jerry miss the party?"

"Why did Linda talk to Professor Delgado?"

Questions about problems:
"What problem does the man have?"

Incomplete sentences beginning with simple forms of verbs or -ing forms
  (A) Call his cousin.
  (B) Take his cousin home.

  (A) Taking a bus to campus.
  (B) Walking to class.

Incomplete sentences beginning with simple forms of verbs
  (A) Park their car.
  (B) Get some gasoline.

Noun phrases:
  (A) The man's new schedule.
  (B) A homework assignment.

Complete sentences or adjective phrases:
  (A) They didn't enjoy it very much.
  (B) They liked it more than they thought they would.

  (A) Angry.
  (B) Enthusiastic.

Complete sentences often containing the auxiliary verbs *would* or *had*:
  (A) She had already finished the paper.
  (B) She wouldn't finish the research on time.

Incomplete sentences beginning with the word *if* or one of the *wh-* words:
  (A) If she is still in her office.
  (B) Where her office is.

  (A) Its location.
  (B) Its hours of operation.

Prepositional phrases of time:
  (A) At the party.
  (B) Before the ceremony.

Complete sentences or incomplete sentences beginning with infinitives (*to* + simple form):
  (A) He didn't receive an invitation.
  (B) He had other plans for the evening.

  (A) To ask him about a grade.
  (B) To explain why she missed class.

Complete sentences:
  (A) He didn't bring enough money for the tickets.
  (B) There were no tickets available.

Questions about activities:
"What are they probably doing?"

Incomplete sentences beginning with *-ing* verbs:
(A) Buying groceries.
(B) Cooking breakfast.

The test-writers sometimes make it more difficult to pick the correct answer by using sound-alike words, homonyms, words with multiple meanings, and other techniques. You'll practice avoiding these traps in this part of the book.

Tactics for Dialogs

- Be familiar with the directions for Part A.
- Remember that the answer for the question is generally contained in what the second speaker says.
- If you are not sure of the answer, eliminate as many answer choices as you can.
- After you have chosen an answer, use the remaining time to preview the choices for the next item. If the answer choices are long, just skim over them quickly. Try to anticipate what the question will be by the form of the answer choices.
- If you don't understand all or part of a conversation, guess and go on.

Lesson 1

ANTICIPATING QUESTIONS ABOUT DIALOGS

Between each dialog in Part A, there is a 12-second pause. During the pause, here's what you should do:

- Answer the question you have just heard as quickly as you can.
- Preview the choices for the next item.

A look at the answer choices may tell you the topic of the upcoming dialog and what question will be asked about it. Consider the answer choices below:

(A) Before she leaves her dormitory.
(B) During the chemistry class.
(C) After the lab period.
(D) While she's eating lunch.

Even a quick glance will tell you that the dialog must be about a student's schedule, and that the question will begin, "When. . . ."

If you have an idea of the topic of the dialog, and if you know what the question about the dialog will be, you will know what to listen for, and your listening task will be easier.

EXERCISE 1

Focus: Guessing which type of question will be asked about dialogs by looking at the four answer choices.

Directions: Quickly look over the five Part A items in each set. Try to guess the topic of the dialog and the type of question that would be asked about it. Then look at the list of questions following each set of items. Put the letter of the appropriate question in the blank provided. One question in each set will NOT be used. The first one is done as an example.

Note: There is no taped material for this exercise.

Set A

1. (A) Pleased.
   (B) Cold.
   (C) Disappointed.
   (D) Hungry.

   Question: ___b___

2. (A) Go to her office.
   (B) Call a taxi.
   (C) Show the man where to find a taxi.
   (D) Get directions.

   Question: _____

3. (A) Cloudy but much warmer.
   (B) Rainy.
   (C) Clear but cold.
   (D) The same as today's.

   Question: _____

4. (A) He left it in the lock.
   (B) It's still in his dorm room.
   (C) He put it in his pocket.
   (D) It doesn't work in this lock.

   Question: _____

5. (A) Playing a game.
   (B) Attending a play.
   (C) Learning some lines.
   (D) Trying to find tickets.

   Question: _____

Questions for Set A

(a) What will tomorrow's weather probably be like?
(b) How does the man feel?
(c) What are these people doing?
(d) Where will the man go tomorrow?
(e) What does John say about the key?
(f) What will the woman do next?

Set B

6. (A) He had given his textbooks to a friend.
   (B) He would receive more money.
   (C) He wouldn't get to the bookstore on time.
   (D) He hadn't sold his textbooks.

   Question: _____

7. (A) She enjoyed it very much.
   (B) She thought it was too long.
   (C) She liked it more than the movie reviewer did.
   (D) She found it confusing.

   Question: _____

8. (A) A tuition increase.
   (B) A policy change.
   (C) A new class.
   (D) A recent proposal.

   Question: _____

9. (A) Buy some new software.
   (B) Get her computer fixed.
   (C) Use the computers at the library.
   (D) Borrow his computer.

   Question: _____

10. (A) He doesn't have the right notebook.
    (B) He forgot to bring a pen.
    (C) He went to the wrong lecture hall.
    (D) He was late for the lecture.

    Question: _____

Questions for Set B

(a) What did the woman think about the movie?
(b) What is the man's problem?
(c) What does the man suggest Ann do?
(d) What had the woman assumed about the man?
(e) What information does the man want?
(f) What are they discussing?

Set C

11. (A) His brother helped him move the piano.
    (B) He moved the piano to his brother's house.
    (C) His brother taught him to play the piano.
    (D) He and his brother hired professional movers.

    Question: _____

12. (A) To ask her a question.
    (B) To get her advice.
    (C) To give her a suggestion.
    (D) To disagree with her idea.

    Question: _____

13. (A) Who Katie is.
    (B) What was said.
    (C) When Katie called.
    (D) What the problem was.

    Question: _____

14. (A) She's probably an expert on modern art.
    (B) She didn't paint the picture herself.
    (C) She's just begun to study painting.
    (D) She probably doesn't like modern art.

    Question: _____

15. (A) At the beginning of the spring semester.
    (B) During spring break.
    (C) During final exams.
    (D) Right after final exams.

    Question: _____

Questions for Set C

(a) How does the man feel about the woman's remark?
(b) Why did the man call Professor Wilkey?
(c) What does the woman want to know?
(d) When does this conversation take place?
(e) What does the man mean?
(f) What can be inferred about the woman?

Lesson 2

DIALOGS WITH SOUND CONFUSION

Some of the items in Part A involve a confusion between words that have similar sounds. Here's how they work: one of the speakers uses a word or phrase that sounds like a word or phrase in one or more of the answer choices. If you don't hear the word clearly, you might incorrectly choose an option with a sound-alike word or phrase.

> **Sample Item**
>
> You will hear:*
>
> M1: I've never had this type of fruit before. I don't even know what to do with it.
>
> F1: You just have to peel it and eat it.
>
> M2: What does the woman mean?
>
> You will read:
>
> (A) She doesn't feel like eating fruit.
> (B) The man should take the pill before eating.
> (C) The fruit shouldn't be eaten until it's been peeled.
> (D) She isn't familiar with this type of fruit either.
>
>
>
> The word *feel* in choice (A) sounds like the word *peel* in the dialog. In a different way, the word *pill* in choice (B) also sounds like the word *peel*. Notice that choice (C)—the correct answer—and choice (D) do not contain sound-alike words.

Many sound-alike expressions in Part A are **minimal pairs**. Minimal pairs are two words that are pronounced alike except for one vowel sound (*peel* and *pill*, *lack* and *lake*, *point* and *paint*) or one consonant sound (*peel* and *feel*, *vine* and *wine*, *mop* and *mob*).

Another sound problem involves two words that sound like one word, such as *mark it* and *market*, *sent her* and *center*, *in tents* and *intense*.

A third type of sound problem involves one word that sounds like part of a longer word, such as *nation* and *imagination*, *mind* and *remind*, *give* and *forgive*.

Hint: If an answer choice contains a word that sounds like a word in the spoken sentence, that choice is probably wrong. For example, if you hear the word *spell* and you read the word *spill* in an answer choice, you can usually eliminate that choice.

When you're taking Part A during an actual exam, you can use the **context** of the dialogs to help you solve problems with sound confusion. If you hear and understand all of the dialog, you won't have much trouble eliminating choices involving sound-alike words. However, if you only understand part of a dialog or if you "mis-hear" one or two words, you may easily choose an incorrect answer.

---

* Note: M1 = first male voice   M2 = second male voice   F1 = first female voice   F2 = second female voice

EXERCISE 2.1

Focus: Discriminating between sound-alike words in dialogs and answer choices.

Directions: Listen to the dialogs. Decide which of the two choices, (A) or (B), best answers the question, and mark the appropriate blank. The first one is done as an example.

Now start the tape.

1. _____ (A) Get in a different lane.
   __X__ (B) Stand in another line.

2. _____ (A) Go down the slide.
   _____ (B) Play on the sled.

3. _____ (A) Put them in a file.
   _____ (B) Throw them in a pile.

4. _____ (A) He can't shut his suitcase.
   _____ (B) His suitcase doesn't fit in the closet.

5. _____ (A) She made bread from whole wheat.
   _____ (B) She baked some white bread.

6. _____ (A) It's being typed.
   _____ (B) Brenda is taping it.

7. _____ (A) Emily bought new clothes.
   _____ (B) Emily recently moved.

8. _____ (A) Its taste has improved.
   _____ (B) It tastes slightly bitter.

9. _____ (A) How much the ticket cost.
   _____ (B) What Ellen might win.

10. _____ (A) It's been chipped.
    _____ (B) There's a ship inside it.

11. _____ (A) He tripped in the aisle.
    _____ (B) He slipped in some oil.

12. _____ (A) For its fast horses.
    _____ (B) For its natural resources.

13. _____ (A) Thinking about the decision.
    _____ (B) Arguing about the issue.

14. _____ (A) The color is too bright.
    _____ (B) It doesn't fit around the neck.

15. _____ (A) Wrote his name on the paper.
    _____ (B) Told his students to write a paper.

EXERCISE 2.2

Focus: Identifying sound-alike expressions in answer choices and choosing correct answers.

Directions: Listen to the dialogs. Each dialog contains a word or phrase that sounds like a word or phrase in two of the answer choices. Underline these words. Underline only those words with similar sounds, **not** words that are exactly the same. Then mark the answer choice that has the same meaning as the spoken sentence. (The correct answer will not contain any sound-alike words.) The first one is done as an example.

Now start the tape. If necessary, repeat this exercise to make sure that you have underlined all the sound-alike words.

1. _____ (A) She went to the <u>center</u> with her friend.
   __X__ (B) She wrote her friend a letter.
   _____ (C) She told her friend to call her <u>later</u>.

2. _____ (A) He has an appointment with the president.
   _____ (B) He was just appointed vice president.
   _____ (C) He's unhappy because he lost the election.

3. _____ (A) It is a study of the life of plants.

_____ (B) It concerns the breeding of cattle.

_____ (C) It deals with life on Earth.

4. _____ (A) They can't leave until the rain is over.

_____ (B) Their drain has stopped up.

_____ (C) He shouldn't board the train until it completely stops.

5. _____ (A) He offered his help to Darlene.

_____ (B) He made an offer to Darlene's sister.

_____ (C) When Darlene was gone, he missed her.

6. _____ (A) Get a copy made.

_____ (B) Buy some cough drops.

_____ (C) Eat in the coffee shop.

7. _____ (A) He didn't hear what the woman said.

_____ (B) He can lend the woman a pen.

_____ (C) He had a pain behind his ear.

8. _____ (A) The food in this town isn't very good.

_____ (B) She needed boots when she left home.

_____ (C) The flooding in her neighborhood was severe.

9. _____ (A) She's been weakened by the sickness.

_____ (B) She was awakened by the coughing.

_____ (C) She missed class because of her cough.

10. _____ (A) Evaluate the texts.

_____ (B) Correct the exams.

_____ (C) Collect the tests.

11. _____ (A) His apartment is more comfortable now.

_____ (B) He recently bought a new van.

_____ (C) He's been feeling fine lately.

12. _____ (A) Her name is not on the list.

_____ (B) The lease is difficult to read.

_____ (C) The lawyer told her to call the police.

End of Tape 1, Side A.

Lesson 3

DIALOGS WITH HOMONYMS AND WORDS WITH MULTIPLE MEANINGS

Two words are **homonyms** if they have the same pronunciation but are spelled differently and have different meanings. The words *flour* and *flower*, *bare* and *bear* are homonyms. In some items in Part A, one or more incorrect answer choices refer to a homonym of a word that is used on the tape, as in the example below.

Sample Item

You will hear:*

M1: Eugene missed a lot of classes last week.
F1: That's because he was sick. I think he had the flu.
M2: What is learned about Eugene?

You will read:

(A) He has been feeling weak for a long time.
(B) Because of sickness, Eugene was absent.
(C) Eugene's eyesight isn't very strong, so he needs glasses.
(D) Eugene flew to another city this week.

(A) ● (C) (D)

The dialog contains the word *week*, meaning a seven-day period. Choices (A) and (C) refer to a homonym of that word, *weak*, which means *not strong*. The dialog also contains the word *flu*, an illness similar to a bad cold. Choice (D) refers to a homonym of that word, *flew* (took a trip by plane).

The dialogs may also contain **words with multiple meanings**. In these items, one or two of the answer choices refer to another definition of a word as it is used in the dialog.

---

* Note: M1 = first male voice   M2 = second male voice   F1 = first female voice   F2 = second female voice

Sample Item

You will hear:*

F1: Are you sure this is how Lois spells her last name?
M1: It doesn't look right, does it? In fact, I'm not even sure it starts with that letter.
M2: What does the man mean?

You will read:

(A) The letter to Lois was incorrectly addressed.
(B) Lois' last name may be incorrectly spelled.
(C) Lois' name appeared on the right side of the page.
(D) Lois hasn't begun writing the letter yet.

Ⓐ ● Ⓒ Ⓓ

The dialog contains the words *right*, meaning "correct," and the word *letter*, meaning a character in the alphabet. Choices (A) and (D) also contain the word *letter*, but in those choices the word has another definition—a message sent through the mail. Choice (C) also contains the word *right*, but in that choice, it refers to a direction—the opposite of left.

You won't be confused by these items if you understand the entire sentence. Again, the **context** of the sentence can help you choose the correct answer. But if you focus only on single words, like *week* and *flu* or *letter* and *right* in the two samples, you can easily make mistakes.

EXERCISE 3.1

Focus: Using the context of dialogs to identify homonyms.

Directions: Listen to the dialogs. Decide which of the pair of homonyms appears in the dialogs and mark the appropriate answer, (A) or (B). The first one is done as an example.

Now start the tape.

1. _____ (A) presence
   __X__ (B) presents

2. _____ (A) overdue
   _____ (B) overdo

3. _____ (A) pain
   _____ (B) pane

4. _____ (A) where
   _____ (B) wear

5. _____ (A) fined
   _____ (B) find

6. _____ (A) right
   _____ (B) write

7. _____ (A) board
   _____ (B) bored

8. _____ (A) brakes
   _____ (B) breaks

9. _____ (A) sail
   _____ (B) sale

10. _____ (A) site
    _____ (B) sight

11. _____ (A) rose
    _____ (B) rows

12. _____ (A) aloud
    _____ (B) allowed

_____
* Note: M1 = first male voice   M2 = second male voice   F1 = first female voice   F2 = second female voice

EXERCISE 3.2

Focus: Using the context of dialogs to identify the definitions of words with multiple meanings.

Directions: Listen to the dialogs. One word from the dialog is given, along with two possible definitions of the word. Choose the definition of the word as it is used in the dialog and mark the appropriate answer, (A) or (B). The first one is done as an example.

Now start the tape.

1. cold

    __X__ (A) minor illness

    _____ (B) chilly weather

2. kind

    _____ (A) type

    _____ (B) considerate

3. light

    _____ (A) not heavy

    _____ (B) not dark

4. wing

    _____ (A) part of an airplane

    _____ (B) part of a building

5. tables

    _____ (A) charts

    _____ (B) furniture

6. coat

    _____ (A) layer

    _____ (B) warm clothing

7. field

    _____ (A) outside the classroom

    _____ (B) area of study

8. playing

    _____ (A) taking part in a game

    _____ (B) appearing

9. party

    _____ (A) celebration

    _____ (B) group

10. period

    _____ (A) punctuation mark

    _____ (B) class time

EXERCISE 3.3

Focus: Using the context of dialogs to answer questions involving both homonyms and words with multiple definitions.

Directions: Listen to the statements. Decide which of the two choices best answers the question, and mark the appropriate answer, (A) or (B). The first one is done as an example.

Now start the tape.

1. __X__ (A) Look for mistakes.

    _____ (B) Write a check.

2. _____ (A) Events in the past.

    _____ (B) The man's performance in class.

3. _____ (A) He'd never heard buffaloes before.

    _____ (B) This was the first herd he'd ever seen.

4. _____ (A) Follow the directions on the sign.

    _____ (B) Sign up for another class.

5. _____ (A) Buy a second suit.

    _____ (B) Consider it for a little while.

6. _____ (A) He can't carry the luggage by himself.

    _____ (B) The handle on the suitcase is broken.

7. _____ (A) He was surprised by the rain.

_____ (B) He just got out of the shower.

8. _____ (A) The class has a better opinion of him.

_____ (B) He was standing in front of the class.

9. _____ (A) She works in an office by herself.

_____ (B) She's in charge of making loans.

10. _____ (A) She's sorry the seminar is over.

_____ (B) She was often absent from the seminar.

11. _____ (A) They can park their car at the zoo.

_____ (B) The park is located near the zoo.

12. _____ (A) If she has some money for a phone call.

_____ (B) If her phone number has changed recently.

Lesson 4

DIALOGS WITH IDIOMATIC EXPRESSIONS

On many TOEFL exams, up to half the dialogs in Part A contain idiomatic expressions. Many of the idiomatic expressions are two- or three-word verbs, such as *call off* and *look out for*.

Sample Item

You will hear:*

F1: I wonder where Mike is.

M1: He'll show up as soon as the work is done, I bet.

M2: What does the man say about Mike?

You will read:

(A) He probably won't arrive until the work is finished.
(B) He went to a show instead of going to work.
(C) He can show them how to do the work.
(D) He'll probably work late today.

The idiom *show up* means "arrive." Choices (B) and (C) contain the word *show* but it is not used in the idiomatic sense.

In most dialogs, the second speaker uses the idiomatic expression. Most questions about this type of dialog are questions about meaning ("What does the man mean?" for example), but some are inference questions or other types of questions. The correct answer often contains a synonym for the idiom (*arrive* for *show up* in choice (A) of the Sample Item). Incorrect choices often contain references to the literal meaning of idioms, as in choices (B) and (D).

The Mini-Lessons for Section 1, at the end of the Listening Comprehension section (pages 93–111), are intended to familiarize you with a large number of idioms. You should work on these lessons and study these expressions as often as possible.

However, memorizing these phrases does not guarantee that you will recognize all the idiomatic expressions that you will hear in the Listening Comprehension section. There are, after all, thousands of these expressions in English. You must develop "a good ear" for guessing the meaning of idioms. The context of the sentence will help you understand the expression, even if you're unfamiliar with it.

---

* Note: M1 = first male voice   M2 = second male voice   F1 = first female voice   F2 = second female voice

EXERCISE 4.1

Focus: Recognizing synonyms for idiomatic expressions.

Directions: Listen to the spoken statements. Each contains an idiomatic or figurative expression that is written out. First decide which of the two choices best answers the question, and mark the appropriate answer, (A) or (B). Then underline the phrase in the correct answer that has the same meaning as the idiom. If necessary, rewind the tape and listen to the exercise again. The first one has been done as an example.

Now start the tape.

1. get in hot water

   X____ (A) She <u>was in trouble</u>.

   _____ (B) She took a warm bath.

2. bump into

   _____ (A) He met Caroline unexpectedly at the coffee shop.

   _____ (B) Caroline and I jogged to the coffee shop.

3. hit it off

   _____ (A) He and Chuck argued as soon as they met.

   _____ (B) He and Chuck quickly became friends.

4. piece of cake

   _____ (A) The exam was simple.

   _____ (B) She had a snack after the test.

5. at the drop of a hat

   _____ (A) He can't leave until he finds his hat.

   _____ (B) He's ready to leave immediately.

6. on edge

   _____ (A) He walks back and forth when he's nervous.

   _____ (B) He likes to walk along the edge.

7. under the weather

   _____ (A) She didn't want to practice because of the bad weather.

   _____ (B) She wasn't there because she felt a little sick.

8. take after

   _____ (A) He looks like his grandfather.

   _____ (B) He takes care of his grandfather.

9. for good

   _____ (A) He doesn't want the professor to quit teaching permanently.

   _____ (B) He hopes Professor Holmes has a good reason for quitting.

10. give a hand with

    _____ (A) Hand her the box.

    _____ (B) Help her carry the box.

11. a stone's throw

    _____ (A) He likes to throw rocks in the park.

    _____ (B) He lives close to the park.

12. not think much of

    _____ (A) She didn't consider it.

    _____ (B) She didn't like it.

EXERCISE 4.2

Focus: Understanding dialogs involving idiomatic and figurative expressions.

Directions: Look over the idiomatic expressions listed before each set of items. If you are unfamiliar with any of the idioms, you may want to look them up in the "Mini-Lessons for Section 1" that follow the Listening Comprehension portion of this book (pages 14–111). The dialogs each contain one of the listed expressions. Listen to the dialogs, and mark the one answer choice, (A) or (B), that best answers the question. The first one has been done as an example.

Now start the tape.

Set A

clear up	push one's luck
get off the ground	run of the mill
hours on end	short for
over one's head	turn in

1. __X__ (A) He's not sure Max's business will succeed.

_____ (B) He doesn't know where Max has gone.

2. _____ (A) Gary is lucky to have such a good car.

_____ (B) It's time for Gary to get some new tires.

3. _____ (A) Go to bed.

_____ (B) Watch a different program.

4. _____ (A) She didn't understand all the jokes.

_____ (B) She left before the performance was over.

5. _____ (A) If the weather gets better.

_____ (B) If she doesn't have any other plans.

6. _____ (A) Elizabeth is taller than Liz.

_____ (B) People call Elizabeth "Liz."

7. _____ (A) She's stopped listening to it.

_____ (B) She listens to it constantly.

8. _____ (A) The service is very fast there.

_____ (B) It's just an average restaurant.

Set B

believe one's eyes   lend a hand
a breeze   look who's talking
chip in   music to one's ears
get in one's blood   what the doctor ordered

9. _____ (A) Ice water sounds perfect.

_____ (B) The doctor told her to drink a lot of water.

10. _____ (A) Skiing can be a dangerous sport.

_____ (B) It's easy to get into the habit of skiing.

11. _____ (A) She enjoys the sound of nature.

_____ (B) She wishes she'd brought a radio.

12. _____ (A) She wants to talk to Norman.

_____ (B) Norman doesn't study much himself.

13. _____ (A) There's not enough wind to go sailing today.

_____ (B) It won't be too hard to learn to sail.

14. _____ (A) Asks the man if he needs some money.

_____ (B) Asks the man if he wants some help.

15. _____ (A) They'll all pay for the gasoline.

_____ (B) Gasoline is very inexpensive.

16. _____ (A) She doesn't think the man is telling he truth.

_____ (B) She was surprised to see the snow.

Set C

by heart   see one off
call it a day   slowly but surely
come around   take a lot of nerve
go without saying   take into account
ring a bell

17. _____ (A) She seems too nervous.

_____ (B) She took a bold approach.

18. _____ (A) He doesn't want to do any more painting today.

_____ (B) He'll phone the woman later today.

19. _____ (A) She spoke the lines in an emotional way.

_____ (B) She's memorized all the lines.

20. _____ (A) At some point, they'll agree to let her go.

_____ (B) They'll come with her to Alaska.

21. _____ (A) Rob Martin hasn't called him yet.

_____ (B) He doesn't think Rob Martin was on the team.

22. _____ (A) He didn't count his money carefully.

_____ (B) He forgot about the tax.

23. _____ (A) She's making steady progress.

_____ (B) She thinks the work is going too slowly.

24. _____ (A) Of course she was sorry that Molly left.

_____ (B) Molly left without saying goodbye.

EXERCISE 4.3

Focus: Using the context of dialogs to understand the meaning of idioms.

Directions: Listen to the following dialog. Decide which of the choices—(A), (B), or (C)—best answers the question about the dialog, and mark the appropriate answer. The first one is done as an example.

Now start the tape.

1. _____ (A) Go to work with Jim.
   _____ (B) Go out for coffee.
   __X__ (C) Get some exercise.

2. _____ (A) If the woman will go to the party with him.
   _____ (B) If the red tie looks good with his shirt.
   _____ (C) If he should wear a tie to the party.

3. _____ (A) She missed Friday's class too.
   _____ (B) They both missed class because they were sailing.
   _____ (C) He should take better notes during Professor Morrison's class.

4. _____ (A) He cut himself while he was preparing food.
   _____ (B) He doesn't want to work in a restaurant.
   _____ (C) He's planning to open up his own restaurant.

5. _____ (A) He wants to know if the woman is joking.
   _____ (B) He wants the woman to leave him alone.
   _____ (C) He'd like to know what the quiz will be about.

6. _____ (A) The program was canceled.
   _____ (B) The shuttle was launched yesterday.
   _____ (C) The launch was delayed.

7. _____ (A) She stood up and left the lecture.
   _____ (B) She was waiting outside the lecture hall.
   _____ (C) Her sweater made her easy to spot.

8. _____ (A) He deserved to get a ticket.
   _____ (B) He was going to a good restaurant.
   _____ (C) He probably wasn't speeding.

9. _____ (A) He'll be glad to help.
   _____ (B) If he helps, it will save the man some money.
   _____ (C) He won't be very cooperative.

10. _____ (A) It's about buying large real estate properties.
    _____ (B) There are too many students in his class.
    _____ (C) In general, he likes his real estate class.

11. _____ (A) The man didn't get Jill a watch.
    _____ (B) The weather will be cool on graduation day.
    _____ (C) Jill won't be graduating.

12. _____ (A) She ordinarily works in a florist shop.
    _____ (B) In the end, she won't have a problem.
    _____ (C) She wears too much perfume to work.

13. _____ (A) She doesn't want any fruit.
    _____ (B) She doesn't want to celebrate her birthday.
    _____ (C) She doesn't like candy.

40

14. _____ (A) He doesn't have any questions for her.

_____ (B) He won't be able to take a trip.

_____ (C) He can't study during spring break.

15. _____ (A) Mick's father told him to go to medical school.

_____ (B) Mick's father studied medicine.

_____ (C) Mick and his father walked to the school.

16. _____ (A) Fred would be upset if he'd lost money.

_____ (B) Fred shouldn't be paid for singing.

_____ (C) Fred is generally very sympathetic.

17. _____ (A) If Wally has been injured.

_____ (B) If Wally has been informed.

_____ (C) If Wally's trip has been canceled.

18. _____ (A) He can't find some of his pictures.

_____ (B) He didn't go to the Grand Canyon.

_____ (C) Not all of his photos were good.

19. _____ (A) She thinks they're certain to do well.

_____ (B) She thinks they're talented but lack experience.

_____ (C) She doesn't like their style of photography.

20. _____ (A) The lake is not very scenic.

_____ (B) Her parents won't let them use the cabin.

_____ (C) The cabin is not luxurious.

End of Tape 1, Side B.

Lesson 5

ANSWERING INFERENCE QUESTIONS ABOUT DIALOGS

Sometimes the answer to a question about a dialog is not directly stated in the dialog. How can you answer this type of question? You must be able to make an **inference** about the dialog. In other words, information in the dialog will indirectly provide you with the answer to the question.

This type of question can be phrased in two ways:

- What does the man/woman imply?
- What can be inferred from the conversation?

Some inference questions involve **overstatement**, or exaggeration.

F: Are you interested in selling your car?
M: Sure—if someone has a million dollars!

Because of the exaggeration, we can infer that the man doesn't want to sell his car at all.

Sample Item

You will hear:*

M1: Can I take this bus to the art museum?
F1: No, this bus goes north to Bank Street. You want a bus that goes the opposite way.
M2: What can be inferred from this conversation?

You will read:

(A) The man needs to take a south-bound bus.
(B) There is no bus to the museum.
(C) It takes a long time to get to the museum by bus.
(D) The art museum is on Bank Street.

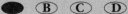

This information can be inferred, because the first bus is going north, but the man must take a bus going in the opposite direction to get to the art museum. Choice (B) is incorrect; it IS possible to get to the museum by bus. There is no information about (C). Choice (D) can't be true because Bank Street is where the first bus is going.

---

* Note: M1 = first male voice   M2 = second male voice   F1 = first female voice   F2 = second female voice

Peterson's TOEFL CBT Success

EXERCISE 5

Focus: Listening to dialogs that are followed by inference questions and identifying the best answers.
Directions: Listen to the following dialogs. Decide which of the three choices—(A), (B), or (C)—best answers the question, and mark the appropriate answer. The first one is done as an example.
Now start the tape.

1. _____ (A) He's not related to Larry.
   _____ (B) He doesn't believe Larry won the contest.
   __X__ (C) He's not a very good dancer.

2. _____ (A) The suit costs a lot of money.
   _____ (B) The man dresses as if he were very wealthy.
   _____ (C) The man already has an expensive suit.

3. _____ (A) There is just enough food.
   _____ (B) Many uninvited guests will come.
   _____ (C) The woman has prepared too much food.

4. _____ (A) Dave is a painter.
   _____ (B) Dave's apartment has been recently painted.
   _____ (C) Dave's brother doesn't like the smell of paint.

5. _____ (A) He's changed his major often.
   _____ (B) He hasn't really changed his major.
   _____ (C) He won't do well in his new major.

6. _____ (A) His lectures put his students to sleep.
   _____ (B) He's a middle-aged man.
   _____ (C) He lectures about history.

7. _____ (A) He hasn't been to the dentist for years.
   _____ (B) He wasn't able to see the dentist yesterday.
   _____ (C) Before he saw the dentist, he had a long wait.

8. _____ (A) They have agreed on it.
   _____ (B) They have different opinions about it.
   _____ (C) It depends on their cooperation.

9. _____ (A) Louis' new boss shouldn't have been promoted.
   _____ (B) Louis and his old boss argued.
   _____ (C) Louis should get a better job.

10. _____ (A) There's not enough snow to cause a cancellation yet.
    _____ (B) It will probably snow all night.
    _____ (C) The university has already decided to cancel classes.

11. _____ (A) He's been interested in folk dancing for a long time.
    _____ (B) He's interested in making new friends.
    _____ (C) He wants to form a new folk-dancing club.

12. _____ (A) She didn't enjoy the music.
    _____ (B) She couldn't see the concert very well.
    _____ (C) She had a good seat near the stage.

13. _____ (A) Last summer was even hotter.
    _____ (B) This is the hottest summer he can remember.
    _____ (C) He didn't live here last year.

14. _____ (A) Students must pay to swim in the pool.
    _____ (B) The public cannot use the pool on campus.
    _____ (C) The pool can be used by students for free.

15. _____
- (A) They can't see the stars clearly.
- (B) They're not in the city tonight.
- (C) They are looking at the lights of the city.

16. _____
- (A) He doesn't know many people at work.
- (B) He wasn't expecting a phone call.
- (C) He's not allowed to get phone calls at work.

17. _____
- (A) Those aren't Shelly's photographs.
- (B) Shelly has begun to take color photographs.
- (C) Shelly took the photographs hanging in the hall.

18. _____
- (A) That scarf looks great on Fran.
- (B) Fran wears that scarf too often.
- (C) In this weather, Fran needs a scarf.

19. _____
- (A) She doesn't have an accent.
- (B) Her parents have very strong accents.
- (C) Her accent is stronger than her parents'.

20. _____
- (A) Robert usually has trouble skiing.
- (B) That's not a difficult slope.
- (C) Robert is an excellent skier.

Lesson 6

DIALOGS INVOLVING AGREEMENT AND DISAGREEMENT

To answer questions about some of the dialogs in Part A, it is necessary to understand if the second speaker agrees or disagrees with the first speaker's ideas or proposals.

There are many ways to express agreement and disagreement:

Agreement

So do I.
Me too.
Neither do I.*
I don't either.*
Who wouldn't?
Isn't he/she/it though! (Didn't he/
   Wasn't she/Hasn't it though!)

I'll second that. I'll say!
You can say that again.
Is/Has/Was it ever!
You bet!
I couldn't agree with you more.
I feel the same way you do about it.

*These two expressions show agreement with a negative statement:

    I don't really like my schedule this term.
    I don't either. *OR* Neither do I.

Disagreement

I don't think so.
That's not what I think.
That's not the way I see it.
I can't say I agree.
I couldn't agree with you less.
I'm afraid I don't agree.

Probably not.
Not necessarily.
Not really.
I'm afraid not.
I'm not so sure.

There are, of course, other expressions that show agreement and disagreement. Some are practiced in the exercises.

Sample Items

You will hear:*

M1: Howard certainly is a talented journalist.

F1: Isn't he though!

M2: What does the woman mean?

You will read:

(A) She doesn't know if Howard is a journalist.
(B) She agrees that Howard is talented.
(C) She read Howard's journal.
(D) She doesn't think Howard is talented.

(A) ● (C) (D)

Although the woman's reply seems negative in form, it actually signals agreement. Therefore, the best answer is (B).

You will hear:*

F1: I thought Cheryl's photographs were the best at the exhibit.

M1: I didn't really see it that way.

M2: What does the man mean?

You will hear:

(A) He thought Cheryl's photos were the best.
(B) He didn't look at Cheryl's photos.
(C) He thought other photos were better than Cheryl's.
(D) He didn't go to the exhibit.

(A) (B) ● (D)

The man's response, "I didn't really see it that way," means that he disagreed with the woman's opinion that Cheryl's photographs were the best. The best answer is therefore (C).

EXERCISE 6.1

Focus: Determining if one speaker agrees or disagrees with the other speaker.

Directions: Listen to the following dialogs. Decide if the second speaker agrees or disagrees with the first speaker, and mark the appropriate blank. The first one is done as an example.

Now start the tape.

1. __X__ (A) Agrees
   _____ (B) Disagrees

2. _____ (A) Agrees
   _____ (B) Disagrees

3. _____ (A) Agrees
   _____ (B) Disagrees

4. _____ (A) Agrees
   _____ (B) Disagrees

5. _____ (A) Agrees
   _____ (B) Disagrees

6. _____ (A) Agrees
   _____ (B) Disagrees

7. _____ (A) Agrees
   _____ (B) Disagrees

8. _____ (A) Agrees
   _____ (B) Disagrees

---

* Note: M1 = first male voice   M2 = second male voice   F1 = first female voice   F2 = second female voice

9. _____ (A) Agrees
   _____ (B) Disagrees

10. _____ (A) Agrees
    _____ (B) Disagrees

11. _____ (A) Agrees
    _____ (B) Disagrees

12. _____ (A) Agrees
    _____ (B) Disagrees

EXERCISE 6.2

Focus: Listening to dialogs that involve agreement and disagreement and answering questions about them.

Directions: Listen to the following dialogs. Decide which choice—(A), (B), or (C)—best answers the question, and mark the appropriate answer. The first one is done as an example.

Now start the tape.

1. __X__ (A) He prefers taking a final exam.
   _____ (B) He thinks an exam takes too much time.
   _____ (C) He'd rather write a research paper.

2. _____ (A) It was difficult, but she understood it.
   _____ (B) It wasn't very useful.
   _____ (C) It's probably easier than the other chapters.

3. _____ (A) He completely disagrees with it.
   _____ (B) He doesn't believe the university will accept it.
   _____ (C) He thinks it's a good one.

4. _____ (A) She doesn't think that Jack wrote it.
   _____ (B) She thinks it had too many details.
   _____ (C) She found it well-written.

5. _____ (A) He thinks it's a good day for bike riding too.
   _____ (B) He doesn't agree with the woman's opinion of the weather.
   _____ (C) He didn't hear what the woman said.

6. _____ (A) Arthur wasn't doing well in the class.
   _____ (B) He's not sure why Arthur dropped the class.
   _____ (C) He believes Arthur dropped the class for no reason.

7. _____ (A) It might work.
   _____ (B) It's very impractical.
   _____ (C) It's unnecessary.

8. _____ (A) He didn't understand it.
   _____ (B) It made him angry.
   _____ (C) He agreed with it.

9. _____ (A) She's never been there during final exam week.
   _____ (B) It's crowded because students will be taking exams soon.
   _____ (C) It's not crowded now, but it soon will be.

10. _____ (A) He likes the costumes Madelyn made.
    _____ (B) He wouldn't recommend the play.
    _____ (C) He doesn't think the costumes are attractive.

11. _____ (A) It was very happy.
    _____ (B) It was exciting.
    _____ (C) It was unhappy.

12. _____ (A) She thinks Pamela is right.
    _____ (B) She thinks the regulations are fair.
    _____ (C) She disagrees with the man's opinion.

Lesson 7

DIALOGS INVOLVING SUGGESTIONS, INVITATIONS, OFFERS, AND REQUESTS

A number of dialogs in Part A involve a speaker making and/or responding to **suggestions**, **invitations**, **offers**, and **requests**. There are many ways to express these language functions. Some are listed in the charts in this lesson, while others are practiced in the exercises.

SUGGESTIONS

These are pieces of advice that one speaker gives another. In most dialogs, the first speaker poses a problem and the second speaker suggests a possible solution to that problem. In some dialogs, the first speaker makes a suggestion, and the second speaker responds to that suggestion positively or negatively.

Making Suggestions

Why don't you/we . . .
Why not . . .
Have you ever thought of . . .
You/We might want to . . .
You/We could always . . .
Maybe you/we could . . .
Try . . .

If I were you . . .
If I were in your shoes . . .
You/We should . . .
Shouldn't you/we . . .
What about . . .
What if you/we . . .
How about . . .

Positive Responses

Why not!
Good idea!
That's an idea.
Sounds good to me.
By all means!
Why didn't I think of that?
That's worth a try.
Thanks, I'll give that a try.

Negative Responses

I don't think so.
I don't believe so.
I already thought of that.
I don't think that will work.
Don't look at me!
Can I take a rain check?*

* This means, "Could we do this some other time?"

Sample Item

You will hear:*

M1: I'm doing so poorly in math class, I think I'm going to have to drop it.

F1: You know, Frank, you should talk to Professor de Marco before you do anything. He's given special help to lots of students who were having trouble.

M2: What does the woman suggest Frank do?

You will read:

(A) Study with a group of students.
(B) Drop his mathematics course.
(C) Discuss the problem with the professor.
(D) Take no action at this time.

The woman suggests that the man talk to Professor de Marco because the professor has helped many students in the past.

INVITATIONS

These are requests for someone to come somewhere or to take part in some activity. The first speaker may invite the second speaker to do something, and the second speaker responds, or the second speaker may invite the first speaker to do something.

Making Invitations

Shall we . . .
Would you like to . . .
Would you care to . . .
Would you be able to . . .
Want to . . .

Let's . . .
Do you want to . . .
Could you . . .
Can you . . .

Positive Responses

Yes, let's.
Sure, thanks.
Sounds good.
All right, I'd love to.
I'd like that.
What a great idea!
Sure. Thanks for inviting me.
If you want me to.
Don't mind if I do.

Negative Responses

I'm sorry, but . . .
I'd like to, but . . .
I'd love to, but . . .
Thanks a lot, but . . .
That sounds nice, but . . .
I'll pass.
Thanks for the invitation, but . . .
I don't think I'll be able to make it this time.

---

* Note: M1 = first male voice   M2 = second male voice   F1 = first female voice   F2 = second female voice

Sample Item

You will hear:*

M1: Would you like to join us on Sunday? We're going to go on a picnic at the lake.
F1: I'd love to, but I have a test Monday, and I have to get ready for it.
M2: What will the woman probably do on Sunday?

You will read:

(A) Study for a test.
(B) Go on a picnic.
(C) Take an exam.
(D) Join a club.

    B **C** **D**

The man invites the woman to come to a picnic. The woman says that she'd love to go, but that she must study for a test she is taking Monday. (If the woman had accepted the man's invitation, choice (B) would have been correct.)

OFFERS

These are proposals to help someone or allow someone to do something. Either speaker in the dialog may make an offer.

Making Offers

Let me . . .
Shall I . . .
Would you like me to . . .
Do you want me to . . .

Can I . . .
May I . . .
Should I . . .
I could . . .

Positive Responses

That would be nice.
Yes, please.
Please do.
Sure, thanks.

Negative Responses

I don't think so.
I'm afraid not.
That won't be necessary.
Thanks anyway.
Please don't.

---

* Note: M1 = first male voice   M2 = second male voice   F1 = first female voice   F2 = second female voice

Peterson's TOEFL CBT Success

Sample Item

You will hear:*

F1: Should I make reservations for dinner Friday night?
M1: Thanks anyway, but I've already made them.
M2: What does the man mean?

You will read:

(A) He can't go to dinner Friday night.
(B) Reservations won't be required.
(C) He made reservations earlier.
(D) He'd like the woman to make reservations.

  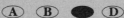

The woman offers to make reservations, but the man replies that he's already made them.

REQUESTS

To make a request is to ask someone to do something, or to ask for help or information.

Making Requests

Would you . . .   Will you . . .
Could you/I . . .   May I . . .
Do you mind if . . .   Can you/I . . .
Would you mind if . . .

Positive Responses

I'd be glad to.
I'd be delighted.
Sure thing.
Certainly.
Why not?
If you want to.
If you'd like.
You bet.
*Not at all.
*Of course not.

Negative Responses

Sorry, but . . .
I'm afraid not.
I'd like to, but . . .
I wish I could, but . . .
*Actually, I do/would.
*I'm afraid I do/would.
*As a matter of fact, I do/would.

* Responses for "Do you mind if . . ." or "Would you mind if . . ."

* Note: M1 = first male voice   M2 = second male voice   F1 = first female voice   F2 = second female voice

Sample Item

You will hear:*

M1: I have to make one more phone call before I go.

F2: Take your time. Would you just lock the door when you finish?

M2: What does the woman want the man to do?

You will read:

(A) Lock the office.
(B) Finish his phone call quickly.
(C) Tell her what time it is.
(D) Look up a phone number.

● Ⓑ Ⓒ Ⓓ

The woman requests that the man lock up the office.

EXERCISE 7.1

Focus: Identifying suggestions, invitations, offers, and requests and responses to them.

Directions: Listen to the following dialogs. Decide which of the two choices best completes the sentence, and mark the appropriate space. The first one is done as an example.

Now start the tape.

1. The man is . . .

   __X__ (A) declining an offer

   _____ (B) making a suggestion

2. The woman is . . .

   _____ (A) accepting an invitation

   _____ (B) making an offer

3. The woman is . . .

   _____ (A) declining an offer

   _____ (B) making a suggestion

4. Mark is . . .

   _____ (A) rejecting a request

   _____ (B) agreeing to a request

5. The woman is . . .

   _____ (A) giving an invitation

   _____ (B) making a suggestion

6. The man is . . .

   _____ (A) agreeing to a request

   _____ (B) turning down an offer

7. Ed is probably going to . . .

   _____ (A) receive a suggestion

   _____ (B) make an offer

8. The woman is . . .

   _____ (A) suggesting a solution

   _____ (B) offering help

9. Cynthia is . . .

   _____ (A) giving an invitation

   _____ (B) accepting an offer

10. The woman is . . .

   _____ (A) declining an offer

   _____ (B) making a request

* Note: M1 = first male voice   M2 = second male voice   F1 = first female voice   F2 = second female voice

Peterson's TOEFL CBT Success

11. The man will probably . . .

_____ (A) do what the woman suggests

_____ (B) turn down the woman's invitation

12. Bob is . . .

_____ (A) agreeing to an offer

_____ (B) refusing a request

13. The man is . . .

_____ (A) making a suggestion

_____ (B) accepting an invitation

14. The man is . . .

_____ (A) requesting that the man do something

_____ (B) giving the woman a suggestion

15. Paul is . . .

_____ (A) rejecting a suggestion

_____ (B) agreeing with a suggestion

16. James tells the woman that . . .

_____ (A) he can't accept her invitation

_____ (B) he'd enjoy another sandwich

EXERCISE 7.2

Focus: Listening to dialogs involving suggestions, invitations, offers, and requests and answering questions about them.

Directions: Listen to the following dialog. Decide which choice—(A), (B), or (C)—best answers the question about the dialogs, and mark the appropriate answer. The first one is done as an example.

1. _____ (A) He would like a cigarette.

    _____ (B) The woman can smoke if she likes.

    __X__ (C) He doesn't want the woman to smoke.

2. _____ (A) The man wears it quite often.

    _____ (B) It needs to be cleaned.

    _____ (C) The man should wear it.

3. _____ (A) Make more popcorn.

    _____ (B) Go to another theater.

    _____ (C) Buy some popcorn.

4. _____ (A) She could plan the trip.

    _____ (B) She may not feel well.

    _____ (C) She can go on the class trip.

5. _____ (A) He doesn't want more coffee.

    _____ (B) He doesn't want to use his credit card.

    _____ (C) He'd like to make coffee.

6. _____ (A) She doesn't think it's warm.

    _____ (B) She'll open the window herself.

    _____ (C) She wants the window closed.

7. _____ (A) The soup is more expensive than sandwiches.

    _____ (B) She doesn't know what kind of soup there is.

    _____ (C) The man might enjoy some soup.

8. _____ (A) The kitchen also needs cleaning.

    _____ (B) The living room doesn't have to be cleaned.

    _____ (C) The man shouldn't do the cleaning.

9. _____ (A) Go with her to the registrar's office.

    _____ (B) Help her find her way to the registrar's office.

    _____ (C) Tell her where to get her own map.

10. _____ (A) Work on their chemistry homework.

    _____ (B) Have breakfast.

    _____ (C) Stop studying for a little while.

11. _____ (A) Buy a new toaster.

    _____ (B) Replace her old shoes.

    _____ (C) Have repairs done.

12. _____ (A) He'd like her to go away.

    _____ (B) She can read his magazine.

    _____ (C) He hasn't finished reading.

13. _____ (A) Get an antique desk.

    _____ (B) Buy a new computer.

    _____ (C) Sit down and get to work.

14. _____ (A) He's already passed the test.

    _____ (B) He doesn't like to study at the library.

    _____ (C) He doesn't plan to study tonight.

15. _____ (A) He hasn't seen the letters.

    _____ (B) He doesn't know the right answers.

    _____ (C) He doesn't want to respond to the letters.

16. _____ (A) She wants to go even though it's raining.

    _____ (B) She can't come to lunch today.

    _____ (C) She'll pay for their lunch.

Lesson 8

DIALOGS INVOLVING CONTRADICTIONS, ASSUMPTIONS, AND QUESTIONS

CONTRADICTIONS

These involve the second speaker correcting what the first speaker says, as in the samples below:

Sample Item

You will hear:*

F2: Amy didn't work overtime last week.
M1: As a matter of fact, she *did*.
M2: What does the man say about Amy?

You will read:

(A) She is always late for work.
(B) She never works overtime.
(C) She worked extra hours last week.
(D) She hasn't had her job very long.

The man's emphatic use of the auxiliary verb *did* shows that he is contradicting what the woman said.

You will hear:*

M1: Martin always talks about how he loves to dance.
F1: Yes, but you don't see him out on the dance floor very often, do you?
M2: What does the woman say about Martin?

You will read:

(A) He is an excellent dancer.
(B) He doesn't like dancing very much.
(C) He doesn't talk about dancing very often.
(D) He goes dancing four times a week.

The woman's use of the word *but* and the tag question ("...do you?") suggest that she doesn't believe that George really loves to dance.

---

* Note: M1 = first male voice   M2 = second male voice   F1 = first female voice   F2 = second female voice

Sampel Items (Continued)

You will hear:*

F1: All of the students voted for the proposal to expand the Student Council.

M1: Well, most of them did, anyway.

M2: What does the man mean?

You will read:

(A) All of the students voted.
(B) Some of the students opposed the proposal.
(C) The proposal was defeated.
(D) The Student Council voted.

The man says that most of the students voted for the proposal, contradicting the idea that all of them did. Therefore, some of the students must have opposed the proposal.

In some dialogs, such as the third Sample Item, the second speaker does not completely contradict what the first speaker says but rather limits the first speaker's idea.

ASSUMPTIONS

These are the beliefs that one speaker has until he or she receives information from a second speaker. You will generally hear dialogs involving assumptions near the end of Part A. These questions are considered difficult, but once you understand how they work and practice answering them, you should find them no more difficult than any other type of question. In this type of dialog, the first speaker makes a statement. The second speaker is surprised because the first statement contradicts what he or she believes to be true. The second speaker's response often begins with the word "Oh" and ends with the phrase " . . . after all." The answer to assumption questions is the reverse of what the second speaker thinks, and so what is "true" according to the first speaker is not the correct choice.

Sample Item

You will hear:*

F1: No, Judy's not here right now. She's at her economics class.

M1: Oh, so she decided to take that course after all.

M2: What had the man assumed about Judy?

You will read:

(A) She wouldn't take the course.
(B) She had already completed that course.
(C) She was busy studying economics.
(D) She wouldn't find economics difficult.

The man is surprised that Judy is in economics class because he thought that she had decided not to take the course. Therefore, he had obviously assumed that Judy was not going to take the course before he spoke to the woman.

---

* Note: M1 = first male voice   M2 = second male voice   F1 = first female voice   F2 = second female voice

QUESTIONS

The second speaker in a dialog sometimes asks about what the first speaker says. The third speaker then asks what the second speaker wanted to know.

Sample Item

You will hear:*

F1: Professor Petrakis said that Mark Twain was his favorite writer.

M1: When did he say that?

M2: What does the man want to know?

You will read:

(A) When Mark Twain lived.
(B) What the professor said about Mark Twain.
(C) When the professor made his remark.
(D) What books Mark Twain wrote.

(A)　(B)　●　(D)

The man asks when Professor Petrakis called Mark Twain his favorite author.

Two question phrases that may give you trouble are *What . . . for?* and *How come . . .?* Both mean *Why . . . ?*

EXERCISE 8

Focus: Answering questions about dialogs involving contradictions, assumptions, and questions.

Directions: Listen to the following dialogs. Decide which one of the answer choices—(A), (B), or (C)—is correct, and mark the appropriate answer. The first one is done as an example.

Now start the tape.

1. _____ (A) Ginny is definitely coming to dinner.

    _____ (B) Ginny likes fish better than chicken.

    ✗ (C) Ginny likes chicken.

2. _____ (A) She had already moved.

    _____ (B) She hadn't found a new apartment yet.

    _____ (C) She'd already made an appointment.

3. _____ (A) What the man's name is.

    _____ (B) Who told the man to see the dean.

    _____ (C) Who the dean is.

4. _____ (A) He wants to take part in the election.

    _____ (B) He's not interested in running for office.

    _____ (C) He wants to get more facts from the president.

5. _____ (A) She couldn't type very fast.

    _____ (B) She had already finished the final draft.

    _____ (C) She hadn't completed the research.

---

* Note:　M1 = first male voice　　M2 = second male voice　　F1 = first female voice　　F2 = second female voice

6. _____ (A) He doesn't really like horse-back riding.

_____ (B) He rides horses whenever possible.

_____ (C) He doesn't talk about riding very much.

7. _____ (A) When his insurance agent called.

_____ (B) What his insurance agent wanted.

_____ (C) What time he should return the call.

8. _____ (A) He was working full-time.

_____ (B) He was eating in the cafeteria.

_____ (C) He didn't want a job.

9. _____ (A) When they returned.

_____ (B) How long their hike was.

_____ (C) Where they hiked.

10. _____ (A) He thinks the clothes are expensive.

_____ (B) He doesn't think the clothes are very nice.

_____ (C) He thinks the woman is being unreasonable.

11. _____ (A) Where the meeting will be held.

_____ (B) When the meeting will start.

_____ (C) Where the recreation center will be built.

12. _____ (A) Joy did not want to study abroad.

_____ (B) The overseas program had been canceled.

_____ (C) Joy would study overseas sooner than next year.

13. _____ (A) If the party was at Ben's house.

_____ (B) What time the party ended.

_____ (C) If the man enjoyed the party.

14. _____ (A) All of Ted's answers were incorrect.

_____ (B) Most of the problems were done correctly.

_____ (C) Ted doesn't have to solve the problems.

15. _____ (A) How she got to the grocery store.

_____ (B) Why she went to the grocery store.

_____ (C) How much she paid for groceries.

16. _____ (A) Robin's brother didn't help her get a job.

_____ (B) Robin didn't get a job.

_____ (C) Robin was able to help her brother.

17. _____ (A) The flashlight had needed batteries.

_____ (B) There had been some other problem with the flashlight.

_____ (C) The woman hadn't changed the batteries.

18. _____ (A) Professor Brennon surely won't lead the seminar.

_____ (B) Professor Brennons' permission is not required.

_____ (C) The man doesn't need to take the seminar.

19. _____ (A) Why Steve is in the Pacific Northwest.

_____ (B) How long Steve has been traveling.

_____ (C) When Steve will return from his trip.

20. _____ (A) It hadn't been released yet.

_____ (B) It wouldn't be very good.

_____ (C) It can no longer be considered new.

Lesson 9

ANSWERING QUESTIONS ABOUT ACTIVITIES, PLANS, TOPICS, AND PROBLEMS

QUESTIONS ABOUT ACTIVITIES

These questions follow dialogs that involve people talking about what they are doing. They are a kind of inference question because the activity itself is not mentioned in the dialog. Instead, you must determine the activity from the special vocabulary used by the speakers.

Sample Item

You will hear:*

F1: Is there room for that box up there?
M1: I can fit it in the trunk. And this suitcase should fit in the back seat.
M2: What are the speakers probably doing?

You will read:

(A) Boarding an airplane.
(B) Unpacking a box.
(C) Loading a car.
(D) Buying a suitcase.

   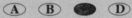

The words *box*, *trunk*, *suitcase*, and *back seat* all indicate that the speakers are putting things into a car.

QUESTIONS ABOUT PLANS

These questions follow dialogs in which two speakers discuss what one or both of them are going to do in the future.

Sample Item

You will hear:*

F2: Are you going to go to Boston with Michael this summer?
M1: Wish I could, but if I want to graduate next year, I've got to stay here and take a couple classes.
M2: What does the man plan to do this summer?

You will read:

(A) Graduate.
(B) Attend classes.
(C) Visit Michael.
(D) Go to Boston.

The man indicates that he must stay where he is and take classes in order to graduate next year.

---

* Note: M1 = first male voice   M2 = second male voice   F1 = first female voice   F2 = second female voice

QUESTIONS ABOUT TOPICS

The third speaker asks what the other two speakers are talking about. The topic is not usually mentioned directly in the dialog; it must be inferred from a general understanding of the dialog. The topic can be a person, a thing, or an activity.

Sample Item

You will hear:*

F1: Have you seen this letter from the bursar's office?

F2: Oh, no! Not another increase! If you ask me, we're already spending too much to go to school here.

M2: What are these speakers talking about?

You will read:

(A) Higher tuition costs.
(B) A poor grade.
(C) Higher postage rates.
(D) A letter from a relative.

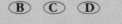 (B) (C) (D)

The fact that the letter comes from the bursar's office (the financial office of a university) and that the second woman is upset about an increase and feels they are spending too much to go to school, it is clear that they are talking about an increase in tuition.

QUESTIONS ABOUT PROBLEMS

These questions follow dialogs in which the speakers are discussing some trouble one or both of them are having. The third speaker asks what the problem is.

Sample Item

You will hear:*

M2: Gordon, what happened to your window?

M1: When I was painting the window last week, I hit it with the ladder.

F1: What problem does Gordon probably have?

You will read:

(A) His house needs painting.
(B) He broke his ladder.
(C) He spilled some paint.
(D) His window is broken.

(A) (B) (C)

Gordon, the second speaker, says that he hit the window with the ladder when he was painting the house. The logical result—a broken window.

---

* Note: M1 = first male voice   M2 = second male voice   F1 = first female voice   F2 = second female voice

Peterson's TOEFL CBT Success

EXERCISE 9

Focus: Answering questions about activities, plans, topics, and problems.

Directions: Listen to the dialogs and the questions about them. Decide which of the answer choices—(A), (B), or (C)—best answers the question, and mark the appropriate blank. The first one is done as an example.

Now start the tape.

1. __X__ (A) Road conditions.
   _____ (B) A weather report.
   _____ (C) Motel reservations.

2. _____ (A) Go to the concert.
   _____ (B) Listen to jazz on the radio.
   _____ (C) Buy more tickets.

3. _____ (A) The man's car is not running.
   _____ (B) The man isn't going to the party.
   _____ (C) The car isn't big enough for four people.

4. _____ (A) Stay inside.
   _____ (B) Find his umbrella.
   _____ (C) Look outside.

5. _____ (A) A store.
   _____ (B) A bridge.
   _____ (C) A street.

6. _____ (A) Shop for groceries.
   _____ (B) Leave for a camping trip.
   _____ (C) Go to a circus.

7. _____ (A) Ask for medicine for his headaches.
   _____ (B) Buy some new frames for his eyeglasses.
   _____ (C) Get different lenses for his glasses.

8. _____ (A) Clothing.
   _____ (B) Hair styling.
   _____ (C) Painting.

9. _____ (A) Take a trip.
   _____ (B) Watch television.
   _____ (C) Examine some documents.

10. _____ (A) He lent it to someone else.
    _____ (B) It was ruined in the rain.
    _____ (C) He forgot where he left it.

11. _____ (A) A car.
    _____ (B) A magazine.
    _____ (C) A computer.

12. _____ (A) Go directly to business school.
    _____ (B) Look for a job with a big company.
    _____ (C) Start her own business.

13. _____ (A) Playing cards.
    _____ (B) Making dinner.
    _____ (C) Repairing a boat.

14. _____ (A) He doesn't have Phyllis' address.
    _____ (B) He's upset with Phyllis.
    _____ (C) He doesn't have a stamp.

15. _____ (A) Order a salad.
    _____ (B) Go to another restaurant.
    _____ (C) Put some salt in her soup.

Lesson 10

DIALOGS WITH SPECIAL VERBS

CAUSATIVE VERBS

These verbs indicate that someone causes someone else to do something. When a dialog contains a causative verb, you must understand who performs the action. The verbs *have*, *get*, *make*, and *let* are the most common causative verbs.

They are used in the following patterns:

Have

have someone do something	Dave had the mechanic fix his car.
have something done	Dave had his car fixed.

The causative verb *have* indicates that one person asks or pays another to do something. The subject of this sentence, *Dave*, does not perform the action. In the first sentence, the mechanic does. In the second sentence, an unnamed person does.

Get

get someone to do something	Jerry got his cousin to cut his hair.
get something done	Jerry got his hair cut.

The causative verb *get* usually means to persuade someone to do something. Again note that the subject, *Jerry*, does not perform the action.

Make

make someone do something	She made her son do his homework.

The causative verb *make* means to force someone or compel someone to do something.

Let

let someone do something	The boss let us go home.

The verb *let* means permit or allow.

Sample Item

You will hear:*

M1: Did you speak to the head of the department.

F1: No, she had her assistant meet with me.

M2: What does the woman mean?

You will read:

(A) She spoke to the head of the department.
(B) The head of the department had a meeting with her assistant.
(C) She met with the assistant to the head of the department.
(D) The assistant will soon become head of the department.

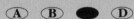

According to the dialog, the head of the department directed her assistant to meet with the woman.

USED TO

The expression *used to* has two forms, each with a different meaning:

    used to + simple form

I used to live in New York.	means →	I once lived in New York (but now I don't).

                   + gerund (*-ing* verb)

  be/get + *used to*

                   + noun phrase

I'm not used to driving on the left side of the road.	means →	I'm not accustomed to driving on the left side.
I've finally gotten used to my new job.	means →	I've finally become accustomed to my new job.

The dialogs in Part A sometimes take advantage of these two functions of *used to*.

---

* Note: M1 = first male voice   M2 = second male voice   F1 = first female voice   F2 = second female voice

Sample Items

You will hear:*

F2: What does Hank's father do for a living?

M1: He's a salesman now, but he used to be a truck driver.

M2: What does the man say about Hank's father?

You will read:

(A) He once drove trucks.
(B) He sells used trucks.
(C) His truck is still useful.
(D) He's accustomed to his job.

 Ⓑ Ⓒ Ⓓ

The man says that Hank's father used to be a truck driver. In other words, Hank's father once drove trucks, but he no longer does so.

You will hear:*

F1: Nancy is working late again today?

M1: Yeah, she must be getting used to it by now.

M2: What does the man say about Nancy?

You will read:

(A) She probably has a more difficult job now.
(B) She once worked later than she does now.
(C) She seldom comes to work late.
(D) She is becoming accustomed to late hours at work.

Ⓐ Ⓑ Ⓒ

The second speaker indicates that Nancy has probably adjusted to working late.

EXERCISE 10

Focus: Listening to dialogs that contain causative verbs or expressions with *used to*.

Directions: Listen to the dialogs and the questions about them. Then decide which of the two answer choices—(A) or (B)—best answers the question, and mark the appropriate blank. The first one is done as an example.

Now start the tape.

1. _____ (A) Doug is happy to be Rose's friend.

__X__ (B) Doug and Rose are no longer good friends.

2. _____ (A) He can do the job as well as a professional.

_____ (B) He should hire an electrician to do the job.

3. _____ (A) This station now plays classical music.

_____ (B) The station doesn't broadcast anything but news.

4. _____ (A) Changing the oil was easy for her.

_____ (B) The oil didn't need to be changed.

---

* Note: M1 = first male voice   M2 = second male voice   F1 = first female voice   F2 = second female voice

Peterson's TOEFL CBT Success

5. _____ (A) He's not accustomed to early classes yet.

_____ (B) His classes are difficult, too.

6. _____ (A) She's finally accustomed to roller skating.

_____ (B) She doesn't go skating as often as she once did.

7. _____ (A) He's going to clean his tie.

_____ (B) He's going to take his tie to the cleaner.

8. _____ (A) He moved the poster.

_____ (B) He no longer likes the poster.

9. _____ (A) She may not be able to take a vacation in August.

_____ (B) She's not sure when the busiest time will be.

10. _____ (A) She asked Greg to explain the point.

_____ (B) She explained the point to Greg.

11. _____ (A) He isn't accustomed to his glasses.

_____ (B) He looks quite different without glasses.

12. _____ (A) This type of weather is not new to him.

_____ (B) He once lived in a very different climate.

13. _____ (A) She's going to take a picture of the members of her club.

_____ (B) Someone is going to photograph her club.

14. _____ (A) He's never cooked with it.

_____ (B) He doesn't feel comfortable using it.

15. _____ (A) If the deer will come near them.

_____ (B) If they can approach the deer.

End of Tape 2, Side A.

Answer Sheet

Mini-Test 1: Dialogs

1. Ⓐ Ⓑ Ⓒ Ⓓ	11. Ⓐ Ⓑ Ⓒ Ⓓ	21. Ⓐ Ⓑ Ⓒ Ⓓ
2. Ⓐ Ⓑ Ⓒ Ⓓ	12. Ⓐ Ⓑ Ⓒ Ⓓ	22. Ⓐ Ⓑ Ⓒ Ⓓ
3. Ⓐ Ⓑ Ⓒ Ⓓ	13. Ⓐ Ⓑ Ⓒ Ⓓ	23. Ⓐ Ⓑ Ⓒ Ⓓ
4. Ⓐ Ⓑ Ⓒ Ⓓ	14. Ⓐ Ⓑ Ⓒ Ⓓ	24. Ⓐ Ⓑ Ⓒ Ⓓ
5. Ⓐ Ⓑ Ⓒ Ⓓ	15. Ⓐ Ⓑ Ⓒ Ⓓ	25. Ⓐ Ⓑ Ⓒ Ⓓ
6. Ⓐ Ⓑ Ⓒ Ⓓ	16. Ⓐ Ⓑ Ⓒ Ⓓ	26. Ⓐ Ⓑ Ⓒ Ⓓ
7. Ⓐ Ⓑ Ⓒ Ⓓ	17. Ⓐ Ⓑ Ⓒ Ⓓ	27. Ⓐ Ⓑ Ⓒ Ⓓ
8. Ⓐ Ⓑ Ⓒ Ⓓ	18. Ⓐ Ⓑ Ⓒ Ⓓ	28. Ⓐ Ⓑ Ⓒ Ⓓ
9. Ⓐ Ⓑ Ⓒ Ⓓ	19. Ⓐ Ⓑ Ⓒ Ⓓ	29. Ⓐ Ⓑ Ⓒ Ⓓ
10. Ⓐ Ⓑ Ⓒ Ⓓ	20. Ⓐ Ⓑ Ⓒ Ⓓ	30. Ⓐ Ⓑ Ⓒ Ⓓ

MINI-TEST 1: DIALOGS

Directions: Listen to the conversations and the questions about them. Decide which of the four answer choices—(A), (B), (C), or (D)—is the best answer to the question. Then mark the appropriate answer on the answer sheet.

Now start the tapes.

1. (A) She met him during the summer.
   (B) She's never liked him very much.
   (C) She warned him of a problem.
   (D) Her impression of him has changed.

2. (A) Review the last point.
   (B) Go on to the next chapter.
   (C) Leave the classroom.
   (D) Point out the teacher's mistake.

3. (A) The weather will not be as nice tomorrow.
   (B) She no longer reads the weather report.
   (C) She went to the store for a newspaper.
   (D) The weather reports will change soon.

4. (A) Writing an advertisement.
   (B) Playing a game.
   (C) Looking at a newspaper.
   (D) Discussing a book.

5. (A) Grace may want to live with the man's sister.
   (B) The woman thinks Grace already has a roommate.
   (C) The woman doesn't know where Grace has moved.
   (D) Grace doesn't know the man's sister.

6. (A) Go to a meeting.
   (B) Keep a budget.
   (C) Reduce his expenses.
   (D) Get some exercise.

7. (A) The man should clean out his closet.
   (B) The lamp will look better in a small space.
   (C) She doesn't like the lamp very much.
   (D) The living room is the best place for the lamp.

8. (A) What Mark is writing.
   (B) Where Mark is living now.
   (C) Why Mark doesn't want to go.
   (D) Why Mark is in a hurry.

9. (A) He certainly likes Ernie's red car.
   (B) The man in the red car resembles Ernie.
   (C) Ernie has a car just like that red one.
   (D) He can't see the man in the red car.

10. (A) The man doesn't need his hat.
    (B) It's not very cold today.
    (C) She likes the way the hat looks.
    (D) The man ought to wear his hat.

11. (A) She's never seen it.
    (B) It was made a long time ago.
    (C) She likes it a lot.
    (D) It's a very unusual movie.

12. (A) He doesn't believe what the woman told him.
    (B) He thinks the team was unprepared too.
    (C) He disagrees with the woman's idea.
    (D) He isn't ready to go to the game either.

13. (A) The man would like to use that computer.
    (B) Becky will need the computer for a long time.
    (C) There are no longer any computers in the library.
    (D) Becky would like the man to go to the library.

14. (A) He hurt his hand while he was scuba diving.
    (B) He hadn't been scuba diving for a long time.
    (C) He's not too old to go scuba diving.
    (D) He's an experienced scuba diver.

15. (A) His shoes hurt his feet.
    (B) He was injured in a skiing accident.
    (C) His shoes are old and in bad shape.
    (D) He walked so far that his legs hurt.

16. (A) She doesn't have time to listen now.
    (B) She doesn't know what song she wants to hear.
    (C) She wants to hear his song right away.
    (D) She prefers old songs to new ones.

17. (A) A television commercial.
    (B) A history class.
    (C) The woman's field of study.
    (D) Some famous artists.

18. (A) She was about to suggest the same thing.
    (B) She doesn't feel like giving a party.
    (C) She's completely surprised by the man's remark.
    (D) She isn't hungry right now.

19. (A) Sophie won't be at her apartment.
    (B) The man can inform Sophie at the meeting.
    (C) The man shouldn't bother Sophie.
    (D) Sophie will think this is bad news.

20. (A) He doesn't go out as often as he once did.
    (B) He doesn't always tell the truth.
    (C) He isn't as friendly as he once was.
    (D) He hasn't always been so sociable.

21. (A) The ring is quite attractive.
    (B) Laura got a bargain on the ring.
    (C) The ring was probably expensive.
    (D) Laura had to sell her ring.

22. (A) She didn't realize Bill had to work.
    (B) Bill has not finished his work.
    (C) The break has not lasted long enough.
    (D) The work didn't take long to complete.

23. (A) The woman has just begun to collect rocks.
    (B) The man is unwilling to help.
    (C) The box is very heavy.
    (D) There's nothing in the box.

24. (A) She doesn't like the length of her hair.
    (B) She thinks the haircut took too long.
    (C) She doesn't know where to get a haircut.
    (D) She thinks haircuts are too expensive.

25. (A) Professor Clayburn is going to speak some other night.
    (B) He's never heard of Professor Clayburn.
    (C) He didn't realize Professor Clayburn was speaking tonight.
    (D) Professor Clayburn is giving his speech in this room.

26. (A) The man may see her drawing.
    (B) She'd like the man to visit.
    (C) The man should draw a second picture.
    (D) She's going to take a guess.

27. (A) The weather has been very warm.
    (B) Her car doesn't need a tune-up.
    (C) She's starting to feel ill.
    (D) She's already too warm.

28. (A) Joe has been making too much noise.
    (B) Dogs are not allowed in the dorm.
    (C) No one understands the parking regulations.
    (D) Joe is not allowed to leave his room.

29. (A) Where the Medical Center is located.
    (B) Which office Dr. Norton is in.
    (C) What Dr. Norton told the man.
    (D) Why the man went to see Doctor Norton.

30. (A) She liked chemistry.
    (B) She would graduate in May.
    (C) She didn't have to repeat a course.
    (D) She hadn't completed the required courses.

Part B

ABOUT EXTENDED CONVERSATIONS

The second part of the Listening Comprehension section consists of longer conversations between a man and a woman or (sometimes) between two men or two women. Each conversation lasts from 30 to 90 seconds. It is preceded by brief introductory comments. After each of the conversations, there are from three to five questions. The questions are separated by a 12-second pause. You must decide which one of the four answer choices in your test book is the best answer for the question, then mark that answer on your answer sheet. You're not permitted to take notes. There are two longer conversations on the standard form, three or four on the long form.

THE INTRODUCTORY COMMENTS

These comments tell you which questions the conversation refers to and provides some brief information about the conversation:

"Questions 31 to 34. Listen to two students talk about their psychology class."
"Questions 31 to 35. Listen to a conversation about plans for a class trip."
"Questions 35 to 38. Listen to two friends discussing a performance that they attended."
"Questions 36 to 39. Listen to a conversation in a student housing office."
"Questions 35 to 39. Listen to a conversation between two teaching assistants."

Not only do these introductory comments tell you to get ready to listen, they also tell you how many questions in your test book to preview at one time. Moreover, they give you a general idea of what to expect as you listen.

Sample Item

You will hear:*

M2: Listen to a conversation between two students.

F1: Bill, you're a physics major, aren't you?

M1: That's right.

F1: I need some advice. I want to take an introductory physics class and I have to choose between two teachers, Professor Hunter and Professor McVey. Do you know much about them?

M1: I've taken classes from both of them. To tell you the truth, I don't really like Hunter's style of teaching. He doesn't seem to care if his students understand or not, and his lectures are pretty dry.

F1: Well then, what about McVey? I've heard his course is difficult.

M1: It's not easy, but you'll learn a lot, and he always encourages his students to ask questions and join in discussions.

You will then hear:*

M2: What does the woman ask Bill to do?

You will read:

(A) Give her information about two teachers.
(B) Help her with a physics assignment.
(C) Speak to a professor for her.
(D) Lead a discussion.

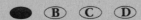 B   C   D

The woman asks Bill for some advice about the two professors who are teaching basic physics courses. Therefore, the best answer is (A).

You will then hear:*

M2: What does Bill imply that the woman should do?

You will read:

(A) Change her major to physics.
(B) Discuss her problem with Professor Hunter.
(C) Sign up for an easy class.
(D) Take Professor McVey's class.

A   B   C

Bill speaks critically of Professor Hunter's teaching methods, but favorably of Professor McVey's, so he would probably advise her to take McVey's course. The best answer is (D).

---

* Note: M1 = first male voice   M2 = second male voice   F1 = first female voice   F2 = second female voice

CONVERSATIONS

The extended conversations are similar to the Part A dialogs in style, but are longer. They frequently take place in a campus setting between two students or between a professor and a student.

THE QUESTIONS

The questions may be overview questions or detail questions. The first question after the conversation is often an overview question. Overview questions require a broad understanding of the entire conversation. To answer them correctly, you must understand what BOTH speakers say. There are several types of overview questions:

Type of Overview Question	Sample Question
Topic question	"What are the speakers discussing?"
Questions about settings (time and location)	"Where did this conversation take place?" "When did this conversation take place?"
Questions about the speakers	"Who are the speakers?" "What is the probable relationship between the speakers?"

It's important to listen carefully to the first few lines of an extended conversation to answer overview questions because this part of the talk often sets the scene. It often establishes the time and location of the conversation, the identity of the speakers, and the main idea of the rest of the conversation.

Detail questions ask about specific points in the conversation. The answer will usually be contained in what ONE speaker says. Detail questions follow the order of information in the conversation. In other words, the first of these questions refers to a point made early in the conversation, and the last asks about a point made near the end of the conversation. Most detail questions are factual questions; the answers are directly stated in the conversation. Many factual questions begin with these phrases:

According to the conversation, . . .
According to the man, . . .
According to the woman, . . .

A few of the detail questions are inference questions. In other words, the information is not directly given by the speakers; it can be concluded from the information that IS stated, however.

What can be inferred from the man's comment about . . . ?
What does the man imply about . . . ?
What will the speakers probably try to do?

THE ANSWER CHOICES

The four choices are all plausible answers for the question. Usually the answer choices are mentioned in some way in the conversation; but, only one, the key, answers that particular question correctly.

Some people prefer to close their eyes or look away while listening to the extended conversations in order to concentrate on the voices on the tape. However, it is better if you read over the answer choices in the test book while listening. This technique is difficult, but it has several advantages:

- It allows you to get an overall sense of what the topic of the conversation will be.
- It enables you to anticipate what the questions will be, then concentrate on listening for those points.
- It permits you to confirm some of the details that you hear by comparing them with the answer choices in the test book.

In the next section of this book, you will practice previewing answer choices, listening to Part B conversations, and answering both overview and detail questions about the conversations.

Tactics for Extended Conversations

- Be familiar with the directions, but remember that you cannot turn the page to look over answer choices while the directions are being read.
- Pay attention to the introductory sentence for each talk. These will tell you which items each talk refers to and may give you an idea of what the talks will be about.
- Preview the answer choices while the talks are being read and during the pauses between questions. Try to guess what the questions will be.
- Listen for overall concepts:
    - Who is taking part in the conversation?
    - Where and when does the conversation take place?
    - What is the main topic of the conversation?
  The answers to these questions are often suggested in the first few lines of the talks.
- You are not permitted to take written notes, but try to take "mental notes" on specific details: facts, figures, dates, places, and so on. You can sometimes check the information you think you hear against information you read in the answer choices while you are previewing.
- Answer items right away.
- Never leave any blanks on your answer sheet. Always guess.

Lesson 11

ANTICIPATING QUESTIONS ABOUT EXTENDED CONVERSATIONS

When you are previewing the items in Part B, you should try to anticipate what the questions will be by the form of the answer choices. You usually won't be able to guess exactly what the question will be, but you can guess what type of question will be asked. For example, if the four answer choices are the names of places, a "Where..." question will be asked; if the answer choices are times of day or dates, you will hear a "When..." question. If you have some idea of what the question will be, you can focus your listening during the talks.

You can also get a good idea of the situation in which the conversation is taking place by previewing the items.

Remember: The introductory comments at the beginning of the conversation tell you which items to preview.

EXERCISE 11

Focus: Guessing the questions that will be asked about an extended conversation and the situation in which the conversation takes place by previewing answer choices.

Directions: Look over the answer choices below. First try to guess the general type of question that will be asked about each item. Then look at the list of questions after each group of items and match the letter of the appropriate question with the item. Then answer the question about the overall topic of the conversation. The first one is done as an example.

There is no taped material for this exercise.

Conversation 1

1. (A) A grade the student received.
   (B) A story about a dance recital.
   (C) The need for correct spelling.
   (D) The role of a reporter.

   Question: ___b___

2. (A) Business.
   (B) Architecture.
   (C) Journalism.
   (D) Dance.

   Question: _____

3. (A) He submitted it too late.
   (B) It was too long.
   (C) Some important details were omitted.
   (D) Almost every word was misspelled.

   Question: _____

4. (A) Rewrite the story.
   (B) Buy a better dictionary.
   (C) Go to more dance recitals.
   (D) Get a job as a reporter.

   Question: _____

Questions for Conversation 1

(a) For what class did the man do the assignment?

(b) What is the main topic of this conversation?

(c) What does the man advise the woman to do?

(d) What problem does the man mention in connection with the story?

Situation Question for Conversation 1

Which of the following best describes the situation in which the first conversation probably takes place?

(A) One student is telling another a story about a dance.

(B) A professor is criticizing a student's story about a dance performance.

(C) An instructor is teaching a student a new dance.

(D) One student is suggesting ways in which the other student can improve his spelling.

Conversation 2

5. (A) He doesn't get enough exercise.
(B) He's nervous about an important test.
(C) He's spending too much time at the Recreation Center.
(D) He doesn't know how to swim.

Question: _____

6. (A) Across campus from the Student Center building.
(B) South of the stadium.
(C) On the north side of campus.
(D) Between the Student Center and the Stadium.

Question: _____

7. (A) Sign up for some classes at the Recreation Center.
(B) Spend more time studying for exams.
(C) Take a break from his studies.
(D) Take a bus to the Recreation Center.

Question: _____

8. (A) Just before the beginning of the semester.
(B) During midterm exams.
(C) Near the end of the semester.
(D) Just after the end of the semester.

Question: _____

Questions for Conversation 2

(a) Where is the Recreation Center?
(b) What does the woman suggest the man do?
(c) What problem does the man complain about?
(d) At what point in the semester does this conversation take place?

Situation Question for Conversation 2

Which of the following best describes the situation in which the conversation probably takes place?

(A) One student recommends that another get some exercise in order to relax during exams.
(B) Two students discuss their plans for a vacation.
(C) A physical-education instructor suggests that a student register for classes in her department.
(D) A student explains to a visitor to campus how to get to the Stadium.

Conversation 3

9. (A) At an art gallery.
(B) At an art museum.
(C) In an artist's studio.
(D) In a special room in the library.

Question: _____

10. (A) Paintings.
(B) Sculptures.
(C) Book covers.
(D) Photographs.

Question: _____

11. (A) A story in a newspaper.
(B) An article in an art magazine.
(C) A class she attended.
(D) A show she saw on television.

Question: _____

12. (A) An art historian and a student.
(B) Two students.
(C) Two visitors to a museum.
(D) A tour guide and a tourist.

Question: _____

13. (A) Primitive.
(B) Life-sized.
(C) Realistic.
(D) Stylized.

Question: _____

Questions for Conversation 3

   (a) Who is taking part in this conversation?

   (b) How would the woman probably describe the works of art that she saw?

   (c) What was the source of the woman's information?

   (d) Where did the exhibit take place?

   (e) What kind of art are the speakers discussing?

Situation Question for Conversation 3

   Which of the following best describes the situation in which the conversation probably takes place?

   (A) One speaker describes his techniques for painting pictures to the other.

   (B) The woman tells the man about a recent book she read.

   (C) An art expert gives some advice to the other speaker about becoming an artist.

   (D) One speaker tells the other about some art she saw at an exhibit.

Lesson 12

ANSWERING OVERVIEW QUESTIONS ABOUT EXTENDED CONVERSATIONS

After each extended conversation in Part B, there are four to five questions. Usually the first and sometimes the last question are **overview questions**. To answer these questions, you need an understanding of the whole lecture or conversation rather than of any specific point.

Overview questions for the Extended Conversations:

- What is the main topic of this conversation?
- What are these people primarily discussing?
- Where does this conversation take place?
- When does this conversation take place?
- What is the relationship between the speakers?
- What is the man's/woman's occupation?
- What is one speaker's attitude toward the other speaker?

Main topic questions must correctly summarize the talk. Incorrect answers for these questions are too general, too specific, or incorrect according to the conversation.

Although these questions require an overall understanding of the conversations, the first few sentences often "set the scene." In other words, the opening lines of the talk establish the time, place, and main topic. Read the opening lines of the extended conversation given below:

M1: (Answering phone) Hello?

F1: Hi, Rod, this is Rita—I'm in your nine o'clock class. I missed class because of a cold, and I was wondering if I could borrow your notes.

M1: I don't know if you could read my notes—I have terrible handwriting. But I can tell you what happened. Professor Phillips went over the material in Chapter 4, about different types of stars in our galaxy. And she talked about what the midterm exam is going to be like.

F1: Uh-oh, you better tell me all about the midterm—I really need to do well on it.

From this portion of a conversation, we learn that:

. . . both of the speakers are students
. . . they are probably taking a course in astronomy
. . . the class is about halfway over (because they are taking midterm exams)
. . . the rest of the talk will probably deal with the material that will be on the examination

Not all conversations begin with so much detail. However, it is important to concentrate on the opening lines to learn this kind of information.

EXERCISE 12

Focus: Listening to the opening lines of extended conversations and answering overview questions about the topics, settings, and speakers.

Directions: Listen to the conversations and the questions about them. Then mark the answer choice—(A), (B), or (C)—that correctly completes the sentence. The first one is done as an example. Now start the tape.

1. _____ (A) Methods of predicting earthquakes.
   __X__ (B) Ways to improve the man's presentation.
   _____ (C) The many new uses of computer graphics.

2. _____ (A) Statistics.
   _____ (B) Computer science.
   _____ (C) Geology.

3. _____ (A) A language teacher and a student.
   _____ (B) A doctor and a patient.
   _____ (C) A teacher and an assistant.

4. _____ (A) The language of the deaf.
   _____ (B) Methods of teaching German.
   _____ (C) Communication networks.

5. _____ (A) Professor Quinn's approach to teaching.
   _____ (B) The process of getting a student identification card.
   _____ (C) Procedures for checking out reserve material.

6. _____ (A) At a university library.
   _____ (B) In a psychology class.
   _____ (C) In a laboratory.

7. _____ (A) Ask for a job.
   _____ (B) Get some advice.
   _____ (C) Discuss medical research.

8. _____ (A) Academic adviser.
   _____ (B) Physician.
   _____ (C) Administrator.

9. _____ (A) Helpful.
   _____ (B) Discouraging.
   _____ (C) Inconsiderate.

10. _____ (A) The art of raising dogs.
    _____ (B) A softball game.
    _____ (C) A dogsled race.

11. _____ (A) An archaeologist.
    _____ (B) An employee at a resort.
    _____ (C) A university student.

12. _____ (A) Their plans for the coming school year.
    _____ (B) Tina's volunteer position.
    _____ (C) Tina's trip to Europe.

13. _____ (A) A clerk at a bookstore.
    _____ (B) A librarian.
    _____ (C) A publisher's sales officer.

14. _____ (A) Before the spring term begins.
    _____ (B) In the middle of the spring term.
    _____ (C) After the spring term ends.

15. _____ (A) In the Student Work-Study Program.
    _____ (B) In the Graduate Admissions Office.
    _____ (C) In the Financial Aid Office.

16. _____ (A) Requirements for graduate admission.
    _____ (B) Directions to another office.
    _____ (C) The man's need for a scholarship.

Lesson 13

ANSWERING DETAIL QUESTIONS ABOUT EXTENDED CONVERSATIONS

Most of the questions in Part B are **detail questions** that require an understanding of specific points in the conversation. A majority of these questions are **factual questions**, asking what, where, when, why, and how much. To answer the question, you need to listen carefully.

Other questions are **inference questions**. As previously explained, the answers to inference questions are not directly stated, but are suggested by information in the lecture. Many of these questions begin, "What do the speakers imply about . . ." or "What can be inferred from the conversation about . . ."

Remember that the order of detail questions follows the order of the conversation. In other words, the first detail question will be about something mentioned early in the conversation while the last one is about something mentioned near the end of the conversation.

If anything in the conversation is emphasized, it will probably be asked about. In other words, if something one speaker says is repeated by the second speaker, or if one speaker talks about something in an emphatic tone of voice, there will probably be a question about that information, as in this section of a conversation:

M1: My project for my filmmaking class took me six weeks to finish.

F1: Six weeks! I can hardly believe it. Doesn't the teacher realize you have other classes too?

You can be fairly sure that there will be a question, "How long did the man's project take to complete?"

EXERCISE 13.1

Focus: Answering detail and inference questions based on specific points in short portions of extended conversations.

Directions: You will hear three extended conversations, each one divided into several short portions. After each portion, there will be a number of questions based on that part of the talk. Mark the best answer choice—(A), (B), or (C)—for each question. The first one is done as an example.

Now start the tape.

1. _____ (A) A doctor.
   _____ (B) A newspaper.
   __X__ (C) A magazine.

2. _____ (A) It's too tiring.
   _____ (B) It can cause injuries.
   _____ (C) It's not demanding enough.

3. _____ (A) Downhill skiing.
   _____ (B) Jogging.
   _____ (C) Cross-country skiing.

4. _____ (A) It doesn't require much snow.
   _____ (B) It is a recently developed sport.
   _____ (C) It can be done in flat areas.

5. _____ (A) Use a cross-country ski machine.
   _____ (B) Travel to ski resorts.
   _____ (C) Take up jogging.

6. _____ (A) The expense.
   _____ (B) The weather conditions.
   _____ (C) The danger.

7. _____ (A) He stayed up most of the night.

_____ (B) He's been studying all morning.

_____ (C) He took an exam last night.

8. _____ (A) It was an improvement.

_____ (B) It was disappointing.

_____ (C) It was unfair.

9. _____ (A) Undergraduate students.

_____ (B) Teachers.

_____ (C) Graduate students.

10. _____ (A) She learned how to do research.

_____ (B) She was prepared for her sociology test.

_____ (C) She learned teaching techniques.

11. _____ (A) Basic scientific research.

_____ (B) Business management.

_____ (C) Test-taking skills.

12. _____ (A) In the library.

_____ (B) In the Physics Tower.

_____ (C) In Staunton Hall.

13. _____ (A) Study for his next exam.

_____ (B) Go to the Study Skills Center.

_____ (C) Get some sleep.

14. _____ (A) To buy something at an auction.

_____ (B) To pay for employees' salaries.

_____ (C) To improve their broadcasts.

15. _____ (A) Apply for a job at the station.

_____ (B) Donate his services for the station's auction.

_____ (C) Direct the construction of a new tower.

16. _____ (A) She must work on her own research project.

_____ (B) She has to help her parents.

_____ (C) She must study for exams.

17. _____ (A) They seldom attend auctions.

_____ (B) They might bid on the man's services.

_____ (C) They use the library often.

EXERCISE 13.2

Focus: Answering detail and inference questions based on specific points in complete extended conversations.

Directions: You will hear four extended conversations. After each conversation, there will be a number of questions based on it. Mark the best answer choice—(A), (B), or (C)—for each question. The first one is done as an example.

Now start the tape.

1. _____ (A) North of Los Angeles.

__X__ (B) Between Los Angeles and San Diego.

_____ (C) East of San Diego.

2. _____ (A) They are a type of insect.

_____ (B) They are a kind of fish.

_____ (C) They are a type of bird.

3. _____ (A) In March.

_____ (B) In early summer.

_____ (C) In October.

4. _____ (A) About 200 miles.

_____ (B) About 1,000 miles.

_____ (C) About 7,000 miles.

5. _____ (A) The swallows' arrival.

_____ (B) The parade.

_____ (C) The swallows' departure.

6. _____ (A) Only during the first week of classes.

_____ (B) Whenever students ask for them.

_____ (C) Only in the afternoon.

7. _____ (A) A tour guide.

_____ (B) A classroom.

_____ (C) A map.

8. _____ (A) In the Science Building.

_____ (B) In the Student Center Building.

_____ (C) In the University Recreation Center.

9. _____ (A) A test in a composition class.

_____ (B) A road test.

_____ (C) The written test for her driver's license.

10. _____ (A) He drove too fast.

_____ (B) He couldn't park well.

_____ (C) He made an improper turn.

11. _____ (A) Drive her to the test site.

_____ (B) Help her get ready for the road test.

_____ (C) Sell her a car.

12. _____ (A) It doesn't belong to her.

_____ (B) She's not a licensed driver.

_____ (C) It isn't running right.

End of Tape 2, Side B.

MINI-TEST 2: EXTENDED CONVERSATIONS

Directions: Listen to the conversations and the questions about them. Decide which one of the four answer choices—(A), (B), (C), or (D)—is the best answer to the question. Then mark the appropriate answer on the answer sheet above.

Now start the tape.

1. (A) To look up some terms.
   (B) To meet Stanley.
   (C) To get a snack.
   (D) To prepare for an exam.

2. (A) His library card.
   (B) A statistics book.
   (C) Some index cards.
   (D) A notebook.

3. (A) Piles of note cards.
   (B) The part of the library where journals are stored.
   (C) The part of the library where books are shelved.
   (D) A place to get something to eat.

4. (A) Behind the main desk.
   (B) The periodicals room.
   (C) A lost and found office.
   (D) The reference room.

5. (A) The sport of mountain climbing.
   (B) Classes the man is taking.
   (C) An exhibit the man saw in a museum.
   (D) A new activity the man is involved in.

6. (A) A means of descending slopes.
   (B) A method of climbing cliffs.
   (C) A way to clean walls.
   (D) A type of graffiti.

7. (A) Educating people about geology.
   (B) Cleaning up after careless people.
   (C) Photographing mountain peaks.
   (D) Rescuing people who are in danger.

8. (A) Explore a cave with him.
   (B) Take some photographs.
   (C) Attend a meeting.
   (D) Examine a crystal.

Part C

ABOUT MINI-TALKS

The third part of Section 1 consists of mini-talks. These are monologues (talks involving only one speaker). Each mini-talk lasts from 30 to 90 seconds. Like the extended conversations, they are preceded by introductory comments. After each talk, there are from three to five questions. The questions are separated by a 12-second pause. You have to decide which of the four answer choices in the test book best answers the question, then mark that answer on your answer sheet. You are not allowed to take notes. There are three mini-talks on the standard form, four on the long form.

THE INTRODUCTORY COMMENTS

These comments tell you which questions the mini-talks refer to and provide some brief information about the conversation:

"Questions 35 to 40: Listen to a lecture given at a botanical garden."
"Questions 31 to 35: Listen to a talk about the university's housing policy."
"Questions 35 to 38: Listen to a lecture given in a history class."

The introductory comments tell you how many questions in your test book to preview at one time and give you a general idea of the topic of the talk.

Sample Item

You will hear:*

M2: Listen to this lecture given in a university classroom.

M1: Students, this evening we'll have a chance to observe a phenomenon that we've discussed several times in class. Tonight there will be a lunar eclipse. As we've said, when an eclipse of the Moon occurs, the Earth passes between the Sun and the Moon. Therefore, the shadow of the Earth moves across the surface of the Moon and obscures it. Because you won't be looking at the Sun, it is not necessary to use the special lenses and filters that you need when observing a solar eclipse. You can observe a lunar eclipse with your unaided eye or with a telescope and photograph it with an ordinary camera. So if the weather's not cloudy tonight, go out and take a look at this eclipse of the Moon. I'm sure you'll find it interesting.

You will hear:*

M2: In what course is this lecture probably being given?

You will read:

(A) Philosophy.
(B) Meteorology.
(C) Astronomy.
(D) Photography.

The lecture concerns a lunar eclipse, a topic that would typically be discussed in an astronomy class.

You will hear:*

M2: According to the speaker, which of the following occurs during a lunar eclipse?

You will read:

(A) The Earth's shadow moves across the Moon.
(B) Clouds block the view of the Moon.
(C) The Moon moves between the Earth and the Sun.
(D) The Sun is too bright to be observed without special equipment.

The speaker says "the shadow of the Earth moves across the surface of the Moon and obscures it." The best answer is therefore (A).

* Note: M1 = first male voice   M2 = second male voice   F1 = first female voice   F2 = second female voice

Peterson's TOEFL CBT Success

THE TALKS

The mini-talks are usually somewhat more formal in style than the extended conversations. Some of the talks resemble lectures given as part of a university course in history, literature, or biology, for example. Other mini-talks resemble talks you would hear at a university, but not in a classroom. For example, you might hear talks about campus organizations, registration procedures, or the services at a campus medical center. Still others have nothing to do with university life; you may hear a tour guide speaking to a group of tourists or a curator speaking to visitors at a museum.

THE QUESTIONS

As with the extended conversations, the questions about mini-talks may be overview questions or detail questions. The first question after the talk is usually an overview question. Overview questions require an understanding of the entire conversation. There are several types of overview questions:

Type of Overview Question	Sample Question
Topic/main idea/purpose questions	"What is the lecture mainly about?" "What is the speaker mainly talking about?" "What is the main idea of this lecture?" "Why is the speaker giving this talk?" "What is the main point of this lecture?"
Questions about settings (course, time, and location)	"In what course was this lecture probably given." "Where was this talk probably given?" "When was this talk probably given?"
Questions about the speaker	"Who is the speaker?" "What is the speaker's occupation?"

You should listen carefully to the first few lines of mini-talk to answer overview questions because this part of the talk often sets the scene. It often establishes the time and location of the conversation, the identity of the speaker, and the main idea of the rest of the conversation.

Detail questions ask about specific points in the talk. Detail questions follow the order of information in the lecture. In other words, the first of these questions refers to a point made early in the lecture; the last asks about a point made near the end of the lecture. Most detail questions are factual questions; the answers are directly stated in the talk. Some factual questions begin with these phrases:

According to the speaker, . . .
According to the lecture, . . .

A few are inference questions. The answers to these are not directly stated in the talk; they are only suggested. These questions usually contain some form of the words *infer* or *imply* or the word *probably*.

What can be inferred about . . . ?
What does the speaker imply about . . . ?
What is probably true about . . . ?

THE ANSWER CHOICES

The four choices are all plausible answers for the question. Usually the answer choices are mentioned in some way in the talk.

As with the conversations, it is better to read over the answer choices in the test book while listening than to look away or close your eyes so that you can preview the answer choices.

In the next section of this book, you will practice previewing answer choices, listening to Part C mini-talks, and answering both overview and detail questions about the talks.

Tactics for Mini-Talks

- Be familiar with the directions, but remember that you cannot turn the page to look over answer choices while the directions are being read.
- Pay attention to the introductory sentence for each talk. These will tell you which items each talk refers to and may give you an idea of what the talks will be about.
- Preview the answer choices while the talks are being read and during the pauses between questions. Try to guess what the questions and the topic will be.
- Listen for overall concepts:
  - Who is giving the talk?
  - Where and when is the talk being given?
  - What is the main topic or purpose of the talk?

The answers to these questions are often suggested in the first few lines of the talks.

- You are not permitted to take written notes, but try to take "mental notes" on specific details: facts, figures, dates, places, and so on. You can sometimes check the information you think you hear against information you read in the answer choices while you are previewing.
- Answer items right away.
- Never leave any blanks on your answer sheet. Always guess.

Lesson 14

As in the other two parts of the Listening Comprehension section, you should preview the items in Part C and try to anticipate what the questions will be by the form of the answer choices. You may not be able to guess exactly what the questions will be, but you can guess what type of question will be asked. For example, if the four answer choices are the names of places, a "Where . . ." question will be asked; if the answer choices are times of day or dates, you will hear a "When . . ." question.

If you have some idea of what the question will be, you can focus your listening during the talks.

✗ EXERCISE 14

Focus: Guessing what Part C questions will be asked by looking at the answer choices.

Directions: Look over the answer choices below. First try to guess the general type of question that will be asked about each item. Then look at the list of questions after each group of items and match the letter of the appropriate question with the item. One question in each set will NOT be used. The first one is done as an example.

There is no taped material for this exercise.

1. (A) The life of Clara Barton.
    (B) A short history of the American Red Cross.
    (C) The role of nurses in the Civil War.
    (D) The writings of Clara Barton.

    Question: ___b___

2. (A) In Virginia.
    (B) In Switzerland.
    (C) In Massachusetts.
    (D) In Texas.

    Question: _____

3. (A) A teacher.
    (B) A superintendent of a hospital.
    (C) A clerk in a government office.
    (D) A diplomatic official.

    Question: _____

4. (A) In 1845.
    (B) During the American Civil War.
    (C) During a trip to Europe.
    (D) In 1881.

    Question: _____

5. (A) To help wounded soldiers.
    (B) To provide relief for hurricane victims.
    (C) To prevent famines.
    (D) To publish books about nursing.

    Question: _____

Questions for Items 1–5

(a) What was Clara Barton's first occupation?
(b) What is this talk mainly about?
(c) Where was Clara Barton born?
(d) When did Clara Barton found the American Red Cross?
(e) What was the original purpose of the American Red Cross?
(f) When was this lecture probably given?

6. (A) To honor a student.
    (B) To introduce a speaker.
    (C) To discuss the creative writing program.
    (D) To criticize a new book.

    Question: _____

7. (A) A science fiction novel.
    (B) Poetry.
    (C) Criticism.
    (D) A collection of short stories.

    Question: _____

8. (A) A cash prize.
    (B) Publication of his works.
    (C) A free trip.
    (D) A scholarship.

    Question: _____

Questions for Items 6–8

(a) How does the speaker feel about Jim McKee?
(b) What award did Jim McKee receive?
(c) What kind of writing has Jim McKee done?
(d) What is the main purpose of this talk?

9. (A) A radio announcer.
    (B) A waitress.
    (C) A television announcer.
    (D) A chef.

    Question: _____

10. (A) Vegetarian food.
    (B) Food from New Mexico.
    (C) Food from Louisiana.
    (D) Fresh seafood.

    Question: _____

11. (A) On Atlantic Avenue.
    (B) On a boat.
    (C) On a dock.
    (D) On First Street.

    Question: _____

12. (A) Most of the dishes are reasonably priced.
    (B) All but a few of the dishes are delicious.
    (C) The service has improved lately.
    (D) It's not too crowded on weekday nights.

    Question: _____

Questions for Items 9–12

(a) What does the speaker say about the Tangerine Café?
(b) What kind of food does the Tangerine Café mainly serve?
(c) What problem did the speaker have when she went to the Tangerine Café?
(d) Who is the speaker?
(e) Where is the Tangerine Café located?

Lesson 15

ANSWERING OVERVIEW QUESTIONS ABOUT MINI-TALKS

After each talk in Part C, there are three or four questions. Usually the first question is an **overview question**. To answer this type of question, you need an understanding of the whole talk rather than of any specific point.

Overview Questions for the Mini-Talks

- What is the main idea/main point/main topic of the lecture?
- What is the purpose of this talk?
- Where was this lecture given?
- When was this talk given?
- In what course was this lecture given?
- What is the speaker's occupation?
- Who is the audience for this talk?

Main idea, main topic, and main point questions must correctly summarize the talk. Incorrect answers for these questions are usually too general, too specific, or incorrect according to the lecture.

Although these questions require an overall understanding of the talks, the first few sentences often "set the scene." In other words, the opening lines of the talk frequently establish the time, place, and main topic. Read the opening lines of the mini-talk given below:

Good morning, everyone. As you probably know, this class is a continuation of a course that began last term. Last term we focused on American writers of the nineteenth century. Today we'll begin our study of twentieth-century novelists with a look at Ernest Hemingway.

From this introduction, we know that:

. . . the speaker is a teacher
. . . the audience is a group of students
. . . the course is in American literature
. . . the talk will concern Ernest Hemingway

Not all talks will begin with so much detail. However, it is important to concentrate on the opening lines to learn this kind of information.

EXERCISE 15

Focus: Listening to the opening lines of mini-talks and answering overview questions about the main ideas, speakers and audiences, settings, and so on.

Directions: Listen to the introductions and the questions about them. Then mark the answer choice—(A), (B), or (C)—that correctly completes the sentence. The first one is done as an example.
Now start the tape.

1. _____ (A) A teacher.
   __X__ (B) A tour guide.
   _____ (C) A photographer.

2. _____ (A) A description of the wildlife preserve.
   _____ (B) Advice about outdoor photography.
   _____ (C) The scientific classification of buffaloes.

3. _____ (A) To explain the traditions of handball.

_____ (B) To give information about the rules of tennis.

_____ (C) To discuss the rules of handball.

4. _____ (A) At the end of a tournament.

_____ (B) Before an exhibition game.

_____ (C) During a game.

5. _____ (A) Factory workers.

_____ (B) Visitors to a factory.

_____ (C) Management trainees.

6. _____ (A) The process of canning soft drinks.

_____ (B) Management-labor teamwork.

_____ (C) The life cycle of plants.

7. _____ (A) The physical rewards of dancing.

_____ (B) The importance of the program to the university.

_____ (C) The disadvantages of being in the program.

8. _____ (A) Director of a dance program.

_____ (B) Professor of psychology.

_____ (C) Athletics coach.

9. _____ (A) A host at a party.

_____ (B) The president of a society.

_____ (C) The captain of a ship.

10. _____ (A) The role of the State Historical Society.

_____ (B) The history of New England.

_____ (C) The story of some shipwrecks.

11. _____ (A) Composition.

_____ (B) Fine arts.

_____ (C) Architecture.

12. _____ (A) The use of blueprints.

_____ (B) Methods of organization.

_____ (C) Editing papers.

13. _____ (A) Experienced skiers.

_____ (B) Ski instructors.

_____ (C) Beginning skiers.

14. _____ (A) The fundamentals of skiing.

_____ (B) Championship skiers.

_____ (C) The development of ski resorts.

15. _____ (A) Law.

_____ (B) Economics.

_____ (C) Classical languages.

16. _____ (A) A few weeks after the beginning of class.

_____ (B) In the first class meeting.

_____ (C) During the final exam.

17. _____ (A) On a boat.

_____ (B) At an aquarium.

_____ (C) On a plane.

18. _____ (A) The habits of whales.

_____ (B) Types of whales.

_____ (C) Efforts to protect whales.

19. _____ (A) Students who own bicycles.

_____ (B) New members of the campus police force.

_____ (C) Pedestrians concerned about safety.

20. _____ (A) To describe some recent accidents.

_____ (B) To introduce a new program.

_____ (C) To provide safety and security hints.

Lesson 16

ANSWERING DETAIL QUESTIONS ABOUT MINI-TALKS

Most of the questions about Part C talks are **detail questions** that ask about specific points in the talk. The majority of these questions are **factual questions**, asking about facts, reasons, places, or dates mentioned by the speaker. This type of question often begins, "According to the speaker,..." Incorrect answers are often mentioned at some point in the talk, but are not appropriate answers to the questions asked.

You are not permitted to take written notes while listening to the lecture.

A few questions about the Part C talks are **inference questions**. Many of these questions begin, "What does the speaker imply about . . ." or "What can be inferred from the lecture about . . ."

As in Part B, if a speaker emphasizes a point in the lecture by going back to it or repeating it, there will probably be a question about it.

> M: . . . Now, in the days of the California Gold Rush, the journey by ship from the East Coast to San Francisco took about six months. Can you imagine that—gold-seekers spent six months at sea just getting to California!

There will almost certainly be a question about how long it took to get from the East Coast to San Francisco during the Gold Rush.

EXERCISE 16.1

Focus: Answering detail and inference questions based on specific points in Part C talks.

Directions: You will hear three talks, each one divided into several short portions. After each portion, there will be a number of questions based on that part of the talk. Mark the best answer choice—(A), (B), or (C)—for each question. The first one is done as an example.

Talk A:

1. _____ (A) It covers some difficult topics.
   __X__ (B) It's unlike other biology courses.
   _____ (C) It has never been offered by this department.

2. _____ (A) By visiting a coral reef.
   _____ (B) By going to the library.
   _____ (C) By going to a farm.

3. _____ (A) Diving.
   _____ (B) Photography.
   _____ (C) Biology.

4. _____ (A) As harmful.
   _____ (B) As easily damaged.
   _____ (C) As frightening.

5. _____ (A) Transportation.
   _____ (B) Housing.
   _____ (C) Basic equipment.

6. _____ (A) Traveling by ship.
   _____ (B) Trying to get financial aid.
   _____ (C) Applying to another university.

Talk B:

7. _____ (A) They have such impressive appetites.
   _____ (B) They sometimes walk on two legs.
   _____ (C) They frequently attack people.

8. _____ (A) They will eat anything except plants.

_____ (B) They eat only honey.

_____ (C) They aren't limited to a few types of food.

9. _____ (A) Five feet.

_____ (B) Ten feet.

_____ (C) Fifteen feet.

10. _____ (A) In Alaska.

_____ (B) In Yellowstone National Park.

_____ (C) All over the United States.

11. _____ (A) The kodiak bear.

_____ (B) The grizzly bear.

_____ (C) The black bear.

12. _____ (A) They are sometimes not as friendly as they seem.

_____ (B) They are much more danger-ous than grizzly bears.

_____ (C) They look dangerous but are usually friendly.

Talk C:

13. _____ (A) In the 1950's.

_____ (B) In the 1970's.

_____ (C) In the 1990's.

14. _____ (A) They fly off into deep space.

_____ (B) They remain in orbit forever.

_____ (C) They burn up in the atmo-sphere.

15. _____ (A) Three to four hundred.

_____ (B) Eight thousand.

_____ (C) Half a million.

16. _____ (A) They are too small.

_____ (B) They are too far away.

_____ (C) They are moving too fast.

17. _____ (A) A large booster rocket.

_____ (B) A piece of metal the size of an aspirin.

_____ (C) A tiny fleck of paint.

18. _____ (A) Their high speed.

_____ (B) Their jagged shape.

_____ (C) Their tremendous size.

19. _____ (A) An aspirin.

_____ (B) A piece of debris.

_____ (C) A model of the debris collector.

20. _____ (A) They detect the debris.

_____ (B) They store the debris.

_____ (C) They collect the debris.

21. _____ (A) It has already been tested on Earth.

_____ (B) It has not been built yet.

_____ (C) It has already been used on a spacecraft.

EXERCISE 16.2

Focus: Answering detail questions about complete Part C talks.

Directions: You will hear a number of Part C mini-talks. After each talk, there will be a number of questions based on that part of the talk. Mark the best answer choice—(A), (B), or (C)—for each question. The first one is done as an example.

1. _____ (A) Two years.
   X (B) Three years.
   _____ (C) Five years.

2. _____ (A) Student fees.
   _____ (B) Room and board charges at the dormitory.
   _____ (C) Student insurance rates.

3. _____ (A) Its tuition rates are going up faster than the ones at Hambleton University.
   _____ (B) It has the highest tuition rates in the state.
   _____ (C) Its tuition rates are still lower than those at Hambleton University.

4. _____ (A) An executive on the Student Council.
   _____ (B) A member of the Board of Regents.
   _____ (C) A spokesperson for the administration.

5. _____ (A) The new dormitory will not be built.
   _____ (B) The proposal to increase student services will not be adopted.
   _____ (C) The tuition will not be raised.

6. _____ (A) A starfish.
   _____ (B) A salamander.
   _____ (C) A mammal.

7. _____ (A) A snake sheds its skin and grows a new one.
   _____ (B) An insect grows a new limb.
   _____ (C) A baby gets its first set of teeth.

8. _____ (A) Embryonic cells.
   _____ (B) Specialized cells.
   _____ (C) Nerve cells.

9. _____ (A) To treat diseases among animals.
   _____ (B) To learn to speed up the process among lower animals.
   _____ (C) To apply what is learned to human medicine.

10. _____ (A) Before the Revolutionary War.
    _____ (B) During the Revolutionary War.
    _____ (C) After American Independence.

11. _____ (A) His military service.
    _____ (B) His political philosophy.
    _____ (C) His dictionary.

12. _____ (A) T-H-E-A-T-R-E instead of T-H-E-A-T-E-R.
    _____ (B) L-A-B-O-U-R instead of L-A-B-O-R.
    _____ (C) N-I-F instead of K-N-I-F-E.

End of Tape 3, Side A.

Answer Sheet

Mini-Test 3: Mini-Talks

1. (A) (B) (C) (D)   5. (A) (B) (C) (D)   9. (A) (B) (C) (D)
2. (A) (B) (C) (D)   6. (A) (B) (C) (D)   10. (A) (B) (C) (D)
3. (A) (B) (C) (D)   7. (A) (B) (C) (D)   11. (A) (B) (C) (D)
4. (A) (B) (C) (D)   8. (A) (B) (C) (D)   12. (A) (B) (C) (D)

MINI-TEST 3: MINI-TALKS

Directions: Listen to the talks and the questions about them. Decide which one of the four answer choices—(A), (B), (C), or (D) —is the best answer to the question. Then mark the appropriate answer on the answer sheet above.

Now start the tape.

1. (A) An improved toothbrush.
   (B) Recent developments in genetics.
   (C) New uses for bacteria.
   (D) A means of fighting tooth decay.

2. (A) They have many side effects.
   (B) They occur naturally in people's mouths.
   (C) They attack one type of bacteria.
   (D) They cause tooth decay.

3. (A) Microbiology.
   (B) Genetic engineering.
   (C) Dentistry.
   (D) Civil engineering.

4. (A) Plan A includes dinner, but Plan B does not.
   (B) Plan B is more expensive than Plan A.
   (C) Plan B includes Sunday dinner, but Plan A does not.
   (D) Plan A provides for three meals on most days while Plan B provides for only two.

5. (A) The Bengal Grill.
   (B) Restaurants near campus.
   (C) The Tiger's Lair.
   (D) The dormitory cafeterias.

6. (A) A receipt.
   (B) A check.
   (C) A student ID card.
   (D) A friend.

7. (A) Selling one's meal tickets to anyone else.
   (B) Eating at a dormitory where one does not live.
   (C) Eating at a cafeteria if one lives off campus.
   (D) Going back for more than one serving of food.

8. (A) They are open longer hours.
   (B) They serve many more students.
   (C) They offer a wider variety of foods.
   (D) They charge lower prices.

9. (A) Visitors to the Bronx Zoo.
   (B) Zoology students.
   (C) Visitors to the City Zoological Gardens.
   (D) New employees at the zoo.

10. (A) They were usually sleeping when visitors were present.
    (B) They were uncomfortable because they were exposed to direct sunlight.
    (C) They couldn't be observed because they were always in darkness.
    (D) They couldn't sleep well and therefore became ill.

11. (A) To make them visible to observers.
    (B) To put them to sleep.
    (C) To simulate natural daylight.
    (D) To allow them to see clearly.

12. (A) Study marsupial mammals.
    (B) Leave the zoo.
    (C) Look at the nocturnal animals.
    (D) Go to the World Down Under exhibit.

Peterson's TOEFL CBT Success

IDIOMATIC EXPRESSIONS

A knowledge of idioms is important for the Listening Comprehension section, especially Part A. These mini-lessons contain lists of some 300 expressions and their definitions as well as exercises to familiarize you with many of these expressions. Many of the expressions listed here have appeared on the Listening Comprehension section of TOEFL exams in the past, some of them several times.

Notes:

1. If a phrase contains a word in parentheses, that word is only used if the phrase is followed by a noun or pronoun.

   Example:
   catch up (with)

   You go ahead. I'll catch up later. (no noun or pronoun)
   I'll catch up with you later. (pronoun)

2. The words *one* and *someone* are used to indicate that any pronoun (or sometimes a noun) can be used in this expression.

   Example:
   on one's own

   How long have you been on *your* own?
   Tom's been on *his* own for several years.

MINI-LESSON 1.1

above all   most importantly
about to   almost ready to
add up   make sense; be logical
all at once   suddenly; without warning
all of a sudden   all at once; suddenly
as a matter of fact   in reality; actually
as a rule   generally; customarily
at the drop of a hat   quickly; without any preparation time
at ease   not nervous; calm
back out (of)   withdraw an offer
bank on   depend on; count on
be my guest   do what you want; feel free; help yourself
be rusty   need practice or review
beats me   I don't know; I have no idea (often used in response to a question)
better off   in an improved condition
bite off more than one can chew   take on more responsibility than one can handle
bound to   certain to; sure to
break down   stop functioning (a machine, for example)
break in (on)   interrupt
break the ice   break through social barriers (as at a party)
break the news (to)   inform; give bad news
break up   end (a meeting, for example)

break up (with)   stop being a couple (a boyfriend and girlfriend, for example)
a breeze   something very simple and easy to do
bring about   cause to happen
bring up   (1) raise (a child); (2) introduce (a topic, for example)
brush up on   review; study; practice
bump into   meet unexpectedly; run into
by and large   mostly; generally; on the whole
by heart   by memory; learned word for word
by no means   in no way; not at all

Exercise: Fill in the blanks in the sentences or dialogs with idioms from the above list. There will be one word per blank. It may be necessary to change the verb forms in order for the sentence to be grammatically correct. The first one is done as an example.

1. "Can you talk now?" "No, I'm __about__ __to__ go to the grocery store, but I'll call you as soon as I get back."

2. "You're probably too tired to play another game of racquetball, right?" "I'm not that tired, really. _____ _____ _____ _____ _____ I'd enjoy another game."

3. "Will you support my proposal at the meeting?" "Certainly. You can _____ _____ my support."

4. I was talking to my aunt when suddenly my cousin George Ann _____ _____ _____ our conversation.

5. "I understand Diane lost her job." "Yes, but she's actually _____ _____. She found a more interesting job with a higher salary."

6. My car _____ _____ last week, and I had to take the bus to work until it was repaired.

7. _____ _____ _____ Carlos is very punctual, but he sure was late tonight.

8. I was taking a quiet walk last night when, _____ _____ _____ _____, there was a loud explosion.

9. Kent is _____ _____ fail that class if he doesn't start studying.

10. They _____ _____ their children to be honest.

11. There were a few things I didn't like about Professor Wong's class, but _____ _____ _____ I enjoyed it.

12. "I think Matthew was cheating on that quiz." "That doesn't _____ _____. Why should the best student in the class cheat?"

13. "Can I have another sandwich?" "Sure, _____ _____ _____. I made plenty."

14. Actors and actresses must know their lines _____ _____.

15. If you don't want to talk about this problem, why did you _____ it _____?

16. Many accidents are _____ _____ by carelessness.

17. Their team won the game, but they _____ _____ _____ dominated it. It was a very close game.

18. "What a boring party. No one is talking to one another." "Maybe we should put on some music and start dancing. That might _____ _____ _____."

19. "Have you studied Spanish before?" "Yes, but it's been years since I took a Spanish class, so I'll need to _____ _____ _____ it before I go to Venezuela."

20. "You're taking five classes this term?" "Yes, and I'm having trouble getting caught up. I'm afraid I _____ _____ _____ _____ I _____ _____ this time."

21. "You're all packed and ready to go, I see." "I could leave _____ _____ _____ _____ _____ _____."

22. "Do you know what the name of this street is?" "_____ _____. This is the first time I've ever been in this town."

23. "How's that biology class you're taking?" "So far, it's been _____ _____. We've just been going over things I studied last semester."

24. "What time did the party _____ _____ last night?" "I don't know. It was still going on when I went home."

25. "I was awfully nervous when I gave that speech." "Really? You hid it well. I thought you were completely _____ _____."

Mini-Lesson 1.2

call it a day   stop working for the day; go home
call off   cancel
call on   visit
calm down   relax
care for   (1) take care of; (2) like; feel affection for
catch on   become popular
catch on (to)   understand, learn
catch up (with)   go as fast as; catch
check in (or **into**)   register (at a hotel)
check out (of)   (1) leave (a hotel); (2) take material (from a library, for example)
cheer up   become cheerful; be happy
chip in (on/for)   contribute
clear up   (1) clarify; make understandable; (2) become nice and sunny (used to talk about the weather)
come across   find; meet; encounter
come around (to)   begin to change one's opinion; begin to agree with
come down with   become sick with (an illness)
come up with   think of (an idea)
cost an arm and a leg   be very expensive
count on   depend on; rely on; bank on
count out   eliminate; no longer consider as a factor
cut off   stop; discontinue (a service, for example)
cut out for   have an aptitude for; be qualified for

Exercise: Fill in the blanks in the sentences or dialogs with idioms from the above list. There will be one word per blank. It may be necessary to change the verb forms in order for the sentence to be grammatically correct.

1. The reception in the garden was _____ _____ because of a thunderstorm.

2. Don't get so excited. Just _____ _____ and tell us what happened.

3. I was looking up some information in the almanac when I _____ _____ an interesting fact.

4. I can _____ _____ my car. It's very dependable and never breaks down.

5. How did you _____ _____ _____ such a strange idea?

6. I arrived in town last night at seven-thirty and _____ _____ my hotel at around eight. This morning I plan to _____ _____ at about nine.

7. "Did you rent this videotape?" "No, I _____ it _____ _____ the library."

8. You look tired. Why don't we _____ _____ _____ _____ and finish up tomorrow?

9. It won't be too expensive to buy Professor McMillen a present if we all _____ _____.

10. If Arthur doesn't pay his electric bill soon, the utilities company might _____ _____ his electricity.

11. "I don't understand this theorem at all." "Talk to Professor Adler. I'll bet she can _____ _____ your confusion."

12. Who _____ _____ your cat while you were out of town?

13. A good stereo system doesn't have to _____ _____ _____ _____ _____ _____. You can find one for a reasonable price.

14. Cauliflower isn't my favorite vegetable. In fact, I don't _____ _____ it at all.

15. "I'm depressed. I didn't do very well on the first quiz." "_____ _____! That quiz only counted for 10 percent of the total grade, and I'm sure you'll do better on the other tests."

16. "How did Eric do in the cross-country ski race?" "He got off to a bad start, and so he never _____ _____ _____ the leading skiers."

17. "Why did Brenda drop out of business school?" "She decided she wasn't _____ _____ _____ a career in business. She's going to study art instead."

18. This song wasn't very popular when it was first recorded, but now it's starting to _____ _____.

19. "Your roommate is still planning to vote for Smithson for president of the Student Council?" "Yes, but I'm going to keep talking to him. I think eventually he'll _____ _____ _____ our point of view and vote for Brannigan."

20. That saleswoman _____ _____ her clients at least once a month because she thinks personal contact is important.

21. "Is it still raining?" "No, the rain has stopped, and it's starting to _____ _____."

MINI-LESSON 1.3

day in and day out   constantly; for a long time
die down   become less severe; quiet down
do over   do again; repeat
do without   not have
down the drain   wasted; done for no reason (work, for example)
dream up   invent; think of; come up with
drop in (on)   visit informally
drop (someone) a line   send someone a letter
drop off   (1) leave something (a package, for example); (2) take (someone) home; let someone out of a car
drop out (of)   stop attending (classes, for example)
easy as pie   very simple; a piece of cake
eyes bigger than one's stomach   said of someone who takes more food than he or she can eat
fall behind   not move as quickly as; lag behind
fall through   fail to happen
a far cry from   not similar to; not as good as
feel free   do something if one wants
feel like   be inclined to; want to
feel like a million dollars   feel very good
feel up to   feel able to do something; ready to
fed up (with)   not able to tolerate; disgusted with; annoyed by
few and far between   uncommon and infrequent
figure out   understand; solve

Exercise: Fill in the blanks in the sentences or dialogs with idioms from the list on page 96. There will be one word per blank. It may be necessary to change the verb forms in order for the sentence to be grammatically correct.

1. It took me hours to _____ _____ how to record programs on my VCR.

2. If you could _____ _____ the laundry on the way to work, I'll pick it up on Monday.

3. "What a wonderful masquerade party!" "People certainly _____ _____ some interesting costumes, didn't they."

4. "Do you _____ _____ going out tonight?" "No, I'd rather stay home and read."

5. "Why have you _____ _____ in your French class?" "I was sick and I missed a few classes. But I'm studying hard to catch up."

6. "Why do we need to get gas now? We have quite a bit left." "This highway goes through some very empty country, and gas stations are _____ _____ _____ _____."

7. Howard's teacher wasn't satisfied with the work he had done, so she asked him to _____ it _____.

8. I'm _____ _____ _____ my roommate's lack of responsibility. He never pays his bills or his share of the rent on time.

9. "Isn't your class picnic today?" "No, our plans for the picnic _____ _____."

10. "The food at that new restaurant isn't bad." "It's all right, but it's _____ _____ _____ _____ the food at Mario's. Now *that* is a great restaurant!"

11. Ben had to _____ _____ _____ the university because of financial problems.

12. After blowing furiously all day, the wind finally _____ _____.

13. "Do you telephone friends before you visit, or just _____ _____ _____ them?" "It depends. If they're close friends, I just visit them. If they're acquaintances, I generally call first."

14. "I'm tired of the same old routine." "I know how you feel. I get tired of doing the same things _____ _____ _____ _____ _____ too."

15. "Ralph really loaded up his tray with food." "He'll never eat it all. Ralph's _____ are _____ _____ his _____."

16. "I need to use a computer for a few hours." "_____ _____ to use my laptop computer. I don't need it this morning."

17. "I've missed James since he moved to Seattle." "You should _____ him _____ _____ and let him know how you're doing. I'm sure he'd love to get a letter from you."

MINI-LESSON 1.4

fill in   write in a blank (on an application form, for example)
fill in (for)   substitute for
fill one in   provide missing information
fill out   complete (an application form, for example)
find out   learn; discover
a fish out of water   someone not in his or her normal surroundings
fix up   repair; renovate
follow in one's footsteps   do what someone else did (especially an older relative)
for good   permanently; forever
for the time being   temporarily; for now
from out of the blue   unexpectedly; without warning

get along with   have good relations with
get carried away   go too far; do too much; buy too much
get in one's blood   become a habit; become customary
get in over one's head   take on too much responsibility; bite off more than one can chew
get in the way   block; obstruct
get in touch with   contact
get the hang of something   learn how to do something
get a kick out of (doing something)   enjoy; have fun doing something
get off   leave (a vehicle)
get off the ground   start to be successful
get on   board (a vehicle)
get over   recover from (a disease)
get rid of   discard; no longer have
get under way   begin; start
give away   distribute (for free)
give (someone) a cold shoulder   act unfriendly toward someone; ignore

Exercise: Fill in the blanks in the sentences or dialog with idioms from the above list. There will be one word per blank. It may be necessary to change the verb forms in order for the sentence to be grammatically correct.

1. "How did you _____ _____ where Warren lives?" "I just looked it up in my address book."

2. "I'm interested in the job that was advertised in the newspaper." "Fine. Just _____ _____ this application form."

3. Don't forget to _____ _____ the date on your check.

4. "Is Agnes still mad at you?" "I suppose so. I saw her at a party last weekend, and she just _____ me _____ _____ it."

5. "Are you moving to Baltimore _____ _____?" "No, just _____ _____ _____ _____. I'll be back here in a month or two."

6. "That old paint that you have stored in your garage is a fire hazard." "You're right. I should _____ _____ _____ it."

7. Some companies _____ _____ free samples of new products in order to familiarize consumers with them.

8. "How's that advanced computer class you're taking, Polly." "Not so good. I can't understand a word that the teacher or any of the students are saying. I really feel like _____ _____ _____ _____ _____."

9. "Don't you just hate all this graffiti?" "It *is* ugly, isn't it? I've never understood why people _____ _____ _____ _____ _____ writing on walls. It doesn't seem like much fun to me."

10. When the train stopped, a mysterious looking woman in a black raincoat _____ _____ the train and found her seat.

11. "Maxwell's project will be very successful, I think." "Oh, I don't know. I'm not sure it will ever _____ _____ _____ _____."

12. Do you _____ _____ _____ your new roommate, or do you two argue?

13. "That run-down old house that David bought looks terrific." "Yes, he's _____ it _____ beautifully, hasn't he?"

14. "Has Edward _____ _____ _____ _____ you lately?" "No, he hasn't. I don't think he has my new telephone number."

15. "Will the concert start soon?" "It should _____ _____ _____ any minute now."

Peterson's TOEFL CBT Success

16. Living by the ocean really _____ _____ your _____. Once you've lived here, you never want to leave.

17. This is the last stop. Everyone has to _____ _____ the bus here.

18. Professor Dunbar came down with the flu, so her teaching assistant _____ _____ _____ her for a few days.

MINI-LESSON 1.5

give a hand   applaud; clap
give a hand (with)   assist
go easy on not punish severely
go on (with)   continue
go with   (1) accompany; (2) look good together; complement (for example, two articles of clothing)
go without saying   be clear; be obvious
grow up   to mature; to become an adult
hand in   give back to; return
hand out   distribute
hang on   wait
hard to come by   difficult to find
have on   wear
have one's hands full   be very busy; have a challenging job
have a heart   be compassionate; show mercy
have a hunch   have an intuitive feeling
have a word with (someone)   talk to someone briefly
have the time of one's life   have fun; have a great time
hear firsthand (from)   get information directly from someone
hear from   be contacted by; be in touch with
hear of   know about; be familiar with
hit it off   become friendly (especially at a first meeting)
hit the road   leave, go away
hold on   wait
hold on (to)   grasp
hold still   not move
hold up   delay

Exercise: Fill in the blanks in the sentences or dialog with idioms from the above list. There will be one word per blank. It may be necessary to change the verb forms in order for the sentence to be grammatically correct.

1. Everett was born in the South but he _____ _____ in Michigan.

2. At the beginning of the class, the instructor _____ _____ the quizzes and told the students they had 10 minutes in which to finish.

3. After 10 minutes, the students _____ _____ their quizzes to the instructor.

4. "Have you ever _____ _____ William Carlos Williams?" "I believe so. He was a poet, wasn't he?"

5. "Hello, is Gina there?" "Yes, _____ _____ a minute and I'll get her."

6. "You're graduating next month, right?" "Yes, but I intend to _____ _____ _____ my studies in graduate school."

7. _____ _____ while I take your photograph. I don't want the picture to be blurry.

8. "I got stopped by the police for speeding. I have to pay a big fine." "Well, you could talk to the judge and ask him to reduce it. Since you've never been stopped for speeding before, maybe he'll _____ _____ _____ you."

9. "Do you like this blouse?" "Yes, but I think the grey silk one would _____ better _____ your jacket."

10. "So, Dave is teaching you how to windsurf?" "Yes, and he's such a good teacher that I'm already _____ _____ _____ _____ it."

11. The audience _____ the cast a big _____ after their wonderful performance.

12. "Do you think Iris will pass the history test?" "That _____ _____ _____. In fact, she'll probably have the best grade in the class."

13. "What _____ _____ your flight?" "There was a big snowstorm in Denver that delayed a lot of flights."

14. "Have you _____ _____ Maureen since she went to Hawaii." "Yeah, I got a postcard from her yesterday. She said she's _____ _____ _____ _____ her _____ and never wants to come home."

15. Can you _____ me _____ _____ _____ this luggage? It's too heavy for me to carry by myself.

16. The wind is starting to blow. You'd better _____ _____ _____ your hat.

17. "Oh, you bought the new book by Richard Stone." "Yes, but that book is _____ _____ _____ _____. I looked for it in three or four bookstores."

18. It's getting late. I'd better _____ _____ _____ if I want to get home by midnight.

19. "Can I _____ _____ _____ _____ you now, Professor Rivera?" "I've got to go to class right now. Drop by my office later and we'll talk then."

20. "You sure bought a lot of groceries." "Yeah, I guess I _____ _____ _____. I should never go grocery shopping when I'm hungry."

MINI-LESSON 1.6

in hot water   in trouble
in the dark   not knowing; confused
in the long run   over a long period of time
in no time   very soon; very quickly
in a nutshell   in summary; in brief
in the same boat   in the same situation; having the same problem
in person   face to face (not by telephone, letter, etc.)
in store   in the future; coming up
iron out   solve (a problem)
join the club   have the same problem
jump to conclusions   form opinions without sufficient evidence
keep an eye on   watch; take care of; look after
keep an eye out (for)   look for
keep on (with)   continue
keep track of   know where something or someone is
keep up (with)   maintain the same speed as
kill time   spend time doing unimportant things (before an appointment, for example)
know like the back of one's hand   be very familiar with
lay off   put out of work
learn the ropes   become familiar with; get used to; get the hang of
leave out   not include; omit

leave someone/something alone   not disturb
let someone down   disappoint
let up   decline in intensity (rain, for example)
look after   take care of; mind
look for   try to locate
look forward to   anticipate (with pleasure)
look into   investigate

Exercise: Fill in the blanks in the sentences or dialogs with idioms from the above list. There will be one word per blank. It may be necessary to change the verb forms in order for the sentence to be grammatically correct.

1. Will you _____ _____ _____ _____ my dog while I go in the drug store?

2. Kathy's daughter has such short legs that she has a hard time _____ _____ _____ the other children.

3. The store had to _____ _____ a number of clerks because sales were down.

4. "You must be anxious to go on your vacation." "I certainly am. I'm really _____ _____ _____ this trip."

5. Don't _____ _____ _____. Maybe your jewelry wasn't stolen after all.

6. "I need to find a new apartment." "There might be some vacancies in the building where I live. I'll _____ _____ _____ _____ _____ one."

7. The company may lose some money now, but _____ _____ _____ _____, this is a good investment.

8. Alex complained that no one invited him to any social events and that he felt _____ _____.

9. "Can you hurry over here? I need to see you right away." "Sure. I'll be there _____ _____ _____."

10. "May I help you, sir?" "No, I'm just looking around and trying to _____ some _____ until my wife finishes shopping."

11. "Has it stopped raining yet?" "No, but it's beginning to _____ _____ a little."

12. "I can't go to Daryl's party this weekend. I have to study." "Guess we're _____ _____ _____ _____. I've got to study too."

13. "Should we stop and spend the night at this motel?" "No, let's _____ _____ driving for a few more miles."

14. If you find a baby animal in the woods, don't touch it. Just _____ it _____.

15. I _____ all over town _____ a good used car, but I couldn't find one.

16. Stella's sister _____ _____ her baby while Stella is at work.

17. "If you don't know how to use this software, why don't you ask Joanne to help?" "I *did* ask her, but I'm still _____ _____ _____. I didn't understand a word she said."

18. The police are _____ _____ the crime.

19. "Did Amanda ever complete her project?" "She's almost finished. She just has a few minor problems left to _____ _____."

20. Alfred is _____ _____ _____ with his boss because he didn't finish an important project by the deadline.

21. "Has Marilyn gotten used to her new job at the bank yet?" "It took her awhile, but I think she's finally _____ _____ _____ there."

22. Are you _____ _____ _____ this proposal or against it?

23. Are you familiar with this neighborhood?" "I grew up here, so I _____ it _____ _____ _____ _____ my _____."

24. "Is your roommate at home now?" "I have no idea. I can never _____ _____ _____ his comings and goings."

25. "I understand that you have a new dean over at the Business School." "Yes, his name is Dean Nishimura. He has a completely different philosophy of business education from the one Dean Woodford had, so I'm sure that some big changes are _____ _____ for us."

MINI-LESSON 1.7

look like   resemble
look out (for)   be careful
look over   examine; read
look up   (1) find information (especially in a reference book); (2) try to locate someone
look up to   respect; admire
make ends meet   balance a budget
make a fool of oneself   act embarrassingly
make a point of   make a special effort
make sense (of)   be logical and clear; understand
make up   invent, create
make up one's mind   decide
make way for   allow space for; provide a path for
mean to   intend to
mixed up   confused
music to one's ears   something that sounds pleasant
a nervous wreck   someone who is very nervous
next to nothing   very little (money, for example); cheap
no doubt about it   certainly; definitely
no harm done   there was no damage done
not at all   not in any way; not to any degree
not believe one's ears (or eyes)   be unable to believe what one hears (or sees)
not think much of   not like; not have a good opinion of
odds and ends   small, miscellaneous items
an old hand (at)   an experienced person
on edge   nervous
on end   consecutively, without a break (*days on end*, for example)
on hand   easily available
on needles and pins   nervous; anxious
on one's own   independent
on second thought   after reconsidering
on the go   always busy; always moving
on the tip of one's tongue   almost able to remember
on the whole   in general
out of (something)   not having something
out of one's mind   insane; illogical; irrational
out of order   broken; not functioning properly
out of the question   definitely not; impossible
over and over   again and again; repeatedly
over one's head   not understandable (a joke, for example); obscure

Peterson's TOEFL CBT Success

Exercise: Fill in the blanks in the sentences or dialogs with idioms from the list on page 102. There will be one word per blank. It may be necessary to change the verb forms in order for the sentence to be grammatically correct.

1. "Have you _____ _____ this contract yet?" "Not yet. I'll try to read it this weekend."

2. "I think I'll have the prime rib, waiter." "All right, sir." "Wait, no—_____ _____ _____ I think I'll have the chicken."

3. Is this story true, or did you just _____ it _____?

4. You can't get a soda from that machine. There's a sign on it that says "_____ _____ _____."

5. Sherry _____ _____ _____ her father because of all the help and good advice he's given her.

6. I don't have much cash _____ _____, but I can get some from an automatic teller machine.

7. What a confusing movie! I couldn't _____ _____ _____ it.

8. "You did a fine job on this research paper, especially on the bibliography." "Thanks. I _____ _____ _____ _____ getting the bibliography exactly right. I did it _____ _____ _____ until it was perfect."

9. "What's Fritz's cousin's name?" "It's _____ _____ _____ _____ my _____, but I can't quite remember."

10. "Hello. I'd like to reserve a room for this weekend." "I'm afraid that's _____ _____ _____ _____. The hotel is fully booked this weekend."

11. "Do you have any fresh peaches?" "Sorry, I'm _____ _____ them. I just sold the last crate of peaches."

12. "Listen to the roar of the engines." "Yeah, it's _____ _____ my _____. I just love going to these car races."

13. The plane was delayed for hours _____ _____. I thought we'd never get off the ground.

14. "Have you finished moving into your new apartment?" "Almost. There are still a few _____ _____ _____ in my old apartment that I need to move today."

15. "Brad sure is busy, isn't he." "Yeah, he's involved in so many activities that he's always _____ _____ _____."

16. There are so many interesting dishes on the menu that it's hard for me to _____ _____ my _____ which one to order.

17. If you go into the swamp, _____ _____ _____ alligators.

18. "When will you be informed of the test results?" "Not until Monday, so I'll be _____ _____ _____ _____ all weekend."

19. "Do you know what the capital of South Dakota is?" "I'm not sure. Let's _____ it _____ in this atlas."

20. They're going to tear down those old warehouses to _____ _____ _____ a big new hotel.

21. "I like that painting you bought. Did it cost much?" "No, the artist sold it to me for _____ _____ _____."

22. "How was your final exam, Laurie?" "A couple of questions were tricky, but _____ _____ _____ it was pretty easy."

23. "I'm sorry I knocked that vase over. I didn't mean to." "_____ _____ _____. It wasn't damaged."

24. I must have been _____ _____ my _____ when I signed the lease on this apartment. I can't afford this much rent.

25. He didn't _____ _____ break the plate; it was an accident.

26. "I didn't know you could play horseshoes so well." "Oh, I'm _____ _____ _____ _____ horseshoes. I've been playing since I was a kid."

27. You must be _____ _____. This isn't River Street; it's Laurel Avenue.

28. "How long have you been living alone?" "I've been _____ my _____ since I graduated from high school."

29. "Did you find that lecture boring?" "_____ _____ _____. In fact, I thought it was fascinating."

30. "Christine is so funny, she should be a stand-up comic." "I suppose, but a lot of her jokes go right _____ my _____. I just don't get them."

Mini-Lesson 1.8

part with   no longer have; get rid of; not be in the company of
pass up   not accept; not choose
pass with flying colors   do very well (on a test)
pat oneself on the back   congratulate oneself
pay attention (to)   concentrate on; focus on
pick out   choose; select
pick up   (1) take something from a surface (for example, a floor); (2) go to a location and get someone or something; (3) learn (especially without formal training)
pick up the tab (for)   pay for
the picture of   a perfect example of something
play it by ear   do something without a definite plan
play it safe   choose a cautious plan
point out   indicate
a pretty penny   a lot of money
pull one's leg   joke with someone; make up a story
push one's luck   to continue doing something too long; to keep taking chances
put aside   save for later; set aside
put away   return something to its proper place
put off   delay; postpone
put on   begin to wear
put together   assemble
put up with   tolerate

Exercise: Fill in the blanks in the sentences or dialogs with idioms from the above list. There will be one word per blank. It may be necessary to change the verb forms in order for the sentence to be grammatically correct.

1. Vanessa is allergic to tobacco smoke, so she can't _____ _____ _____ smoking.

2. "That conference you attended in Honolulu must have been very expensive." "Yes, but fortunately, the company I work for _____ _____ _____ _____ _____ it."

3. I asked my teacher to _____ _____ the mistakes that I made in my essay so that I could correct them.

4. "What do you want to do tomorrow?" "I don't know. Let's just _____ _____ _____ _____."

5. "You should get rid of that old leather jacket." "I know, but I hate to _____ _____ it. I've had it for years."

6. "How did you learn to make such beautiful pottery? Did you take a class in ceramics?" "No, I just _____ it _____ on my own."

7. "Can you read that sign?" "Just a minute. Let me _____ my glasses _____."

8. It took Linda weeks to _____ _____ that thousand-piece jigsaw puzzle.

9. This bike cost _____ _____ _____, but I think it was worth it.

10. "I passed the first two quizzes in this class and I scarcely studied for them at all." "Well, if I were you, I wouldn't _____ my _____ any further. You should study for the next quiz because it's going to be a lot harder."

11. I'll _____ _____ the laundry that you dropped off at the cleaners this morning.

12. The child _____ _____ her toys from the floor and then _____ them _____ in her toy box.

13. Bert and Mary had to _____ _____ their dinner party until next weekend because Bert wasn't feeling well.

14. "Who _____ _____ that tie for you?" "No one. I chose it myself."

15. "Are you going to take that job?" "No, I decided to _____ it _____ because I don't want to relocate."

16. _____ _____ as I read the directions or you won't understand what to do.

17. "I finally finished collecting all the materials I need to write my report." "Great, but don't be too quick to _____ yourself _____ _____ _____. You still have to write the report and then word process it."

18. "How did you do on your final exams?" "Great! I _____ them all _____ _____ _____."

19. I'm going to _____ this magazine _____ for now and read it later.

20. I wouldn't believe a word Lynn told you. She's just _____ your _____.

MINI-LESSON 1.9

right away   immediately
ring a bell (with)   sound familiar to
rough it   experience somewhat difficult or primitive conditions
rule out   say something is impossible; eliminate
run a temperature   have a fever
run for office   try to get elected
run into   (1) meet unexpectedly; bump into; (2) collide with
run late   be late; be in a hurry
run of the mill   ordinary
run out of   exhaust the supply of
save one's breath   don't bother asking someone
search me   I don't know; I have no idea; beats me
see eye to eye (with someone) (on something)   have the same opinion; be in agreement
see (someone) off   accompany (to an airport or train station, for example)
see to   take care of; check on; fix
serve one right   receive the proper punishment; get the penalty one deserves
short for   a nickname for
show around   orient; give a tour

show off   try to attract attention by unusual behavior
show up   arrive
shut down   close
sign up (for)   enroll (for a class, for example)
sing another tune   change one's opinion; feel differently
size up   measure; estimate
sleep on it   postpone a decision until the next day
slowly but surely   gradually; steadily but not quickly
snowed under   very busy
so far, so good   up until now, there are no problems
sooner or later   at some indefinite future time
speak one's mind   say what one is thinking
speak up   speak more loudly
speak up for   support verbaly
spell out (for)   make something very clear; explain in detail

Exercise: Fill in the blanks in the sentences or dialogs with idioms from the above list. There will be one word per blank. It may be necessary to change the verb forms in order for the sentence to be grammatically correct.

1. "Has John gone back to Minneapolis yet?" "Yes, I just _____ him _____ at the airport."

2. "This pipe is leaking again." "We'd better have a plumber _____ _____ it."

3. I was late because I _____ _____ _____ gasoline.

4. Write down your ideas _____ _____. If you wait to write them down, you may forget them.

5. When the factory _____ _____, hundreds of workers were laid off.

6. "Did you _____ _____ _____ Professor Carmichael's class?" "No, I decided to take Professor Knudson's class instead."

7. "Vicki, how's that project you're working on coming along?" "_____ _____, _____ _____, but the tricky part will be next week."

8. "Have you ever heard of a actor named Anthony Reed?" "Hmmm. I don't think so. The name doesn't _____ _____ _____ _____ me at all."

9. "Frank doesn't take a hint very well, does he?" "No, you have to _____ things _____ _____ Frank. He likes everything crystal clear."

10. I'd heard that the clothes in this store were very nice, but I found them _____ _____ _____ _____.

11. "Bennet thought those stories Tina told about you were pretty funny." 'They weren't funny, they were embarrassing. Bennet would be _____ _____ _____ if Tina had told that kind of story about him."

12. Norman doesn't like to _____ _____ when he goes on vacation. He prefers to stay at luxury hotels.

13. I don't like to go to parties too early. I'd rather _____ _____ a little bit late.

14. It's expensive to _____ _____ _____ these days. Political campaigns cost a lot of money.

15. "So, do you plan to buy this motorcycle or not?" "I'm still not sure. Can I _____ _____ _____ and let you know tomorrow morning?"

16. "Have you seen the campus yet?" "Yes, my cousin Melissa is a student there, and she _____ me _____."

17. "I'm collecting money for the Red Cross. I think I'll ask Pat to contribute." "_____ your _____. Pat never contributes to anything."

18. "Are you going to medical school?" "Not this year, but I wouldn't _____ it _____ in the future."

19. I _____ _____ my old friend Leslie downtown yesterday. I hadn't seen her for months.

20. "I understand you're learning how to speak Russian." "Yes, and it was really hard for me, especially at first. Now, though, I'm _____ _____ _____ getting the hang of it."

21. "Your sister's name is Jessie?" "That's what everyone calls her—it's _____ _____ Jessica."

22. "Have a busy night at the restaurant?" "We weren't just busy—we were _____ _____! I've never seen so many customers!"

23. "I feel terrible. I have a terrible cold or maybe even the flu." "Are you _____ _____ _____? If you have a fever, then you probably have the flu."

24. My brother and I agree on most issues, but I sure don't _____ _____ _____ _____ _____ him _____ this proposal to build a new stadium.

Mini-Lesson 1.10

spick and span   extremely clean; spotless
stack up against   compare with
stamp out   eliminate; wipe out
stand for   (1) tolerate; put up with; (2) symbolize; represent
stand out   be noticeable
stay out   not come home
stay out (or up) to all hours   come home (or go to bed) very late
stay up   not go to bed
stick with   not change; stay with
stock up on   get a large supply of something
a stone's throw from   not far away from; close to
stop by   visit informally; go to see
straighten up   clean up; make tidy
stuck with   have something one cannot get rid of
take a break   stop working for a short time
take a lot of nerve   require a lot of courage
take a lot out of (someone)   be hard on someone; drain energy from someone
take advantage of   utilize; make use of; exploit
take after   resemble; look like (especially an older relative)
take apart   disassemble
take it easy   relax; calm down

Exercise: Fill in the blanks in the sentences or dialogs with idioms from the above list. There will be one word per blank. It may be necessary to change the verb forms in order for the sentence to be grammatically correct.

1. Vaccines have permitted doctors to virtually _____ _____ a number of diseases, including smallpox and polio.

2. "How late do you usually _____ _____?" "I'm normally in bed by eleven on weekdays."

3. "How late do you usually _____ _____ on weekends?" "I sometimes don't come home until two or three in the morning."

4. "Do you _____ _____ your mother or father?" "I don't think I look much like either one of them."

5. Earl had no trouble _____ _____ the engine on the lawn mower, but then he couldn't put it back together.

6. You look a little tired. Why don't you _____ _____ _____ and finish your homework later?

7. The teacher won't _____ _____ cheating. When she caught one student cheating on the midterm exam, she gave him a zero on that test.

8. "I tried and tried to find a buyer for this old car." "Looks like you're _____ _____ it for now."

9. "My brother is going to invest all his savings in a new business venture." "That _____ _____ _____ _____ _____. I'd be afraid to take a risk like that."

10. "I give up. I can't solve this chemistry problem." "_____ _____ it. Eventually, you'll figure it out."

11. We have to leave the apartment _____ _____ _____. The landlord said that if it wasn't clean when we moved out, we'd lose part of our security deposit.

12. Don was wearing jeans and a tee shirt while all the other guests had on formal dinner wear. He really _____ _____.

13. "I'm nervous about my interview." "_____ _____ _____. You'll make a better impression if you're relaxed."

14. The fifty stars on the American flag _____ _____ the fifty states.

15. "Do you _____ _____ your apartment before guests _____ _____?" "A little bit. I don't mind if it's a little messy, but I don't want it to look like a disaster area."

16. "My new roommate is from Italy." "You should _____ _____ _____ this opportunity to learn some Italian."

17. "I just heard on the news that the Florida orange crop was damaged by the hurricane last week, and that orange juice prices are going to go way up." "If we had a big freezer, we could _____ _____ _____ frozen orange juice now and we wouldn't have to pay those prices."

18. "Do you live near Cecilia?" "Oh, sure. My apartment building is just _____ _____ _____ _____ hers."

19. "So you ran in that 10-kilometer race?" "Yes, but it _____ _____ _____ _____ _____ me. I can hardly move."

20. "Tim, you've eaten at both these restaurants—how does Chez Michelle _____ _____ _____ the Oak Room?" "Oh, they're both good. I think the Oak Room has slightly better food, but the service is better at Chez Michelle."

MINI-LESSON 1.11

take off   (1) remove (clothing, for example); (2) ascend (a plane, for example); (3) become popular quickly
take over   assume control or responsibility
take part in   participate in
take a shortcut   take a more direct or faster route than usual
take the plunge   finally take action; do something different
take time off (from)   take a vacation or a break from work or school
take up   begin to study some topic or engage in some activity
talk down to   speak to someone as if he or she were a child; patronize
talk into   persuade; convince
talk out of   dissuade; convince not to do something
talk over   discuss
tear oneself away from something   stop doing something interesting

Peterson's TOEFL CBT Success

tear up   rip into small pieces
tell apart   distinguish
things are looking up   the situation is improving
think over   consider
throw away   discard; get rid of
throw cold water on   discourage; force to cancel (a plan, for example)
throw the book at someone   give someone the maximum punishment
try on   test clothing before buying (for size, style, and so on)
try out   test a product before buying
try out (for)   audition for (a role in a play, for example); attempt to join (a team, for example)

Exercise: Fill in the blanks in the sentences or dialogs with idioms from the above list. There will be one word per blank. It may be necessary to change the verb forms in order for the sentence to be grammatically correct.

1. You'd better _____ _____ these gloves before you buy them; they may not fit.

2. At first, I didn't want to go to the party, but I'm glad Annette _____ me _____ it. It was fun.

3. The spy _____ _____ the document so that no one else could read it.

4. The twins look so much alike that almost no one can _____ them _____.

5. "I need more excitement in my life." "Why don't you give up stamp collecting and _____ _____ skydiving instead?"

6. "Who made the final decision?" "All of the people who were at the meeting _____ _____ _____ the decision-making process."

7. Most air accidents take place when a plane is _____ _____ or landing.

8. "Will your friend Scott be coming to the reception?" "If he can _____ himself _____ _____ those computer games he's always playing."

9. Dan was afraid the judge would _____ _____ _____ _____ him because he had been charged with the same offense several times.

10. _____ _____ your boots before you go into the house.

11. I wish I'd _____ _____ this calculator before I bought it. It doesn't seem to be working right.

12. Marvin was going to drop out of school, but his grandfather_____ him _____ _____ it.

13. I'm not sure if this is a suitable topic for a research paper. I need to _____ it _____ with my teacher before I start writing.

14. "I'm going to _____ _____ those old newspapers." "Don't just put them in the trash—recycle them instead."

15. "Are you going on the class trip?" "I need to _____ it _____ before I decide."

16. "How did you get home so quickly?" "I _____ _____ _____ through the fields."

17. "So, Louisa, you decided to _____ _____ for a part in the play?" "Yes, I've been interested in acting for quite a while, so I finally decided to _____ _____ _____."

18. Akiko is going to _____ some _____ _____ _____ teaching to finish writing her dissertation.

MINI-LESSON 1.12

turn around   face in a different direction
turn down   (1) reject an offer; (2) decrease in intensity
turn in   (1) return; give back; hand in; (2) go to bed
turn into   change to; transform into
turn off   stop the operation (of an appliance, for example); shut off
turn on   start the operation (of an appliance, for example)
turn out   (1) result; end up; be the final product; (2) produce; (3) arrive; gather (for a meeting, for example)
turn up   (1) increase in intensity; (2) arrive
under the weather   slightly ill
use up   use completely
wait on   serve
walk on air   be very happy
warm up   (1) heat; (2) practice; prepare for
warm up (to)   become friendly with; start to enjoy
watch out (for)   be alert; look out for
wear out   become no longer useful because of wear
what the doctor ordered   exactly what was needed; the perfect thing
wipe out   eliminate; stamp out
without a hitch   without a problem
work out   (1) exercise; (2) bring to a successful conclusion; solve

Exercise: Fill in the blanks in the sentences or dialogs with idioms from the above list. There will be one word per blank. It may be necessary to change the verb forms in order for the sentence to be grammatically correct.

1. The story of Dr. Jekyll and Mr. Hyde is about a scientist who _____ _____ a monster after drinking a chemical potion.

2. _____ _____ the water or the tub will overflow.

3. It's warm in here. Could you _____ _____ the heater a little?

4. I love that song. Could you _____ _____ the radio a little?

5. I can't see a thing. Please _____ _____ the light.

6. This sweater looked nice when it was new, but now it's _____ _____.

7. "I'm hungry!" "Why don't you _____ _____ some of the leftovers that are in the refrigerator? You can use the microwave oven."

8. Not many people _____ _____ for the meeting last night.

9. It's been a rough day. I'm going to _____ _____ early and get a good night's sleep.

10. "How about a nice cup of hot tea?" "That's exactly what I'm in the mood for. It's just _____ _____ _____ _____."

11. "How was your presentation." "Great. It went off _____ _____ _____."

12. I'm going to the gym to _____ _____ on the exercise machines.

13. If you're on a crowded bus or subway car, you must _____ _____ _____ pickpockets.

14. "A bear! I don't see a bear! Where is it?" "_____ _____ slowly. It's right behind you."

15. Maria had quite a few problems last year, but she _____ them all _____.

16. Don't ask me to _____ _____ you! I'm not your servant.

17. Brian was offered the manager's job but he _____ it _____. He said he didn't want the responsibility.

18. Before the game starts, the players need to _____ _____.

19. "This cake Holly baked for the wedding _____ _____ very well, don't you think?" "Yes, indeed. It was delicious."

20. "Mitchell looked pale and tired." "He told me he was feeling a little _____ _____ _____."

21. "You must be happy about getting that scholarship." "Are you kidding? I'm still _____ _____ _____."

Section 2:

STRUCTURE AND
WRITTEN EXPRESSION

RED ALERT

The second section of TOEFL tests your understanding of English grammar and usage. This section is divided into two parts: structure and written expression. The length of these parts varies depending on the form of the test.

	Standard Form	Long Form
Structure (Sentence Completion)	15 items	23 items
Written Expression (Error Identification)	25 items	37 items
Totals	40 items	60 items
Time	25 minutes	35 minutes

Section 2 is important! Your best chance for improving your score on TOEFL in a short time is to improve your score on this section, and therefore pull up your total score. Although a wide range of grammar points are tested, there are certain points that appear again and again, and you can master these points with the information and practice this book provides. Also, there are fewer items in this part than in the other two, so each item that you answer correctly adds more to your total score.

Section 2 may seem less stressful for you than Section 1 because you don't have to divide your attention between the tape and the test book. It may seem less stressful than Section 3 because it is easier to finish all the items before time is called.

Section 2 sentences are generally about academic subjects: the physical sciences (such as astronomy or geology), the social sciences (such as psychology or economics), or the humanities (such as music or literature). You will NOT see sentences that deal with "controversial" subjects such as abortion, drugs, or sensitive political issues.

Any cultural references in the sentences are to the culture of the United States or Canada. Many of the sentences contain references to people, places, and institutions that you will not be familiar with. (In fact, many North Americans are not familiar with these either!) It's not necessary to know these references; you should simply concentrate on the structure of the sentences. It's also not necessary to understand all the vocabulary in a sentence; you can often answer a question correctly without a complete understanding of that sentence.

There are two possible approaches to Section 2 problems: an analytical approach and an intuitive approach. A test-taker who uses the analytical approach quickly analyzes the grammar of a sentence to see what element is missing (in structure) or which element is incorrect (in written expression). Someone who uses the second approach simply chooses the answer that "sounds right" (in structure) or the one that "sounds wrong" (in written expression). Although this book emphasizes the first approach, the second can be useful too, especially for people who learned English primarily by speaking it and listening to it rather than by studying grammar and writing. If you aren't sure which approach works best for you, take Section 2 of one of the Practice Tests using the first method, and Section 2 of another test using the second approach. Did one approach give you a significantly better score? You can also combine the two approaches: if you get "stuck" (unable to choose an answer) using one method, you can switch to another.

Hint: An excellent way to prepare for Section 2 is to write your own structure and written expression items. Write several items for each of the lessons in this part of the book. There's no better way to start thinking like a test-writer.

Strategies for Section 2

- Be familiar with the directions for both parts. Don't waste time reading the directions or examples. Begin immediately with question 1.
- You can spend an average of about thirty seconds on each item. If an item seems difficult, make a guess and lightly mark the item on your answer sheet so that you can come back to it later. Erase all such marks before time is up. Don't spend too much time working on difficult items; it's better to work on items that you will probably get correct.

- Never answer any item too quickly, even if it seems easy. Always consider all four answer choices. On both parts of this section, it's easy to make mistakes because of carelessness.
- Never leave any answers blank. Always guess even if you have no idea what the answer is.
- If you finish before time is called, go back and work on items that you found difficult. You are not permitted go ahead to Section 3.

Now begin your preparation for Section 2 by taking the Sample Structure and Written Expression Test. Be sure to observe the 25-minute time limit.

WAIT

SAMPLE STRUCTURE AND WRITTEN EXPRESSION TEST
TIME—25 MINUTES

This section tests your ability to recognize grammar and usage suitable for standard written English. This section is divided into two parts, each with its own directions.

STRUCTURE

Directions: Items in this part are incomplete sentences. Following each of these sentences, there are four words or phrases. You should select the *one* word or phrase—(A), (B), (C), or (D)—that best completes the sentence. Then fill in the space on your answer sheet that matches the letter of the answer that you have selected.

Example I

Pepsin _____ an enzyme used in digestion.

(A) that
(B) is
(C) of
(D) being

Sample Answer

Ⓐ ● Ⓒ Ⓓ

This sentence should properly read, "Pepsin is an enzyme used in digestion." You should fill in (B) on your answer sheet.

Example II

_____ large natural lakes are found in the state of South Carolina.

(A) There are no
(B) Not the
(C) It is not
(D) No

Sample Answer

Ⓐ Ⓑ Ⓒ ●

This sentence should properly read, "No large natural lakes are found in the state of South Carolina." You should fill in (D) on your answer sheet.

As soon as you understand the directions, begin work on this part.

Answer Sheet

Sample Structure and Written Expression Test

1. Ⓐ Ⓑ Ⓒ Ⓓ 21. Ⓐ Ⓑ Ⓒ Ⓓ 31. Ⓐ Ⓑ Ⓒ Ⓓ
2. Ⓐ Ⓑ Ⓒ Ⓓ 22. Ⓐ Ⓑ Ⓒ Ⓓ 32. Ⓐ Ⓑ Ⓒ Ⓓ
3. Ⓐ Ⓑ Ⓒ Ⓓ 23. Ⓐ Ⓑ Ⓒ Ⓓ 33. Ⓐ Ⓑ Ⓒ Ⓓ
4. Ⓐ Ⓑ Ⓒ Ⓓ 24. Ⓐ Ⓑ Ⓒ Ⓓ 34. Ⓐ Ⓑ Ⓒ Ⓓ
5. Ⓐ Ⓑ Ⓒ Ⓓ 25. Ⓐ Ⓑ Ⓒ Ⓓ 35. Ⓐ Ⓑ Ⓒ Ⓓ
6. Ⓐ Ⓑ Ⓒ Ⓓ 26. Ⓐ Ⓑ Ⓒ Ⓓ 36. Ⓐ Ⓑ Ⓒ Ⓓ
7. Ⓐ Ⓑ Ⓒ Ⓓ 27. Ⓐ Ⓑ Ⓒ Ⓓ 37. Ⓐ Ⓑ Ⓒ Ⓓ
8. Ⓐ Ⓑ Ⓒ Ⓓ 28. Ⓐ Ⓑ Ⓒ Ⓓ 38. Ⓐ Ⓑ Ⓒ Ⓓ
9. Ⓐ Ⓑ Ⓒ Ⓓ 29. Ⓐ Ⓑ Ⓒ Ⓓ 39. Ⓐ Ⓑ Ⓒ Ⓓ
10. Ⓐ Ⓑ Ⓒ Ⓓ 30. Ⓐ Ⓑ Ⓒ Ⓓ 40. Ⓐ Ⓑ Ⓒ Ⓓ

11. Ⓐ Ⓑ Ⓒ Ⓓ
12. Ⓐ Ⓑ Ⓒ Ⓓ
13. Ⓐ Ⓑ Ⓒ Ⓓ
14. Ⓐ Ⓑ Ⓒ Ⓓ
15. Ⓐ Ⓑ Ⓒ Ⓓ
16. Ⓐ Ⓑ Ⓒ Ⓓ
17. Ⓐ Ⓑ Ⓒ Ⓓ
18. Ⓐ Ⓑ Ⓒ Ⓓ
19. Ⓐ Ⓑ Ⓒ Ⓓ
20. Ⓐ Ⓑ Ⓒ Ⓓ

1. Martha Graham, _____ of the pioneers of modern dance, didn't begin dancing until she was 21.

   (A) who, as one
   (B) she was
   (C) one
   (D) was one

2. Tiger moths _____ wings marked with stripes or spots.

   (A) have
   (B) with
   (C) their
   (D) whose

3. Platinum is harder than copper and is almost as pliable _____.

   (A) gold
   (B) than gold
   (C) as gold
   (D) gold is

4. Most of Annie Jump Cannon's career as an astronomer involved the observation, classification, and _____.

   (A) she analyzed stars
   (B) the stars' analysis
   (C) stars were analyzed
   (D) analysis of stars

5. Many communities are dependent on groundwater _____ from wells for their water supply.

   (A) that obtained
   (B) obtained
   (C) is obtained
   (D) obtain it

6. _____ experimental studies of the aging process, psychologist Ross McFarland determined that people could work productively much longer than had previously been thought.

   (A) In that
   (B) Through
   (C) Since
   (D) Into

7. _____ often raise funds from the sale of stock.

   (A) For corporations to operate
   (B) The operations of corporations
   (C) Corporations operate by
   (D) To operate, corporations

8. While all birds are alike in that they have feathers and lay eggs, _____ great differences among them in terms of size, structure, and color.

   (A) there are
   (B) but are
   (C) if there are
   (D) to be

9. There were _____ federal laws regulating mining practices until 1872.

   (A) none
   (B) not
   (C) no
   (D) nor

10. The Masters, one of the most important of all golf tournaments, _____ every year in Augusta, Georgia.

    (A) has held
    (B) being held
    (C) is held
    (D) holding

11. Not only _____ places of beauty, they serve scientific and educational purposes as well.

    (A) are botanical gardens
    (B) botanical gardens to be
    (C) botanical gardens are
    (D) to be botanical gardens

12. _____ quicksand can be found all over the world, little was known about its composition until recently.

    (A) Except
    (B) Although
    (C) Even
    (D) Despite

13. In 1791, Quebec was divided into two sections, Upper Canada and Lower Canada, _____ were ruled by elected assemblies.

    (A) they both
    (B) both of them
    (C) in which both
    (D) both of which

14. _____ are a form of carbon has been known since the late eighteenth century.

    (A) Diamonds
    (B) Because diamonds
    (C) That diamonds
    (D) Diamonds, which

15. Designed by Frederic Auguste Batholde, _____.

    (A) the United States was given the Statue of Liberty by the people of France
    (B) the people of France gave the Statue of Liberty to the United States
    (C) the Statue of Liberty was given to the United States by the people of France
    (D) the French people presented the United States with a gift, the Statue of Liberty

WRITTEN EXPRESSION

Directions: The items in this part have four underlined words or phrases, (A), (B), (C), and (D). You must identify the *one* underlined expression that must be changed for the sentence to be correct. Then find the number of the question on your answer sheet and fill in the space corresponding to the letter.

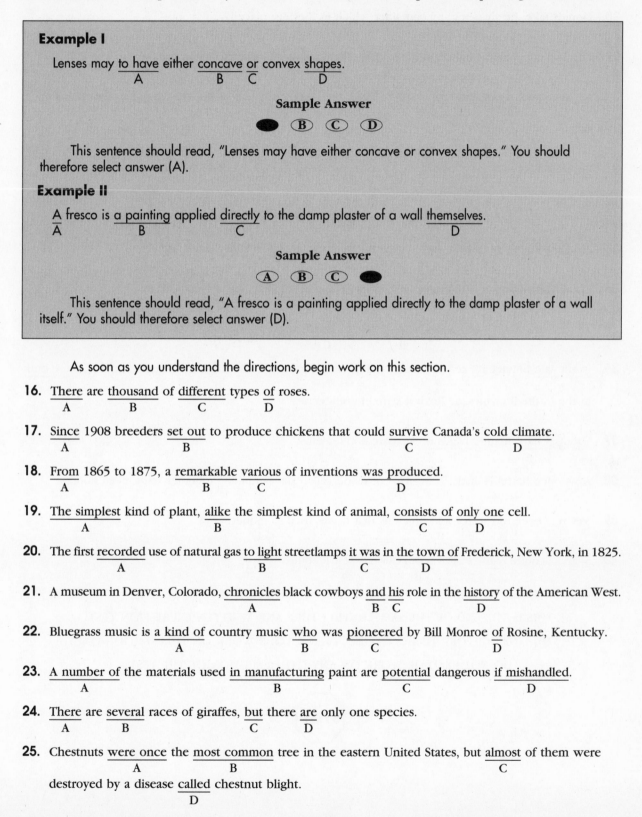

Example I

Lenses may <u>to have</u> either <u>concave</u> or <u>convex</u> <u>shapes</u>.
      A   B   C   D

Sample Answer

● Ⓑ Ⓒ Ⓓ

This sentence should read, "Lenses may have either concave or convex shapes." You should therefore select answer (A).

Example II

<u>A</u> fresco is <u>a painting</u> applied <u>directly</u> to the damp plaster of a wall <u>themselves</u>.
A   B   C   D

Sample Answer

Ⓐ Ⓑ Ⓒ ●

This sentence should read, "A fresco is a painting applied directly to the damp plaster of a wall itself." You should therefore select answer (D).

As soon as you understand the directions, begin work on this section.

16. There are <u>thousand</u> of <u>different</u> types <u>of</u> roses.
     A   B   C   D

17. <u>Since</u> 1908 breeders <u>set out</u> to produce chickens that could <u>survive</u> Canada's <u>cold climate</u>.
    A   B   C   D

18. <u>From</u> 1865 to 1875, a <u>remarkable</u> <u>various</u> of inventions <u>was produced</u>.
    A   B   C   D

19. <u>The simplest</u> kind of plant, <u>alike</u> the simplest kind of animal, <u>consists of</u> <u>only one</u> cell.
       A   B   C   D

20. The first <u>recorded</u> use of natural gas <u>to light</u> streetlamps <u>it was</u> in <u>the</u> town of Frederick, New York, in 1825.
           A   B   C   D

21. A museum in Denver, Colorado, <u>chronicles</u> black cowboys <u>and</u> <u>his</u> role in the <u>history</u> of the American West.
                            A   B C   D

22. Bluegrass music is <u>a kind of</u> country music <u>who</u> was <u>pioneered</u> by Bill Monroe <u>of</u> Rosine, Kentucky.
               A   B   C   D

23. <u>A number of</u> the materials used <u>in manufacturing</u> paint are <u>potential</u> dangerous <u>if mishandled</u>.
      A   B   C   D

24. There are <u>several</u> races of giraffes, <u>but</u> there <u>are</u> only one species.
     A   B   C   D

25. Chestnuts <u>were once</u> the <u>most common</u> tree in the eastern United States, but <u>almost</u> of them were
            A   B   C
destroyed by a disease <u>called</u> chestnut blight.
                      D

26. Despite they are <u>small</u>, ponies are <u>strong</u> and <u>have</u> great stamina.
    A   B   C   D

27. Physical therapists help patients <u>relearn</u> how <u>to use</u> their bodies <u>after</u> disease or <u>injure</u>.
                                A   B   C   D

28. Liquids take <u>the shape</u> of <u>any</u> container <u>which in</u> they are <u>placed</u>.
              A   B   C   D

29. <u>The Sun</u> supplies the light and <u>the warmth</u> that permit <u>life</u> on earth <u>existing</u>.
    A   B   C   D

30. For seventeen years, between 1932 <u>to</u> 1949, Fred Allen <u>was</u> <u>one of the</u> most popular comedians <u>on</u>
                            A   B   C

radio.
<u></u>
D

31. Boolean algebra is <u>most often</u> used <u>to solve</u> problems in <u>logic</u>, probability, and <u>engineer</u>.
                        A   B   C   D

32. Attorney Clarence Darrow <u>is knowing</u> for <u>his</u> <u>defense of</u> unpopular persons and <u>causes</u>.
                               A   B   C   D

33. Phi Beta Kappa is <u>a</u> honor <u>society</u> that encourages <u>scholarship</u> in science and <u>art</u>.
                  A   B   C   D

34. The French Quarter is <u>the</u> most <u>famous</u> and the <u>most old</u> section <u>of</u> New Orleans.
                      A   B   C   D

35. <u>There was</u> once a widespread <u>believe</u> that <u>all lizards</u> were <u>poisonous</u>.
    A   B   C   D

36. <u>In the late</u> nineteenth century, many public buildings, especially <u>that</u> on college campuses, <u>were built</u>
    A   B   C
in the in the Romanesque Revival style of <u>architecture</u>.
                                           D

37. Sponges <u>have</u> neither <u>heads</u> <u>or</u> separate body <u>organs</u>.
                  A   B C   D

38. A <u>wooden</u> barrel is made from <u>strips</u> of wood called staves <u>holding</u> together with <u>metal</u> hoops.
     A   B   C   D

39. Salt was once <u>too</u> scarce <u>and</u> precious that it <u>was used</u> as <u>money</u>.
                    A   B   C   D

40. Sharks acquire <u>many</u> sets of <u>tooth</u> <u>during</u> their lifetimes.
              A   B C   D

THIS IS THE END OF THE SAMPLE STRUCTURE AND WRITTEN EXPRESSION TEST.

IF YOU FINISH BEFORE TIME IS CALLED, CHECK YOUR WORK ON THIS SECTION ONLY.

DO NOT READ OR WORK ON ANY OTHER SECTION OF THE TEST.

Peterson's TOEFL CBT Success

Part A

ABOUT STRUCTURE

This part of the test consists of fifteen incomplete sentences (twenty-three on the long form). Some portion of each sentence has been replaced by a blank. Under each sentence, four words or phrases are listed. One of these completes the sentence grammatically and logically.

Sample Item

Pepsin _____ an enzyme used in digestion.
(A) that
(B) is
(C) of
(D) being

Sample Answer

Ⓐ ● Ⓒ Ⓓ

The sentence consists of a single clause (*Pepsin is an enzyme*) and a reduced (shortened) adjective clause (*used in digestion*). Each clause must contain a subject and a verb. There is a subject but no main verb. (The verbal form *used* is NOT the main verb in this sentence; it is a past participle.) Therefore a main verb is needed. Only choices (B) and (D) are verb forms. However, an *-ing* verb can never be used alone as a main verb. The only possible choice is (B), the main verb *is*.

WHAT IS TESTED IN THIS SECTION?

In general, there are five main points tested. The chart below shows how these are presented in the next section of this book.

Main Testing Points	Lesson
Sentence Structure	Lesson 17: Incomplete Independent Clauses
	Lesson 18: Incomplete Adjective Clauses
	Lesson 19: Incomplete/Missing Participial Phrases
	Lesson 20: Incomplete/Missing Appositives
	Lesson 21: Incomplete Adverb Clauses
	Lesson 22: Incomplete Noun Clauses
	Lesson 23: Incomplete/Missing Prepositional Phrases
Word Order	Lesson 24: Word Order Problems
Verbs and Verbals	Lesson 25: Items Involving Verb Problems
	Lesson 26: Incomplete/Missing Infinitive and Gerund Phrases
Proper Style	Lesson 27: Items Involving Parallel Structures
	Lesson 28: Items Involving Misplaced Modifiers
Word Choice	Lesson 29: Incomplete/Missing Comparisons
	Lesson 30: Missing Conjunctions
	Lesson 31: Missing Negative Words

The points practiced in the first group of lessons (Lessons 17 to 23) are tested on almost every TOEFL exam. The points in the second group (Lessons 24 to 31) are tested on some TOEFL exams.

WHAT IS THE BEST WAY TO ANSWER STRUCTURE ITEMS?

If the answer choices are fairly short, you should begin by taking a quick look at the answer choices to get an idea of what to look for when you read the sentence. A look at the answer choices can often tell you that you are looking at a problem involving verb forms, word order, parallel structure, misplaced modifiers, or others.

If the answer choices are long or complicated, begin by reading the stem. Don't analyze it word for word, but as you are reading, try to form a picture of the sentence's overall structure. How many clauses will there be in the complete sentence? Does each clause have a complete subject and verb? Is there a connecting word to join clauses? Are any other elements obviously missing?

Then look at the answer choices. If you're not sure of the answer, try to eliminate as many distractors as possible. Distractors in structure are generally incorrect for one of the following reasons:

- A necessary word or phrase is missing, so the sentence is still incomplete.
- An unnecessary word or phrase is included.
- Part of the answer choice is ungrammatical when put into the stem.

Never choose an answer until you've read the sentence completely; sometimes an option seems to fit in the sentence unless you read every word.

After you have eliminated as many answer choices as possible, read the sentence quickly to yourself with the remaining choice or choices in place of the blank. If an answer doesn't "sound right," it probably isn't. If you still can't decide, guess and go on. If you have time, come back to these more difficult items later.

Punctuation clues can sometimes help you solve structure problems. For example, if there are a series of items in a sentence separated by commas (A, B, and C) you will probably see a problem involving parallel structures.

Tactics for Structure

- If the answer choices are short, look them over before you read the sentence. Try to get an idea of what type of problem you are working with.
- Read the sentence, trying to determine which elements are missing. Never choose an answer until you have read the entire sentence; sometimes an answer will seem to fit until you have read the last few words of the sentence.
- Mark your choice immediately if the answer is obvious.
- If you're not sure, try to eliminate incorrect answers.
- Read the sentence with the remaining answer choices in place of the blank. Choose the option that sounds best.
- If you are still unable to decide on an answer, guess and and go on. Lightly mark these items on your answer sheet and come back to them if time permits.
- Go on to the second part of this section (Written Expression) as soon as you've finished Structure. Don't spend so much time working on Structure that you don't have enough time to finish Written Expression.

Lesson 17

INCOMPLETE INDEPENDENT CLAUSES

The structures practiced in this lesson are the ones that are most often tested in the Structure section. About 20 percent of all problems in the section (usually three or four per test) involve incomplete main clauses.

ABOUT CLAUSES

All sentences consist of one or more clauses. A **simple sentence** consists of one clause.

People need vitamins.
The man took a vitamin pill.
Judy lives in northern California.
In the summer, Tom walks to his office.

A **compound sentence** consists of two independent clauses joined by a coordinating conjunction (such as *and* and *but*).

The man took a vitamin pill, and he drank a glass of orange juice.
Judy lives in northern California now, but she was raised in Ohio.

A **complex sentence** consists of an independent clause (called the main clause) and a subordinate (dependent) clause. Subordinate clauses may be adverb clauses, noun clauses, or adjective clauses. In the sentences below, the independent clauses are italicized.

The man took a vitamin pill because he had a cold. (independent clause + adverb clause)
I didn't realize that Nancy was here. (noun clause)
Tom walks to his office, which is located on Broadway, *every day during the summer*.
(independent clause + adjective clause)

All three types of subordinate clauses are commonly seen in the Structure part of the test, and each is considered in separate lessons (Lessons 18, 21, and 22). The emphasis in this chapter, however, is on the basic components of independent clauses.

MISSING SUBJECTS, VERBS, OBJECTS, AND COMPLEMENTS

All clauses have a **subject** and a **verb**. Clauses with an action verb often take a **direct object** as well.

Subject	Verb	Object
People	need	vitamins.

The verb missing from an independent clause may be a single-word verb (*need, was, took, had, walked*) or a verb phrase consisting of one or more auxiliary verbs and a main verb (*will need, has been, should take, would have had, had walked*). The verbs may be active (*need, take*) or passive (*was needed, is taken*).

The missing subject and direct object may be a noun (*people, vitamins, Tom*), a noun phrase (*some famous people, a vitamin pill, my friend Tom*), or a pronoun. (*He, she, it,* and *they* are subject pronouns; *him, her, it,* and *them* are object pronouns.)

After the verb *to be* and certain other nonaction verbs, a **subject complement** is used rather than a direct object. (Subject complements are also known as predicate nominatives and predicate adjectives.)

Subject	Verb	Complement
She	is	an architect.
The teacher	seemed	upset.

In the Structure section of TOEFL, it is common for any of these elements or a combination of two or more of these elements to be missing from the stem. The most common problem in structure involves a missing verb. A missing subject and a missing subject-verb combination are common as well. The missing element may also be part of rather than all of the verb or noun phrase.

Sample Items

The art of storytelling _____ almost as old as humanity.

(A) that is
(B) is
(C) it is
(D) being

(A) ● (C) (D)

The correct answer supplies the missing verb. Choice (A) is incorrect because the word *that* is used to connect a relative clause to a main clause; in this sentence, there is only one verb, so there can only be one clause. Choice (C) is incorrect because there is an unnecessary repetition of the subject (*The art of storytelling it...*). Choice (D) is not correct because an *-ing* form (*being*) cannot be the main verb of a clause.

_____ a few of the sounds produced by insects can be heard by humans.

(A) Only
(B) There are only
(C) That only
(D) With only

● (B) (C) (D)

The correct answer completes the noun phrase that is the subject of the sentence. The expletive *There* in choice (B) is incorrectly used. In (C), the word *That* creates a noun clause, but each clause must have its own verb. (*Produced* is used as a participle, not a main verb in this sentence.) Choice (D) is incorrect because a preposition may not be used directly before the subject.

_____ when lava cools very rapidly.

(A) Because pumice is formed
(B) To form pumice
(C) Pumice is formed
(D) Forming pumice

(A) (B) ● (D)

The best answer supplies an independent clause to join to the adverb clause *when lava cools very rapidly*. Choice (A) consists of an adverb clause; two adverb clauses cannot be joined to form a complete sentence. Choices (B) and (D) are incorrect because they do not contain main verbs, and an independent clause must contain a main verb. (*To form* and *forming* are not main verbs.) Only choice (C) could serve as an independent clause because it contains a subject (*Pumice*) and a full verb; the passive verb *is formed*.

Sample Items (Continued)

Duke Ellington wrote _____ during his career.

(A) that over a thousand songs
(B) over a thousand songs
(C) over a thousand songs were
(D) there were over a thousand songs

The direct object is missing from this sentence. In choice A, the connecting word *that* is used unnecessarily. In (C), the verb *were* is used unnecessarily because there is only one clause and it has a verb (*wrote*). In choice (D) the phrase *there were* is not needed between a verb and its direct object.

Before the invention of the printing press, books _____.

(A) that were very rare
(B) were very rarely
(C) were very rare
(D) as very rare

Choice (A) incorrectly forms an adjective clause; an adjective must be joined to a main clause. Choice (B) contains an adverb; after the verb *to be,* an adjective is required. Choice (D) lacks a verb. Choice (C) correctly supplies a verb (*were*).

CLAUSES WITH *THERE* AND *IT*

Some clauses begin with the introductory words *there* or *it* rather than with the subject of the sentence. These introductory words are sometimes called **expletives**.

The expletive *there* shows that someone or something exists, usually at a particular time or place. These sentences generally follow the pattern *there* + verb *to be* + subject.

There are many skyscrapers in New York City.
There was a good movie on television last night.

The expletive *it* is used in a number of different situations and patterns:

It is important to be punctual for appointments. (with the verb *to be* + adjective + infinitive)
It was in 1959 that Alaska became a state. (with the verb *to be* + adverbial + noun clause)
It takes a long time to learn a language. (with the verb *to take* + time phrase + infinitive)
It was David who did most of the work. (with the verb *to be* + noun + relative clause)

It and *there*, along with the verb and other sentence elements, may be missing from the stem.

Sample Items

In Michigan, _____ over six hundred feet deep.

(A) salt deposits
(B) where salt deposits are
(C) having salt deposits
(D) there are salt deposits

Ⓐ Ⓑ Ⓒ ⬤

Choice (D) correctly supplies an introductory word (*there*), a verb, and a subject. Choice (A) lacks a verb. Choice (B) contains a subordinator, used to introduce a clause; there is only one verb, however, so there can only be one clause. Choice (C) also lacks a main verb.

_____ a tomato plant from seventy-five to eighty-five days to develop into a mature plant with ripe fruit.

(A) It takes
(B) To take
(C) That takes
(D) By taking

⬤ Ⓑ Ⓒ Ⓓ

Choice (A) correctly completes the sentence with the introductory word *It* and a verb. Choices (B) and (D) do not supply main verbs. Choice (C) incorrectly creates a noun clause.

EXERCISE 17

Focus: Completing structure problems involving incomplete independent clauses. (Note: Three or four items in this exercise do NOT focus on missing subjects, verbs, complements, or introductory words; these items are marked in the answer key with asterisks.)

Directions: Choose the one option—(A), (B), (C), or (D)—that correctly completes the sentences, then mark the appropriate blank.

1. In the United States, _____ is generally the responsibility of municipal governments.

   _____ (A) for water treatment

   _____ (B) water treatment

   _____ (C) where water treatment

   _____ (D) in which water treatment

2. Crop rotation _____ of preserving soil fertility.

   _____ (A) it is one method

   _____ (B) one method

   _____ (C) a method is one

   _____ (D) is one method

3. _____ the dollar as its monetary unit in 1878.

   _____ (A) Canada adopted

   _____ (B) Adopted by Canada,

   _____ (C) It was adopted by Canada

   _____ (D) The Canadian adoption of

4. _____ almost impossible to capture the beauty of the aurora borealis in photographs.

   _____ (A) Being

   _____ (B) It is

   _____ (C) There is

   _____ (D) Is

126

5. Usually political cartoons _____ on the editorial page of a newspaper.

_____ (A) appear

_____ (B) whose appearance

_____ (C) by appearing

_____ (D) when they appear

6. _____ two major art museums, the Fogg and the Sadler.

_____ (A) Harvard University has

_____ (B) At Harvard University

_____ (C) Harvard University, with its

_____ (D) There at Harvard University

7. American actress and director Margaret Webster _____ for her production of Shakespearean plays.

_____ (A) who became famous

_____ (B) famous as she became

_____ (C) becoming famous

_____ (D) became famous

8. _____ gas tanks connected to welding equipment, one full of oxygen and the other full of acetylene.

_____ (A) It is two

_____ (B) Of the two

_____ (C) There are two

_____ (D) Two

9. _____ is more interested in rhythm than in melody is apparent from his compositions.

_____ (A) That Philip Glass

_____ (B) Philip Glass, who

_____ (C) Philip Glass

_____ (D) Because Philip Glass

10. Compressed air _____ the power to drive pneumatic tools.

_____ (A) by providing

_____ (B) provides

_____ (C) that provides

_____ (D) the provision of

11. _____ by cosmic rays.

_____ (A) The Earth is constantly bombarded

_____ (B) Bombarded constantly, the Earth

_____ (C) Bombarding the Earth constantly

_____ (D) The Earth's constant bombardment

12. _____ primary colors are red, blue, and yellow.

_____ (A) There are three

_____ (B) The three

_____ (C) Three of them

_____ (D) That the three

13. _____ who was elected the first woman mayor of Chicago in 1979.

_____ (A) It was Jane Byrne

_____ (B) Jane Byrne

_____ (C) That Jane Byrne

_____ (D) When Jane Byrne

14. Every computer consists of a number of systems _____ together.

_____ (A) by working

_____ (B) work

_____ (C) they work

_____ (D) that work

15. On the Moon, _____ air because the Moon's gravitational field is too weak to retain an atmosphere.

_____ (A) there is no

_____ (B) where no

_____ (C) no

_____ (D) is no

16. The Glass Mountains of northwestern Oklahoma _____ with flecks of gypsum, which shine in the sunlight.

    _____ (A) they are covered

    _____ (B) covered them

    _____ (C) that are covered

    _____ (D) are covered

17. In some cases, _____ to decide if an organism is a plant or an animal.

    _____ (A) difficult if

    _____ (B) it is difficult

    _____ (C) the difficulty

    _____ (D) is difficult

18. The first American novelist to have a major impact on world literature _____ .

    _____ (A) who was James Fenimore Cooper

    _____ (B) James Fenimore Cooper was

    _____ (C) it was James Fenimore Cooper

    _____ (D) was James Fenimore Cooper

19. _____ important railroad tunnel in the United States was cut through the Hoosac Mountains in Massachusetts.

    _____ (A) At first

    _____ (B) It was the first

    _____ (C) The first

    _____ (D) As the first of

20. Generally, _____ in the valleys and foothills of the Pacific Coast ranges.

    _____ (A) the California poppy grown

    _____ (B) the growth of the California poppy

    _____ (C) the California poppy grows

    _____ (D) growing the California poppy

21. When bats are at rest, _____ hang upside-down.

    _____ (A) they

    _____ (B) and

    _____ (C) to

    _____ (D) as

22. _____ that the capital of South Carolina was moved from Charleston to Columbia.

    _____ (A) In 1790 was

    _____ (B) There was in 1790

    _____ (C) In 1790

    _____ (D) It was in 1790

23. Although not as important as they once were, _____ a major form of transportation in North America.

    _____ (A) there are still railroads

    _____ (B) railroads, which are still

    _____ (C) railroads are still

    _____ (D) railroads still being

24. The Loop, which is the commercial heart of Chicago, _____ within a rectangular loop of elevated train tracks.

    _____ (A) that is enclosed

    _____ (B) enclosing it

    _____ (C) is enclosed

    _____ (D) it is enclosed

25. _____ amino acids that serve as the basic building blocks of all proteins.

    _____ (A) It was about twenty

    _____ (B) For about twenty of

    _____ (C) About twenty are

    _____ (D) There are about twenty

Lesson 18

As mentioned in the previous lesson, there are three types of dependent clauses, all of which are tested in structure.

Adjective clauses—also called **relative clauses**—are the most commonly tested of the three. You will see one or two items involving adjective clauses on most tests.

Adjective clauses are a way of joining two sentences. In the joined sentence, the adjective clause modifies (describes) a noun (called the **head noun**) in another clause of the sentence. It begins with an **adjective clause marker**.

I wanted the book. The book had already been checked out.
The book *that I wanted* had already been checked out.

The adjective clause in this example begins with the marker *that* and modifies the head noun *book*. Adjective clause markers are relative pronouns such as *who*, *that*, or *which* or the relative adverbs *when* or *where*.

Adjective Clause Marker	Use	Example
who	Subject (people)	A neurologist is a doctor *who* specializes in the nervous system.
whom	Object (people)	This is the patient *whom* the doctor treated.
whose	Possessive (people/things)	Mr. Collins is the man *whose* house I rented.
which	Subject/Object (things)	That is a topic *which* interests me. (*which* as subject)
		That is the topic *on which* I will write. (*which* as object of preposition)
that	Subject/Object (people/things)	Art *that* is in public places can be enjoyed by everyone. (*that* as subject)
		The painting *that* Ms. Wallace bought was very expensive. (*that* as object)
where	Adverb (place)	Here is the site *where* the bank plans to build its new headquarters.
when	Adverb (time)	This is the hour *when* the children usually go to bed.

Like all clauses, adjective clauses must have a subject and a verb. In some cases the adjective-clause marker itself is the subject; in some cases, there is another subject.

The painting was very expensive. Ms. Wallace bought it.
The painting *which Ms. Wallace bought* was very expensive.

The adjective-clause marker in the joined sentence replaces *it*, the object of the verb *bought*. In the joined sentence, the adjective clause keeps the subject—*Ms. Wallace*—that it had in the original sentence.

This is a topic. It interests me.
This is a topic *that interests me*.

The adjective-clause marker in the joined sentence replaces *it*, the subject of the second original sentence. In the joined sentence, the marker itself is the subject of the adjective clause. Notice that the inclusion of the pronoun *it* in the joined sentences above would be an error.

Incorrect:

    *The painting which Ms. Wallace bought *it* was very expensive.

    *This is a topic which *it* interests me.

This type of mistake is sometimes seen in distractors.

When the markers *which*, *that*, and *whom* are used as objects in relative clauses, they can correctly be omitted.

The painting Ms. Wallace bought is very expensive. (*which* omitted)

The adjective-clause markers *which* and *whom* can also be used as objects of prepositions:

That is the topic. I will write on it.
That is the topic *on which I will write*.

You may also see sentences with adjective clauses used in this pattern:

quantity word + *of* + relative clause

He met with two advisers. He had known both of them for years.
He met with two advisers, *both of whom he had known for years*.

I read a number of articles. Most of them were very useful.
I read a number of articles, most of which were very useful.

Any part of a relative clause can be missing from the stem of Structure items, but most often, the marker and the subject (if there is one) and the verb are missing. Any word or phrase from another clause—usually the head noun—may also be missing from the stem.

Sample Items

Cable cars are moved by cables _____ underground and are powered by a stationary engine.

(A) they run
(B) that they run
(C) run
(D) that run

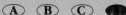

    Choice (A) is incorrect because the pronoun *they* cannot be used to join two clauses. Choice (B) is not appropriate because the subject *they* is not needed in the adjective clause; the marker *that* serves as the subject of the clause. Choice (C) is incorrect because there is no marker to join the adjective clause to the main clause.

Sample Items (Continued)

The melting point is the temperature _____ a solid changes to a liquid.

(A) which
(B) at which
(C) which at
(D) at

Ⓐ ● Ⓒ Ⓓ

Choice (A) is incorrect because a preposition is needed before the adjective clause. Choice (C) is incorrect because the relative pronoun comes before the preposition. Choice (D) is incorrect because the relative pronoun has been omitted.

There are six types of flamingos, all _____ have long legs, long necks, and beaks that curve sharply downward.

(A) of them
(B) that
(C) of which
(D) they

Ⓐ Ⓑ ● Ⓓ

Choices (A) and (D) do not contain connecting words needed to join clauses. Choice (B) does not follow the correct pattern of relative clauses after a quantity word (all). The correct pattern needed to complete this sentence is quantity word + of + marker. Only (C) follows this pattern.

EXERCISE 18

Focus: Answering structure problems involving incomplete adjective clauses. (Note: One or two items in this exercise do NOT focus on adjective clauses; these items are marked in the answer key with asterisks.)

Directions: Choose the one option—(A), (B), (C), or (D)—that correctly completes the sentence, then mark the appropriate blank.

1. Most folk songs are ballads _____ have simple words and tell simple stories.

_____ (A) what
_____ (B) although
_____ (C) when
_____ (D) that

2. After its introduction in 1969, the float process _____ the world's principal method of manufacturing flat sheets of glass.

_____ (A) by which it became
_____ (B) it became
_____ (C) became
_____ (D) which became

3. In 1850, Yale University established Sheffield Scientific School, _____ .

_____ (A) engineers were educated there
_____ (B) where engineers were educated
_____ (C) in which were engineers educated
_____ (D) where were engineers educated

4. Many of Louise Nevelson's sculptures consisted of a number of large wooden structures _____ in complex patterns.

   _____ (A) which she arranged

   _____ (B) she arranged them

   _____ (C) which arranged

   _____ (D) arranged them

5. In addition to being a naturalist, Stewart E. White was a writer _____ the struggle for survival on the American frontier.

   _____ (A) whose novels describe

   _____ (B) he describes in his novels

   _____ (C) his novels describe

   _____ (D) who, describing in his novels

6. Diamonds are often found in rock formations called pipes, _____ the throats of extinct volcanoes.

   _____ (A) in which they resemble

   _____ (B) which resemble

   _____ (C) there is a resemblance to

   _____ (D) they resemble

7. William Samuel Johnson, _____ helped write the Constitution, became the first president of Columbia College in 1787.

   _____ (A) whom he had

   _____ (B) and he had

   _____ (C) who had

   _____ (D) had

8. Seals appear clumsy on the land, _____ are able to move short distances faster than most people can run.

   _____ (A) but they

   _____ (B) which they

   _____ (C) they

   _____ (D) which

9. The instrument panel of a light airplane has at least a dozen instruments _____ .

   _____ (A) the pilot must watch

   _____ (B) what the pilot must watch

   _____ (C) which the pilot must watch them

   _____ (D) such that the pilot must watch them

10. A keystone species is a species of plants or animals _____ absence has a major effect on an ecological system.

    _____ (A) that its

    _____ (B) its

    _____ (C) whose

    _____ (D) with its

11. The size and shape of a nail depends primarily on the function _____ intended.

    _____ (A) which it is

    _____ (B) for which it is

    _____ (C) which it is for

    _____ (D) for which is

12. In geometry, a tangent is a straight line _____ a curve at only one point.

    _____ (A) it touches

    _____ (B) whose touching

    _____ (C) its touching

    _____ (D) that touches

13. It was the ragtime pianist Scott Joplin _____ the *Maple Leaf Rag*, perhaps the best known of all ragtime tunes.

    _____ (A) wrote

    _____ (B) the writer of

    _____ (C) who wrote

    _____ (D) writing

14. There are over 2,000 varieties of snakes, _____ are harmless to humans.

_____ (A) mostly they

_____ (B) most of them

_____ (C) most of which

_____ (D) which most

15. Smokejumpers are _____ descend into remote areas by parachute to fight forest fires.

_____ (A) firefighters

_____ (B) when firefighters

_____ (C) who, as firefighters

_____ (D) firefighters who

16. Charlotte Gilman's best known book _____ she urges women to become financially independent.

_____ (A) is *Women and Economics*, in which

_____ (B) *Women and Economics*, in which

_____ (C) is *Women and Economics*, which

_____ (D) *Women and Economics*, which

Lesson 19

INCOMPLETE/MISSING PARTICIPIAL PHRASES

Participial phrases generally occur after nouns. They are actually **reduced** (shortened) **relative clauses**. **Present participles** (which always end in *-ing*) are used to reduce adjective clauses that contain active verbs.

Minnesota, *which joined the Union in 1858*, became the thirty-second state. (adjective clause with active verb) Minnesota, *joining the Union in 1858*, became the thirty-second state. (participial phrase with a present participle)

Most **past participles** end in *-ed*, but there are also many irregular forms. Past participles are used to reduce adjective clauses with passive verbs.

William and Mary College, *which was founded in 1693*, is the second-oldest university in the United States. (adjective clause with a passive verb)

William and Mary College, *founded in 1693*, is the second-oldest university in the United States. (participial phrase with a past participle)

Participial phrases can also come before the subject of a sentence.

Joining the Union in 1858, Minnesota became the thirty-second state. *Founded in 1693*, William and Mary College is the second-oldest university in the United States.

Usually, the participle itself is missing from this type of structure item, but any part of a participial phrase as well as parts of a main clause may be missing.

Sample Item

Natural resources provide the raw materials _____ to produce finished goods.

(A) needed
(B) are needed
(C) which need
(D) needing

Option (B) is a passive verb; the sentence cannot contain two main verbs (*are needed* and *provide*) in the same clause. Choice (C) creates an adjective clause, but the verb in the clause is active and a passive verb is needed. (However, a relative clause with a passive verb (*which are needed*) would be a correct answer. Choice (D) is a present participle and has an active meaning; a past participle is needed.

134
Peterson's TOEFL CBT Success

EXERCISE 19

Focus: Structure problems involving incomplete or missing participial phrases. (Note: One or two items in this exercise do NOT focus on participial phrases; these items are marked on the answer key with asterisks.)

Directions: Choose the one option—(A), (B), (C), or (D)—that correctly completes the sentence, then mark the appropriate blank.

1. Aerodynamics is the study of the forces _____ on an object as it moves through the atmosphere.

   _____ (A) acting

   _____ (B) act

   _____ (C) are acting

   _____ (D) acted

2. _____ for their strong fiber include flax and hemp.

   _____ (A) Plants are grown

   _____ (B) Plants grown

   _____ (C) Plants that grow

   _____ (D) To grow plants

3. _____, Jose Limon's dance troupe often toured abroad.

   _____ (A) The U.S. State Department sponsored it

   _____ (B) Sponsored by the U.S. State Department

   _____ (C) The U.S. State Department, which sponsored it

   _____ (D) The sponsorship of the U.S. State Department

4. Elfreth's Alley in Philadelphia is the oldest residential street in the United States, with _____ from 1728.

   _____ (A) houses are dated

   _____ (B) the dates of the houses

   _____ (C) the dating of houses

   _____ (D) houses dating

5. In 1821, the city of Indianapolis, Indiana, was laid out in a design _____ after that of Washington, D.C.

   _____ (A) patterned

   _____ (B) was patterned

   _____ (C) a pattern

   _____ (D) that patterned

6. _____ in front of a camera lens changes the color of the light that reaches the film.

   _____ (A) Placed a filter

   _____ (B) A filter is placed

   _____ (C) A filter placed

   _____ (D) When a filter placed

7. The Massachusetts State House, _____ in 1798, was the most distinguished building in the United States at that time.

   _____ (A) completing

   _____ (B) which was completed

   _____ (C) was completed

   _____ (D) to be completed

8. Barbara McClintock _____ for her discovery of the mobility of genetic elements.

   _____ (A) known

   _____ (B) who knows

   _____ (C) knowing

   _____ (D) is known

9. The solitary scientist _____ by himself
has in many instances been replaced by a
cooperative scientific team.

_____ (A) to make important discoveries

_____ (B) important discoveries were
made

_____ (C) has made important discoveries

_____ (D) making important discoveries

10. Geometry is the branch of mathematics
_____ the properties of lines, curves,
shapes, and surfaces.

_____ (A) that concerned with

_____ (B) it is concerned with

_____ (C) concerned with

_____ (D) its concerns are

11. _____ an average of 471 inches of rain a
year, Mount Waialeale in Hawaii is the
wettest spot in the world.

_____ (A) It receives

_____ (B) Receiving

_____ (C) To receive

_____ (D) Received

12. Amber is a hard, yellowish-brown _____
from the resin of pine trees that lived
millions of years ago.

_____ (A) substance formed

_____ (B) to form a substance

_____ (C) substance has formed

_____ (D) forming a substance

Lesson 20

INCOMPLETE/MISSING APPOSITIVES

An **appositive** is a noun phrase that explains or rephrases another noun phrase. It usually comes after the noun that it rephrases. It may also come before the subject of a sentence.

Buffalo Bill, *a famous frontiersman*, operated his own Wild West Show. (appositive following a noun)

A famous frontiersman, Buffalo Bill operated his own Wild West Show. (appositive before the subject)

Appositives are actually reduced adjective clauses that contain the verb *to be*. However, unlike adjective clauses, they do not contain a marker or a verb.

Oak, *which is one of the most durable hard woods*, is often used to make furniture. (adjective clause)

Oak, *one of the most durable hard woods*, is often used to make furniture. (appositive)

Appositives are usually separated from the rest of the sentence by commas, but short appositives (usually names) are not.

Economist *Paul Samuelson* won a Nobel Prize in 1970.

In Structure items, all or part of an appositive phrase may be missing. In addition, the noun that the appositive refers to or other parts of the main clause may be missing.

Sample Item

The National Road, _____ of the first highways in North America, connected the East Coast to the Ohio Valley.

(A) which one
(B) it was one
(C) one
(D) was one

    Choice (A) is incorrect; there is no verb in the relative clause. Choice (B) has no connecting word to join the clause to the rest of the sentence. Choice (D) is incorrect because a verb cannot be used in an appositive phrase. Note: *which was one* would also be a correct answer for this problem.

EXERCISE 20

Focus: Completing structure problems involving appositives. (Note: The focus for one or two items in this exercise is NOT appositives; these sentences are marked in the answer key with asterisks.)

Directions: Choose the one option—(A), (B), (C), or (D)—that correctly completes the sentences, then mark the appropriate blank.

1. The Democratic party is older than the other major American political party, _____.

    _____ (A) which the Republican party

    _____ (B) the Republican party

    _____ (C) it is the Republican party

    _____ (D) the Republican party is

2. _____ relations with friends and acquaintances, play a major role in the social development of adolescents.

    _____ (A) What are called peer group relations are

    _____ (B) Peer group relations are

    _____ (C) Peer group relations, the

    _____ (D) By peer group relations, we mean

3. Joseph Henry, _____ director of the Smithsonian Institution, was President Lincoln's adviser on scientific matters.

    _____ (A) the first

    _____ (B) to be the first

    _____ (C) was the first

    _____ (D) as the first

4. The Wassatch Range, _____ extends from southeastern Idaho into northern Utah.

    _____ (A) which is a part of the Rocky Mountains,

    _____ (B) a part of the Rocky Mountains that

    _____ (C) is a part of the Rocky Mountains

    _____ (D) a part of the Rocky Mountains, it

5. _____ Ruth St. Dennis turned to Asian dances to find inspiration for her choreography.

    _____ (A) It was the dancer

    _____ (B) The dancer

    _____ (C) That the dancer

    _____ (D) The dancer was

6. The organs of taste are the _____ that are mainly located on the tongue.

    _____ (A) groups of cells, are taste buds

    _____ (B) taste buds, are groups of cells

    _____ (C) taste buds, these are groups of cells

    _____ (D) taste buds, groups of cells

7. In 1878, Frederick W. Taylor invented a concept called scientific management, _____ of obtaining as much efficiency from workers and machines as possible.

    _____ (A) it is a method

    _____ (B) a method which

    _____ (C) a method

    _____ (D) called a method

8. A group of Shakers, _____ settled around Pleasant Hill, Kentucky, in 1805.

    _____ (A) members of a strict religious sect which

    _____ (B) whose members of a strict religious sect

    _____ (C) members of a strict religious sect,

    _____ (D) were members of a strict religious sect

9. In physics, _____ "plasma" refers to a gas that has a nearly equal number of positively and negatively charged particles.

_____ (A) the term

_____ (B) by the term

_____ (C) is termed

_____ (D) terming

10. Norman Weiner, _____ mathematician and logician, had an important role in the development of the computer.

_____ (A) who, as a

_____ (B) was a

_____ (C) whom a

_____ (D) a

11. Jerome Kern's most famous work is *Showboat*, _____ most enduring musical comedies.

_____ (A) it is one of the finest,

_____ (B) one of the finest,

_____ (C) the finest one

_____ (D) as the finest of the

12. _____ a marshland that covers over 750 square miles in North Carolina and Virginia.

_____ (A) In the Great Dismal Swamp,

_____ (B) The Great Dismal Swamp, which

_____ (C) The Great Dismal Swamp,

_____ (D) The Great Dismal Swamp is

Lesson 21

INCOMPLETE ADVERB CLAUSES

FULL ADVERB CLAUSES

An **adverb clause** consists of a connecting word, called an **adverb clause marker** (or subordinate conjunction), and at least a subject and a verb.

The demand for economical cars increases *when gasoline becomes more expensive*.

In this example, the adverb clause marker *when* joins the adverb clause to the main clause. The adverb clause contains a subject (*gasoline*) and a verb (*becomes*).

An adverb clause can precede the main clause or follow it. When the adverb clause comes first, it is separated from the main clause by a comma.

When gasoline becomes more expensive, the demand for economical cars increases.

The following markers are commonly seen in the Structure section:

Adverb Clause Marker	Use	Example
because	cause	*Because* the speaker was sick, the program was canceled.
since	cause	*Since* credit cards are so convenient, many people use them.
although	opposition (contrary cause)	*Although* he earns a good salary, he never saves any money.
even though	opposition (contrary cause)	*Even though* she was tired, she stayed up late.
while	contrast	Some people arrived in taxis *while* others took the subway.
if	condition	*If* the automobile had not been invented, what would people use for basic transportation?
unless	condition	I won't go *unless* you do.
when	time	Your heart rate increases *when* you exercise.
while	time	Some people like to listen to music *while* they are studying.
as	time	One train was arriving *as* another was departing.
since	time	We haven't seen Professor Hill *since* she returned from her trip.
until	time	Don't put off going to the dentist *until* you have a problem.
once	time	*Once* the dean arrives, the meeting can begin.
before	time	*Before* he left the country, he bought some traveler's checks.
after	time	She will give a short speech *after* she is presented with the award.

In structure items, any part of a full adverb clause—the marker, the subject, the verb, and so on—can be missing from the stem.

Peterson's TOEFL CBT Success

CLAUSE MARKERS WITH *-EVER*

Words that end with *-ever* are sometimes used as adverb clause markers. (In some sentences, these words are actually noun-clause markers, but they are seldom used that way in structure items.)

The three *-ever* words that you are likely to see in the Structure section are given in the chart below:

Adverb clause marker with *-ever*	Meaning	Example
wherever	any place that . . .	Put that box *wherever* you can find room for it.
whenever	any time that . . .	They stay at that hotel *whenever* they're in Boston.
however	any way that . . .	*However* you solve the problem, you'll get the same answer.

REDUCED ADVERB CLAUSES

When the subject of the main clause and the subject of the adverb clause are the same person or thing, the adverb clause can be reduced (shortened). Reduced adverb clauses do not contain a main verb or a subject. They consist of a marker and a participle (either a present or a past participle) or a marker and an adjective.

When astronauts are orbiting the Earth, they don't feel the force of gravity. (full adverb clause)
When orbiting the Earth, astronauts don't feel the force of gravity. (reduced clause with present participle)

Although it had been damaged, the machine was still operational. (full adverb clause)
Although damaged, the machine was still operational. (reduced clause with a past participle)
Although he was nervous, he gave a wonderful speech. (full adverb clause)
Although nervous, he gave a wonderful speech. (reduced clause with an adjective)

You will most often see reduced adverb clauses with the markers *although*, *while*, *if*, *when*, *before*, *after*, and *until*. Reduced adverb clauses are NEVER used after *because*.

PREPOSITIONAL PHRASES WITH THE SAME MEANING AS ADVERB CLAUSES

There are also certain prepositions that have essentially the same meaning as adverb-clause markers but are used before noun phrases or pronouns, not with clauses.

Preposition	Related marker	Example
because of	because/since	He chose that university *because of* its fine reputation.
due to	because/since	The accident was *due to* mechanical failure.
on account of	because/since	Visibility is poor today *on account of* air pollution.
in spite of	although/even though	He enjoys motorcycle riding *in spite of* the danger.
despite	although/even though	*Despite* its loss, the team is still in first place.
during	when/while	Her father lived in England *during* the war.

In structure items where the correct answer is an adverb-clause marker, one of these words often appears as a distractor.

Sample Items

No one knows what color dinosaurs were _____ no sample of their skin has survived.

(A) because of
(B) because that
(C) it is because
(D) because

(A) (B) (C) ●

Choice (A) is incorrect; *because of* can only be used before nouns or pronouns. In choice (B), *that* is unnecessary. In (C), the phrase *it is* is used unnecessarily.

_____ rises to the surface of the Earth, a volcano is formed.

(A) Liquid magma
(B) Whenever liquid magma
(C) Liquid magma, which
(D) That liquid magma

(A) ● (C) (D)

Choice (A) creates two clauses, but there is no connecting word to join them. Choice (C) creates a sentence with a main clause and an adjective clause, but the main clause has two subjects (*liquid magma* and *a volcano*). Choice (D) creates a noun clause. In a correct sentence, when a noun clause begins a sentence, the clause itself is the subject of the verb in the main clause, but this sentence already has a subject (*volcano*).

_____ invisible to the unaided eye, ultraviolet light can be detected in a number of ways.

(A) Although is
(B) Despite
(C) Even though it
(D) Although

(A) (B) (C) ●

The best answer completes a reduced adverb clause. In choice (A), the adverb clause lacks a subject and is not a correct reduction because it contains a verb. In choice (B), *despite* cannot be used with an adjective (only with a noun phrase or pronoun). Choice (C) does not supply a verb for the adverb clause and is not a correct reduction because it contains a subject.

Because _____, alabaster can be easily carved.

(A) is soft
(B) softness
(C) of its softness
(D) of soft

(A) (B) ● (D)

Choice (A) lacks a subject in the adverb clause. Choice (B), a noun, could only be used with *because of*. In (D), *because of* is followed by an adjective; to be correct, it must be followed by a noun phrase or pronoun.

EXERCISE 21

Focus: Completing structure problems involving adverb clauses, reduced adverb clauses, and prepositional expressions. (Note: Two or three items do NOT focus on one of these structures. These items are marked in the answer key with an asterisk.)

Directions: Choose the one option—(A), (B), (C), or (D)—that correctly completes the sentences, then mark the appropriate blank.

1. Small sailboats can easily capsize _____ they are not handled carefully.

   _____ (A) but

   _____ (B) which

   _____ (C) if

   _____ (D) so

2. _____ they are tropical birds, parrots can live in temperate or even cold climates.

   _____ (A) Despite

   _____ (B) Even though

   _____ (C) Nevertheless

   _____ (D) But

3. _____ added to a liquid, antifreeze lowers the freezing temperature of that liquid.

   _____ (A) That

   _____ (B) As is

   _____ (C) It is

   _____ (D) When

4. _____ advertising is so widespread in the United States, it has had an enormous effect on American life.

   _____ (A) Why

   _____ (B) The reason

   _____ (C) On account of

   _____ (D) Since

5. _____ toward shore, its shape is changed by its collision with the shallow sea bottom.

   _____ (A) During a wave rolls

   _____ (B) As a wave rolls

   _____ (C) A wave rolls

   _____ (D) A wave's rolling

6. _____ are increasingly linked over long distances by electronic communications, but many of them still prefer face-to-face encounters.

   _____ (A) Although people

   _____ (B) Despite people

   _____ (C) Today people

   _____ (D) The fact that people

7. _____ together in one place, they form a community.

   _____ (A) When people who live

   _____ (B) When people living

   _____ (C) Whenever people live

   _____ (D) Whenever living people

8. _____ managed by an independent governor and board of directors, the Bank of Canada is owned by the Canadian government.

   _____ (A) And yet

   _____ (B) In spite of it

   _____ (C) Although

   _____ (D) It is

9. _____ pieces of rope are of different thickness, the weaver's knot can be used to join them.

   _____ (A) Two of

   _____ (B) What two

   _____ (C) Two such

   _____ (D) If two

10. _____, the seeds of the Kentucky coffee plant are poisonous.

   _____ (A) Until they have been cooked

   _____ (B) Cooking them

   _____ (C) They have been cooked

   _____ (D) Cooked until

11. Natural silk is still highly prized _____ similar artificial fabrics.

_____ (A) although is available

_____ (B) despite there are available

_____ (C) in spite of the availability of

_____ (D) even though an availability of

12. Cattle ranches are found almost _____ in Utah.

_____ (A) wherever

_____ (B) everywhere

_____ (C) overall

_____ (D) somewhere

13. _____ through a prism, a beam of white light breaks into all the colors of the rainbow.

_____ (A) When shines

_____ (B) It shines

_____ (C) It is shone

_____ (D) When shone

14. _____ most people think of freezing as a relatively modern method of food preservation, it is actually one of the oldest.

_____ (A) Even

_____ (B) As though

_____ (C) However

_____ (D) Although

15. _____ large bodies of water never freeze solid is that the sheet of ice on the surface protects the water below it from the cold air.

_____ (A) Because

_____ (B) Why do

_____ (C) The reason that

_____ (D) For the reason

16. _____ granted by the Patent Office, it becomes the inventor's property and he or she can keep it, sell it, or license it to someone else.

_____ (A) Once a patent is

_____ (B) When a patent

_____ (C) A patent, once

_____ (D) A patent, whenever it

17. Owls can hunt in total darkness _____ their remarkably keen sense of smell.

_____ (A) since

_____ (B) because of

_____ (C) the result

_____ (D) that

18. _____ most bamboo blooms every year, there are some species that flower only two or three times a century.

_____ (A) Whenever

_____ (B) That

_____ (C) While

_____ (D) However

Lesson 22

INCOMPLETE NOUN CLAUSES

Noun clauses are the third type of subordinate clause. They begin with **noun-clause markers**. Noun clauses that are formed from statements begin with the noun-clause marker *that*. Noun clauses formed from *yes/no* questions begin with the noun-clause markers *whether* or *if*. Those formed from information questions begin with *wh-* words: *what*, *where*, *when*, and so on.

Dr. Hopkins' office is in this building. (statement)
I'm sure *that* Dr. Hopkins' office is in this building.
Is Dr. Hopkins' office on this floor? (yes/no question)
I don't know *if* (*whether*) Dr. Hopkins' office is on this floor.
Where is Dr. Hopkins' office? (information question)
Please tell me *where* Dr. Hopkins' office is.

Notice that the word order in direct questions is not the same as it is in noun clauses. The noun clause follows statement word order (subject + verb), not question word order (auxiliary + subject + main verb). Often one of the distractors for noun-clause items will incorrectly follow question word order.

*I don't know what *is her name*. (incorrect use of question word order)
    I don't know what *her name is*. (correct word order)
*She called him to ask what time *did his party start*. (incorrect use of question word order)
    She called him to ask what time *his party started*. (correct word order)

Noun clauses function exactly as nouns do: as subjects, as direct objects, or after the verb *to be*.

When the meeting will be held has not been decided. (noun clause as subject)
The weather announcer said *that there will be thunderstorms*. (noun clause as direct object)
This is *what you need*. (noun clause after *to be*)

Notice that when the noun clause is the subject of a sentence the verb in the main clause does not have a noun or pronoun subject.

In structure items, the noun-clause marker, along with any other part of the noun clause—subject, verb, and so on—may be missing from the stem, or the whole noun clause may be missing.

Sample Items

_____ was caused by breathing impure air was once a common belief.

(A) Malaria
(B) That malaria
(C) Why malaria
(D) Because malaria

Ⓐ ● Ⓒ Ⓓ

Choice (A) is incorrect because there are two verbs (*was caused* and *was*) but only one subject. Choice (C) is incorrect because *Why* is not the appropriate noun-clause marker in this sentence; the noun clause is based on a statement, not on an information question. Choice (D) is incorrect because it forms an adverb clause, but the main clause lacks a subject. In the correct answer the noun clause itself (*That malaria was caused by breathing impure air*) is the subject of the verb *was* in the main clause.

One basic question psychologists have tried to answer is _____ .

(A) people learn
(B) how do people learn
(C) people learn how
(D) how people learn

Ⓐ Ⓑ Ⓒ ●

Choice (A) is incorrect; there is no connector between the first clause and the second. Choice (B) incorrectly follows question word order. Choice (C) is incorrect because *how* is in the wrong position.

EXERCISE 22

Focus: Completing structure problems involving incomplete noun clauses. (Note: Two or three items in this exercise do NOT focus on noun clauses. These items are marked in the answer key with asterisks.)

Directions: Choose the one option—(A), (B), (C), or (D)—that correctly completes the sentences, then mark the appropriate blank.

1. _____ begin their existence as ice crystals over most of the earth seems likely.

   _____ (A) Raindrops
   _____ (B) If raindrops
   _____ (C) What if raindrops
   _____ (D) That raindrops

2. Scientists cannot agree on _____ related to other orders of insects.

   _____ (A) that fleas are
   _____ (B) how fleas are
   _____ (C) how are fleas
   _____ (D) fleas that are

3. It was in 1875 _____ joined the staff of the astronomical observatory at Harvard University.

   _____ (A) that Anna Winlock
   _____ (B) Anna Winlock, who
   _____ (C) as Anna Winlock
   _____ (D) Anna Winlock then

4. _____ is a narrow strip of woods along a stream in an open grassland.

  _____ (A) Ecologists use the term "gallery forest"

  _____ (B) What do ecologists call a "gallery forest"

  _____ (C) "Gallery forest" is the term ecologists use

  _____ (D) What ecologists call a "gallery forest"

5. _____ developed so rapidly in Alabama primarily because of its rich natural resources.

  _____ (A) That heavy industry

  _____ (B) Heavy industry

  _____ (C) Heavy industry that was

  _____ (D) When heavy industry

6. _____ so incredible is that these insects successfully migrate to places that they have never even seen.

  _____ (A) That makes the monarch butterflies' migration

  _____ (B) The migration of the monarch butterflies is

  _____ (C) What makes the monarch butterflies' migration

  _____ (D) The migration of the monarch butterflies, which is

7. Art critics do not all agree on what _____ a painting great.

  _____ (A) qualities make

  _____ (B) are the qualities for making

  _____ (C) qualities to make

  _____ (D) do the qualities that make

8. In order to grow vegetables properly, gardeners must know _____.

  _____ (A) what the requirements for each vegetable are

  _____ (B) that the requirements for each vegetable

  _____ (C) what are each vegetable's requirements

  _____ (D) that is required by each vegetable

9. When _____ is not known.

  _____ (A) was the wheel invented

  _____ (B) the invention of the wheel

  _____ (C) inventing the wheel

  _____ (D) the wheel was invented

10. For many years people have wondered _____ exists elsewhere in the universe.

  _____ (A) that life

  _____ (B) life which

  _____ (C) whether life

  _____ (D) life as it

11. _____ of all modern domestic poultry is the red jungle fowl is widely believed.

  _____ (A) The ancestor

  _____ (B) The ancestor is

  _____ (C) How the ancestor

  _____ (D) That the ancestor

12. _____ the right side of a person's brain is dominant, that person is left-handed.

  _____ (A) That

  _____ (B) If

  _____ (C) Which

  _____ (D) For

Lesson 23

INCOMPLETE/MISSING PREPOSITIONAL PHRASES

A **prepositional phrase** consists of a **preposition** (*in*, *at*, *with*, *for*, *until*, and so on) followed by a noun phrase or pronoun, which is called the **prepositional object**. Prepositional phrases often describe relationships of time and location, among others.

> *In the autumn* maple leaves turn red.
> Beacon Hill is one of the most famous neighborhoods *in Boston*.
> *With luck*, there won't be any more problems.
> This house was built *by John's grandfather*.

Often prepositional phrases come at the beginning of sentences, but they may appear in other parts of the sentence as well.

The correct answer for this type of item may be a preposition, its object, or both, as well as other parts of the sentence.

You may see prepositions in distractors, especially before the subject of a sentence. Remember, the object of a preposition cannot correctly be the subject of a sentence, as in these examples:

> *In the autumn* is my favorite season.
> *Without a pencil* is no way to come to a test.

Sample Items

_____ the unaided eye can see about 6,000 stars.

(A) A clear night
(B) It's a clear night
(C) On a clear night
(D) When a clear night

Choice (A) is incorrect because there is no connector to join the noun phrase *A clear night* to the rest of the sentence. Choice (B) consists of an independent clause, but there is no connector to join it to the other clause. Choice (D) seems to form a subordinate clause, but the clause lacks a verb.

_____ all the field crops grown in the United States are harvested with machines called combines.

(A) Of nearly
(B) Nearly
(C) That nearly
(D) Nearly of

Choices (A) and (D) are incorrect because the subject of a sentence (*all the field crops*) cannot be the object of a preposition (*of*). Choice (C) creates a noun clause, but the noun clause lacks a verb.

148

EXERCISE 23

Focus: Completing structure problems involving prepositional phrases. (Note: One or two items in this exercise do NOT focus on prepositional phrases. These items are marked in the answer key with asterisks.)

Directions: Choose the one option—(A), (B), (C), or (D)— that correctly completes the sentence, then mark the appropriate blank.

1. _____ seed of a flowering plant is covered by a dense protective coat.

    _____ (A) On each

    _____ (B) Each

    _____ (C) Each of

    _____ (D) That each

2. Dynamite is ordinarily detonated _____ called a blasting cap.

    _____ (A) a device is used

    _____ (B) that a device

    _____ (C) with a device

    _____ (D) the use of a device

3. _____ 1900 there were some 300 bicycle factories in the United States, and they produced over a million bicycles.

    _____ (A) In

    _____ (B) Because in

    _____ (C) It was in

    _____ (D) That in

4. A thick layer of fat called blubber keeps whales warm even _____ coldest water.

    _____ (A) although the

    _____ (B) in the

    _____ (C) the

    _____ (D) of the

5. _____ the United States, the general movement of air masses is from west to east.

    _____ (A) Across

    _____ (B) To cross

    _____ (C) They cross

    _____ (D) It's across

6. The bark of a tree thickens _____.

    _____ (A) with age

    _____ (B) it gets older

    _____ (C) as older

    _____ (D) by age

7. A substance that is harmless to a person who has no allergies can cause mild to serious reactions in a person _____ allergies.

    _____ (A) has

    _____ (B) which having

    _____ (C) can have

    _____ (D) with

8. In 1886 a number of national unions formed the American Federation of Labor _____.

    _____ (A) Samuel Gompers was its leader

    _____ (B) under the leadership of Samuel Gompers

    _____ (C) which, under Samuel Gompers' leadership

    _____ (D) Samuel Gompers led it

9. Harmonicas, autoharps, and kazoos _____ folk instruments.

    _____ (A) are examples

    _____ (B) for example

    _____ (C) are examples of

    _____ (D) as examples of

10. _____ charming shops and restaurants, Old Town is the most picturesque section of Albuquerque.

    _____ (A) With its

    _____ (B) Its

    _____ (C) Because its

    _____ (D) For its

11. _____ such as banking and travel, in which computers are not a convenience but a necessity.

_____ (A) Where some industries,

_____ (B) In some industries,

_____ (C) Some industries,

_____ (D) There are some industries,

12. One of the oldest large suspension bridges still _____ today is the George Washington Bridge between New York City and Fort Lee, New Jersey.

_____ (A) uses

_____ (B) is used

_____ (C) the use of

_____ (D) in use

Answer Sheet

Mini-Test 4: Structure

1. (A) (B) (C) (D)	6. (A) (B) (C) (D)	11. (A) (B) (C) (D)
2. (A) (B) (C) (D)	7. (A) (B) (C) (D)	12. (A) (B) (C) (D)
3. (A) (B) (C) (D)	8. (A) (B) (C) (D)	13. (A) (B) (C) (D)
4. (A) (B) (C) (D)	9. (A) (B) (C) (D)	14. (A) (B) (C) (D)
5. (A) (B) (C) (D)	10. (A) (B) (C) (D)	15. (A) (B) (C) (D)

MINI-TEST 4: STRUCTURE

Directions: The following sentences are incomplete. Beneath each of these sentences, there are four words or phrases marked (A), (B), (C), and (D). Choose the one word or phrase that best completes the sentence and fill in the appropriate answer above.

Time: 12 minutes

1. _____ by Anna Baldwin in 1878.

_____ (A) The invention of the vacuum milking machine

_____ (B) That the vacuum milking machine was invented

_____ (C) The vacuum milking machine, which was invented

_____ (D) The vacuum milking machine was invented

2. Dry cleaning is the process _____ clothes are cleaned in liquids other than water.

_____ (A) by

_____ (B) which through

_____ (C) by which

_____ (D) through

3. Sand dunes are made of loose sand _____ up by the action of the wind.

_____ (A) it builds

_____ (B) builds

_____ (C) is building

_____ (D) built

4. _____ book *Jubilee*, which was based on the life of her great-grandmother, Margaret Walker was awarded the Pulitzer Prize.

_____ (A) For her

_____ (B) Her

_____ (C) It was her

_____ (D) That her

5. Job specialization takes place _____ of production is separated into occupations.

_____ (A) whenever the work is

_____ (B) when the work

_____ (C) is when the work

_____ (D) whenever working

6. _____ are hot is a common misconception.

_____ (A) All deserts

_____ (B) All deserts which

_____ (C) Of all deserts

_____ (D) That all deserts

7. _____ imaginative stories about the origin of the game of chess.

_____ (A) Many of the

_____ (B) Many

_____ (C) There are many

_____ (D) Of the many

8. _____ one of Canada's greatest engineering projects, is a 27-mile-long waterway between Lake Erie and Lake Ontario.

_____ (A) Because the Welland Ship Canal is

_____ (B) The Welland Ship Canal is

_____ (C) That the Welland Ship Canal is

_____ (D) The Welland Ship Canal,

9. A deep-tissue massage is a type of massage therapy _____ on one part of the body, such as the lower back.

_____ (A) its concentration is

_____ (B) concentrating

_____ (C) why it concentrates

_____ (D) to be concentrated

10. One of the most powerful optical telescopes, the ''Big Eye'' at Mt. Palomar, _____ a 200-inch mirror.

_____ (A) has

_____ (B) that has

_____ (C) with

_____ (D) which

11. Elfego Baca, _____ legendary Mexican-American folk hero, was a lawman in New Mexico in the late 1880s.

_____ (A) a

_____ (B) who, as a

_____ (C) was a

_____ (D) and he was a

12. _____ relatively inexpensive, the metal pewter can be fashioned into beautiful and useful objects.

_____ (A) Even it is

_____ (B) Despite

_____ (C) Nevertheless, it is

_____ (D) Although

13. _____ is a general category that includes all mental states and activities.

_____ (A) What do psychologists call cognition

_____ (B) Psychologists call it cognition

_____ (C) What psychologists call cognition

_____ (D) Cognition, as it is called by psychologists, which

14. Nathaniel Hawthorne wrote four novels, _____ The Scarlet Letter, became an American literary classic.

_____ (A) of which one,

_____ (B) which one

_____ (C) one of which,

_____ (D) one was

15. _____ about four years for a new aircraft model to move from the preliminary design stage to the full-production stage.

_____ (A) It takes

_____ (B) Taking

_____ (C) That takes

_____ (D) To take

Lesson 24

WORD ORDER PROBLEMS

All of the answer choices for a structure item involving **word order** contain more or less the same words, but they are arranged in four different orders. The word order is "scrambled" in three choices; one is correct. Most items consist of three or four words.

(A) X Y Z
(B) Y X Z
(C) Z Y X
(D) X Z Y

Word order problems are easy to identify because the answer choices are exactly—or almost exactly—the same length, so the answer choices form a rectangle.

(A) so far away from
(B) away so far from
(C) from so far away
(D) away from so far

Many different types of structures are used in word order problems. One of the most common is a phrase with a superlative adjective or adverb.

Word order items are the only structure items in which the distractors can be ungrammatical. In other structure problems, distractors are always correct in some context. However, at least two of the choices may be grammatical. The correct choice depends on the context of the sentence.

It sometimes is easy to eliminate distractors in word order items by making sure they "fit" with the rest of the sentence. If you are not sure which remaining answer is correct, use your "ear." Say the sentence to yourself (silently) to see which sounds best. Sometimes in word order problems, the answer that looks best doesn't always sound best. Don't, however, go just by the sound of the answer choices; you must consider them as part of the whole sentence.

A special type of word order problem involves **inversions**. This type of sentence uses question word order even though the sentence is not a question. When are inversions used?

- When the negative words listed below are placed at the beginning of a clause for emphasis

not only	never
not until	seldom
not once	rarely
at no time	scarcely
by no means	no sooner
nowhere	

Not once *was he* on time.
Seldom *have I heard* such beautiful music.
Not only *did the company* lose profits, but it also had to lay off workers.

- When the following expressions beginning with *only* occur at the beginning of a sentence (with these expressions, the subject and verb in that clause are inverted)

only in (on, at, by, etc.)   only recently
only once

Only in an emergency *should you use* this exit.
Only recently *did she return* from abroad.
Only by asking questions *can you learn*.

- When the following expressions beginning with *only* occur at the beginning of a sentence (with these expressions, the subject and verb of the second clause are inverted)

only if	only when
only because	only after
only until	

Only if you have a serious problem *should you* call Mr. Franklin at home.
Only when you are satisfied *is the sale* considered final.

- When clauses beginning with the word *so* + an adjective or participle occur at the beginning of a sentence

So rare *is this coin* that it belongs in a museum.
So confusing *was the map* that we had to ask a police officer for directions.

- When clauses beginning with expressions of place or order occur at the beginning of a sentence (in these cases, the subject and main verb are inverted since auxiliary verbs are not used as they would be in most questions)

In front of the museum *is a statue*.
Off the coast of California *lie the Channel Islands*.
First *came a police car*, then *came an ambulance*.

Sample Items

Andromeda is a galaxy containing millions of individual stars, but it is _____ Earth that it looks like a blurry patch of light.

(A) so far away from
(B) away so far from
(C) from so far away
(D) away from so far

● Ⓑ Ⓒ Ⓓ

Only choice (A) involves the correct word order for this sentence. Choices (B) and (D) are incorrect word orders in any sentence. Choice (C) could be correct in certain sentences, but is not correct in the context of this sentence.

Not only _____ shade and beauty, but they also reduce carbon dioxide.

(A) do trees provide
(B) trees provide
(C) provide trees
(D) trees do provide

● Ⓑ Ⓒ Ⓓ

Only choice (A) correctly uses question word order after *not only*. Choices (B) and (C) do not use an auxiliary verb, which is required after *not only*. Choice (D) does not follow the correct word order: auxiliary + adjective + main verb.

EXERCISE 24

Focus: Completing structure problems involving word order. (Note: ALL the items in this exercise focus on word order problems.)

Directions: Choose the one option—(A), (B), (C), or (D)—that correctly completes the sentence, then mark the appropriate blank.

1. Hills known as land islands, or salt domes, are _____ Louisiana's marshlands.

   _____ (A) extremely interesting features of

   _____ (B) of extremely interesting features

   _____ (C) interesting extremely features of

   _____ (D) extremely interesting of features

2. _____ of chamber music is the string quartet.

   _____ (A) The famous most form

   _____ (B) The most famous form

   _____ (C) The form most famous

   _____ (D) Most the form famous

3. Not until the seventeenth century _____ to measure the speed of light.

   _____ (A) did anyone even attempt

   _____ (B) anyone did even attempt

   _____ (C) did anyone attempt even

   _____ (D) did even attempt anyone

4. Alfalfa is _____ for livestock.

   _____ (A) a primarily grown crop

   _____ (B) grown primarily a crop

   _____ (C) a crop grown primarily

   _____ (D) a grown crop primarily

5. The Franklin stove, which became common in the 1790s, burned wood _____ an open fireplace.

   _____ (A) efficiently more than much

   _____ (B) much more efficiently than

   _____ (C) much more than efficiently

   _____ (D) more efficiently much than

6. Reinforced concrete is concrete that is strengthened by metal bars _____ .

   _____ (A) in it that are embedded

   _____ (B) embedded that are in it

   _____ (C) are that it embedded in

   _____ (D) that are embedded in it

7. The type of clothing people wear tells others a lot about _____ .

   _____ (A) who they are

   _____ (B) are they who

   _____ (C) they are who

   _____ (D) who are they

8. Most southern states had set up primary school systems by the late eighteenth century, but only in New England _____ and open to all students.

   _____ (A) primary schools were free

   _____ (B) were primary schools free

   _____ (C) free were primary schools

   _____ (D) were free primary schools

9. Fungi, _____, do not produce chlorophyll.

   _____ (A) as such mushrooms

   _____ (B) mushrooms as such

   _____ (C) such as mushrooms

   _____ (D) mushrooms such as

10. Seldom _____ more than 20 minutes a night.

   _____ (A) sleep giraffes

   _____ (B) do giraffes sleep

   _____ (C) giraffes do sleep

   _____ (D) giraffes sleep

11. _____ of the early years of space exploration was the discovery of the Van Allen radiation belt in 1958.

_____ (A) Perhaps the greatest triumph

_____ (B) The triumph perhaps greatest

_____ (C) The greatest perhaps triumph

_____ (D) The triumph greatest perhaps

12. Today _____ major new products without conducting elaborate market research.

_____ (A) corporations hardly introduce ever

_____ (B) hardly ever corporations introduce

_____ (C) hardly ever introduce corporations

_____ (D) corporations hardly ever introduce

13. Across the Chesapeake Bay from the rest of the state _____, whose farms produce beans, tomatoes, and other garden vegetables.

_____ (A) there lies Maryland's Eastern Shore

_____ (B) lies Maryland's Eastern Shore

_____ (C) Maryland's Eastern Shore lies there

_____ (D) Maryland's Eastern Shore lies

14. Acidophilus bacteria are _____ in an acid medium.

_____ (A) those that grow best

_____ (B) those grow best that

_____ (C) that those grow best

_____ (D) grow best those that

15. _____ of great apes, the gibbon is the smallest.

_____ (A) Four of the types

_____ (B) The four of types

_____ (C) Four types of the

_____ (D) Of the four types

16. It is difficult _____ through swamps because of tangled roots and shallow waterways.

_____ (A) to navigate even for small boats

_____ (B) for even small boats to navigate

_____ (C) even small boats for to navigate

_____ (D) even to navigate for small boats

17. A lodestone is _____ .

_____ (A) an occurring naturally magnet

_____ (B) a magnet naturally occurring

_____ (C) naturally a magnet occurring

_____ (D) a naturally occurring magnet

18. So complicated _____ that consumers who use a product are seldom aware of where all its components come from.

_____ (A) today trade is international

_____ (B) today international trade is

_____ (C) is international trade today

_____ (D) international trade is today

19. The snow bunting is _____ winter birds in Canada.

_____ (A) one most of the common

_____ (B) the most common one of

_____ (C) one of the most common

_____ (D) the one of most common

20. Nashville has _____ the capital of country music.

_____ (A) as long been known

_____ (B) been known long as

_____ (C) long been known as

_____ (D) long as been known

Lesson 25

ITEMS INVOLVING VERB PROBLEMS

The answer choices for this type of problem are all or almost all different forms of the same verb. From the context of the sentence stem, you'll have to decide which form works best in the sentence. Distractors are generally incorrect for one of these reasons:

- **The "verb" is not really a verb.** Used alone, an infinitive, gerund, or participle cannot be a main verb.
- **The verb is active, but it should be passive, or it is passive but it should be active.** If the subject of the sentence *performs* the action, the verb must be in the active voice. If the subject of the sentence *receives* the action, the verb must be in the passive.

  The architect *designed* the building. (active verb)
  The building *was designed* by the architect. (passive verb)

- **The verb does not agree with its subject.** Singular subjects require singular verbs; plural subjects require plural verbs.
- **The verb is not in the right tense.** According to the time words or ideas in the sentence, the appropriate tense must be used.
- **An unnecessary element comes before the verb.** Personal pronouns (*he*, *she*, *it*), relative pronouns (*who*, *which*, *that*, and so on), or conjunctions (*and*, *but*, and so on) may be used unnecessarily before verbs in some sentences.

Sample Item

Before the late eighteenth century, most textiles _____ at home.

(A) produced
(B) was produced
(C) producing
(D) were produced

   Choice (D) is the best answer. (A) can be considered either an active verb in the past tense or a past participle; both are incorrect. An active verb is incorrect because a passive verb is needed; a past participle is incorrect because a past participle cannot serve as a main verb. (B) is incorrect because the plural subject *textiles* requires a plural verb, *were*. (C) is incorrect because, by itself, an *-ing* form can never be a main verb.

EXERCISE 25

Focus: Completing structure problems involving verb forms. (Note: One or two items in this exercise do NOT focus on finite verb forms. These items are marked in the answer key with asterisks.)

Directions: Choose the one option—(A), (B), (C), or (D)—that correctly completes the sentence, then mark the appropriate blank.

1. R. M. Bartlett of Philadelphia _____ the first private business college in the United States in 1843.

    _____ (A) founding

    _____ (B) founded

    _____ (C) was founded

    _____ (D) founds

2. In 1989, the space probe Voyager 2 _____ by the planet Neptune.

    _____ (A) fly

    _____ (B) having flown

    _____ (C) flying

    _____ (D) flew

3. A cupful of stagnant water may _____ millions of microorganisms.

    _____ (A) contains

    _____ (B) to contain

    _____ (C) contain

    _____ (D) containing

4. Computers and new methods of communication _____ revolutionized the modern office.

    _____ (A) have

    _____ (B) to have

    _____ (C) that have

    _____ (D) has

5. Sarah Knight _____ a fascinating account of a journey she made from Boston to New York in 1704.

    _____ (A) written

    _____ (B) write

    _____ (C) wrote

    _____ (D) writing

6. All animals _____ on other animals or plants.

    _____ (A) feed

    _____ (B) feeds

    _____ (C) fed

    _____ (D) feeding

7. Chromium _____ in the manufacture of stainless steel.

    _____ (A) using

    _____ (B) is used

    _____ (C) uses

    _____ (D) is using

8. The Baltimore and Ohio Railroad _____ the first air conditioning system for trains in 1931.

    _____ (A) has installed

    _____ (B) installed

    _____ (C) to have installed

    _____ (D) installing

9. Porous rocks such as chalk and sandstone allow water _____ through them.

    _____ (A) soaks

    _____ (B) is soaked

    _____ (C) to soak

    _____ (D) can soak

10. By 1790, rice _____ an important crop in the South.

    _____ (A) being

    _____ (B) has been

    _____ (C) was

    _____ (D) was being

11. Weavers are social birds that _____ complex nests housing hundreds of families.

_____ (A) build

_____ (B) are built

_____ (C) are building

_____ (D) built

12. The American dancer Maria Tallchief first _____ prominent in Europe.

_____ (A) to become

_____ (B) become

_____ (C) has become

_____ (D) became

Peterson's TOEFL CBT Success

Lesson 26

INCOMPLETE/MISSING INFINITIVE AND GERUND PHRASES

An **infinitive** is a verbal form that consists of the word *to* and the simple form of the verb: *to be, to go, to give, to build*. Infinitives are often followed by an object: *to give directions, to build a house*. Together, an infinitive and its object form an **infinitive phrase**.

Infinitives can be used in a variety of ways. They may be the subjects or objects of verbs or used after *to be* + adjective.

To read the directions is important. (infinitive as subject of a verb)
He forgot *to read* the directions. (infinitive as object of a verb)
It's important *to read* the directions. (infinitive after *to be* + adjective)

Infinitives can be used as adjective phrases after noun phrases. You will often see this in structure problems after noun phrases containing the word *first*. These infinitive phrases often come at the end of a sentence and are set off by commas.

John Glenn was the first American *to orbit* the Earth.

Infinitives can also be used to show purpose. In other words, they explain why an action takes place. (The phrase *in order* + infinitive also shows purpose.)

To learn how to dance, he took lessons.
In order to learn how to dance, he took lessons.

You may see structure items that focus on **passive infinitives**. A passive infinitive consists of the word *to* + *be* + past participle.

Roberta was the first person *to be asked* to speak at the meeting.

A **gerund** is a verbal form that ends in *-ing*: *being, going, giving, building*. Like infinitives, gerunds are often followed by objects: *giving directions, building a house*. Together, a gerund and its object form **a gerund phrase**.

Gerunds are verbal nouns and are used as other nouns are used. You will generally see gerunds as subjects or objects of verbs or as objects of prepositions. (Note: Infinitives can also be subjects and objects but NEVER objects of prepositions.)

Playing cards is enjoyable. (gerund as subject of a verb)
He enjoys *playing* cards. (gerund as object of a verb)
He passes the time by *playing* cards. (gerund as object of a preposition)

Sample Items

_____ the eggs of most birds must be kept warm.

(A) Proper development
(B) By properly developing,
(C) They develop properly
(D) To develop properly,

Ⓐ Ⓑ Ⓒ ⬤

The only one of these four phrases listed here that can show purpose is choice (D), an infinitive. This expression means, *In order to develop properly.*

In 1959 the political philosopher Hannah Arendt became the first woman _____ a full professor at Princeton University.

(A) to appoint
(B) was appointed
(C) to be appointed
(D) an appointment as

Ⓐ Ⓑ ⬤ Ⓓ

After a noun phrase such as *the first woman* an infinitive is used as an adjective phrase. Because a passive form is needed (Hannah Arendt receives the action; she doesn't perform the action), choice (A) is not the correct infinitive form. Choice (C), a passive infinitive, is best.

The ear is the organ of hearing, but it also plays a role in _____ balance.

(A) maintaining
(B) it maintains
(C) to maintain
(D) maintained

⬤ Ⓑ Ⓒ Ⓓ

A gerund is used correctly after a preposition. Choices (B), (C), and (D) would not be appropriate after a preposition.

EXERCISE 26

Focus: Completing structure problems involving infinitive and gerund phrases. (Note: One or two of the items in this exercise do NOT focus on infinitives or gerunds. These items are marked in the answer key with asterisks.)

Directions: Choose the one option—(A), (B), (C), or (D)—that correctly completes the sentence, then mark the appropriate blank.

1. _____ for a career in dance generally begins at an early age.

    _____ (A) People train

    _____ (B) That people train

    _____ (C) If training

    _____ (D) Training

2. A baby's first teeth _____ are generally the lower incisors.

    _____ (A) appearance

    _____ (B) appear

    _____ (C) to appear

    _____ (D) in appearing

3. A climbing helmet _____ protection for a rock-climber's head from falling rocks and other hazards.

    _____ (A) to provide

    _____ (B) provides

    _____ (C) providing

    _____ (D) that provides

4. Power tools require careful handling _____ injuries.

    _____ (A) by avoiding

    _____ (B) they avoid

    _____ (C) to avoid

    _____ (D) that avoid

5. An electromagnet is created _____ electrical current through a coil of wire.

    _____ (A) by passing

    _____ (B) passes by

    _____ (C) to be passed

    _____ (D) passed

6. _____ at home requires only three types of chemicals, several pieces of simple equipment, and running water.

    _____ (A) For the development of film

    _____ (B) To develop film

    _____ (C) When film is developed

    _____ (D) In developing film

7. The purpose of cost accounting is _____ involved in producing and selling a good or service.

    _____ (A) as a determination of its costs

    _____ (B) the costs determined

    _____ (C) that determines the costs

    _____ (D) to determine the costs

8. _____ was one of the most difficult tasks pioneers faced on their journeys west.

    _____ (A) Crossing rivers

    _____ (B) While crossing rivers

    _____ (C) Rivers being crossed

    _____ (D) By crossing rivers

9. Energy can be defined as the ability _____ .

    _____ (A) do working

    _____ (B) to do work

    _____ (C) doing work

    _____ (D) work to be done

10. The process of _____ by hand has changed little since the fifteenth century.

    _____ (A) to bind books

    _____ (B) binding books

    _____ (C) books are bound

    _____ (D) bound books

11. A crescent wrench has adjustable jaws for
    _____ a nut, bolt, or pipe.

    _____ (A) to grip

    _____ (B) they grip

    _____ (C) gripping

    _____ (D) gripped

12. Compressed air is _____ air brakes,
    pneumatic tools, and other machinery.

    _____ (A) used to powering

    _____ (B) to use powering

    _____ (C) used to power

    _____ (D) in use by powering

13. Some people believe that the crystals of
    certain minerals _____ curative powers.

    _____ (A) have

    _____ (B) having

    _____ (C) that have

    _____ (D) to have

14. The narrow blades of speed skates allow
    _____ speeds of up to 30 miles per
    hour.

    _____ (A) for skaters maintaining

    _____ (B) skaters to maintain

    _____ (C) skaters maintain

    _____ (D) maintenance by skaters

15. The first library _____ in the Nebraska
    Territory was built in Fort Atkinson in 1870.

    _____ (A) to be established

    _____ (B) was established

    _____ (C) could establish

    _____ (D) to establish

Lesson 27

ITEMS INVOLVING PARALLEL STRUCTURES

In certain structure items, the correct use of **parallel structures** is tested. Parallel structures have the same grammatical form and function. Look at the following sentences:

She spends her leisure time *hiking*, *camping*, and *fishing*.
He *changed* the oil, *checked* the tire pressure, and *filled* the tank with gas.
Nancy plans to either *study* medicine or *major* in biology.
Nancy plans to study either *medicine* or *biology*.

All of the structures in italics are parallel. In the first, three gerunds are parallel; in the second, three main verbs; in the third, two simple forms; and in the fourth, two nouns. Many other structures must be parallel in certain sentences: adjectives, adverbs, infinitives, prepositional phrases, noun clauses, and others.

The most common situation in which parallel structures are required is in a sequence (*A*, *B*, and *C*) as in the first two sentences above. Parallel structures are also required with correlative conjunctions such as *either...or* or *not only...but also*. (Correlative conjunctions are presented in Lesson 30.)

Sample Item

San Francisco has a pleasant climate, _____ and many fascinating neighborhoods.

(A) exciting scenery,
(B) has exciting scenery
(C) that the scenery is exciting
(D) the scenery is exciting,

This sentence contains a series of three objects after the verb *has*: the first and third are noun phrases (*a pleasant climate* and *many fascinating neighborhoods*). To be parallel, the second object must also be a noun phrase. Therefore, choice (A) is the correct answer; (B), (C), and (D) are not parallel.

EXERCISE 27

Focus: Completing structure problems involving parallelism. (Note: One or two items in the exercise do NOT focus on items involving parallel structures. These items are marked in the answer key with asterisks.)

Directions: Choose the one option—(A), (B), (C), or (D)—that correctly completes the sentence, then mark the appropriate blank.

1. Insects provide many beneficial services, such as _____, breaking down dead-wood, and pollinating plants.

   _____ (A) they condition soils

   _____ (B) to condition soil

   _____ (C) conditioning the soil

   _____ (D) soil conditioned

2. Frozen orange juice must be packed, _____, and stored when the fruit is ripe.

   _____ (A) be frozen

   _____ (B) must be frozen

   _____ (C) frozen

   _____ (D) it must be frozen

3. The Sioux language is spoken not only _____ Sioux but also by the Crow and Osage tribes.

   _____ (A) by the

   _____ (B) the

   _____ (C) do the

   _____ (D) and the

4. In 1900 electrically powered cars were more popular than gasoline powered cars because they were quiet, operated smoothly, and _____ .

   _____ (A) handled easily

   _____ (B) ease of handling

   _____ (C) handling easily

   _____ (D) easy to handle

5. Roger Williams was a clergyman, _____ the colony of Rhode Island, and an outspoken advocate of religious and political freedom.

   _____ (A) founded

   _____ (B) the founder of

   _____ (C) was the founder of

   _____ (D) he founded

6. Paint can be applied to a surface with rollers, _____, or spray guns.

   _____ (A) brushes

   _____ (B) brushes can be used

   _____ (C) with brushes

   _____ (D) by brush

7. The use of labor-saving devices in homes, _____, and in factories added to the amount of leisure time people had.

   _____ (A) at office

   _____ (B) used in offices

   _____ (C) offices

   _____ (D) in offices

8. A dulcimer can be played by either striking its strings with a hammer or _____ .

   _____ (A) to pluck them with the fingers

   _____ (B) fingers are used to pluck them

   _____ (C) they are plucked with the fingers

   _____ (D) plucking them with the fingers

9. Throughout history, trade routes have increased contact between people, _____, and greatly affected the growth of civilization.

    _____ (A) have resulted in an exchange of ideas

    _____ (B) an exchange of ideas has resulted

    _____ (C) resulted in an exchange of ideas

    _____ (D) resulting in an exchange of ideas

10. Walt Disney made many technical advances in the use of sound, color, and _____ in animated films.

    _____ (A) photographing

    _____ (B) using photography

    _____ (C) photography

    _____ (D) use of photographs

11. Artist Paul Kane traveled throughout Northwest Canada on foot, by canoe, and _____ to sketch Native Canadians going about their ordinary lives.

    _____ (A) on horseback

    _____ (B) riding a horse

    _____ (C) was on horseback

    _____ (D) by a horse

12. Barbara Jordan was the first woman in the South to win an election to the House of Representatives, _____ as Congresswoman from Texas from 1973 to 1979.

    _____ (A) to serve

    _____ (B) served

    _____ (C) serving

    _____ (D) has served

13. Photographers' choice of a camera depends on what kind of pictures they want to take, how much control they want over exposure, and _____ they want to spend.

    _____ (A) the amount of money

    _____ (B) what money

    _____ (C) how much money

    _____ (D) so much money that

14. Atlanta is the commercial, financial, and _____ of Georgia.

    _____ (A) center of administration

    _____ (B) administrative center

    _____ (C) center for administering

    _____ (D) administering center

15. Even after the Revolutionary War, American importers obtained merchandise from Britain because British merchants understood American tastes, offered attractive prices, and _____ .

    _____ (A) easy credit was provided

    _____ (B) because of easy credit

    _____ (C) easy credit

    _____ (D) provided easy credit

Lesson 28

ITEMS INVOLVING MISPLACED MODIFIERS

A **misplaced modifier** is a participial phrase or other modifier that comes before the subject, but does NOT refer to the subject.
Look at this sentence:

*Driving down the road, a herd of sheep suddenly crossed the road in front of Liza's car. (INCORRECT)

This sentence is incorrect because it seems to say that a herd of sheep—rather than Liza—was driving down the road. The participial phrase is misplaced. The sentence could be corrected as shown:

As Liza was driving down the road, a herd of sheep suddenly crossed the road in front of her. (CORRECT)

This sentence now correctly has Liza in the driver's seat instead of the sheep.
The following sentence structures are often misplaced:

Misplaced Structure	Example	Correction
present participle	Walking along the beach, the ship was spotted by the men.	Walking along the beach, the men spotted the ship.
past participle	Based on this study, the scientist could make several conclusions.	Based on this study, several conclusions could be made by the scientist.
appositive	A resort city in Arkansas, the population of Hot Springs is about 35,000.	A resort city in Arkansas, Hot Springs has a population of about 35,000.
reduced adjective clause	While peeling onions, his eyes began to water.	While he was peeling onions, his eyes began to water.
adjective phrases	Warm and mild, everyone enjoys the climate of the Virgin Islands.	Everyone enjoys the warm, mild climate of the Virgin Islands.
expressions with like or unlike	Like most cities, parking is a problem in San Francisco.	Like most cities, San Francisco has a parking problem.

Structure items with misplaced modifiers are usually easy to spot. They generally consist of a modifying element at the beginning of the sentence followed by a comma, with the rest or most of the rest of the sentence missing. The answer choices tend to be long. To find the answer, you must decide what subject the modifier correctly refers to.

Sample Item

Using a device called a cloud chamber, _____ .

(A) experimental proof for the atomic theory was found by Robert Millikin
(B) Robert Millikin's experimental proof for the atomic theory was found
(C) Robert Millikin found experimental proof for the atomic theory
(D) there was experimental proof found for the atomic theory by Robert Millikin

Ⓐ Ⓑ ⬤ Ⓓ

　　Choice (A) and (B) are incorrect because the modifier (*Using a device called a cloud chamber...*) could not logically refer to the subjects (*experimental proof* and *Robert Millikin's experimental proof*). (D) is incorrect because a modifier can never properly refer to the introductory words *there* or *it*.

EXERCISE 28

Focus: Completing structure problems involving misplaced modifiers. (Note: ALL the items in this exercise focus on misplaced modifiers.)

Directions: Choose the one option—(A), (B), (C), or (D)—that correctly completes the sentences, then mark the appropriate blank.

1. Fearing economic hardship, _____.

_____ (A) many New Englanders emigrated to the Midwest in the 1820s

_____ (B) emigration from New England to the Midwest took place in the 1820s

_____ (C) it was in the 1820s that many New Englanders emigrated to the Midwest

_____ (D) an emigration took place in the 1820s from New England to the Midwest

2. Rich and distinctive in flavor, _____.

_____ (A) there is in the United States a very important nut crop, the pecan

_____ (B) the most important nut crop in the United States, the pecan

_____ (C) farmers in the United States raise pecans, a very important nut crop

_____ (D) pecans are the most important nut crop in the United States

3. Orbiting from 2.7 to 3.6 billion miles from the sun, _____.

_____ (A) the astronomer Clyde Tombaugh discovered Pluto in 1930

_____ (B) Pluto was discovered by the astronomer Clyde Tombaugh in 1930

_____ (C) it was in 1930 that the astronomer Clyde Tombaugh discovered Pluto

_____ (D) the discovery of Pluto was made by Clyde Tombaugh in 1930

4. A popular instrument, _____.

_____ (A) only a limited role has been available to the accordion in classical music

_____ (B) there is only a limited role for the accordion in popular music

_____ (C) classical music provides only a limited role for the accordion

_____ (D) the accordion has played only a limited role in classical music

5. Unlike most birds, _____.

_____ (A) the heads and necks of vultures lack feathers

_____ (B) feathers are not found on the heads and necks of vultures

_____ (C) vultures do not have feathers on their heads and necks

_____ (D) there are no feathers on vultures' heads and necks

6. Widely reproduced in magazines and books, _____.

_____ (A) Ansel Adams depicted the Western wilderness in his photographs

_____ (B) the Western wilderness was depicted in the photographs of Ansel Adams

_____ (C) Ansel Adams' photographs depicted the Western wilderness

_____ (D) it was through his photographs that Ansel Adams depicted the Western wilderness

7. Smaller and flatter than an orange, _____.

_____ (A) a tangerine is easy to peel and its sections separate readily

_____ (B) the peel of a tangerine is easily removed and its sections are readily separated

_____ (C) it's easy to peel a tangerine and to separate its sections

_____ (D) to peel a tangerine is easy, and its sections can be readily separated

8. Like the federal government, _____.

_____ (A) taxation provides most of the funds for state and local governments as well

_____ (B) state and local governments obtain most of their funds through taxation

_____ (C) through taxation is how state and local governments obtain most of their funds

_____ (D) funds are provided from taxation for state and local governments

9. Originally settled by Polynesians around 700 AD, _____.

_____ (A) Hawaii received its first European visitor in 1778, when Captain James Cook landed there

_____ (B) Hawaii's first European visitor, Captain James Cook, landed there in 1778

_____ (C) in 1778 the first European, Captain James Cook, visited Hawaii

_____ (D) the first European to visit Hawaii was Captain James Cook, landing there in 1778

10. Unlike most modernist poets, _____ based on ordinary speech.

_____ (A) Robert Frost's poems were

_____ (B) the works of Robert Frost were

_____ (C) Robert Frost wrote poems that were

_____ (D) the poetry written by Robert Frost was

11. Named for its founder, _____ in Ithaca, New York.

_____ (A) in 1865 Ezra Cornell established Cornell University

_____ (B) Cornell University was established in 1865 by Ezra Cornell

_____ (C) it was in 1865 that Cornell University was established by Ezra Cornell

_____ (D) Ezra Cornell established Cornell University in 1865

12. While living in New Orleans, _____ the Creole people of Louisiana.

_____ (A) a book of folklore, *Bayou Folk,* was written by Kate Chapin about

_____ (B) *Bayou Folk*, a book of folklore, was written by Kate Chapin about

_____ (C) the subject of Kate Chapin's book *Bayou Folk* was the folklore of

_____ (D) Kate Chapin wrote *Bayou Folk,* a book about the folklore of

Lesson 29

MISSING OR INCOMPLETE COMPARISONS

You may see sentences on the Structure section that contain comparisons. Many of these involve the comparative forms of adjectives.

On the average, the Pacific Ocean is *deeper than* the Atlantic.
Rhonda is a *more experienced* performer *than* Theresa.
This show is *less interesting than* the one we watched last night.

Be sure that the sentence compares similar things or concepts.

The ears of African elephants are bigger than *Indian elephants*. (INCORRECT)
The ears of African elephants are bigger than *those of Indian elephants*. (CORRECT)

The first sentence above is incorrect because it compares two dissimilar things: an African elephant's ears and an Indian elephant. In the second, the word *those* refers to ears, so the comparison is between similar things.

Another type of comparison involves the phrase *as...as.*

The lab lasted *as long as* the class did.
There weren't *as many people at the meeting as* I had thought there would be.

The words *like/alike* and *unlike/not alike* can also be used to express comparison:

Like A, B, . . .   Unlike X, Y, . . .
A, like B, . . .   X, unlike Y, . . .
A is like B.   X is unlike Y.

A and B are alike.   X and Y are not alike.

In these sentences, similar-looking words such as *likely*, *likewise*, *dislike,* and *unlikely* may appear as distractors.

Other phrases can be used in making comparisons:

A is the same as B   X is different from Y
A and B are the same   X and Y are different
A is similar to B   X differs from Y

A special kind of comparison is called a **proportional statement**. A proportional statement follows this pattern: *The more A...the more B.*

The higher the humidity, *the more uncomfortable* people feel.

Sample Items

Subtropical zones _____ temperate zones, but they still have distinct summer and winter seasons.

(A) that are warmer
(B) warmer
(C) are warmer as
(D) are warmer than

Ⓐ   Ⓑ   Ⓒ   ⬤

   Choice (A) creates a relative clause, which is not appropriate in this sentence; also, the choice lacks the word *than*. Choice (B) lacks both a verb and the word *than*. (C) incorrectly uses *as* in place of *than*.

_____ other mammals, whales do not have a sense of smell.

(A) Not alike
(B) Unlike
(C) Unlikely
(D) Dislike

Ⓐ   ⬤   Ⓒ   Ⓓ

   Choice (A) is only used in the pattern, "A and B are not alike." (C) and (D) are not used in comparisons; *unlikely* is an adjective meaning "not probable;" *dislike* is a verb meaning "not enjoy, not admire."

_____ the diameter of a circle, the larger its circumference is.

(A) Greater than
(B) The greater
(C) Great as
(D) As great as

Ⓐ   ⬤   Ⓒ   Ⓓ

   The correct pattern for a proportional statement is *the more A...the more B*. Only choice (B) follows this pattern.

EXERCISE 29

Focus: Completing structure problems involving comparisons. (Note: All the items in this exercise focus on comparisons.)

Directions: Choose the option—(A), (B), (C), or (D)— that correctly completes the sentence, then mark the appropriate blank.

1. Wild strawberries are _____ as cultivated strawberries.

   _____ (A) not so sweet

   _____ (B) not as sweet

   _____ (C) less sweeter

   _____ (D) not as sweeter

2. Sea bass _____ freshwater bass.

   _____ (A) are larger than

   _____ (B) are larger the

   _____ (C) are as large

   _____ (D) are larger

3. Automobiles, airplanes, and buses use more energy per passenger _____ .

_____ (A) as do trains

_____ (B) than trains do

_____ (C) trains do

_____ (D) like trains

4. The larger a drop of water, _____ freezing temperature.

_____ (A) the higher its

_____ (B) its higher

_____ (C) higher than its

_____ (D) higher of its

5. _____ San Diego and San Francisco, Los Angeles has no natural harbor.

_____ (A) Dissimilar

_____ (B) Unlike

_____ (C) Dislike

_____ (D) Different

6. The water of the Great Salt Lake is _____ seawater.

_____ (A) saltier than that of

_____ (B) as salty as that of

_____ (C) saltier than

_____ (D) so salty as

7. A psychosis is a severe mental disorder, _____ than a neurosis.

_____ (A) the most serious

_____ (B) as serious

_____ (C) more serious

_____ (D) as though serious

8. The social system of bumblebees is not as complex _____ .

_____ (A) than honeybees

_____ (B) as honeybees

_____ (C) that honeybees are

_____ (D) as that of honeybees

9. The administration of private colleges is nearly _____ that of public colleges.

_____ (A) same

_____ (B) just as

_____ (C) the same as

_____ (D) similar

10. _____ a river on land, an ocean current does not flow in a straight line.

_____ (A) Alike

_____ (B) Like

_____ (C) Likewise

_____ (D) Likely

11. The skin temperature of humans is _____ their internal temperature.

_____ (A) not high as

_____ (B) not so high

_____ (C) as low

_____ (D) lower than

12. A butterfly _____ a moth in a number of ways.

_____ (A) is different from

_____ (B) is different

_____ (C) the difference is

_____ (D) differing from

Lesson 30

MISSING CONJUNCTIONS

Conjunctions are connecting words; they join parts of a sentence. In this lesson, we'll look at two main types of conjunctions.

Coordinate conjunctions are used to join equal sentence parts: single words, phrases, and independent clauses. When two full clauses are joined, they are usually separated by a comma. The coordinate conjunctions you will most often see in structure problems are listed in the chart below.

Coordinate Conjunctions	Use	Examples
and	addition	Hereford cows are brown *and* white. He washed his car *and* cleaned up the garage.
or	choice, possibility	This plant can be grown in a house *or* in a garden. Her action was very brave *or* very foolish.
but	contrast, opposition	He brought his wallet *but* forgot his checkbook. The book discussed some interesting ideas *but* it wasn't very well written.
nor	negation	He's never taken a class in sociology, *nor* does he intend to. I didn't have breakfast *nor* lunch.
so	effect	It was a bright day, *so* she put on her sunglasses.

(The conjunction *so* is used to join only clauses—not single words or phrases.)

Conjunctive adverbs (*moreover, therefore, however, nevertheless,* and so on) are also used to join clauses, but in structure problems, these words are most often used as distractors—they seldom appear as correct answers.

Correlative conjunctions are two-part conjunctions. Like coordinate conjunctions, they are used to join clauses, phrases, and words.

Correlative Conjunction	Use	Example
both . . . and	addition	*Both* wolves *and* coyotes are members of the dog family.
not only . . . but also	addition	Dominic studied *not only* mathematics *but also* computer science.
either . . . or	choice, possibility	We need *either* a nail *or* a screw to hang up this picture.
neither . . . nor	negation (Not A and not B)	*Neither* the television *nor* the stereo had been turned off.

Peterson's TOEFL CBT Success

Sample Items

The automobile began as a toy _____ developed into a powerful force for social change.

(A) it
(B) but
(C) when
(D) or

Ⓐ ⬛ Ⓒ Ⓓ

There is a contrast in this sentence; the role of the automobile as a toy in its early days is contrasted with its later role as a force for social change. The only word among the four choices that indicates contrast is choice (B), *but*.

Singer Marian Anderson trained _____ in the United States and abroad.

(A) not just
(B) and
(C) both
(D) not only

Ⓐ Ⓑ ⬛ Ⓓ

The correct structure for this sentence is *both . . . and*. Choices (A), (B), and (D) do not follow this pattern. (In choice (D), *not only* must be paired with *but also* to be correct.)

EXERCISE 30

Focus: Completing structure problems involving conjunctions. (Note: One or two of the items in this exercise do NOT focus on conjunctions. These items are marked in the answer key with asterisks.)

Directions: Choose the one option—(A), (B), (C), or (D)—that correctly completes the sentence, then mark the appropriate blank.

1. Blindfish, which spend their whole lives in caves, have _____ eyes nor body pigments.

   _____ (A) not any

   _____ (B) neither

   _____ (C) nor

   _____ (D) without

2. Specialty stores, unlike department stores, handle only one line of merchandise _____ a limited number of closely related lines.

   _____ (A) either

   _____ (B) but

   _____ (C) instead

   _____ (D) or

3. Thomas Eakins studied not only painting _____ anatomy when he was training to become an artist.

   _____ (A) moreover

   _____ (B) but also

   _____ (C) as well

   _____ (D) and

4. Although topology is the youngest branch of geometry, _____ is considered the most sophisticated.

   _____ (A) but it

   _____ (B) so it

   _____ (C) it

   _____ (D) however it

5. In 1923 Jean Toomer wrote a book titled *Cane* which combined fiction _____ poetry to describe the experience of being Black in the United States.

_____ (A) and

_____ (B) to

_____ (C) also

_____ (D) or

6. Endive can be used _____ as a salad green or as a cooking vegetable.

_____ (A) such

_____ (B) both

_____ (C) either

_____ (D) neither

7. Glucose does not have to be digested, _____ it can be put directly into the bloodstream.

_____ (A) so

_____ (B) while

_____ (C) and since

_____ (D) nor

8. Natural fiber comes from either animal _____ plant sources.

_____ (A) or

_____ (B) otherwise

_____ (C) and

_____ (D) nor

9. Paint is _____ used to protect wood.

_____ (A) not only the substance

_____ (B) the substance which is not only

_____ (C) not only a substance which is

_____ (D) not the only substance

10. An acoustic engineer's purpose in designing a factory is to suppress sound, _____ his purpose in designing a concert hall is to transmit sound faithfully.

_____ (A) or

_____ (B) so

_____ (C) but

_____ (D) which

11. Demographers believe most metropolitan areas will continue to grow in _____ population and area in the future.

_____ (A) moreover

_____ (B) both

_____ (C) together

_____ (D) besides

12. Must crustaceans live in the sea, _____ some live in fresh water and a few have ventured onto land.

_____ (A) both

_____ (B) also

_____ (C) but

_____ (D) and

Lesson 31

MISSING NEGATIVE WORDS

The answer choices for this type of item are four negative expressions, such as the ones listed below:

Negative Word	Use	Meaning	Example
no	adjective	not any	There was *no* milk in the refrigerator.
none	pronoun	not one	They took a lot of pictures, but almost *none* of them turned out.
nothing	pronoun	not anything	There was *nothing* in his briefcase.
no one	pronoun	not anyone	*No one* arrived at the meeting on time.
nor	conjunction	and . . . not	He's never been fishing, *nor* does he plan to go.
without	preposition	not having	She likes her coffee *without* milk or sugar.
never	adverb	at no time	I've *never* been to Alaska.

The negative word *not* is used to make almost any kind of word or phrase negative: verbs, prepositional phrases, infinitives, adjectives, and so on.

Both *no* and *not* can be used before nouns, depending on meaning:

There is *no* coffee in the pot. (It's empty.)
This is *not* coffee. (It's tea.)

The adjective *no* is also used before the word *longer* to mean "not anymore":

I no longer read the afternoon paper.

Sample Item

There is almost _____ vegetation in the Badlands, a barren region of South Dakota.

(A) not
(B) nor
(C) none
(D) no

Ⓐ Ⓑ Ⓒ ⬤

Choices (A), (B), and (C) cannot be used before nouns as adjectives.

By the way, probably the most common correct answer for this type of problem is the adjective *no*.

EXERCISE 31

Focus: Completing structure problems involving negative words. (Note: ALL the items in this exercise focus on negative words.)

Directions: Choose the one option—(A), (B), (C), or (D)—that correctly completes the sentence, then mark the appropriate blank.

1. Early carpenters, having _____ nails, had to use wooden pegs to secure their constructions.

    _____ (A) no

    _____ (B) not

    _____ (C) without

    _____ (D) neither

2. Old Faithful is the most famous but _____ the most powerful geyser in Yellowstone National Park.

    _____ (A) none of

    _____ (B) no

    _____ (C) nothing

    _____ (D) not

3. Joseph Priestly, the discoverer of oxygen, had little _____ interest in science until he met Benjamin Franklin in Paris.

    _____ (A) and not

    _____ (B) or no

    _____ (C) but not

    _____ (D) nor any

4. Mobile homes were _____ counted as permanent houses until the 1960 census.

    _____ (A) not

    _____ (B) nor

    _____ (C) no

    _____ (D) none

5. Most solo musicians play _____ sheet music in front of them.

    _____ (A) without

    _____ (B) not having

    _____ (C) lacking

    _____ (D) and no

6. Desertification is the creation of deserts where _____ had existed before.

    _____ (A) never

    _____ (B) no one

    _____ (C) none

    _____ (D) not one

7. Glass snakes are actually legless lizards, _____ snakes.

    _____ (A) no

    _____ (B) not

    _____ (C) nor

    _____ (D) none

8. There is _____ truth to the old expression "Lightning never strikes the same place twice."

    _____ (A) without

    _____ (B) none

    _____ (C) no

    _____ (D) not

9. _____ single person can be said to have invented the automobile.

    _____ (A) There was not a

    _____ (B) Nor a

    _____ (C) Not one of

    _____ (D) No

10. A serious study of physics is impossible _____ some knowledge of mathematics.

    _____ (A) not with

    _____ (B) no

    _____ (C) not having

    _____ (D) without

11. _____ two fingerprints have ever been found to be exactly the same.

_____ (A) No

_____ (B) Never

_____ (C) Not

_____ (D) None

12. One of the few stands of forest on the East Coast of the United States that has _____ been harvested is Hutcheson Forest in New Jersey.

_____ (A) no

_____ (B) never

_____ (C) none

_____ (D) nothing

13. Customers could, until the 1960s, open small savings accounts at U.S. Post Offices, but that service is _____ offered.

_____ (A) no longer

_____ (B) not longer

_____ (C) no long

_____ (D) not along

14. _____ the reptiles alive today is capable of flight.

_____ (A) No

_____ (B) None of

_____ (C) Not one

_____ (D) Not

Answer Sheet

Mini-Test 5: Structure

1. (A) (B) (C) (D)   6. (A) (B) (C) (D)   11. (A) (B) (C) (D)
2. (A) (B) (C) (D)   7. (A) (B) (C) (D)   12. (A) (B) (C) (D)
3. (A) (B) (C) (D)   8. (A) (B) (C) (D)   13. (A) (B) (C) (D)
4. (A) (B) (C) (D)   9. (A) (B) (C) (D)   14. (A) (B) (C) (D)
5. (A) (B) (C) (D)   10. (A) (B) (C) (D)   15. (A) (B) (C) (D)

MINI-TEST 5: STRUCTURE

Directions: The following sentences are incomplete. Beneath each of these sentences, there are four words or phrases, marked (A), (B), (C), and (D). Choose the one word or phrase that best completes the sentence and fill in the appropriate answer above.

Time: 12 minutes

1. _____, an organism must be able to adapt to changing factors in its environment.

    _____ (A) If survival

    _____ (B) For surviving

    _____ (C) To survive

    _____ (D) It survives

2. The art of landscape architecture is _____ that of architecture itself.

    _____ (A) almost as old as

    _____ (B) as almost old

    _____ (C) almost as old than

    _____ (D) old as almost

3. The Mummers' Parade has _____ every year in Philadelphia on New Year's Day since 1901.

    _____ (A) holding

    _____ (B) been holding

    _____ (C) held

    _____ (D) been held

4. Rarely _____ more than 50 miles from the coast.

    _____ (A) redwood trees grow

    _____ (B) redwood trees do grow

    _____ (C) grow redwood trees

    _____ (D) do redwood trees grow

5. Microorganisms live in extreme conditions of heat and cold where _____ other organisms can survive.

    _____ (A) not

    _____ (B) never

    _____ (C) no

    _____ (D) none

6. The higher one rises in the atmosphere, _____ the temperature generally becomes.

    _____ (A) colder than

    _____ (B) the colder

    _____ (C) the colder as

    _____ (D) is colder

7. Medical researchers are constantly looking for ways to control, _____, and cure diseases.

_____ (A) prevention

_____ (B) preventing

_____ (C) prevent

_____ (D) to prevent

8. Nerve cells, or neurons, _____ in the human body.

_____ (A) the most complex cells are

_____ (B) are the most complex cells

_____ (C) most complex the cells are

_____ (D) most are the complex cells

9. Released in 1915, _____.

_____ (A) D. W. Griffith made an epic film about the Civil War, *Birth of a Nation*

_____ (B) the Civil War was the subject of D. W. Griffith's epic film, *Birth of a Nation*

_____ (C) D. W. Griffith's epic film *Birth of a Nation* was about the Civil War

_____ (D) the subject of D. W. Griffith's epic film *Birth of a Nation* was the Civil War

10. _____ on barren slopes can help prevent erosion.

_____ (A) Planting trees

_____ (B) For trees to be planted

_____ (C) In order to plant trees

_____ (D) Trees are planted

11. Vermont is the only state in New England _____ an Atlantic coastline.

_____ (A) without

_____ (B) not with

_____ (C) which not having

_____ (D) doesn't have

12. In 1867, Hiram R. Revels _____ the first Black to be elected to the U.S. Senate.

_____ (A) becoming

_____ (B) became

_____ (C) to have become

_____ (D) has become

13. Jupiter's moons can be easily seen through _____ binoculars or a small telescope.

_____ (A) either

_____ (B) if

_____ (C) whether

_____ (D) or

14. The Colorado beetle is a beautiful insect, _____ it causes a great deal of damage to food crops.

_____ (A) but

_____ (B) what

_____ (C) or

_____ (D) that

15. Judge Francis Hopkins is probably best known as a signer of the Declaration of Independence, but he also excelled as a poet, _____, and an orator.

_____ (A) as a musician

_____ (B) by playing music

_____ (C) a musician

_____ (D) he played music

Part B

ABOUT WRITTEN EXPRESSION

In this part of the test, there are twenty-five sentences (thirty-seven on the long form). In each sentence, four expressions—single words or two-or-three word phrases—are underlined. Your job is to identify which of these phrases must be rewritten (it can't simply be omitted) in order for the sentence to be correct. All the errors involve grammar or usage—never punctuation or spelling.

Sample Items

Music, <u>dramatic</u>, and <u>art</u> contribute to <u>the culture</u> of <u>any</u> community.
   A   B   C   D

● Ⓑ Ⓒ Ⓓ

This sentence should correctly read, "Music, *drama*, and art contribute to the culture of any community." Choice (B) would have to be rewritten to correct the sentence, and so (A) is the best answer.

Lenses may <u>having</u> either <u>concave</u> or <u>convex</u> <u>shapes</u>.
              A   B   C   D

● Ⓑ Ⓒ Ⓓ

The correct verb form after a modal auxiliary is the simple form *have*. This sentence should read, "Lenses may have either concave or convex shapes." The best answer is (A).

WHAT'S THE BEST WAY TO ANSWER WRITTEN EXPRESSION ITEMS?

You should begin with a quick reading of each sentence to find any obvious errors. **Don't** simply read the underlined portions, because in most items, the underlined expression is incorrect only in the context of the sentence. **Don't** answer the question until you've read the entire sentence.

Easier questions can be answered after the first reading; mark your answer and go on. If you don't find the error immediately, reread the sentence, now concentrating on the underlined expressions. You can't use the same techniques for reading these items as you would to read other materials, such as newspapers or magazine articles. Usually, a person's eyes move very quickly over "little words" like articles and prepositions because these words don't contain much information. However, in this part of the test, these expressions may be used incorrectly. It would be helpful, in fact, if you could read these sentences aloud, but of course that isn't permitted. You **can**, however, train your eyes to move slowly and to pronounce the sentences in your mind exactly as if you were speaking them.

If you haven't identified the error after a careful reading of the sentence, go through a mental checklist of the six most common errors: word form, word choice, verb error, parallelism, pronoun errors, and singular/plural noun errors. Do the underlined expressions seem to fit into any of these categories?

If you still can't find an error, eliminate expressions that seem to be used correctly, then make a guess from any items that remain.

Frequency of Errors in Written Expression*

Type of Error	Percentage
Word Form	21
Word Choice	15
Verbs	10
Parallel Structures	9
Pronouns	8
Singular/Plural Nouns	8
Verbals (Infinitives, Gerunds, and Participles)	6
Prepositions	6
Articles	5
Word Order	5
Comparatives and Superlatives	3
Conjunctions	2
Other Types of Errors	2

* Based on an analysis of 20 different exams that test-takers were allowed to keep after Disclosed Test Admissions.

In this section of the book, the lessons follow the same order as given in the chart above. The most common error, which involves incorrect word forms, is considered first, and so on. Each type of error is explained and examples are provided. There are exercises to help you practice identifying all these types of errors.

When taking actual exams, once you've found an error, don't worry about how to correct it. However, while working the exercises in this book, it's important to understand **why** an item is incorrect, and therefore most of the exercises ask you not just to identify errors but to supply corrections as well.

Tactics for Written Expression

- Skim each sentence, looking for obvious errors.
- If you haven't found the error, read the sentence again carefully, concentrating on the underlined parts. Go through a mental checklist of the most common types of errors (those involving word form, word choice, parallelism, verbs, pronouns, and singular/plural nouns) to see if any of the underlined expressions seem to fall into those categories.
- If you are still unable to find an error, try eliminating options that seem to be correct. If more than one option remains, put a mark by the number of that item on your answer sheet, then take a guess and go on.
- If you finish before time is called, go back and work on Section 2 problems that you marked as difficult. Make sure you have an answer for every problem. Don't go on to Section 3.

Lesson 32

ERRORS WITH WORD FORMS

By far the most common type of written expression error involves word forms. As many as eight or nine items per test may be word form problems. Most errors of this type involve using one part of speech in place of another. Both the incorrect word and the correction come from the same root *(rapid* and *rapidly*, for example, or *inform* and *information)*. The four parts of speech generally involved are verbs, nouns, adjectives, and adverbs. The most common problems are adjectives in place of adverbs and adverbs in place of adjectives. Nouns in place of adjectives and adjectives in place of nouns are also commonly seen. In some word form problems, different forms of the same form of speech may be involved. For example, a noun that refers to a person *(leader)* may be used in place of the field *(leadership)*. A gerund (a verbal noun) may also be used in place of an ordinary noun *(judging* and *judgment,* for example).

Parts of speech can often be identified by their suffixes (word endings).

Common Noun Endings

-tion	information	-ery	recovery
-sion	provision	-ship	scholarship
-ence	independence	-tude	multitude
-ance	acceptance	-ism	capitalism
-ity	creativity	-cracy	democracy
-hood	childhood	-logy	biology
-dom	wisdom	-ness	happiness
-th	health	-ment	experiment

Endings for nouns that refer to persons

-er	explorer	-ee	employee
-or	sailor	-ic	comic
-ist	psychologist	-ian	technician
-ent	student	-ant	attendant

Common Verb Endings

-ize	realize	-ify	justify
-en	shorten	-ate	incorporate
-er	recover		

Common Adjective Endings

-ate	moderate	-y	sunny
-ous	dangerous	-ic	economic
-al	normal	-ical	logical
-ial	remedial	-ory	sensory
-able	comfortable	-less	hopeless
-ible	sensible	-ive	competitive
-ish	sluggish	-ly	friendly
-ant	resistant	-ful	colorful

Common Adverb Endings

-ly	quickly	-ally	historically

ADJECTIVE/ADVERB ERRORS

The most common type of word form problem involves the use of an adverb in place of an adjective or an adjective in place of an adverb. A few points to keep in mind:

- Adjectives modify nouns, noun phrases, and pronouns.

  - Adjectives often come before nouns.

  an *important* test
  a *quiet* evening
  a *long* letter

  - They often answer the question *What kind?*

  She is a *brilliant* doctor. (What kind of a doctor is she? *A brilliant one.*)

- Adjectives also follow the verb *to be* and other linking verbs.

  The glass was *empty*.
  That song sounds *nice*.
  They look *upset*.

- Adverbs may modify verbs, participles, adjectives, prepositions, adverb clause markers, and other adverbs.

  Ann *eagerly* accepted the challenge. (adverb modifying the main verb *accepted*)
  It was a *rapidly* changing situation. (adverb modifying the present participle *changing*)
  She wore a *brightly* colored scarf. (adverb modifying the past participle *colored*)
  Ted seemed *extremely* curious about that topic. (adverb modifying the adjective *curious*)
  We arrived at the airport *shortly* before our flight left. (adverb modifying the adverb-clause marker *before*)
  We arrived at the airport *shortly* before noon. (adverb modifying the preposition *before*)
  The accident occurred *incredibly* quickly. (adverb modifying the adverb *quickly*)

  - Sometimes adverbs are used at the beginning of sentences, usually followed by a comma. These adverbs sometimes modify the entire sentence rather than one word in the sentence.

  Generally, I like my classes.
  Usually, Professor Ingram's lectures are more interesting.

  - Most adverbs tested in this section are adverbs of manner. They are formed by adding the suffix *-ly* or *-ally* to an adjective.

  quick quickly
  comic comically
  comfortable comfortably
  historic historically

  - Adverbs of manner answer the question *How?*

  She treated her employees *honestly*. (How did she treat her employees? *Honestly*.)

  - A few adverbs (*fast*, *hard*, *high*, for example) have the same form as adjectives.

  He bought a *fast* car. (adjective)
  He was driving so *fast* that he got a speeding ticket. (adverb)

  - *Well* is the irregular adverb form of the adjective *good*.

  Juan is an exceptionally *good* student.
  He did very *well* on the last test.

  - Some adjectives also end in *-ly*: *friendly*, *yearly*, *costly*, and *lively*, for example.

  That was a *costly* mistake.
  I found Houston a very *friendly* city.

Sample Items

The Black Hills of South Dakota are covered with densely pine forests.
  A   B   C   D

(A) (B) (C) ●

The best answer is (D). An adjective, *dense*, not an adverb is required to modify the noun phrase *pine forests*.

Crows and ravens are members of a family of birds that includes exact 100 species.
                  A   B   C   D

(A) (B) ● (D)

The adverb *exactly* is needed in place of the adjective *exact*.

INCORRECT FORMS OF WORDS CONNECTED WITH CERTAIN FIELDS

This error involves a confusion between the names of fields (*biology*, for example) and the name of a person who practices in that field (*biologist*), or between one of those terms and the adjective that describes the field (*biological*).

Sample Item

First specializing in industrial photography, Margaret Bourke-White later became a famous
         A   B

news photographer and editorial.
     C   D

(A) (B) (C) ●

The adjective *editorial* is used to describe the field of editing. However, a noun referring to a person (*editor*) is needed in this sentence.

OTHER WORD FORM PROBLEMS

There are many other word form problems. Some examples are given here:

Sample Items

Corn played <u>an</u> important <u>role in</u> the <u>cultural</u> of the <u>cliff-dwelling</u> Indians of the Southwest.
         A   B   C   D

Ⓐ   Ⓑ   ⬤   Ⓓ

The noun *culture*, not the adjective *cultural* is needed.

<u>The galaxy</u> Andromeda is the most <u>distance</u> object <u>visible</u> to <u>observers</u> in the Northern
A   B   C   D

Hemisphere.

Ⓐ   ⬤   Ⓒ   Ⓓ

The adjective *distant* is needed in place of the noun *distance*.

Scientists <u>belief</u> that the continents once <u>formed</u> a single continent surrounded <u>by</u> an
        A   B   C

<u>enormous</u> sea.
D

⬤   Ⓑ   Ⓒ   Ⓓ

In this sentence, the verb *believe* is needed in place of the noun *belief*.

Bunsen burners <u>are used</u> to <u>hot</u> materials <u>in</u> a <u>chemistry</u> lab.
              A   B   C   D

Ⓐ   ⬤   Ⓒ   Ⓓ

The verb *heat* is needed in place of the adjective *hot*.

A <u>sudden</u> <u>freezing</u> can <u>destroy</u> citrus <u>crops</u>.
   A   B   C   D

Ⓐ   ⬤   Ⓒ   Ⓓ

Rather than the gerund (*-ing*) form, the noun *freeze* is required.

EXERCISE 32.1

Focus: Correctly providing word forms for different parts of speech are commonly confused in written expression problems.

Directions: Fill in the lines in the blanks below with the appropriate word forms. In some cases, there may be more than one correct answer. The first one is done as an example.

	Verb	Noun	Adjective	Adverb
1.	differ	difference	different	differently
2.			inventive	
3.	compete			
4.	fertilize			
5.				deeply
6.		decision		
7.	beautify			
8.	prohibit			
9.	originate			
10.			emphatic	
11.			inconvenient	
12.		glory		
13.	mystify			
14.				equally
15.			general	
16.				simply
17.			familiar	
18.			pure	
19.	free			
20.	restrict			

Peterson's TOEFL CBT Success

EXERCISE 32.2

Focus: Providing word forms related to the names of fields, to adjectives describing those fields, and to people involved in those fields.

Directions: Fill in the blanks in the chart below with the appropriate form. The first one is done as an example.

	Field	Person	Adjective
1.	music	musician	musical
2.		surgeon	
3.			poetic
4.		architect	
5.	administration		
6.			financial
7.		photographer	
8.	theory		
9.			athletic
10.	editing		
11.		philosopher	
12.		criminal	
13.			political
14.		lawyer	
15.	humor		

EXERCISE 32.3

Focus: Identifying errors and recognizing correct use of adjectives and adverbs.
Directions: Underline the form that correctly completes the sentence.

1. In any animal community, herbivores (great/greatly) outnumber carnivores.

2. Floods cause billions of dollars worth of property damage (annual/annually).

3. (Regular/Regularly) airmail service in the United States began in 1918.

4. Writer Ernest Hemingway was known for his (simple/simply) language and his lively dialog.

5. The tiny coral snake is (beautiful/beautifully) but deadly.

6. Skyscrapers developed (simultaneous/simultaneously) in Chicago and New York City.

7. (General/Generally), bauxite is found near the surface, so it is relatively (simple/simply) to mine.

8. A good proofreader (painstaking/painstakingly) examines a manuscript for errors in spelling and grammar as well as for factual mistakes.

9. The colony of New Hampshire was (permanent/permanently) separated from the Massachusetts Bay Colony in 1692.

10. The most numerous and (wide/widely) distributed of all insectivorous animals are the shrews.

11. The endocrine system functions in (close/closely) relationship with the nervous system.

12. A gap in the Coast Range of California provides (easy/easily) access to the San Francisco Bay Area.

13. Mushrooms are found in an (incredible/incredibly) range of sizes, colors, and shapes.

14. Some airplanes have an automatic pilot that is connected to the airplane's controls and (automatic/automatically) keeps the plane on course.

15. Winslow Homer, who had no (formal/formally) training in art, became famous for his paintings of the sea.

16. The potter's wheel was an invention of (profound/profoundly) importance.

17. The nuclear-powered cargo ship *Savannah* proved (commercial/commercially) impractical.

18. Sojourner Truth spoke (persuasively/persuasive) in opposition to slavery.

19. In 1948, Stan Getz made a (masterful/masterfully) solo recording of the song *Early Autumn,* which (deep/deeply) influenced younger musicians.

20. The planet Venus was once believed to be two (distinct/distinctly) objects: the morning star Phosphorous and the evening star Hesperus.

EXERCISE 32.4

Focus: Identifying which parts of speech are appropriate in sentences.

Directions: Underline the form that correctly completes the sentence. Then identify the parts of speech of the words in parentheses. You can use these abbreviations for parts of speech:

N = noun	G = gerund (*-ing*) noun
V = verb	ADJ = adjective
PN = "person" noun	ADV = adverb

The first one is done as an example.

1. Sinclair Lewis' novel *Babbitt* is set in the (fiction/*fictional*) town of Zenith. (___N___ / ___ADJ___)

2. By-products from chicken eggs are used by (industry/industrial) in manufacturing such (produces/products) as soap and paint. (_____/_____) (_____/_____)

3. The daylily is an attractive, (fragrance/fragrant) flower. (_____/_____)

4. An equation is a (mathematics/mathematical) statement that says that two expressions are (equal/equality). (_____/_____) (_____/_____)

5. The Supreme Court has ruled that (evidence/evident) obtained from (illegal/illegally) searches cannot be used in court. (_____/_____) (_____/_____)

6. The Richter scale measures the (severely/severity) of earthquakes. (_____/_____)

7. Justin Winsom promoted the (developing/development) of libraries throughout the United States in the nineteenth century. (_____/_____)

8. Pipelines (transportation/transport) huge quantities of natural gas and liquid petroleum products. (_____/_____)

9. Scientists (differ/different) in their opinions of how snow crystals (originate/origin).
   (_____/_____) (_____/_____)

10. Harry Blackstone was a famous (magic/magician). (_____/_____)

11. Glass sponges are found in oceans at a (deep/depth) of 300 feet or more. (_____/_____)

12. Colorado shares with Wyoming the (distinction/distinctly) of having four (perfect/perfectly) straight
    borders. (_____/_____) (_____/_____)

13. Yale's Peabody Museum has a world-famous (collection/collecting) of fossils. (_____/_____)

14. Pronghorns, which are American antelopes, are (present/presence) in large numbers on the (open/
    openly) plains of Wyoming. (_____/_____) (_____/_____)

15. The President's (chooses/choices) for the members of the Cabinet must be (approved/approval) by
    the Congress. (_____/_____) (_____/_____)

16. Rose Han Lee wrote a number of (scholar/scholarly) accounts about the effects of (immigrant/
    immigration) on mining towns in the western United States. (_____/_____)
    (_____/_____)

17. Most snails venture out to look for (feed/food) only after sunset or on (rain/rainy) days.
    (_____/_____) (_____/_____)

18. Hats may (symbolic/symbolize) social status or (occupation/occupational) as well as being fashion
    items. (_____/_____) (_____/_____)

19. Analgesics are used to (relieve/relief) pain and reduce fever. (_____/_____)

20. The process of (respire/respiration) in plants involves a complex series of (chemistry/chemical)
    reactions. (_____/_____) (_____/_____)

21. A (member/membership) of the Paiute tribe of Nevada, Sarah Winnemuca worked as a guide and
    (interpret/interpreter). (_____/_____) (_____/_____)

22. The Earth's (out/outer) shell is divided into sections called plates, which are (constant/constantly) in
    motion. (_____/_____) (_____/_____)

23. The Nassau grouper is a (tropics/tropical) fish that is noted for its (able/ability) to change color.
    (_____/_____) (_____/_____)

24. Alpha rays (loss/lose) energy (rapidity/rapidly) as they pass through matter. (_____/_____)
    (_____/_____)

25. The cherry is one of the only fruits that will not (ripe/ripen) if it is removed from the tree.
    (_____/_____)

EXERCISE 32.5

Focus: Identifying errors involving word form problems. (Note: One or two items in this exercise do not focus on word form errors. These are marked in the answer key with an asterisk.)

Directions: Decide which of the four underlined words or phrases —(A), (B), (C), or (D)—would not be considered correct, and write the letter of the expression in the blank. Then, on the line at the end of the sentence, write the correction for the underlined phrase. The first one is done as an example.

_B_ 1. Liberal arts colleges <u>cultivate</u> general <u>intellectually</u> <u>abilities</u> rather than technical or
              A   B   C

professional skills.   intellectual
D

_____ 2. Goats are extremely <u>destruction</u> to <u>natural</u> <u>vegetation</u> and are often <u>responsible</u> for soil
                          A   B   C   D

erosion. _____

_____ 3. <u>Wild</u> plants were of <u>considerable</u> <u>important</u> to early settlers, and many are still used
          A   B   C

<u>medicinally</u> and as foods. _____
D

_____ 4. One important <u>branch</u> of <u>linguistics</u> is semantics, which <u>analysis</u> the <u>meaning</u> of words.
                        A   B   C   D

_____

_____ 5. Unlike folk <u>dancers</u>, which are the <u>product</u> of a single <u>culture</u>, ballet is an <u>international</u> art
                      A   B   C   D

form. _____

_____ 6. The <u>strong</u> of a rope is <u>directly</u> <u>proportional</u> to its <u>cross-sectional</u> area. _____
              A   B   C   D

_____ 7. Black bears can move <u>rapidly</u> when <u>necessary</u> and are <u>skillful</u> tree-climbers for their size and
                              A   B   C

<u>weigh</u>. _____
D

_____ 8. In an arboretum, trees are <u>cultivated</u> for <u>scientific</u> and <u>educational</u> <u>purpose</u>. _____
                                  A   B   C   D

_____ 9. In most Western states, the first major <u>industry</u> was mining, which was <u>gradually</u>
                                              A   B

<u>supplemented</u> by <u>ranches</u>. _____
C   D

_____ 10. Peach trees <u>grow</u> <u>good</u> in a <u>variety</u> of soil types, but do best in <u>sandy</u> loam. _____
                      A   B   C   D

_____ 11. The <u>unit</u> of <u>measuring</u> called the foot was <u>originally</u> based on the <u>length</u> of the human foot.
              A   B   C   D

_____

_____ 12. <u>Philosopher</u> Theodore A. Langerman was <u>interested</u> in the fields of <u>literary</u> and
              A   B   C

<u>music</u>. _____
D

_____ **13.** Pure nitric acid is colorless, but it <u>acquires</u> a yellow <u>color</u> when it is <u>exposed of</u> air.

               A   B   C   D

_____

_____ **14.** A <u>chemical</u> <u>react</u> that <u>absorbs</u> <u>heat</u> is called endothermic. _____
          A   B   C   D

_____ **15.** One <u>characteristic</u> of the <u>poems</u> of Emily Dickinson is the <u>sharp</u> of her <u>images</u>. _____
                 A   B   C   D

_____ **16.** Luther Gulick was a <u>teacher</u> and <u>physician</u> who spent much of his <u>live</u> promoting <u>physical</u>
                             A   B   C

      <u>fitness</u>. _____
      D

_____ **17.** A dog should be checked <u>regularly</u> by a veterinarian <u>to ensure</u> that it <u>remains</u> in good
                                 A   B   C

      <u>healthy</u>. _____
      D

_____ **18.** <u>Southwestern</u> Boston is made up of Hyde Park, West Roxbury, and other <u>pleasant</u> <u>residential</u>
      A   B   C

      <u>neighbors</u>. _____
      D

_____ **19.** Hunting and fishing techniques were <u>highly developed</u> among the North American Indians,
                                         A

      <u>particularly</u> in regions where <u>agriculture</u> was less <u>success</u>. _____
      B   C   D

_____ **20.** Science requires the <u>careful</u> <u>collect</u> and <u>organization</u> of data. _____
                      A   B   C   D

_____ **21.** The Natchez Trace was <u>an important</u> <u>commercial</u> and <u>military route</u> between Nashville,
                               A   B   C

      Tennessee <u>to</u> Natchez, Mississippi. _____
             D

_____ **22.** Some games rely <u>mainly</u> on <u>skill</u> and practice while others <u>primarily</u> involve <u>lucky</u>. _____
                        A   B   C   D

_____ **23.** In the <u>absent</u> of <u>natural</u> enemies, the gypsy moth has <u>become</u> a <u>serious</u> pest in North
             A   B   C   D

      America. _____

_____ **24.** Huey Long and his <u>brother</u> Earl were the two most <u>powerful</u> <u>politics</u> in the <u>history</u> of
                     A   B   C   D

      Louisiana. _____

_____ **25.** To make candles, pioneers <u>twisted</u> string into wicks, dipped the wicks into <u>hot</u> fat, then
                       A   B

      <u>hung</u> the candles to cool and <u>hard</u>. _____
      C   D

Lesson 33

ERRORS IN WORD CHOICE

Word choice errors involve the incorrect use of one word in place of another. These two words may be related forms (*other* and *another*, for example) or they may be completely different (*do* and *make*, for example).

Descriptions of some of the most common word choice errors are given below:

WRONG CHOICE OF *MAKE* OR *DO*

The verb *to do* is often used in place of *to make*, and *to make* in place of *to do*. In its basic sense, *to make* means to produce, to create, to construct, while *to do* means to perform, to act, to accomplish. These verbs are also used in a number of set expressions:

Common Expressions with *Make*

make advances in	make an investment
make an attempt	make a plan
make a comparison	make a prediction
make a contribution	make a profit
make a decision	make a promise
make a distinction	make an offer
make a forecast	make a suggestion
make a law	make a sound/noise
make a point	

be made of (= be composed of)
make up (= compose)

To make is also used in this pattern: *make* + someone + adjective (The gift *made* her happy.)

Common Expressions with *Do*

do an assignment	do a job (errand, chore)
do business with	do research
do one's duty	do one's work
do someone a favor	

The auxiliary verb *do* is used rather than repeat main verbs: (My computer doesn't operate as fast as theirs *does*.)

Anytime you see the verb *make* or *do* underlined in the Written Expression section, suspect a word choice error.

Sample Items

Cement is <u>done</u> from <u>varying</u> <u>amounts</u> of limestone, clay, <u>and</u> gypsum.
        A   B   C   D

● Ⓑ Ⓒ Ⓓ

The verb *done* is incorrect in this sentence. The correct word choice is *made*.

Small town <u>newspapers</u> often <u>urge</u> readers to <u>make business</u> with <u>local</u> merchants.
            A   B   C   D

Ⓐ Ⓑ ● Ⓓ

The phrase should read *do business with*.

WRONG CHOICE OF *LIKE* OR *ALIKE* AND *LIKE* OR *AS*

The word *alike* is incorrectly used in place of *like*, or *like* is used in place of *alike*.
These words are used correctly in the following patterns:

Like A, B ...	Like birds, mammals are warm-blooded.
A, like B, ...	Birds, like mammals, are warm-blooded.
A is like B ...	Birds are like mammals in that they are both warm-blooded.
A and B are alike ...	Birds and mammals are alike in that they are both warm-blooded.

Whenever you see the words *alike* or *like* underlined, you should suspect a word choice error.

The word *like* is also sometimes confused with the word *as*. When *like* is used in a comparison, it is followed by a noun or pronoun. When *as* is used in a comparison, it is followed by a clause containing a subject and a verb.

I did my experiment just *as* Paul did.
My results were much *like* Paul's.

The word *as* is also used before nouns when it means *in place of* or *in the role of*. This is particularly common after certain verbs: *serve*, *function*, and *use*, among others.

The vice-president served *as* president when the president was sick.

Sample Items

<u>Alike</u> their <u>close</u> relative the <u>frogs</u>, toads <u>are</u> amphibians.
 A   B   C   D

● Ⓑ Ⓒ Ⓓ

Choice (A) doesn't follow the pattern *Like A, B ...*

Asters, <u>as</u> <u>most</u> perennial plants, <u>bloom</u> once <u>a year</u>.
     A B   C   D

● Ⓑ Ⓒ Ⓓ

The word *like* should be used in place of the word *as* before a noun phrase (*most perennial plants*).

WRONG CHOICE OF *SO, SUCH, TOO, AND AS*

The words *so*, *such*, and *too* are used in the following patterns:

so + adjective + *that* clause
>These boxes are *so* heavy that we can't lift them.

(*So* is also used with *many ... that* and *much ... that*.)
>There were *so* many people in the auditorium that we could barely get in the front door.

such + adjective + noun + *that* clause
>It was *such* a pretty view that he took a photograph.

too + adjective + infinitive
>It's *too* cold to go swimming today.

Notice that *so* and *such* are both followed by *that* clauses, but *too* is followed by an infinitive.

The words *as* and *so* are also sometimes confused:

>Jane did *so* well as I did on the economics exam. (INCORRECT)
>The coffee was *as* hot that I couldn't drink it. (INCORRECT)

In the first sentence, the word *as* should be used in place of *so*; in the second, *so* should be used in place of *as*.

Also look for *so much* or *too much* used in place of *so* or *too*.

Sample Items

>The sun is so bright to look at directly.
>$\overline{A}$ $\quad$ $\overline{B}$ $\qquad$ $\overline{C}$ $\quad$ $\overline{D}$

>Ⓐ ● Ⓒ Ⓓ

The correct pattern *too* + adjective + infinitive.

>In much of Alaska, the growing season is as short that crops can't be raised.
>$\underline{}$ $\qquad$ $\underline{}$ $\qquad$ $\underline{}$ $\qquad$ $\underline{}$
>A $\qquad$ B $\qquad$ C $\qquad$ D

>Ⓐ Ⓑ ● Ⓓ

The correct pattern is *so* + adjective + *that* clause.

>The giant squid is so an elusive animal that at one time it was believed to be purely mythical.
>$\overline{A}$ $\qquad\qquad\qquad$ B $\qquad$ C $\qquad$ D

>● Ⓑ Ⓒ Ⓓ

Before an adjective + noun + *that* clause, the word *such* should be used.

>The mineral grains in basalt are so much small that they cannot be seen with the unaided eye.
>$\underline{}$ $\qquad$ $\underline{}$ $\qquad$ $\underline{}$ $\qquad$ $\underline{}$
>A $\qquad$ B $\qquad$ C $\qquad$ D

>Ⓐ ● Ⓒ Ⓓ

The phrase should read *so small* rather than *so much small*.

Peterson's TOEFL CBT Success

WRONG CHOICE OF *ANOTHER* OR *OTHER*

	Another	Other
Used as an adjective	*another* + singular noun (Have *another* sandwich.)	*other* + plural noun (I wonder if there is life on *other* planets.) determiner + *other* + noun (There may be life on some *other* planets.)
Used as a pronoun	*another* (Thanks. I'll have *another*.)	determiner + *other* ("I have one book." "I have the *other*.")

Another means "one more, an additional one." It can be used as an adjective before a singular noun or alone as a pronoun.

He needs *another* piece of paper.
I have one class in that building and *another* in the building across the quadrangle.

Other is used as an adjective before a plural noun. It is also used as an adjective before a singular noun when preceded by a determiner such as *the*, *some*, *any*, *one*, *no*, and so on. It can also be used alone as a pronoun when preceded by a determiner.

There are *other* matters I'd like to discuss with you.
One of the books was a novel; the *other* was a collection of essays.
There's no *other* place I'd rather visit.

Sample Items

Willa Cather is known for *My Antonia* and another novels of the American frontier.
      A   B   C   D

(A) ● (C) (D)

Before a plural noun, *other* must be used.

An understudy is an actor who can substitute for other actor in case of an emergency.
A   B   C   D

(A) (B) ● (D)

Other is used incorrectly in place of *another* before a singular noun.

WRONG CHOICE OF *BECAUSE* OR *BECAUSE OF; IN SPITE OF/DESPITE* OR *ALTHOUGH; DURING* OR *WHEN/WHILE*

Certain expressions, such as *because*, are adverb clause markers and are used only before clauses. Other expressions, such as *because of*, are prepositions and are used before noun phrases or pronouns.

Adverb-clause Markers (Used with clauses)	Prepositions (Used with noun phrases)
because	because of
although	despite
	in spite of
when	
while	during

Sample Items

Because migration to the suburbs, the population of many large American cities declined
    A   B   C   D
between 1950 and 1960.

● Ⓑ Ⓒ Ⓓ

Before a noun phrase (*migration*), the preposition *because of* must be used.

Despite most people consider the tomato a vegetable, botanists classify it as a fruit.
  A   B   C   D

● Ⓑ Ⓒ Ⓓ

Before a full clause (*most people consider the tomato a vegetable*), the adverb marker *although* must be used.

WRONG CHOICE OF *MUCH* OR *MANY* AND SIMILAR EXPRESSIONS

Certain expressions can only be used in phrases with plural nouns; others can be used in expressions only with uncountable nouns.

Used with plural nouns	Used with uncountable nouns
many	much
few, a few	little, a little
fewer, the fewest	less, the least
number	amount

Peterson's TOEFL CBT Success

Sample Items

Pearls are <u>found</u> in <u>much</u> colors, <u>including</u> cream, <u>blue</u>, lavender, and black.
        A   B   C   D

        Ⓐ   ●   Ⓒ Ⓓ

Many must be used with a plural noun (*colors*).

Even <u>during</u> <u>economic</u> booms, there is a small <u>number</u> of <u>unemployment</u>.
      A   B   C   D

        Ⓐ Ⓑ ● Ⓓ

The word *amount* must be used to refer to an uncountable noun such as *unemployment*.

OTHER WORD FORM PROBLEMS

Other pairs of words are sometimes confused in written expression, including those listed below. (NOTE: If one of the words appears in **boldface print**, that word is generally used incorrectly in Written Expression sentences; the other word is the correction for the error.) All of the starred sentences are examples of errors and are INCORRECT.

no	Used as an adjective before nouns; means "not any." Also used in the expression *no longer*.
not	Used to make all other words negatives.

    * *Not* gasoline was left in the tank.
    * This is *no* the station I usually listen to.
    * I *not* longer listen to that station.

most	Used in superlative adjective phrases; also used to mean "the majority."
almost	Used as an adverb to mean "nearly."

    * This is the *almost* interesting chapter in the book.
    * I've read *almost* of the chapters in the book.
    * I've solved *most* all of the problems in the book.

twice	Used as an adjective to mean "two times."
double	Used as an adjective to mean "make twice as large."

    * Henry has *double* as much money as he did before he invested it.
    * Henry *twice* his money.

earliest	Used as a superlative adjective to mean "most distant in time."
soonest	Used as a superlative adverb to mean "most promptly."

    * These are the *soonest* examples of the artist's works.

(You will probably not see *earliest* used incorrectly in place of *soonest*.)

percent	Used after a number.
percentage	Not used after a number.

    * Fifty *percentage* of the people voted in favor of the initiative.
    * The *percent* of people who approve of the initiative has been steadily growing.

after	Used as a preposition before a noun or as an adverb-clause marker before a clause.
afterward	Used as an adverb, means "after that."

    * We'll go to dinner *afterward* the play.
    * We'll go to dinner *afterward* the play is over.
    * First the performer played the guitar and *after* she played the flute.

ago	Used to talk about a time earlier than the present.
before	Used to talk about a time earlier than some other point in time.

     * Harold won a gold medal in the Olympics last year, and four years *ago* that, he won a silver medal.

(You will probably not see *before* used incorrectly in place of *ago*.)

tell	Used with an object; also used in certain set expressions: *tell a story*, *tell the truth*, *tell a secret*.
say	Used without an object.

     *Mr. Hunter *said* us that he'd had a good trip.
     *Joe *said* a wonderful story.
     *Mr. Hunter *told* that he'd had a good trip.

ever	Means "at any time." Used with *not* to mean "never." Also used in some set expressions such as *ever since* and *hardly ever*.
never	Means "at no time." Not used with a negative word.

     *He hardly *never* goes to that club.

(You will probably not see *ever* used incorrectly in place of *never*.)

alive	Used after a verb.
live	Used before a noun.

     * Sue likes to have *alive* plants in her apartment.
     * Although she forgot to water it for a week, the plant was still *live*.

around	Used as a preposition to mean "in a circular path."
round	Used as an adjective to mean "circular in shape."

     * The new office building will be an *around* glass tower.

(You will probably not see *round* used incorrectly in place of *around*.)

age	Used as a noun, often in these patterns: at the age of 21, 21 years of age.
old	Used as an adjective, often in this pattern: 21 years old.

     * Harriet will be thirty years *age* next week.
     * Operators of motor vehicles must be thirty years of *old* in this state.

near	Used as an adjective; means "close to."
nearly	Used as an adverb; means "almost."

     * Lynn is looking for an apartment *nearly* the Medical Center.
     * The two-bedroom apartment she looked at cost *near* a thousand dollars a month.

some	Used as a determiner before a noun to mean "an indefinite amount."
somewhat	Used as an adverb to mean "slightly."

     * This bicycle is *some* more expensive that the one I looked at yesterday.

(You will probably not see *somewhat* used incorrectly in place of *some*.)

You can practice the distinctions between many of these words in Exercise 44.7.

     NOTE: The distinctions between words such as *desert* and *dessert*, *stationary* and *stationery*, *capital* and *capitol*, which are really spelling problems, are NOT tested on TOEFL. (One reason is that native-speakers of English often make mistakes with these words!)

Peterson's TOEFL CBT Success

EXERCISE 33.1

Focus: Correctly choosing between *do* and *make*.
Directions: Underline the word that correctly completes each sentence below.

1. The tips of high-speed dental drills are (done/made) of tungsten steel and often contain diamonds.

2. A cottage industry is a form of manufacturing (done/made) at home.

3. Margaret Mead (did/made) fundamental contributions to both the theory and fieldwork of anthropology.

4. Many universities receive grants to (do/make) research for the federal government.

5. Research in genetics in the early nineteenth century (did/made) much to improve agriculture.

6. Futurologists study current trends to (do/make) predictions about the future.

7. Filmmaker George Lucas has (done/made) many advances in the production of motion pictures, especially in the use of special effects.

8. The distinction between wildflowers and weeds is one that is often difficult to (do/make).

9. The helicopter can (do/make) jobs that no other aircraft can.

10. Yeast is added to dough to (do/make) bread light and porous.

EXERCISE 33.2

Focus: Correctly choosing between *like* and *alike* and *like* and *as*.
Directions: Underline the word that correctly completes each sentence below.

1. The government of the United States and that of Canada are (alike/like) in that both conduct a complete census every ten years.

2. Fashion design, (as/like) all types of design, has been greatly aided by computers.

3. (Alike/Like) stars, galaxies tend to congregate in clusters.

4. Fungi are the most important decomposers of forest soil just (as/like) bacteria are the most important decomposers of grassland soil.

5. The spinal column is (alike/like) the brain in that its main functions can be classified as either sensory or motor functions.

6. A peanut is not actually a nut but a legume (alike/like) peas and beans.

7. The stately Government House in Annapolis serves (as/like) the residence of the governor of Maryland.

8. The cetosaur was a dinosaur that looked much (as/like) the whales of today.

9. Fats are made up of carbon, hydrogen, and carbon atoms just (like/as) carbohydrates are.

10. One way pumpkins and watermelons are (like/alike) is that both grow on vines trailing along the surface of the ground.

EXERCISE 33.3

Focus: Correctly choosing between *so*, *such*, *too*, and *as*.
Directions: Underline the word that correctly completes each sentence below.

1. The mineral talc is (so/such) soft that it can be scratched with a fingernail.

2. Oceanographers use robots and unmanned submarines to explore parts of the ocean that are (so/too) deep for people to explore safely.

3. (So/As) much paper money was printed during the Revolutionary War that it became almost worthless.

4. The walking stick is an insect with (so/such a) close resemblance to a twig that it escapes the notice of its enemies.

5. At present, solar cells are (so/too) expensive and inefficient to be used in the commercial generation of electricity.

6. Acrylic plastics are very hard and are (so/as) clear as glass.

7. Founded in 1682, Norfolk developed (so/such a) prosperous sea trade that it quickly became the largest town in the colony of Virginia.

8. Continental islands are (so/so much) close to continents that their plant and animal life are identical to life on the mainland.

9. Timberline is the elevation on a mountainside above which temperatures become (so/too) cold for most trees to grow.

10. A few people have (such/too) good eyesight that they can actually see the brightest stars during full daylight.

EXERCISE 33.4

Focus: Correctly choosing between *other* and *another*.
Directions: Underline the word that correctly completes each sentence below.

1. Lightning is a rush of electrical current from a cloud to the ground or from one cloud to (another/ other).

2. A ballet dancer's techniques and skills are very different from those of (another/other) dancers.

3. The commercial center of New York City, the island of Manhattan is joined to the (another/other) boroughs by bridges and tunnels.

4. The legal surrender of a criminal suspect from one state or country to (another/other) is called extradition.

5. Rocky Mountain spotted fever is one type of disease that is carried by ticks, and Colorado tick fever is (another/other).

6. The art of photography has often been influenced by—and has influenced—(another/other) fine arts.

7. William O. Douglas was a Supreme Court Justice for thirty-six years, longer than any (another/other) justice in the history of the Court.

8. In physics, diffusion is the spread of one substance's molecules or atoms through those of (another/ other).

9. A basketball player may advance the ball by dribbling it or passing it to (another/other) player.

10. Limkins are water birds that eat snails and (another/other) mollusks.

EXERCISE 33.5

Focus: Correctly choosing between *because of* or *because* and similar expressions.
Directions: Underline the words that correctly complete the sentences below.

1. (Although/Despite) cats cannot see in complete darkness, their eyes are much more sensitive to light than humans' eyes.

2. (Because/Because of) cheese is essentially a concentrated form of milk, it contains the same nutrients as milk.

3. (Although/In spite of) its frightening appearance, the octopus is shy and completely harmless.

4. (Because/Because of) its acute sense of smell, the bloodhound is often used in tracking.

5. (When/During) the female oriole is absent from the nest, the male oriole stands guard.

6. (Although/Despite) their light weight, aluminum alloys can be very strong.

7. (Although/In spite of) Adlai Stevenson was never elected president, he was one of the preeminent American politicians of the mid-twentieth century.

8. Snakebirds were not given their name because they eat snakes, but (because/because of) their long, slender necks resemble snakes.

9. In the sixteenth century, it was thought that a compass needle pointed north (because/because of) some mysterious influence of the stars.

10. (Although/Despite) it can occur in adults, chicken pox is classified as a disease of childhood.

11. Opinion polls are often used (while/during) political campaigns to find out how voters feel about candidates and issues.

12. Geneticists often experiment with bacteria and viruses (because/because of) those organisms reproduce so quickly.

EXERCISE 33.6

Focus: Correctly choosing between *much* or *many* and similar words.
Directions: Underline the words that correctly complete each sentence below.

1. (Many/Much) industrial products can be made from soybeans.

2. Desert plants compete fiercely for the (few/little) available water.

3. The American designer Louis Comfort Tiffany took (many/much) of his inspiration from nature.

4. A (few/little) simple precautions can prevent accidents at home and on the job.

5. In a formal debate, the same (number/amount) of persons speak for each team, and both teams are granted an equal (number/amount) of time in which to make their arguments.

6. Bats do (few/little) damage to people, livestock, or crops.

7. Even small (numbers/amounts) of zinc can have a significant effect on the growth of plants.

8. The adrenal glands, one on top of each kidney, secrete (many/much) important hormones.

9. (Many/Much) of the stories in John Weems' biography of George Washington are difficult to believe.

10. Folk artists have (few/little) or no formal art training.

EXERCISE 33.7

Focus: Correctly choosing between other commonly confused words.
Directions: Underline the words that correctly complete each sentence below.

1. In 1941, nylon was first used to make stockings, and the year (ago/before), it was first used to make toothbrush bristles.

2. The Missouri River is about (double/twice) as long as the Colorado River.

3. Catherine Esther Beacher established schools in Connecticut and Ohio, and (after/afterward) founded the American Women's Educational Association.

4. (Most/Almost) antibiotics are antibacterial agents, but some are effective against fungal, protozoal, or yeast infections.

5. At eight weeks of (age/old), red foxes begin to get their adult markings.

6. Chuck Berry was one of the (soonest/earliest) and most influential performers of rock music.

7. Long before Columbus, various thinkers believed that the Earth was (around/round).

8. Apricots, (some/somewhat) smaller than peaches, are known for their delicate taste.

9. Huge radio telescopes aimed into space may someday (say/tell) us whether intelligent life exists elsewhere in the universe.

10. One of Canada's most beautiful botanical gardens is Butchart Gardens (near/nearly) Victoria, British Columbia.

11. Since 1945, the average size of American farms has more than (doubled/twice).

12. When the Hopi Indians perform the Snake Dance, the dancers handle (alive/live) rattlesnakes.

13. Around 85 (percentage/percent) of the bauxite produced in the United States is mined in Arkansas.

14. Artist Clementine Hunter continued to paint until she was more than 100 years (age/old).

15. The period immediately (after/afterward) the Civil War is known as Reconstruction.

16. (No/Not) plant has a nervous system, and most respond very slowly to stimuli in their environment.

17. (Most/Almost) every county in the United States has agricultural extension agents who provide help to farmers.

18. Murals (say/tell) narrative stories through visual images.

19. Forests cover (near/nearly) half the land area of Tennessee.

20. Giraffes hardly (ever/never) sleep more than 20 minutes a night.

EXERCISE 33.8

Focus: Identifying a variety of word choice errors. (Note: One or two items in this exercise do not focus on word choice errors. These are marked in the answer key with an asterisk.)

Directions: Decide which of the four underlined words or phrases—(A), (B), (C), or (D)—would not be considered correct, and write the letter of the expression in the blank. Then, on the line at the end of the sentence, write the correction for the underlined phrase.

_____ 1. When a spacecraft is operating <u>beyond</u> the atmosphere, its fins and wings <u>not longer</u> serve
       A   B   C
     to stabilize it. _____
     D

_____ 2. The University of Chicago is <u>unlike</u> <u>most other</u> U.S. universities in that it has emphasized
                                   A   B
     graduate student programs <u>so much</u> as undergraduate programs <u>ever since</u> it opened.
                           C   D

       _____

_____ 3. The mass <u>production</u> of paper bags cut costs <u>so much</u> that a bag <u>soon</u> became a routine part
                  A   B   C
     of <u>near</u> every purchase. _____
       D

_____ 4. A person <u>must be</u> at <u>least</u> thirty years <u>age</u> in order to <u>serve</u> as a U.S. senator. _____
                  A   B   C   D

_____ 5. <u>No</u> <u>other</u> state receives as <u>few</u> rainfall <u>as</u> the state of Nevada. _____
        A B   C   D

_____ 6. <u>Because of</u> refraction, the water in a tank <u>ever</u> looks as <u>deep</u> as it <u>actually</u> is. _____
        A   B   C   D

_____ 7. Molds <u>grow</u> on bread, fruit, paper, and <u>much</u> <u>other</u> <u>substances.</u> _____
        A   B C D

_____ 8. The *lei*, which is <u>made</u> of flowers, shells, and <u>other</u> materials, is presented to visitors <u>as</u> a
                          A   B   C
     <u>symbolize</u> of Hawaiian hospitality. _____
       D

_____ 9. The <u>botanists</u> Katherine Hunter and Emily Fose spent <u>many</u> difficult months <u>making</u> research
             A   B   C
     in the Rocky Mountains. _____
       D

_____ 10. Early explorers in Utah named the cliffs they <u>encountered</u> "reefs" <u>because</u> they thought
      A   B   C
     these cliffs looked <u>alike</u> coral formations. _____
                     D

_____ 11. Today oysters are grown and harvested <u>much</u> <u>like</u> any <u>another</u> crop. _____
      A   B C   D

_____ **12.** Walter Hunt invented an enormous <u>amount</u> of devices, <u>including</u> the safety pin and a

  A B

<u>machine</u> for <u>making</u> nails. _____

  C D

_____ **13.** Connecticut, <u>like</u> the <u>other</u> New England states, <u>are</u> dotted with <u>many</u> little lakes. _____

  A B C D

_____ **14.** The <u>soonest</u> parachutes were <u>made of</u> canvas, but <u>later</u>, silk and then nylon <u>were used</u>.

  A B C D

_____

_____ **15.** <u>When</u> vigorous exercise, muscles require a <u>much greater</u> <u>amount</u> of oxygen than <u>when they</u>

  A B C D

are at rest. _____

_____ **16.** One should <u>never</u> throw water on <u>an alive</u> <u>electrical</u> fire. _____

  A B C D

Lesson 34

ERRORS WITH VERBS

Whenever the verb is underlined in a Written Expression problem, you should check for the common verb errors outlined in this lesson:

ERRORS IN SUBJECT/VERB AGREEMENT

If a subject is singular, the verb must be singular. If the subject is plural, the verb must be plural. Most problems involving subject-verb agreement on TOEFL are simple, but a few are tricky.

Sample Items

Minerals in seawater exists in the same proportions in all of the oceans of the world.
    A   B   C   D

Ⓐ ● Ⓒ Ⓓ

The plural subject *minerals* requires a plural verb, *exist*. You might have found this question tricky because the singular noun *seawater* comes between the subject and the verb, and you may have mistaken that word for the true subject.

Bowling, one of the most popular indoor sports, are popular all over the United States and in
    A   B   C

other countries.
D

Ⓐ Ⓑ ● Ⓓ

The subject of the sentence is *bowling*, not *sports*. The singular verb form *is* should therefore be used.

There are some special rules about subject-verb agreement that you should be familiar with:

- A sentence with two subjects joined by *and* takes a plural verb.

    The chemistry lab and the physics lab *are* . . .

- Some words end in *-s* but are singular in form. Many of these words are the names of fields of study (*economics*, *physics*, and so on). *News* is another word of this kind.

    Economics *is* . . .
    The news *was* . . .

- Irregular plurals (*children*, *feet*, *mice*, and so on) do not end in *-s* but take plural verbs.

    The women *were* . . .
    His feet *are* . . .

- When a clause begins with the expletive *there*, the verb may be singular or plural, depending on the grammatical subject.

    There *was* a loud noise . . .
    There *were* a few problems . . .

- Subjects with *each* and *every* take singular verbs. (This includes compound words like *everyone* and *everything*.)

    Each state *has* . . .
    Each of the representatives *was* . . .
    Every person *was* . . .
    Everyone *wants* . . .

- The verb in relative clauses depends on the noun that the relative pronoun refers to.

    The house that *was* built . . .
    The students who *were* selected . . .

- The phrase *the number of* + plural noun takes a singular verb. The phrase *a number of* + plural noun takes a plural verb.

    The number of trees *is* . . .
    A number of important matters *have* . . .

- Singular subjects used with phrases such as *along with*, *accompanied by*, *together with*, *as well as*, and *in addition to* take singular verbs.

    The mayor, along with the city council, *is* . . .
    Together with his friends, Mark *has* . . .

- Quantities of time, money, distance, and so on usually take a singular verb.

    Five hundred dollars *was* . . .
    Two years *has* . . .
    Ten miles *is* . . .

ERRORS INVOLVING TENSE

Most tense errors involve the simple present tense, the simple past tense, and the present perfect tense.

- The simple present tense is a general-time tense. It usually indicates that a condition is always true or that an action always occurs. It may also indicate that an action regularly occurs.

    The atmosphere *surrounds* the earth.
    Dana often *stays* at this hotel.
    Generally, the lectures in this class *are* very interesting.

- The simple past tense indicates that an action took place at a specific time in the past.

    They *moved* to Phoenix five years ago.
    This house *was built* in the 1920s.
    Dinosaurs *lived* millions of years ago.

- The present perfect tense usually indicates that an action began at some time in the past and continues to the present. It may also indicate that an action took place at an unspecified time in the past.

    Mr. Graham *has worked* for this company since 1990.
    She *hasn't been* to a doctor for a year.
    Jennifer *has* recently *returned* from Europe.

Sample Items

The <u>most important</u> period of physical <u>growth</u> in humans <u>occurred</u> during <u>their</u> first two years.
　　　　　A　　　　　　　　　　　　B　　　　　　　C　　　　　　D

Ⓐ　Ⓑ　●　Ⓓ

Choice (C) is best. The simple present tense, not the past tense, should be used because the situation described in this sentence always occurs.

<u>Personal</u> taxes <u>for</u> Americans <u>rose</u> <u>sharply</u> since 1945.
　A　　　　　　B　　　　　C　　　D

Ⓐ　Ⓑ　●　Ⓓ

Option (C) is again best. The time phrase *since 1945* means *from 1945 until now*. Therefore, the present perfect (*have risen*) is required in place of the past tense.

INCORRECT VERB FORMS

Some of the verb errors are errors in form. Most verb form problems involve main verb forms: An *-ing* form may be used in place of a past participle, a past participle in place of a past tense form, a simple form in place of an -ing form, an infinitive in place of a simple form, and so on. Some involve irregular verbs that have different forms for the past tense and the past participle—*took* and *taken*—for example. The following information may help you chose the correct form of the main verb.

- The simple form follows all modal auxiliaries.

might be	can remember	should study
must know	could go	may follow

  (Certain similar auxiliary verbs require infinitives.)

ought to attend	used to play	have to hurry

- The past participle is used after a form of *have* in all perfect forms of the verb.

has done	had called	should have said
have run	will have read	could have made

- The *-ing* form is used after a form of *be* in all progressive forms of the verb.

is sleeping	has been writing	should have been wearing
was working	had been painting	will be waiting

- The past participle is used after a form of *be* in all passive forms of the verb.

is worn	has been shown	would have been lost
is being considered	had been promised	might have been canceled
were told	will have been missed	

Verb form problems may also involve auxiliary verbs: *has* may be used in place of *did*, *is* in place of *does*, and so on.

Sample Item

The first bicycle race on record in the United States taken place in 1883.
    A   B   C   D

Ⓐ Ⓑ ● Ⓓ

The correct verb is the past tense form (*took*), not a past participle.

The Michigan Dunes, located on Lake Michigan's eastern shore, may to reach a height of 200 feet.
                   A   B   C   D

Ⓐ Ⓑ ● Ⓓ

After a modal auxiliary, the simple form of the verb (*reach*) should be used in place of the full infinitive (*to reach*).

Dextrose does not taste as sweet as table sugar is.
           A   B C   D

Ⓐ Ⓑ Ⓒ ●

The correct auxiliary verb in this sentence is *does*, not *is*. The auxiliary *does* replaces the present tense verb *tastes*.

EXERCISE 34.1

Focus: Written Expression problems involving subject-verb agreement.

Directions: Underline the form that correctly completes each sentence. Then circle the subject with which the underlined verb agrees. The first one is done as an example.

1. The first (bridge) to be built with electric lights (was/were) the Brooklyn Bridge.

2. Ethics (is/are) the study of moral duties, principles, and values.

3. There (is/are) two types of calculus, differential and integral.

4. George Gershwin, together with his brother Ira, (was/were) the creator of the first musical comedy to win a Pulitzer Prize.

5. In a chess game, the player with the white pieces always (moves/move) first.

6. The Earth and Pluto (is/are) the only two planets believed to have a single moon.

7. A number of special conditions (is/are) necessary for the formation of a geyser.

8. Each of the Ice Ages (was/were) more than a million years long.

9. The battery, along with the alternator and starter, (makes/make) up the electrical system of a car.

10. Teeth (is/are) covered with a hard substance called enamel.

11. The more-or-less rhythmic succession of economic booms and busts (is/are) referred to as the business cycle.

12. The number of protons in the nucleus of an atom (varies/vary) from element to element.

13. All trees, except for the tree fern, (is/are) seed-bearing plants.

14. Fifteen hundred dollars a year (was/were) the per capita income in the United States in 1950.

15. Everyone who (goes/go) into the woods should recognize common poisonous plants such as poison ivy and poison oak.

         Peterson's TOEFL CBT Success

EXERCISE 34.2

Focus: Recognizing and correcting errors in verb tense and form.

Directions: If the underlined form is correct, mark the sentence *C*. If the underlined form is incorrect, mark the sentence *X*, and write a correction for the underlined form in the blank at the end of the sentence.

_____   1. Coal, grain, steel, and other products are often *shipping* by barge on inland waterways. _____

_____   2. The first cotton mill in Massachusetts *has built* in the town of Beverly in 1787. _____

_____   3. Physician Alice Hamilton *is known* for her research on industrial diseases. _____

_____   4. When scientists search a site for fossils, they begin by examining places where the soil has *wore* away from the rock. _____

_____   5. The popularity of recreational vehicles *has been grown* over the last few decades. _____

_____   6. Experts have estimated that termites cause as much property damage every year as fire *has*. _____

_____   7. In music, a chord is the sound of two or more notes that *are playing* together. _____

_____   8. The white pine *is* the most commercially important forest tree in North America until the beginning of the twentieth century. _____

_____   9. In 1846, the Swiss naturalist Louis Agassiz *come* to the United States to give a series of lectures. _____

_____   10. Parrots and crows *are considered* the most intelligent birds. _____

_____   11. Portable fire extinguishers generally *containing* liquid carbon dioxide. _____

_____   12. The first experimental telegraph line in the United States *run* from Baltimore to Washington, D.C., a distance of forty miles. _____

_____   13. The first seven American astronauts *were chose* in 1959. _____

_____   14. Since ancient times, farmers *used* scarecrows to protect their crops from hungry birds. _____

_____   15. In the late nineteenth century, many important theories in both the biological and the physical sciences *have been produced*. _____

EXERCISE 34.3

Focus: Identifying and correcting errors involving verb forms. (Note: One or two items in this exercise do not focus on word form errors. These are marked in the answer key with an asterisk.)

Directions: Decide which of the four underlined words or phrases—(A), (B), (C), or (D)—would *not* be considered correct, and write the letter of the expression in the blank. Then, on the line at the end of the sentence, write a correction for the underlined phrase.

_____   1. Medical students must to study both the theory and practice of medicine. _____
                          A   B   C   D

_____   2. The seal, like the sea lion and the walrus, is a descendant of ancestors that once live on the
                      A   B   C   D
            land. _____

_____ 3. The top layer of the ocean stores as much heat as does gases in the atmosphere. _____
              A   B   C   D

_____ 4. Every one of the body's billions of cells require a constant supply of food and oxygen.
                                    A   B   C   D

_____

_____ 5. In science, the results of an experiment are not generally accepted until they had been
              A   B   C

          duplicated in other laboratories. _____
             D

_____ 6. In Colonial times, flax and wool required months of preparation before they could be dyed
           A   B   C

          and spin into cloth. _____
             D

_____ 7. Although some people find bats terrifying, they are actually beneficial because they ate
                          A   B   C   D

          harmful insects. _____

_____ 8. Each of the four types of human tooth are suited for a specific purpose. _____
               A   B   C   D

_____ 9. Mathematicians taken centuries to develop the methods that now are used in arithmetic.
                        A   B   C   D

          _____

_____ 10. Electric milking machines have made dairy farming a much easier job than it once did.
                   A   B   C   D

           _____

_____ 11. Playwright Frank Shin has often describes the lives of Chinese Americans in his dramas.
                 A   B   C   D

           _____

_____ 12. Cans of paint must be shaking to mix the pigments with the medium in which they are
                                A   B   C

           suspended. _____
              D

_____ 13. Beavers continuously repair the dams they have build. _____
                    A   B   C   D

_____ 14. The emphasize on team sports has become even stronger in this century than it was in the
                A   B   C   D

           last. _____

_____ 15. Sheep are often dip in liquid chemicals to eliminate ticks and other external parasites.
                A   B   C   D

           _____

Lesson 35

ERRORS WITH PARALLEL STRUCTURES

Written Expression items involving errors with parallel structures are similar to those in the Structure part of the test (Lesson 24). These sentences most often contain a series of three expressions: *X, Y,* and *Z.* One of these expressions is *not* grammatically parallel to the other two items in the series.

Structures that are often involved in parallelism are nouns, adjectives, verbs, prepositional phrases, gerunds, and infinitives.

Some problems with parallelism are actually word form problems similar to those in Lesson 32.

Sample Item

As a young <u>man</u>, George Washington liked <u>boating</u>, <u>to hunt</u>, and <u>fishing</u>.
      A   B   C   D

                        (A) (B) ● (D)

Option (C) is not parallel with the other items in the series: *to hunt* is an infinitive, while the other items are gerunds. You may have considered the other options that are part of the series, (B) and (D), but if you rewrote only one of these, the three expressions would still not be parallel.

In general, errors involving parallelism are easy to identify.

EXERCISE 35.1

Focus: Identifying and correcting errors involving parallelism.

Directions: If the underlined form is parallel to other forms in the sentence, mark the sentence *C.* If the underlined form is not parallel, mark the sentence *X,* and write a correction for the underlined form in the blank at the end of the sentence.

_____ 1. Steel is alloyed with manganese to increase its strength, hardness, and *resistance* to wear. _____

_____ 2. Sacramento is the commercial, *industry*, and financial center of California's Central Valley, as well as being the state capital. _____

_____ 3. Philosophers are concerned with questions about nature, *human behavior*, society, and reality. _____

_____ 4. When taking part in winter sports, one should wear clothing that is lightweight, *warmth*, and suitable for the activity. _____

_____ 5. Folklore consists of the beliefs, customs, traditions, and *telling stories* that people pass from generation to generation. _____

_____ 6. Major sources of noise pollution include automobiles and other vehicles, industrial plants, and *heavy construction equipment*. _____

_____ 7. Because of their hardness, industrial diamonds can be used for cutting, *grind*, and drilling. _____

_____ 8. Scholar John Fiske wrote on history, *religious*, and social issues. _____

_____ 9. Electricity is used to light, *hot*, and cool buildings. _____

_____ **10.** T. S. Eliott was equally distinguished as a poet, *he wrote criticism*, and a dramatist. _____

_____ **11.** Jute is a glossy fiber that is strong, does not easily stretch, and *inexpensive*. _____

_____ **12.** Wetlands were once considered useless areas, but they have been found to purify water, nurture wildlife, and *flood control*. _____

EXERCISE 35.2

Focus: Identifying and correcting errors with parallel structures. (Note: One or two items in this exercise do not focus on errors involving parallel structures. These are marked in the answer key with an asterisk.)

Directions: Decide which of the four underlined words or phrases—(A), (B), (C), or (D)—would not be considered correct, and write the letter of that expression in the blank. Then, on the line at the end of the sentence, write a correction for the underlined phrase.

_____ **1.** The bellflower is a wildflower that grows in shady fields, in marshes, and mountain slopes.
      A   B   C   D

_____

_____ **2.** Computers are often used to control, adjustment, and correct complex industrial operations.
         A   B   C   D

_____

_____ **3.** Eggs may be boiled in the shell, scrambled, fried, and cooked in countless another ways.
         A   B   C   D

_____

_____ **4.** Many places of history, scientific, cultural, or scenic importance have been designated
         A   B   C

national monuments. _____
   D

_____ **5.** R. Buckminster Fuller was a design, an architect, an inventor, and an engineer. _____
         A   B   C   D

_____ **6.** Modern motorcycles are lighter, faster, and specialized than motorcycles of twenty-five years
         A   B   C   D
ago. _____

_____ **7.** Many people who live near the ocean depend on it as a source of food, recreation, and
                                       A   B   C

to have economic opportunities. _____
   D

_____ **8.** Large commercial fishing vessels are equipped to clean, packaging, and freeze the fish that
                                       A   B   C

they catch at sea. _____
         D

_____ **9.** As a breed, golden retrievers are intelligent, loyally, and friendly dogs. _____
         A   B   C   D

_____ **10.** Mathematics can be considered a language, an art, a science, a tool, or playing a game.
                             A   B   C   D

_____

Peterson's TOEFL CBT Success

_____ 11. Paper may contain vegetable, minerals, or man-made fibers. _____
           A   B   C   D

_____ 12. According to Susan Sontag, our concepts of art, beauty, and nature has been changed by
                                        A   B   C   D

photography. _____

_____ 13. The economist Kenneth Boulding proposed a single social science that would unify
                                            A   B

economic, sociology, and political science. _____
   C   D

_____ 14. The teeth front are used to bite food, the canines to tear it, and the molars to grind it.
                A   B   C   D

_____

_____ 15. An ant's antennae provide it with the senses of hear, smell, touch, and taste. _____
                                    A   B   C   D

Lesson 36

ERRORS WITH PRONOUNS

Pronoun errors in written expression involve several types of pronouns:

- **Personal pronouns**
  (*he, she, it, they,* and so on)

- **Reflexive pronouns**
  (*himself, herself, itself, themselves,* and so on)

- **Relative pronouns** (adjective-clause markers)
  (*who, whose, which, that,* and so on)

- **Demonstrative pronouns**
  (*this, that, these, those*)

For the purposes of this lesson, possessive adjectives (*his* house, *their* bicycles) are considered personal pronouns, and demonstrative adjectives (*that* book, *those* horses) are considered demonstrative pronouns.

The greatest number of errors involve personal pronouns.

ERRORS IN PRONOUN/NOUN AGREEMENT

A pronoun must agree with the noun to which it refers (the pronoun's **referent**).

Most agreement errors with personal pronouns, reflexive pronouns, and demonstrative pronouns consist of a singular pronoun referring to a plural noun or a plural pronoun referring to singular nouns.

Agreement errors with relative pronouns usually involve the use of *who* to refer to things or *which* to refer to persons. (Note: The relative pronoun *that* can be used in certain sentences to refer to both persons and things.)

Another error involves the use of *this* or *these* in place of *that* and *those.* (*This* and *these* are used to refer to things that are perceived as close in time or space; *that* and *those* are used to refer to things that are perceived as distant in time or space.)

Sample Items

Jackrabbits <u>have</u> powerful <u>rear legs</u> that enable <u>it</u> to leap long <u>distances</u>.
A   B   C   D

       Ⓐ   Ⓑ   ⬤   Ⓓ

The pronoun referring to the plural noun *Jackrabbits* must be plural.

The <u>best way</u> for children to learn <u>science</u> is for them <u>to perform</u> experiments <u>himself</u>.
A   B   C   D

       Ⓐ   Ⓑ   Ⓒ   ⬤

The referent is plural (*children*), so the reflexive pronouns must also be plural (*themselves*) to agree with it. Therefore, the best answer is (D).

The Canadian Shield is <u>a huge</u>, rocky region <u>who curves</u> <u>around</u> Hudson Bay <u>like</u> a giant
A   B   C   D

horseshoe.

       Ⓐ   ⬤   Ⓒ   Ⓓ

The referent for the pronoun *who* is *region*. To agree with the referent, the relative pronoun *that* must be used. The pronoun *who* can refer only to a person.

Trademarks <u>enable</u> a company to distinguish <u>its</u> products from <u>these</u> of <u>another</u> company.
A   B   C   D

       Ⓐ   Ⓑ   ⬤   Ⓓ

The demonstrative *these* cannot be used to refer to the products of another company. The demonstrative *those* should be used instead.

ERRORS IN PRONOUN FORM

These errors involve personal pronouns. A subject form like *he* might be used in place of an object form like *him*, or a possessive pronoun like *hers* might be used in place of a possessive adjective like *her*. This type of pronoun error is usually easy to spot.

Sample Item

Herman Melville <u>gathered</u> material for <u>him</u> novels, including Moby Dick, <u>during his</u> years
A   B   C

<u>at sea</u>.
D

       Ⓐ   ⬤   Ⓒ   Ⓓ

The possessive form *his*, not the object form *him*, is required.

INCORRECT TYPE OF PRONOUN

In some sentences, the wrong type of pronoun is used. For example, a reflexive pronoun might be used when a personal pronoun is needed, or a personal pronoun used when a relative pronoun is required.

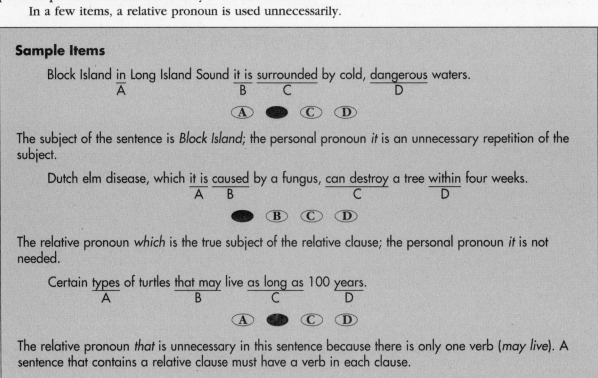

INCORRECT INCLUSION OF PRONOUNS

Some errors involve the unnecessary use of pronouns. Often, this type of error occurs when a personal pronoun is used as a subject in a sentence that already has a noun subject. Or it may involve a personal pronoun used unnecessarily in a relative clause.

In a few items, a relative pronoun is used unnecessarily.

Sample Items

> Block Island in Long Island Sound it is surrounded by cold, dangerous waters.
> A   B   C   D

Ⓐ ● Ⓒ Ⓓ

The subject of the sentence is *Block Island*; the personal pronoun *it* is an unnecessary repetition of the subject.

> Dutch elm disease, which it is caused by a fungus, can destroy a tree within four weeks.
>   A   B   C   D

● Ⓑ Ⓒ Ⓓ

The relative pronoun *which* is the true subject of the relative clause; the personal pronoun *it* is not needed.

> Certain types of turtles that may live as long as 100 years.
>   A   B   C   D

Ⓐ ● Ⓒ Ⓓ

The relative pronoun *that* is unnecessary in this sentence because there is only one verb (*may live*). A sentence that contains a relative clause must have a verb in each clause.

Peterson's TOEFL CBT Success

EXERCISE 36.1

Focus: Identifying and correcting pronoun agreement.
Directions: If the underlined form is correct, mark the sentence *C*. If the underlined form is incorrect, mark the sentence *X,* and write a correction for the underlined form in the blank at the end of the sentence. Then circle the referent (the noun to which the pronoun refers).

_____ 1. Unlike other cats, the cheetah cannot fully extract *their* claws. _____

_____ 2. One cannot see through translucent materials, but light can pass through *it*. _____

_____ 3. Investment banking is concerned with the sale of government bonds, and *they* also deals with corporate stocks and bonds. _____

_____ 4. The oldest known forms of fossils are *those* of microscopic plants similar to algae. _____

_____ 5. Gene Krupa had one of the few big bands *who* was centered around a drummer. _____

_____ 6. Emeralds get *its* beautiful green color from titanium and chromium impurities in the stone. _____

_____ 7. The viola is larger and heavier than the violin, and *she* has a darker, somewhat nasal tone. _____

_____ 8. The Ringling Brothers were five brothers *which* built a small group of performers into the world's largest circus. _____

_____ 9. Storms on the planet Saturn may be larger than the planet Earth *itself*. _____

_____ 10. The molecules of a liquid are held together tighter than *that* of a gas. _____

_____ 11. Ducks make nests out of leaves and *its* own feathers. _____

_____ 12. The clipper ship *Flying Cloud* was one of the fastest ships of *their* kind. _____

_____ 13. There are thousands of kinds of bacteria, many of *whom* are beneficial. _____

_____ 14. When babies reach the age of 1, *her* growth begins to slow down. _____

_____ 15. The arrangement of keys on the keyboard of a personal computer is almost the same as *those* on a standard typewriter. _____

EXERCISE 36.2

Focus: Identifying and correcting errors involving incorrect types and forms of pronouns.
Directions: If the underlined form is correct, mark the sentence *C*. If the underlined form is incorrect, mark the sentence *X,* and write a correction for the underlined form in the blank at the end of the sentence.

_____ 1. Artist Margaret Leng Tan combined dance and piano-playing in *her* performances. _____

_____ 2. Over the years, the intensive breeding of domestic rabbits has given *their* softer, finer fur than wild rabbits. _____

_____ 3. New England poet Edwin A. Robinson moved to New York City in 1896 and devoted *himself* to his writing. _____

_____ 4. Yellow journalism was a form of news reporting *it* emphasized the spectacular aspects of the news. _____

_____ 5. There are between 100 and 400 billion stars in *ours* galaxy, the Milky Way. _____

_____   **6.** The atoms of a crystal always arrange *them* into a specific array, called a lattice. _____

_____   **7.** Fred Astaire and Gene Kelly were basically tap dancers, but *their* both added some ballet movements to their dance steps. _____

_____   **8.** The Pritzken Prize is given every year to architects *their* work benefits humanity and the environment. _____

_____   **9.** Charleston, South Carolina, has preserved to a remarkable degree *it* historic houses and famous gardens. _____

_____   **10.** Ice fishermen sometimes build small, movable huts to protect *them* from the cold winds. _____

EXERCISE 36.3

Focus: Identifying errors involving the incorrect inclusion of pronouns.

Directions: If the sentence contains a pronoun that is incorrectly included, mark that sentence *X*, and underline the pronoun. If the sentence does not contain a pronoun inclusion, mark that sentence *C*. The first one is done as an example.

_X_   **1.** The first great public library in the United States <u>it</u> was founded in Boston in the 1830s.

_____   **2.** Floods which cause billions of dollars worth of property damage in the United States annually.

_____   **3.** As a class, percussion instruments such as drums that are the simplest in construction of any musical instruments.

_____   **4.** Richard G. Hatcher of Gary, Indiana, he was one of the first black mayors of a sizable American city.

_____   **5.** Active stocks are stocks which are frequently bought and sold.

_____   **6.** There are many species of plants and animals that they are peculiar to Hawaii.

_____   **7.** Pipettes are glass tubes, open at both ends, which chemists use them to transfer small volumes of liquid.

_____   **8.** When molten basalt cools, it forms six-sided columns.

_____   **9.** Elizabeth Peabody, founder of the first American kindergarten, she helped gain acceptance of that institution as a regular part of public education.

_____   **10.** Today scientists obtain the information which they use to make weather prediction chiefly from satellites.

_____   **11.** Cells often obtain water through which the process of osmosis.

_____   **12.** The lighting of large outdoor arenas it first became feasible in the 1930s.

EXERCISE 36.4

Focus: Identifying and correcting errors involving pronouns. (Note: One or two items in this exercise do not focus on pronoun errors. These are marked in the answer key with an asterisk.)

Directions: Decide which of the four underlined words or phrases—(A), (B), (C), or (D)—would not be considered correct, and write the letter of the expression in the blank. Then, on the line at the end of the sentence, write a correction for the underlined phrase.

_____ 1. A beaver uses <u>its strong</u> front <u>teeth</u> to cut down trees and <u>peel off</u> <u>its</u> bark. _____
                      A   B   C D

_____ 2. A caricature is a picture <u>in which</u> the subject's <u>distinctive</u> features <u>they are</u> deliberately
                                  A   B   C
<u>exaggerated</u>. _____
D

_____ 3. Ants are blind to red light, so <u>it is</u> possible to observe <u>themselves</u> in an artificial nest <u>without</u>
                                        A   B   C
disturbing <u>their</u> activities. _____
               D

_____ 4. An auger is <u>a tool</u> which a carpenter <u>uses</u> <u>it</u> to bore holes <u>in</u> wood. _____
                          A   B   C   D

_____ 5. The glaciers in Olympia National Park are <u>unusually</u> because <u>they</u> are found at altitudes
                                                       A   B
lower than <u>those</u> at <u>which</u> glaciers are usually found. _____
           C   D

_____ 6. In <u>his</u> novels, Sinclair Lewis <u>drew</u> critical portraits of Americans <u>who</u> thought of <u>them</u> as
                 A   B   C   D
model citizens. _____

_____ 7. Jaguars <u>which resemble</u> leopards but <u>they</u> are larger and are <u>marked</u> with rosettes <u>rather</u>
                          A   B   C
<u>than</u> spots. _____
D

_____ 8. Most bacteria <u>have</u> strong cell walls <u>much</u> <u>like</u> <u>that</u> of plants. _____
                            A   B C D

_____ 9. Bees <u>collect</u> pollen, <u>which</u> <u>furnishes</u> protein for <u>its</u> diet. _____
                  A   B   C   D

_____ 10. A small business <u>often</u> limits <u>their</u> operations to a single <u>neighborhood</u> or a group of
                             A   B   C
neighboring <u>communities</u>. _____
                D

_____ 11. Louisa May Alcott, <u>she</u> is best known for <u>her books</u> for children, <u>served</u> as a nurse <u>during</u>
                                 A   B   C   D
the Civil War. _____

_____ 12. The <u>principles</u> used in air-conditioning are <u>basically</u> the same as <u>those</u> used by the human
                 A   B   C
body to cool <u>himself</u>. _____
              D

_____ **13.** In that age of computers, it is difficult to imagine how tedious the work of accountants and
      A   B   C

clerks must have been in the past. _____
           D

_____ **14.** In general, the only kind of cells that cannot replace itself are nerve cells. _____
       A   B   C   D

_____ **15.** The naturalist Edwin Teal illustration his books with photographs he had taken
                                         A   B   C

himself. _____
   D

Lesson 37

ERRORS WITH SINGULAR AND PLURAL NOUNS

PLURAL NOUNS IN PLACE OF SINGULAR NOUNS AND SINGULAR NOUNS IN PLACE OF PLURAL NOUNS

Underlined nouns in the Written Expression section may be incorrect because they are plural but should be singular, or because they are singular but should be plural.

Sometimes it is clear that a singular subject is incorrectly used because the verb is plural, or that a plural noun is used incorrectly because the verb is singular. In this type of item, the verb will NOT be underlined, because this is not a verb error.

Sometimes it is obvious that a plural or a singular noun is needed because of the determiners that precede the noun. Certain determiners are used only before singular nouns while other determiners are used only before plural nouns.

Determiners used with singular nouns	Determiners used with plural nouns
a/an	two, three, four, etc.
one	dozens of
a single	hundreds of
each	thousands of
every	a few (of)
this	many (of)
that	a number of
	the number of
	a couple (of)
	every one of
	each one of
	each of
	one of
	these
	those

Each *contestant* won a prize.
Each of the *contestants* won a prize.
This *flower* is a yellow rose.
These *flowers* are yellow roses.
I only attended one *game* this season.
It was one of the most exciting *games* that I ever attended.

Sample Items

Several of Washington Irving's story have become classics in American literature.
   A   B   C   D

Ⓐ ⬤ Ⓒ Ⓓ

In this item, both the determiner before the noun (*Several of*) and the plural verb (*have*) indicate that a plural noun (*stories*) should be used.

Mauna Loa, an active volcano on the island of Hawaii, usually has one eruptions every three
              A   B   C   D

years.

Ⓐ Ⓑ Ⓒ ⬤

A singular noun must be used after the determiner *one*.

One of the most beautiful state capitol is the Utah Sate Capitol, located in Salt Lake City.
  A   B   C   D

Ⓐ Ⓑ ⬤ Ⓓ

The correct pattern is *one of the* + superlative adjective + plural noun. The plural noun *capitols* must therefore be used.

ERRORS INVOLVING IRREGULAR PLURALS

Most plural nouns in English end in *-s*, but a few are irregular. Only the most common irregular plurals are tested on TOEFL. (Irregular plurals that come to English from Latin or Greek—*data*, *cacti*, *alumnae*, or *phenomena*, for example—will NOT be tested on TOEFL.)

Common Irregular Plural Nouns

Singular Noun	Plural Noun
child	children
man	men
woman	women
foot	feet
tooth	teeth
mouse	mice
fish	fish

Sample Item

As childs grow older, their bones become thicker and longer.
   A   B C   D

⬤ Ⓑ Ⓒ Ⓓ

The correct plural form of *child* is *children*.

ERRORS WITH PLURAL FORMS OF NON-COUNT NOUNS

In some items a non-count noun (such as *furniture, research, sunshine, information, bread,* and so on) is incorrectly given as a plural noun.

Sample Item

<u>Some</u> encyclopedias <u>deal</u> with specific fields, such as <u>music</u> or philosophy, and provide
  A   B   C
<u>informations</u> only on subject.
  D

                          (A)   (B)   (C)   ●

Information is an uncountable noun and cannot be pluralized.

ERRORS WITH PLURAL COMPOUND NOUN

Compound nouns consist of two nouns used together to express a single idea: *grocery store, travel agent, dinner party,* and *house cat* for example. Only the second noun of compounds is pluralized: *grocery stores, travel agents, dinner parties,* and *house cats.*

(There are rare exceptions to this rule—*sports cars* and *women doctors,* for example—but these won't be tested.)

Sample Item

Raymond Chandler's <u>detectives stories</u> are <u>admired</u> both by critics <u>and</u> general <u>readers.</u>
                            A   B   C   D

                          ●   (B)   (C)   (D)

The correct plural form of this compound noun is *detective stories.*

ERRORS INVOLVING PLURAL FORMS OF NUMBERS AND MEASUREMENT

Some errors involve numbers + measurements:

They went for a *6-mile* walk.
They walked *6 miles*.

In the first sentence, the number + measurement is used as an adjective, and the measurement is singular. In the second, the measurement is a noun, and is therefore plural.

Numbers like *hundred, thousand,* and *million* may be pluralized when they are used indefinitely—in other words, when they do not follow other numbers:

seven thousand   thousands
five million dollars   millions of dollars

Sample Items

The U.S. president serves a maximum of two four-years terms.
A   B   C   D

Ⓐ   Ⓑ   Ⓒ   ⬤

When used before a noun, a number + measurement is singular.

Thousand of antibiotics have been developed, but only about thirty are in common use today.
A   B   C   D

⬤   Ⓑ   Ⓒ   Ⓓ

The plural form *thousands* should be used.

EXERCISE 37

Focus: Identifying and correcting errors involving singular and plural nouns. (Note: One or two items in this exercise do not focus on singular-plural errors. These are marked in the answer key with an asterisk.)

Directions: Decide which of the four underlined words or phrases—(A), (B), (C), or (D)—would not be considered correct, and write the letter of the expression in the blank. Then, on the line at the end of the sentence, write a correction for the underlined phrase.

_____ **1.** The male mandril baboon is one of the most colorful of all mammal. _____
       A   B   C   D

_____ **2.** Zoonoses are diseases that can be transmitted to humans beings by animals. _____
         A   B   C   D

_____ **3.** Many championship automobiles and motorcycle races take place in Daytona Beach,
     A   B   C D

     Florida. _____

_____ **4.** The Newberry Award is granted every years to the authors of outstanding books for
               A   B   C

     children. _____
     D

_____ **5.** The major source of air pollution vary from city to city. _____
       A   B C   D

_____ **6.** Around 75 percents of the earth's surface is covered by water. _____
       A   B   C   D

_____ **7.** All college and universities get their funds from a variety of sources. _____
       A   B   C D

_____ **8.** Russell Cave in northeastern Alabama was the home of cliff-dwelling Indians thousand of
         A   B   C

     years ago. _____
     D

_____ **9.** In 1792 a corporation constructed a 60-miles toll road from Philadelphia to Lancaster,
     A   B   C   D

     Pennsylvania. _____

_____ 10. The mathematician and astronomer David Rittenhouse was one of the first man of science in
                                        A   B   C   D
the American colonies. _____

_____ 11. Publishers of modern encyclopedias employ hundreds of specialists and large editorials
                A   B   C   D
staffs. _____

_____ 12. The electric toaster was one of the earliest appliance to be developed for the
                A   B   C
kitchen. _____
                D

_____ 13. Tornadoes can pick up objects as heavy as automobiles and carry them for hundreds of
                                          A   B   C

foot. _____
    D

_____ 14. Many kinds of vegetables are growth in California's Imperial Valley. _____
                    A   B   C   D

_____ 15. In typical pioneers settlements, men, women, and children worked from morning until night
                        A   B   C
at farm and household tasks. _____
    D

_____ 16. Some engineers have predicted that, within twenty years,
                    A   B
automobiles will be make almost completely of plastic. _____
                    C   D

_____ 17. The pine tree is probably the more important lumber tree in the world. _____
                A   B   C   D

_____ 18. Mary Lyon founded Mount Holyoke College, the first permanent institution of higher
                        A   B
learning for woman in the United States. _____
        C   D

_____ 19. Adult humans have more than a trillions cells in their bodies. _____
                A   B   C   D

_____ 20. Phytoplankton is found only in the upper layers of the ocean, where sunlights can
                            A   B   C   D
reach. _____

Answer Sheet

Mini-Test 6: Written Expression

1. Ⓐ Ⓑ Ⓒ Ⓓ   11. Ⓐ Ⓑ Ⓒ Ⓓ   21. Ⓐ Ⓑ Ⓒ Ⓓ
2. Ⓐ Ⓑ Ⓒ Ⓓ   12. Ⓐ Ⓑ Ⓒ Ⓓ   22. Ⓐ Ⓑ Ⓒ Ⓓ
3. Ⓐ Ⓑ Ⓒ Ⓓ   13. Ⓐ Ⓑ Ⓒ Ⓓ   23. Ⓐ Ⓑ Ⓒ Ⓓ
4. Ⓐ Ⓑ Ⓒ Ⓓ   14. Ⓐ Ⓑ Ⓒ Ⓓ   24. Ⓐ Ⓑ Ⓒ Ⓓ
5. Ⓐ Ⓑ Ⓒ Ⓓ   15. Ⓐ Ⓑ Ⓒ Ⓓ   25. Ⓐ Ⓑ Ⓒ Ⓓ
6. Ⓐ Ⓑ Ⓒ Ⓓ   16. Ⓐ Ⓑ Ⓒ Ⓓ
7. Ⓐ Ⓑ Ⓒ Ⓓ   17. Ⓐ Ⓑ Ⓒ Ⓓ
8. Ⓐ Ⓑ Ⓒ Ⓓ   18. Ⓐ Ⓑ Ⓒ Ⓓ
9. Ⓐ Ⓑ Ⓒ Ⓓ   19. Ⓐ Ⓑ Ⓒ Ⓓ
10. Ⓐ Ⓑ Ⓒ Ⓓ   20. Ⓐ Ⓑ Ⓒ Ⓓ

MINI-TEST 6: WRITTEN EXPRESSION

Directions: The sentences below have four underlined words or phrases, (A), (B), (C), and (D). Identify the *one* underlined expression that must be changed for the sentence to be correct. Then find the number of the question on your answer sheet above and circle the corresponding letter.

Time: 12 minutes

1. Bricks <u>can be</u> made from <u>many</u> <u>difference</u> types of <u>clay</u>.
          A   B   C   D

2. <u>Despite</u> most mushrooms are <u>edible</u>, some species <u>cause</u> serious <u>poisoning</u>.
      A   B   C   D

3. Judges in <u>dog shows</u> rate dogs on <u>such points</u> as their <u>colorful</u>, posture, shape, and <u>size</u>.
            A   B   C   D

4. The <u>medicine</u> of prehistoric people probably consisted of a <u>mixture of</u> scientific practices,
       A   B
   <u>superstitions</u>, and <u>religous</u> <u>believes</u>.
      C   D

5. <u>The game</u> backgammon <u>has</u> been <u>playing</u> since ancient <u>times</u>.
       A   B   C   D

6. One of the <u>greatest</u> of American automobile <u>designer</u> <u>was</u> Harley Earl.
     A   B   C   D

7. <u>Before</u> the late eighteenth century, most <u>textiles</u> were <u>done</u> at home.
      A   B   C   D

8. Political science, <u>alike</u> the <u>other</u> social <u>sciences</u>, is not <u>an exact</u> science.
                 A   B   C   D

9. <u>About 8,000 years</u> ago, people <u>began</u> using animals to carry <u>themselves</u> and their belongings.
       A   B   C   D

10. Storks <u>constantly</u> rearrange their nests to keep <u>their</u> eggs <u>safety</u>, dry, and <u>warm</u>.
             A   B   C   D

Peterson's TOEFL CBT Success

11. In its <u>purely</u> state, hydrochloric acid is <u>a gas</u>, but <u>it</u> is <u>almost</u> always used as a solution in water.
        A   B   C   D

12. Animals <u>that</u> hibernate <u>usually</u> eat large <u>numbers</u> of food <u>in the</u> autumn.
              A   B   C   D

13. <u>Many</u> folk <u>songs</u> have been <u>written</u> about railroads and <u>railroads</u> workers.
      A   B   C   D

14. Some plants and <u>insects</u> exhibit <u>so</u> high degree of interdependence that the elimination of one <u>results</u>
                  A   B   C

    in the elimination of <u>the other</u>.
                        D

15. <u>Lightly</u>, sandy soil <u>absorbs</u> water more <u>quickly</u> than clay <u>or</u> loam.
      A   B   C   D

16. Fannie Farmer, an <u>educator</u> and <u>cooking</u> expert, <u>she wrote</u> the first <u>distinctively</u> American cookbook.
                      A   B   C   D

17. The rhesus monkey <u>has</u> been <u>widely</u> used in <u>biological</u>, psychological, and <u>medicine</u> research.
                 A   B   C   D

18. <u>During</u> the Depression of the 1930s, <u>many</u> artists <u>were giving</u> <u>jobs</u> by the Federal Arts Project.
      A   B   C   D

19. Crocodiles are sometimes <u>confused</u> with alligators, but are <u>different</u> from <u>they</u> in <u>a number</u> of ways.
                           A   B   C   D

20. As a concert <u>violinist</u>, conductor, and <u>he composed</u> both serious and popular <u>music</u>, Leonard Bern-
                  A   B   C

    stein achieved a series of <u>remarkable</u> successes.
                                D

21. It is a <u>chemical</u> called capsaicin <u>that gives</u> hot peppers <u>their</u> <u>spice</u> flavor.
              A   B   C D

22. Flying snakes <u>can launch</u> <u>itself</u> from <u>the top of</u> one tree and glide to <u>another</u>.
                 A   B   C   D

23. A <u>basic</u> knowledge of social studies, such as <u>history</u> and geography, <u>are</u> considered a basic part of the
       A   B   C

    education of every <u>child</u>.
                      D

24. The black walnut tree <u>is grown</u> principally for <u>its</u> lumber, <u>which is</u> used for cabinets and <u>furnitures</u>.
                       A   B   C   D

25. Plymouth was the <u>soonest</u> of the five <u>colonies</u> <u>established</u> by the Pilgrims <u>in</u> Massachusetts.
                   A   B   C   D

Lesson 38

ERRORS WITH VERBALS

Verbals are participles, gerunds, infinitives, and—for the purpose of this lesson—simple forms of the verb.

Participles are verbal adjectives. In this part of the test, participles are often seen before nouns as one-word adjectives. **Present participles** end with *-ing*. When used before a noun, present participles have an active meaning. **Past participles** of regular verbs end in *-ed*; the past participles of many common verbs are irregular. Before nouns, past participles have a passive meaning.

> It was an *exhausting* 10-kilometer race. (present participle)
> The *exhausted* runners were too tired to move after the race. (past participle)

In the first sentence, the race exhausts the runners. The race "performs" the action. In the second sentence, the runners are exhausted by the race. They receive the action.

Participles are also used in phrases after nouns as reduced (shortened) relative clauses. Again, present participles imply an active idea, past participles a passive one.

> The man *stealing* the money was arrested. (present participle; means "who stole")
> The money *stolen* from the bank was recovered. (past participle; means "which was stolen")

Gerunds are verbal nouns. Like present participles, gerunds end in *-ing*. They can be the subjects of verbs, the objects of prepositions, and the objects of certain verbs. (See the list on the following page.)

> *Dancing* is good exercise. (gerund as subject)
> You can solve this problem *by using* a calculator. (gerund as object of a preposition)
> He enjoys *going* to good restaurants. (gerund as object of a verb)

All two- and three-word verb phrases that can be followed by verbals are used with gerunds, not infinitives. This is true even when the verb phrase ends with the word *to*. (This can be tricky because infinitives always begin with the word *to*.)

> I'm looking forward to *going* to New Orleans.
> John is opposed to our *participating*.

Infinitives consist of the word *to* and the simple form of the verb. Like gerunds, infinitives can be the subjects of verbs and the objects of certain verbs (see list). Unlike gerunds, infinitives can NEVER be the objects of prepositions.

> *To help* others is rewarding. (infinitive as subject)
> He attempted *to swim* across the river. (infinitive as object of a verb)

Infinitives are used in several other ways:

> It's important *to change* the oil in your car frequently. (infinitive after an adjective)
> The first man *to land* on the moon was Neil Armstrong. (infinitive used as an adjective after a noun)
> She must take this class *to graduate*. (infinitive used to show purpose)

Simple forms are the base forms of verbs; they consist of the infinitive without the word *to*. Simple forms are used after the causative verbs *have*, *make*, and *let*:

> He had the carpenter *repair* the door.
> His father makes him *study* hard.
> She let her son *go* on the trip.

Common Verbs That Take Verbal Objects

Verbs Used with Gerunds	Verbs Used with Infinitives	Verbs Used with Simple Forms
admit	agree	have
avoid	allow	let
deny	arrange	make
enjoy	attempt	
finish	cause	
justify	choose	
quit	decide	
recommend	enable	
suggest	hope	
understand	instruct	
	know (how)	
	learn (how)	
	permit	
	persuade	
	require	
	seem	
	teach (how)	
	tell	
	use	
	warn	

Watch for the following errors involving verbals:

INCORRECT CHOICE OF VERBAL

Any of these verbals—participle, gerund, infinitive, or simple form—may be incorrectly used when another one of them is required.

Sample Items

The writer Edgar Allen Poe is usually credited with invent the short story.
           A   B   C   D

Ⓐ　Ⓑ　●　Ⓓ

After a preposition (*with*), a simple form cannot be used. The correct form is a gerund (*inventing*).

A single-lens reflex camera allows a photographer seeing exactly what the camera will
    A   B   C
photograph.
  D

Ⓐ　Ⓑ　●　Ⓓ

After the verb *allow*, a gerund (*seeing*) cannot be used. An infinitive (*to see*) is correct.

INCORRECT CHOICE OF PARTICIPLE

You may see past participles used incorrectly for present participles or present participles used incorrectly for past participles.

You may also see a main verb used when a participle is required.

Sample Items

There <u>are</u> probably <u>around</u> 3,000 languages <u>speaking</u> in <u>the</u> world.
    A   B   C   D

            Ⓐ Ⓑ ● Ⓓ

A past participle (*spoken*) is required because the idea is passive. The sentence means, "...3,000 languages *which are spoken. . . .*"

For <u>decades</u>, journalist Theodore H. White <u>wrote</u> books <u>described</u> American <u>presidential</u>
    A   B   C   D
elections.

            Ⓐ Ⓑ ● Ⓓ

The past participle *described* is used incorrectly because the idea is active: the books described the elections. Therefore a present participle, *describing* should be used. (The sentence could also be corrected by adding a relative pronoun: *that described*.)

Nutmeg, widely <u>is used</u> as a <u>spice</u>, is <u>actually</u> the kernel of a <u>tropical</u> spice.
                    A   B   C   D

            ● Ⓑ Ⓒ Ⓓ

Rather than the main verb *is used*, a past participle (*used*) is required.

INCORRECT FORMS OF INFINITIVES

Incorrect infinitive forms such as *for go* or *to going* may be used in place of the correct form, *to go*.

Sample Item

Viral infections <u>are</u> generally <u>more difficult</u> to <u>treating</u> than bacterial <u>infections</u>.
               A   B   C   D

          Ⓐ Ⓑ ● Ⓓ

The correct form of the infinitive is *to treat*.

EXERCISE 38.1

Focus: Identifying errors and correct forms of gerunds, infinitives, and simple forms.
Directions: Underline the form that best completes each sentence.

1. Sports parachutes are relatively easy (controlling/to control).

2. Sleeve bearings allow pistons (to move/move) back and forth.

3. One of the most important steps in (producing/to produce) a motion picture is film editing.

4. An opera singer is required (having/to have) a powerful and beautiful voice.

5. The Wampanoag Indians taught the Pilgrims how (growing/to grow) corn.

6. Frogs and certain kinds of birds use their tongues (to catch/catch) insects.

7. Isadora Martinez invented a knee implant that lets people with arthritis (to bend/bend) their knees easily.

8. Smells can be more effective than any other sensory stimuli in vividly (bringing/bring) back memories.

9. Modems permit computers (communicating/to communicate) with one another over telephone lines.

10. A sudden sound can make a golfer (to miss/miss) a shot.

11. Heavy spring snows may cause the branches of trees (snap/to snap).

12. Modern race cars store fuel in rubber bladders that are almost impossible (rupturing/to rupture).

13. New words are constantly being invented (describe/to describe) new objects and concepts.

14. Dr. Mary Walker, a surgeon in the Union Army during the Civil War, was the first, and so far only woman (to be awarded/awarding) the Congressional Medal of Honor.

15. In 1957 Ralph Abernathy founded an organization devoted to (achieve/achieving) racial equality for black Americans.

EXERCISE 38.2

Focus: Identifying errors and correct forms of participles.
Directions: Underline the form that best completes each sentence.

1. The largest (knowing/known) insects are found in tropical rain forests.

2. A bill of lading is a (writing/written) receipt for goods that are sent by public transportation.

3. A hummingbird's heart beats at the (astonishing/astonished) rate of 615 beats per minute.

4. At the peak of his jump, a pole-vaulter performs a series of (twisting/twisted) body motions to clear the bar.

5. Anyone (working/worked) under conditions that cause a heavy loss of perspiration can suffer heat exhaustion.

6. A mosquito (filled/is filled) with blood is carrying twice its own body weight.

7. The state of Wisconsin has seventy-two counties, many (naming/named) after Indian tribes.

8. Sunspots occur in cycles, with the greatest number generally (appearing/are appearing) every eleven years.

9. A delta is a more-or-less triangular area of sediments (depositing/deposited) at the mouth of a river.

10. William H. Kilpatrick was a philosopher and scholar now generally (regarding/regarded) as the father of progressive education.

11. Checkerboard Mesa in Utah features a strangely (cracked/cracking) expanse of stone.

12. It has been known since the third century that coffee has a (stimulated/stimulating) effect.

EXERCISE 38.3

Focus: Identifying and correcting a variety of errors involving verbals. (Note: One or two items in this exercise do not focus on errors involving verbals. These are marked in the answer key with an asterisk.)

Directions: Decide which of the four underlined words or phrases—(A), (B), (C), or (D)—would not be considered correct, and write the letter of that expression in the blank. Then, on the line at the end of the sentence, write a correction for the underlined phrase.

_____ 1. The most widely used material for package consumer goods is cardboard. _____
                A   B   C   D

_____ 2. One of the latest methods of quarrying stone is to cutting the stone with a jet
                     A   B   C   D
torch. _____

_____ 3. In 1944, biologist Charles Michener devised a system for to classify the approximate 20,000
                                         A   B   C
species of bees. _____
    D

_____ 4. Most candles are made of paraffin wax mix with compounds that have higher melting points
                                      A   B
to keep them from melting in hot weather. _____
  C   D

_____ 5. Machines used to harvest tree crops such as cherries or almonds can be classified either as
                  A   B   C
shakers and as pick-up machines. _____
      D

_____ 6. Fishing cats, found in Southeast Asia, are distinguished by their webbed feet that enable
                A   B   C
them catching fish. _____
      D

_____ 7. Geothermal energy is energy to obtain by using heat from the Earth's interior. _____
                A   B   C   D

_____ 8. Bathe in mineral water has long been believed to have beneficial effects. _____
      A   B   C   D

_____ 9. It is the facets cut into a diamond that make it to sparkle. _____
      A   B   C   D

_____ 10. Ralph Blakelock specialized in paint wild, lonely nighttime landscapes, usually with black
                   A   B   C
trees silhouetted against the moon. _____
    D

_____ 11. The Farallon Islands are a group of uninhabited islands lying about 40 mile west of
                      A   B   C   D
San Francisco. _____

_____ 12. The crushing leaves of yarrow plants can serve as a traditional medicine for cleansing
      A   B   C   D
wounds. _____

_____ 13. Robert A. Moog developed an electronic device that could be used for play synthesized
                A   B   C   D
music. _____

_____ 14. Hypnosis is sometimes employed as a means of helping people to quit to smoke. _____
        A   B   C   D

_____ 15. Throughout his long career, Pete Seeger has been a lead figure in reviving folk
                A   B   C   D
music. _____

Lesson 39

ERRORS WITH PREPOSITIONS

Errors with **prepositions** are among the most difficult errors to catch. Preposition use in English is very complex. For every rule, there seems to be an exception. Recently, there have been more errors involving prepositions in the Written Expression part of TOEFL, and the errors have been more difficult to spot.

Prepositions are used in the following ways:

- In adverbial phrases that show time, place, and other relationships.
  in the morning   on Pennsylvania Avenue   to the park
  by a student

- After certain nouns.
  a cause of   a reason for   a solution to

- After certain adjectives and participles
  different from   aware of   disappointed in

- After certain verbs
  combine with   rely on   refer to

- In phrasal prepositions (two- or three-word prepositions)
  according to   together with   instead of

- In certain set expressions
  by far   in general   on occasion   at last

Note: In Mini-Lessons for Section 2, found at the end of this section of the book, all of these uses for prepositions are explained, and practice exercises are provided.

There are two main types of preposition errors that you may see in the Written Expression part of the test:

ERRORS IN PREPOSITION CHOICE

The wrong preposition is used according to the context of the sentence.

Some of the rules for choosing the correct prepositions are given in the mini-lessons, but you will never be able to memorize all the rules for preposition use in English. The more you practice, though, the more you will develop a "feel" for determining which preposition is correct in any given situation.

There are two particular situations involving preposition choice that are often tested in Written expression:

- Errors with *from . . . to* and *between . . . and*

Both these expressions are used to give the starting time and ending time. They can also be used to show relationships of place and various other relationships.

He lived in Seattle *from* 1992 *to* 1997.
He lived in Seattle *between* 1992 *and* 1997.

Route 66 ran *from* Chicago *to* Los Angeles.
Route 66 ran *between* Chicago *and* Los Angeles.

Errors usually involve an incorrect pairing of those words, or the incorrect use of other prepositions:

    * *between* A *to* B   * *from* X *and* Y

    * *between* A *with* B   * *since* X *to* Y

- Errors with *since*, *for*, and *in*

Since is used before a point in time with the present perfect tense—but never with the past tense. *For* is used before a period of time with the present perfect and other tenses. *In* is used before certain points in time (years, centuries, decades) with the past tense and other tenses—but never with the present perfect tense.

> He's lived here *since* 1995.
> He's lived here *for* two years.
> He moved here *in* 1995.

Errors involve the use of one of these prepositions for another:

> * He's lived here *in* 1995.
> * He's lived here *since* two years.
> * He moved here *since* 1995.

Sample Items

The pitch of a <u>tuning fork</u> depends <u>of</u> the <u>size</u> and shape of <u>its</u> arms.
             A   B   C   D

(A) ● (C) (D)

The correct preposition after the verb *depend* is *on*, not *of*.

The Alaskan Pipeline <u>runs</u> <u>between</u> Prudhoe Bay on the Arctic Coastal Plain to the <u>port</u> of
                 A   B   C
Valdez, a <u>distance</u> of 789 miles.
        D

(A) ● (C) (D)

The correct pattern is *from . . . to*.

Candles were <u>mankind's</u> chief <u>source</u> of illumination <u>since</u> at <u>least</u> 2,000 years.
            A   B   C   D

(A) (B) ● (D)

Before a period of time (*2,000 years*) the preposition *for* should be used.

INCORRECT INCLUSION OR OMISSION OF PREPOSITIONS

A preposition is used when one is not needed, or not used when one is needed.

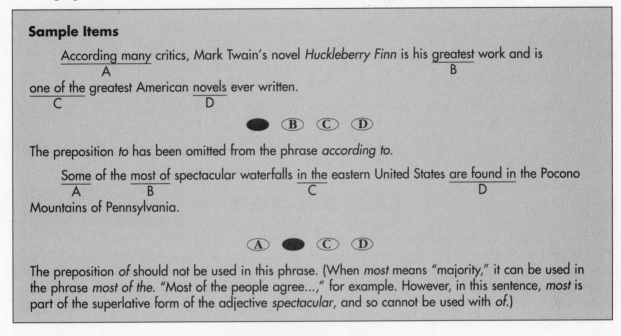

Sample Items

According many critics, Mark Twain's novel *Huckleberry Finn* is his greatest work and is
     A   B

one of the greatest American novels ever written.
    C   D

● Ⓑ Ⓒ Ⓓ

The preposition *to* has been omitted from the phrase *according to.*

Some of the most of spectacular waterfalls in the eastern United States are found in the Pocono
  A   B   C   D

Mountains of Pennsylvania.

Ⓐ ● Ⓒ Ⓓ

The preposition *of* should not be used in this phrase. (When *most* means "majority," it can be used in the phrase *most of the.* "Most of the people agree...," for example. However, in this sentence, *most* is part of the superlative form of the adjective *spectacular,* and so cannot be used with *of.*)

EXERCISE 39.1

Focus: Identifying correct and incorrect preposition choice.
Directions: Underline the prepositions that correctly complete the sentences below.

1. Wage rates depend (in/on) part (from/on) the general prosperity (of/for) the economy.

2. (For/To) an injection to be effective (on/against) tetanus, it must be administered (by/within) 72 hours (of/for) the injury.

3. The invention (of/for) the hand-cranked freezer opened the door (for/to) commercial ice-cream production, and (for/since) then, the ice-cream industry has grown (in/into) a four-billion-dollar-a-year industry.

4. (At/On) the time (of/in) the Revolutionary War, the North American colonies were merely a long string (with/of) settlements (along/among) the Atlantic Coast (between/from) Maine and Georgia.

5. The probability (of/for) two people (in/on) a group (of/for) ten people having birthdays (in/on) the same day is about one (in/of) twenty.

6. Showboats were floating theaters that tied up (at/to) towns (in/on) the Ohio and Mississippi Rivers to bring entertainment and culture (to/at) the people (on/in) the frontier.

7. Scrimshaw, the practice (of/for) carving ornate designs (in/on) ivory, was first practiced (by/of) sailors working (by/with) sail needles while (in/on) long sea voyages.

8. Assateague Island, (off/of) the coast (off/of) Virginia, is famous (for/to) its herds (of/with) wild ponies.

9. (In/On) order (for/to) an object to be visible, light must travel (from/for) that object (at/to) a person's eyes.

10. (In/On) the 1930s and 1940s, when train travel was (on/at) its peak, passengers could look forward (for/to) wonderful meals (on/at) trains.

11. (In/Since) the 1960s, op art, which was based (in/on) scientific theories (of/for) optics, employed patterns (of/in) lines and colors that seemed to change shape as the viewer looked (on/at) them.

12. The first national convention devoted (for/to) the issue (of/with) women's rights, organized partly (of/by) Elizabeth Cady Stanton, was held (in/on) her hometown (in/of) Seneca Falls, New York, (in/on) 1848.

13. (In/Since) 1716, a party (of/for) explorers led (by/with) Lieutenant Governor Spotswood (of/in) Virginia tried (in/on) vain to find a route (through/of) the Appalachian Mountains.

14. Dolphins rely (in/on) echolocation, a form (of/for) navigation similar (with/to) the sonar systems used (on/at) submarines.

15. Analytical geometry, (in/on) which algebraic ideas are used (for/to) the description (of/for) geometric objects, has been (in/on) use (for/since) the seventeenth century.

EXERCISE 39.2

Focus: Identifying and correcting errors involving the inclusion or omission of prepositions.

Directions: If there is a preposition unnecessarily included in a sentence, mark that sentence X, and underline the preposition. If there is a preposition incorrectly omitted from a sentence, mark that sentence X, underline the words before and after the missing preposition, and write the correct preposition on the line at the end of the sentence. If the sentence is correctly written, mark that sentence C. The first is done as an example.

__X__ 1. According polls taken throughout the twentieth century, Lincoln and Washington are the preeminent American presidents. _to_

_____ 2. Today, many varieties of fruit are available all year thanks improved storage and shipping techniques. _____

_____ 3. The origin of the Moon remains a mystery. _____

_____ 4. Traffic jams can cause of pollution, delays, and short tempers. _____

_____ 5. The Sun's rays heat the Earth's surface, on which then radiates the heat into the air. _____

_____ 6. A warm-blooded animal is one that keeps the same body temperature regardless the air temperature. _____

_____ 7. Charlie Parker, considered by many the greatest improviser in the history of jazz, influenced many other jazz musicians. _____

_____ 8. Most the people are aware of the need to visit dentists regularly. _____

_____ 9. Muscle fibers are attached bones by tendons. _____

_____ 10. In his essay "Self Reliance," Ralph W. Emerson told to his readers why they should not depend on the ideas of others. _____

_____ 11. The crayfish is a freshwater crustacean related the lobster. _____

_____ 12. Charles Goren was an expert the game of bridge. _____

_____ 13. Stomata are the tiny openings in the leaves of plants through which oxygen and carbon dioxide pass. _____

_____ 14. Ducks have small oil glands by which keep their feathers oily and repel water. _____

_____ **15.** The tail of a comet always points away the Sun. _____

_____ **16.** Lichens grow in extreme environments in where no other plant can exist. _____

_____ **17.** Not all of waterfalls are formed in the same way. _____

_____ **18.** The pulmonary artery carries blood from the right side the heart to the lungs. _____

_____ **19.** In addition to the twelve constellations of the zodiac, thirty other constellations were familiar people of ancient times. _____

_____ **20.** Rainbows always appear in that part of the sky opposite the sun. _____

EXERCISE 39.3

Focus: Identifying and correcting preposition errors. (Note: One or two items in this exercise do not focus on preposition errors. These are marked in the answer key with an asterisk.)

Directions: Decide which of the four underlined words or phrases—(A), (B), (C), or (D)—would not be considered correct, and write the letter of that expression in the blank at the beginning of the sentence. Then, in the blank at the end of the sentence, write a correction for the underlined phrase.

_____ **1.** Water polo is a game in which is played in the water by two teams, each with seven
        A   B   C   D

    players. _____

_____ **2.** Dynamics is a branch of physics that deals for the relationship between motion
            A   B   C

    and force. _____
      D

_____ **3.** Many of radio stations began broadcasting baseball games during the 1920s. _____
      A   B   C   D

_____ **4.** The economy of Maine is based to a great extent in its forests, which cover 80 percent of its
        A   B   C   D

    surface area. _____

_____ **5.** The removal of waste materials is essential to all forms of live. _____
        A   B   C   D

_____ **6.** John Diefenbaker, Prime Minister of Canada during 1957 to 1963, is given much of the
                                  A   B   C

    credit for the adoption of the Canadian Bill of Rights. _____
        D

_____ **7.** The first stage on the manufacturing of all types of clothing is the cutting of the
             A   B   C   D

    material. _____

_____ **8.** All of the wheat grown throughout the world belongs one of fourteen species. _____
      A   B   C   D

_____ **9.** There are approximately 600 different species of trees native of the continental United
        A   B   C   D

    States. _____

_____ **10.** Waterwheels, <u>which</u> appeared <u>on</u> the fourth century B.C., were probably <u>the first</u> machines
         A   B   C

not powered <u>by</u> humans or animals. _____
     D

_____ **11.** <u>Since</u> centuries, Southwestern Indian tribes have <u>valued</u> turquoise and have <u>used</u> it <u>in</u>
     A   B   C

<u>jewelry</u>. _____
  D

_____ **12.** Loggerhead turtles lay <u>thousands eggs</u> at <u>a single</u> time, but only a <u>few</u> survive
            A   B   C

to adulthood. _____
  D

_____ **13.** <u>In nowadays</u>, commercial bakeries use complex, automated machines, but the basic prin-
     A

ciples <u>of baking</u> have changed <u>little</u> <u>for</u> thousands of years. _____
     B   C D

_____ **14.** It takes <u>over</u> four years <u>for</u> light <u>from</u> the nearest star <u>reaching</u> the earth. _____
      A   B C   D

_____ **15.** <u>In</u> the mid-1900s, an <u>increasing</u> number <u>of jobs</u> in the United States have involved the
    A   B   C

<u>handling of</u> information. _____
   D

Lesson 40

ERRORS WITH ARTICLES

Like errors with prepositions, errors with articles are sometimes hard to catch. This is partly because of the complexity of the article system in English, and partly because articles, like prepositions, are "small words," and one's eye tends to skip over errors involving these words.

The basic uses of articles are explained in the chart:

Indefinite Articles *a* and *an*	Definite Article *the*	No Article (ø)
A or *an* is used before singular nouns when one does not have a specific person, place, thing, or concept in mind: an orange a chair	*The* is used before singular, plural, and noncount nouns when one does not have a specific person, place, thing, or concept in mind: the orange the oranges the fruit the chair the chairs the furniture	No article is used before noncount nouns or plural nouns when one does not have specific persons, places, concepts, or things in mind: ø orange ø oranges ø fruit ø chair ø chairs ø furniture

The indefinite article *a* is used before words that begin with a consonant sound (*a chair, a book*); *an* is used before words that begin with a vowel sound (*an orange, an ocean liner*). Before words that begin with the letters *h-* and *u-*, either *a* or *an* can be used, depending on the pronunciation of the words.

Vowel Sounds	Consonant Sounds
an honor	a hat
an umbrella	a university

There are also some specific rules for using (or not using) articles that you should be aware of.

- An indefinite article can be used to mean "one." It is also used to mean "per."

    a half, a quarter, a third, a tenth
    a mile a minute (one mile per minute)
    an apple a day (one apple per day)

- A definite article is used when there is only one example of the thing or person, or when the identity of the thing or person is clear.

    The Moon went behind some clouds. (There's only one moon.)
    Please open *the door*. (You know which door I mean.)

- A definite article is usually used before these expressions of time and position.

the morning	the front	the beginning
the afternoon	the back	the middle
the evening*	the center	the end
	the top	
the past	the bottom	
the present		
the future		

---

* No article is used in the expression "at night."

- A definite article comes before a singular noun that is used as a representative of an entire class of things. This is especially common with the names of animals, trees, inventions, musical instruments, and parts of the body.

  The tiger is the largest cat.
  My favorite tree is *the oak*.
  The Wright bothers invented *the airplane*.
  The oboe is a woodwind instrument.
  The heart pumps blood.

- A definite article is used before expressions with a ordinal number. No article is used before expressions with cardinal numbers.

the first	one
the fourth chapter	Chapter Four
the seventh volume	Volume Seven

- A definite article is used before decades and centuries.

the 1930s	the 1800s
the fifties	the twenty-first century

- A definite article is usually used before superlative forms of adjectives.

the widest river	the most important decision

- A definite article is used in quantity expressions in this pattern: quantifier + *of* + *the* + noun.

many of the textbooks	not much of the paper
some of the water	most of the students
all of the people	a few of the photographs

  These expressions can also be used without the phrase *of the*.

many textbooks	not much paper
some water	most students
all people	a few photographs

- A definite article is used before the name of a group of people or a nationality. No article is used before the name of a language.

  The Swedish are proud of their ancestors, *the Vikings*.
  She learned to speak *Swedish* when she lived in Stockholm.

- A definite article is used when an adjective is used without a noun to mean "people who are. . . ."

  Both the *young and the old* will enjoy this movie.
  The poor have many problems.

- A definite article is used before a noncount noun or a plural noun when it is followed by a modifier. No article is used when these nouns appear alone.

  The rice that I bought today is in the bag.
  Rice is a staple in many countries.
  Trees provide shade.
  The trees in this park are mostly evergreens.

- A definite article is used before the name of a field of study followed by an *of* phrase. If a field is used alone, or is preceded by an adjective, no article is used.

the literature of the twentieth century	literature
the history of the United States	American history

- Definite articles are used before the "formal" names of nations, states, and cities. (These usually contain *of* phrases.) No articles are used before the common names of nations, states, and cities.

  the United States of America   America

  the state of Montana   Montana

  the city of Philadelphia   Philadelphia

- Definite articles are used before most plural geographic names: the names of groups of lakes, mountains, and islands. No article is used before the names of individual lakes, mountains, and islands.

  the Great Lakes   Lake Powell

  the Rocky Mountains   Mount Washington

  the Hawaiian Islands   Long Island

In the Written Expression section, there are three main types of errors involving articles:

INCORRECT ARTICLE CHOICE

One of the most common errors is the use of *a* in place of *an* or vice versa. Fortunately, this is also the easiest type of error to detect. Another error is *a* or *an* used in place of *the*, or *the* in place of *a* or *an*.

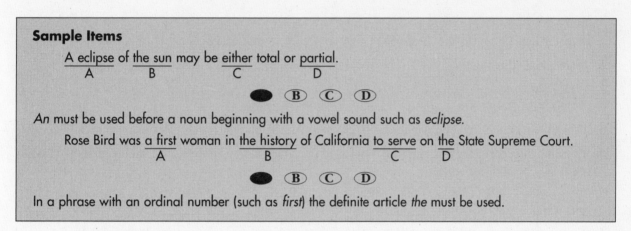

Sample Items

A eclipse of the sun may be either total or partial.
  A   B   C   D

● Ⓑ Ⓒ Ⓓ

An must be used before a noun beginning with a vowel sound such as *eclipse*.

Rose Bird was a first woman in the history of California to serve on the State Supreme Court.
      A   B   C   D

● Ⓑ Ⓒ Ⓓ

In a phrase with an ordinal number (such as *first*) the definite article *the* must be used.

INCORRECT OMISSION OR INCLUSION OF AN ARTICLE

Sometimes an article is used when none is needed, or one is omitted when one is required.

Sample Items

Slag consists of waste materials and impurities which rise to top of melted metals.
        A   B   C   D

Ⓐ Ⓑ ● Ⓓ

The definite article *the* should not be omitted from the phrase *the top of*.

The most asteroids are beyond the orbit of the planet Mars.
  A   B   C   D

● Ⓑ Ⓒ Ⓓ

Definite articles are used only before quantity expressions that contain *of* phrases. (*Most asteroids* or *Most of the asteroids* are both correct in this sentence.)

USE OF A DEFINITE ARTICLE IN PLACE OF A POSSESSIVE

A definite article may be incorrectly used in place of a possessive word—*its*, *his*, *her*, or *their*.

Sample Item

The Ozark Mountains of Arkansas are famous for the rugged beauty.
<u>A</u>   <u>B</u>   <u>C</u>   <u>D</u>

Ⓐ Ⓑ Ⓒ ●

The should correctly read *their* because the sentence refers to the beauty belonging to the Ozark Mountains.

EXERCISE 40.1

Focus: Identifying the correct and incorrect use of articles.
Directions: Underline the forms that correctly complete the sentence.

1. Only about (the one/one) percent of (the water/water) on Earth is (the fresh/fresh) water.

2. (The mineral/Mineral) phosphate is (the most/most) common ingredient of all types of (the fertilizers/fertilizers).

3. (The/A) process of refining minerals requires (a/an) huge amount of (an electrical/electrical) energy.

4. (A humor/Humor) runs through (the American/American) literature from (the earliest/earliest) times until (the present/present).

5. (The ozone/Ozone) layer acts as (a/an) umbrella against (the most/most) of (the Sun's/Sun's) dangerous rays.

6. In (the early/early) 1800s, Sequoia, (a Cherokee/Cherokee) leader, created (the/a) first written form of (a North/North) American Indian language.

7. (The Goddard/Goddard) family of (the New/New) England produced some of (the/a) finest furniture made in (the United/United) States in (the seventeenth/seventeenth) century.

8. (The popcorn/Popcorn) has (a/the) same food value as any other kind of (a corn/corn).

9. One of (the most/most) important tools for (a research/research) in social science is (a well-written/well-written) questionnaire.

10. Native to (the American/American) West, (the/a) coyote came east early in (the twentieth/twentieth) century when its chief natural competitor, (the/a) wolf, died out.

11. (The nineteenth/Nineteenth) century astronomer Alvin G. Clarke built hundreds of (the refracting/refracting) telescopes during (the/his) lifetime.

12. (The Hawaiian/Hawaiian) Islands are among (the most/most) geographically isolated islands on (the Earth/Earth).

EXERCISE 40.2

Focus: Identifying and correcting errors with articles. (Note: One or two items in this exercise do not focus on article errors. These are marked in the answer key with an asterisk.)

Directions: Decide which of the four underlined words or phrases—(A), (B), (C), or (D)—would not be considered correct, and write the letter of the expression in the blank. Then, on the line at the end of the sentence, write a correction for the underlined phrase.

_____ **1.** The most butterfly eggs are coated with a sticky substance that holds them to
                        A   B   C

plants. _____
D

_____ **2.** A number of large insurance companies have the headquarters in Hartford,
                 A   B   C   D

Connecticut. _____

_____ **3.** To be effective, an advertisement must first attract an attention. _____
                        A   B   C   D

_____ **4.** Virgin Islands National Park features a underwater preserve with coral reefs and colorful
                                                                 A   B   C

tropical fish. _____
               D

_____ **5.** Arthritis, a painful swelling of the joints, is often associated with elderly people, but can
                         A   B   C

afflict young as well. _____
            D

_____ **6.** Wilmington is an only large city in the state of Delaware. _____
                              A   B   C   D

_____ **7.** About the third of the Earth's land surface is covered by relatively flat plains. _____
                       A   B   C   D

_____ **8.** In the 1920s, gasoline companies began giving away free road maps to
                    A   B   C

the customers. _____
       D

_____ **9.** The Tropic of Cancer is imaginary line that marks the northern boundary of the Earth's
                  A   B   C   D

tropical zone. _____

_____ **10.** Hereford cows are one of most common breeds of cattle raised for beef. _____
                  A   B   C   D

_____ **11.** American soprano Kathleen Battle taught music in elementary school before beginning the
                                                        A   B

career as a professional singer. _____
C   D

_____ **12.** In 1891, first state law to help local communities pay for highways was passed in New
                         A   B   C   D

Jersey. _____

_____ **13.** Lumber is dried and seasoned in an heated chamber called a dry kiln. _____
              A   B   C   D

_____ **14.** Grandfather Mountain, a highest mountain in the Blue Ridge mountain range, is in North
                                          A   B   C   D
Carolina. _____

_____ **15.** The term "baritone" refers to the range of male voice that lies between tenor to
              A   B   C   D
bass. _____

_____ **16.** It was around 1925 that accurate, convenient system for recording the choreography of
                        A   B   C
ballet was developed. _____
     D

_____ **17.** Richard Byrd was the first person in the history to fly over the North Pole. _____
                            A   B   C   D

_____ **18.** At beginning of the Civil War, Matthew Brady was authorized to accompany the Union Army
              A   B   C
and take photographs. _____
          D

_____ **19.** In 1878 in San Francisco, Kate Wiggins open the first kindergarten on
                    A   B   C
the West Coast. _____
     D

_____ **20.** The tulip tree, the tallest broadleaf plant in the eastern United States, may reach height of
              A   B   C   D
over 200 feet. _____

Lesson 41

ERRORS WITH COMPARATIVES AND SUPERLATIVES

Most adjectives have three forms: the absolute (the basic adjective form), the comparative, and the superlative. Comparatives are used to show that one item has more of some quality that another does.

George is *taller* than his brother.

Superlatives are used to show that one item in a group of three or more has the greatest amount of some quality.

He was the *tallest* man in the room.

The chart explains how comparatives and superlatives are formed:

	Absolute	Comparative	Superlative
One-syllable adjectives	warm	warmer	the warmest
Two-syllable adjectives ending with -y	funny	funnier	the funniest
Other two-syllable adjectives	common	more common	the most common
Adjectives with three or more syllables	important	more important	the most important

Some two-syllable adjectives have two correct forms of both the comparative and the superlative:

narrower	clever	polite
more narrow	more clever	more polite

narrowest	cleverest	politest
most narrow	most clever	most polite

A "negative" comparison can be expressed with the words *less* and *least*. *Less* and *least* are used no matter how many syllables an adjective has.

less bright	less expensive
the least bright	the least expensive

The absolute form of a few adjectives ends in *-er* (*tender, bitter, slender, clever*, and so on.) Don't confuse these with the comparative forms (*more bitter* or *bitterer*, for example).

Many adverbs also have comparative and superlative forms. The comparative and superlative forms of all *-ly* adverbs are formed with *more* and *most*.

more brightly	more importantly
most brightly	most importantly

A few adjectives and adverbs have irregular comparative and superlative forms:

Irregular Comparatives and Superlatives

good/well	better	the best
bad/badly	worse	the worst
far	farther	the farthest
	further	the furthest

(*Far* has two comparative and superlative forms, depending on how the word is used, but the distinction between these two forms will not be tested.)

There are two main types of errors involving comparatives and superlatives:

INCORRECT CHOICE OF THE THREE FORMS

Any of the three forms—absolute, comparative, or superlative—may be incorrectly used in place of one of the other forms.

Sample Items

> Basketball is played at a much fast pace than baseball.
>   A   B   C   D
>
>   Ⓐ Ⓑ ● Ⓓ

The comparative form *faster* is needed because two concepts—the pace of *basketball* and the pace of *baseball*—are being compared.

> The deep oceans contain some of the stranger of all living creatures.
>   A   B   C   D
>
>   Ⓐ Ⓑ ● Ⓓ

This sentence does not compare two groups; a superlative form (*strangest*) is required.

INCORRECT FORMS OF COMPARATIVES AND SUPERLATIVES

Incorrect forms such as *more bigger*, *most hot*, and so on, may appear.

Sample Item

> The most small vessels in the circulatory system are capillaries.
>   A   B   C   D
>
>   ● Ⓑ Ⓒ Ⓓ

The correct form is *smallest* because *small* is a one-syllable adjective.

Peterson's TOEFL CBT Success

EXERCISE 41

Focus: Identifying and correcting errors and correct forms of comparatives and superlatives.

Directions: If the underlined form is correct, mark the sentence *C*. If the underlined form is incorrect, mark the sentence *X*, and write a correction for the underlined form in the blank at the end of the sentence.

_____ 1. The period is probably *the most easiest* punctuation mark to use. _____

_____ 2. When metal replaced wood in the construction of ships' hulls, *more strong and large* ships could be built. _____

_____ 3. Charcoal is *the most commonly* used cooking fuel in the world. _____

_____ 4. Soft solder melts at a *low* temperature than ordinary solder. _____

_____ 5. Many of the nation's *most important* documents are stored in the National Archives Building in Washington, D.C. _____

_____ 6. The surfboards used twenty-five years ago were *more heavier* than the ones used by surfers today. _____

_____ 7. Few American politicians have spoken *more eloquently* than William Jennings Bryan. _____

_____ 8. Subterranean termites are the *more destructive* type of termites in the United States. _____

_____ 9. Prince Edward Island is the *less* populous of Canada's ten provinces. _____

_____ 10. During a depression, economic conditions are far *worst* than they are during a recession. _____

_____ 11. One of *the most basic* American contributions to technology was the so-called "American system" of interchangeable machine parts. _____

_____ 12. The horse chestnut has a stronger, *bitter* taste than other chestnuts. _____

_____ 13. Chicago's Field Museum is one of the largest and *better known* natural history museums in the United States. _____

_____ 14. Baltimore has one of the world's *most finest* natural harbors. _____

_____ 15. The Kennedy-Nixon race of 1960 was *the closest* presidential election of this century. _____

_____ 16. The finback whale is the fastest of all whales, and only the blue whale is *largest*. _____

_____ 17. The cello is shorter and *more slender* than the double bass. _____

_____ 18. Oil floats on water because oil is *less dense* than water. _____

Lesson 42

ERRORS IN WORD ORDER

Most word order errors in written expression consist of two words in reverse order. Some of the most common examples of this type of error are given below:

Error	Example	Correction
Noun + adjective	drivers careful	careful drivers
Noun + possessive	clothing women's	women's clothing
Main verb + auxiliary	finished are	are finished
Adjective + adverb	a basic extremely idea	an extremely basic idea
Verb + subject (in an indirect question or other *wh-* clause)	Tell me where is it. I spoke to John when was he here.	Tell me where it is. I spoke to John when he was here.
Preposition/adverb clause marker + adverb	after immediately	immediately after
Participle + adverb	baked freshly bread	freshly baked bread
Relative pronoun + preposition	the house which in she lives	the house in which she lives
adverb, adjective, or quantifier + *almost*	totally almost, late almost, all almost	almost totally, almost late, almost all
enough + adjective*	enough good	good enough

* Enough can correctly be used before nouns: *enough money, enough time. Enough* may also be used before an adjective when the adjective comes before a noun. (There weren't *enough good seats* at the concert.)

Sample Items

Goods such as flowers fresh and seafood are often shipped by air.
 A   B   C   D

Ⓐ ● Ⓒ Ⓓ

The adjective *fresh* must come before the noun *flowers: fresh flowers.*

Visitors to Vancouver often comment on how beautiful its setting is and on how clean is it.
       A   B   C   D

Ⓐ Ⓑ Ⓒ ●

The correct word order is subject + verb: *it is.*

EXERCISE 42.1

Focus: Identifying and correcting word order in sentences.

Directions: If the word order of the underlined form is correct, mark the sentence *C*. If the word order is incorrect, mark the sentence *X*, and write a correction in the blank at the end of the sentence.

_____ 1. The Douglas fir is the *source chief* of lumber in the state of Oregon. _____

_____ 2. The painted turtle is a *colored brightly*, smooth-shelled turtle. _____

_____ 3. Trained in Europe, John Sargent became *an extremely successful* portrait painter in the United States. _____

_____ 4. Insects lived on the Earth *before long* the first mammal appeared. _____

_____ 5. The freezing point is the temperature *which at* a liquid becomes a solid. _____

_____ 6. Ammonia, a compound of nitrogen and hydrogen, has many *industrial uses*. _____

_____ 7. The Atlantic coastline of the United States is about 400 *longer miles* than the Gulf coastline. _____

_____ 8. Zoos provide an opportunity to study a wide range of animals, often in their *habitats natural*. _____

_____ 9. A test pilot tries out new kinds of aircraft to determine if *are they* safe. _____

_____ 10. The air of the upper atmosphere is just *enough dense* to ignite meteors by friction. _____

_____ 11. More pigs are raised in Iowa than in *other any* state. _____

_____ 12. Cirrus clouds are composed *entirely almost* of ice crystals. _____

_____ 13. Many sailboats are equipped with small engines for times when there is not *enough wind*. _____

_____ 14. Few of the doctors in the thirteen Colones had any *training formal* as physicians. _____

_____ 15. Margaret Wise Brown was a successful writer of *books children's*. _____

EXERCISE 42.2

Focus: Identifying errors involving word-order. (Note: One or two items in this exercise do not focus on word order errors. These are marked in the answer key with an asterisk.)

Directions: Decide which of the four underlined words or phrases—(A), (B), (C), or (D)—would not be considered correct, and write the letter of the expression in the blank. Then, on the line at the end of the sentence, write the correction for the underlined phrase.

_____ 1. During <u>pioneer times</u>, the Allegheny Mountains <u>were</u> a <u>barrier major</u>
             A   B   C
    <u>to transportation</u>. _____
      D

_____ 2. In Philadelphia's Franklin Institute, <u>there is a</u> <u>working model</u> of a <u>human heart</u> <u>enough large</u>
                                       A   B   C   D
    for visitors to walk through. _____

_____ **3.** The task of the cartographer is to represent the Earth's surface at a reduced greatly
                              A   B   C   D
scale. _____

_____ **4.** Mutualism is a relationship between animal species which in both benefit. _____
                                A   B   C   D

_____ **5.** To grow well, a tree must be well-suited to the area where is it planted. _____
                    A   B   C   D

_____ **6.** The development of transistors made possible it to reduce the size of many electronic
                    A   B   C
devices. _____
    D

_____ **7.** Twelve drawings usually have to be prepared for second each of animated film. _____
                                A   B   C   D

_____ **8.** During solar storms, the Earth is bombarded with abnormally high amounts
                    A   B   C
of radiate. _____
    D

_____ **9.** Sloths are moving slow, shaggy mammals that are often seen hanging upside down from
                          A   B   C
tree limbs. _____
    D

_____ **10.** Carbohydrates as such sugar or starches are important energy sources for humans and
                                  A   B   C
animals. _____
    D

_____ **11.** An umbra is a shadow's darkest central part where is light totally excluded. _____
                                A   B   C   D

_____ **12.** Frank Lloyd Wright is known for his original highly methods of harmonizing buildings with
                                        A   B   C
their surroundings. _____
    D

_____ **13.** Some algae are microscopic and consist of one only cell, but others are large plants contain-
                                A   B   C
ing many cells. _____
    D

_____ **14.** A fully grown male mountain lion may be eight long feet. _____
                    A   B   C   D

_____ **15.** Stone fruits are fruits such as peaches and plums in which a hard pit surrounded is by
                                        A   B   C
soft pulp. _____
    D

_____ **16.** Job enrichment is a technique used to increase satisfaction workers' by giving them
                                  A   B   C
more responsibilities. _____
    D

_____ **17.** The first permanent European settlement in what is now Mississippi was a center trading in
                          A   B   C   D
Biloxi. _____

_____ **18.** In the early 1800s, a dispute developed among geologists how about rocks are
               A   B   C   D
formed. _____

_____ **19.** Most country music songs are deeply personal and deal with themes of love, lonely, and
                 A   B   C   D
separation. _____

_____ **20.** On nights when is the sky clear and the air calm, the Earth's surface rapidly radiates heat
                            A   B   C   D
into the atmosphere. _____

Lesson 43

ERRORS WITH CONJUNCTIONS

You may encounter errors with either **correlative conjunctions** or **coordinate conjunctions**.

ERRORS WITH CORRELATIVE CONJUNCTIONS

Correlative conjunctions are two-part adjectives. Errors usually involve an incorrect combination of the two parts, such as *neither . . . or* or *not only . . . and*. Anytime you see a sentence containing correlative conjunctions you should be on the lookout for this type of error. This is an easy error to spot!

Correlative Conjunctions

either...or
neither...nor
both...and
not only...but also
whether...or

Another error is the use of *both . . . and* to join three elements.

Sample Items

X rays <u>have</u> important <u>applications</u>, not only in medicine <u>and</u> in <u>industry</u>.
    A   B   C   D

Ⓐ   Ⓑ   ●   Ⓓ

The correct pattern is *not only . . . but also.*

The air that surrounds our planet is both odorless, colorless, and invisible.
   A   B   C   D

Ⓐ   Ⓑ   Ⓒ   ●

Because *both . . . and* can only be used to join two elements, the word *both* must be eliminated to correct the sentence.

ERRORS WITH COORDINATE CONJUNCTIONS

The conjunction *and* is correctly used to show addition; *or* is used to show choice between alternatives; *but* is used to show contrast or opposition.

Sample Item

Brakes and clutches <u>serve</u> very different <u>functions</u> in an automobile, <u>and</u> their principles of
           A   B   C

operation are <u>nearly</u> the same.
          D

(A) (B) ● (D)

The first clause discusses how brakes and clutches are different; the second clause discusses how they are the same. Therefore, the conjunction joining them must show contrast. Choice (C) should read *but*.

EXERCISE 43

Focus: Identifying errors involving conjunctions.

Directions: If the underlined form is correct, mark the sentence *C*. If the underlined form is incorrect, mark the sentence *X*, and write a correction for the underlined form in the blank at the end of the sentence.

_____ 1. Model airplanes can be guided *both* by control wires or by radio transmitters. _____

_____ 2. Information in a computer can be lost because it is no longer stored or because it is stored *but* cannot be retrieved. _____

_____ 3. John Lancaster Spaulding was not only a religious leader *and also* a social reformer. _____

_____ 4. Although fish can hear, they have neither external ears *or* eardrums. _____

_____ 5. In all animals, whether simple *and* complex, enzymes aid in the digestion of food. _____

_____ 6. The two most common methods florists use to tint flowers are the spray method *or* the absorption method. _____

_____ 7. Beekeepers can sell *either* the honey and the beeswax that their bees produce. _____

_____ 8. The alloys brass *and* bronze both contain copper as their principle metals. _____

_____ 9. The human brain is often compared to a computer, *and* such an analogy can be misleading. _____

_____ 10. Rust both corrodes the surface of metal *but also* weakens its structure. _____

_____ 11. A work of science fiction generally uses scientific discoveries and advanced technology, either real *or* imaginary, as part of its plot. _____

_____ 12. Community theater *both* provides entertainment for local audiences but also furnishes a creative outlet for amateurs interested in drama. _____

_____ 13. The heron is a long-legged wading bird that preys on *both frogs*, fish, and eels. _____

_____ 14. For over twenty years after winning the World Chess Championship in 1972, Bobby Fischer played in *either* a tournament nor an exhibition game. _____

_____ 15. Designing fabric requires not only artistic talent but also a knowledge of fiber *and* of textile machinery. _____

Answer Sheet

Mini-Test 7: Written Expression

1. Ⓐ Ⓑ Ⓒ Ⓓ	10. Ⓐ Ⓑ Ⓒ Ⓓ	18. Ⓐ Ⓑ Ⓒ Ⓓ
2. Ⓐ Ⓑ Ⓒ Ⓓ	11. Ⓐ Ⓑ Ⓒ Ⓓ	19. Ⓐ Ⓑ Ⓒ Ⓓ
3. Ⓐ Ⓑ Ⓒ Ⓓ	12. Ⓐ Ⓑ Ⓒ Ⓓ	20. Ⓐ Ⓑ Ⓒ Ⓓ
4. Ⓐ Ⓑ Ⓒ Ⓓ	13. Ⓐ Ⓑ Ⓒ Ⓓ	21. Ⓐ Ⓑ Ⓒ Ⓓ
5. Ⓐ Ⓑ Ⓒ Ⓓ	14. Ⓐ Ⓑ Ⓒ Ⓓ	22. Ⓐ Ⓑ Ⓒ Ⓓ
6. Ⓐ Ⓑ Ⓒ Ⓓ	15. Ⓐ Ⓑ Ⓒ Ⓓ	23. Ⓐ Ⓑ Ⓒ Ⓓ
7. Ⓐ Ⓑ Ⓒ Ⓓ	16. Ⓐ Ⓑ Ⓒ Ⓓ	24. Ⓐ Ⓑ Ⓒ Ⓓ
8. Ⓐ Ⓑ Ⓒ Ⓓ	17. Ⓐ Ⓑ Ⓒ Ⓓ	25. Ⓐ Ⓑ Ⓒ Ⓓ
9. Ⓐ Ⓑ Ⓒ Ⓓ		

MINI-TEST 7: WRITTEN EXPRESSION

Directions: The sentences below have four underlined words or phrases, (A), (B), (C), and (D). You must identify the *one* underlined expression that must be changed for the sentence to be correct. Then find the number of the question on your answer sheet above and fill in the appropriate letter.

Time: 12 minutes

1. Commercial bakeries <u>can make</u> thousands of <u>loaves</u> of bread <u>on one time</u> by <u>using</u> automated
                 A   B   C   D
   equipment.

2. North America is <u>a third-largest</u> <u>of the seven</u> <u>continents</u>.
                A   B   C   D

3. Neither humans <u>or</u> dogs <u>can hear</u> as <u>well</u> as <u>cats</u>.
              A   B   C   D

4. <u>The astronomer</u> George Hale was <u>a pioneer</u> in <u>the art</u> of <u>photograph</u> the Sun.
          A   B   C   D

5. Trucks <u>can be</u> used <u>transport</u> <u>a wide</u> <u>variety</u> of cargoes.
             A   B   C   D

6. Pikes Peak, <u>named for</u> explorer Zebulon Pike, is Colorado's <u>most famous</u> <u>but</u> not its <u>most highest</u>
              A   B   C   D
   mountain.

7. Identical colors <u>may appear</u> to be quite different when <u>are they</u> viewed <u>against</u> different backgrounds.
                   A   B   C   D

8. Oceanography is not <u>a single</u> science <u>and</u> rather a group of disciplines <u>with</u> a common <u>focus</u>.
                       A   B   C   D

9. <u>Until 1960</u>, Maine was unique in that <u>it held</u> presidential and congressional elections <u>on</u> September,
   A   B   C
   two months <u>earlier</u> than the rest of the nation.
              D

10. Snowshoes allow a person <u>to walking</u> on snow without <u>sinking</u> into it because <u>they</u> distribute <u>the</u>
                                 A   B   C
<u>person's</u> weight over a wide area.
 D

11. Fuel injection engines <u>employ</u> injectors <u>instead</u> a carburetor <u>to spray</u> fuel <u>into</u> the cylinders.
                            A   B   C   D

12. <u>Ocean</u> currents have <u>a</u> enormous effect <u>on life</u> on <u>this planet</u>.
    A   B   C   D

13. Hydraulic elevators are <u>still used</u> in some <u>old</u> buildings, but <u>all almost</u> new buildings are <u>equipped</u>
                              A   B   C
<u>with</u> electrical elevators.
 D

14. Diaries <u>and</u> journals <u>writing</u> during Colonial times provide <u>the best</u> records of <u>that era</u>.
            A   B   C   D

15. Frequently, the <u>combination of</u> several spices will <u>result of</u> a more <u>pleasing</u> flavor <u>than</u> the use of just
                       A   B   C   D
one.

16. Gold topaz is <u>much rare</u> <u>than</u> <u>either</u> white or <u>blue</u> topaz.
               A   B   C   D

17. A mosaic is <u>picture</u> <u>made</u> from small bits of <u>colored</u> glass colored glass <u>or</u> tile.
               A   B   C   D

18. Reclamation is <u>the successful</u> attempt <u>to make</u> deserts, marshlands, or other unusable land <u>suitable of</u>
                   A   B   C
farming or <u>building</u>.
        D

19. A <u>successful</u> salesperson <u>must have</u> an intuitive <u>understanding</u> of <u>psychology human</u>.
           A   B   C   D

20. The University of Wisconsin was <u>the first</u> school <u>to make</u> a serious effort <u>teach</u> students <u>public</u>
                                   A   B   C
administration.
     D

21. <u>Some</u> underground water is <u>enough safe</u> to drink, <u>but</u> all surface water must be <u>treated</u>.
     A   B   C   D

22. <u>A feeding</u> animal will usually allow competitors <u>approaching</u> only <u>within</u> a certain distance, the
     A   B   C
<u>boundaries</u> <u>of which</u> are called its feeding territory.
               D

23. Most familiar <u>type of</u> pump <u>in use</u> today is <u>the</u> piston pump.
     A   B   C   D

24. <u>The term</u> "forgetting" refers <u>to</u> the loss, whether temporary <u>and</u> long-term, of material <u>that</u> has
     A   B   C   D
previously been learned.

25. Dietitians urge people <u>to eat</u> <u>the banana</u> a day to get <u>enough potassium</u> in <u>their diet</u>.
                       A   B   C   D

MINI-LESSONS FOR SECTION 2

PREPOSITION USE

It is important for the Structure and especially the Written Expression parts of the test that you be familiar with the correct usage of prepositions. The mini-lessons for this section consist of lists of prepositions in combination with other words and in various set expressions. The exercises allow you to practice using these prepositions in sentences.

MINI-LESSON 2.1

Adjectives/Participles + Prepositions, Part A

acceptable to	characteristic of	eligible for
accustomed to	close to	equipped with
adequate for	composed of	equal to
afraid of	contrary to	essential to/for
aware of	dependent on	familiar with
based on	different from	famous for
capable of	disappointed in/with	

Exercise: Fill in the blanks in the sentences below with the correct prepositions.

1. I was disappointed _____ the grade I received on my last essay.

2. The Medical Center is close _____ campus.

3. Now that she has graduated, Anne is no longer dependent _____ her parents for financial support.

4. Catherine became accustomed _____ spicy foods when she was traveling.

5. Table salt is composed _____ two elements, sodium and chlorine.

6. Is your bicycle equipped _____ a light?

7. This computer isn't capable _____ running this software.

8. Bluegrass music is somewhat different _____ other types of country music.

9. Washington State is famous _____ its apples.

10. Was your choice of research topic acceptable _____ your instructor?

11. People who are afraid _____ heights are called acrophobes.

12. Water is essential _____ all life.

13. Were you aware _____ the regulation against smoking in this area?

14. Tepees are characteristic _____ the Indian tribes of the Great Plains.

15. Will this office be adequate _____ your needs?

16. I'm not familiar _____ that song.

17. One meter is approximately equal _____ a yard.

18. This movie is based _____ a true story.

19. This summer, he'll be eligible _____ a three-week vacation.

20. What he said is contrary _____ common sense.

MINI-LESSON 2.2

Adjectives/Participles + Prepositions, Part B

free of

independent of

inferior to

married to

native to

necessary for/to

next to

opposed to

opposite of*

perfect for

possible for

preferable to

related to

relevant to

satisfied with

suitable for

surprised at/by

typical of

---

* *Opposite of* is used for words or concepts that are completely different, such as "large" and "small." When *opposite* means "across from," it is not used with *of*. "The bank is *opposite* the post office on Cedar Street."

Exercise: Fill in the blanks in the sentences below with the correct prepositions.

1. The art museum is located next _____ the museum of natural history on State Street.

2. Many vegetables, including tomatoes, potatoes, and corn, are native _____ the New World.

3. This style of architecture is typical _____ the Colonial period.

4. Oxygen, fuel, and heat are all necessary _____ combustion.

5. Two people would find this apartment too crowded, but it's perfect _____ one.

6. This variety of seed is inferior _____ the type I planted last year.

7. Were you surprised _____ the grade you received?

8. The opposite _____ *old fashioned* is *modern*.

9. House cats are distantly related _____ lions and tigers.

10. Is this type of soil suitable _____ growing tomatoes?

11. The point that Murray brought up wasn't really relevant _____ the discussion.

12. Organically raised crops are free _____ chemical pesticides and herbicides.

13. A grade of A- is preferable _____ one of B+.

14. If you're not satisfied _____ your essay, then I suggest that you rewrite it.

15. Abolitionists were people who were opposed _____ the practice of slavery.

16. The United States became independent _____ England in 1776.

17. Is it possible _____ me to get an appointment sometime next week?

18. President James Madison was married _____ one of the most famous of all first ladies, Dolley Madison.

MINI-LESSON 2.3

Nouns + Prepositions

approach to	exception to	origin of
attention to	experience with	price of
cause of	expert on	probability of
contribution to	form of	quality of
component of	group of	reason for
cure for	improvement in	reliance on
decrease in	increase in	result of
demand for	influence on	solution to
effect of/on*	interest in	supply of
example of	native of	

_____
* *effect + of + cause*
effect + on + thing or person affected (The effect *of* heat *on* rocks...)

Exercise: Fill in the blanks in the sentences below with the correct prepositions.

1. A decrease _____ the supply _____ a good usually results in an increase _____ the price _____ that good.

2. Once scientists fully understand the cause _____ a disease, it becomes easier for them to find a cure _____ it.

3. Professor Lyle noticed a distinct improvement _____ the quality _____ her students' work.

4. It is believed that sunspots have an influence _____ the Earth's weather patterns.

5. Have you had much experience _____ computers?

6. I'm sorry; I wasn't paying close attention _____ what you said.

7. The professor gave us several examples _____ that phenomenon.

8. Do you know the reason _____ the delay?

9. Interest _____ physical fitness increased during the 1980s.

10. The Dorothy Chandler pavilion is part _____ the Los Angeles Music Center.

11. Linguists have many theories about the origin _____ language.

12. This is an exception _____ the general rule.

13. What approach should I take _____ this problem?

14. The Ivy League is a group _____ eight prestigious universities in the Northeast.

15. People's reliance _____ automobiles as their chief form _____ transportation has increased over the years.

16. I've tried and tried, but I simply can't find a solution _____ this dilemma.

17. The demand _____ personal computers continues to grow.

18. Only a native _____ the United States can serve as president.

19. Economists don't agree on what effects government spending has _____ the economy.

20. Margaret Knight designed some of the components _____ the rotary engine.

MINI-LESSON 2.4

Verbs + Prepositions

account for
adjust to
agree with/on*
attach to
attribute to
begin with
believe in
belong to
combine with
_____

compete with
concentrate on
consist of
contribute to
cooperate with
deal with
depend on
devote to
engage in

insist on
interfere with
plan on
participate in
refer to
rely on
result in
search for

* *agree with* is used with people
   agree on is used with an issue, plan, etc. (I *agreed with* Mary *on* that issue.)

Exercise: Fill in the blanks in the sentences below with the correct prepositions.

1. Do you belong _____ any campus clubs or organizations?

2. Cytology is the branch of biology that deals _____ the structure, form, and life of cells.

3. Maybe you should begin your speech _____ some jokes.

4. Let's concentrate _____ solving this problem before we discuss the other ones.

5. People want friends they can rely _____.

6. Most essays consist _____ an introduction, a body, and a conclusion.

7. We didn't plan _____ such a long delay.

8. If you are engaged _____ any extracurricular activities, you should mention that fact on your résumé.

9. Iron combines _____ oxygen to form rust.

10. After several hours of discussion, the council finally agreed _____ a plan.

11. The accident resulted _____ several minor injuries.

12. Storms on the Sun can interfere _____ radio broadcasts on the Earth.

13. By the late 1940s, television had begun to seriously compete _____ radio for audience and advertisers.

14. That theatrical company can always be depended _____ to deliver a good performance.

15. James didn't have any trouble adjusting _____ the climate in Atlanta because he'd grown up in the South.

16. William insists _____ getting up early, even on weekends.

17. What does this symbol refer _____?

18. Occupational physicians search _____ the causes of injury and sickness at the workplace.

19. Many companies participated _____ the trade fair.

20. How do you account _____ this discrepancy?

21. Do you believe _____ any superstitions?

22. Workaholics devote too much of their time _____ their jobs.

MINI-LESSON 2.5

Phrasal Prepositions

according to	due to	on account of
ahead of	except for	prior to
along with	in favor of	regardless of
because of	in spite of	thanks to
by means of	instead of	together with

Exercise: Fill in the blanks in the sentences below with the correct prepositions.

1. The new highway will be finished ahead _____ schedule.

2. _____ spite _____ the warnings, Phil dove off the cliff.

3. The chairman, along _____ his staff, attended the conference.

4. According _____ my dictionary, you're mispronouncing that word.

5. Prior _____ her wedding, Nicole's last name was Brooks.

6. Are you _____ favor _____ that amendment or against it?

7. _____ account _____ a lack of funds, the university library will now close at nine instead _____ at eleven.

8. Sunsets may appear more colorful because _____ air pollution.

9. Due _____ a computer error, $100,000 was transferred into Judy's checking account.

10. Regardless _____ the final score, I'm sure this will be an exciting game.

11. Glider pilots can actually increase their altitude _____ means _____ hot air currents called thermals.

12. Thanks _____ the financial aid he received, he was able to attend the university.

MINI-LESSON 2.6

In, On, and At, Part A

Expressions of time

in
+ century (*in the eighteenth century*)
+ decade (*in the 1990s*)
+ year (*in 1975*)
+ season (*in the summer*)
+ month (*in July*)
+ parts of the day (*in the morning, in the evening, in the afternoon*)

on
+ days of the week (*on Wednesday*)
+ dates (*on October 7*)

at
+ time of day (*at 6 pm; at noon*)
+ night

Expressions of place

in
+ continent (*in Africa*)
+ country (*in Mexico*)
+ state (*in Pennsylvania*)
+ city (*in Los Angeles*)
+ building (*in the bank*)
+ room (*in the auditorium*)
+ the world

on
+ street (*on Maxwell Street*)
+ floor of a building (*on the fourth floor*)
+ Earth

at
+ address (*at 123 Commonwealth Avenue*)

Exercise: Fill in the blanks in the sentences below with the prepositions *in*, *on*, or *at*.

1. John F. Kennedy was the first president of the United States to be born _____ the twentieth century.

2. Fruit trees generally bloom _____ April or May.

3. Gettysburg, the greatest battle ever fought _____ North America, took place _____ July 1863.

4. I like to shower _____ the morning, but my roommate likes to shower _____ night.

5. The president lives _____ the White House, which is located _____ 1600 Pennsylvania Avenue _____ Washington, D.C.

6. Many advertising agencies are located _____ Madison Avenue _____ New York City.

7. Jazz was so popular _____ the 1920s that the decade is sometimes called the Jazz Age.

8. Leaves turn red and gold _____ the autumn.

9. Most college football games are played _____ Saturdays.

10. Both Washington and Lincoln were born _____ February. Washington was born _____ February 22, Lincoln _____ February 12.

11. About 90 percent of all the people _____ New Jersey live _____ cities.

12. The New Year is celebrated _____ midnight _____ January 1.

13. Dean Hughes' office is _____ the Administration Building _____ the third floor.

14. Quebec is the largest province _____ Canada.

MINI-LESSON 2.7

In, On, and At, Part B

The prepositions *in*, *on*, and *at* are also used in a number of set expressions:

in a book/magazine/newspaper	on a bus/train/etc.	at best/worst
in charge (of)	on fire	at first/last
in common (with)	on the other hand	at once
in danger (of)	on purpose	at the peak (of)
in detail	on radio/television	at present
in existence	on the whole	at the moment
in the front/middle/back		at birth
in general		at death
in practice		at random
in the past/future		
in a row		
in style		
in theory		

Exercise: Fill in the blanks in the sentences below with the prepositions *in*, *on*, or *at*.

1. Did you hear that news _____ television or read it _____ the newspaper?

2. The members of a jury are chosen _____ random from a list of voters.

3. Videophones are not practical _____ present, but they may be _____ the near future.

4. Mr. Grigsby is _____ charge of the marketing department.

5. Please come here _____ once.

6. I'm sure he didn't break the plate _____ purpose.

7. Air travel is _____ its peak _____ the summer.

8. _____ the whole, I enjoyed the movie, but there were a few scenes I didn't like.

9. Corn is planted _____ rows.

10. Claudia has gotten so many speeding tickets that she's _____ danger of losing her driver's license.

11. The story _____ the magazine described the incident _____ great detail.

12. There must be _____ least one vowel in every English word.

13. Five oak trees were planted _____ a row _____ front of the school.

14. This type of music is no longer _____ style.

15. _____ general, I found zoology to be an easier subject than botany.

16. The American Constitution has been _____ existence for over two hundred years.

17. Like many other baby birds, ducklings are blind _____ birth.

18. This book is based _____ part on fact.

19. The ship was _____ fire.

20. _____ theory, this idea is quite difficult to understand; _____ the other hand, it is quite simple _____ practice.

MINI-LESSON 2.8

Other Prepositions

By is often used with forms of communication and transportation:

> *by car, by plane, by phone, by express mail*

(Note: if the noun is plural or is preceded by a determiner, the prepositions *in* or *on* must be used:

> *in cars, on a boat, on the telephone, in a taxi*

By is also used with gerunds to show how an action happened:

> How did you get an appointment with Dr. Blish?
> *By calling his secretary.*

With is used to indicate the idea of accompaniment or possession:

> Melanie came to the party *with her friend.*
> He wanted a house *with a garage.*

Without indicates the opposite relationship:

> Melanie came to the party *without her friend.*
> He bought a house *without a garage.*

With also indicates that an instrument was used to perform an action:

> He opened the door *with a key.*

Without indicates the opposite relationship:

> He opened the door *without a key.*

By and *for* are also used in the following expressions:

by chance	for example
by far	for free
by hand	for now

For is sometimes used to show purpose; it means "to get."

> She went to the store *for toothpaste and shampoo.*

Exercise: Fill in the blanks in the sentences below with the correct prepositions.

1. Magnetic compasses are not very useful on ships _____ steel hulls.

2. Penicillin was discovered more or less _____ chance.

3. Legal aid organizations provide legal advice for poor people for small fees or _____ free.

4. Alaska is _____ far the largest state.

5. Amoebas are so small that they can't be seen _____ a microscope; they can't be seen _____ the naked eye.

6. Fruits, vegetables, and other agricultural products are generally shipped _____ truck.

7. Semaphore operators communicate _____ using flags.

8. The most expensive rugs are made _____ hand.

9. Ice hockey is played _____ a hard rubber disk called a puck.

10. They traveled to the island _____ a boat.

Section 3

READING COMPREHENSION

RED ALERT

INTRODUCTION TO READING COMPREHENSION

INTRODUCTION

This part of the exam tests your ability to read and answer questions about passages written in formal written English. It usually contains five passages (eight on the long form). After each passage there are usually from eight to twelve questions referring to that passage for a total of fifty questions (approximately 75 on the long form). The passages vary in length from about seven lines to about thirty-five.

In July 1995, Section 3 of TOEFL changed somewhat. The first part of the section, which consisted of thirty individual vocabulary items, was eliminated. More vocabulary-in-context items have been added. These ask about the meaning of words in the passages. The passages have become somewhat longer, and the time limit has been extended by 10 minutes.

Sample Items

A bird's territory may be small or large. Some males claim only their nest and the area right around it, while others claim far larger territories that include their feeding area. Gulls, penguins, and other
(5) waterfowl nest in huge colonies, but even in the biggest colonies, each male and his mate have small territories of their own immediately around their nests.

Males defend their territory chiefly against other males of the same species. In some cases, a warning call
(10) or threatening pose may be all the defense needed, but in other cases, intruders may refuse to leave peacefully.

1. What is the main topic of this passage?

(A) Birds that live in colonies
(B) How birds defend their territory
(C) The behavior of birds
(D) Territoriality in birds

Choice (A) deals with particular types of birds—gulls, penguins, and others—but the passage concerns all birds. Choice (B) deals only with the concept of defending a territory. This is the topic of the second paragraph, but not of the passage as a whole. Choice (C) is too general; there are many types of bird behavior that this passage does not examine. Choice (D) is best, because all the aspects of the passage deal with some factors of birds' territories.

Sample Items (Continued)

2. According to the passage, male birds defend their territories primarily against

   (A) female birds
   (B) birds of other species
   (C) males of their own species
   (D) carnivorous mammals

Lines 8–9 state that male birds "defend their territory chiefly against other males of the same species." There is no mention in the passage of any of the other options.

3. It can be inferred from the passage that gulls and penguins

   (A) do not claim a feeding area as part of their territories
   (B) share their territories with many other birds
   (C) leave their colonies during their nesting season
   (D) do not build nests

The passage says that birds that claim their feeding areas have large territories compared to those that do not. Birds living in colonies have "small territories . . . immediately around their nests," indicating that their feeding areas would not be part of their territories. Choice (B) contradicts lines 6-7, which state that "each male and his mate have small territories of their own." Choice (C) is unlikely because the passage indicates that these birds' nests are part of large colonies; they would not leave during nesting season. Choice (D) is incorrect because these birds' nests are part of their territories.

4. In line 4, the word "their" refers to

   (A) male birds'
   (B) a male bird and his mate's
   (C) gulls'
   (D) the colonies'

Substitute all four answer choices for the word *their* in line 4; as you'll see, only (A) is a logical choice.

5. The word "intruders" in line 11 is closest in meaning to

   (A) invaders
   (B) youngsters
   (C) defenders
   (D) guests

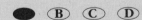

It is clear from the passage that the "intruders" mentioned in this line are male birds that "refuse to leave peacefully." Of the four answer choices, only "invaders" (persons or creatures that attack from the outside) could be substituted for the word "intruders" with no major change in meaning.

THE PASSAGES

The passages cover a wide range of topics, but in general can be classified as follows:

1. **Science and technology (40 percent)** Includes astronomy, geology, chemistry, physics, mathematics, zoology, botany, medicine, engineering, mechanics, and so on.

2. **North American history, government, geography, and culture (20 percent)**

3. **Art (15 percent)** Includes literature, painting, architecture, dance, drama, and so on.

4. **Social science (10 percent)** Includes anthropology, economics, psychology, urban studies, sociology, and so on.

5. **Biography (15 percent)**

Some passages may be classified in more than one way. For example, a biography might be about the life of a historical figure, an artist, or a scientist.

If there is a national context for any of the passages, it is American or occasionally Canadian. Therefore, if a passage is about history, it will be about the history of the United States or Canada.

Although the passages deal with various topics, the style in which they are written is similar, and they usually follow fairly simple patterns of organization.

The vocabulary used in the Reading Comprehension portion is fairly sophisticated. There will almost certainly be words that you do not recognize. Sometimes you can guess the meaning of these words by context. However, it is not necessary to understand all the vocabulary in the passages in order to answer the questions.

THE QUESTIONS

The main types of questions asked can be categorized as shown below:

Type of question/ Percentage on test	Explanation	Example
Main Idea/ Main Topic/ Main Purpose questions (10 percent)	These ask you to identify an answer choice that correctly summarizes the author's main idea, the subject of the whole passage, or the author's reason for writing the passage.	"What is the main idea of the passage?" "What is the passage primarily about?" "Why did the author write the passage?"
Factual questions (24 percent)	These ask you to locate and identify answers to questions about specific information and details in the passage.	"According to the passage, where did . . .?" "According to the author, why did . . .?" "Which of the following is true, according to the passage?"
Negative questions (9 percent)	These ask which of the answer choices is NOT discussed in the passage.	"Which of the following is NOT true about . . ." "All of the following are true EXCEPT . . ."
Scanning questions (4 percent)	These ask you to find the place in the passage that some topic is mentioned.	"Where in the passage does the author first discuss . . ."
Inference questions (12 percent)	These ask you to draw conclusions based on information in the passage.	"The author implies that which of the following is true?" "Which of the following can be inferred from the passage?"
Vocabulary-in-Context questions (26 percent)	These ask you identify the meaning of a word or phrase as used in the passage.	"The word '——' in line 5 is closest in meaning to . . ."
Reference questions (10 percent)	These ask you to identify the noun to which a pronoun or other expression refers.	"The word 'it' in line 15 refers to . . ." "In line 20, the word 'there' refers to which of the following?"

There are a few other types of questions that are occasionally asked about the readings. These make up the remaining 5 percent of the question types.

About half the reading items have **closed stems**; they begin with direct questions. The others have **open stems**; they begin with incomplete sentences.

CLOSED STEM
Which of the following is the main topic of the passage?

OPEN STEM
The main topic of the passage is

THE ANSWER CHOICES

For all questions in this part, the four options are equally grammatical and, in most cases, would be equally logical choices for someone who has not carefully read the passage. Incorrect choices are generally based on information that is found in the passage, but does not correctly answer the question.

WHAT IS THE BEST WAY TO APPROACH THE PASSAGES?

First, take a quick look at the questions (NOT at the answer choices) to see what will be asked about. Try to keep these in the back of your mind as you read the passage. Then read the article at a comfortable speed. Try NOT to read one word at a time, like this:

A bird's territory may be small or large. Some males claim only their nest and the area right around it.

Word-by-word reading slows you down and interferes with your comprehension. Try to read in units of thought. In other words, group words into related phrases.

A bird's territory may be small or large. Some males claim only their nest and the area right aroun d it.

The paragraph is the primary unit of meaning in all reading. Most passages consist of from one to five paragraphs. If you can form a clear idea of what each paragraph is about, you can put these ideas together and come up with the main idea of the entire passage. The main idea of each paragraph is often contained in one sentence, called the topic sentence. Try to locate topic sentences. Often, the topic sentence is the first sentence of a paragraph, but it may also be the last sentence. Occasionally a paragraph has no topic sentence; the topic is stated indirectly.

If there is more than one paragraph in the passage, try to understand the relationship between the paragraphs. Form a mental "map" of the passage. Watch for words that signal special relationships and transitions, such as *however*, *therefore*, *first*, *next*, *then*, and so on.

WHAT IS THE BEST WAY TO ANSWER THE QUESTIONS?

It depends on the type of question. The best tactics for answering each type of question are given in the next five lessons. In the exercises, you will read passages similar to the ones found on actual TOEFL tests to develop the reading skills needed to do well on this section.

WHAT ARE SOME IMPORTANT FACTORS IN SCORING HIGH IN THIS SECTION?

Timing is an important factor. Most test-takers find this the hardest to complete because reading the passages takes up so much time. Near the end of the test, you may realize that you won't have enough time to finish. Don't panic! When there is only about 4 or 5 minutes remaining, this is what you should do: If you have not read one of the passages, skim it over very quickly to get the main idea. Answer the first question about it (which will probably be a main idea or topic question). Then answer any of the questions that provide line numbers (vocabulary-in-context and reference questions) because these require less time to locate the information you need. Then answer any remaining questions, referring back to the passage as little as possible. If you can't find the information needed to answer the question in about 10 seconds, just pick the choice that seems the most logical.

Then, in the last few seconds, fill in any empty blanks with your "guess answer."

On the other hand, if you *do* finish the test before time is called, go back and work on items that you had trouble with the first time. Don't just sit back and relax, and don't turn back to Sections 1 or 2.

Concentration is another important factor. This is the last section of the test. It's also the longest and, for some people, the most difficult. You may be starting to get tired. However, you've got to maintain your concentration until the end of the test and not waste any time.

WHAT IS THE BEST WAY TO PREPARE FOR THIS PART OF TOEFL?

After completing the exercises in *TOEFL CBT Success* and taking the practice tests in this book, read as much on your own as you can. A recent study showed that **extracurricular reading** (readings done outside of classes) was the single most important factor in improving overall TOEFL scores. Material from textbooks, magazines, newspapers, and encyclopedias will be useful. You might also want to try writing TOEFL-style questions about passages that you read. This technique not only increases your comprehension, but it also helps you think like the people who write TOEFL tests.

Strategies for Section 3

- As with the other sections, be familiar with the directions and examples for Section 3 so that you can begin work immediately.
- For each passage, begin by briefly looking over the questions (but not the answer choices). Try to keep these questions in mind during your reading.
- Read each passage at a comfortable speed.
- Answer the questions, referring to the passage when necessary.
- Eliminate answers that are clearly wrong or do not answer the questions. If more than one option remains, guess.
- Mark difficult or time-consuming answers so that you can come back to them later if you have time. Erase all these marks before the end of the test.
- Don't spend more than about 10 minutes on any one reading and the questions about it.
- When only a few minutes remain, **don't** start guessing blindly. Skim the remaining passage or passages quickly, then answer the first question in each set. Then answer any questions with line numbers. After that, read the remaining questions, and if you can't find the question quickly, choose the one that seems most logical to you.
- When there are only a few seconds left, fill in all remaining blanks with your guess letter.

SAMPLE VOCABULARY AND READING COMPREHENSION TEST
TIME—55 MINUTES

This section of the test measures your ability to understand the meaning of words and to comprehend written materials.

Directions: The remainder of this section contains several passages, each followed by a number of questions. Read the passages and, for each question, choose the *one* best answer—(A), (B), (C), or (D)—based on what is stated in or on what can be inferred from the passage. Then fill in the space on your answer sheet that matches the letter of the answer that you have selected.

Read the following passage:

Line   Like mammals, birds claim their own territories. A bird's territory may be small or large. Some birds claim only their nest and the area right around it, while others claim far larger territories that include their feeding areas. Gulls, penguins, and other waterfowl nest in huge colonies, but even in the biggest colonies, each male and his mate have small territories of their own immediately around their nests.

  Male birds defend their territory chiefly against other males of the same species. In some cases, a warning call or threatening pose may be all the defense needed, but in other cases, intruders may refuse to leave peacefully.

Example I

What is the main topic of this passage?

(A) Birds that live in colonies
(B) Birds' mating habits
(C) The behavior of birds
(D) Territoriality in birds

Sample Answer

 Ⓐ Ⓑ Ⓒ ●

The passage mainly concerns the territories of birds. You should fill in (D) on your answer sheet.

Example II

According to the passage, male birds defend their territory primarily against

(A) female birds
(B) birds of other species
(C) males of their own species
(D) mammals

Sample Answer

 Ⓐ Ⓑ ● Ⓓ

The passage states that "Male birds defend their territory chiefly against other males of the same species." You should fill in (C) on your answer sheet.

As soon as you understand the directions, begin work on this part.

Answer Sheet

Sample Vocabulary and Reading Comprehension Test

1. Ⓐ Ⓑ Ⓒ Ⓓ	21. Ⓐ Ⓑ Ⓒ Ⓓ	41. Ⓐ Ⓑ Ⓒ Ⓓ
2. Ⓐ Ⓑ Ⓒ Ⓓ	22. Ⓐ Ⓑ Ⓒ Ⓓ	42. Ⓐ Ⓑ Ⓒ Ⓓ
3. Ⓐ Ⓑ Ⓒ Ⓓ	23. Ⓐ Ⓑ Ⓒ Ⓓ	43. Ⓐ Ⓑ Ⓒ Ⓓ
4. Ⓐ Ⓑ Ⓒ Ⓓ	24. Ⓐ Ⓑ Ⓒ Ⓓ	44. Ⓐ Ⓑ Ⓒ Ⓓ
5. Ⓐ Ⓑ Ⓒ Ⓓ	25. Ⓐ Ⓑ Ⓒ Ⓓ	45. Ⓐ Ⓑ Ⓒ Ⓓ
6. Ⓐ Ⓑ Ⓒ Ⓓ	26. Ⓐ Ⓑ Ⓒ Ⓓ	46. Ⓐ Ⓑ Ⓒ Ⓓ
7. Ⓐ Ⓑ Ⓒ Ⓓ	27. Ⓐ Ⓑ Ⓒ Ⓓ	47. Ⓐ Ⓑ Ⓒ Ⓓ
8. Ⓐ Ⓑ Ⓒ Ⓓ	28. Ⓐ Ⓑ Ⓒ Ⓓ	48. Ⓐ Ⓑ Ⓒ Ⓓ
9. Ⓐ Ⓑ Ⓒ Ⓓ	29. Ⓐ Ⓑ Ⓒ Ⓓ	49. Ⓐ Ⓑ Ⓒ Ⓓ
10. Ⓐ Ⓑ Ⓒ Ⓓ	30. Ⓐ Ⓑ Ⓒ Ⓓ	50. Ⓐ Ⓑ Ⓒ Ⓓ
11. Ⓐ Ⓑ Ⓒ Ⓓ	31. Ⓐ Ⓑ Ⓒ Ⓓ	
12. Ⓐ Ⓑ Ⓒ Ⓓ	32. Ⓐ Ⓑ Ⓒ Ⓓ	
13. Ⓐ Ⓑ Ⓒ Ⓓ	33. Ⓐ Ⓑ Ⓒ Ⓓ	
14. Ⓐ Ⓑ Ⓒ Ⓓ	34. Ⓐ Ⓑ Ⓒ Ⓓ	
15. Ⓐ Ⓑ Ⓒ Ⓓ	35. Ⓐ Ⓑ Ⓒ Ⓓ	
16. Ⓐ Ⓑ Ⓒ Ⓓ	36. Ⓐ Ⓑ Ⓒ Ⓓ	
17. Ⓐ Ⓑ Ⓒ Ⓓ	37. Ⓐ Ⓑ Ⓒ Ⓓ	
18. Ⓐ Ⓑ Ⓒ Ⓓ	38. Ⓐ Ⓑ Ⓒ Ⓓ	
19. Ⓐ Ⓑ Ⓒ Ⓓ	39. Ⓐ Ⓑ Ⓒ Ⓓ	
20. Ⓐ Ⓑ Ⓒ Ⓓ	40. Ⓐ Ⓑ Ⓒ Ⓓ	

QUESTIONS 1-12

Line   The technology of the North American Colonies did not differ strikingly from that of Europe, but in one respect, the colonists enjoyed a great advantage. Especially by comparison with Britain, Americans had a wonderfully plentiful supply of wood.

The first colonists did not, as many people imagine, find an entire continent covered by a
5   climax forest. Even along the Atlantic seaboard, the forest was broken at many points. Nevertheless, all sorts of fine trees abounded, and through the early colonial period, those who pushed westward encountered new forests. By the end of the Colonial era, the price of wood had risen slightly in eastern cities, but wood was still extremely abundant.

The availability of wood brought advantages that have seldom been appreciated. Wood was a
10   foundation of the economy. Houses and all manner of buildings were made of wood to a degree unknown in Britain. Secondly, wood was used as a fuel for heating and cooking. Thirdly, it was used as the source of important industrial compounds, such as potash, an industrial alkali; charcoal, a component of gunpowder; and tannic acid, used for tanning leather.

The supply of wood conferred advantages, but had some negative aspects as well. Iron at that
15   time was produced by heating iron ore with charcoal. Because Britain was so stripped of trees, she was unable to exploit her rich iron mines. But the American Colonies had both iron ore and wood; iron production was encouraged and became successful. However, when Britain developed coke smelting, the Colonies did not follow suit because they had plenty of wood and besides, charcoal iron was stronger than coke iron. Coke smelting led to technological innovations and was linked to
20   the emergence of the Industrial Revolution. In the early nineteenth century, the former Colonies lagged behind Britain in industrial development because their supply of wood led them to cling to charcoal iron.

1. What does the passage mainly discuss?

   (A) The advantages of using wood in the colonies.
   (B) The effects of an abundance of wood on the colonies.
   (C) The roots of the Industrial Revolution.
   (D) The difference between charcoal iron and coke iron.

2. The word "strikingly" in line 1 is closest in meaning to

   (A) realistically
   (B) dramatically
   (C) completely
   (D) immediately

3. Which of the following is a common assumption about the forests of North America during the Colonial period?

   (A) They contained only a few types of trees.
   (B) They existed only along the Atlantic seaboard.
   (C) They had little or no economic value.
   (D) They covered the entire continent.

4. The word "abounded" in line 6 is closest in meaning to

   (A) were present in large numbers
   (B) were restricted to certain areas
   (C) were cut down
   (D) were cultivated

5. According to the passage, by the end of the Colonial period, the price of wood in eastern cities

   (A) rose quickly because wood was becoming so scarce
   (B) was much higher than it was in Britain
   (C) was slightly higher than in previous years
   (D) decreased rapidly because of lower demand for wood

6. What can be inferred about houses in Britain during the period written about in the passage?

   (A) They were more expensive than American houses.
   (B) They were generally built with imported materials.
   (C) They were typically smaller than homes in North America.
   (D) They were usually built from materials other than wood.

7. Why does the author mention gunpowder in line 13?

   (A) To illustrate the negative aspects of some industrial processes.
   (B) To give an example of a product made with wood compounds.
   (C) To remind readers that the Colonial era ended in warfare.
   (D) To suggest that wood was not the only important product of the Colonies.

8. The word "conferred" in line 14 is closest in meaning to

   (A) consulted
   (B) gathered
   (C) provided
   (D) restricted

9. The phrase "follow suit" in line 18 means

   (A) do the same thing
   (B) make an attempt
   (C) have the opportunity
   (D) take a risk

10. According to the passage, why was the use of coke smelting advantageous?

    (A) It led to advances in technology.
    (B) It was less expensive than wood smelting.
    (C) It produced a stronger type of iron than wood smelting.
    (D) It stimulated the demand for wood.

11. The phrase "cling to" in line 21 is closest in meaning to

    (A) try to develop
    (B) avoid
    (C) continue to use
    (D) reconsider

12. Where in the passage does the author begin to discuss in detail the disadvantages that an abundant supply of wood brought to the Colonies?

    (A) Lines 1–2
    (B) Lines 4–5
    (C) Lines 9–11
    (D) Line 14

QUESTIONS 13–22

Line The Peales were a distinguished family of American artists. Charles Wilson Peale is best remembered for his portraits of leading figures of the American Revolution. He painted portraits of Franklin and Jefferson, and over a dozen of George Washington. His life-size portrait of his sons Raphaelle and Titian was so realistic that George Washington reportedly once tipped his hat to the figures in the

5 picture.

Charles Wilson Peale gave up painting in his middle age and devoted his life to the Peale Museum, which he founded in Philadelphia. The world's first popular museum of art and natural science, it featured paintings by Peale and his family as well as displays of animals in their natural settings. Peale found the animals himself and devised a method of taxidermy to make the exhibits

10 more lifelike. The museum's most popular display was the skeleton of a mastodon—a huge, extinct elephant—which Peale unearthed on a New York farm in 1801.

Three of Peale's seventeen children were also famous artists. Raphaelle Peale often painted still lifes of flowers, fruit, and cheese. His works show the same luminosity and attention to detail that the works of the Dutch masters show. In the late eighteenth century, however, portraiture was the rage,

15 and so Raphaelle Peale found few buyers for his still lifes at the time. His brother Rembrandt studied under his father and painted portraits of many noted people, including one of George Washington. Another brother, Rubens Peale, painted mostly landscapes and portraits.

James Peale, the brother of Charles Wilson Peale, specialized in miniatures. His daughter Sarah Miriam Peale was probably the first professional female portrait painter in America.

13. What is the main topic of the passage?

(A) The life of Charles Wilson Peale.
(B) Portraiture in the 18th century.
(C) The Peale Museum.
(D) A family of artists.

14. The author probably mentions that Washington "tipped his hat to the figures in the painting" (lines 4–5) to indicate that

(A) Charles Wilson Peale's painting was very lifelike.
(B) Washington respected Charles Wilson Peale's work.
(C) Washington was friendly with Raphaelle and Titian Peale.
(D) The painting of the two brothers was extremely large.

15. The word "settings" in line 9 is closest in meaning to which of the following?

(A) environments
(B) categories
(C) positions
(D) requirements

16. For which of the following terms does the author give a definition in the second paragraph?

(A) natural science
(B) skeleton
(C) taxidermy
(D) mastodon

17. Which of the following questions about the Peale Museum does the passage NOT supply enough information to answer?

(A) Who found and prepared its animal exhibits?
(B) In what city was it located?
(C) Where did its most popular exhibit come from?
(D) In what year was it founded?

18. The word "unearthed" in line 11 is closest in meaning to

(A) displayed
(B) dug up
(C) located
(D) looked over

19. Which of the following words could best be substituted for the word "rage" in line 14?

(A) fashion
(B) anger
(C) conflict
(D) desire

20. According to the passage, Rembrandt Peale and his father both painted

(A) miniatures
(B) portraits of George Washington
(C) paintings of flowers, fruit, and cheese
(D) pictures of animals

Peterson's TOEFL CBT Success

21. Which of the following is NOT one of the children of Charles Wilson Peale?

(A) Titian Peale
(B) Rubens Peale
(C) Raphaelle Peale
(D) Sarah Miriam Peale

22. The author's attitude toward the Peales is generally

(A) envious
(B) puzzled
(C) admiring
(D) disappointed

QUESTIONS 23–34

Line According to the best evidence gathered by space probes and astronomers, Mars is an inhospitable planet, more similar to Earth's Moon than to Earth itself—a dry, stark, seemingly lifeless world. Mars' air pressure is equal to Earth's at an altitude of 100,000 feet. The air there is 95 percent carbon dioxide.

Mars has no ozone layer to screen out the sun's lethal radiation. Daytime temperatures may reach
5 above freezing, but because the planet is blanketed by the mere wisp of an atmosphere, the heat radiates back into space. Even at the equator, the temperature drops to −50C (−60F) at night. Today there is no liquid water, although valleys and channels on the surface show evidence of having been carved by running water. The polar ice caps are made of frozen water and carbon dioxide, and water may be frozen in the ground as permafrost.

10 Despite these difficult conditions, certain scientists believe that there is a possibility of transforming Mars into a more Earth-like planet. Nuclear reactors might be used to melt frozen gases and eventually build up the atmosphere. This in turn could create a "greenhouse effect" that would stop heat from radiating back into space. Liquid water could be thawed to form a polar ocean. Once enough ice has melted, suitable plants could be introduced to build up the level of oxygen in the
15 atmosphere so that, in time, the planet would support animal life from Earth and even permanent human colonies. "This was once thought to be so far in the future as to be irrelevant," said Christopher McKay, a research scientist at the National Aeronautics and Space Administration. "But now it's starting to look practical. We could begin work in four or five decades."

The idea of "terra-forming" Mars, as enthusiasts call it, has its roots in science fiction. But as
20 researchers develop a more profound understanding of how Earth's ecology supports life, they have begun to see how it may be possible to create similar conditions on Mars. Don't plan on homesteading on Mars any time soon, though. The process could take hundreds or even thousands of years to complete and the cost would be staggering.

23. With which of the following is the passage primarily concerned?

(A) The possibility of changing the Martian environment.
(B) The challenge of interplanetary travel.
(C) The advantages of establishing colonies on Mars.
(D) The need to study the Martian ecology.

24. The word "stark" in line 2 is closest in meaning to

(A) harsh
(B) unknown
(C) dark
(D) distant

25. The word "there" in line 3 refers to

(A) a point 100 miles above the Earth
(B) the Earth's Moon
(C) Mars
(D) outer space

26. Which of the following does the author NOT list as a characteristic of the planet Mars that would make colonization difficult?

(A) There is little liquid water.
(B) Daytime temperatures are dangerously high.
(C) The sun's rays are deadly.
(D) Nighttime temperatures are extremely low.

27. According to the passage, the Martian atmosphere today consists mainly of

(A) carbon dioxide
(B) oxygen
(C) ozone
(D) water vapor

28. It can be inferred from the passage that the "greenhouse effect" mentioned in line 12 is

   (A) the direct result of nuclear reactions
   (B) the cause of low temperatures on Mars
   (C) caused by the introduction of green plants
   (D) a possible means of warming Mars

29. The word "suitable" in line 14 is closest in meaning to

   (A) resistant
   (B) altered
   (C) appropriate
   (D) native

30. According to Christopher McKay, the possibility of transforming Mars

   (A) could only occur in science fiction stories
   (B) will not begin for hundreds, even thousands of years
   (C) is completely impractical
   (D) could be started in forty to fifty years

31. As used in line 19, the term "terra-forming" refers to

   (A) a process for adapting plants to live on Mars
   (B) a means of transporting materials through space
   (C) a method of building housing for colonists on Mars
   (D) a system of creating Earth-like conditions on other planets

32. The phrase "more profound" in lines 19–20 is closest in meaning to

   (A) deeper
   (B) more practical
   (C) more up-to-date
   (D) brighter

33. According to the article, the basic knowledge needed to transform Mars comes from

   (A) the science of astronomy
   (B) a knowledge of Earth's ecology
   (C) data from space probes
   (D) science fiction stories

34. The word "staggering" in line 23 is closest in meaning to

   (A) astonishing
   (B) restrictive
   (C) increasing
   (D) unpredictable

QUESTIONS 35–43

Line   Another critical factor that plays a part in susceptibility to colds is age. A study done by the University of Michigan School of Public Health revealed particulars that seem to hold true for the general population. Infants are the most cold-ridden group, averaging more than six colds in their first year. Boys have more colds than girls up to age three. After the age of three, girls are more susceptible
5   than boys, and teenage girls average three colds a year to boys' two.

The general incidence of colds continues to decline into maturity. Elderly people who are in good health have as few as one or two colds annually. One exception is found among people in their twenties, especially women, who show a rise in cold infections, because people in this age group are most likely to have young children. Adults who delay having children until their thirties and forties
10   experience the same sudden increase in cold infections.

The study also found that economics plays an important role. As income increases, the frequency at which colds are reported in the family decreases. Families with the lowest income suffer about a third more colds than families at the lower end. Lower income generally forces people to live in more cramped quarters than those typically occupied by wealthier people, and crowding increases
15   the opportunities for the cold virus to travel from person to person. Low income may also adversely influence diet. The degree to which poor nutrition affects susceptibility to colds is not yet clearly established, but an inadequate diet is suspected of lowering resistance generally.

276

35. The paragraph that precedes this passage most probably deals with

(A) minor diseases other than colds
(B) the recommended treatment of colds
(C) a factor that affects susceptibility to colds
(D) methods of preventing colds among elderly people

36. Which of the following is closest in meaning to the word "particulars" in line 2?

(A) minor errors
(B) specific facts
(C) small distinctions
(D) individual people

37. What does the author claim about the study discussed in the passage?

(A) It contains many inconsistencies.
(B) It specializes in children.
(C) It contradicts the results of earlier studies in the field.
(D) Its results apparently are relevant for the population as a whole.

38. It may be inferred from the passage that which of the following groups of people is most likely to catch colds?

(A) Infant boys.
(B) Young girls.
(C) Teenage boys.
(D) Elderly women.

39. There is information in the second paragraph of the passage to support which of the following conclusions?

(A) Men are more susceptible to colds than women.
(B) Children infect their parents with colds.
(C) People who live in a cold climate have more colds than those who live in a warm one.
(D) People who don't have children are more susceptible to colds than those who do.

40. The phrase "in this age group" (line 8) refers to

(A) infants
(B) people in their twenties
(C) people in their thirties and forties
(D) elderly people

41. The author's main purpose in writing the last paragraph of the passage is to

(A) explain how cold viruses are transmitted
(B) prove that a poor diet causes colds
(C) discuss the relationship between income and frequency of colds
(D) discuss the distribution of income among the people in the study

42. The word "cramped" in line 14 is closest in meaning to

(A) cheap
(B) crowded
(C) depressing
(D) simple

43. The author's tone in this passage could best be described as

(A) neutral and objective
(B) humorous
(C) tentative but interested
(D) highly critical

QUESTIONS 44–50

Line   About fifty years ago, plant physiologists set out to grow roots by themselves in solutions in laboratory flasks. The scientists found that the nutrition of isolated roots was quite simple. They required
sugar and the usual minerals and vitamins. However, they did not require organic nitrogen compounds. These roots got along fine on mineral inorganic nitrogen. Roots are capable of making their
5   own proteins and other organic compounds. These activities by roots require energy, of course. The
process of respiration uses sugar to make the high energy compound ATP, which drives the biochemical reactions. Respiration also requires oxygen. Highly active roots require a good deal of
oxygen.
        The study of isolated roots has provided an understanding of the relationship between shoots
10   and roots in intact plants. The leaves of the shoots provide the roots with sugar and vitamins, and the
roots provide the shoots with water and minerals. In addition, roots can provide the shoots with
organic nitrogen compounds. This comes in handy for the growth of buds in the early spring when
leaves are not yet functioning. Once leaves begin photosynthesizing, they produce protein, but only
mature leaves can "export" protein to the rest of the plant in the form of amino acids.

44. What is the main topic of the passage?

(A) The relationship between a plant's
roots and its shoots.
(B) What can be learned by growing roots
in isolation.
(C) How plants can be grown without
roots.
(D) What elements are necessary for the
growth of plants.

45. The word "themselves" in line 1 refers to

(A) plant physiologists
(B) solutions
(C) laboratory flasks
(D) roots

46. According to the passage, what is ATP?

(A) A biochemical process.
(B) The tip of a root.
(C) A chemical compound.
(D) A type of plant cell.

47. The word "intact" in line 10 is closest in
meaning to

(A) mature
(B) wild
(C) whole
(D) tiny

48. The use of the phrase "comes in handy" in
line 12 indicates that the process is

(A) useful
(B) predictable
(C) necessary
(D) successful

49. It can be inferred from the passage that, in
the early spring, the buds of plants

(A) "export" protein in the form of amino
acids
(B) do not require water
(C) have begun photosynthesizing
(D) obtain organic compounds from the
roots

50. Which of the following best describes the
organization of the passage?

(A) The results of two experiments are
compared.
(B) A generalization is made and several
examples of it are given.
(C) The findings of an experiment are
explained.
(D) A hypothesis is presented, and several
means of proving it are suggested.

THIS IS THE END OF THE SAMPLE READING COMPREHENSION SECTION.
IF YOU FINISH BEFORE TIME IS CALLED, GO BACK AND CHECK YOUR WORK.

Lesson 44

MAIN IDEA, MAIN TOPIC, AND MAIN PURPOSE QUESTIONS

After almost every passage, the first question is an **overview question** about the main idea, main topic, or main purpose of a passage. **Main idea questions** ask you to identify the most important thought in the passage.

Sample Questions

- What is the main idea of the passage?
- The primary idea of the passage is. . . .
- Which of the following best summarizes the author's main idea?

When there is not a single, readily identified main idea, **main topic questions** may be asked. These ask you what the passage is generally "about."

Sample Questions

- The main topic of the passage is. . . .
- What does the passage mainly discuss?
- The passage is primarily concerned with. . . .

Main purpose questions ask *why* an author wrote a passage. The answer choices for these questions usually begin with infinitives.

Sample Questions

- The author's purpose in writing is. . . .
- What is the author's main purpose in the passage?
- The main point of this passage is. . . .
- Why did the author write the passage?

Sample Answer Choices

- To define . . .
- To relate . . .
- To discuss . . .
- To propose . . .
- To illustrate . . .
- To support the idea that . . .
- To distinguish between _____ and _____
- To compare _____ and _____

Don't answer the initial overview question about a passage until you have answered the other questions. The process of answering the detail questions may give you a clearer idea of the main idea, topic, or purpose of the passage.

The correct answers for main idea, main topic, and main purpose questions correctly summarize the main points of the passage; they must be more general than any of the supporting ideas or details, but not so general that they include ideas outside the scope of the passages.

Distractors for this type of question have one of these characteristics:

1. They are too specific.

2. They are too general.

3. The are incorrect according to the passage.

4. They are irrelevant (unrelated) to the main idea of the passage.

If you're not sure of the answer for one of these questions, go back and quickly scan the passage. You can usually infer the main idea, main topic, or main purpose of the entire passage from an understanding of the main ideas of the paragraphs that make up the passage and the relationship between them.

OTHER OVERVIEW QUESTIONS

A number of other questions are asked that require an overall understanding of the passage. These are often the last question in a set of questions.

Tone questions ask you to determine the author's feelings about the topic by the language that he or she uses in writing the passage. Look for vocabulary that indicates if the author's feelings are positive, negative, or neutral.

Sample Questions

- What tone does the author take in writing this passage?
- The tone of this passage could best be described as. . . .

Sample Answer Choices

- Positive
- Favorable
- Optimistic
- Amused
- Pleased
- Respectful

- Humorous
- Negative
- Critical
- Unfavorable
- Angry
- Defiant

- Worried
- Outraged
- Neutral
- Objective
- Impersonal

If you read the following sentences in passages, would the tone of those passages most likely be positive or negative?

1. That was just the beginning of a *remarkable* series of performances by this *brilliant* actress.

2. Despite some minor problems, this device has a number of *admirable* features.

3. This practice is *a waste of time and money*.

4. At the time his poems were first published, they were very popular, but today most critics find them *simplistic and rather uninteresting*.

The italicized words in sentences 1 and 2 show a positive tone; in 3 and 4, the italicized words indicate a negative attitude. Notice that sentence 2 contains negative words ("minor problems") but the overall meaning of the sentence is positive. Sentence 4 contains positive language ("very popular") but overall, the tone is negative. (Words like *despite*, *but*, *although*, *however*, and similar words can "reverse" the tone of the passage.)

Most TOEFL reading passages have a neutral tone, but sometimes an author may take a position for or against some point. However, answer choices that indicate strong emotion—*angry, outraged, sad*, and so forth—will seldom be correct.

Attitude questions are very similar to tone questions. Again, you must understand the author's opinion. The language that the author uses will tell you what his or her position is.

What is the author's attitude toward smoking on airplanes as expressed in the sentence below?

Although some passengers may experience a slight discomfort from not smoking on long flights, their smoking endangers the health of all the passengers and crew.

Peterson's TOEFL CBT Success

The author opposes smoking during flights. He admits that there is some argument in favor of smoking—some passengers may feel discomfort—but this is not as important as the fact that smoking can be dangerous to everyone on the flight. The use of the word *although* shows this.

Sample Questions

- What is the author's attitude toward. . . .
- The author's opinion of _____ is best described as. . . .
- The author's attitude toward _____ could best be described as one of. . . .
- How would the author probably feel about. . . .

Another type of attitude question presents four statements and asks how the author would feel about them.

- Which of the following recommendations would the author most likely support?
- The author would be LEAST likely to agree with which of the following statements?
- The author of the passage would most likely be in favor of which of the following policies?

Organization questions ask about the overall structure of a passage or about the organization of a particular paragraph.

Sample Question

- Which of the following best describes the organization of the passage?

Sample Answer Choices

- A general concept is defined and examples are given.
- Several generalizations are presented, from which a conclusion is drawn.
- The author presents the advantages and disadvantages of _____.
- The author presents a system of classification for _____.
- Persuasive language is used to argue against _____.
- The author describes _____.
- The author presents a brief account of _____.
- The author compares _____ and _____.

Questions about previous or following paragraphs ask you to assume that the passage is part of a longer work: what would be the topic of the hypothetical paragraph that precedes or follows the passage? To find the topic of the previous paragraph, look for clues in the first line or two of the passage; for the topic of the following passage, look in the last few lines. Sometimes incorrect answer choices mention topics that have already been discussed in the passage.

Sample Questions

- With what topic would the following/preceding paragraph most likely deal?
- The paragraph prior to/after the passage most probably discusses. . . .
- It can be inferred from the passage that the previous/next paragraph concerns. . . .
- What most likely precedes/follows the passage?

EXERCISE 44.1

Focus: Identifying correct answers and recognizing distractors in main idea/main topic/main purpose questions.

Directions: Read the passages. Then mark each answer choice according to the following system:

S Too specific
G Too general
X Incorrect
I Irrelevant
C Correct

The first one is done as an example.

There are two main types of cell division. Most cells are produced by a process called mitosis. In mitosis, a cell divides and forms two identical daughter cells, each with an identical number of chromosomes. Most one-celled creatures reproduce by this method, as do most of the cells in multi-celled plants and animals. Sex cells, however, are formed in a special type of cell division called meiosis. This process reduces the number of chromosomes in a sex cell to half the number found in other kinds of cells. Then, when sex cells unite, they produce a single cell with the original number of chromosomes.

1. What is the main topic of this passage?

    S   (A) The method by which one-celled organisms reproduce

    C   (B) A comparison between mitosis and meiosis

    X   (C) Meiosis, the process by which identical cells are produced

The last gold rush belongs as much to Canadian history as it does to American. The discovery of gold along the Klondike River, which flows from Canada's Yukon Territory into Alaska, drew some 30,000 fortune hunters to the north. The Yukon became a territory and its capital of the time, Dawson, would not have existed without the gold rush. The gold strike furnished material for a dozen of Jack London's novels; it inspired Robert Service to write "The Shooting of Dan McGrew" and other poems, and it provided the background for the wonderful Charlie Chaplin movie, *The Gold Rush*. It also marked the beginnings of modern Alaska.

2. This author's main purpose in writing is to

    _____ (A) discuss the significance of mining in Canada and the United States
    _____ (B) show the influence of the Klondike gold strike on the creative arts
    _____ (C) point out the significance of the Klondike gold strike

The keystone arch was used by almost every early civilization. To build a keystone arch, stones are cut so that the opposite sides taper toward each other sightly. The upper and lower surfaces are carved so that when several stones are placed side by side, the upper and lower surfaces meet in smooth, continuous curves. Some form of scaffolding is built under the arch and shaped to accept the curved underside of the stones. Then the stones are fitted in place one by one. The keystone is the top center stone, the last to be dropped into position. Afterwards, the scaffolding is removed and the arch is self-supporting.

3. The passage mainly concerns

    _____ (A) the basic principles of building keystone arches
    _____ (B) the uses of arches in modern architecture
    _____ (C) the role of scaffolding in building keystone arches

Circumstantial evidence is evidence not drawn from the direct observation of a fact. If, for example, there is evidence that a piece of rock embedded in a wrapped chocolate bar is the same type of rock found in the vicinity of the candy factory, and that rock of this type is found in few other places, then there is circumstantial evidence that the stone found its way into the candy during manufacture and suggests that the candy maker was negligent. Despite a popular notion to look down on the quality of circumstantial evidence, it is of great usefulness if there is enough of it and if it is properly interpreted. Each circumstance, taken singly, may mean little, but a whole chain of circumstances can be as conclusive as direct evidence.

4. What is the main idea of the passage?

_____ (A) A manufacturer's negligence can be shown by direct evidence only.

_____ (B) Enough circumstantial evidence is as persuasive as direct evidence.

_____ (C) Circumstantial evidence can be very useful in science.

The Northwest Ordinance was passed by Congress in 1787. It set up the government structure of the region north of the Ohio River and west of Pennsylvania, then called the Northwest Territory. It set the conditions under which parts of the territory could become states having equality with the older states. But the ordinance was more than just a plan for government. The law also guaranteed freedom of religion and trial by jury in the Territory. It organized the territory into townships of 36 square miles and ordered a school to be built for each township. It also abolished slavery in the Territory. The terms were so attractive that thousands of pioneers poured into the Territory. Eventually, the Territory became the states of Ohio, Indiana, Illinois, Michigan, and Wisconsin.

5. What is the main topic of this passage?

_____ (A) The structure of government

_____ (B) The provisions of an important law

_____ (C) The establishment of schools in the Northwest Territory

The story of the motel business from 1920 to the start of World War II in 1941 is one of uninterrupted growth. Motels spread from the west and the midwest all the way to Maine and Florida. They clustered along transcontinental highways such as U.S. Routes 40 and 66 and along the north-south routes running up and down both the East and West Coasts. There were 16,000 motels by 1930 and 24,000 by 1940. The motel industry was one of the few industries that was not hurt by the Depression of the 1930s. Their cheap rates attracted travelers who had very little money.

6. What does the passage mainly discuss?

_____ (A) How the Depression hurt U.S. motels

_____ (B) The impact of transcontinental highways

_____ (C) Two decades of growth for the motel industry

An old proverb states, "Beware of oak, it draws the stroke." This saying is handy during thunderstorm season. In general, trees with deep roots that tap into groundwater attract more lightning than do trees with shallow, drier roots. Oaks are around 50 times more likely to be struck than beeches. Spruces are nearly as safe as beeches. Pines are not as safe as these two, but are still much safer than oaks.

7. What is the author's main point?

_____ (A) Old proverbs often contain important truths.

_____ (B) Trees with shallow roots are more likely to avoid lightning than those with deep roots.

_____ (C) The deeper a tree's roots, the safer it is during a thunderstorm.

Alternative history is generally classified as a type of science fiction, but it also bears some relation to historical fiction. This type of writing describes an imaginary world that is identical to ours up to a certain point in history, but at that point, the two worlds diverge; some important historical event takes place in one world but not in the other, and they go in different directions. Alternative histories might describe worlds in which the Roman Empire had never fallen, in which the Spanish Armada had been victorious, or in which the South had won the Civil War. Or they may suppose that some technology had been introduced earlier in the world's history than actually happened. For example: What if computers had been invented in Victorian times? Many readers find these stories interesting because of the way they stimulate the imagination and get them thinking about the phenomenon of cause and effect in history.

8. What is the main idea of this passage?

_____ (A) Alternative histories describe worlds in which history has taken another course.
_____ (B) Alternative histories are a type of historical novel.
_____ (C) Science fiction writers have accurately predicted certain actual scientific developments.

Until the late 1700s, metal could not be turned on a lathe to make it uniformly smooth and round. The operator could not guide the cutting tool evenly by hand against the turning piece. This problem was solved by David Wilkinson of Pawtucket, Rhode Island. In 1798 he invented a machine in which the cutter was clamped into a moveable slide that could be advanced precisely, by hand crank, parallel to the work. The slide rest, as it came to be called, has many uses. It permits the manufacture of parts so uniform that they can be interchanged. Without it, mass production would not have been possible. As it turns out, the great English machinist Henry Maudsley developed nearly the same mechanism a few years before, but this was unknown to Wilkinson and does not diminish his accomplishment.

9. Why did the author write this passage?

_____ (A) To prove that Wilkinson's invention was based on Maudsley's.
_____ (B) To demonstrate the importance of mass production to American society.
_____ (C) To show the usefulness of Wilkinson's invention.

Almost every form of transportation has given someone the idea for a new type of toy. After the Montgolfier brothers flew the first balloon, toy balloons became popular playthings. In the nineteenth century, soon after railroads and steamships were developed, every child had to have model trains and steamboats. The same held true for automobiles and airplanes in the early twentieth century. Toy rockets and missiles became popular at the beginning of the space age, and by the 1980s, there were many different versions of space-shuttle toys.

10. The main idea of this passage is that

_____ (A) inventors have been inspired by toys to build new forms of transportation
_____ (B) toy automobiles and airplanes were very popular in the early 1900s
_____ (C) toy design has followed developments in transportation

EXERCISE 44.2

Focus: Answering a variety of overview questions about short passages.
Directions: Read the passages and mark the best answer choice—(A), (B), (C), or (D).

American folk music originated with ordinary people at a time when the rural population was isolated and music was not yet spread by radio, records, or music videos. It was transmitted by oral tradition and is noted for its energy, humor, and emotional impact. The major source of early American folk songs was music from the British Isles, but songs from Africa as well as songs of the American Indians have a significant part in its heritage. Later settlers from other countries also contributed songs. In the nineteenth century, composer Steven Foster wrote some of the most enduringly popular of all American songs, which soon became part of the folk tradition. Beginning in the 1930s, Woody Guthrie gained great popularity by adapting traditional melodies and lyrics and supplying new ones as well. In the 1950s and 1960s, signer-composers such as Pete Seeger, Bob Dylan, and Joan Baez continued this tradition by creating "urban" folk music. Many of these songs dealt with important social issues, such as racial integration and the war in Vietnam.

1. The primary purpose of this passage is to

_____ (A) trace the development of American folk music
_____ (B) explain the oral tradition
_____ (C) contrast the styles of folk musicians
_____ (D) point out the influence of social issues on "urban" folk music

Every scientific discipline tends to develop its own special language because it finds ordinary words inadequate, and psychology is no different. The purpose of this special jargon is not to mystify non-psychologists; rather, it allows psychologists to accurately describe the phenomena they are discussing and to communicate with each other effectively. Of course, psychological terminology consists in part of everyday words such as *emotion*, *intelligence*, and *motivation*, but psychologists use these words some-what differently. For example, laymen use the term *anxiety* to mean nervousness or fear, but most psychologists reserve the term to describe a condition produced when one fears events over which one has no control.

2. The main topic of this passage is

_____ (A) effective communication
_____ (B) the special language of psychology
_____ (C) two definitions of the word "anxiety"
_____ (D) the jargon of science

Gifford Pinchot was the first professionally trained forester in the United States. After he graduated from Yale in 1889, he studied forestry in Europe. In the 1890s he managed the forest on the Biltmore estate in North Carolina (now Pisgah National Forest) and became the first to practice scientific forestry. Perhaps his most important contribution to conservation was persuading President Theodore Roosevelt to set aside millions of acres in the West as forest reserves. These lands now make up much of the national parks and national forests of the United States. Pinchot became the chief forester of the U.S. Forest Service in 1905. Although he held that post for only five years, he established guidelines that set forest policy for decades to come.

3. The passage primarily deals with

_____ (A) Gifford Pinchot's work on the Biltmore Estate
_____ (B) the practice and theory of scientific forestry
_____ (C) the origin of national parks and national forests in the United States
_____ (D) the contributions Gifford Pinchot made to American forestry

Off-Broadway theater developed in New York City in about 1950 as a result of dissatisfaction with conditions on Broadway. Its founders believed that Broadway was overly concerned with producing safe, commercially-successful hit plays rather than drama with artistic quality. Off-Broadway producers tried to assist playwrights, directors, and performers who could not find work on Broadway. Off-Broadway theaters were poorly equipped, had limited seating, and provided few conveniences for audiences. But the original-ity of the scripts, the creativity of the performers, and the low cost of tickets made up for these disadvan-tages, and off-Broadway theater prospered. However, by the 1960s, costs began to rise, and by the 1970s, off-Broadway theater was encountering many of the difficulties of Broadway and had lost much of its vitality. With its decline, a experimental movement called *off-off-Broadway* theater developed.

4. What is the main idea of this passage?

_____ (A) After initial success, off-Broadway theater began to decline.
_____ (B) Off-Broadway theaters produced many hit commercial plays.
_____ (C) Theaters on Broadway were not well equipped.
_____ (D) Off-Broadway plays were highly creative.

5. The paragraph that follows this passage most likely deals with

_____ (A) the help off-Broadway producers provided directors, playwrights, and performers
_____ (B) methods off-broadway theaters used to cope with rising prices
_____ (C) the development of off-off-Broadway theater
_____ (D) the decline of Broadway theater

At the time of the first European contact, there were from 500 to 700 languages spoken by North American Indians. These were divided into some 60 language families, with no demonstrable genetic relationship among them. Some of these families spread across several of the seven cultural areas. The

Algonquin family, for instance, contained dozens of languages and occupied a vast territory. Speakers of Algonquin languages included the Algonquins of the Eastern Woodland, the Blackfoots of the Plains, and the Wiyots and Yuroks of California. Other language families, like the Zuni family of the Southwest, occupy only a few square miles of area and contain only a single tribal language.

6. What is the main idea of this passage?

    _____ (A) Each of the cultural areas was dominated by one of the language families.

    _____ (B) The Zuni language is closely related to the Algonquin language.

    _____ (C) There is considerable diversity in the size and the number of languages in language families of the North American Indians.

    _____ (D) Contact with Europeans had an extraordinary effect on the languages of the Indian tribes of North America.

Other major changes in journalism occurred around this time. In 1846, Richard Hoe invented the steam cylinder rotary press, making it possible to print newspapers faster and cheaper. The development of the telegraph made possible much speedier collection and distribution of news. Also in 1846, the first wire service was organized. A new type of newspaper appeared around this time, one that was more attuned to the spirit and needs of the new America. Although newspapers continued to cover politics, they came to report more human interest stories and to record the most recent news, which they could not have done before the telegraph. New York papers, and those of other northern cities, maintained corps of correspondents to go into all parts of the country to cover newsworthy events.

7. The main purpose of the passage is to

    _____ (A) present a brief history of American journalism

    _____ (B) outline certain developments in mid-nineteenth-century journalism

    _____ (C) explain the importance of the steam cylinder rotary press

    _____ (D) present some biographical information about Richard Hoe

8. What is the most probable topic of the paragraph preceding this one?

    _____ (A) Other types of rotary presses

    _____ (B) Alternatives to using wire services

    _____ (C) Newspapers that concentrated on politics

    _____ (D) Other developments in journalism

9. The tone of the passage could best be described as

    _____ (A) objective

    _____ (B) optimistic

    _____ (C) angry

    _____ (D) humorous

In the western third of North America, the convoluted folds of the Earth's surface and its fractured geologic structure tend to absorb the seismic energy of an earthquake. Even if an earthquake measuring 8.5 on the Richter scale struck Los Angeles, its force would fade by the time it reached San Francisco, some 400 miles away. But in the eastern two thirds of the continent the same energy travels more easily. The earthquake that struck New Madrid, Missouri, in 1811, estimated at 8 on the Richter scale, shook Washington, D.C., about 800 miles away, and was felt as far as Boston and Toronto.

10. Which of the following best expresses the main idea of this passage?

    _____ (A) If a major earthquake strikes Los Angeles, it will probably damage San Francisco as well.

    _____ (B) The New Madrid earthquake of 1811 was felt in Boston and Toronto.

    _____ (C) The geology of the western United States is much more complex than that of the East.

    _____ (D) Earthquakes travel farther in the East than in the West.

There has never been an adult scientist who has been half as curious as any child between the ages of four months and four years. Adults sometimes mistake this superb curiosity about everything as a lack of ability to concentrate. The truth is that children begin to learn at birth, and by the time they begin formal schooling at the age of 5 or 6, they have already absorbed a fantastic amount of information, perhaps more, fact for fact, than they will learn for the rest of their lives. Adults can multiply by many times the knowledge children absorb if they appreciate this curiosity while simultaneously encouraging the children to learn.

11. With which of the following statements would the author probably agree?

_____ (A) Children lack the ability to concentrate.
_____ (B) Young children have a much greater curiosity than adult scientists do.
_____ (C) The first few years of school are the most important ones for most children.
_____ (D) Adults can utilize children's intense curiosity to help children learn more.

12. The paragraph following this one most likely deals with

_____ (A) ways in which adults can help children learn by stimulating their curiosity
_____ (B) the learning habits of children over the age of 4
_____ (C) the methods adult scientists use to study the curiosity of young children
_____ (D) ways in which adults can become as curious as children about their environments

Settlement houses were institutions established to improve living conditions in poor city neighborhoods in the late 1800s and early 1900s. They offered health, educational, recreational, and cultural activities. The first to open in the United States was University Settlement in New York City. It was established by the social reformer Stanton Coit in 1886. The most famous example was Hull House, established by the famous reformer Jane Addams in Chicago in 1890. Settlement houses were usually staffed by idealistic young college graduates who were eager to improve the condition of the poor.

13. The passage mainly discusses

_____ (A) American cities in the late nineteenth century
_____ (B) the idealism of college graduates
_____ (C) settlement houses in the late 1800s and early 1900s
_____ (D) the life of several American social reformers

The dancer Isadora Duncan was a daring, dynamic innovator in dance. While she was not very successful in teaching her highly personal style of dance to others, she taught a generation of dancers to trust their own forms of expression. She rebelled against the rigid, formal style of classical ballet. Inspired by the art of Greece, she usually danced barefoot in a loose, flowing Greek tunic. She found further inspiration in nature and used dance movements to mirror the waves of the sea and passing clouds.

Isadora Duncan was born in San Francisco in 1878. She gave her first performance in 1899. Early failures gave way to triumphant performances in Budapest, Berlin, London, and finally, in 1908, back in the United States. She lived in Europe most of her life, establishing dancing schools for children there. She died in 1927 near Nice, France, in a freak accident, her long scarf being caught in the wheel of an open sports car in which she was riding.

14. The author's attitude toward Isadora Duncan could best be described as one of

_____ (A) displeasure
_____ (B) admiration
_____ (C) compassion
_____ (D) amazement

15. Which of the following best describes the organization of the passage?

_____ (A) The author first discusses Isadora Duncan's style of dance and then her life history.

_____ (B) The first paragraph deals with Isadora Duncan's role as a teacher; the second, her role as a performer.

_____ (C) The author first discusses Isadora Duncan's shortcomings and then her positive points.

_____ (D) First there is an analysis of Isadora Duncan's influences and then of her lasting contributions to dance.

Through the centuries, the dream of medieval alchemists was to discover how to turn lead and other "base" metals into gold. Some were fakes, but many were learned men with philosophical goals. Their quest was based on the ancient idea that all matter consists of different proportions of just four substances—earth, water, fire, and air. They believed that it was possible to adjust the proportions of the elements that made up lead by chemical means so that it turned into gold, a process called transmutation. Their experiments were concerned with finding the substance—which they called the *philosopher's stone*—that, when added to lead, would cause this astonishing change to take place. Alchemists also searched for the *elixir of life*, a substance that could cure diseases and prolong life. They failed on both counts. However, their techniques for preparing and studying chemicals helped lay the foundation for the modern science of chemistry.

16. Which of the following statements best summarizes the author's attitude toward medieval alchemists?

_____ (A) Although they were all fakes, they made important contributions to science.

_____ (B) Their discovery of the philosopher's stone was more important than the achievements of modern chemists.

_____ (C) Although their theories were sound, they lacked the equipment needed to accomplish their goals.

_____ (D) They were unable to realize their goals, but they helped prepare the way for modern chemistry.

EXERCISE 44.3

Focus: Understanding the meaning of multi-paragraph passages by identifying the main point of each of the paragraphs.

Directions: Read the following passages and the questions about them. Decide which of the choices best answers the question, and mark the answer.

QUESTIONS 1–3

In most of Europe, farmers' homes and outbuildings are generally located within a village, and tools and animals are housed there. Every morning, the farmers and farm laborers leave their village to work their land or tend their animals in distant fields and return to the village at the end of the day. Social life is thus centripetal; that is, it is focused around the community center, the village. Only in certain parts of Quebec has this pattern been preserved in North America.

Throughout most of North America, a different pattern was established. It was borrowed from northern Europe, but was pushed even further in the New World where land was cheap or even free. It is a centrifugal system of social life, with large isolated farms whose residents go to the village only to buy goods and procure services. The independence associated with American farmers stems from this pattern of farm settlement. The American farmer is as free of the intimacy of the village as the urbanite.

1. The main topic of the first paragraph is

_____ (A) European farm products

_____ (B) social life in Quebec

_____ (C) the European pattern of rural settlement

2. The main topic of the second paragraph is

_____ (A) the relative isolation of North American farm families

_____ (B) the relationship between farmers and urbanites in North America

_____ (C) the low cost of farmland in North America

3. The main topic of the entire passage is

_____ (A) a comparison of farming in northern and southern Europe

_____ (B) the difference between farming in Quebec and the rest of North America

_____ (C) European influence on American agriculture

_____ (D) a contrast between a centripetal system of rural life and a centrifugal system

QUESTIONS 4–7

While fats have lately acquired a bad image, one should not forget how essential they are. Fats provide the body's best means of storing energy, far more efficient energy sources than either carbohydrates or proteins. They act as insulation against cold, as cushioning for the internal organs, and as lubricants. Without fats, energy would be no way to utilize fat soluble vitamins. Furthermore, some fats contain fatty acids that contain necessary growth factors and help with the digestion of other foods.

An important consideration of fat intake is the ratio of saturated fats to unsaturated fats. Saturated fats, which are derived from dairy products, animal fats, and tropical oils, increase the amount of cholesterol in the blood. Cholesterol may lead to coronary heart disease by building up in the arteries of the heart. However, unsaturated fats, derived from vegetable oils, tend to lower serum cholesterol if taken in a proportion twice that of saturated fats.

The consumption of a variety of fats is necessary, but the intake of too much fat may lead to a variety of health problems. Excessive intake of fats, like all nutritional excesses, is to be avoided.

4. The main idea of the first paragraph is that

_____ (A) fats have a bad image

_____ (B) fats serve important functions in the body

_____ (C) fats store food more efficiently than proteins or carbohydrates

5. What is the main idea of the second paragraph?

_____ (A) Unsaturated fats may reduce cholesterol levels.

_____ (B) The consumption of any type of fat leads to heart disease.

_____ (C) Fats taken in the proper proportion may reduce serum cholesterol.

6. The main idea of the third paragraph is that

_____ (A) people are eating less and less fat today

_____ (B) fats should be gradually eliminated from the diet

_____ (C) excessive consumption of fats may be dangerous to one's health

7. With which of the following is the whole passage primarily concerned?

_____ (A) The role of fats in human health

_____ (B) The dangers of cholesterol

_____ (C) The benefits of fats in the diet

_____ (D) The importance of good nutrition

QUESTIONS 8–10

The term *weathering* refers to all the ways in which rock can be broken down. It takes place because minerals formed in a particular way (say at high temperatures, in the case of igneous rocks) are often unstable when exposed to various conditions. Weathering involves the interaction of the lithosphere (the Earth's crust) with the atmosphere and hydrosphere (air and water). It occurs at different rates and in different ways, depending on the climactic and environmental conditions. But all kinds of weathering ultimately produce broken minerals and rock fragments and other products of the decomposition of stone.

Soil is the most obvious and, from the human point of view, the most important result of the weathering process. Soil is the weathered part of the Earth's crust that is capable of sustaining plant life. The character of soil depends on the nature of rock from which it is formed. It also depends on the climate and on the relative "age" of the soil. Immature soils are little more than broken rock fragments. Over time, immature soil develops into mature soil, which contains quantities of humus, formed from decayed plant matter. Mature soil is darker, richer in microscopic life, and more conducive to plant growth.

8. The first paragraph primarily describes

_____ (A) the process by which rocks are broken down
_____ (B) the weathering of igneous rocks
_____ (C) gradual changes in the Earth's weather patterns

9. The main topic of the second paragraph is

_____ (A) a description of immature soil
_____ (B) the growth of plants
_____ (C) the evolution of soil

10. The main topic of the entire passage is that

_____ (A) weathering breaks down rocks and leads to the development of soil
_____ (B) soils may be classified as mature or immature
_____ (C) the process of soil development is more important to humans than that of weathering
_____ (D) the Earth's crust is constantly changing

QUESTIONS 11–16

The first Dutch outpost in New Netherlands was made at Fort Orange (now Albany) in 1624; it became a depot of the fur trade. But the most important settlement was at the southern tip of Manhattan, commanding the great harbor at the mouth of the Hudson River. Peter Minuit, first governor-general of New Netherlands, "purchased" title to the island from the Canarsie Indians for the equivalent of $24 worth of trinkets. However, the Canarsie Indians might be described as tourists from Brooklyn; Minuit had to make a later payment to the group that was actually resident there.

In 1626, engineers from Holland arrived in Manhattan to construct Fort Amsterdam. Within its rectangular walls, permanent houses were built, replacing the thatched dwellings of the original Manhattanites. The fort became the nucleus of the town of New Amsterdam. Soon Manhattan had its first skyline: the solid outline of the fort; the flagstaff; the silhouette of a giant windmill; and the masts of trading ships.

The Dutch West India company established dairy farms in the vicinity of New Amsterdam. Each morning, the cattle were driven to the "Bouwerie" (now the Bowery), a large open common in the city. Just southwest of the Bouwerie was the Bowling Green, a level area where the burghers played ninepins, the ancestor of modern bowling. The Bowling Green became the site of a cattle fair where livestock were marketed; beer and sausage were available from booths; cheese, lace, and linen were sold by farmers' wives; and Indian women sold baskets and other handicrafts. These colorful gatherings and other aspects of everyday life in New Amsterdam are described in Washington Irving's rollicking book, *Diedrich Knickerbocker's* "History of New York."

The last and most powerful governor-general of New Netherlands was Peter Stuyvesant, famous for his temper and his wooden leg. He annexed the Swedish colony of Delaware and ordered the streets of New Amsterdam laid out in an orderly manner and numbered. He did his best to obtain military and financial aid from Holland against the British. When the British sent emissaries demanding the surrender of the colony, he wanted to fight.

Four British warships, commanded by Colonel Richard Nicolls, sailed into the harbor in 1664. The fort was long out of repair, and there was a shortage of ammunition. Stuyvesant had no choice but to surrender. New Netherlands became the British colony of New York, and New Amsterdam became New York City.

11. What is the main topic of the first paragraph?

_____ (A) The first Dutch settlement in New Netherlands
_____ (B) Peter Minuit's acquisition of Manhattan
_____ (C) Tourism in Manhattan

12. The second paragraph deals primarily with

_____ (A) the establishment of Fort Amsterdam
_____ (B) the skyline of Manhattan
_____ (C) the thatched houses of the Indians

13. The third paragraph mainly describes

_____ (A) aspects of everyday life in New Amsterdam
_____ (B) the origin of the game of modern bowling
_____ (C) Washington Irving's book about New Amsterdam

14. What does the fourth paragraph mainly discuss?

_____ (A) The annexation of the Swedish colony of Delaware
_____ (B) The ordering of the streets in New Amsterdam
_____ (C) A description of Peter Stuyvesant and his accomplishments

15. What is the primary topic of the entire passage?

_____ (A) A history of the British colony of New York
_____ (B) The origin and importance of the cattle fair
_____ (C) European colonization in the New World
_____ (D) Forty years of Dutch rule in New Amsterdam

Lesson 45

FACTUAL QUESTIONS, NEGATIVE QUESTIONS, AND SCANNING QUESTIONS

FACTUAL QUESTIONS

Factual questions ask about explicit facts and details given in the passage. They often contain one of the *wh-* question words: *who, what, when, where, why, how much,* and so on.

Factual questions often begin with the phrases "According to the passage,..." or "According to the author. . . ." When you see these phrases, you know that the information needed to answer the question is directly stated somewhere in the passage (unlike answers for inference questions).

To answer factual questions, you have to locate and identify the information that the question asks about. If you are not sure from your first reading where to look for specific answers, use the following **scanning** techniques.

- Focus on one or two key words as you read the stem of each question. Lock these words in your mind.
- Scan the passage looking for the key words or their synonyms. Look only for these words. Do NOT try to read every word of the passage.
- It may help to use the eraser end of your pencil as a pointer to focus your attention. Don't reread the passage completely—just look for these words.
- When you find the key words in the passage, carefully read the sentence in which they occur. You may have to read the sentence preceding or following that sentence as well.
- Compare the information you read with the four answer choices.

The order of detail questions about a passage almost always follows the order in which ideas are presented in the passage. In other words, the information you need to answer the first detail question will usually come near the beginning of the passage; the information for the second will follow that, and so on. Knowing this should help you locate the information you need.

Correct answers for detail questions are seldom the same, word for word, as information in the passage; they often contain synonyms and use different grammatical structures.

There are generally more factual questions—twelve to eighteen per reading section—than any other type except (on some tests) vocabulary-in-context questions.

NEGATIVE QUESTIONS

These questions ask you to determine which of the four choices is not given in the passage. These questions contain the words NOT, EXCEPT, or LEAST (which are always capitalized).

- According to the passage, all of the following are true EXCEPT
- Which of the following is NOT mentioned in the passage?
- Which of the following is the LEAST likely . . .

Scan the passage to find the answers that ARE correct or ARE mentioned in the passage. Sometimes the three distractors are clustered in one or two sentences; sometimes they are scattered throughout the passage. The correct answer, of course, is the one that does not appear.

Negative questions often take more time than other questions. Therefore, you may want to guess and come back to these questions if you have time.

There are generally from three to six negative questions per reading section.

SCANNING QUESTIONS

These questions ask you to find where in the passage some particular information or transition is located. They are easy to identify: the answers are usually line numbers. They are usually easy to answer too. Scanning questions are often the last question in a set of questions about a passage. Use the same techniques for scanning given in Part A about detail questions.

Sample Questions

- In what line does the author shift his focus to _____?
- Where in the passage does the author first discuss _____?
- A description of _____ can be found in . . .
- Where in the passage does the author specifically stress _____?
- In what paragraph does the author first mention the concept of _____?

In each reading section, there are generally from one to three scanning questions.

EXERCISE 45.1

Focus: Scanning passages to locate answers for factual and scanning questions.

Directions: For each question, locate that part of the passage in which the answer will probably be found, and write down the line numbers in the blank at the end of the passage. Don't worry about answering the question itself, only about finding the information. The first one is done as an example. Do these scanning exercises as fast as you can.

QUESTIONS 1–7

Line Antlers grow from permanent knoblike bones on a deer's skull. Deer use their antlers chiefly to fight for mates or for leadership of a herd. Among most species of deer, only the males have antlers, but both male and female reindeer and caribou have antlers. Musk deer and Chinese water deer do not have antlers at all.

5   Deer that live in mild or cold climates lose their antlers each winter. New ones begin to grow the next spring. Deer that live in tropical climates may lose their antlers and grow new ones at other times of year.

      New antlers are soft and tender. Thin skin grows over the antlers as they develop. Short, fine hair on the skin makes it look like velvet. Full-grown antlers are hard and strong. The velvety skin

10 dries up and the deer rubs the skin off by scraping its antlers against trees. The antlers fall off several months later.

      The size and shape of a deer's antlers depend on the animal's age and health. The first set grows when the deer is from 1 to 2 years old. On most deer, the first antlers are short and straight. As deer get older, their antlers grow larger and form intricate branches.

1. How do deer primarily use their antlers?   **1-2**

2. In what way are reindeer and caribou different from other types of deer? _____

3. When do deer that live in temperate climates begin to grow their antlers? _____

4. According to the article, which of the following does the skin on deer's antlers most closely resemble? _____

5. Which of the following factors influences the size and shape of a deer's antlers? _____

6. At what age do deer get their first antlers? _____

7. What happens to deer's antlers as the deer grow older? _____

QUESTIONS 8–13

Line   The trumpet player Louis Armstrong, or Satchmo as he was usually called, was among the first jazz
musicians to achieve international fame. He is known for the beautiful, clear tone of his trumpet-
playing and for his gruff, gravelly singing voice. He was one of the first musicians to sing in the scat
style, using rhythmic nonsense syllables instead of lyrics.

5   Armstrong was born into a poor family in New Orleans. He first learned to play the cornet at
the age of 13, taking lessons while living in a children's home. As a teenager, he played in a number
local jazz bands in New Orleans' rollicking nightlife district, Storyville.

            In 1922, Armstrong moved to Chicago to play in Joe "King" Oliver's band. Two years later, he
joined Fletcher Henderson's band. Then, from 1925 to 1928, Armstrong made a series of records with
10   groups called the Hot Five, the Hot Seven, and the Savoy Ballroom Five. These records rank among
the greatest recordings in the history of jazz. They include "Cornet Chop Suey," "Potato Head
Blues," and "West End Blues."

            Armstrong led a big band during the 1930s and 1940s, but in 1947, returned to playing with
small jazz groups. He performed all over the world and made a number of hit records, such as
15   "Hello, Dolly" and "Mack the Knife." Armstrong also appeared in a number of movies, first in *New
Orleans* in 1947, *High Society* in 1956, and *Hello, Dolly* in 1969.

8. What was Armstrong's nickname? _____

9. Which of the following phrases best describes Armstrong's singing voice? _____

10. Where did Armstrong first learn to play the cornet? _____

11. In what city was Joe "King" Oliver's band based? _____

12. During what period did Armstrong record some of jazz's greatest records? _____

13. What was the first movie Armstrong appeared in? _____

QUESTIONS 14–23

Line   In 1862, during the Civil War, President Lincoln signed the Morrill Act. The measure was named for
its sponsor, Congressman (later Senator) Justin S. Morrill of Vermont. Popularly called the Land Grant
Act, it provided each state with 30,000 acres of public land for each senator and each representative
it had in Congress. It required that the land be sold, the proceeds invested, and the income used to
5   create and maintain colleges to teach agriculture and engineering.

            Although not all states used the money as planned in the act, some thirty states did establish
new institutions. Purdue University, the University of Illinois, Texas A & M, Michigan State, and the
University of California all trace their roots to the Morrill Act. Eighteen states gave the money to
existing state universities to finance new agricultural and engineering departments. A few gave their
10   money to private colleges. For example, Massachusetts used much of its funds to endow the Massachusetts Institute of Technology. One state changed its mind. Yale University was chosen to be
funded in Connecticut, but farmers protested, and the legislature moved the assets to the University
of Connecticut.

            Most students chose to study engineering. Agriculture was not even considered a science until
15   it had been dignified by the work of research stations. These were established at land-grant institutions in 1887 by the Hatch Act. Gradually, universities broke away from the narrow functions
Congress had assigned them and presented a full range of academic offerings from anthropology to
zoology.

            Today there are some sixty-nine land-grant institutions in all fifty states, the District of Columbia,
20   and Puerto Rico. About one in five college students in the United States attends land-grant schools.

14. When was the Morrill Act signed? _____

15. Who sponsored the Morrill Act? _____

16. What position did the sponsor of the Morrill Act have at the time it was passed? _____

17. How much land did each state receive under the Morrill Act? _____

18. How many states used the money in the way it was intended by Congress? _____

19. Which of these states used its money to fund a private university? _____

20. Who objected to the way the Connecticut legislature initially decided to spend its funds? _____

21. What was one effect of the Hatch Act of 1887? _____

22. How many land-grant institutions are in operation at present? _____

23. What percent of college students in the United States currently attend land-grant institutions? _____

EXERCISE 45.2

Focus: Answering factual, negative, and scanning questions about reading passages.

Directions: Read the following passages and the questions about them. Decide which of the choices—(A), (B), (C), or (D)—best answers the question, and mark the answer.

QUESTIONS 1–9

Line   Mesa Verde is the center of the prehistoric Anasazi culture. It is located in the high plateau lands
near Four Corners, where Colorado, Utah, New Mexico, and Arizona come together. This high
ground is majestic but not forbidding. The climate is dry but tiny streams trickle at the bottom of
deeply cut canyons, where seeps and springs provided water for the Anasazi to irrigate their crops.
5   Rich red soil provided fertile ground for their crops of corn, beans, squash, tobacco, and cotton. The
Anasazi domesticated the wild turkey and hunted deer, rabbits, and mountain sheep.

For a thousand years the Anasazi lived around Mesa Verde. Although the Anasazi are not related
to the Navajos, no one knows what these Indians called themselves, and so they are commonly
referred to by their Navajo name, Anasazi, which means "ancient ones" in the Navajo language.

10   Around 550 A.D., early Anasazi—then a nomadic people archaeologists call the Basketmakers—
began constructing permanent homes on mesa tops. In the next 300 years, the Anasazi made rapid
technological advancements, including the refinement of not only basket-making but also pottery-
making and weaving. This phase of development is referred to as the Early Pueblo Culture.

By the Great Pueblo Period (1100–1300 A.D.), the Anasazi population swelled to more than
15   5,000 and the architecturally ambitious cliff dwellings came into being. The Anasazi moved from the
mesa tops onto ledges on the steep canyon walls, creating two- and three-story dwellings. They used
sandstone blocks and mud mortar. There were no doors on the first floor and people used ladders to
reach the first roof. All the villages had underground chambers called *kivas*. Men held tribal councils
there and also used them for secret religious ceremonies and clan meetings. Winding paths, ladders,
20   and steps cut into the stone led from the valleys below to the ledges on which the villages stood.
The largest settlement contained 217 rooms. One might surmise that these dwellings were built for
protection, but the Anasazi had no known enemies and there is no sign of conflict.

But a bigger mystery is why the Anasazi occupied these structures such a short time. By 1300,
Mesa Verde was deserted. It is conjectured that the Anasazi abandoned their settlements because of
25   drought, overpopulation, crop failure, or some combination of these. They probably moved south-
ward and were incorporated into the pueblo villages that the Spanish explorers encountered 200
years later. Their descendants still live in the Southwest.

1. The passage does NOT mention that the Anasazi hunted

    _____ (A) sheep

    _____ (B) turkeys

    _____ (C) deer

    _____ (D) rabbits

2. The name that the Anasazi used for themselves

    _____ (A) means "Basketmakers" in the Navajo language

    _____ (B) is unknown today

    _____ (C) was given to them by archaeologists

    _____ (D) means "ancient ones" in the Anasazi language

3. How long did the Early Pueblo Culture last?

    _____ (A) 200 years

    _____ (B) 300 years

    _____ (C) 550 years

    _____ (D) 1,000 years

4. Where did the Anasazi move during the Great Pueblo Period?

    _____ (A) to settlements on ledges of canyon walls

    _____ (B) to pueblos in the South

    _____ (C) onto the tops of the mesas

    _____ (D) onto the floors of the canyons

5. According to the passage, the Anasazi buildings were made primarily of

    _____ (A) mud

    _____ (B) blocks of wood

    _____ (C) sandstone

    _____ (D) the skins of animals

6. According to the passage, the Anasazi entered their buildings on the ledges

    _____ (A) by means of ladders

    _____ (B) from underground chambers

    _____ (C) by means of stone stairways

    _____ (D) through doors on the first floor

7. According to the passage, *kivas* were used for all the following purposes EXCEPT

    _____ (A) clan meetings

    _____ (B) food preparation

    _____ (C) religious ceremonies

    _____ (D) tribal councils

8. According to the passage, the LEAST likely reason that the Anasazi abandoned Mesa Verde was

    _____ (A) drought

    _____ (B) overpopulation

    _____ (C) war

    _____ (D) crop failure

9. Where in the passage does the author mention specific accomplishments of the Basketmakers?

    _____ (A) Lines 5–6

    _____ (B) Lines 11–13

    _____ (C) Lines 15–16

    _____ (D) Lines 18–20

QUESTIONS 10–15

Line Dulcimers are musical instruments that basically consist of wooden boxes with strings stretched over
them. In one form or another, they have been around since ancient times, probably originating with
the Persian santir. Today there are two varieties: the hammered dulcimer and the Appalachian, or
mountain dulcimer. The former is shaped like a trapezoid, has two or more strings, and is played
5   with wooden mallets. It is the same instrument played in a number of Old World countries. The
Appalachian dulcimer is classified by musicologists as a box zither. It is a descendant of the Pennsylvania Dutch scheitholt and the French epinette. Appalachian dulcimers are painstakingly fashioned by
artisans in the mountains of West Virginia, Kentucky, Tennessee, and Virginia. These instruments
have three or four strings and are plucked with quills or the fingers. They are shaped like teardrops
10   or hourglasses. Heart-shaped holes in the sounding board are traditional. Most performers play the
instruments while seated with the instruments in their laps, but others wear them around their necks
like guitars or place them on tables in front of them. Originally used to play dance music, Appalachian dulcimers were popularized by performers such as John Jacob Niles and Jean Ritchie during the
folk music revival of the 1960s.

10. According to the passage, a hammered dulcimer is made in the shape of

_____ (A) an hourglass

_____ (B) a heart

_____ (C) a trapezoid

_____ (D) a teardrop

11. According to the passage, which of the following is NOT an ancestor of the Appalachian dulcimer?

_____ (A) the box zither

_____ (B) the santir

_____ (C) the scheitholt

_____ (D) the epinette

12. According to the passage, how many strings does the Appalachian dulcimer have?

_____ (A) one or two

_____ (B) three or four

_____ (C) four or five

_____ (D) six or more

13. According to the author, most performers play the Appalachian dulcimer

_____ (A) while sitting down

_____ (B) with the instrument strapped around their neck

_____ (C) while standing at a table

_____ (D) with wooden hammers

14. According to the author, what are John Jacob Niles and Jean Ritchie known for?

_____ (A) playing dance music on Appalachian dulcimers

_____ (B) are artisans who design Appalachian dulcimers

_____ (C) helped bring Appalachian dulcimers to the public's attention

_____ (D) began the folk music revival of the 1960s

15. Where in the passage does the author describe the hammered dulcimer?

_____ (A) Lines 1–2

_____ (B) Lines 3–4

_____ (C) Lines 4–5

_____ (D) Lines 8–10

QUESTIONS 16–20

Line Humanitarian Dorothea Dix was born in Hampden, Maine, in 1802. At the age of 19, she established
a school for girls, the Dix Mansion School, in Boston, but had to close it in 1835 due to her poor
health. She wrote and published the first of many books for children in 1824. In 1841, Dix accepted
an invitation to teach classes at a prison in East Cambridge, Massachusetts. She was deeply disturbed
5   by the sight of mentally-ill persons thrown in the jail and treated like criminals. For the next eighteen
months, she toured Massachusetts institutions where other mental patients were confined and
reported the shocking conditions she found to the state legislature. When improvements followed in
Massachusetts, she turned her attention to the neighboring states and then to the West and South.
Dix's work was interrupted by the Civil War; she served as superintendent of women hospital
10   nurses for the federal government.
Dix saw special hospitals for the mentally ill built in some fifteen states. Although her plan to
obtain public land for her cause failed, she aroused concern for the problem of mental illness all over
the United States as well as in Canada and Europe.
Dix's success was due to her independent and thorough research, her gentle but persistent
15   manner, and her ability to secure the help of powerful and wealthy supporters.

16. In what year was the Dix Mansion School closed?

_____ (A) 1821

_____ (B) 1824

_____ (C) 1835

_____ (D) 1841

17. Why did Dorothea Dix first go to a prison?

_____ (A) She taught classes there.

_____ (B) She was sent there by the state legislature.

_____ (C) She was convicted of a crime.

_____ (D) She was doing research for a book.

18. Where was Dorothea Dix first able to bring about reforms in the treatment of the mentally ill?

_____ (A) Canada

_____ (B) Massachusetts

_____ (C) The West and South

_____ (D) Europe

19. Dorothea Dix was NOT successful in her attempt to

_____ (A) become superintendent of nurses

_____ (B) publish books for children

_____ (C) arouse concern for the mentally ill

_____ (D) obtain public lands

20. At what point of the passage does the author discuss specific reasons for Dix's success?

_____ (A) Lines 7–8

_____ (B) Lines 9–10

_____ (C) Lines 11–13

_____ (D) Lines 14–15

QUESTIONS 21–26

Line   A quilt is a bed cover made of squares of material pieced together. Each square consists of two layers filled with a layer of wool or cotton cloth, feathers, or down. Often, the squares are decorated with fancy stitches and designs. According to legend, the earliest pieced quilt was stitched in 1704 by Sarah Sedgewick Everett, wife of the governor of the Massachusetts colony. By 1774 George Washing-
5   ton was buying quilts in Belvoir, Virginia, to take back to Martha in Mount Vernon. As the frontier moved westward, quilting went along. In addition to sleeping under them, homesteaders kept out drafts by hanging quilts over doors and windows. And if the money ran out, quilts were used to pay debts.

For isolated pioneer women, quilts were a source of comfort. Mary Wilman, whose family
10   moved to Texas from Missouri in 1890, recalled the first time she and her mother had to spend a week alone and a dust storm came up. "The wind blew for three days and the dust was so thick that you couldn't see the barn. My mother quilted all day, and she taught me how to quilt. If it hadn't been for quilting, I think we would have gone crazy."

Quilting provided an important social function for the women of the frontier as well. At quilting
15   bees, women met to work on quilts and to share the latest news.

Today, however, the homely quilt has become a costly cultural phenomenon. The International Quilt Festival in Houston, Texas, "world's fair of quilting," attracted only 2,500 people and displayed only 200 quilts when it began a dozen years ago. This year there were more than 20,000 visitors and 5,000 quilts, some of which sold for as much as $50,000.

21. According to legend, who made the first American quilt?

_____ (A) Sarah Sedgewick Everett

_____ (B) the governor of the colony of Massachusetts

_____ (C) Martha Washington

_____ (D) Mary Wilman

22. Which of the following is NOT mentioned in the passage as one of the benefits of quilts for pioneers?

_____ (A) They could be used to pay debts.

_____ (B) They could be used to help insulate houses.

_____ (C) They could provide psychological comfort.

_____ (D) They could be worn as warm clothing.

23. According to the passage, what is a "quilting bee?"

_____ (A) a type of insect

_____ (B) a gathering where women socialize and make quilts

_____ (C) a type of quilt

_____ (D) a place where people buy and sell quilts

24. Where is the International Quilt Festival held?

_____ (A) Massachusetts

_____ (B) Houston, Texas

_____ (C) Belvoir, Virginia

_____ (D) Missouri

25. How many quilts were displayed at the first International Quilt Festival?

_____ (A) 200

_____ (B) 2,500

_____ (C) 5,000

_____ (D) 20,000

26. Where in the passage does the author first begin to discuss the way in which the public's perception of quilts has changed in modern times?

_____ (A) Lines 5-6

_____ (B) Line 9

_____ (C) Lines 16

_____ (D) Lines 18-19

QUESTIONS 27–32

Line   Ambient divers are, unlike divers who go underwater in submersible vehicles or pressure resistant
suits, exposed to the pressure and temperature of the surrounding (*ambient*) water. Of all types of
diving, the oldest and simplest is free diving. Free divers may use no equipment at all, but most use a
face mask, foot fins, and a snorkel. Under the surface, free divers must hold their breath. Most free
5   divers can only descend 30 to 40 feet, but some skilled divers can go as deep as 100 feet.

    Scuba diving provides greater range than free diving. The word *scuba* stands for *s*elf-*c*ontained
*u*nderwater *b*reathing *a*pparatus. Scuba divers wear metal tanks with compressed air or other
breathing gases. When using open-circuit equipment, a scuba diver simply breathes air from the tank
through a hose and releases the exhaled air into the water. A closed-circuit breathing device, also
10   called a rebreather, filters out carbon dioxide and other harmful gases and automatically adds oxygen.
This enables the diver to breathe the same air over and over.

    In surface-supplied diving, divers wear helmets and waterproof canvas suits. Today, sophisti-
cated plastic helmets have replaced the heavy copper helmets used in the past. These divers get their
air from a hose connected to compressors on a boat. Surface-supplied divers can go deeper than any
15   other type of ambient diver.

27. Ambient divers are ones who

_____ (A) can descend to extreme depths

_____ (B) use submersible vehicles

_____ (C) use no equipment

_____ (D) are exposed to the surrounding water

28. According to the passage, a free diver may use any of the following EXCEPT

_____ (A) a rebreather

_____ (B) a snorkel

_____ (C) foot fins

_____ (D) a mask

29. According to the passage, the maximum depth for free divers is around

_____ (A) 40 feet

_____ (B) 100 feet

_____ (C) 200 feet

_____ (D) 1,000 feet

30. When using closed-circuit devices, divers

_____ (A) exhale air into the water

_____ (B) hold their breath

_____ (C) breathe the same air over and over

_____ (D) receive air from the surface

31. According to the passage, surface-supplied divers today use helmets made from

_____ (A) glass

_____ (B) copper

_____ (C) plastic

_____ (D) canvas

32. Where in the passage does the author mention which type of diver can make the deepest descents?

_____ (A) Lines 2–3

_____ (B) Lines 4–5

_____ (C) Lines 11

_____ (D) Lines 14–15

Lesson 46

INFERENCE QUESTIONS AND PURPOSE QUESTIONS

INFERENCE QUESTIONS

As in the Listening Comprehension section, there are questions in the Reading Comprehension section that require you to make **inferences.** The answers to these questions are not directly provided in the passage—you must "read between the lines." In other words, you must make conclusions based indirectly on information in the passage. Many test-takers find these questions the most difficult type of reading question.

Inference questions may be phrased in a number of ways. Many of these questions contain some form of the words *infer* or *imply.*

- Which of the following can be inferred from the passage?
- It can be inferred from the passage that . . .
- The author implies that . . .
- Which of the following does the passage imply?
- Which of the following would be the most reasonable guess about _____?
- The author suggests that . . .
- It is probable that . . .

There will probably be from five to eight of these questions per reading section.

Sample Item

A star very similar to the Sun is one of the nearest stars to Earth. That star is Alpha Centauri, just 4.3 light-years away. Other than our own Sun, the nearest star to the Earth is a tiny red star, not visible without a telescope, called Proxima Centauri.

It can be inferred from this passage that

(A) Proxima Centauri is similar to the Earth's Sun.
(B) Proxima Centauri is the closest star to the Earth.
(C) Alpha Centauri is invisible from the Earth.
(D) Proxima Centauri is less than 4.3 light-years from the Earth.

Choice (A) is not a valid inference; Alpha Centauri is similar to the Earth, but Proxima Centauri is "a tiny red star." Choice (B) also cannot be inferred; the closest star to the Earth is our own Sun. Nor can (C) be inferred; Proxima Centauri is invisible, but there is no information as to whether Alpha Centauri is. Since Alpha Centauri is 4.3 light-years away, it can be inferred that Alpha Centauri, the closest star, is less than that.

PURPOSE QUESTIONS

These questions ask why the author of a passage mentions some piece of information, or includes a quote from a person or a study, or uses some particular word or phrase.

Sample Questions

- Why does the author mention _____?
- The author refers to _____ to indicate that . . .
- The author quotes _____ in order to show . . .
- The phrase _____ in line _____ is mentioned to illustrate the effect of . . .

Sample Answer Choices

- To strengthen the argument that _____
- To provide an example of _____
- To challenge the idea that _____
- To contradict _____
- To support the proposal to _____

There are usually from one to four purpose questions per reading section.

EXERCISE 46.1

Focus: Identifying valid inferences based on sentences.

Directions: Read each sentence, then mark the one answer choice—(A), (B), or (C)—that is a valid inference based on that sentence.

1. A metal-worker of 3,000 years ago would recognize virtually every step of the lost-wax process used to cast titanium for jet engines.

    _____ (A) Titanium has been forged for thousands of years.
    _____ (B) The lost-wax method of casting is very old.
    _____ (C) Metal working has changed very little in 3,000 years.

2. When apple growers talk about new varieties of apples, they don't mean something developed last month, last year, or even in the last decade.

    _____ (A) Apple growers haven't developed any new varieties in recent decades.
    _____ (B) Some varieties of apples can be developed in a short time, but others take a long time.
    _____ (C) New varieties of apples take many years to develop.

3. Blood cholesterol used to be thought of as a problem only for adults.

    _____ (A) Blood cholesterol is no longer a problem for adults.
    _____ (B) Only children have a problem with blood cholesterol.
    _____ (C) Blood cholesterol affects both adults and children.

4. Cities founded around the turn of the eighteenth century, such as Williamsburg, Annapolis, and especially Philadelphia, were laid out on a regular grid with public squares, while cities laid out in the mid-seventeenth century, such as Boston, remain chaotic to this day.

    _____ (A) Philadelphia is today laid out more regularly than either Williamsburg or Annapolis.
    _____ (B) Boston was not originally laid out according to a logical plan.
    _____ (C) Philadelphia, Williamsburg, and Annapolis were founded before Boston.

5. There is more quartz in the world than any one kind of feldspar, but the feldspars as a group are five times more common than quartz.

    _____ (A) One type of quartz is five times more plentiful than feldspar.

    _____ (B) Quartz is less common than the feldspars.

    _____ (C) The most common type of feldspar is as plentiful as quartz.

6. Compared with the rest of its brain, the visual area of a turtle's brain is comparatively small since turtles, like all other reptiles, depend on senses other than sight.

    _____ (A) No reptile uses sight as its primary sense.

    _____ (B) Animals that depend on sight all have larger visual areas in their brains than turtles do.

    _____ (C) The visual areas of other reptile brains are comparatively smaller than those of turtles.

7. Contrary to popular belief, there is no validity to the stories one hears of initials carved in a tree by a young boy becoming elevated high above his head when he visits the tree as an old man.

    _____ (A) Trees don't grow the way many people think they do.

    _____ (B) If a child carves initials in a tree, it won't grow.

    _____ (C) Over time, initials that are carved into a tree will be elevated.

8. That composer Philip Glass is more interested in rhythm than in melody or harmony becomes obvious when one listens to his works.

    _____ (A) Most of Glass's listeners prefer melody and harmony to rhythm.

    _____ (B) It is not clear what Glass's musical interests are.

    _____ (C) Rhythm is more important in Glass' works than melody or harmony.

9. Illegible handwriting does not indicate weakness of character, as even a quick glance at the penmanship of George Washington, Franklin D. Roosevelt, or John Kennedy reveals.

    _____ (A) Washington, Roosevelt, and Kennedy all had handwriting that was difficult to read.

    _____ (B) A person's handwriting reveals a lot about that person.

    _____ (C) The author believes that Washington, Roosevelt, and Kennedy all had weak characters.

10. William Faulkner set many of his novels in and around an imaginary town, Jefferson, Mississippi, which he closely patterned after his hometown of Oxford, Mississippi.

    _____ (A) William Faulkner wrote many of his novels while living in Jefferson, Mississippi.

    _____ (B) The town of Oxford, Mississippi, exists only in Faulkner's novels.

    _____ (C) Faulkner actually wrote about his hometown but did not use its real name.

11. Most fish take on, to a certain degree, the coloration of their natural surroundings, so it is not surprising that the fish inhabiting warm, shallow waters around tropical reefs are colored all the brilliant tints of the rainbow.

    _____ (A) Tropical fish are unlike other fish because they take on the coloration of their environment.

    _____ (B) Tropical fish are brightly colored because they inhabit warm waters.

    _____ (C) Tropical reefs are brightly colored environments.

12. Although sheepherding is an older and more beloved occupation, shepherds never caught the attention of American filmmakers the way cowboys did.

    _____ (A) There have been more American films about cowboys than about shepherds.

    _____ (B) Films about shepherds were popular before films about cowboys.

    _____ (C) Cowboys are generally younger than shepherds.

13. The Okefenokee Swamp is a fascinating realm that both confirms and contradicts popular notions of a swamp, because along with huge cypresses, dangerous quagmires, and dim waterways, the Okefenokee has sandy pine islands, sunlit prairies, and clear lakes.

    _____ (A) People generally feel that swamps are fascinating places.

    _____ (B) The Okefenokee has features that most people do not associate with swamps.

    _____ (C) Most swamps do not have huge cypresses, dangerous quagmires, and dim water-ways.

14. As an architect, Thomas Jefferson preferred the Roman style, as seen in the University of Virginia, to the English style favored by Charles Bullfinch.

    _____ (A) The University of Virginia was influenced by the Roman style.

    _____ (B) Bullfinch was an English architect.

    _____ (C) Jefferson preferred to build in the English style of architecture.

15. In all cultures, gestures are used as a form of communication, but the same gestures may have very different meanings in different cultures.

    _____ (A) No two cultures use the same gestures.

    _____ (B) One gesture will never have the same meaning in two cultures.

    _____ (C) A person from one culture may misunderstand the gestures used by a person from another culture.

16. Even spiders that do not build webs from silk use it for a variety of purposes, such as constructing egg sacs and nursery tents.

    _____ (A) All spiders build webs.

    _____ (B) Spiders that build webs don't build egg sacs or nursery tents.

    _____ (C) Silk is used by all spiders.

EXERCISE 46.2

Focus: Recognizing valid inferences based on longer passages.

Directions: Read the passages. If the statements following the passages are valid inferences based on those passages, mark the items *I*. If the statements cannot be inferred from the passage, mark those items *X*.

QUESTIONS 1-7

Line   The term "neon light" was originally applied to a particular type of vapor lamp using the inert gas neon. A long tube was filled with neon, which then became luminous at low pressure when an electric current was passed through it. The lamp then emitted the characteristic reddish-orange light of neon. Today, the term "neon light" is given to lamps of this general type that may be filled with a
5   variety of gasses, depending on the color that is desired. Argon, for example, is used to produce blue light.

Colors can also be altered by changing the color of the glass tube. The tubes must be quite long in all these lamps to produce light efficiently. As a result, high voltages are required. Neon tube lamps are not practical for indoor illumination, but they have found widespread outdoor use in glowing, colorful advertising signs.

_____ **1.** The inert gas neon is reddish-orange in color.

_____ **2.** The meaning of the term "neon light" has changed over time.

_____ **3.** Today's "neon lights" never actually contain neon.

_____ **4.** All types of "neon lights" work on the same general principles.

_____ **5.** When stimulated by electricity, different types of gas produce different colors.

_____ **6.** Modern "neon lights" are more efficient than those used in the past.

_____ **7.** The primary market for neon lights is businesses rather than private households.

QUESTIONS 8–15

Line   Natural flavorings and fragrances are often costly and limited in supply. For example, the vital ingredient in a rose fragrance is extracted from natural rose oil at a cost of thousands of dollars a pound; an identical synthetic substance can be made for 1 percent of this cost. Since the early twentieth century, success in reproducing these substances has created a new industry that today
5   produces hundreds of artificial flavors and fragrances.

Some natural fragrances are easily synthesized; these include vanillin, the aromatic ingredient in vanilla, and benzaldehyde, the aromatic ingredient in wild cherries. Other fragrances, however, have dozens, even hundreds of components. Only recently has it been possible to separate and identify these ingredients by the use of gas chromatography and spectroscopy. Once the chemical identity is
10   known, it is often possible to synthesize them. Nevertheless, some complex substances, such as the aroma of fresh coffee, have still not been duplicated satisfactorily.

Many of the chemical compounds making up these synthetics are identical to those found in nature and are as harmless or harmful as the natural substances. New products must be tested for safety, and when used in food, must be approved by the U.S. Food and Drug Administration.
15   The availability of synthetic flavors and fragrances has made possible a large variety of products, from inexpensive beverages to perfumed soap to used cars with applied "new car odor."

_____   **8.** Natural rose fragrance is 100 times more expensive to produce than artificial rose fragrance.

_____   **9.** Vanillin is easier to synthesize than benzaldehyde.

_____   **10.** In general, the more components there are in a fragrance, the harder it is to synthesize.

_____   **11.** Once a substance has been chemically analyzed, it can always be easily synthesized.

_____   **12.** Only recently has it been possible to satisfactorily synthesize the aroma of fresh coffee.

_____   **13.** Not all synthetic flavors are harmless.

_____   **14.** Synthesized substances must be tested for safety only if they are used in food.

_____   **15.** Synthetic fragrances can be used to make a used car smell like a new one.

QUESTIONS 16–20

Line   A legend is a popular type of folk tale. In some ways, legends resemble myths, another type of folk tale. But myths describe events from antiquity and usually deal with religious subjects, such as the birth of a god. Legends tell of recognizable people, places, and events and often take place in comparatively recent times. Some legends are based on real persons or events but many are entirely
5   fictional. The legends of the superhuman accomplishments of Paul Bunyan and Pecos Bill are imaginary, while the legends about Washington and Lincoln are mostly exaggerations of real qualities those two presidents had.

All societies have legends. Most legends began as stories about the heroes of a particular region, occupation, or ethnic group. For example, John Henry was a legendary hero of black Americans, and Casey Jones of railroad workers. Over time, however, these figures have become national heroes.

_____   **16.** Both legends and myths can be classified as folk tales.

_____   **17.** Myths generally take place in comparatively recent times.

_____   **18.** The stories of Paul Bunyan and Pecos Bill are not true but they are based on actual people.

_____   **19.** Legends about Washington and Lincoln are not entirely fictional.

_____   **20.** John Henry and Casey Jones are today well known only by certain groups of people.

Peterson's TOEFL CBT Success

EXERCISE 46.3

Focus: Answering inference and purpose questions.

Directions: Read the following passages and the questions about them. Decide which of the choices—(A), (B), (C), or (D)—best answers the question, and mark the answer.

QUESTIONS 1–4

Line   Pigeons have been taught to recognize human facial expressions, upsetting long-held beliefs that only humans had evolved the sophisticated nervous systems to perform such a feat. In recent experiments at the University of Iowa, eight trained pigeons were shown photographs of people displaying emotions of happiness, anger, surprise, and disgust. The birds learned to distinguish between these
5   expressions. Not only that, but they were also able to correctly identify the same expressions on photographs of unfamiliar faces. Their achievement does not suggest, of course, that the pigeons had any idea what the human expressions meant.

      Some psychologists have theorized that because of the importance of facial expression to human communication, humans developed special nervous systems capable of recognizing subtle
10   expressions. The pigeons cast doubt on that idea, however.

      In fact, the ability to recognize facial expressions of emotion is not necessarily innate even in human babies, but may have to be learned in much the same way pigeons learn. In experiments conducted several years ago at the University of Iowa, it was found that pigeons organize images of things into the same logical categories that humans do.

15   None of this work would come as any surprise to Charles Darwin, who long ago wrote about the continuity of mental development from animals to humans.

1. From the passage, which of the following can be inferred about pigeons?

_____ (A) They can show the same emotions humans can.

_____ (B) They can understand human emotions.

_____ (C) They can only identify the expressions of people they are familiar with.

_____ (D) They have more sophisticated nervous systems than was once thought.

2. The passage implies that, at birth, human babies

_____ (A) have nervous systems capable of recognizing subtle expressions

_____ (B) can learn from pigeons

_____ (C) are not able to recognize familiar faces

_____ (D) may not be able to identify basic emotions through facial expressions

3. Why does the author mention the experiments conducted several years ago at the University of Iowa?

_____ (A) They proved that pigeons were not the only kind of animal with the ability to recognize facial expressions.

_____ (B) They were contradicted by more recent experiments.

_____ (C) They proved that the ability to recognize human expressions was not innate in human babies.

_____ (D) They showed the similarities between the mental organization of pigeons and that of humans.

4. If Charles Darwin could have seen the results of this experiment, his most probable response would have been one of

_____ (A) rejection

_____ (B) surprise

_____ (C) agreement

_____ (D) amusement

QUESTIONS 5–7

Line   The spectacular eruptions of Old Faithful geyser in Yellowstone National Park do not occur like
clockwork. Before the earthquake of 1959, eruptions came every 60 to 65 minutes; today they are as
little as 30 minutes or as much as 90 minutes apart. The geyser usually gives a warning: a short burst
of steam. Then a graceful column rises up to 150 feet in the air. The water unfurls in the sunlight
5   with the colors of the rainbow playing across it.

This eruption is only the visible part of the spectacle. The geyser is linked by an intricate
plumbing network to some extremely hot rocks. As water seeps into the underground system, it is
heated at the bottom like water in a tea kettle. But while water in a kettle rises because of convec-
tion, the narrow tubes of the geyser system prevent free circulation of the water. Thus, the water in
10   the upper tubes is far cooler than the water at the bottom. The weight of the water puts pressure on
the column, and this raises the boiling point of the water near the bottom. Finally, the water in the
upper part of the column warms and expands, some of it welling out of the mouth of the geyser.
This decreases the pressure on the superheated water, which abruptly turns to steam. This in turn
forces all the water and vapor out of the geyser.

5. It can be inferred from the passage that the earthquake of 1959 made Old Faithful geyser erupt

_____ (A) more frequently

_____ (B) less regularly

_____ (C) more suddenly

_____ (D) less spectacularly

6. Why does the author mention a rainbow in line 5?

_____ (A) The column of water forms an arc in the shape of a rainbow.

_____ (B) In the sunlight, the column of water may produce the colors of the rainbow.

_____ (C) Rainbows can be seen quite frequently in Yellowstone National Park.

_____ (D) The rainbow, like the geyser, is an example of the beauty of nature.

7. The passage implies that Old Faithful would probably not erupt at all if

_____ (A) the tubes of the geyser system were very wide

_____ (B) the climate suddenly changed

_____ (C) there had not been an earthquake in 1959

_____ (D) the underground tubes were longer

QUESTIONS 8–12

Line In 1881, a new type of weed began spreading across the northern Great Plains. Unlike other weeds, the
tumbleweed did not spend its life rooted to the soil; instead, it tumbled and rolled across fields in the
wind. The weed had sharp, spiny leaves that could lacerate the flesh of ranchers and horses alike. It ex-
ploited the vast area of the plains, thriving in regions too barren to support other plants. With its ability
5   to generate and disseminate numerous seeds quickly, it soon became the scourge of the prairies.

To present-day Americans, the tumbleweed symbolizes the Old West. They read the Zane Grey novels in which tumbleweeds drift across stark western landscapes and see classic western movies in which
tumbleweeds share scenes with cowboys and covered wagons. Yet just over a century ago, the tumbleweed was a newcomer. The first sign of the invasion occurred in North and South Dakota in the late
10   1870s.

Farmers had noticed the sudden appearance of the new, unusual weed. One group of immigrants,
however, did not find the weed at all unfamiliar. The tumbleweed, it turns out, was a native of southern
Russia, where it was known as Tartar thistle. It was imported to the United States by unknown means.

Frontier settlers gave the plants various names: saltwort, Russian cactus, and wind witch. But bota-
15   nists at the Department of Agriculture preferred the designation *Russian thistle* as the plant's common
name. However, these botanists had a much harder time agreeing on the plant's scientific name. Generally, botanists compare a plant to published accounts of similar plants, or to samples kept as specimens.
Unfortunately, no book described the weed and no samples existed in herbaria in the United States.

8. Which of the following can be inferred about tumbleweeds?

_____ (A) They have strong, deep roots.

_____ (B) They require a lot of care.

_____ (C) They reproduce efficiently.

_____ (D) They provided food for ranchers and animals.

9. The passage suggests that most present-day Americans

_____ (A) consider the tumbleweed beneficial

_____ (B) don't know when tumbleweeds came to North America

_____ (C) have never heard of tumbleweeds

_____ (D) believe tumbleweeds are new-comers to the United States

10. The author mentions the novels of Zane Grey and classic western movies (lines 6–8) because they

_____ (A) tell the story of the invasion of tumbleweeds

_____ (B) are sources of popular informa-tion about tumbleweeds

_____ (C) present very inaccurate pictures of tumbleweeds

_____ (D) were written long before tumbleweeds were present in the United States

11. It is probable that the "group of immigrants" mentioned in line 11

_____ (A) was from southern Russia

_____ (B) had lived in North and South Dakota for many years

_____ (C) imported tumbleweeds into the United States

_____ (D) wrote a number of accounts about tumbleweeds

12. From the passage it can be inferred that the botanists at the Department of Agriculture

_____ (A) could not find any tum-bleweeds on the plains

_____ (B) gave the names saltwort, Russian cactus, and wind witch to the tumbleweed

_____ (C) could not decide on a com-mon designation for the tumbleweed

_____ (D) found it difficult to classify the plant scientifically

QUESTIONS 13–17

Line For most modern airports, the major design problem is scale—how to allow adequate space on the
ground for maneuvering wide-body jets while permitting convenient and rapid movement of passengers departing, arriving, or transferring from one flight to another.

5   Most designs for airport terminals take one of four approaches. In the linear plan, the building
may be straight or curved. The passengers board aircraft parked next to the terminal. This plan works
well for small airports that need to provide boarding areas for only a few aircraft at a time.

     In the pier plan, narrow corridors or piers extend from a central building. This plan allows
many aircraft to park next to the building. However, it creates long walking distances for passengers.

     In the satellite plan, passengers board aircraft from small terminals that are separated from the
10   main terminals. Passengers reach the satellites by way of shuttle trains or underground passageways
that have shuttle trains or moving sidewalks.

     The transporter plan employs some system of transport to move passengers from the terminal
building to the aircraft. If buses are used, the passengers must climb a flight of stairs to board the
aircraft. If mobile lounges are used, they can link up directly with the aircraft and protect passengers
from the weather.

13. It can be inferred that scale would not pose a major design problem at airports if

    _____ (A) airports were larger

    _____ (B) aircraft did not need so much space to maneuver on the ground

    _____ (C) other forms of transportation were more efficient

    _____ (D) airplanes could fly faster

14. The linear plan would probably be best at

    _____ (A) a busy airport

    _____ (B) an airport used by many small aircraft

    _____ (C) an airport with only a few arrivals or departures

    _____ (D) an airport that serves a large city

15. The passage implies that the term "satellite plan" is used because

    _____ (A) satellites are launched and tracked from these sites

    _____ (B) small terminals encircle the main terminal like satellites around a planet

    _____ (C) the plan makes use of the most modern, high-technology equipment

    _____ (D) airports that make use of this plan utilize data from weather satellites

16. The passage suggests that shuttle trains transfer passengers to satellite terminals from

    _____ (A) the main terminal

    _____ (B) airplanes

    _____ (C) downtown

    _____ (D) other satellite terminals

17. It can be inferred that mobile lounges would be more desirable than buses when

    _____ (A) passengers are in a hurry

    _____ (B) flights have been delayed

    _____ (C) the weather is bad

    _____ (D) passengers need to save money

QUESTIONS 18–20

Line The sea has been rising relative to the land for at least 100 years, geologists say. During that same period, the Atlantic Coast has eroded an average of 2 to 3 feet per year, the Gulf Coast even faster. Many engineers maintain that seawalls and replenished beaches are necessary to protect the nation's shoreline. Too many people live or vacation in Miami Beach, Atlantic City, or Martha's Vineyard to
5 allow their roads and buildings to simply fall into the sea.

The problem with seawalls is that they simply don't work. One study has shown that, in fact, seawalls accelerate the erosion of beaches.

Faced with the loss of their beaches, other communities have tried a simple but expensive solution: replace the lost sand. These replenishment programs, however, are costly and of dubious
10 value. Another study has shown that only 10 percent of replenished beaches lasted more than five years.

18. It can be inferred from the passage that the author

_____ (A) opposes the use of both seawalls and beach replenishment

_____ (B) believes beach replenishment would be more effective than seawalls

_____ (C) opposes any actions to protect the shoreline

_____ (D) denies that beach erosion is a problem

19. Why does the author mention Miami Beach, Atlantic City, and Martha's Vinyard?

_____ (A) These are communities with sea walls.

_____ (B) These are communities that have implemented replenishment programs.

_____ (C) These are communities in danger of beach erosion.

_____ (D) These are communities that have lost roads and buildings to erosion.

20. The author quotes the two studies in the passage in order to

_____ (A) suggest that the sea is not rising as fast as was originally believed

_____ (B) strengthen the engineers' contention that seawalls and replenished beaches are necessary

_____ (C) propose two new solutions to beach erosion

_____ (D) support his own position

Lesson 47

VOCABULARY-IN-CONTEXT QUESTIONS

When ETS eliminated the first section of Section 3, which consisted of 30 discrete vocabulary items, it replaced them with an increased number of questions (from 12 to 18) about the vocabulary in the reading passages. Most test-takers find that, in general, it is easier to answer vocabulary questions based on the context of a passage than it is to answer questions about vocabulary in single, isolated sentences.

In vocabulary-in-context questions, you must determine which of four words or phrases can best substitute for a word or words in the passage.

Most of the questions ask about single words (usually nouns, verbs, adjectives, and adverbs). Some ask about two- or three-word phrases.

Sometimes two of the answer choices for these items might be "correct" definitions of the word that is asked about. In those cases, you must decide which of the two is correct in the context of the passage.

In ordinary reading, there are a number of clues that can help you determine the meaning of an unknown word:

- **Synonyms**
  The first state to institute *compulsory* education was Massachusetts, which made it mandatory for students to attend school twelve weeks a year.
  The word *mandatory* is a synonym for the word *compulsory*.

- **Examples**
  Many gardeners use some kind of *mulch*, such as chopped leaves, peat moss, grass clippings, pine needles, or wood chips, in order to stop the growth of weeds and hold in moisture.
  From the examples given, it is clear that *mulch* is plant matter.

- **Contrast**
  In the 1820s, the Southern states supported improvements in the national transportation system, but the Northern states *balked*.
  Since the Southern states supported improvements, and since a word signaling contrast (*but*) is used, it is clear that the Northern states disagreed with this idea, and that the word *balked* must mean *objected or refused*.

- **General context**
  In a desert, vegetation is so *scanty* as to be incapable of supporting any large human population.
  As is generally known, deserts contain little vegetation, so clearly the word *scanty* must mean *scarce* or *barely sufficient*.

When answering vocabulary-in-context questions, you must most often depend on the general context of the sentence to help you choose the correct answer.

You should follow these steps to answer vocabulary-in-context items.

1. Look at the word being asked about and the four answer choices. If you are familiar with the word, guess which answer is correct. Do NOT mark your answer sheet yet.

2. Read the sentence in which the word appears. If you were familiar with the word and guessed at the answer, make sure that the word that you chose fits with the word as it is used in the sentence. If you were unfamiliar with the word, see if context clues in the sentence or in the sentences before or after help you guess the meaning.

3. If you are not sure which answer is correct, read the sentence with each of the four answer choices in place. Does one seem more logical, given the context of the sentence, than the other three? If not, do any seem illogical? (Those you can eliminate.)

4. If you're still not sure, make the best guess you can and go on.

Sample Items

In Britain's North American colonies, university-trained physicians were at a premium. At the time of the Revolution, there were probably only around 400 and some 3,000 practitioners who had on-the-job training

(5) as barber-surgeons or physicians' apprentices. Whether university trained or not, none had much knowledge of the causes of disease, and the "cures" they often recommended—bleeding, blistering, and the use of violent purgatives—were at best ineffective and at

(10) worst lethal.

1. The phrase "at a premium" in line 2 is closest in meaning to

   (A) well-paid
   (B) not very numerous
   (C) very experienced
   (D) not well-respected

The phrase "only around 400" indicates that there was a shortage of university-trained physicians.

2. Which of the following words could best be substituted for the word "lethal" in line 10?

   (A) Impractical
   (B) Brutal
   (C) Impossible
   (D) Deadly

The phrase "at best ineffective and at worst lethal" indicates that the correct answer must describe a situation much worse than ineffective. Choices (A) and (C) don't create logical sentences when substituted for *lethal*. Choice (B), *brutal* (which means savage or violent), is more logical, but only choice (D) is synonymous with the word that is asked about.

EXERCISE 47.1

Focus: Using context clues to answer vocabulary-in-context questions involving words with multiple definitions.

Directions: Read each item. Then mark the answer choice that could best be used in place of the underlined expression as it appears in the sentence.

Every atlas has its own <u>legend</u>.

1. _____ (A) mythical story
   _____ (B) famous person
   _____ (C) explanation of symbols

The planet Mercury is visible to the <u>naked</u> eye but is not the easiest planet to spot.

2. _____ (A) unclothed
   _____ (B) unaided
   _____ (C) unarmed

Above the snow line, any mountain hollow is permanently <u>occupied</u> with snow.

3. _____ (A) filled
   _____ (B) busy

The glass factories of Toledo, Ohio, <u>boomed</u> after Michael Owens invented a process that turned out bottles by the thousands.

4. _____ (A) exploded
   _____ (B) resounded
   _____ (C) prospered

Dr. Rene Dubos, a French physician who came to the United States in 1924, searched for substances that would <u>check</u> the growth of bacteria.

5. _____ (A) restrict
   _____ (B) investigate

The root of the horseradish plant has a <u>biting</u> taste.

6. _____ (A) chewing
   _____ (B) sharp
   _____ (C) sarcastic

The double-bass is shaped like a viola and has a deep, <u>rich</u> tone.

7. _____ (A) valuable
   _____ (B) resonant
   _____ (C) abundant

A public library is a resource the entire community can <u>draw on</u>.

8. _____ (A) illustrate
   _____ (B) approach
   _____ (C) utilize

A business <u>concern</u> with two or more owners is referred to as a partnership.

9. _____ (A) firm
   _____ (B) worry

Table salt is <u>finer</u> than rock salt.

10. _____ (A) made up of smaller particles
    _____ (B) of better quality
    _____ (C) freer of impurities

Shirley Jackson's sometimes <u>chilling</u>, sometimes hilarious stories were largely ignored by critics at the time they were published.

11. _____ (A) freezing
    _____ (B) frightening

As a child, the sharpshooter Annie Oakley hunted <u>game</u> with such success that, by selling it, she was able to pay off the mortgage on her family's farm.

12. _____ (A) animals
    _____ (B) athletic competition

All chimpanzees are extremely curious about their surroundings.

13. _____ (A) strange

_____ (B) inquisitive

Furniture design and manufacture were originally the work of individuals, but by the eighteenth century, many furniture makers had teams of craftsmen to help them carry out their plans.

14. _____ (A) transport

_____ (B) obey

_____ (C) implement

Samuel Latham Mitchell helped found Rutgers Medical College in New Jersey in 1826, and he produced several important works in chemistry and geology.

15. _____ (A) books

_____ (B) accomplishments

_____ (C) factories

EXERCISE 47.2

Focus: Answering vocabulary-in-context questions about words or phrases in reading passages.

Directions: Answer the questions about the vocabulary in the passages, and mark the words or phrases that are closest in meaning to the words or phrases that are asked about.

QUESTIONS 1–11

Line The Civil War created feverish manufacturing activity to supply critical material, especially in the North. When the fighting stopped, the stage was set for dramatic economic growth. Wartime taxes on production had vanished, and the few taxes that remained leaned heavily on real estate, not on business. The population flow from farm to city increased, and the labor force it provided was

5 buttressed by millions of newly arrived immigrants willing to work for low wages in the mills of the North and on the railroad crews of the Midwest and West.

Government was nothing if not accommodating. It established tariff barriers, provided loans and grants to build a transcontinental railroad, and assumed a studied posture of nonintervention in private enterprise. The social-Darwinism of British philosopher Herbert Spencer and American

10 economist William Graham Summer prevailed. The theory was that business, if left to its own devices, would cull out the weak and nurture the strong. But as business expanded, the rivalry heated up. In the 1880s, five railroads operating between New York and Chicago were vying for traffic, and two more were under construction. As a result of the battle, the fare between the cities decreased to $1. The petroleum industry suffered from similar savage competition, and in the 1870s, many oil industries failed.

1. The word "feverish" in line 1 is closest in meaning to

_____ (A) extremely rapid

_____ (B) sickly and slow

_____ (C) very dangerous

_____ (D) understandable

2. Which of the following is closest in meaning to the word "critical" in line 1?

_____ (A) industrial

_____ (B) serious

_____ (C) crucial

_____ (D) insulting

3. The phrase "the stage was set" in line 2 is closest in meaning to which of the following?

_____ (A) The play was over

_____ (B) The progress continued

_____ (C) The foundation was laid

_____ (D) The direction was clear

4. The phrase "real estate" in line 3 refers to

_____ (A) tools and machines

_____ (B) actual income

_____ (C) new enterprises

_____ (D) land and buildings

5. The word "buttressed " in line 5 is closest in meaning to

_____ (A) concerned

_____ (B) supplemented

_____ (C) restructured

_____ (D) enriched

6. The word "accommodating" in line 7 is closest in meaning to

_____ (A) persistent

_____ (B) indifferent

_____ (C) balanced

_____ (D) helpful

7. Which of the following could best be substituted for the word "posture" in line 8?

_____ (A) stature

_____ (B) predicament

_____ (C) position

_____ (D) situation

8. The word "prevailed" in line 10 is closest in meaning to

_____ (A) influenced

_____ (B) triumphed

_____ (C) premiered

_____ (D) evolved

9. The phrase "left to its own devices" in lines 10–11, means

_____ (A) forced to do additional work

_____ (B) allowed to do as it pleased

_____ (C) made to change its plans

_____ (D) encouraged to produce more goods

10. The word "vying" in line 12 is closest in meaning to

_____ (A) competing

_____ (B) hoping

_____ (C) arranging

_____ (D) caring

11. The word "savage" in line 14 is closest in meaning to

_____ (A) fierce

_____ (B) growing

_____ (C) surprising

_____ (D) genuine

QUESTIONS 12-19

Line   All birds have feathers, and all animals with feathers are birds.

No other major group of animals is so easy to categorize. All birds have wings, too, but wings are not peculiar to birds.

Many adaptations are found in both feathers and wings. Feathers form the soft down of geese

5   and ducks, the long decorative plumes of ostriches, and the strong flight feathers of eagles and hawks. Wings vary from the short, broad ones of chickens, which seldom fly, to the long, slim ones of albatrosses, which spend almost all their lives soaring on air currents. In penguins, wings have been modified into flippers and feathers into a waterproof covering. In kiwis, the wings are almost impossible to detect.

10   Yet diversity among birds is not so striking as it is among mammals. The difference between a hummingbird and a penguin is immense, but hardly as startling as that between a bat and a whale. It is variations in details rather than in fundamental patterns that has been important in the adaptation of birds to many kinds of ecosystems.

12. The word "categorize" in line 2 is closest in meaning to

_____ (A) appreciate

_____ (B) comprehend

_____ (C) classify

_____ (D) visualize

13. Which of the following is closest in meaning to the phrase "peculiar to" in line 3?

_____ (A) unusual for

_____ (B) common to

_____ (C) necessary for

_____ (D) unique to

14. The word "slim" in line 6 is closest in meaning to

_____ (A) slender

_____ (B) powerful

_____ (C) graceful

_____ (D) soft

15. The word "detect" in line 9 is closest in meaning to

_____ (A) utilize

_____ (B) extend

_____ (C) observe

_____ (D) describe

16. Which of the following is closest in meaning to the word "diversity" in line 10?

_____ (A) function

_____ (B) heredity

_____ (C) specialty

_____ (D) variety

17. The word "hardly" in line 11 is closest in meaning to

_____ (A) definitely

_____ (B) not nearly

_____ (C) possibly

_____ (D) not always

18. The word "startling" in line 11 is closest in meaning to

_____ (A) initial

_____ (B) exciting

_____ (C) tremendous

_____ (D) surprising

19. The word "fundamental" in line 12 is closest in meaning to

_____ (A) basic

_____ (B) shifting

_____ (C) predictable

_____ (D) complicated

QUESTIONS 20–27

Line   Manufactured in the tranquil New England town of Concord, New Hampshire, the famous Concord
Coach came to symbolize the Wild West. Its rugged body and a suspension system of leather straps
could handle the hard jolts from rough roads. A journalist in 1868, describing a railroad shipment of
30 coaches bound for Wells, Fargo and Company, wrote, "They are splendidly decorated . . . the
5   bodies red and the running parts yellow. Each door has a handsome picture, mostly landscapes, and
no two coaches are exactly alike."

Wells, Fargo and Company was founded in 1852 to provide mail and banking services for the
gold camps of California and later won a monopoly on express services west of the Mississippi. A
Wells, Fargo Concord Coach carried nine to fourteen passengers plus baggage and mail. The accom-
10   modations were by no means plush. However, the stagecoach was the swiftest method of travel
through much of the Far West.

20. The word "tranquil" in line 1 is closest in meaning to

_____ (A) peaceful

_____ (B) bustling

_____ (C) industrial

_____ (D) tiny

21. The word "symbolize" in line 2 is closest in meaning to

_____ (A) recollect

_____ (B) fulfill

_____ (C) deny

_____ (D) represent

22. Which of the following could best substitute for the word "rugged" in line 2?

_____ (A) streamlined

_____ (B) roomy

_____ (C) sturdy

_____ (D) primitive

23. Which of the following is closest in meaning to the word "jolts" in line 3?

_____ (A) signs

_____ (B) shocks

_____ (C) sights

_____ (D) shots

24. The phrase "bound for" in line 4 is closest in meaning to

_____ (A) belonged to

_____ (B) destined for

_____ (C) built by

_____ (D) paid for

25. The word "splendidly" in line 4 is closest in meaning to

_____ (A) superbly

_____ (B) deliberately

_____ (C) specifically

_____ (D) slightly

26. The word "plush" in line 10 is closest in meaning to

_____ (A) normal

_____ (B) luxurious

_____ (C) memorable

_____ (D) unpleasant

27. Which of the following is closest in meaning to the word "swiftest" in line 10?

_____ (A) most comfortable

_____ (B) cheapest

_____ (C) most direct

_____ (D) fastest

QUESTIONS 28–35

Line The Hopi people of Arizona stress the institutions of family and religion in a harmonious existence that makes the self-sacrificing individual the ideal. The Hopi individual is trained to feel his or her responsibility to and for the Peaceful People—the Hopi's own term for themselves. Fighting, bullying, or attempting to surpass others bring automatic rebuke from the community.

5   Implicit in the Hopi view is an original and integrated theory of the universe. With this they organize their society in such a way to obtain a measure of security from a harsh and hazardous environment made up of human foes, famine, and plagues. They conceive of the universe—humans, animals, plants, and supernatural spirits—as an ordered system functioning under a set of rules known to them alone. These rules govern their behavior, emotions, and thoughts in a prescribed way.

28. The word "stress" in line 1 is closest in meaning to

_____ (A) emphasize

_____ (B) define

_____ (C) describe

_____ (D) persuade

29. Which of the following could best substitute for the word "harmonious" in line 1?

_____ (A) cooperative

_____ (B) dangerous

_____ (C) philosophical

_____ (D) exclusive

30. The word "term" in line 3 is closest in meaning to

_____ (A) era

_____ (B) name

_____ (C) area

_____ (D) law

31. The word "bullying" in line 3 is closest in meaning to

_____ (A) lying

_____ (B) organizing

_____ (C) entertaining

_____ (D) tormenting

32. Which of the following can replace the word "rebuke" in line 4 with the least change in meaning?

_____ (A) prestige

_____ (B) criticism

_____ (C) reaction

_____ (D) acknowledgment

33. Which of the following could best be substituted for the word "hazardous" in line 6?

_____ (A) changing

_____ (B) random

_____ (C) familiar

_____ (D) dangerous

34. The word "foes" in line 7 is closest in meaning to

_____ (A) fears

_____ (B) needs

_____ (C) enemies

_____ (D) failures

35. Which of the following is closest in meaning to the word "prescribed" in line 9?

_____ (A) set

_____ (B) disorderly

_____ (C) legal

_____ (D) compatible

QUESTIONS 36–42

Line   Canadian researchers have discovered a set of genes that determine the lifespan of the common
nematode, a type of worm. This finding sheds new light on the aging process that may eventually
allow them to delay the inexorable process of aging and death.

        By manipulating the newly discovered genes, the team at McGill University in Montreal was able
5   to increase the lifespan of the nematode fivefold. Altering the genes apparently slowed the metabolism of the worms to a more leisurely pace. This in turn may slow the accumulation of the DNA
defects thought to cause aging.

        Although the causes of aging in humans are undoubtedly more involved, researchers are
confident that the discoveries will provide invaluable clues about this heretofore mysterious process.

36. The word "determine" in line 1 is closest in meaning to

_____ (A) control

_____ (B) modify

_____ (C) maintain

_____ (D) shorten

37. Which of the following is closest in meaning to the phrase "sheds new light on" in line 2?

_____ (A) contradicts what is known about

_____ (B) gives new meaning to

_____ (C) provides new information about

_____ (D) calls more attention to

38. The word "inexorable" in line 3 is closest in meaning to

_____ (A) cruel

_____ (B) unstoppable

_____ (C) essential

_____ (D) incomprehensible

39. Which of the following could best be used in place of the phrase "more leisurely" in line 6?

_____ (A) more relaxed

_____ (B) livelier

_____ (C) easier

_____ (D) more irregular

40. The word "involved" in line 8 is closest in meaning to

_____ (A) committed

_____ (B) serious

_____ (C) apparent

_____ (D) complicated

41. Which of the following is closest in meaning to the word "clues" in line 9?

_____ (A) plans

_____ (B) secrets

_____ (C) signals

_____ (D) hints

42. The word "heretofore" in line 9 is closest in meaning to

_____ (A) universally

_____ (B) almost

_____ (C) previously

_____ (D) somewhat

Lesson 48

Reference questions ask what noun (called the **referent**) a pronoun or some other expression refers to. The correct answer is NOT always the noun that is closest to the pronoun in the passage. Incorrect choices are usually other nouns that appear in the passage. If you are unable to decide immediately which answer is correct, substitute the four choices for the word that is being asked about. Which one is the most logical substitute?

In general, reference questions tend to be the easiest type of reading question.

Sample Items

            There is a poisonous, plant-like animal called the anemone that lives among coral reefs. When small fish venture too close to the tentacles of these "living flowers," they are stung and eaten. For unknown reasons,

(5)   the anemone makes an exception of the clownfish, which swims through its deadly tentacles in safety. When in danger, the clownfish dashes among the anemone's tentacles where other fish are afraid to follow. The clownfish even builds its nest where the anemone can

(10)   protect it.

1. The word "they" in line 4 refers to

   (A) coral reefs
   (B) small fish
   (C) tentacles
   (D) flowers

Of the four choices, only "small fish" is a logical answer.

2. The word "it" in line 10 is a reference to the

   (A) clownfish
   (B) nest
   (C) anemone
   (D) exception

Only the words "a nest" is a logical substitute for "it."

EXERCISE 48.1

Focus: Identifying the referents for pronouns and other expressions in sentences and very short passages.

Directions: Read the items. Decide which choice is the correct referent for the underlined expression, and mark the answer.

Detergents clean clothes by first removing particles of dirt from the fabric, then suspending the particles until <u>they</u> can be washed away.

1. _____ (A) clothes

   _____ (B) particles of dirt

   _____ (C) detergents

Wooly mammoths were hunted by big cats called sabertooth tigers that also became extinct by the end of the last Ice Age. <u>They</u> were also hunted by early men armed with spears and clubs.

2. _____ (A) sabertooth tigers

   _____ (B) early men

   _____ (C) wooly mammoths

X rays allow art historians to examine paintings internally without damaging <u>them</u>.

3. _____ (A) x rays

   _____ (B) art historians

   _____ (C) paintings

There is a New England influence in southern Ohio, manifesting <u>itself</u> in white churches and village greens.

4. _____ (A) a New England influence

   _____ (B) southern Ohio

Florists often refrigerate cut flowers to protect <u>their</u> fresh appearance.

5. _____ (A) florists'

   _____ (B) flowers'

A flat kite needs a tail to supply drag and to keep the kite pointed toward the sky. A simple <u>one</u> consists of cloth strips tied end to end.

6. _____ (A) kite

   _____ (B) tail

   _____ (C) sky

A number of sculptors have rejected the abstractions of minimalist artists. <u>These sculptors</u> have developed a style of extreme realism involving ordinary subjects.

7. _____ (A) extreme realists

   _____ (B) minimalists

Water is an exception to many of nature's rules because of <u>its</u> unusual properties.

8. _____ (A) nature's

   _____ (B) water's

Compound bows are popular with bow hunters but <u>they</u> are not permitted in international archery competitions.

9. _____ (A) bow hunters

   _____ (B) compound bows

Ropes are cords at least .15 inches in diameter and are made of three or more strands which are <u>themselves</u> formed of twisted yarns.

10. _____ (A) yarns

    _____ (B) ropes

    _____ (C) strands

    _____ (D) cords

Grocers slice sides, quarters, and what are called primal cuts of beef into smaller pieces. <u>These pieces</u> are called retail cuts.

11. _____ (A) smaller pieces

    _____ (B) sides, quarters, and primal cuts

Leaves are found on all deciduous trees, but <u>they</u> differ greatly in size and shape.

12. _____ (A) trees

    _____ (B) leaves

Yasuo Kuniyashi was born in Japan in 1883 and studied art at the Los Angeles School of Art and Design. He also studied art in New York City, where he gave his first one-man show. In 1925 he moved from there to Paris where he was influenced by the works of Chagall and other artists.

13. _____ (A) Japan

_____ (B) Paris

_____ (C) Los Angeles

_____ (D) New York City

In the past, biologists considered mushrooms and other fungi as a type of non-green plant. Today, however, they are most commonly regarded as a separate kingdom of living things.

14. _____ (A) mushrooms and other fungi

_____ (B) biologists

_____ (C) plants

William Dean Howells, a contemporary and friend of Mark Twain, wrote a number of books that realistically portrayed life on farms in midwestern America. One of his followers, Hamlin Garland, was even more bitter in his criticism of rural America than his mentor.

15. _____ (A) William Dean Howells

_____ (B) Mark Twain

_____ (C) Hamlin Garland

The Wisconsin Dells is a region where the Wisconsin River cuts through soft sandstone. The strange formations that have been carved out of the rocks are a delight to tourists. They have names such as Devil's Elbow, Grand Piano, and Fat Man's Misery.

16. _____ (A) strange formations

_____ (B) tourists

_____ (C) rocks

The lives of beetles are divided into four stages, as are those of wasps, ants, and butterflies.

17. _____ (A) lives

_____ (B) stages

_____ (C) insects

After electron microscopes were invented, scientists found many new viruses. Some of them were round, some oval, and some corkscrew-shaped.

18. _____ (A) electron microscopes

_____ (B) viruses

_____ (C) scientists

The detailed information in maps is now produced almost entirely from satellite photography rather than by ground surveying because this method is faster, cheaper, and more accurate.

19. _____ (A) satellite photography

_____ (B) ground surveying

An elephant is bigger than a mouse because it has trillions more cells, not because its cells are any bigger.

20. _____ (A) a mouse's

_____ (B) an elephant's

EXERCISE 48.2

Focus: Answering reference questions based on longer passages.

Directions: Read the following passages and the questions about them. Decide which of the choices—(A), (B), (C), or (D)—best answers the question, and mark the answer.

QUESTIONS 1-6

Line   In addition to these various types of deep mining, several types of surface mining may be used when minerals lie relatively close to the surface of the Earth. One type is open-pit mining. The first step is to remove the overburden, the layers of rock and earth lying above the ore, with giant scrapers. The ore is broken up in a series of blasting operations. Power shovels pick up the pieces and load them
5   into trucks or, in some cases, ore trains. These carry it up ramps to ground level. Soft ores are removed by drilling screws, called augers.

   Another type is called "placer" mining. Sometimes heavy metals, such as gold, are found in soil deposited by streams and rivers. The soil is picked up by a power shovel and transferred to a long trough. Water is run through the soil in the trough. This carries soil particles away with it. The metal
10   particles are heavier than the soil and sink to the bottom where they can be recovered.

   The finishing-off process of mining is called mineral concentration. In this process, the desired substances are removed from the waste in various ways. One technique is to bubble air through a liquid in which ore particles are suspended. Chemicals are added that make the minerals cling to the air bubbles. The bubbles rise to the surface with the mineral particles attached, and they can be skimmed off and saved.

1. The word "them" in line 4 refers to

   _____ (A) power shovels

   _____ (B) layers of rock and earth

   _____ (C) giant scrapers

   _____ (D) pieces of ore

2. To which of the following does the word "these" in line 5 refer?

   _____ (A) ramps

   _____ (B) trucks or ore trains

   _____ (C) augers

   _____ (D) blasting operations

3. The phrase "another type" in line 7 is a reference to another type of

   _____ (A) deep mining

   _____ (B) ore

   _____ (C) metal

   _____ (D) surface mining

4. The word "this" in line 9 refers to

   _____ (A) a power shovel

   _____ (B) gold

   _____ (C) running water

   _____ (D) a long trough

5. In line 11, the phrase "this process" refers to

   _____ (A) surface mining

   _____ (B) the depositing of soil

   _____ (C) mineral concentration

   _____ (D) placer mining

6. The word "they" in line 14 refers to

   _____ (A) the processes

   _____ (B) the air bubbles

   _____ (C) the chemicals

   _____ (D) the minerals

QUESTIONS 7–10

Line Mount Rainier, the heart of Mt. Rainier National Park, is the highest mountain in the state of Washington and in the Cascade Range. The mountain's summit is broad and rounded. It is 14,410 feet above
sea level and has an area of about one square mile.

5   Numerous steam and gas jets occur around the crater, but the volcano has been sleeping for
many centuries.

    Mount Rainier has a permanent ice cap and extensive snow fields, which give rise to more than
forty glaciers. These feed swift streams and tumbling waterfalls that race through the glacial valleys.
Forests extend to 4,500 feet. There are alpine meadows between the glaciers and the forests, which
contain beautiful wild flowers. The Nisqually Glacier is probably the ice region that is most often
10 explored by visitors. Paradise Valley, where hotel accommodations are available, perches on the
mountains slope at 5,400 feet. The Wonderland Trail encircles the mountain. Its 90-mile length can
be covered in about a week's time.

7. To which of the following does the word "it" in line 2 refer?

_____ (A) Mt. Rainier

_____ (B) the summit

_____ (C) the Cascade Range

_____ (D) the national park

8. The word "these" in line 7 refers to which of the following?

_____ (A) snow fields

_____ (B) steam and gas jets

_____ (C) glaciers

_____ (D) streams and waterfalls

9. The word "which" in line 8 refers to

_____ (A) forests

_____ (B) wild flowers

_____ (C) alpine meadows

_____ (D) glacial valleys

10. What does the word "its" in line 11 refer to?

_____ (A) the trail's

_____ (B) an ice region's

_____ (C) the mountain's

_____ (D) a week's

QUESTIONS 11–15

Line Some people associate migration mainly with birds. Birds do travel vast distances, but mammals also
migrate. An example is the caribou, reindeer that graze on the grassy slopes of northern Canada.
When the weather turns cold, they travel south until spring. Their tracks are so well-worn that they
are clearly visible from the air. Another migrating mammal is the Alaskan fur seal. These seals breed
5   only in the Pribilof Islands in the Bering Sea. The young are born in June and by September are
strong enough to go with their mothers on a journey of over 3,000 miles. Together they swim down
the Pacific Coast of North America. The females and young travel as far as southern California. The
males do not journey so far. They swim only to the Gulf of Alaska. In the spring, males and females
all return to the islands, and there the cycle begins again. Whales are among the greatest migrators of
10   all. The humpback, fin, and blue whales migrate thousands of miles each year from the polar seas to
the tropics. Whales eat huge quantities of tiny plants and animals (called plankton). These are most
abundant in cold polar waters. In winter, the whales move to warm waters to breed and give birth to
their young.

11. The phrase "an example" in line 2 refers to an example of

_____ (A) a migratory mammal

_____ (B) a place where animals migrate

_____ (C) a bird

_____ (D) a person who associates migration with birds

12. In line 3, the word "their" is a reference to

_____ (A) the caribou's

_____ (B) the grassy slopes'

_____ (C) the birds'

_____ (D) the seals'

13. To what does the word "they" in line 8 refer?

_____ (A) female seals

_____ (B) young seals

_____ (C) the islands

_____ (D) male seals

14. In line 9, the word "there" refers to

_____ (A) the Gulf of Alaska

_____ (B) the Pribilof Islands

_____ (C) southern California

_____ (D) the Pacific Coast of North America

15. The word "these" in line 11 refers to

_____ (A) three types of whales

_____ (B) tiny plants and animals

_____ (C) cold waters

_____ (D) quantities

QUESTIONS 16–19

Line Design is the arrangement of materials to produce certain effects. Design plays a role in visual arts and in the creation of commercial products as well. Designers are concerned with the direction of lines, the size of shapes, and the shading of colors. They arrange these patterns in ways that are satisfying to viewers. There are various elements involved in creating a pleasing design.

5   *Harmony*, or *balance,* can be obtained in a number of ways. It may be either symmetrical (in balance) or asymmetrical (out of balance, but still pleasing to the eye). Or a small area may balance a large area if it has an importance to the eye (because of color or treatment) that equals that of the larger area.

      Contrast is the opposite of harmony. The colors red and orange harmonize, since orange 10 contains red. A circle and oval harmonize, as they are both made up of curved lines. But a short line does not harmonize with a long line. It is in contrast.

      Unity occurs when all the elements in a design combine to form a consistent whole. Unity resembles balance. A design has balance if its masses are balanced, or if its tones and colors harmonize. But unity differs from balance because it implies that balance elements work together to form harmony in the design as a whole.

16. The word "they" in line 3 refers to

     _____ (A) designers

     _____ (B) lines, shapes, and colors

     _____ (C) directions, size, and shape

     _____ (D) visual artists

17. The word "that" in line 7 is used as a reference to

     _____ (A) color

     _____ (B) area

     _____ (C) importance

     _____ (D) balance

18. The word "it" in line 11 is used as a reference to

     _____ (A) a circle

     _____ (B) the color red

     _____ (C) a long line

     _____ (D) a short line

19. In line 14, the word "it" refers to

     _____ (A) unity

     _____ (B) balance

     _____ (C) a design

     _____ (D) a consistent whole

QUESTIONS 20–22

Line Although they had been used to haul freight and passengers between the Eastern Seaboard and the
Ohio Valley since 1812, wagon trains were first used extensively in the 1820s on the Santa Fe Trail.
Long trains of covered wagons drawn by oxen or mules carried manufactured goods to trade for fur,
gold, and silver in Santa Fe. The independent traders who pooled their resources to form these trains
5 elected a captain and several lieutenants who commanded the parallel columns in which the wagons
usually moved. They enforced the rules, selected the routes, and designated stopping places.

20. To what does the word "they" in line 1
refer?

_____ (A) the Eastern Seaboard and the
Ohio Valley

_____ (B) wagon trains

_____ (C) freights and passengers

_____ (D) oxen and mules

21. The word "their" in line 4 refers to

_____ (A) the covered wagons'

_____ (B) the oxen and mules'

_____ (C) the independent traders'

_____ (D) the captain and lieutenants'

22. To what does the word "they" in line 6
refer?

_____ (A) the leaders

_____ (B) the traders

_____ (C) the parallel columns

_____ (D) the stopping places

QUESTIONS 23-26

Line In most of the earliest books for children, illustrations were an afterthought. But in the Caldecott "toy books," pictures took up as much space as the lines of copy, and they occupied far more space. One can almost read the nursery rhymes from the dramatic action in the pictures.

5   Since then, thousands of successful picture books have been published in the United States and in many countries around the world. In the best, the text and illustrations seem to complement each other perfectly. Often one person is the author and illustrator—for example, Robert McCloskey (*Make Way for Ducklings*) and Arnold Loebel (*Frog and Toad Together*). Many others have been produced by an author-artist team, as in *The Happy Lion*, written by Louise Fatio and illustrated by Roger Duvoisin.

10   Wordless picture books have also become popular. With a little help, 3- or 4-year olds can follow the sequence of events and they can understand the stories suggested in them. One of the most delightful examples of a wordless book is Jan Ormerod's *Sunshine*.

American publishers have also drawn on artists from other countries whose original, imaginative works have brought their different visions to American children's book illustration. Among them are Leo Lionni from Italy, Feoddor Rojankowski from Russia, and Taro Yashima of Japan.

23. The word "they" in line 2 refers to

_____ (A)   the earliest books for children

_____ (B)   lines of copy

_____ (C)   the Caldecott "toy books"

_____ (D)   pictures

24. The phrase "the best" in line 5 refers to the best

_____ (A)   picture books

_____ (B)   illustrations

_____ (C)   authors

_____ (D)   nursery rhymes

25. The word "they" in line 11 refers to

_____ (A)   delightful examples

_____ (B)   events

_____ (C)   3- and 4-year olds

_____ (D)   wordless picture books

26. The word "them" in line 14 refers to

_____ (A)   American publishers

_____ (B)   original, imaginative works

_____ (C)   artists from other countries

_____ (D)   American children

Answer Sheet

Mini-Test 8: Reading Comprehension

1. (A) (B) (C) (D)	11. (A) (B) (C) (D)	21. (A) (B) (C) (D)
2. (A) (B) (C) (D)	12. (A) (B) (C) (D)	22. (A) (B) (C) (D)
3. (A) (B) (C) (D)	13. (A) (B) (C) (D)	23. (A) (B) (C) (D)
4. (A) (B) (C) (D)	14. (A) (B) (C) (D)	24. (A) (B) (C) (D)
5. (A) (B) (C) (D)	15. (A) (B) (C) (D)	25. (A) (B) (C) (D)
6. (A) (B) (C) (D)	16. (A) (B) (C) (D)	26. (A) (B) (C) (D)
7. (A) (B) (C) (D)	17. (A) (B) (C) (D)	27. (A) (B) (C) (D)
8. (A) (B) (C) (D)	18. (A) (B) (C) (D)	28. (A) (B) (C) (D)
9. (A) (B) (C) (D)	19. (A) (B) (C) (D)	29. (A) (B) (C) (D)
10. (A) (B) (C) (D)	20. (A) (B) (C) (D)	30. (A) (B) (C) (D)

31. (A) (B) (C) (D)	41. (A) (B) (C) (D)
32. (A) (B) (C) (D)	42. (A) (B) (C) (D)
33. (A) (B) (C) (D)	43. (A) (B) (C) (D)
34. (A) (B) (C) (D)	44. (A) (B) (C) (D)
35. (A) (B) (C) (D)	45. (A) (B) (C) (D)
36. (A) (B) (C) (D)	46. (A) (B) (C) (D)
37. (A) (B) (C) (D)	47. (A) (B) (C) (D)
38. (A) (B) (C) (D)	48. (A) (B) (C) (D)
39. (A) (B) (C) (D)	49. (A) (B) (C) (D)
40. (A) (B) (C) (D)	50. (A) (B) (C) (D)

MINI-TEST 8: READING COMPREHENSION

Directions: In this mini-test, there are several passages, each followed by a number of questions. Read the passages and, for each question, choose the *one* best answer, (A), (B), (C), or (D). Then fill in the space on your answer sheet above that corresponds to the answer you have chosen. All of your answers should be based on what is stated or implied in the passages.

Time: 55 minutes

Questions 1–12

Line   Humans have struggled against weeds since the beginnings of agriculture. Marring our gardens is one of
         the milder effects of weeds—any plants that thrive where they are unwanted. They clog waterways,
         destroy wildlife habitats, and impede farming. Their spread eliminates grazing areas and accounts for
         one-third of all crop loss. They compete for sunlight, nutrients, and water with useful plants.
5   The global need for weed control had been answered mainly by the chemical industry. Its
         herbicides are effective and sometimes necessary, but some pose serious problems, particularly if
         misused. Toxic compounds threaten animal and public health when they accumulate in food plants,
         groundwater, and drinking water. They also harm workers who apply them.
             In recent years, the chemical industry has introduced several herbicides that are more ecologi-
10   cally sound. Yet new chemicals alone cannot solve the world's weed problems. Hence, scientists are
         exploring the innate weed-killing powers of living organisms, primarily insects and microorganisms.
             The biological agents now in use are environmentally benign and are harmless to humans. They
         can be chosen for their ability to attack selected targets and leave crops and other plants untouched.
         In contrast, some of the most effective chemicals kill virtually all the plants they come in contact
15   with, sparing only those that are naturally resistant or have been genetically modified for resistance.
         Furthermore, a number of biological agents can be administered only once, after which no added
         applications are needed. Chemicals typically must be used several times per growing season.

1. With what topic does this passage primarily deal?

   (A) The importance of the chemical industry.
   (B) The dangers of toxic chemicals.
   (C) Advantages of biological agents over chemical ones.
   (D) A proposal to ban the use of all herbicides.

2. The word "marring" in line 1 is closest in meaning to

   (A) spoiling
   (B) dividing
   (C) replacing
   (D) planting

3. The word "clog" in line 2 is closest in meaning to

   (A) drain
   (B) float on
   (C) obstruct
   (D) grow along

4. Which of the following terms does the author define in the first paragraph?

   (A) grazing areas
   (B) weeds
   (C) wildlife habitats
   (D) nutrients

5. Which of the following statements about the use of chemical agents as herbicides would the author most likely agree?

   (A) It should be increased.
   (B) It has become more dangerous recently.
   (C) It is safe but inefficient.
   (D) It is occasionally required.

6. Which of the following is NOT given as an advantage of using biological agents over chemical herbicides?

   (A) They are less likely to destroy desirable plants.
   (B) They are safer for workers.
   (C) They are more easily available.
   (D) They do not have to be used as often.

7. Which of the following is closest in meaning to the word "Hence" in line 10?

   (A) in addition
   (B) consequently
   (C) subsequently
   (D) in contrast

8. The word "innate" in line 11 is closest in meaning to

   (A) natural
   (B) effective
   (C) organic
   (D) active

9. According to the passage, biological agents mainly consist of

    (A) insects and microorganisms
    (B) useful plants
    (C) weeds
    (D) herbicides

10. The word "those" in line 15 refers to

    (A) chemicals
    (B) targets
    (C) plants
    (D) agents

11. The word "applications" in line 17 could best be replaced by which of the following?

    (A) requests
    (B) special purposes
    (C) treatments
    (D) qualifications

12. Which of the following best describes the organization of the passage?

    (A) A general idea is introduced and several specific examples are given.
    (B) A recommendation is analyzed and rejected.
    (C) A problem is described and possible solutions are discussed.
    (D) Two possible causes for a phenomenon are compared.

QUESTIONS 13–21

Line   *West Side Story* is a musical tragedy based on William Shakespeare's play *Romeo and Juliet*. It is set in the early 1950s, when gang warfare in big cities led to injuries and even death. *West Side Story* transformed the Montagues and Capulets of Shakespeare's play into feuding street gangs, the Jets and the Sharks, one consisting of newly-arrived Puerto Ricans and the other of native-born New Yorkers.

5   The plot, tightly choreographed by Jerome Robbins, tells the story of the love of Maria, a Puerto Rican, for Tony who, while attempting to stop a street fight, kills Maria's brother and is ultimately killed himself. Leonard Bernstein's musical score is brilliant, and Stephen Sondheim, making his Broadway debut, revealed a remarkable talent for writing lyrics. Among the hit songs of the play are "Tonight," "Maria," "America," and "I Feel Pretty."

10   The play opened on September 26, 1957. It ran for 734 performances, toured for ten months, then returned to New York for an additional 246 performances. A film version was released in 1961, and a successful New York revival opened in 1980.

13. The author's attitude toward the play is generally

    (A) regretful
    (B) critical
    (C) emotional
    (D) favorable

14. According to the passage, when does the action of the play *West Side Story* take place?

    (A) Shakespeare's time
    (B) the early 1950s
    (C) 1957
    (D) 1980

15. It can be inferred from the passage that the Capulets and Montagues

    (A) were rival groups in Shakespeare's play
    (B) were 1950s street gangs
    (C) fought against the Jets and Sharks
    (D) were groups of actors, dancers, and singers

16. The word "feuding" in line 3 is closest in meaning to

    (A) growing
    (B) hostile
    (C) organized
    (D) criminal

17. Which of the following is closest in meaning to the word "ultimately" in line 6?

(A) evidently
(B) immediately
(C) eventually
(D) savagely

18. According to the article, the words to the songs of *West Side Story* were written by

(A) Jerome Robbins
(B) Leonard Bernstein
(C) William Shakespeare
(D) Stephen Sondheim

19. The word "score" in line 7 could best be replaced by which of the following?

(A) talent
(B) music
(C) performance
(D) dialog

20. During its initial appearance in New York, how many times was *West Side Story* performed?

(A) 10
(B) 26
(C) 246
(D) 734

21. Where in the passage is the basic story of *West Side Story* summarized?

(A) Lines 1-2
(B) Lines 2-4
(C) Lines 5-7
(D) Lines 10-11

QUESTIONS 22–33

Line About 8,000 people looked over the horseless carriages on November 3, 1900, the opening day of the New York Auto Show, and the first opportunity for the automobile industry to show off its wares to a sizeable audience.

By happenstance, the number of people at the show equalled the entire car population at that
5   time. At that time, 10 million bicycles and an unknown number of horse-and-buggies provided the prime means of transportation. Only about 4,000 cars were assembled in the United States in 1900, and only a quarter of those were gasoline powered. (The rest ran on steam or electricity.)

After viewing the cars made by 32 carmakers, the show's audience favored electric cars because they were quiet. The risk of a boiler explosion turned people away from steamers, and the gasoline
10   powered cars produced smelly fumes. The Duryea Motor Wagon Company, which launched the American auto industry in 1892, offered an additive designed to mask the smell of the naphtha that it burned.

The prices were not that different than they are today. Most cost between $800 and $1500, or roughly $11,000 to $18,500 in today's prices. Many of the 1900 models were cumbersome—the
15   Gasmobile, the Franklin, and the Orient, for example, steered with tillers like boats rather than with steering wheels.

The black-tie audience at the show viewed the display more as a social outing than as the extravaganza that auto shows were about to become.

22. Approximately how many cars were there in the United States in 1900?

(A) 4,000
(B) 8,000
(C) 10 million
(D) An unknown number

23. Which of the following is closest in meaning to the phrase "by happenstance" as used in line 4?

(A) generally
(B) for example
(C) coincidentally
(D) by design

24. Approximately how many of the cars assembled in the year 1900 were gasoline powered?

(A) 32
(B) 1,000
(C) 2,000
(D) 4,000

25. According to the passage, people at the 1900 New York Auto Show favored cars powered by

(A) electricity
(B) naphtha
(C) gasoline
(D) steam

26. The word "fumes" in line 10 is closest in meaning to

(A) fuels
(B) grains
(C) fires
(D) gases

27. Which of the following is closest in meaning to the word "launched" in line 10?

(A) joined
(B) designed
(C) initiated
(D) anticipated

28. The purpose of the additive mentioned in line 11 was to

(A) increase the speed of cars
(B) make engines run more efficiently
(C) hide offensive smells
(D) make cars look better

29. What was the highest price asked for a car at the 1900 New York Auto Show in the dollars of that time?

(A) $800
(B) $1500
(C) $11,300
(D) $18,500

30. The word "cumbersome" in line 14 is closest in meaning to

(A) clumsy
(B) unshapely
(C) fragile
(D) inconvenient

31. Which of the following is NOT mentioned in the passage as steering with a tiller rather than with a steering wheel?

(A) a Franklin
(B) a Duryea
(C) an Orient
(D) a Gasmobile

32. The passage implies that the audience viewed the 1900 New York Auto Show primarily as

(A) a formal social affair
(B) a chance to buy automobiles at low prices
(C) an opportunity to learn how to drive
(D) a chance to invest in one of thirty-two automobile manufacturers

33. It can be inferred from the passage that auto shows held after 1900

(A) were more spectacular
(B) involved fewer manufacturers
(C) were more formal
(D) involved less expensive cars

QUESTIONS 34–41

Line   When drawing human figures, children often make the head too large for the rest of the body. A
recent study offers some insights into this common disproportion in children's illustrations. As part of
the study, researchers asked children between 4 and 7 years old to make several drawings of men.
When they drew front views of male figures, the size of the heads was markedly enlarged. However,
5   when the children drew rear views of men, the size of the heads was not so exaggerated. The
researchers suggest that children draw bigger heads when they know they must leave room for facial
details. Therefore, the odd head size in children's illustrations is a form of planning ahead and not an
indication of a poor sense of scale.

34. The main subject of the passage is

    (A) what the results of an experiment revealed

    (B) how children learn to draw

    (C) how researchers can gather data from works of art

    (D) what can be done to correct a poor sense of scale

35. It can be inferred that, during the research project, the children drew

    (A) pictures of men from different angles

    (B) figures without facial expression

    (C) sketches of both men and women

    (D) only the front view of men

36. The word "they" in line 4 refers to

    (A) researchers

    (B) men

    (C) illustrations

    (D) children

37. The word "markedly" in line 4 is closest in meaning to

    (A) modestly

    (B) noticeably

    (C) merely

    (D) newly

38. The findings of the experiment described in the passage would probably be of LEAST interest to which of the following groups?

    (A) teachers of art to children

    (B) commercial artists

    (C) experts in child development

    (D) parents of young children

39. The word "odd" in line 7 is closest in meaning to

    (A) unusual

    (B) huge

    (C) average

    (D) expected

40. The word "scale" in line 8 is closest in meaning to

    (A) measurement

    (B) proportion

    (C) balance

    (D) property

41. The passage provides information to support which of the following conclusions?

    (A) Children under the age of 7 do not generally have a good sense of scale.

    (B) With training, young children can be taught to avoid disproportion in their art.

    (C) Children enlarge the size of the head because they sense that it is the most important part of the body.

    (D) Children plan ahead when they are drawing pictures.

QUESTIONS 42–50

Line Georgia O'Keefe was born in Sun Prairie, Wisconsin, in 1887. She studied art in Chicago and New York from 1904 to 1908. Beginning as an advertising illustrator, she supported herself until 1918 by teaching in various schools and colleges in Texas. After that date, she devoted herself entirely to painting. Her paintings were first exhibited in 1916 at "291," an experimental art gallery in New

5 York City owned by Alfred Steiglitz, which was frequented by some of the most influential artists of the time. O'Keefe married Steiglitz in 1924.

O'Keefe's early paintings were mostly abstract designs. In the 1920s she produced depictions of flowers and precise cityscapes of New York City. Whether painting flowers or buildings, she captured their beauty by intuitively magnifying their shapes and simplifying their details.

10 O'Keefe's style changed dramatically in 1929 during a visit to New Mexico. She was enchanted by the stark but beautiful landscapes under the bright Southwestern sun, and she then adopted her characteristic style. Thereafter, she most often painted desert landscapes, often with the blanched skull of a longhorn in the foreground.

O'Keefe's paintings were exhibited annually at several New York galleries until 1946, and she is

15 represented in the permanent collections of most major American museums. In her later years, she settled in Taos, New Mexico, becoming the dean of Southwestern painters and one of the best known of American artists.

42. The author's main purpose in writing this passage was to

(A) criticize Georgia O'Keefe's style of painting
(B) discuss the early career of an important American artist
(C) compare abstract art and landscape art
(D) give the highlights of Georgia O'Keefe's artistic career

43. According to the article, where did Georgia O'Keefe receive her formal art training?

(A) Sun Prairie, Wisconsin
(B) Chicago and New York
(C) Texas
(D) Taos, New Mexico

44. The expression "that date" in line 3 refers to

(A) 1887
(B) 1908
(C) 1916
(D) 1918

45. The word "frequented" in line 5 is closest in meaning to

(A) visited
(B) supported
(C) founded
(D) favored

46. The word "intuitively" in line 9 is closest in meaning to

(A) deliberately
(B) defiantly
(C) instinctively
(D) intuitively

47. Which of the following had the greatest influence on changing O'Keefe's style of painting?

(A) a trip to the Southwest
(B) Alfred Steiglitz's photographs
(C) her job as an advertising illustrator
(D) meeting influential artists

48. The word "blanched" in line 12 is closest in meaning to

(A) shattered
(B) prominent
(C) whitened
(D) inexplicable

49. Which of the following became the most common subject of O'Keefe's paintings after 1929?

(A) city scenes
(B) desert scenes
(C) flowers
(D) abstract patterns

50. It can be inferred from the passage that, in her later years, O'Keefe

(A) continued to be successful
(B) returned to New York City
(C) could not match the successes of her early career
(D) took up photography

MINI-LESSONS FOR SECTION 3

VOCABULARY BUILDING

These mini-lessons consist of lists of more than 500 words and their synonyms as well as practice exercises. Although vocabulary is no longer tested in discrete items in Section 3, there are vocabulary-in-context questions in the Reading Comprehension section. These exercises will improve your ability to use context to chose the word that best fits into a sentence.

MINI-LESSON 3.1

abandon *v.* desert, leave behind
able *adj.* capable, qualified, fit
abolish *v.* end, eliminate
abrupt *adj.* sudden, hasty, unexpected
acclaim *v.* applaud, praise, honor
          n. praise, applause, honor
acrid *adj.* bitter, sharp, biting
adapt *v.* adjust, modify
adept *adj.* skillful, expert
adhere *v.* stick, cling
admonish *v.* warn, caution, advise
adorn *v.* decorate, ornament
advent *n.* coming, arrival
adverse *adj.* hostile, negative, contrary
affluent *adj.* rich, wealthy, prosperous, well-to-do
aggravate *v.* (1) annoy, irritate; (2) intensify, worsen
aggregate *adj.* entire, total, combined
agile *adj.* graceful, nimble, lively
ailment *n.* sickness, illness
allot *v.* divide, distribute
amazing *adj.* astonishing, astounding, surprising, startling
amiable *adj.* agreeable, congenial, pleasant
anticipate *v.* foresee, expect, predict
anxious *adj.* (1) worried, nervous, apprehensive; (2) eager, avid
appraise *v.* evaluate, estimate, assess
apt *adj.* (1) appropriate, suitable, correct, relevant, proper; (2) likely, prone
arduous *adj.* difficult, exhausting
arid *adj.* dry, barren
aroma *n.* fragrance, smell, odor, scent
artificial *adj.* synthetic, imitation, man-made
astonishing *adj.* surprising, amazing, astounding
astute *adj.* intelligent, clever, perceptive
attain *v.* accomplish, achieve
augment *v.* supplement, increase, strengthen, expand
austere *adj.* strict, harsh, severe, stern
authentic *adj.* genuine, true
aversion *n.* dislike, hostility, fear
awkward *adj.* clumsy

Exercise: Complete the following sentences by filling in the blanks with vocabulary items (A), (B), or (C) according to the context of the sentences. The first one is done as an example.

1. Penicillin can have an ___A___ effect on a person who is allergic to it.

    (A) adverse
    (B) anxious
    (C) awkward

2. Burning rubber produces an _____ smoke.

    (A) austere
    (B) arid
    (C) acrid

3. Rationing is a system for _____ scarce resources.

    (A) allotting
    (B) adapting
    (C) appraising

4. Anthrax is generally an _____ of sheep and cattle, but may also be transmitted to humans.

    (A) ailment
    (B) aroma
    (C) aversion

5. The head of an academic department at a university should be not only a distinguished scholar but also an _____ administrator.

    (A) agile
    (B) able
    (C) abrupt

6. Mountain climbing is an _____ sport.

    (A) austere
    (B) arduous
    (C) anxious

7. Turtles _____ their eggs after they lay them and never see their young.

    (A) abandon
    (B) appraise
    (C) adorn

8. Scholarships allow some students from less _____ families to attend college.

    (A) artificial
    (B) affluent
    (C) amiable

9. Jewelers are sometimes asked to _____ jewelry for insurance purposes.

    (A) attain
    (B) abandon
    (C) appraise

10. Acrobats must be extremely _____.

    (A) awkward
    (B) affluent
    (C) agile

11. In a domed stadium such as Seattle's King Dome, natural grass cannot be grown. _____ turf is used on the playing field.

    (A) Artificial
    (B) Arid
    (C) Austere

12. Southern Arizona has an _____ climate.

    (A) arid
    (B) astute
    (C) acrid

13. A person suffering from claustrophobia has an _____ to confined spaces.

    (A) ailment
    (B) aversion
    (C) acclaim

14. I didn't care for the play because it ended so _____.

    (A) amiably
    (B) abruptly
    (C) anxiously

15. The ballerina was _____ for her wonderful performances.

    (A) augmented
    (B) anticipated
    (C) acclaimed

MINI-LESSON 3.2

baffle *v.* confuse, puzzle, mystify
balmy *adj.* mild, warm
ban *v.* prohibit, forbid
bar *v.* prevent, obstruct, block
barren *adj.* sterile, unproductive, bleak, lifeless
barter *v.* trade, exchange
beckon *v.* summon, call, signal
belligerent *adj.* hostile, aggressive
beneficial *adj.* helpful, useful, advantageous
benevolent *adj.* benign, kind, compassionate
bias *n.* prejudice, leaning
bland *adj.* mild, tasteless, dull
blatant *adj.* flagrant, obvious, overt
blend *v.* mix, mingle, combine
       n. mixture, combination
bloom *v.* blossom, flower, flourish
blunder *v.* make a mistake
       n. error, mistake
blunt *adj.* (1) unsharpened, dull; (2) rude, abrupt, curt
blurry *adj.* unfocused, unclear, indistinct
bold *adj.* brave, courageous
bolster *v.* support, sustain
bond *v.* join, connect
       n. tie, link, connection
boom *v.* expand, prosper
       n. expansion, prosperity, growth
brace *v.* support, reinforce
brilliant *adj.* (1) bright, shiny, radiant, dazzling; (2) talented, gifted, intelligent
brisk *adj.* (1) lively, quick, vigorous; (2) cool, chilly, invigorating
brittle *adj.* fragile, breakable, weak
bulky *adj.* huge, large, clumsy

Exercise: Complete the following sentences by filling in the blanks with vocabulary items (A), (B), or (C) according to the context of the sentences.

1. Most flowers _____ in the spring.

   (A) blend
   (B) brace
   (C) bloom

2. The Virgin Islands, located in the Caribbean, have a _____ climate.

   (A) blurry
   (B) brittle
   (C) balmy

3. Before currency came into use, people used the _____ system, exchanging goods directly for goods.

   (A) barter
   (B) blunder
   (C) bias

4. The airline _____. It sent me to Atlanta but my luggage to Montreal.

   (A) beckoned
   (B) bartered
   (C) blundered

5. People with ulcers must eat _____ foods.

   (A) bold
   (B) bland
   (C) bulky

6. Steel is not as _____ as cast iron; it doesn't break as easily.

   (A) brisk
   (B) brittle
   (C) brilliant

7. Some people feel that violent sports such as boxing should be _____ because they are too dangerous.

    (A) banned
    (B) bloomed
    (C) braced

8. Many people think of deserts as _____ regions, but many species of plants and animals have adapted to life there.

    (A) bland
    (B) barren
    (C) balmy

9. An autocratic ruler who serves his people well is sometimes called a _____ dictator.

    (A) blatant
    (B) belligerent

    (C) benevolent

10. Robert Goddard was a _____ pioneer in the field of rocketry.

    (A) brilliant
    (B) balmy
    (C) brisk

11. I enjoy taking walks on _____ autumn mornings.

    (A) barren
    (B) brisk
    (C) blurry

12. The victim was apparently struck by a club or some other _____ object.

    (A) bland
    (B) brittle
    (C) blunt

Mini-Lesson 3.3

calamity *n.* disaster, catastrophe
capable *adj.* competent, able, efficient, skillful
carve *v.* cut, sculpt, slice
casual *adj.* (1) informal, relaxed; (2) accidental, chance
caustic *adj.* biting, harsh, sarcastic
cautious *adj.* careful, alert, prudent
celebrated *adj.* distinguished, famous, prominent
charming *adj.* delightful, lovely, attractive
cherish *v.* appreciate, esteem, treasure
choice *n.* selection, option
　　　adj. exceptional, superior
cite *v.* quote, mention, refer to, list
clash *v.* argue, dispute, quarrel
　　　n. argument, conflict, dispute
classify *v.* categorize
clever *adj.* smart, sharp, witty, bright
cling *v.* stick, adhere, hold
clumsy *adj.* awkward, inept
coax *v.* persuade, urge
colossal *adj.* huge, enormous, gigantic
commence *v.* begin, initiate, start
commerce *n.* trade, business
commodity *n.* good, product, merchandise
compel *v.* force, require, coerce
competent *adj.* adept, skillful, capable, able

Peterson's TOEFL CBT Success

Exercise: Complete the following sentences by filling in the blanks with vocabulary items (A), (B), or (C) according to the context of the sentences.

1. The Red Cross provides relief in case of _____ such as floods, earthquakes, and hurricanes.

   (A) challenges
   (B) commodities
   (C) calamities

2. Spoken language is generally more _____ than written language.

   (A) casual
   (B) capable
   (C) cautious

3. When writing research papers, writers must _____ the sources they use.

   (A) coax
   (B) cite
   (C) clash

4. Monkeys are _____ as primates.

   (A) compelled
   (B) classified
   (C) coaxed

5. _____ remarks can offend people.

   (A) Casual
   (B) Caustic
   (C) Clever

6. Sculptors use hammers and chisels to _____ statues out of stone.

   (A) clash
   (B) compel
   (C) carve

7. The Space Age _____ in October 1957 when Sputnik, the first artificial satellite, was launched by the Soviet Union.

   (A) commenced
   (B) coaxed
   (C) cited

8. Workers must be very _____ when dealing with toxic substances.

   (A) caustic
   (B) casual
   (C) cautious

9. In seaside communities, building sites that have a view of the ocean are considered _____.

   (A) choice
   (B) clever
   (C) competent

10. With the growth of international _____, the economies of the world have become more interdependent.

    (A) commodity
    (B) commerce
    (C) choice

11. The Lincoln Memorial features a _____ statue of the sixteenth president.

    (A) colossal
    (B) caustic
    (C) casual

12. Corn, cotton, sugar, and many other goods are bought and sold in _____ markets.

    (A) clash
    (B) commerce
    (C) commodity

Mini-Lesson 3.4

complement *v.* supplement, complete
         n. supplement, addition
compliment *v.* praise, flatter, commend
         n. praise, flattery, commendation
comprehensive *adj.* complete, thorough, exhaustive
compulsory *adj.* necessary, obligatory, mandatory
concede *v.* admit, acknowledge, recognize
concise *adj.* brief, short, abbreviated
concrete *adj.* tangible, specific, real, perceptible
congregate *v.* assemble, gather
conspicuous *adj.* noticeable, obvious, prominent
contemplate *v.* think about, ponder, speculate
controversial *adj.* disputable, debatable
convenient *adj.* accessible, available, handy
cope with *v.* deal with, manage, handle
copious *adj.* abundant, ample, plentiful
cordial *adj.* congenial, warm, friendly
courteous *adj.* polite, refined, gracious
covert *adj.* secret, hidden
cozy *adj.* (1) comfortable, warm; (2) friendly, intimate, close
crave *v.* desire, long for, hope for
crooked *adj.* (1) curved, twisted, zigzag; (2) dishonest, corrupt
crucial *adj.* critical, decisive, key
crude *adj.* (1) rude, impolite, vulgar; (2) unprocessed, raw, unrefined
cruel *adj.* brutal, vicious, ruthless
cryptic *adj.* secret, hidden, mysterious
curb *v.* restrict, limit, control
curious *adj.* (1) inquisitive; (2) odd, strange, unusual
curt *adj.* abrupt, blunt, impolite

Exercise: Complete the following sentences by filling in the blanks with vocabulary items (A), (B), or (C) according to the context of the sentences.

1. The use of seat belts is _____ in many states; failure to wear them may result in fines.

   (A) covert
   (B) cruel
   (C) compulsory

2. Every summer, bears from all over southern Alaska _____ along the McNeil River.

   (A) crave
   (B) curb
   (C) congregate

3. An abstract is a _____ form of an academic article. Many journals publish abstracts so readers can decide if it is worthwhile to read the full version of the article.

   (A) concise
   (B) comprehensive
   (C) concrete

4. Before 1754, Britain and the North American colonies had a _____ relationship, but after that, their relationship became strained.

   (A) conspicuous
   (B) cozy
   (C) curt

5. Automatic teller machines provide a
_____ means of banking 24 hours a day.

(A) cordial
(B) crooked
(C) convenient

6. Lombard Street in San Francisco, which
zigzags its way up a steep hill, is known as
the most _____ street in the world.

(A) controversial
(B) crooked
(C) cryptic

7. A good writer supports his or her generalizations with _____ examples.

(A) concrete
(B) curious
(C) crude

8. Many hunters wear orange and other bright
colors in order to be as _____ as

possible, and therefore avoid being shot by
other hunters by mistake.

(A) covert
(B) cruel
(C) conspicuous

9. Movie directors use music to _____ the
action on the screen.

(A) contemplate
(B) complement
(C) compliment

10. Workers in the service sector should be
trained to act as _____ as possible.

(A) crudely
(B) courteously
(C) curtly

MINI-LESSON 3.5

damp *adj.* moist, wet, humid
daring *adj.* bold, courageous, brave
dazzling *adj.* shining, sparkling, blinding, bright
declare *v.* announce, proclaim
deem *v.* believe, consider, regard, judge
defective *adj.* flawed, faulty, broken, malfunctioning
defiant *adj.* rebellious, insubordinate
delicate *adj.* exquisite, fragile
delightful *adj.* charming, attractive, enchanting
delusion *n.* illusion, dream, fantasy
demolish *v.* tear down, destroy, wreck
dense *adj.* thick, solid
desist *v.* stop, cease, discontinue
device *n.* instrument, tool, mechanism
devise *v.* invent, plan, figure out
dim *adj.* unclear, faint, indistinct
din *n.* noise, clamor, commotion
dire *adj.* desperate, grievous, serious
dismal *adj.* gloomy, depressing, dreary
disperse *v.* scatter, distribute, spread
dispute *n.* argument, quarrel, debate, clash, feud
distinct *adj.* discrete, separate, different
distinguished *adj.* celebrated, notable, famous, well-known
divulge *v.* reveal, admit, disclose
dogged *adj.* stubborn, determined, persistent
dominate *v.* rule, control, govern
dot *v.* located, scattered around
    n. spot, point
downfall *n.* collapse, ruin, destruction

doze *v.* sleep, nap
drawback *n.* disadvantage, weakness, flaw
dreary *adj.* dismal, gloomy, bleak
drench *v.* wet, soak
drowsy *adj.* sleepy, tired
dubious *adj.* doubtful, skeptical, uncertain
durable *adj.* lasting, enduring, resistant
dwell *v.* live, reside, inhabit
dwelling *n.* house, home, residence
dwindle *v.* decrease, diminish
dynamic *adj.* energetic, forceful, active, vibrant

Exercise: Complete the following sentences by filling in the blanks with vocabulary items (A), (B), or (C) according to the context of the sentences.

1. The snow on the mountaintop was
   _____ in the bright morning sun.

   (A) dazzling
   (B) dogged
   (C) dim

2. A person who has been accused of a crime
   cannot be forced to _____ any information that is self-incriminating.

   (A) divulge
   (B) desist
   (C) disperse

3. Roses have a _____ beauty.

   (A) dense
   (B) delicate
   (C) dire

4. An odometer is a _____ for measuring
   distance.

   (A) device
   (B) delusion
   (C) dwelling

5. The amount of open space has _____ as
   more and more land is developed.

   (A) dominated
   (B) dwindled
   (C) dispersed

6. A _____ battery can cause an electrical
   device to malfunction.

   (A) dogged
   (B) durable
   (C) defective

7. Richard Bird and his pilot Floyd Bennet
   undertook a _____ flight to the North
   Pole in May 1926.

   (A) daring
   (B) defiant
   (C) distinct

8. Steep, round hills called knobs _____
   southern Indiana.

   (A) demolish
   (B) dot
   (C) dwell

9. Artists Nathaniel Currier and J. Merritt Ives
   produced some _____ prints of nineteenth-century New England scenes, which
   collectors prize for their charm.

   (A) dreary
   (B) dim
   (C) delightful

10. Economists define _____ goods as ones
    intended to last more than four months.

    (A) durable
    (B) dense
    (C) delicate

11. One cause of the American Revolution was
    a _____ over taxation.

    (A) drawback
    (B) delusion
    (C) dispute

12. Florida has a humid climate. Summers there
    are particularly hot and _____.

    (A) dynamic
    (B) damp
    (C) dogged

Peterson's TOEFL CBT Success

MINI-LESSON 3.6

eerie *adj.* strange, odd, unusual, frightening
elderly *adj.* old, aged
elegant *adj.* sophisticated, polished
eligible *adj.* suitable, qualified, acceptable
eminent *adj.* celebrated, distinguished, famous
emit *v.* send out, discharge
enchanting *adj.* delightful, charming, captivating
encounter *v.* meet, find, come across
          n. meeting, confrontation
endeavor *n.* attempt, venture
endorse *v.* authorize, approve, support
enhance *v.* intensify, amplify, strengthen
ensue *v.* follow, result
entice *v.* lure, attract, tempt
era *n.* period, age
essential *adj.* critical, vital, crucial, key
esteem *v.* cherish, honor, admire
evade *v.* escape, avoid, elude
exhaustive *adj.* thorough, complete, comprehensive
exhilarating *adj.* exciting, thrilling, stimulating
extravagant *adj.* excessive, lavish
fable *n.* story, tale
fabled *adj.* legendary, mythical, famous
facet *n.* aspect, point, feature
faint *adj.* dim, pale, faded, indistinct
falter *v.* hesitate, waver
fancy *adj.* decorative, ornate, elaborate
fasten *v.* attach, secure
fatal *adj.* mortal, lethal, deadly
fatigue *v.* tire, exhaust
        n. exhaustion, weariness
faulty *adj.* flawed, inferior
feasible *adj.* possible
feeble *adj.* weak, fragile, frail
ferocious *adj.* fierce, savage, violent
fiery *adj.* (1) blazing, burning; (2) passionate, fervent
fitting *adj.* suitable, proper, apt, appropriate
flagrant *adj.* blatant, obvious
flaw *n.* defect, imperfection, fault
flee *v.* escape, go away, elude
flimsy *adj.* fragile, frail, weak, feeble
forego *v.* abandon, give up
foremost *adj.* chief, principal, leading
fragment *n.* particle, piece, bit
fragrant *adj.* aromatic, scented
fraudulent *adj.* false, deceptive, deceitful
fundamental *adj.* basic, integral, elemental
fusion *n.* blend, merger, union
futile *adj.* useless, pointless, vain

Exercise: Complete the following sentences by filling in the blanks with vocabulary items (A), (B), or (C) according to the context of the sentences.

1. In 1906, much of San Francisco was destroyed by an earthquake and the fires that _____.

   (A) evaded
   (B) ensued
   (C) encountered

2. The writer H. P. Lovecraft wrote many _____ stories about the supernatural.

   (A) essential
   (B) eerie
   (C) exhilarating

3. A new _____ of aviation began in 1947 when Chuck Yaeger became the first pilot to fly faster than the speed of sound.

   (A) fable
   (B) endeavor
   (C) era

4. Vance Packard's book *The Hidden Persuaders* deals with the tactics advertisers use to _____ consumers.

   (A) endorse
   (B) entice
   (C) enhance

5. Riding a roller coaster is an _____ experience.

   (A) exhilarating
   (B) elegant
   (C) exhaustive

6. Before the plane takes off, passengers must _____ their seat belts.

   (A) flee
   (B) emit
   (C) fasten

7. In the United States, citizens are _____ to vote at the age of eighteen.

   (A) essential
   (B) elderly
   (C) eligible

8. Barracudas are _____ predators, sometimes called the "tigers" of tropical waters.

   (A) elegant
   (B) futile
   (C) ferocious

9. Certain gases such as neon _____ light when exposed to an electrical current.

   (A) emit
   (B) evade
   (C) esteem

10. People make more mistakes when they are _____ than when they are fresh.

    (A) exhaustive
    (B) eminent
    (C) fatigued

11. A _____ in a jewel makes it less valuable.

    (A) fragment
    (B) facet
    (C) flaw

12. Honeysuckle is a shrub that has _____ white or yellowish blossoms.

    (A) elegant
    (B) fatal
    (C) exhilarating

MINI-LESSON 3.7

gala *adj.* festive, happy, joyous
gap *n.* break, breach, opening
garrulous *adj.* talkative
gaudy *adj.* showy, flashy, ostentatious
genial *adj.* pleasant, cordial, agreeable
gentle *adj.* mild, kind, considerate
genuine *adj.* authentic, real, valid
glitter *v.* sparkle, shine, glisten
glory *n.* grandeur, majesty, fame
gorgeous *adj.* attractive, beautiful
graphic *adj.* clear, explicit, vivid
grasp *v.* (1) grab, seize, grip; (2) understand
grave *adj.* serious, grievous, solemn, somber
gregarious *adj.* sociable, friendly
grim *adj.* severe, dreary, bleak, somber
grip *v.* hold, grasp, seize
grueling *adj.* exhausting, difficult
gullible *adj.* innocent, naive, trusting, credulous
hamper *v.* delay, obstruct, hinder, block
haphazard *adj.* random, chance, aimless, unplanned
hardship *n.* difficulty, trouble
harm *v.* injure, damage
harmony *n.* accord, agreement, peace
harness *v.* control, utilize
harsh *adj.* severe, rough, strict
hasty *adj.* quick, rushed, hurried
hazardous *adj.* dangerous, risky
heed *v.* obey, listen to, mind, follow
hinder *v.* block, obstruct, hamper
hoist *v.* lift, raise, pick up
hue *n.* color, tint, shade
huge *adj.* enormous, giant, colossal, immense
hurl *v.* pitch, throw, fling

Exercise: Complete the following sentences by filling in the blanks with vocabulary items (A), (B), or (C) according to the context of the sentences.

1. During the construction of skyscrapers, cranes are used to _____ building materials to the upper floors.

   (A) hurl
   (B) harness
   (C) hoist

2. The 23-mile-long Boston Marathon is a _____ foot race.

   (A) gorgeous
   (B) grueling
   (C) hasty

3. Dams can _____ the power of rivers, but they may also destroy their beauty.

   (A) heed
   (B) harness
   (C) hurl

4. The more facets a diamond has, the more it _____.

   (A) glitters
   (B) harms
   (C) hinders

5. Many people celebrate the new year with _____ parties.

   (A) gala
   (B) grueling
   (C) haphazard

6. Think it over for awhile; don't make a _____ decision.

   (A) genuine
   (B) gullible
   (C) hasty

7. Bad weather _____ the rescue crews trying to locate the life rafts.

   (A) hampered
   (B) grasped
   (C) harnessed

8. Gorillas look ferocious but are actually quite _____ creatures.

   (A) gaudy
   (B) gentle
   (C) gorgeous

9. Con artists are criminals who take advantage of _____ people by tricking them and taking their money.

   (A) garrulous
   (B) grim
   (C) gullible

10. Working with toxic materials is a _____ occupation.

   (A) hazardous
   (B) genial
   (C) haphazard

11. Most minnows are tiny fish, but squawfish, which can weigh as much as 30 pounds, are actually _____ minnows.

   (A) gregarious
   (B) gaudy
   (C) huge

12. At first, the results of the experience seemed _____, but finally a pattern emerged.

   (A) haphazard
   (B) grave
   (C) genuine

MINI-LESSON 3.8

idea *n.* concept, notion, thought
ideal *n.* model, standard
     adj. perfect, model, standard
idle *adj.* (1) inactive, unused, inert; (2) lazy
illusion *n.* fantasy, delusion
imaginary *adj.* unreal, fantastic, fictitious
imaginative *adj.* creative, original, clever
immense *adj.* huge, enormous, massive, colossal
impair *v.* damage, injure, spoil
impartial *adj.* fair, unbiased, neutral
implement *v.* realize, achieve, put into practice, execute
         n. tool, utensil, instrument
incessant *adj.* constant, ceaseless, continuous
increment *n.* increase, amount
indifferent *adj.* uncaring, apathetic, unconcerned
indigenous *adj.* native
indispensable *adj.* necessary, essential, vital, critical
indistinct *adj.* unclear, blurry, hazy
induce *v.* persuade, convince, coax
inept *adj.* incompetent, awkward, clumsy

inexorable *adj.* unstoppable
infamous *adj.* notorious, shocking
infinite *adj.* limitless, endless, boundless
infinitesimal *adj.* tiny, minute, minuscule
ingenious *adj.* brilliant, imaginative, clever, inventive
ingenuous *adj.* naive, trusting
inhabit *v.* live, dwell, reside, populate
inhibit *v.* control, limit, restrain
initial *adj.* original, first, beginning, introductory
innate *adj.* natural, inborn
intense *adj.* powerful, heightened, concentrated
intricate *adj.* complicated, complex, involved
irate *adj.* angry, furious, upset
jagged *adj.* rough, rugged, uneven, irregular
jeopardy *n.* danger, hazard, risk, threat
jolly *adj.* joyful, happy, cheerful, jovial
jolt *v.* shock, jar, shake up, surprise
    n. blow, surprise, shock
keen *adj.* (1) sharp; (2) shrewd, clever, bright; (3) eager, enthusiastic
key *adj.* principal, crucial, important
knack *n.* skill, ability, aptitude, talent

    Exercise: Complete the following sentences by filling in the blanks with vocabulary items (A), (B), or (C) according to the context of the sentences.

1. Many people feel that Hawaii has an almost _____ climate.

   (A) idle
   (B) impartial
   (C) ideal

2. A plow is a farm _____ used to break up soil and prepare the land for planting.

   (A) increment
   (B) knack
   (C) implement

3. A laser uses a synthetic ruby to concentrate light into an extremely _____ high-energy beam.

   (A) intense
   (B) indistinct
   (C) imaginary

4. Jesse James was an _____ outlaw, well-known as a bank robber and gunfighter.

   (A) inept
   (B) ingenuous
   (C) infamous

5. Antibiotics _____ the growth of bacteria.

   (A) inhabit
   (B) jolt
   (C) inhibit

6. Optical _____ deceive the eye with tricks of perception.

   (A) illusions
   (B) ideals
   (C) increments

7. Stockholders may be too _____ to vote in corporate elections, so they let management vote for them by proxy.

   (A) infamous
   (B) indifferent
   (C) ingenious

8. The heavily populated states of Ohio, Pennsylvania, Illinois, and Michigan are _____ states for any candidate in a presidential election.

   (A) initial
   (B) impartial
   (C) key

9. A virus is so _____ that it can be seen only with an electron microscope.

   (A) infinite
   (B) imaginary
   (C) infinitesimal

10. The _____ character Falstaff is one of Shakespeare's finest comic creations.

    (A) keen
    (B) jolly
    (C) irate

11. Anyone can learn basic cooking skills; you don't need a special _____.

    (A) knack
    (B) idea
    (C) implement

12. Alcohol can _____ one's ability to drive.

    (A) jolt
    (B) impair
    (C) induce

13. The _____ people of Australia were called Aborigines by the English settlers.

    (A) indigenous
    (B) ingenuous
    (C) innate

14. The rhinoceros has a poor sense of sight but _____ sense of smell.

    (A) an impartial
    (B) an inept
    (C) a keen

15. The equator is _____ line running around the center of the Earth.

    (A) an imaginative
    (B) a jagged
    (C) an imaginary

16. A glacier's progress is slow but _____.

    (A) inexorable
    (B) impartial
    (C) infinite

MINI-LESSON 3.9

lack *v.* need, require, not have
    n. shortage, absence, scarcity
lag *v.* fall behind, go slowly
lavish *adj.* luxurious, plentiful, abundant
lax *adj.* careless, negligent, loose
legendary *adj.* mythical, fabled, famous
legitimate *adj.* proper, authentic, valid
lethargic *adj.* slow, listless, sluggish, lazy
likely *adj.* probable, plausible
linger *v.* remain, stay
link *v.* join, connect, fasten, bind
    n. connection, tie
long *v.* desire, wish for
lucid *adj.* clear, plain, understandable
lull *v.* soothe, calm, quiet
    n. pause, break
lure *v.* attract, tempt, entice
lurid *adj.* shocking, sensational, graphic
lurk *v.* prowl, sneak, hide
luster *n.* shine, radiance, brightness
luxurious *adj.* lavish, elegant, plush
magnificent *adj.* majestic, impressive, splendid
magnitude *n.* size, extent, amount
mandatory *adj.* necessary, obligatory, compulsory
mar *v.* damage, ruin, deface, spoil
memorable *adj.* unforgettable, impressive, striking
mend *v.* fix, repair
mild *adj.* gentle, moderate, calm

mingle *v.* blend, combine, mix
minute *adj.* tiny, minuscule, infinitesimal
monitor *v.* observe, watch
moral *adj.* honorable, ethical
morale *n.* spirit, confidence, attitude
murky *adj.* unclear, cloudy
mysterious *adj.* puzzling, strange
mythical *adj.* legendary, imaginary, fictional

Exercise: Complete the following sentences by filling in the blanks with vocabulary items (A), (B), or (C) according to the context of the sentences.

1. It's difficult for scuba divers to see when the water is _____.

   (A) murky
   (B) lucid
   (C) magnificent

2. In most cultures, it is traditional to prepare _____ meals to celebrate holidays.

   (A) lurid
   (B) lethargic
   (C) lavish

3. Parents often sing to children to _____ them to sleep.

   (A) lurk
   (B) mingle
   (C) lull

4. Julius Caesar is known not only for his military and political skills but also for his _____, informative writing.

   (A) lucid
   (B) lurid
   (C) lethargic

5. A cobbler _____ damaged shoes.

   (A) mars
   (B) mends
   (C) lacks

6. One of the _____ exhibits of Impression-ist art is found at the Art Institute of Chicago.

   (A) mildest
   (B) most memorable
   (C) most lucid

7. The USO is a service organization that entertains U.S. troops and improves their _____.

   (A) morale
   (B) luster
   (C) lack

8. Quarks are _____ particles that are believed to be the fundamental unit of matter.

   (A) massive
   (B) minute
   (C) mythical

9. Some people like to _____ after dinner over coffee and dessert.

   (A) lag
   (B) long
   (C) linger

10. Paperback novels in the 1940s and 1950s often had _____ covers to attract readers' attention.

    (A) lurid
    (B) murky
    (C) legitimate

11. One problem caused by a rising crime rate is a _____ of space in prisons.

    (A) lag
    (B) lack
    (C) link

12. The _____ lumberjack Paul Bunyan and his giant blue ox Babe are two of the most famous characters in American folklore.

    (A) legendary
    (B) moral
    (C) minute

MINI-LESSON 3.10

negligible *adj.* unimportant, trivial
nimble *adj.* graceful, agile
notable *adj.* remarkable, conspicuous, striking
notify *v.* inform
notion *n.* idea, concept, thought
notorious *adj.* infamous, disreputable
novel *adj.* new, innovative
objective *n.* goal, purpose, aim
        adj. fair, impartial, unbiased, neutral
oblong *adj.* oval
obscure *adj.* unfamiliar, ambiguous, little-known
obsolete *adj.* antiquated, out of date, outmoded
odd *adj.* strange, unusual, peculiar, curious
offspring *n.* young, children, descendants
ominous *adj.* threatening, menacing, dangerous
opulent *adj.* luxurious, plush, affluent
ornamental *adj.* ornate, decorative, elaborate
outgoing *adj.* (1) open, friendly; (2) departing, leaving
outlook *n.* (1) opinion, view; (2) prospect, forecast
outstanding *adj.* excellent, exceptional, notable, well-known
overall *adj.* general, comprehensive
overcast *adj.* cloudy, gloomy
overcome *v.* subdue, defeat, overwhelm
overlook *v.* ignore, disregard, neglect
oversee *v.* supervise, manage, direct
oversight *n.* error, mistake, omission
overt *adj.* open, obvious
overtake *v.* catch up with, reach
overwhelm *v.* (1) astonish, astound; (2) inundate, overcome, engulf; (3) conquer, defeat, overpower

Exercise: Complete the following sentences by filling in the blanks with vocabulary items (A), (B), or (C) according to the context of the sentences.

1. Who should be _____ in case you are involved in an accident?

   (A) overlooked
   (B) notified
   (C) overtaken

2. Many of the world's most _____ restaurants are located in luxury hotels.

   (A) outgoing
   (B) opulent
   (C) overt

3. The black clouds of a gathering thunderstorm look quite _____.

   (A) ominous
   (B) negligible
   (C) overcast

4. Pulitzer Prizes are awarded to _____ journalists, novelists, poets, and other writers.

   (A) objective
   (B) outstanding
   (C) notorious

5. An _____ plant is cultivated chiefly for its beauty.

   (A) opulent
   (B) obscure
   (C) ornamental

6. Franklin D. Roosevelt was able to _____ his physical handicaps; he didn't permit them to interfere with his living a vigorous life.

   (A) oversee
   (B) overcome
   (C) overtake

7. The poetry of Ezra Pound is sometimes difficult to understand because it contains so many _____ references.

   (A) notable
   (B) obscure
   (C) objective

8. The Bessemer process was once the most common method of making steel, but today this process is considered _____.

   (A) odd
   (B) novel
   (C) obsolete

9. Gregarious people are friendly and _____.

   (A) overcast
   (B) nimble
   (C) outgoing

10. The town planning commission said that its financial _____ for the next fiscal year was optimistic; it expects increased tax revenues.

    (A) outlook
    (B) oversight
    (C) notion

11. The new play was so successful that the demand for tickets was _____.

    (A) odd
    (B) overwhelming
    (C) negligible

12. A book's table of contents provides readers with an _____ idea of what the book is about.

    (A) outgoing
    (B) overt
    (C) overall

13. Because ultraviolet light from the Sun can penetrate clouds, it is possible to get a sunburn on an _____ day.

    (A) obscure
    (B) overcast
    (C) opulent

14. Although the accident appeared serious, only a _____ amount of damage was done.

    (A) novel
    (B) notable
    (C) negligible

MINI-LESSON 3.11

pace *n.* rate, speed
painstaking *adj.* careful, conscientious, thorough
pale *adj.* white, colorless, faded
paltry *adj.* unimportant, minor, trivial
particle *n.* piece, bit, fragment
path *n.* trail, track, way, route
peculiar *adj.* (1) strange, odd, puzzling; (2) distinctive, characteristic, unique, special
penetrate *v.* enter, go through, pierce, puncture
perceive *v.* observe, sense, notice
peril *n.* danger, hazard, risk, threat
perpetual *adj.* constant, endless, eternal
perplexing *adj.* puzzling, mystifying, confusing
pierce *v.* penetrate, puncture, stab
plausible *adj.* likely, credible, believable
plead *v.* appeal, beg

plush *adj.* opulent, luxurious, elegant
ponder *v.* consider, think about, reflect on
portion *n.* share, part, section, segment
postpone *v.* delay, put off, defer
potent *adj.* strong, powerful, effective
pounce *v.* jump, leap, spring
precious *adj.* expensive, costly, rare
precise *adj.* accurate, exact, definite
premier *adj.* (1) first, opening, earliest, initial; (2) chief, leading, foremost
pressing *adj.* urgent, crucial, compelling
pretext *n.* excuse, pretense, justification
prevail *v.* succeed, win, triumph
prevalent *adj.* common, widespread, popular
prior *adj.* earlier, preceding, former
probe *v.* investigate, inquire into
procure *v.* obtain, acquire, secure
profound *adj.* important, significant, deep
prompt *adj.* punctual, timely
prosper *v.* flourish, thrive, succeed
provoke *v.* (1) irritate, anger, annoy; (2) cause, trigger
prudent *adj.* careful, sensible, cautious
pulverize *v.* crush, grind, powder
pungent *adj.* (1) bitter, harsh, biting, sharp; (2) spicy, sour, tart
pursue *v.* chase, follow, seek
puzzling *adj.* mystifying, confusing, baffling

Exercise: Complete the following sentences by filling in the blanks with vocabulary items (A), (B), or (C) according to the context of the sentences.

1. Turquoise is not valuable enough to be classified as a _____ stone.

   (A) perpetual
   (B) pale
   (C) precious

2. Employers often require job applicants to have _____ experience in the field.

   (A) premier
   (B) prior
   (C) plush

3. Hospitals define *urgent care* as medical care given to somewhat less _____ medical problems than emergency care.

   (A) perplexing
   (B) pressing
   (C) prudent

4. Toolmakers must have the ability to work very _____ in order to meet exact specifications.

   (A) precisely
   (B) profoundly
   (C) plausibly

5. NASA _____ the launch of space vehicles on account of bad weather or technical problems.

   (A) ponders
   (B) postpones
   (C) probes

6. _____ of dust in the air may trigger allergies in some people.

   (A) Portions
   (B) Pretexts
   (C) Particles

7. The Appalachian Trail, extending from Maine to Georgia, is the longest continuous hiking _____ in the world.

   (A) pace
   (B) peril
   (C) path

8. When a tiger spots its prey, it crouches down and then _____.

   (A) pleads
   (B) ponders
   (C) pounces

Peterson's TOEFL CBT Success

9. X rays cannot _____ lead.

   (A) provoke
   (B) penetrate
   (C) pursue

10. Morphine, a form of synthetic heroin, is a _____ painkiller.

    (A) potent
    (B) pungent
    (C) paltry

11. Sherlock Holmes, a fictional detective, solved many _____ crimes.

    (A) puzzling
    (B) prevalent
    (C) prompt

12. Mallows are a type of wildflower that grows _____ in prairies, woods, and marshes.

    (A) profusely
    (B) profoundly
    (C) preciously

13. Certain spices give foods a _____ taste.

    (A) prudent
    (B) pungent
    (C) pale

14. Trade with Britain and the West Indies allowed Colonial seaports such as Boston to _____.

    (A) postpone
    (B) provoke
    (C) prosper

15. A _____ investor never takes unnecessary financial risks.

    (A) perplexing
    (B) prudent
    (C) premier

MINI-LESSON 3.12

quaint *adj.* charming, picturesque, curious, old-fashioned
quake *v.* shiver, shake, tremble
quandary *n.* problem, dilemma, predicament
quarrel *n.* argument, dispute, disagreement
quest *n.* search, journey, venture
radiant *adj.* bright, shiny, glowing
ragged *adj.* torn, tattered, worn
range *n.* scope, extent, spectrum
       v. (1) extend, vary, fluctuate; (2) roam, wander
rash *adj.* thoughtless, careless, reckless
raw *adj.* (1) uncooked; (2) unprocessed, unrefined, crude
raze *v.* demolish, level, knock down
recede *v.* retreat, go back, subside, withdraw
reckless *adj.* careless, rash
recollect *v.* recall, remember
recount *v.* narrate, tell
refine *v.* improve, process, purify
refuge *n.* shelter, haven, retreat
rehearse *v.* practice, train, go over
reliable *adj.* dependable, trustworthy
relish *v.* enjoy, savor, like
remedy *n.* treatment, cure
remnant *n.* remainder, balance, fragment
remote *adj.* isolated, distant
renowned *adj.* famous, celebrated, notable
resent *v.* dislike, take offense at
retract *v.* withdraw, pull back
riddle *n.* puzzle, mystery

rigid *adj.* (1) stiff, unbending; (2) harsh, severe, strict
rip *v.* tear, cut, slash
ripe *adj.* mature, developed, grown
risky *adj.* dangerous, hazardous, treacherous
roam *v.* travel, wander, range
rough *adj.* (1) uneven, jagged, rugged; (2) difficult; (3) impolite
route *n.* way, course, path, road
rudimentary *adj.* elementary, fundamental, primary
rugged *adj.* (1) jagged, rough, uneven; (2) strong, sturdy
rumor *adj.* gossip, hearsay, story
rural *adj.* agricultural
ruthless *adj.* cruel, brutal, vicious

Exercise: Complete the following sentences by filling in the blanks with vocabulary items (A), (B), or (C) according to the context of the sentences.

1. Motorists can be fined for driving _____.

   (A) recklessly
   (B) reliably
   (C) ruthlessly

2. Millions of bison once _____ the plains of North America.

   (A) recollected
   (B) ripped
   (C) roamed

3. Musicians have to _____ before performing.

   (A) rehearse
   (B) resent
   (C) recount

4. At the end of the Ice Age, glaciers began to _____.

   (A) quake
   (B) raze
   (C) recede

5. Big Sur, a wild section of California's coastline, is known for its _____ beauty.

   (A) ragged
   (B) rash
   (C) rugged

6. Wetlands provide _____ for many species of birds, reptiles, mammals, and amphibians.

   (A) riddles
   (B) refuge
   (C) rumors

7. The pirate Blackbeard had a reputation for being a harsh, _____ man.

   (A) ruthless
   (B) quaint
   (C) reliable

8. Wrecking balls are used to _____ buildings.

   (A) rip
   (B) quake
   (C) raze

9. The northernmost section of the Rocky Mountains, the Brooks Range, is located in a _____ section of Alaska.

   (A) remote
   (B) reliable
   (C) radiant

10. Dogs can hear a greater _____ of sounds than humans.

    (A) remnant
    (B) quandary
    (C) range

11. Patent medicine salesmen have claimed to have _____ for all types of ailments, from cancer to baldness to the common cold.

    (A) remedies
    (B) quandaries
    (C) riddles

Peterson's TOEFL CBT Success

12. Visitors to Vermont delight in the beautiful scenery and picturesque villages and enjoy staying in some of the _____ country inns there.

(A) rudimentary
(B) ragged
(C) quaint

13. _____ materials have less economic value than processed materials.

(A) Raw
(B) Rash
(C) Renowned

14. Many medieval stories dealt with _____, such as the story of the search for the Grail.

(A) quarrels
(B) quandaries
(C) quests

15. The Tennessee Valley Authority helped bring cheap electricity to farmers in the _____ South.

(A) reliable
(B) rural
(C) rugged

MINI-LESSON 3.13

salvage *v.* save, rescue, recover, retrieve
scale *v.* climb
    n. (1) range, spectrum; (2) proportion
scarce *adj.* rare, sparse, unusual
scatter *v.* disperse, spread
scent *n.* aroma, fragrance, odor, smell
scrap *v.* abandon, get rid of
    n. piece, fragment
seasoned *adj.* experienced, veteran
secluded *adj.* hidden, isolated, secret
sensational *adj.* thrilling, exciting, shocking
serene *adj.* quiet, peaceful, calm, tranquil
sever *v.* cut, slice off
severe *adj.* (1) harsh, strict, austere; (2) undecorated, plain
shatter *v.* break, smash, fragment
sheer *adj.* (1) steep, sharp, abrupt; (2) transparent, thin, filmy
shimmer *v.* shine, glow, glisten, gleam
shred *v.* rip up, tear up
shrewd *adj.* clever, sly
shrill *adj.* piercing, high-pitched
shun *v.* avoid, stay away from
shy *adj.* timid, reserved
significant *adj.* important, vital, major
signify *v.* symbolize, stand for, indicate
sketch *v.* draw
    n. drawing, picture, diagram
slender *adj.* thin, slim, slight
sluggish *adj.* slow, listless, lazy, lethargic
sly *adj.* cunning, clever, shrewd
soak *v.* wet, drench, saturate
solace *n.* comfort, consolation, relief
somber *adj.* serious, grave, solemn
sort *v.* classify, categorize
    n. type, kind, variety
sound *n.* noise
    adj. safe, solid, secure

Exercise: Complete the following sentences by filling in the blanks with vocabulary items (A), (B), or (C) according to the context of the sentences.

1. Skunks use a pungent _____ as their first line of defense.

   (A) scent
   (B) scrap
   (C) sound

2. One of the most popular peaks for mountain climbers to _____ is El Capitan in Yosemite National Park.

   (A) scale
   (B) soak
   (C) shun

3. Foxes are not particularly rare, but they are not often seen because they are so

   _____.

   (A) sluggish
   (B) somber
   (C) shy

4. The Civil Rights Act of 1964 was a particularly _____ piece of legislation.

   (A) serene
   (B) significant
   (C) slender

5. _____ workers are more valuable to employers than beginners.

   (A) Shrill
   (B) Seasoned
   (C) Sluggish

6. The Shakers were a strict religious group that _____ all types of pleasure.

   (A) scrapped
   (B) shunned
   (C) sketched

7. Denver's plan to build a subway system was _____ in the 1970s.

   (A) scattered
   (B) sorted
   (C) scrapped

8. Even after a ship has sunk, its cargo can often be _____.

   (A) severed
   (B) shattered
   (C) salvaged

9. Some economists believe that the best way to get a _____ economy moving again is to cut taxes.

   (A) sensational
   (B) sluggish
   (C) shrewd

10. Government bonds and blue-chip stocks are _____ investments.

    (A) sound
    (B) shy
    (C) scarce

11. If a person's spinal cord is _____, paralysis results.

    (A) soaked
    (B) severed
    (C) salvaged

12. Silk is a _____ fabric.

    (A) sheer
    (B) shrewd
    (C) slender

MINI-LESSON 3.14

span *v.* extend, bridge, connect
    n. length, extent, range
spawn *v.* generate, create, produce
      n. offspring, descendants
specific *adj.* definite, particular, exact
specimen *n.* example, sample
spectacular *adj.* dramatic, sensational, impressive
spell *n.* interval, period, time
spirited *adj.* lively, energetic, vigorous
splendid *adj.* excellent, superb, wonderful
spoil *v.* (1) ruin, mar; (2) decay, deteriorate, decompose, rot
spot *v.* locate, find, see
    n. (1) location, site; (2) mark, stain, speck
spur *v.* stimulate, impel, encourage, provoke
    n. inducement, stimulus
stable *adj.* steady, secure, stationary, fixed
stage *v.* present, put on
    n. grade, step, level, phase
stain *v.* color, tint, discolor, dye
    n. spot, mark, blemish
stale *adj.* (1) old, dry; (2) dull, trite, uninteresting
stall *v.* halt, delay, put off
stately *adj.* dignified, grand, magnificent, elegant
steep *adj.* sheer, perpendicular
stern *adj.* firm, severe, strict, harsh
strife *n.* conflict, dispute, struggle
strive *v.* attempt, try
struggle *v.* fight, argue, dispute
      n. conflict, strife, battle, effort
stubborn *adj.* rigid, uncompromising, obstinate
sturdy *adj.* strong, rugged, well-built
subsequent *adj.* later, succeeding, following, ensuing
subtle *adj.* indirect, suggestive, implied
suitable *adj.* appropriate, correct, apt
summit *n.* peak, apex, zenith
sundry *adj.* miscellaneous, diverse, various
superb *adj.* excellent, splendid
supplant *v.* replace, substitute for
supple *adj.* pliable, flexible, bendable
sway *v.* (1) wave, rock, swing, bend; (2) persuade, influence
sweeping *adj.* complete, exhaustive, general, comprehensive
swift *adj.* fast, quick, rapid
swivel *v.* rotate, spin, turn

Exercise: Complete the following sentences by filling in the blanks with vocabulary items (A), (B), or (C) according to the context of the sentences.

1. High-pressure cells may bring brief warm _____ even in the middle of winter.

   (A) struggles
   (B) spells
   (C) spans

2. The _____ cliffs of the Na Pali Coast of Kauai Island, Hawaii, rise some 4,000 feet from the sea.

   (A) still
   (B) steep
   (C) subtle

3. The process of refining oil involves a number of _____.

   (A) specimens
   (B) spots
   (C) stages

4. In high winds, skyscrapers will _____ slightly.

   (A) swivel
   (B) sway
   (C) stall

5. One invention often _____ many others.

   (A) spoils
   (B) strives
   (C) spawns

6. The snow-covered _____ of Mount Hood is the highest point in the state of Oregon.

   (A) spur
   (B) summit
   (C) span

7. D. W. Griffith was the first director of _____ films. These were movies made on a colossal scale.

   (A) specific
   (B) suitable
   (C) spectacular

8. Cheetahs are the _____ of all land mammals, with top speeds of up to 70 miles per hour.

   (A) stalest
   (B) subtlest
   (C) swiftest

9. Salt can be used to keep meat from _____.

   (A) struggling
   (B) spoiling
   (C) stalling

10. Because they must be able to break a path through icebound waters, icebreakers have to be very _____ boats.

    (A) stern
    (B) sturdy
    (C) supple

11. Most people who divorce _____ remarry.

    (A) specifically
    (B) subsequently
    (C) stubbornly

12. A roadbed supplies a _____ base for a highway.

    (A) stable
    (B) sundry
    (C) sweeping

13. The geographical center of the North American continent is a _____ near Balta, North Dakota.

    (A) spot
    (B) stage
    (C) summit

14. Many medical tests require a blood _____.

    (A) spell
    (B) specimen
    (C) stain

15. Because of their protective coloration, ghost crabs are hard to _____.

    (A) spur
    (B) spawn
    (C) spot

16. Severe thunderstorms may _____ tornadoes.

    (A) spot
    (B) spawn
    (C) span

Peterson's TOEFL CBT Success

MINI-LESSON 3.15

tact *n.* diplomacy, discretion, poise
tale *n.* story
tame *v.* domesticate, master
    adj. docile, domesticated, gentle
tamper (with) interfere (with)
tangle *v.* knot, twist
tart *adj.* sour, tangy, piquant
taunt *v.* insult, mock, torment
tedious *adj.* boring, dull, tiresome
telling *adj.* effective, convincing, forceful
temperate *adj.* mild, moderate
tempting *adj.* alluring, attractive, enticing
tender *adj.* (1) delicate, soft; (2) gentle, loving; (3) sore, painful
thaw *v.* melt
thorough *adj.* complete, comprehensive
thoroughfare *n.* street, boulevard
thrifty *adj.* economical, inexpensive
thrilling *adj.* exciting, stimulating, stirring
thrive *v.* prosper, flourish
thwart *v.* prevent, impede, obstruct
tidings *n.* news, message
tilt *v.* incline, slope
timid *adj.* fearful, shy, retiring
tint *v.* color, hue, shade, tone
    n. color, stain, dye
tiresome *adj.* tedious, dull, boring
toil *v.* labor, work
    n. exertion, labor, work
tolerant *adj.* patient, impartial, open-minded
torment *v.* taunt, abuse, bully
torrent *n.* flood, deluge
tow *v.* haul, draw, pull, drag
toxic *adj.* poisonous, noxious
trait *n.* characteristic, feature, quality
treacherous *adj.* dangerous, hazardous
trickle *n.* drip, leak
triumph *n.* victory, success, achievement
trivial *adj.* unimportant, minor
trying *adj.* demanding, difficult, troublesome
tug *v.* pull, draw

Exercise: Complete the following sentences by filling in the blanks with vocabulary items (A), (B), or (C) according to the context of the sentences.

1. Citric acid gives citrus fruit their _____ taste.

   (A) temperate
   (B) toxic
   (C) tart

2. The use of robots and automated machinery has eliminated certain _____ factory jobs.

   (A) tedious
   (B) thrilling
   (C) timid

3. One should never buy a food or medicine if the packaging has obviously been _____.

   (A) tangled
   (B) thwarted
   (C) tampered with

4. Alfred Hitchcock directed a number of _____ psychological dramas; among the most exciting were *Psycho* and *North by Northwest*.

   (A) timid
   (B) trivial
   (C) thrilling

5. Tides are caused by the _____ of the moon's gravity.

   (A) tangle
   (B) torrent
   (C) tug

6. Many people find chocolate _____.

   (A) tempting
   (B) tender
   (C) temperate

7. Peachtree Street is the main _____ in Atlanta.

   (A) triumph
   (B) thoroughfare
   (C) tilt

8. In her book *Silent Spring*, Rachel Carson wrote about insecticides and their _____ effects on animal life.

   (A) tiresome
   (B) tender
   (C) toxic

9. In the desert, dry creek beds may turn into raging _____ after heavy rainstorms.

   (A) trickles
   (B) torrents
   (C) toils

10. Barley can be grown almost anywhere in the temperate zone. Unlike most other grains, it even _____ at high altitudes.

    (A) tampers
    (B) thrives
    (C) thaws

11. _____ such as hair color and eye color are inherited genetically from one's parents.

    (A) Traits
    (B) Triumphs
    (C) Tints

12. Washington Irving collected and interpreted many famous old _____, including the legends of *Rip Van Winkle* and the *Headless Horseman*.

    (A) tales
    (B) tidings
    (C) traits

MINI-LESSON 3.16

ultimate *adj.* (1) conclusive, definite, final; (2) maximum, highest, best

unbearable *adj.* intolerable, agonizing

uncouth *adj.* impolite, rude, vulgar

undertake *v.* try, attempt

ungainly *adj.* awkward, unskillful

uniform *adj.* consistent, regular

unique *adj.* singular, one of a kind, special

unruly *adj.* unmanageable, disorganized, disorderly

unsound *adj.* defective, faulty, unsafe

uphold *v.* support, sustain

upkeep *n.* maintenance

uproar *n.* disorder, disturbance, commotion

urge *v.* encourage, advise, implore

urgent *adj.* pressing, compelling

utensil *n.* tool, implement, device

utter *v.* say, speak
      adj. total, absolute, complete

vacant *adj.* empty, unoccupied

vague *adj.* unclear, uncertain, ambiguous

vain *adj.* (1) useless, pointless; (2) conceited, proud

valid *adj.* genuine, authentic, legitimate

vanish *v.* disappear

variable *adj.* changeable, shifting

vast *adj.* huge, enormous, extensive, immense

venomous *adj.* poisonous

verbose *adj.* talkative, wordy

verge *n.* brink, edge, threshold

vessel *n.* (1) container, bottle; (2) ship

vex *v.* irritate, anger, annoy

viable *adj.* (1) alive, living; (2) feasible, practical, possible

vicinity *n.* area, proximity, zone

vigorous *adj.* dynamic, energetic, spirited

vital *adj.* critical, crucial, key, essential

vivid *adj.* clear, distinct, graphic

vow *v.* promise, pledge, swear
      n. oath, promise, pledge

Exercise: Complete the following sentences by filling in the blanks with vocabulary items (A), (B), or (C) according to the context of the sentences.

1. To be fair, laws must be _____ applied to all persons.

   (A) urgently
   (B) vaguely
   (C) uniformly

2. The rattlesnake is the most common _____ snake in the United States.

   (A) ungainly
   (B) venomous
   (C) variable

3. The League of Women Voters _____ all citizens to vote.

   (A) urges
   (B) vexes
   (C) upholds

4. In his novel *The Red Badge of Courage*, Stephen Crane _____ describes a Civil War battle.

   (A) vividly
   (B) uniformly
   (C) vitally

5. An Erlenmeyer flask is a glass _____ used in chemistry labs.

   (A) vessel
   (B) vow
   (C) verge

6. Aerobics is _____ form of exercise.

   (A) a viable
   (B) an uncouth
   (C) a vigorous

7. A metropolitan area consists of a central city and any suburban areas in its _____.

   (A) vicinity
   (B) vessel
   (C) upkeep

8. Special police tactics are required to deal with riots or _____ crowds.

   (A) ungainly
   (B) unruly
   (C) unsound

9. The kidneys play a _____ role in maintaining health by removing impurities from the bloodstream.

   (A) vivid
   (B) viable
   (C) vital

10. The myth of Narcissus tells the story of a handsome but _____ young man who stares at his reflection in a pool of water for so long that he turns into a flower.

    (A) vain
    (B) ungainly
    (C) verbose

11. The fork has been used as an eating _____ at least since the twelfth century.

    (A) vessel
    (B) utensil
    (C) verge

12. The Great Plains cover _____ area.

    (A) a vast
    (B) a viable
    (C) an ultimate

MINI-LESSON 3.17

wage *n.* salary, pay, earnings
wander *v.* roam, travel, range
wane *v.* shrink, decrease, decline
ware *n.* good, merchandise
warp *v.* deform, bend, twist
wary *adj.* careful, cautious, alert
weary *adj.* tired, exhausted, fatigued
well-to-do *adj.* rich, wealthy, affluent
wholesome *adj.* healthy, nutritious, beneficial
wicked *adj.* evil, corrupt, immoral
widespread *adj.* extensive, prevalent, sweeping
wily *adj.* crafty, cunning, shrewd
wise *adj.* astute, prudent, intelligent
withdraw *v.* retreat, pull out, remove
wither *v.* dry, shrivel, wilt
withhold *v.* reserve, retain, hold back
witty *adj.* comic, clever, amusing
woe *n.* trouble, distress, sorrow
wonder *v.* think about, speculate, ponder
　　　　 n. marvel, miracle
wound *v.* injure, hurt
　　　　 n. injury
yearn *v.* desire, crave, want
yield *v.* (1) give up, surrender; (2) produce, supply
　　　　 n. production, output, crop
zealous *adj.* enthusiastic, eager
zenith *n.* peak, tip, apex
zone *n.* area, vicinity, region

Exercise: Complete the following sentences by filling in the blanks with vocabulary items (A), (B), or (C) according to the context of the sentences.

1. If boards become wet, they may _____.

   (A) wither
   (B) yield
   (C) warp

2. Whole grains and fresh fruit and vegetables are _____ foods.

   (A) wicked
   (B) wholesome
   (C) well-to-do

3. You must be _____ when buying a used car; be sure the engine is in good condition.

   (A) weary
   (B) zealous
   (C) wary

4. In the past, many salesmen tried to sell their _____ door-to-door.

   (A) wares
   (B) woes
   (C) yields

5. Humorist Will Rogers wrote many _____ newspaper columns.

   (A) wily
   (B) weary
   (C) witty

6. Congress sets the minimum _____, which is the lowest amount of money workers may be paid per hour.

   (A) wage
   (B) yield
   (C) zone

7. Intelligent policies are needed so that public funds are used _____.

(A) wholesomely
(B) zealously
(C) wisely

8. Fertilizers can increase farmers' _____.

(A) wonders
(B) yields
(C) woes

9. Some superstitions are familiar to many cultures. For example, there is a _____ belief that black cats bring bad luck.

(A) widespread
(B) wily
(C) wicked

10. A green belt is a parklike _____ around a city in which no development is permitted.

(A) zenith
(B) wound
(C) zone

Guide to the
Test of Written English
(TWE)

INTRODUCTION

The TWE is given before the other three sections of TOEFL. It is currently given five times a year: in February, May, August, September, and October. There is no additional fee required to take TWE. This part of the test was added at the request of a number of universities that wanted an assessment of their prospective students' writing skills.

TWE differs from the rest of TOEFL in that it is **productive**. Instead of choosing one of four answer choices, you must write your own short essay. TWE consists of a single essay topic; there is no choice as to what to write about. You have 30 minutes in which to write an essay based on the topic. A typical TWE answer is about 200 to 300 words long and is divided into four or five paragraphs.

The most common type of TWE topic asks you to write a contrast/opinion essay. In this type of essay, you must contrast two points of view, then defend one of those positions. Another type of essay asks you to select some development, invention, or phenomenon and explain its importance. Essay topics that ask you to interpret the information given in a graph or chart are no longer given. Topics are carefully chosen to avoid anything controversial, upsetting, or unfair to a particular group.

At ETS, your essay is read by at least two trained readers who score it "holistically." In other words, the essay is not judged according to individual errors you might make but by the overall organization, development, clarity, and effectiveness of your writing. The score is based on a scale of 1 to 6; half point scores (5.5, 4.5, and so on) are also given. The scoring system ETS uses is similar to the one that follows. (You can use this chart to estimate your TWE score when you take the TWE Practice Tests.)

Score	Explanation of Score
6	Strongly indicates the ability to write a well-organized, well-developed, and logical essay. Specific examples and details support the main ideas. All the elements of the essay are unified and cohesive. A variety of sentence structures are used successfully, and sophisticated vocabulary is employed. Grammatical errors are infrequent but a few minor mistakes may occur.
5	Indicates the ability to write an organized, developed, and logical essay. The main ideas are adequately supported by examples and details. Sentence structure may be less varied than that of a level 6 essay, and vocabulary less sophisticated. Some grammatical errors will appear.
4	Indicates a moderate ability to write an acceptable essay. Although main ideas may be adequately supported, weaknesses in organization and development will be apparent. Sentence structure and vocabulary may lack sophistication or be used inappropriately. Grammatical errors may be frequent.
3	Indicates some minimal ability in writing an acceptable essay, but involves serious weaknesses in organization and development. Significant sentence-structure and vocabulary problems occur, and there are frequent grammatical errors that sometimes make the writer's ideas difficult to comprehend.
2	Indicates the inability to write an acceptable essay. Organization and development are very weak or nonexistent. Lacks unity and cohesion. Few if any specific details may be given in support of the writer's ideas. If details are given, they may seem inappropriate. Significant and frequent errors in grammar occur throughout the essay. Writer may not have fully understood the essay topic.
1	Strongly indicates the inability to write an acceptable essay. No apparent development or organization. Sentences may be brief and fragmentary and unrelated to one another. Significant grammatical errors occur throughout the essay and make it difficult to understand any of the author's ideas. Writer may have completely misunderstood the essay topic.
OFF	Did not write on the topic assigned.
1NR	Did not write the essay.

The average score TWE score is between 3.5 and 4.0. TWE is scored separately from the rest of the test and has no effect on your overall TOEFL score.

IMPORTANT: Don't take TWE if you don't need to! Many universities that require TOEFL scores do NOT require TWE scores. There is no way to cancel your TWE score without canceling your TOEFL score, and a low TWE score may have a negative effect on your application *even though you were not required to take the test*. If you are certain that you won't need a TWE score, then try to sign up for a test administration when TWE is not given if at all possible.

Following are two sample TWE topics and essays that respond to those topics. (Note: These essays are based on composite student essays. They have been edited to correct errors in grammar and mechanics.)

SAMPLE TWE TOPIC A

Some people believe that money spent on space research benefits all of humanity. Others take the opposite view and say that money for this type of research is wasted. Discuss these two positions, using examples. Tell which view you agree with and explain why.

Notes

Intro: Space research + 50 years: expensive—$ well spent or wasted?

– ideas	+ ideas
costs billions; also human resources; no real benefits e.g., trip to Moon—only brought back rocks	consumer products; e.g., PCs, freeze-dried foods, pacemakers weather and communication satellites
many important uses for this $ on Earth: e.g., education, environment, housing	scientific knowledge about planets, Moon, even Earth

Conclusion: As shown, many benefits—also, human race needs challenge just as individuals do—therefore, space research is worth all the money spent

For over fifty years, a number of nations have been involved in the exploration of outer space. This research has been very costly, of course. Has this money been well-spent or wasted?

Some people believe that all or most space research should be eliminated because of its incredible expense, not only in terms of money, but also in terms of scientific and human resources. These people point out the fact that it cost billions of dollars to send astronauts to the moon, but all they brought back were some worthless rocks. These people say that the money and effort now being wasted in outer space could be spent on more important projects right here on earth, such as providing housing for homeless people, improving the education system, saving the environment, and finding cures for diseases.

However, other people believe that space research has provided many benefits to mankind. They point out that hundreds of useful products, from personal computers to heart pacemakers to freeze-dried foods, are the direct or indirect results of space research. They say that weather and communication satellites, which are also products of space programs, have benefitted people all over the globe. In addition to these practical benefits, supporters of the space program point to the scientific knowledge that has been acquired about the sun, the moon, the planets, and even our own earth as a result of space research.

I agree with those people who support space research and want it to continue. Space research, as shown, has already brought many benefits to humanity. Perhaps it will bring even more benefits in the future, ones that we can't even imagine now. Moreover, just as individual people need challenges to make their lives more interesting, I believe the human race itself needs a challenge, and I think that the peaceful exploration of outer space provides just such a challenge.

Notice that in the first Sample TWE, the writer organized the essay in the following way:

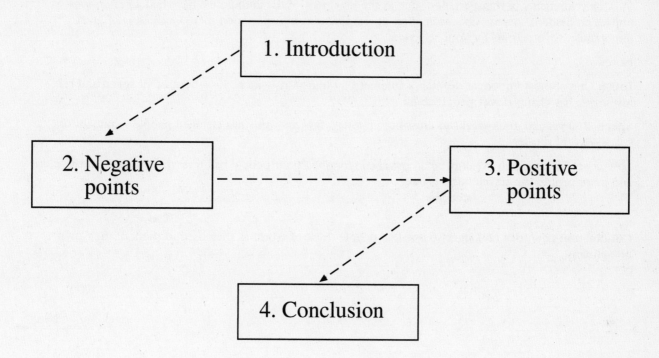

SAMPLE TWE TOPIC B

Developments in transportation such as the invention of the automobile have had an enormous impact on modern society. Choose another development in transportation that you think is of great importance. Give reasons for your selection.

Notes

Intro: One of most important develop is internat'l jet transport—since '50s—because of speed and rel. low costs, has changed way people think

Speed: 100 yrs ago, took weeks to cross ocean: today, few hrs—this has changed people's concept of space—world smaller

Low costs: In past, only wealthy could travel comfortably; poor people had to save for years—today, more and more people can travel: businessmen
                           students
                           tourists

Conclusion: countries no longer so isolated; people think of world as they used to think of their own hometowns

INTRODUCTION

I believe that one of the most important developments in transportation has been the development of international jet transport. Since this style of transportation appeared in the 1950s, it has had some revolutionary effects. Because of the high speeds and the relatively low costs of this type of travel, it has changed the way people look at the world.

The most obviously important characteristic of jet travel is the high speed involved. A hundred years ago, it took weeks to cross the Atlantic or Pacific Oceans by ship. Today, those same trips can be completed in a matter of hours. One can attend a meeting in Paris and have dinner in New York the same day. These amazing speeds have changed people's concepts of space. Today the world is much smaller than it was in the past.

Another important aspect of jet travel is its relatively low cost. An international journey one hundred years ago was extremely expensive. Only wealthy people could afford to travel comfortably, in first class. Poor people had to save for years to purchase a ticket, and the conditions in which they traveled were not very good. Today it is possible for more and more people in every country to travel in comfort.

Thus it is possible for businessmen to do business all over the world, for students to attend universities in other countries, and for tourists to take vacations anywhere in the world.

In conclusion, the speed and low cost of international jet travel have changed the world. Individual nations are not as isolated as they were in the past, and people now think of the whole planet as they once thought of their own hometowns.

Notice that the writer organized the second sample essay as follows:

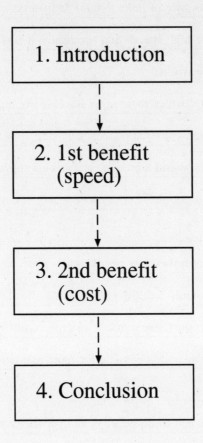

TEN KEYS TO WRITING THE TWE ESSAY

Key #1: Budget your time carefully.

You have only a half hour in which to complete your work. You should use your time more or less as shown below:

Reading and thinking about the topic	2 minutes
Planning and taking notes	3 minutes
Writing the essay	22 minutes
Checking the essay	3 minutes

As with all parts of TOEFL, be familiar with the directions for TWE so that you don't have to waste time reading them.

Key #2: Read the question carefully.

You must write on the topic exactly as it is given, so be sure that you understand it. If you write about another topic, you won't receive a score at all. If you don't completely address the topic, you will receive a lower score.

Key #3: Brainstorm.

Before you begin to write, spend a minute or two jotting down any ideas you have while you're brainstorming in the section marked notes. Think about the topic and the best way to approach it. Remember: there is no "correct" answer for TWE questions. You can choose to support any position as long as you can adequately support your choice.

Key #4: Plan your essay before you write.

You don't have to write out a formal outline with Roman numerals, capital letters, and so on. However, you SHOULD make some notes. By following your notes, you can organize your essay BEFORE you write, leaving you free to concentrate on the task of writing.

When making notes, don't worry about writing complete, grammatical sentences; use abbreviations if possible. You may choose to make a simple chart similar to the ones on pages 371 and 374. The point of taking notes is to simply get your ideas down on paper as quickly as possible.

Key #5: Be sure your handwriting is as clear and legible as possible.

Handwriting that is hard to read may unconsciously prejudice the readers who are grading your essay. Be sure your handwriting is not too small or too large.

Key #6: Follow a clear, logical organization.

All TWE essays should consist of three basic parts: an **introductory paragraph**, a **body** that consists of two or three paragraphs, and a **concluding paragraph**. You need to include all of these elements in your essay. The introduction states the main idea of the essay in one sentence called the **thesis statement** and may provide some background about that idea. The body develops the main idea brought up in the introduction. Specific examples are given to make the thesis statement seem stronger and believable to the reader. The conclusion evaluates and summarizes the material that is in the body. It provides the reader with a sense of closure—the feeling that the essay is really finished, not that the writer simply ran out of time.

The exact plan of organization you use depends on the type of topic you are given. The following patterns could be used for the two main types of topics commonly given. Of course, these are not the only patterns that could be used in writing TWE essays, but they are effective plans for organizing your ideas.

TOPIC TYPE A: CONTRAST/OPINION

Introduction:	Paragraph 1:	Present the two sides of the issue; give a brief amount of background information.
Body:	Paragraph 2:	Discuss the negative side of the issue; give examples.
	Paragraph 3:	Discuss the positive side of the issue; give examples.
Conclusion:	Paragraph 4:	Express your own opinion about the issue; give specific reasons for your decision.

TOPIC TYPE B: EXPLAIN THE IMPORTANCE OF A DEVELOPMENT, INVENTION, OR PHENOMENON

Introduction:	Paragraph 1:	Explain what development you have chosen to write about and why.
Body:	Paragraph 2:	Discuss one aspect of why this development is important; give examples.
	Paragraph 3:	Discuss another aspect of why this development is important; give examples.
Conclusion:	Paragraph 4:	Summarize the points made in paragraphs 2 and 3.

Now look back at the two TWE sample essays to see if they follow these patterns of organization.

Key #7: Use concrete examples and specific reasons.

Whenever you make a general statement, you should support it with specific examples. Don't just say, "Computers are important to modern business." Give specific examples of how computers can benefit businesses. If you state an opinion, give reasons. Don't just say, "I believe television is harmful to children." Explain exactly why you think television hurts children.

Key #8: Use signal words to indicate transitions.

Signal words can be used to join paragraph to paragraph and sentence to sentence. These words make your essay clearer and easier to follow. Some of these expressions and their meanings are given below:

Expressions used to list points, examples, or reasons

First example or reason

> First, . . .
> The first example is . . .
> The first reason for this is that . . .

Additional examples or reasons

> Second . . . (Third, Fourth)
> A second (third, fourth) example is that . . .
> Another example is . . .
> Another reason is that . . .
> In addition, . . .
> Furthermore, . . .
> Moreover, . . .

Final examples or reasons

> Finally, . . .

To give individual examples

> For example, . . .
> For instance, . . .
> To give a specific example, . . .
> X is an example of Y.

To show contrast

> However, . . .
> On the other hand, . . .
> Nevertheless, . . .

To show a conclusion

> Therefore, . . .
> Consequently, . . .

To show similarity

> Likewise, . . .
> Similarly, . . .

To begin a concluding paragraph

> In conclusion, . . .
> In summary, . . .

Examples of the use of signal words

> I agree with the idea of stricter gun control for a number of reasons. *First*, statistics show that guns are not very effective in preventing crime. *Second*, accidents involving guns frequently occur. *Finally*, guns can be stolen and later used in crimes.

> I believe that a good salary is an important consideration when looking for a career. *However*, the nature of the work is more important to me. *Thus*, I would not accept a job that I did not find rewarding.

> For me, the reasons for living in an urban area are stronger than the reasons for living in a rural community. *Therefore*, I agree with those people who believe it is an advantage to live in a big city.

> Look back at the sample essays again. Did the authors use signal words to show transitions?

Key #9: Use a variety of sentence types.

Good writing in English consists of a more or less equal balance between short, simple sentences consisting of only one clause and longer sentences containing two or more clauses. Therefore, make an effort to use sentences of various lengths.

You should also vary sentence structures. Begin some sentences with prepositional phrases or subordinate clauses.

Examples of various sentence types

> Instead of . . .
> I agree with this idea for several reasons.
> Try . . .
> For several reasons, I agree with this idea.
> Instead of . . .
> I support Idea A even though Idea B has some positive attributes.
> Try . . .
> Even though Idea B has some positive attributes, I support Plan B.

Key #10: Check your essay for errors.

Allow a few minutes to proofread the essay. However, don't make any major changes at this time. Don't cross out long sections or try to add a lot of new material. Look for obvious errors in punctuation, spelling, and capitalization, as well as common grammatical mistakes: subject-verb agreement, wrong tense use, incorrect use of plurals, incorrect word forms, and so on. If you have ever taken a writing class in English, look at the corrections the teacher made on your papers to see what types of mistakes you commonly make, and look for these.

THREE PRACTICE TWE TESTS

The following exams are very similar to actual TWE tests. Time yourself carefully while taking these practice tests. You can use the scoring chart on pp. 368 to estimate your score. If you are taking an English course, you may want to ask your English teacher to score your test and to make recommendations for improving your essay.

Practice TWE Directions—30 Minutes

1. When you are ready, turn the page and carefully read the essay topic.

2. Before you begin writing, think about the topic. You will probably want to make some notes to organize your thoughts. Use only the space marked NOTES to write notes or an outline.

3. Write on only *one* topic. If you do not write on the topic given, you will not receive a score.

4. Your essay should be clear and precise. Support your ideas with facts. The quality of your writing is of more importance than the quantity, but you will probably want to write more than one paragraph.

5. Begin your essay on the first line of the essay page. Use the next page if you need to. Write as neatly as possible. Don't write in large letters. Don't skip lines or leave large margins.

6. Check your essay after you have finished. Give yourself enough time to read over your essay and make minor revisions *before* the end of the exam.

7. After 30 minutes, stop writing and put your pencil down.

TWE ESSAY TOPIC 1

Some people believe that advertising on television is generally beneficial to viewers. Others take the position that television advertising has primarily negative effects. Which position do you agree with? Explain your decision, using specific examples.

Notes

Use this space for essay notes only. Write the final version of your essay on the next two pages.

_____

_____

_____

_____

_____

_____

_____

_____

_____

_____

_____

_____

_____

_____

_____

_____

_____

_____

_____

Name: _____

Write your essay here.

_____

_____

_____

_____

_____

_____

_____

_____

_____

_____

_____

_____

_____

_____

_____

_____

_____

_____

_____

_____

_____

_____

_____

TWE ESSAY TOPIC 2

Some people say that university students should concentrate on their own field of study, and that all the classes they take should be closely related to that subject. Others believe that university students should get a general education, taking classes in many fields before concentrating on a single field. Discuss both points of view, using concrete examples. Which view do you support? Give reasons for your choice.

Notes

Use this space for essay notes only. Write the final version of your essay on the next two pages.

_____

_____

_____

_____

_____

_____

_____

_____

_____

_____

_____

_____

_____

_____

_____

_____

_____

_____

_____

_____

_____

_____

_____

Name: _____

Write your essay here.

_____

_____

_____

_____

_____

_____

_____

_____

_____

_____

_____

_____

_____

_____

_____

_____

_____

_____

_____

_____

_____

_____

TWE ESSAY TOPIC 3

Good, affordable housing is one of the factors that make a community a desirable place to live. Choose one other factor that you feel is important. Give specific reasons for your choice.

Notes

Use this space for essay notes only. Write the final version of your essay on the next two pages.

_____

_____

_____

_____

_____

_____

_____

_____

_____

_____

_____

_____

_____

_____

_____

_____

_____

_____

_____

_____

Name: _____

Write your essay here.

_____

_____

_____

_____

_____

_____

_____

_____

_____

_____

_____

_____

_____

_____

_____

_____

_____

_____

_____

_____

_____

_____

Three Complete Practice Tests

TAKING THE PRACTICE TESTS

One of the best ways to ensure success on TOEFL is to take realistic practice exams. The three tests in this book are accurate and up to date, reflecting the changes in format that ETS instituted in 1995. They duplicate actual exams in terms of format, content, and level of difficulty. They cover all the types of items that commonly appear on actual exams. All items have been pretested.

These tests can be used in the classroom or by self-study learners. In order to get the most from these practice tests, suggestions for both types of users are given below.

Using the Tests in the Classroom

- The tests should be given under actual testing conditions—for example, desks should be arranged as they would be during a test, and no talking should be allowed. If possible, each test should be given in its entirety rather than section by section.
- Sections 2 and 3 should be carefully timed and students should not work ahead.
- Students should mark answers on the answer sheets provided at the end of the book.
- An analysis and a discussion of all three parts of the exam is an important follow-up for the practice tests. These activities can be done as a class or in small groups. Test-takers should understand *why* a choice is correct.

Using the Tests for Self-Study

- Take each test all at one time rather than section by section.
- Use a watch to time yourself carefully during Sections 2 and 3. Do not go ahead to the next section even if you finish early. Do not give yourself extra time even if you haven't finished the section.
- Sit at a desk or table, not in an easy chair or on a sofa, and work away from distractions such as a television or a stereo.
- Mark your answers on the answer sheets rather than in the book.
- After completing the test, mark incorrect answers but do not write in the corrections. Instead, go back and answer these questions a second time.
- Read the explanations in the Written Expression section and the Reading Comprehension section for all items that you you answer incorrectly.
- If you have time, take the entire test over again on another answer sheet. (You may want to make photocopies of the answer sheets in the back of the book before you begin.)
- Use the scoring charts in the back of this book to calculate your scores for each practice test.
- Keep track of your scores in the Personal Score Record in the Scoring section of this book. If you have consistently lower scores on one section of the test, you might want to review the related section in *TOEFL CBT Success*. If you have enough time, take the entire test over on a separate answer sheet.

SCORING THE PRACTICE TESTS

The level of difficulty varies slightly from one TOEFL test to another. ETS uses a statistical process called "test equating" to adjust each set of scores. The chart given here can only be used to determine a range of scores. ETS, of course, reports your score as a single number, not as a range.

After completing each test, obtain a raw score for each of the three sections by counting the number of correct answers in the three sections. Then look at the conversion chart to determine the range of scaled scores for each section. Add the three low scores from the range of scores for each section, then the three high scores. Multiply both totals by 10 and divide by 3. Your "actual" TOEFL score will lie somewhere in that range of numbers.

For example, suppose that you had 32 correct answers in Listening Comprehension, 29 in Structure and Written Expression, and 37 in Reading Comprehension:

Peterson's TOEFL CBT Success

	Raw Score (number correct)	Range of Scaled Scores (from conversion chart)
Section 1	32	49-50
Section 2	29	50-52
Section 3	37	53-54

$49 + 50 + 53 = 152$
$50 + 52 + 54 = 156$

$152 \times 10 = 1{,}520 \div 3 = 507$
$156 \times 10 = 1{,}560 \div 3 = 520$

Your score on the practice test would be between 507 and 520.

Score Conversion Chart

Section 1		Section 2		Section 3	
Raw Scores	Range of Scaled Scores	Raw Scores	Range of Scaled Scores	Raw Scores	Range of Scaled Scores
48-50	65-68	39-40	64-68	48-50	65-67
45-47	57-64	36-38	60-64	45-47	57-64
42-44	55-57	34-35	57-59	42-44	56-57
39-41	54-55	31-33	53-56	39-41	55-56
36-38	52-54	29-30	50-52	36-38	53-54
33-35	50-52	27-28	49-50	33-35	51-52
30-32	49-50	24-26	48-49	30-32	50-51
27-29	47-48	21-23	46-48	27-29	48-49
24-26	45-47	18-20	43-45	24-26	46-47
21-23	44-45	15-17	39-42	21-23	44-45
18-20	42-44	12-14	36-38	18-20	42-44
15-17	39-41	9-11	32-35	15-17	39-41
12-14	36-38	6-8	28-32	12-14	36-38
9-11	33-36	3-5	24-27	9-11	33-36
6-8	29-32	0-2	20-23	6-8	29-32
3-5	25-28			3-5	25-28
0-2	23-24			0-2	21-24

PERSONAL SCORE RECORD

Practice Test 1			
Section 1 Range of Scores	Section 2 Range of Scores	Section 3 Range of Scores	Total Range of Scores

Practice Test 2			
Section 1 Range of Scores	Section 2 Range of Scores	Section 3 Range of Scores	Total Range of Scores

Practice Test 3			
Section 1 Range of Scores	Section 2 Range of Scores	Section 3 Range of Scores	Total Range of Scores

Practice Test 1

SECTION 1: LISTENING COMPREHENSION

This section tests your ability to comprehend spoken English. It is divided into three parts, each with its own directions. You are *not* permitted to turn the page during the reading of the directions or to take notes at any time.

PART A

Directions: Each item in this part consists of a brief conversation involving two speakers. Following each conversation, a third voice will ask a question. You will hear the conversations and questions only once, and they will *not* be written out.

When you have heard each conversation and question, read the four answer choices and select the one—(A), (B), (C), or (D)—that best answers the question based on what is directly stated or on what can be inferred. Then fill in the space on your answer sheet (on page 414) that matches the letter of the answer that you have selected.

Here is an example.

You will hear:*

M1: Do you think I should leave this chair against the wall or put it somewhere else?

F1: Over by the window, I'd say.

M2: What does the woman think the man should do?

You will read:

(A) Open the window.
(B) Move the chair.
(C) Leave the room.
(D) Take a seat.

Sample Answer

From the conversation you find out that the woman thinks the man should put the chair over by the window. The best answer to the question, "What does the woman think the man should do?" is (B), "Move the chair." You should fill in (B) on your answer sheet.

(WAIT)

---

* Note: M1 = first male voice   M2 = second male voice   F1 = first female voice   F2 = second female voice

1. (A) She doesn't have an apartment.
   (B) Her problem is complicated.
   (C) She must live somewhere else.
   (D) Her apartment isn't far away.

2. (A) She can use his phone if she wants.
   (B) There's no charge for phone calls.
   (C) His phone is out of order too.
   (D) She can call him later if she likes.

3. (A) He couldn't find it.
   (B) It was too hard to solve.
   (C) It was simpler than he'd thought.
   (D) He solved it even though it was hard.

4. (A) He cleaned up after cooking.
   (B) He forgot to put the pots and pans away.
   (C) He was out in a terrible storm.
   (D) He put some plants in the kitchen.

5. (A) He studied forestry in school.
   (B) He worked in a forest.
   (C) He read a lot of books about trees.
   (D) His father taught him.

6. (A) How many pages he must write.
   (B) What Professor Barclay discussed.
   (C) How long the class lasted.
   (D) When the paper is due.

7. (A) She doesn't like any music except classical.
   (B) There is some classical music she doesn't like.
   (C) She likes classical music but she can't play it.
   (D) Classical music doesn't interest her at all.

8. (A) He was too busy to take the test.
   (B) He did well on the test.
   (C) He left some questions unanswered.
   (D) He took the test twice.

9. (A) Breaking the glass.
   (B) Warming the lid.
   (C) Hitting the lid.
   (D) Filling the jar.

10. (A) It was too expensive.
    (B) She bought it at the shop next door.
    (C) It was given to her as a gift.
    (D) She paid very little for it.

11. (A) She doesn't want to discuss the traffic.
    (B) She didn't have to go downtown today.
    (C) She was in the traffic herself.
    (D) She thinks the traffic was better today.

12. (A) The classes aren't interesting.
    (B) Classes have been canceled.
    (C) The weather is pleasant.
    (D) It isn't very sunny today.

13. (A) Gary doesn't need a tape player.
    (B) She wants her tape player back.
    (C) She's glad Gary is finally here.
    (D) Gary can keep her tape player.

14. (A) Stay inside and read it.
    (B) Look in it for advertisements for umbrellas.
    (C) Cover her head with it.
    (D) Throw it away.

15. (A) She originally supported Margaret.
    (B) She can no longer support Ed.
    (C) Ed has dropped out of the race.
    (D) She's not interested in the election.

16. (A) She and her brother painted the apartment.
    (B) Her brother owes her some money.
    (C) Her brother painted the apartment by himself.
    (D) She painted her brother's apartment.

17. (A) Give him a map.
    (B) Cut his hair for him.
    (C) Drive him to the lake.
    (D) Show him another route.

18. (A) Hanging it.
    (B) Buying it.
    (C) Painting it.
    (D) Framing it.

19. (A) Borrow Stephanie's computer.
    (B) Buy her own computer.
    (C) Save some money.
    (D) Stay home and complete her assignment.

20. (A) He doesn't need to practice anymore.
    (B) His team has won a lot of games.
    (C) He doesn't want to play volleyball.
    (D) His team needs to improve.

21. (A) She seems to be feeling better.
    (B) She has quite an imagination.
    (C) She takes beautiful pictures.
    (D) She's too sick to go out.

22. (A) Lou has been here once before.
    (B) They'll start when Lou arrives.
    (C) Lou has already started.
    (D) Everyone is getting hungry.

23. (A) She thinks they're reasonably priced.
    (B) She doesn't like them at all.
    (C) She'd buy them if she had enough money.
    (D) She doesn't need them, but she still likes them.

24. (A) To improve his game quickly.
    (B) To take more lessons.
    (C) To train with a professional.
    (D) To teach people to play tennis.

25. (A) Wrap the present.
    (B) Play a game.
    (C) Point out a problem.
    (D) End the discussion.

26. (A) He wants to buy some books.
    (B) Two of the books are the same.
    (C) He needs some matches.
    (D) The couple is a good match.

27. (A) Neither street goes downtown.
    (B) California Street is better than Oak Street.
    (C) There's not enough time to go downtown.
    (D) He can take either street.

28. (A) It was hard to hear.
    (B) It wasn't true.
    (C) It was surprising.
    (D) It wasn't very interesting.

29. (A) The handle on the suitcase is broken.
    (B) His hands are already full.
    (C) The luggage is too heavy for him.
    (D) He'll be happy to help.

30. (A) She had to prepare for an exam.
    (B) She'd passed the physics test.
    (C) She was going camping.
    (D) She'd dropped the physics class.

PART B

Directions: This part of the test consists of extended conversations between two speakers. After each of these conversations, there are a number of questions. You will hear each conversation and question only once, and the questions are *not* written out.

When you have heard the questions, read the four answer choices and select the *one*—(A), (B), (C), or (D)—that best answers the question based on what is directly stated or on what can be inferred. Then fill in the space on your answer sheet that matches the letter of the answer that you have selected.

Don't forget: During actual exams, taking notes or writing in your test book is *not* permitted.

31. (A) They are both studying social anthropology.
(B) Both of them are going to the museum on Saturday.
(C) They both have the same teacher.
(D) Both of them have studied anthropology before.

32. (A) In the morning.
(B) In the afternoon.
(C) In the evening.
(D) Only on Saturdays.

33. (A) Relationships between parents and children.
(B) The tools used by ancient people.
(C) Leadership in contemporary society.
(D) Marriage customs.

34. (A) He found it uninteresting.
(B) He found it useful.
(C) He found it fascinating.
(D) He found it difficult.

35. (A) At a university.
(B) At a television station.
(C) At a newspaper office.
(D) At a hospital.

36. (A) He needs a well-paying position.
(B) He was told to by a professor.
(C) He wants the experience.
(D) He recently lost another job.

37. (A) Drama.
(B) Journalism.
(C) Telecommunications.
(D) History.

38. (A) Talk to Ms. Wagner.
(B) Drop a class.
(C) Change his major.
(D) Complete a form.

PART C

Directions: This part of the test consists of several talks, each given by a single speaker. After each of these talks, there are a number of questions. You will hear each talk and question only once, and the questions are *not* written out.

When you have heard each question, read the four answer choices and select the *one*—(A), (B), (C), or (D)—that best answers the question based on what is directly stated or on what can be inferred. Then fill in the space on your answer sheet that matches the letter of the answer that you have selected.

Here is an example.

You will hear:*

M1: Students, this evening we'll have a chance to observe a phenomenon that we've discussed several times in class. Tonight there will be a lunar eclipse. As we've said, when an eclipse of the Moon occurs, the Earth passes between the Sun and the Moon. Therefore, the shadow of the Earth moves across the surface of the Moon and obscures it. Because you won't be looking at the Sun, it is not necessary to use the special lenses and filters that you need when observing a solar eclipse. You can observe a lunar eclipse with your unaided eye or with a telescope, and photograph it with an ordinary camera. So if the weather's not cloudy tonight, go out and take a look at this eclipse of the Moon. I'm sure you'll find it interesting.

Now here is a sample question.

You will hear:

In what course is this lecture probably being given?

You will read:

(A) Philosophy
(B) Meteorology
(C) Astronomy
(D) Photography

Sample Answer

The lecture concerns a lunar eclipse, a topic that would typically be discussed in an astronomy class. The choice that best answers the question, "In what course is this lecture probably being given?" is (C), "Astronomy." You should fill in (C) on your answer sheet.

---

* Note: M1 = first male voice   M2 = second male voice   F1 = first female voice   F2 = second female voice

Here is another sample question.

You will hear:*

　　According to the speaker, which of the following occurs during a lunar eclipse?

You will read:

(A) The Earth's shadow moves across the Moon.
(B) Clouds block the view of the Moon.
(C) The Moon moves between the Earth and the Sun.
(D) The Sun can be observed without special equipment.

Sample Answer

From the lecture you learn that a lunar eclipse occurs when the Earth moves between the Sun and the Moon, and the shadow of the Earth passes across the Moon. The choice that best answers the question, "According to the speaker, which of the following occurs during a lunar eclipse?" is (A), "The Earth's shadow moves across the Moon."

Don't forget: During actual exams, taking notes or writing in your test book is *not* permitted.

* Note:　M1 = first male voice　　M2 = second male voice　　F1 = first female voice　　F2 = second female voice

39. (A) A football game.
    (B) Jet transportation.
    (C) The *Von Hindenburg* disaster.
    (D) Lighter-than-air-craft.

40. (A) Early twentieth-century airships.
    (B) Blimps.
    (C) Jet aircraft.
    (D) Modern airships.

41. (A) The age of zeppelins ended in disaster there.
    (B) It was there that the first blimp was designed.
    (C) Helium was first substituted for hydrogen there.
    (D) It was there that the last zeppelin was built.

42. (A) They would be safer.
    (B) They would use less fuel.
    (C) They would be faster.
    (D) They could fly higher.

43. (A) The Uniform Time Act.
    (B) The role of daylight savings time in wartime.
    (C) Ways to save energy.
    (D) The history of daylight savings time.

44. (A) In the spring.
    (B) In the summer.
    (C) In the fall.
    (D) In the winter.

45. (A) As confusing.
    (B) As innovative.
    (C) As amusing.
    (D) As wasteful.

46. (A) To standardize daylight savings time.
    (B) To establish year-round daylight savings time.
    (C) To abolish daylight savings time.
    (D) To shorten daylight savings time.

47. (A) A program the city is starting.
    (B) The uses of recycled materials.
    (C) A proposed schedule.
    (D) A recent newspaper article.

48. (A) Newspapers.
    (B) Aluminum cans.
    (C) Plastic bottles.
    (D) Glass containers.

49. (A) The north.
    (B) The east.
    (C) The south.
    (D) The central.

50. (A) Look in the local newspaper.
    (B) Keep listening to radio.
    (C) Stop by the recycling center.
    (D) Call the radio station.

THIS IS THE END OF SECTION 1, LISTENING COMPREHENSION.

STOP WORK ON SECTION 1.

End of Tape 3, Side B.

Peterson's TOEFL CBT Success

SECTION 2: STRUCTURE AND WRITTEN EXPRESSION
TIME—25 MINUTES

This section tests your ability to recognize grammar and usage suitable for standard written English. This section is divided into two parts, each with its own directions.

STRUCTURE

Directions: Items in this part are incomplete sentences. Following each of these sentences, there are four words or phrases. You should select the *one* word or phrase—(A), (B), (C), or (D)—that best completes the sentence. Then fill in the space on your answer sheet (on page 415) that matches the letter of the answer that you have selected.

Example I

Pepsin _____ an enzyme used in digestion.

(A) that
(B) is
(C) of
(D) being

Sample Answer

(A) ● (C) (D)

This sentence should properly read, "Pepsin is an enzyme used in digestion." You should fill in (B) on your answer sheet.

Example II

_____ large natural lakes are found in the state of South Carolina.

(A) There are no
(B) Not the
(C) It is not
(D) No

Sample Answer

(A) (B) (C) ●

This sentence should properly read, "No large natural lakes are found in the state of South Carolina." You should fill in (D) on your answer sheet.

As soon as you understand the directions, begin work on this part.

1. _____ team sports require cooperation.

   (A) Of all
   (B) They are all
   (C) All
   (D) Why are all

2. A medical emergency is a sudden or unexpected condition _____ immediate care to prevent death or serious harm.

   (A) it requires
   (B) to require
   (C) that requires
   (D) a requirement of

3. Centuries of erosion have exposed _____ rock surfaces in the Painted Desert of northern Arizona.

   (A) in colors of the rainbow
   (B) colored like a rainbow
   (C) rainbow-colored
   (D) a rainbow's coloring

4. The higher the temperature of a molecule, _____.

   (A) the more energy it has
   (B) than it has more energy
   (C) more energy has it
   (D) it has more energy

5. Frontier surgeon Ephraim MacDonald had to perform operations _____ anesthesia.

   (A) no
   (B) not having
   (C) without
   (D) there wasn't

6. _____ young, chimpanzees are easily trained.

   (A) When are
   (B) When
   (C) They are
   (D) When they

7. A person of _____ age may suffer from defects of vision.

   (A) every
   (B) any
   (C) certain
   (D) some

8. _____ have settled, one of their first concerns has been to locate an adequate water supply.

   (A) Wherever people
   (B) There are people who
   (C) Whether people
   (D) People

9. If a bar magnet is _____, the two pieces form two complete magnets, each with a north and south pole.

   (A) broken
   (B) broke
   (C) breaking
   (D) break

10. The type of plant and animal life living in and around a pond depends on the soil of the pond, _____, and the pond's location.

    (A) what the quality of the water is
    (B) how is the water quality
    (C) the quality of the water
    (D) what is the water quality

11. Clifford Holland, _____ civil engineer, was in charge of the construction of the first tunnel under the Hudson River.

    (A) he was a
    (B) a
    (C) being a
    (D) who was, as a

12. _____ parrots are native to tropical regions is untrue.

    (A) That all
    (B) All
    (C) Why all
    (D) Since all

13. A major concern among archaeologists today is the preservation of archaeological sites, _____ are threatened by development.

    (A) of which many
    (B) many of them
    (C) many of which
    (D) which many

14. In 1775, Daniel Boone opened the Wilderness Trail and made _____ the first settlements in Kentucky.

    (A) possibly it was
    (B) as possible
    (C) possible
    (D) it possible

15. Rarely _____ seen far from water.

    (A) spotted turtles
    (B) spotted turtles are
    (C) have spotted turtles
    (D) are spotted turtles

402

WRITTEN EXPRESSION

Directions: The items in this part have four underlined words or phrases, (A), (B), (C) and (D). You must identify the *one* underlined expression that must be changed for the sentence to be correct. Then find the number of the question on your answer sheet and fill in the space corresponding to the letter.

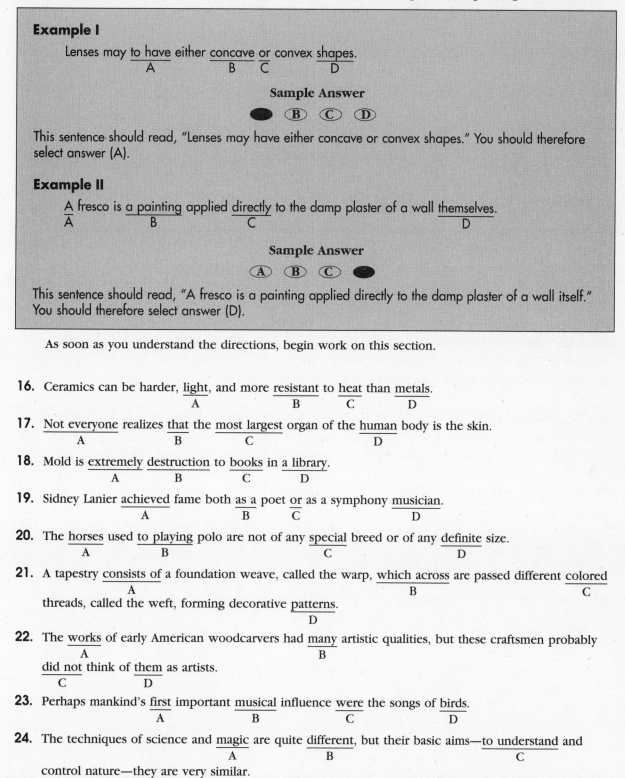

Example I

Lenses may to have either concave or convex shapes.
     A   B C   D

Sample Answer

● Ⓑ Ⓒ Ⓓ

This sentence should read, "Lenses may have either concave or convex shapes." You should therefore select answer (A).

Example II

A fresco is a painting applied directly to the damp plaster of a wall themselves.
A   B   C   D

Sample Answer

Ⓐ Ⓑ Ⓒ ●

This sentence should read, "A fresco is a painting applied directly to the damp plaster of a wall itself." You should therefore select answer (D).

As soon as you understand the directions, begin work on this section.

16. Ceramics can be harder, light, and more resistant to heat than metals.
        A   B   C   D

17. Not everyone realizes that the most largest organ of the human body is the skin.
  A   B   C   D

18. Mold is extremely destruction to books in a library.
      A   B   C D

19. Sidney Lanier achieved fame both as a poet or as a symphony musician.
      A   B   C   D

20. The horses used to playing polo are not of any special breed or of any definite size.
   A   B   C   D

21. A tapestry consists of a foundation weave, called the warp, which across are passed different colored
     A   B   C

  threads, called the weft, forming decorative patterns.
               D

22. The works of early American woodcarvers had many artistic qualities, but these craftsmen probably
   A   B

  did not think of them as artists.
   C   D

23. Perhaps mankind's first important musical influence were the songs of birds.
        A   B   C   D

24. The techniques of science and magic are quite different, but their basic aims—to understand and
           A   B   C

  control nature—they are very similar.
        D

25. It was in a cave near Magdalena, New Mexico, <u>when</u> the <u>oldest</u> <u>known</u> ears of cultivated corn were
                                           A   B   C

<u>discovered</u>.
D

26. The fossil remains of <u>much</u> extinct <u>mammals</u> have been <u>found</u> in the tar pits at Rancho La Brea <u>in</u>
                    A   B   C   D
Los Angeles.

27. Sharks <u>can detect</u> minute <u>electrical</u> discharges <u>coming</u> from <u>its</u> prey.
           A   B   C   D

28. A dark nebula consists of <u>a cloud of</u> interstellar dust <u>enough dense</u> <u>to obscure</u> the stars <u>beyond</u> it.
                              A   B   C   D

29. <u>Commercially</u> honey is heated and <u>filtered</u> in order to <u>stabilize</u> and clarify <u>it</u>.
       A   B   C   D

30. The <u>various</u> parts of the body require <u>so</u> different <u>surgical</u> skills that <u>many</u> surgical specialties have
          A   B   C   D
developed.

31. One reason birds <u>have been</u> so successful is <u>because of</u> their <u>able</u> to escape from danger <u>quickly</u>.
                      A   B   C   D

32. The <u>wood</u> of the rosewood tree <u>is used</u> <u>to do</u> fine <u>musical</u> instruments.
       A   B   C   D

33. Chemical engineering is based <u>on</u> the <u>principles</u> of physics, <u>chemists</u>, and <u>mathematics</u>.
                               A   B   C   D

34. Ballet performers <u>must be</u> believable <u>actors</u> and actresses <u>as well as</u> <u>experts</u> dancers.
                      A   B   C   D

35. Venus, <u>the second</u> planet <u>from</u> the Sun, is <u>exactly almost</u> the <u>same size as</u> the Earth.
           A   B   C   D

36. P. T. Barnum opened <u>his own</u> circus in 1871 and <u>become</u> the <u>most famous</u> showman of his <u>time</u>.
                    A   B   C   D

37. The way a child <u>plays with</u> other children reveals <u>a lots</u> about <u>the child's</u> emotional <u>development</u>.
                  A   B   C   D

38. Sheep <u>have been</u> <u>domesticated</u> for <u>over</u> 5,000 <u>years</u> ago.
       A   B   C   D

39. Chemical compounds <u>with</u> barium, cobalt, and strontium <u>are</u> responsible <u>to</u> many of the vivid <u>colors</u>
                     A   B   C   D
in fireworks.

40. Duke University in North Carolina <u>has</u> an outstanding <u>collecting</u> of documents <u>concerning</u> Southern
                                 A   B   C

<u>history</u>.
D

THIS IS THE END OF SECTION 2, STRUCTURE AND WRITTEN EXPRESSION.
IF YOU FINISH BEFORE TIME IS CALLED, CHECK YOUR WORK ON SECTION 2 ONLY.
DO NOT READ OR WORK ON ANY OTHER SECTION OF THE TEST.

STOP

SECTION 3: READING COMPREHENSION
TIME—55 MINUTES

This section of the test measures your ability to comprehend written materials.

Directions: This section contains several passages, each followed by a number of questions. Read the passages and, for each question, choose the *one* best answer—(A), (B), (C), or (D)—based on what is stated in or on what can be inferred from the passage. Then fill in the space on your answer sheet (on page 412) that matches the letter of the answer that you have selected.

Read the following passage:

> Like mammals, birds claim their own territories. A
> bird's territory may be small or large. Some birds
> claim only their nest and the area right around it,
> while others claim far larger territories that include
> (5)   their feeding areas. Gulls, penguins, and other waterfowl
> nest in huge colonies, but even in the biggest colonies,
> each male and his mate have small territories of their
> own immediately around their nests.
>   Male birds defend their territory chiefly against other
> (10)   males of the same species. In some cases, a warning call
> or threatening pose may be all the defense needed, but in
> other cases, intruders may refuse to leave peacefully.

Example I

What is the main topic of this passage?

(A) Birds that live in colonies
(B) Birds' mating habits
(C) The behavior of birds
(D) Territoriality in birds

Sample Answer

The passage mainly concerns the territories of birds. You should fill in (D) on your answer sheet.

Example II

According to the passage, male birds defend their territory primarily against

(A) female birds
(B) birds of other species
(C) males of their own species
(D) mammals

Sample Answer

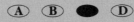

The passage states that "Male birds defend their territory chiefly against other males of the same species." You should fill in (C) on your answer sheet.

As soon as you understand the directions, begin work on this part.

QUESTIONS 1–11

Line   The Sun today is a yellow dwarf star. It is fueled by thermonuclear reactions near its center that convert hydrogen to helium. The Sun has existed in its present state for about 4 billion, 600 million years and is thousands of times larger than the Earth.

     By studying other stars, astronomers can predict what the rest of the Sun's life will be like.
5   About 5 billion years from now, the core of the Sun will shrink and become hotter. The surface temperature will fall. The higher temperature of the center will increase the rate of thermonuclear reactions. The outer regions of the Sun will expand approximately 35 million miles, about the distance to Mercury, which is the closest planet to the Sun. The Sun will then be a red giant star. Temperatures on the Earth will become too hot for life to exist.

10   Once the Sun has used up its thermonuclear energy as a red giant, it will begin to shrink. After it shrinks to the size of the Earth, it will become a white dwarf star. The Sun may throw off huge amounts of gases in violent eruptions called nova explosions as it changes from a red giant to a white dwarf.

     After billions of years as a white dwarf, the Sun will have used up all its fuel and will have lost
15   its heat. Such a star is called a black dwarf. After the sun has become a black dwarf, the Earth will be dark and cold. If any atmosphere remains there, it will have frozen onto the Earth's surface.

1. What is the primary purpose of this passage?

    (A) To alert people to the dangers posed by the Sun.
    (B) To discuss conditions on Earth in the far future.
    (C) To present a theory about red giant stars.
    (D) To describe changes that the Sun will go through.

2. The word "fueled" in line 1 is closest in meaning to

    (A) powered
    (B) bombarded
    (C) created
    (D) propelled

3. The word "state" in line 2 is closest in meaning to

    (A) shape
    (B) condition
    (C) location
    (D) size

4. It can be inferred from the passage that the Sun

    (A) is approximately halfway through its life as a yellow dwarf
    (B) has been in existence for 10 billion years
    (C) is rapidly changing in size and brightness
    (D) will continue as a yellow dwarf for another 10 billion years

5. What will probably be the first stage of change as the Sun becomes a red giant?

   (A) Its core will cool off and use less fuel.
   (B) Its surface will become hotter and shrink.
   (C) It will throw off huge amounts of gases.
   (D) Its center will grow smaller and hotter.

6. When the Sun becomes a red giant, what will conditions be like on Earth?

   (A) Its atmosphere will freeze and become solid.
   (B) It will be enveloped in the expanding surface of the Sun.
   (C) It will become too hot for life to exist.
   (D) It will be nearly destroyed by nova explosions.

7. As a white dwarf, the Sun will be

   (A) the same size as the planet Mercury
   (B) thousands of times smaller than it is today
   (C) around 35 million miles in diameter
   (D) cold and dark

8. According to the passage, which of the following best describes the sequence of stages that the Sun will probably pass through?

   (A) yellow dwarf, white dwarf, red giant, black giant
   (B) red giant, white dwarf, red dwarf, nova explosion
   (C) yellow dwarf, red giant, white dwarf, black dwarf
   (D) white dwarf, red giant, black dwarf, yellow dwarf

9. The phrase "throw off" in line 11 is closest in meaning to

   (A) eject
   (B) burn up
   (C) convert
   (D) let in

10. The word "there" in line 16 refers to

    (A) our own planet
    (B) the outer surface of the Sun
    (C) the core of a black dwarf
    (D) the planet Mercury

11. Which of the following best describes the tone of the passage?

    (A) alarmed
    (B) pessimistic
    (C) comic
    (D) objective

QUESTIONS 12–23

Line It is said that George Washington was one of the first to realize how important the building of canals would be to the nation's development. In fact, before he became president, he headed the first company in the United States to build a canal that was to connect the Ohio and Potomac Rivers. It was never completed, but it showed the nation the feasibility of canals. As the country expanded
5 westward, settlers in western New York, Pennsylvania, and Ohio needed a means to ship goods. Canals linking natural waterways seemed to offer an effective solution.

In 1791, engineers commissioned by the state of New York investigated the possibility of a canal between Albany on the Hudson River and Buffalo on Lake Erie, which would link the Great Lakes area with the Atlantic seacoast. It would avoid the mountains that served as a barrier to canals
10 from the Delaware and Potomac rivers.

The first attempt to dig the canal, to be called the Erie Canal, was made by private companies but only a comparatively small portion was built before the project was halted for lack of funds. The cost of the project was an estimated five million dollars, an enormous amount for those days. There was some on-again, off-again federal funding, but the War of 1812 put an end to this. In 1817, DeWitt
15 Clinton was elected governor of New York and persuaded the state to finance and build the Canal. It was completed in 1825, costing two million dollars more than expected.

The canal rapidly lived up to its sponsor's faith, quickly paying for itself through tolls. It was far more economical than any other form of transportation at the time. It permitted trade between the Great Lake region and East Coast, robbing the Mississippi River of much of its traffic. It allowed New
20 York to supplant Boston, Philadelphia, and other eastern cities as the chief center of both domestic and foreign commerce. Cities sprang up along the Canal. It also contributed in a number of ways to the North's victory over the South in the Civil War.

An expansion of the canal was planned in 1849. Increased traffic would undoubtedly have warranted its construction had it not been for the development of the railroads.

12. Why does the author most likely mention George Washington in the first paragraph?

(A) He was president at the time the Erie Canal was built.
(B) He was involved in pioneering efforts to build canals.
(C) He successfully opened the first canal in the United States.
(D) He commissioned engineers to study the possibility of building the Erie Canal.

13. The word "feasibility" in line 4 is closest in meaning to

(A) profitability
(B) difficulty
(C) possibility
(D) capability

14. According to the passage, the Erie Canal connected the

(A) Potomac and Ohio Rivers
(B) Hudson River and Lake Erie
(C) Delaware and Potomac Rivers
(D) Atlantic Ocean and the Hudson River

15. Which of the following is closest in meaning to the word "comparatively" in line 12?

(A) relatively
(B) contrarily
(C) incredibly
(D) considerably

16. The phrase "on-again, off-again" in line 14 could be replaced by which of the following with the least change in meaning?

(A) intermittent
(B) unsolicited
(C) ineffectual
(D) gradual

17. The completion of the Erie Canal was financed by

(A) the state of New York
(B) private companies
(C) the federal government
(D) DeWitt Clinton

Peterson's TOEFL CBT Success

18. The actual cost of building the Erie Canal was

    (A) five million dollars
    (B) less than had been estimated
    (C) seven million dollars
    (D) more than could be repaid

19. The word "tolls" in line 17 is closest in meaning to which of the following?

    (A) jobs
    (B) grants
    (C) links
    (D) fees

20. Which of the following is NOT given as an effect of the building of the Erie Canal in the fourth paragraph?

    (A) It allowed the East Coast to trade with the Great Lakes area.
    (B) It took water traffic away from the Mississippi River.
    (C) It helped determine the outcome of the Civil War.
    (D) It established Boston and Philadelphia as the most important centers of trade.

21. What can be inferred about railroads in 1849 from the information in the last paragraph?

    (A) They were being planned but had not yet been built.
    (B) They were seriously underdeveloped.
    (C) They had begun to compete with the Erie Canal for traffic.
    (D) They were weakened by the expansion of the Canal.

22. The word "warranted" in line 24 is closest in meaning to

    (A) guaranteed
    (B) justified
    (C) hastened
    (D) prevented

23. At what point in the passage does the author focus on the beginning of construction of the Erie Canal?

    (A) Lines 1-4
    (B) Lines 5-6
    (C) Lines 11-16
    (D) Lines 17-22

QUESTIONS 24–33

Line It's a sound you will probably never hear, a sickened tree sending out a distress signal. But a group of
scientists has heard the cries, and they think some insects also hear the trees and are drawn to them
like vultures to a dying animal.

5   Researchers with the U.S. Department of Agriculture's Forest Service fastened sensors to the
bark of drought-stricken trees and clearly heard distress calls. According to one of the scientists, most
parched trees transmit their plight in the 50- to 500-kilohertz range. (The unaided human ear can
detect no more than 20 kilohertz.) Red oak, maple, white pine, and birch all make slightly different
sounds in the form of vibrations at the surface of the wood.

10 The scientists think that the vibrations are created when the water columns inside tubes that
run the length of the tree break, a result of too little water flowing through them. These fractured
columns send out distinctive vibration patterns. Because some insects communicate at ultrasonic
frequencies, they may pick up the trees' vibrations and attack the weakened trees. Researchers are
now running tests with potted trees that have been deprived of water to see if the sound is what
attracts the insects. "Water-stressed trees also smell differently from other trees, and they experience
thermal changes, so insects could be responding to something other than sound," one scientist said.

24. Which of the following is the main topic of
the passage?

(A) the vibrations produced by insects
(B) the mission of the U.S. Forest Service
(C) the effect of insects on trees
(D) the sounds made by trees

25. The word "them" in line 2 refers to

(A) trees
(B) scientists
(C) insects
(D) vultures

26. The word "parched" in line 6 is closest in
meaning to which of the following?

(A) burned
(B) dehydrated
(C) recovered
(D) damaged

27. The word "plight" in line 6 is closest in
meaning to

(A) cry
(B) condition
(C) need
(D) agony

28. It can be inferred from the passage that the
sounds produced by the trees

(A) serve as a form of communication
among trees
(B) are the same no matter what type of
tree produces them
(C) cannot be heard by the unaided human
ear
(D) fall into the 1–20-kilohertz range

29. The word "fractured" in line 10 is closest
in meaning to

(A) long
(B) blocked
(C) hollow
(D) broken

30. Which of the following could be considered
a cause of the trees' distress signals?

(A) torn roots
(B) attacks by insects
(C) experiments by scientists
(D) lack of water

31. In line 12, the phrase "pick up" could best
be replaced by which of the following?

(A) perceive
(B) lift
(C) transmit
(D) attack

32. All of the following are mentioned as
possible factors in drawing insects to
weakened trees EXCEPT

(A) thermal changes
(B) smells
(C) sounds
(D) changes in color

33. It can be inferred from the passage that research concerning the distress signals of trees

(A) was conducted many years ago
(B) has been unproductive up to now
(C) is continuing
(D) is no longer sponsored by the govern-
ment

QUESTIONS 34–41

Line The concepts of analogy and homology are probably easier to exemplify than to define. When
different species are structurally compared, certain features can be described as either analogous or
homologous. For example, flight requires certain rigid aeronautical principles of design, yet birds,
bats, and insects have all conquered the air. The wings of all three types of animals derive from
5   different embryological structures, but they perform the same functions. In this case, the flight organs
of these creatures can be said to be analogous. In contrast, features that arise from the same structures in the embryo but are used in different functions are said to be homologous. The pectoral fins
of a fish, the wings of a bird, and the forelimbs of a mammal are all homologous structures. They are
genetically related in the sense that both the forelimb and the wing evolved from the fin.

34. Which of the following best describes the organization of the passage?

(A) A contrast is drawn between two concepts by means of examples.
(B) A general concept is introduced, examples are given, and a conclusion is offered.
(C) Two definitions of the same concept are compared.
(D) Two proposals are suggested and support for both is offered.

35. According to the passage, the concepts of analogy and homology are

(A) difficult to understand
(B) easier to understand through examples than through definitions
(C) impossible to explain
(D) simple to define but hard to apply

36. The word "rigid" in line 3 is closest in meaning to

(A) inflexible
(B) ideal
(C) unnatural
(D) steep

37. According to the information provided in the passage, which of the following would most probably be considered analogous?

(A) A shark's fin and a tiger's claws.
(B) A man's arms and a bird's wings.
(C) A monkey's tail and an elephant's tail.
(D) A spider's legs and a horse's legs.

38. According to the passage, one way in which homologous organs differ from analogous organs is that they

(A) are genetically related
(B) are only found in highly developed animals
(C) perform the same general functions
(D) come from different embryological structures

39. As used throughout the passage, the term "structures" most nearly means

(A) buildings
(B) features of an animal's anatomy
(C) organizational principles
(D) units of grammar

40. The word "sense" in line 9 is closest in meaning to

(A) feeling
(B) logic
(C) meaning
(D) perception

41. Where in the passage does the author focus his discussion on the concept of homology?

(A) Line 6–8
(B) Line 1–3
(C) Line 4–5
(D) Line 8–9

QUESTIONS 42–50

Line Probably the most famous film commenting on twentieth-century technology is *Modern Times*, made in 1936. Charlie Chaplin was motivated to make the film by a reporter who, while interviewing him, happened to describe working conditions in industrial Detroit. Chaplin was told that healthy young farm boys were lured to the city to work on automotive assembly lines. Within four or five years,
5 these young men's health was destroyed by the stress of work in the factories.

      The film opens with a shot of a mass of sheep making their way down a crowded ramp. Abruptly the scene shifts to a scene of factory workers jostling one another on their way to a factory. However, the rather bitter note of criticism in the implied comparison is not sustained. It is replaced by a gentler note of satire. Chaplin prefers to entertain rather than lecture.

10   Scenes of factory interiors account for only about one third of the footage of *Modern Times*, but they contain some of the most pointed social commentary as well as the most comic situations. No one who has seen the film can ever forget Chaplin vainly trying to keep pace with the fast-moving conveyor belt, almost losing his mind in the process. Another popular scene involves an automatic feeding machine brought to the assembly line so that workers need not interrupt their
15 labor to eat. The feeding machine malfunctions, hurling food at Chaplin who is strapped into his position on the assembly line and cannot escape. This serves to illustrate people's utter helplessness in the face of machines that are meant to serve their basic needs.

      Clearly, *Modern Times* has its faults, but it remains the best film treating technology within a social context. It does not offer a radical social message, but it does accurately reflect the sentiments of many who feel they are victims of an over-mechanized world.

42. The author's main purpose in writing this passage is to

(A) criticize the factory system of the 1930s
(B) analyze an important film
(C) explain Chaplin's style of acting
(D) discuss how film reveals the benefits of technology

43. According to the passage, Chaplin got the idea for the film *Modern Times* from

(A) a newspaper article
(B) a scene in a movie
(C) a job he had once held
(D) a conversation with a reporter

44. The word "abruptly" in line 7 is closest in meaning to

(A) suddenly
(B) mysteriously
(C) finally
(D) predictably

45. It can be inferred from the passage that two thirds of the film *Modern Times*

(A) is extremely unforgettable
(B) takes place outside a factory
(C) is more critical than the other third
(D) entertains the audience more than the other third

46. Which of the following could best replace the phrase "losing his mind" in line 13?

(A) getting fired
(B) doing his job
(C) going insane
(D) falling behind

47. The word "This" in line 16 refers to which of the following?

(A) the machine
(B) the food
(C) the assembly line
(D) the scene

Peterson's TOEFL CBT Success

48. According to the passage, the purpose of the scene involving the feeding machine is to show people's

(A) ingenuity
(B) adaptability
(C) helplessness
(D) independence

49. The word "utter" in line 16 is closest in meaning to which of the following?

(A) notable
(B) complete
(C) regrettable
(D) necessary

50. The author would probably use all of the following words to describe the film *Modern Times* EXCEPT

(A) revolutionary
(B) entertaining
(C) memorable
(D) satirical

THIS IS THE END OF SECTION 3, READING COMPREHENSION.
IF YOU FINISH BEFORE TIME IS CALLED, GO BACK AND CHECK YOUR WORK IN THIS SECTION ONLY.

Answer Sheet

Practice Test 1

Section 1: Listening Comprehension

1. Ⓐ Ⓑ Ⓒ Ⓓ	21. Ⓐ Ⓑ Ⓒ Ⓓ	31. Ⓐ Ⓑ Ⓒ Ⓓ
2. Ⓐ Ⓑ Ⓒ Ⓓ	22. Ⓐ Ⓑ Ⓒ Ⓓ	32. Ⓐ Ⓑ Ⓒ Ⓓ
3. Ⓐ Ⓑ Ⓒ Ⓓ	23. Ⓐ Ⓑ Ⓒ Ⓓ	33. Ⓐ Ⓑ Ⓒ Ⓓ
4. Ⓐ Ⓑ Ⓒ Ⓓ	24. Ⓐ Ⓑ Ⓒ Ⓓ	34. Ⓐ Ⓑ Ⓒ Ⓓ
5. Ⓐ Ⓑ Ⓒ Ⓓ	25. Ⓐ Ⓑ Ⓒ Ⓓ	35. Ⓐ Ⓑ Ⓒ Ⓓ
6. Ⓐ Ⓑ Ⓒ Ⓓ	26. Ⓐ Ⓑ Ⓒ Ⓓ	36. Ⓐ Ⓑ Ⓒ Ⓓ
7. Ⓐ Ⓑ Ⓒ Ⓓ	27. Ⓐ Ⓑ Ⓒ Ⓓ	37. Ⓐ Ⓑ Ⓒ Ⓓ
8. Ⓐ Ⓑ Ⓒ Ⓓ	28. Ⓐ Ⓑ Ⓒ Ⓓ	38. Ⓐ Ⓑ Ⓒ Ⓓ
9. Ⓐ Ⓑ Ⓒ Ⓓ	29. Ⓐ Ⓑ Ⓒ Ⓓ	39. Ⓐ Ⓑ Ⓒ Ⓓ
10. Ⓐ Ⓑ Ⓒ Ⓓ	30. Ⓐ Ⓑ Ⓒ Ⓓ	40. Ⓐ Ⓑ Ⓒ Ⓓ

11. Ⓐ Ⓑ Ⓒ Ⓓ
12. Ⓐ Ⓑ Ⓒ Ⓓ
13. Ⓐ Ⓑ Ⓒ Ⓓ
14. Ⓐ Ⓑ Ⓒ Ⓓ
15. Ⓐ Ⓑ Ⓒ Ⓓ
16. Ⓐ Ⓑ Ⓒ Ⓓ
17. Ⓐ Ⓑ Ⓒ Ⓓ
18. Ⓐ Ⓑ Ⓒ Ⓓ
19. Ⓐ Ⓑ Ⓒ Ⓓ
20. Ⓐ Ⓑ Ⓒ Ⓓ

Section 2: Structure and Written Expression

1. Ⓐ Ⓑ Ⓒ Ⓓ   21. Ⓐ Ⓑ Ⓒ Ⓓ   31. Ⓐ Ⓑ Ⓒ Ⓓ
2. Ⓐ Ⓑ Ⓒ Ⓓ   22. Ⓐ Ⓑ Ⓒ Ⓓ   32. Ⓐ Ⓑ Ⓒ Ⓓ
3. Ⓐ Ⓑ Ⓒ Ⓓ   23. Ⓐ Ⓑ Ⓒ Ⓓ   33. Ⓐ Ⓑ Ⓒ Ⓓ
4. Ⓐ Ⓑ Ⓒ Ⓓ   24. Ⓐ Ⓑ Ⓒ Ⓓ   34. Ⓐ Ⓑ Ⓒ Ⓓ
5. Ⓐ Ⓑ Ⓒ Ⓓ   25. Ⓐ Ⓑ Ⓒ Ⓓ   35. Ⓐ Ⓑ Ⓒ Ⓓ
6. Ⓐ Ⓑ Ⓒ Ⓓ   26. Ⓐ Ⓑ Ⓒ Ⓓ   36. Ⓐ Ⓑ Ⓒ Ⓓ
7. Ⓐ Ⓑ Ⓒ Ⓓ   27. Ⓐ Ⓑ Ⓒ Ⓓ   37. Ⓐ Ⓑ Ⓒ Ⓓ
8. Ⓐ Ⓑ Ⓒ Ⓓ   28. Ⓐ Ⓑ Ⓒ Ⓓ   38. Ⓐ Ⓑ Ⓒ Ⓓ
9. Ⓐ Ⓑ Ⓒ Ⓓ   29. Ⓐ Ⓑ Ⓒ Ⓓ   39. Ⓐ Ⓑ Ⓒ Ⓓ
10. Ⓐ Ⓑ Ⓒ Ⓓ   30. Ⓐ Ⓑ Ⓒ Ⓓ   40. Ⓐ Ⓑ Ⓒ Ⓓ

11. Ⓐ Ⓑ Ⓒ Ⓓ
12. Ⓐ Ⓑ Ⓒ Ⓓ
13. Ⓐ Ⓑ Ⓒ Ⓓ
14. Ⓐ Ⓑ Ⓒ Ⓓ
15. Ⓐ Ⓑ Ⓒ Ⓓ
16. Ⓐ Ⓑ Ⓒ Ⓓ
17. Ⓐ Ⓑ Ⓒ Ⓓ
18. Ⓐ Ⓑ Ⓒ Ⓓ
19. Ⓐ Ⓑ Ⓒ Ⓓ
20. Ⓐ Ⓑ Ⓒ Ⓓ

Section 3: Reading Comprehension

1. Ⓐ Ⓑ Ⓒ Ⓓ	21. Ⓐ Ⓑ Ⓒ Ⓓ	41. Ⓐ Ⓑ Ⓒ Ⓓ
2. Ⓐ Ⓑ Ⓒ Ⓓ	22. Ⓐ Ⓑ Ⓒ Ⓓ	42. Ⓐ Ⓑ Ⓒ Ⓓ
3. Ⓐ Ⓑ Ⓒ Ⓓ	23. Ⓐ Ⓑ Ⓒ Ⓓ	43. Ⓐ Ⓑ Ⓒ Ⓓ
4. Ⓐ Ⓑ Ⓒ Ⓓ	24. Ⓐ Ⓑ Ⓒ Ⓓ	44. Ⓐ Ⓑ Ⓒ Ⓓ
5. Ⓐ Ⓑ Ⓒ Ⓓ	25. Ⓐ Ⓑ Ⓒ Ⓓ	45. Ⓐ Ⓑ Ⓒ Ⓓ
6. Ⓐ Ⓑ Ⓒ Ⓓ	26. Ⓐ Ⓑ Ⓒ Ⓓ	46. Ⓐ Ⓑ Ⓒ Ⓓ
7. Ⓐ Ⓑ Ⓒ Ⓓ	27. Ⓐ Ⓑ Ⓒ Ⓓ	47. Ⓐ Ⓑ Ⓒ Ⓓ
8. Ⓐ Ⓑ Ⓒ Ⓓ	28. Ⓐ Ⓑ Ⓒ Ⓓ	48. Ⓐ Ⓑ Ⓒ Ⓓ
9. Ⓐ Ⓑ Ⓒ Ⓓ	29. Ⓐ Ⓑ Ⓒ Ⓓ	49. Ⓐ Ⓑ Ⓒ Ⓓ
10. Ⓐ Ⓑ Ⓒ Ⓓ	30. Ⓐ Ⓑ Ⓒ Ⓓ	50. Ⓐ Ⓑ Ⓒ Ⓓ
11. Ⓐ Ⓑ Ⓒ Ⓓ	31. Ⓐ Ⓑ Ⓒ Ⓓ	
12. Ⓐ Ⓑ Ⓒ Ⓓ	32. Ⓐ Ⓑ Ⓒ Ⓓ	
13. Ⓐ Ⓑ Ⓒ Ⓓ	33. Ⓐ Ⓑ Ⓒ Ⓓ	
14. Ⓐ Ⓑ Ⓒ Ⓓ	34. Ⓐ Ⓑ Ⓒ Ⓓ	
15. Ⓐ Ⓑ Ⓒ Ⓓ	35. Ⓐ Ⓑ Ⓒ Ⓓ	
16. Ⓐ Ⓑ Ⓒ Ⓓ	36. Ⓐ Ⓑ Ⓒ Ⓓ	
17. Ⓐ Ⓑ Ⓒ Ⓓ	37. Ⓐ Ⓑ Ⓒ Ⓓ	
18. Ⓐ Ⓑ Ⓒ Ⓓ	38. Ⓐ Ⓑ Ⓒ Ⓓ	
19. Ⓐ Ⓑ Ⓒ Ⓓ	39. Ⓐ Ⓑ Ⓒ Ⓓ	
20. Ⓐ Ⓑ Ⓒ Ⓓ	40. Ⓐ Ⓑ Ⓒ Ⓓ	

Practice Test 2

This section tests your ability to comprehend spoken English. It is divided into three parts, each with its own directions. You are *not* permitted to turn the page during the reading of the directions or to take notes at any time.

PART A

Directions: Each item in this part consists of a brief conversation involving two speakers. Following each conversation, a third voice will ask a question. You will hear the conversations and questions only once, and they will *not* be written out.

When you have heard each conversation and question, read the four choices and select the *one*—(A), (B), (C), or (D)—that best answers the question based on what is directly stated or on what can be inferred. Then fill in the space on your answer sheet (on page 437) that matches the letter of the answer that you have selected.

Here is an example.

You will hear:*

M1: Do you think I should leave this chair against the wall or put it somewhere else?

F1: Over by the window, I'd say.

F2: What does the woman think the man should do?

You will read:

(A) Open the window.
(B) Move the chair.
(C) Leave the room.
(D) Take a seat.

Sample Answer

Ⓐ ● Ⓒ Ⓓ

From the conversation you find out that the woman thinks the man should put the chair over by the window. The best answer to the question, "What does the woman think the man should do?" is (B), "Move the chair." You should fill in (B) on your answer sheet.

WAIT

---

* Note: M1 = first male voice   M2 = second male voice   F1 = first female voice   F2 = second female voice

1. (A) The plane hasn't taken off yet.
   (B) The cost of flying has increased.
   (C) More flights will soon be scheduled.
   (D) He hasn't changed his vacation plans.

2. (A) All of the books are cheap.
   (B) None of the books is required.
   (C) Half of the books should be returned.
   (D) Only four of the books are expensive.

3. (A) It will probably rain tonight.
   (B) She likes to watch the rain come down.
   (C) She'll play even if it rains.
   (D) It has rained a lot lately.

4. (A) Nearly all of the students can meet.
   (B) The meeting time must be changed.
   (C) Only Lisa will be at the library.
   (D) Lisa dropped the class on Friday.

5. (A) He was the first person to get tickets.
   (B) He has good seats for the concert.
   (C) The performance has already been held.
   (D) The group may perform somewhere else.

6. (A) He intends to see Michelle.
   (B) Michelle may visit him anytime.
   (C) He has to return some money to Michelle.
   (D) Michelle owes him some money.

7. (A) Buying some red chairs.
   (B) Renting a bigger auditorium.
   (C) Moving chairs from the auditorium.
   (D) Getting more chairs.

8. (A) He can't read the sign.
   (B) He didn't make the sign.
   (C) He didn't sign his name.
   (D) He doesn't like the sign.

9. (A) Housing near campus is getting cheaper and cheaper.
   (B) She doesn't need to live close to campus.
   (C) It's not easy to find inexpensive housing near campus.
   (D) The man could find housing if he looked carefully.

10. (A) To a game.
    (B) To buy tickets.
    (C) To get some groceries.
    (D) To a party.

11. (A) The bucket has been broken.
    (B) The water was spilled.
    (C) They still need more money.
    (D) They have run out of time.

12. (A) He is kind.
    (B) He is impolite.
    (C) He is somewhat busy.
    (D) She doesn't want to say.

13. (A) It's not surprising that Tony went fishing.
    (B) He already knew Tony had caught only one fish.
    (C) He doesn't think Tony is a good fisherman.
    (D) Tony usually catches a lot of fish.

14. (A) Don't complete the form.
    (B) Don't waste time.
    (C) Take a form.
    (D) There's no hurry.

15. (A) He is telling her the truth.
    (B) He's never been to Seattle.
    (C) He has visited Seattle once.
    (D) She's only spoken to him once.

16. (A) Disapproved of her plan.
    (B) Watered Lily's plants.
    (C) Traveled overseas.
    (D) Caught colds.

17. (A) It should have been turned up.
    (B) The people across town enjoy it.
    (C) It's extremely popular.
    (D) It was much too loud.

18. (A) It was quite relaxing.
    (B) The weather wasn't good.
    (C) It was unexpectedly busy.
    (D) It was perfectly planned.

19. (A) The lab is generally locked on Saturdays.
    (B) The man doesn't have a key to the lab.
    (C) Something strange happened in the lab on Saturday.
    (D) The lab should never be locked.

20. (A) He needs the insurance no matter how much it costs.
    (B) There are other types of insurance he should buy.
    (C) The man doesn't have enough money to buy insurance.
    (D) The cost of insurance is becoming more reasonable.

Peterson's TOEFL CBT Success

21. (A) She's an art student.
    (B) She's afraid of flying.
    (C) She did well on the test.
    (D) She got her pilot's license.

22. (A) An elevator.
    (B) A television.
    (C) An automobile.
    (D) A telephone.

23. (A) Meg's sister took it to the cleaner's.
    (B) Meg cleaned it.
    (C) Meg wore it to class.
    (D) Meg's sister borrowed it.

24. (A) They must go to an orientation session.
    (B) They are not new students.
    (C) They won't be allowed to register.
    (D) They were given the wrong schedule.

25. (A) He doesn't mind moving.
    (B) His brother won't move for two weeks.
    (C) He'd rather not help his brother move.
    (D) His brother decided not to move.

26. (A) She has a coin like his.
    (B) She knows a lot about coins.
    (C) She thinks the coin is worthless.
    (D) She's never seen this type of coin.

27. (A) Its lyrics are hard to understand.
    (B) It needs a stronger melody.
    (C) It has become very popular.
    (D) Its melody is hard to forget.

28. (A) He hadn't been smiling.
    (B) His picture hadn't been taken.
    (C) It wasn't a good picture.
    (D) The woman wouldn't show him the picture.

29. (A) They're always expensive.
    (B) They haven't been cleaned.
    (C) They're inexpensive now.
    (D) There aren't any available.

30. (A) From college.
    (B) Through her roommate.
    (C) From the reception.
    (D) Through her sister.

PART B

Directions: This part of the test consists of extended conversations between two speakers. After each of these conversations, there are a number of questions. You will hear each conversation and question only once, and the questions are *not* written out.

When you have heard the questions, read the four answer choices and select the *one*—(A), (B), (C), or (D)—that best answers the question based on what is directly stated or on what can be inferred. Then fill in the space on your answer sheet that matches the letter of the answer that you have selected.

Don't forget: During actual exams, taking notes or writing in your test book is *not* permitted.

WAIT

31. (A) At a newspaper.
    (B) At an advertising agency.
    (C) At a furniture store.
    (D) At a real estate office.

32. (A) A two-bedroom apartment.
    (B) A sofa.
    (C) A chair.
    (D) A roommate.

33. (A) Her phone number.
    (B) The location of the apartment.
    (C) The best time to call her.
    (D) Her first name.

34. (A) $5
    (B) $15
    (C) $30
    (D) $250

35. (A) From a newspaper advertisement.
    (B) From a magazine article.
    (C) From a television program.
    (D) From an automobile dealer.

36. (A) To warn of dangers.
    (B) To explain traffic regulations.
    (C) To wake up drivers who are falling asleep.
    (D) To give directions.

37. (A) He has a good sense of direction.
    (B) He owns a "smart" car.
    (C) He doesn't know how to drive.
    (D) He doesn't know the way to the woman's house.

38. (A) He got lost.
    (B) He ran out of gas.
    (C) He was in an accident.
    (D) His car broke down.

PART C

Directions: This part of the test consists of several talks, each given by a single speaker. After each of these talks, there are a number of questions. You will hear each talk and question only once, and the questions are *not* written out.

When you have heard each question, read the four answer choices and select the *one*—(A), (B), (C), or (D)—that best answers the question based on what is directly stated or on what can be inferred. Then fill in the space on your answer sheet that matches the letter of the answer that you have selected.

Here is an example.

You will hear:*

M1: Students, this evening we'll have a chance to observe a phenomenon that we've discussed several times in class. Tonight there will be a lunar eclipse. As we've said, when an eclipse of the Moon occurs, the Earth passes between the Sun and the Moon. Therefore, the shadow of the Earth moves across the surface of the Moon and obscures it. Because you won't be looking at the Sun, it is not necessary to use the special lenses and filters that you need when observing a solar eclipse. You can observe a lunar eclipse with your unaided eye or with a telescope, and photograph it with an ordinary camera. So if the weather's not cloudy tonight, go out and take a look at this eclipse of the Moon. I'm sure you'll find it interesting.

Now here is a sample question.

You will hear:

In what course is this lecture probably being given?

You will read:

(A) Philosophy
(B) Meteorology
(C) Astronomy
(D) Photography

Sample Answer

The lecture concerns a lunar eclipse, a topic that would typically be discussed in an astronomy class. The choice that best answers the question, "In what course is this lecture probably being given?" is (C), "Astronomy." You should fill in (C) on your answer sheet.

Here is another sample question.

You will hear:*

According to the speaker, which of the following occurs during a lunar eclipse?

You will read:

(A) The Earth's shadow moves across the Moon.
(B) Clouds block the view of the Moon.
(C) The Moon moves between the Earth and the Sun.
(D) The Sun can be observed without special equipment.

Sample Answer

From the lecture you learn that a lunar eclipse occurs when the Earth moves between the Sun and the Moon, and the shadow of the Earth passes across the Moon. The choice that best answers the question, "According to the speaker, which of the following occurs during a lunar eclipse?" is (A), "The Earth's shadow moves across the Moon."

Don't forget: During actual exams, taking notes or writing in your test book is *not* permitted.

* Note: M1 = first male voice   M2 = second male voice   F1 = first female voice   F2 = second female voice

39. (A) To present an award.
 (B) To say goodbye to Professor Callaghan.
 (C) To explain computer models.
 (D) To welcome a new college president.

40. (A) An administrator.
 (B) A faculty member.
 (C) A chancellor of the college.
 (D) A graduate student.

41. (A) Computer science.
 (B) History.
 (C) Economics.
 (D) Physics.

42. (A) Two.
 (B) Four.
 (C) Six.
 (D) Eight.

43. (A) A bicycle racer.
 (B) A radio announcer.
 (C) A coach.
 (D) A television reporter.

44. (A) The benefits of bicycle commuting.
 (B) Local traffic problems.
 (C) A bicycle race.
 (D) The American university system.

45. (A) On the college campus.
 (B) On downtown streets.
 (C) In Woodland Park.
 (D) In the nearby countryside.

46. (A) Take part in the race.
 (B) Travel to the country.
 (C) Avoid the downtown area.
 (D) Ride a bicycle to work.

47. (A) In an art history class.
 (B) In a painter's studio.
 (C) In a photography class.
 (D) In an art museum.

48. (A) A famous person.
 (B) A beautiful landscape.
 (C) An empty phone booth.
 (D) Geometric shapes.

49. (A) They are very valuable.
 (B) They are quite large.
 (C) They are highly abstract.
 (D) They are extremely lifelike.

50. (A) Paint pictures.
 (B) Write papers.
 (C) View some slides.
 (D) Discuss their reactions.

THIS IS THE END OF SECTION 1, LISTENING COMPREHENSION.

STOP WORK ON SECTION 1.

End of Tape 4, Side A.

SECTION 2: STRUCTURE AND WRITTEN EXPRESSION
TIME—25 MINUTES

This section tests your ability to recognize grammar and usage suitable for standard written English. This section is divided into two parts, each with its own directions.

STRUCTURE

Directions: Items in this part are incomplete sentences. Following each of these sentences, there are four words or phrases. You should select the *one* word or phrase—(A), (B), (C), or (D)—that best completes the sentence. Then fill in the space on your answer sheet (on page 438) that matches the letter of the answer that you have selected.

Example I

Pepsin _____ an enzyme used in digestion.

(A) that
(B) is
(C) of
(D) being

Sample Answer

Ⓐ ● Ⓒ Ⓓ

This sentence should properly read, "Pepsin is an enzyme used in digestion." You should fill in (B) on your answer sheet.

Example II

_____ large natural lakes are found in the state of South Carolina.

(A) There are no
(B) Not the
(C) It is not
(D) No

Sample Answer

Ⓐ Ⓑ Ⓒ ●

This sentence should properly read, "No large natural lakes are found in the state of South Carolina." You should fill in (D) on your answer sheet.

As soon as you understand the directions, begin work on this part.

1. Sharp knives are actually safer to use
   _____.

   (A) as dull ones
   (B) as ones that are dull
   (C) than dull ones
   (D) that are dull ones

2. Daniel Webster, Thadeus Stevens, and many
   others _____ prominent in public life
   began their careers by teaching school.

   (A) they became
   (B) once they became
   (C) became
   (D) who became

3. As coal mines became deeper, the problems
   of draining water, bringing in fresh air, and
   _____ to the surface increased.

   (A) transporting ore
   (B) to transport ore
   (C) how ore is transported
   (D) ore is transporting

4. _____ because of the complexity of his
   writing, Henry James never became a
   popular writer, but his works are admired
   by critics and other writers.

   (A) It may be
   (B) Perhaps
   (C) Besides
   (D) Why is it

5. Piedmont glaciers are formed _____
   several valley glaciers join and spread out
   over a plain.

   (A) by
   (B) when
   (C) from
   (D) that

6. As late as 1890, Key West, with a population of 18,000, _____ Florida's largest
   city.

   (A) that was
   (B) to be
   (C) was
   (D) it was

7. A mastery of calculus depends on _____
   of algebra.

   (A) an understanding
   (B) is understood
   (C) to understand
   (D) understand

8. _____ he was not a musician himself,
   Lawrence Hammond developed an elec-
   tronic keyboard instrument called the
   Hammond organ.

   (A) Although
   (B) That
   (C) Despite
   (D) For

9. Agnes De Mille's landmark musical play
   Oklahoma! was _____ of story, music,
   and dance.

   (A) successfully combined
   (B) a successful combination
   (C) to combine successfully
   (D) successful combining

10. _____ single dialect of American English
    has ever become dominant.

    (A) No
    (B) Not only a
    (C) Not
    (D) Nor a

11. In 1837 the University of Michigan became
    the first state university _____ by a
    board of regents elected by the voters of
    the state.

    (A) under the control
    (B) it was controlled
    (C) being controlled
    (D) to be controlled

12. Indoor heating systems have made _____
    for people to live and work comfortably in
    temperate climates.

    (A) it is possible
    (B) possible
    (C) it possible
    (D) possibly

13. Certain fish eggs contain droplets of oil,
    _____ to float on the surface of the
    water.

    (A) allowing them
    (B) allows them
    (C) they are allowed
    (D) this allows them

14. Considered America's first great architect, _____.

    (A) many of the buildings at Harvard University were designed by Henry Hobson Richardson

    (B) Henry Hobson Richardson designed many of the buildings at Harvard University

    (C) Harvard University has many buildings that were designed by Henry Hobson Richardson

    (D) it was Henry Hobson Richardson who designed many of the buildings at Harvard University

15. _____ is caused by a virus was not known until 1911.

    (A) That measles

    (B) As measles

    (C) Measles

    (D) What if measles

WRITTEN EXPRESSION

Directions: The items in this part have four underlined words or phrases, (A), (B), (C), and (D). You must identify the *one* underlined expression that must be changed for the sentence to be correct. Then find the number of the question on your answer sheet and fill in the space corresponding to the letter.

Example I

Lenses may to have either concave or convex shapes.
      A   B   C D

Sample Answer

● Ⓑ Ⓒ Ⓓ

This sentence should read, "Lenses may have either concave or convex shapes." You should therefore select answer (A).

Example II

A fresco is a painting applied directly to the damp plaster of a wall themselves.
A   B   C   D

Sample Answer

Ⓐ Ⓑ Ⓒ ●

This sentence should read, "A fresco is a painting applied directly to the damp plaster of a wall itself." You should therefore select answer (D).

As soon as you understand the directions, begin work on this section.

16. Dreams are <u>commonly</u> <u>made up of</u> <u>either</u> visual <u>and</u> verbal images.
             A   B   C   D

17. The Yale *Daily News* is <u>oldest than</u> any <u>other</u> college newspaper <u>still</u> <u>in operation</u> in the United
                  A   B   C   D
States.

18. Mary Rinehart was <u>a pioneer</u> in the <u>field</u> of <u>journalist</u> <u>in the early</u> twentieth century.
                    A   B   C   D

19. The Dave Brubek Quartet, one of <u>the most popular</u> jazz bands of the 1950s, had a <u>particularly</u> loyal
                              A   B
<u>following</u> on <u>campuses college</u>.
  C   D

20. <u>In the</u> architecture, a <u>capital</u> is <u>the top</u> portion of a <u>column</u>.
   A   B   C   D

21. Today successful farmers are experts not only in <u>agriculture</u>, <u>but also</u> in <u>market</u>, finance, and
                                        A   B   C
<u>accounting</u>.
  D

22. In the <u>early</u> days of jet development, jet engines <u>used</u> great <u>numbers</u> of <u>fuel</u>.
       A   B   C   D

23. Georgia has <u>too</u> many types of <u>soil</u> that <u>virtually</u> any temperate-zone crop can be grown <u>there</u>.
          A   B   C   D

24. The sum of <u>all</u> chemical reactions in <u>an organism's</u> living cells <u>are</u> called <u>its</u> metabolism.
         A   B   C   D

25. River <u>transportation</u> in the United States <u>consists</u> <u>primarily</u> of barges <u>pull</u> by towboats.
           A   B   C   D

26. <u>Most modern</u> barns are <u>both insulated</u>, ventilated, and <u>equipped with</u> <u>electricity</u>.
     A   B   C   D

27. <u>Many</u> bridges in New England <u>were covered</u> with wooden roofs to protect <u>it</u> from <u>rain and snow</u>.
   A   B   C   D

28. It is their <u>nearly perfect</u> crystal structure <u>that gives</u> diamonds their <u>hardness</u>, brilliance, and
               A   B   C
<u>transparent</u>.
  D

29. Needles are <u>simple-looking</u> tools, <u>but</u> they are <u>very relatively</u> difficult <u>to make</u>.
           A   B   C   D

30. Ducks are <u>less</u> susceptible <u>to</u> infection <u>than</u> <u>another</u> types of poultry.
           A   B   C   D

31. <u>Unlike</u> competitive <u>running</u>, race walkers must always keep some portion of <u>their</u> feet <u>in contact with</u>
   A   B   C   D
the ground.

32. One of the <u>most beautiful</u> botanical <u>gardens</u> in the United States is the <u>wildly</u> and lovely Magnolia
             A   B   C
Gardens <u>near</u> Charleston, South Carolina.
       D

33. Composer John Cage used many <u>unusual</u> objects as <u>instrument</u> in his music, <u>including</u> cowbells,
                        A   B   C

flower pots, <u>tin cans,</u> and saw blades.
           D

34. Woody Guthrie wrote <u>thousands</u> of songs during <u>the lifetime</u>, many of <u>which</u> became classic <u>folk</u>
                     A   B   C

<u>songs.</u>
 D

35. Runner Wilma Rudolf <u>win</u> three gold medals <u>at the 1960</u> Olympics, and <u>she set the</u> <u>world record</u> for
                         A   B   C   D

the 100-meter dash in 1961.

36. Some critics <u>have called</u> Theodore Dreiser's book *Sister Carrie* <u>a first</u> modern novel <u>because</u> it broke
                 A   B   C

<u>so many</u> traditions.
    D

37. Abigail Adams' <u>letters</u> to <u>her</u> husband present <u>a graphic</u> picture of the <u>age which</u> she lived.
                  A   B   C   D

38. Viscosity is a measurement <u>describing</u> the <u>relative</u> difficulty or <u>easy</u> <u>with which</u> liquids flow.
                                A   B   C   D

39. <u>More than</u> 10,000 years ago, glaciers <u>moved</u> across the Minnesota region four <u>time</u>, levelling <u>most of</u>
    A   B   C   D

the land.

40. The <u>discover</u> of gold and silver in the rugged <u>mountains</u> of Nevada in 1858 <u>attracted</u> many fortune-
        A   B   C

seekers <u>to that area.</u>
     D

THIS IS THE END OF SECTION 2, STRUCTURE AND WRITTEN EXPRESSION.
IF YOU FINISH BEFORE TIME IS CALLED, CHECK YOUR WORK ON SECTION 2 ONLY.
DO NOT READ OR WORK ON ANY OTHER SECTION OF THE TEST.

SECTION 3: READING COMPREHENSION
TIME—55 MINUTES

This section of the test measures your ability to comprehend written materials.

Directions: This section contains several passages, each followed by a number of questions. Read the passages and, for each question, choose the *one* best answer—(A), (B), (C), or (D)—based on what is stated in or on what can be inferred from the passage. Then fill in the space on your answer sheet (on page 437) that matches the letter of the answer that you have selected.

Read the following passage:

> Like mammals, birds claim their own territories. A
> bird's territory may be small or large. Some birds
> claim only their nest and the area right around it,
> while others claim far larger territories that include
> (5) their feeding areas. Gulls, penguins, and other waterfowl
> nest in huge colonies, but even in the biggest colonies,
> each male and his mate have small territories of their
> own immediately around their nests.
>   Male birds defend their territory chiefly against other
> (10) males of the same species. In some cases, a warning call
> or threatening pose may be all the defense needed, but in
> other cases, intruders may refuse to leave peacefully.

Example I

What is the main topic of this passage?

(A) Birds that live in colonies
(B) Birds' mating habits
(C) The behavior of birds
(D) Territoriality in birds

Sample Answer

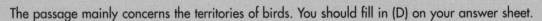

The passage mainly concerns the territories of birds. You should fill in (D) on your answer sheet.

Example II

According to the passage, male birds defend their territory primarily against

(A) female birds
(B) birds of other species
(C) males of their own species
(D) mammals

Sample Answer

 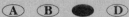

The passage states that "Male birds defend their territory chiefly against other males of the same species." You should fill in (C) on your answer sheet.

As soon as you understand the directions, begin work on this part.

QUESTIONS 1–11

Line   The time when humans crossed the Arctic land bridge from Siberia to Alaska seems remote to us today, but actually represents a late stage in the prehistory of humans, an era when polished stone implements and bows and arrows were already being used and dogs had already been domesticated.

      When these early migrants arrived in North America, they found the woods and plains domi-

5   nated by three types of American mammoths. These elephants were distinguished from today's elephants mainly by their thick, shaggy coats and their huge, upward-curving tusks. They had arrived on the continent hundreds of thousands of years before their human followers. The wooly mammoth in the North, the Columbian mammoth in middle North America, and the imperial mammoth of the South, together with their distant cousins the mastodons, dominated the land. Here, as in the Old

10   World, there is evidence that humans hunted these elephants, as shown by the numerous spear points found with mammoth remains.

      Then, at the end of the Ice Age, when the last glaciers had retreated, there was a relatively sudden and widespread extinction of elephants. In the New World, both mammoths and mastodons disappeared. In the Old World, only Indian and African elephants survived.

15   Why did the huge, seemingly successful mammoths disappear? Were humans connected with their extinction? Perhaps, but at that time, although they were cunning hunters, humans were still widely scattered and not very numerous. It is difficult to see how they could have prevailed over the mammoth to such an extent.

1. With which of the following is the passage primarily concerned?

    (A) Migration from Siberia to Alaska.
    (B) Techniques used to hunt mammoths.
    (C) The prehistory of humans.
    (D) The relationship between man and mammoth in the New World.

2. The word "implements" in line 3 is closest in meaning to

    (A) tools
    (B) ornaments
    (C) houses
    (D) carvings

3. The phrase "these early migrants" in line 4 refers to

    (A) mammoths
    (B) humans
    (C) dogs
    (D) mastodons

4. Where were the imperial mammoths the dominant type of mammoth?

    (A) Alaska
    (B) the central portion of North America
    (C) the southern part of North America
    (D) South America

5. It can be inferred that when humans crossed into the New World, they

   (A) had previously hunted mammoths in Siberia
   (B) had never seen mammoths before
   (C) brought mammoths with them from the Old World
   (D) soon learned to use dogs to hunt mammoths

6. Which of the following could best substitute for the word "remains" in line 11?

   (A) bones
   (B) drawings
   (C) footprints
   (D) spear points

7. The word "seemingly" in line 15 is closest in meaning to

   (A) tremendously
   (B) apparently
   (C) formerly
   (D) obviously

8. The passage supports which of the following conclusions about mammoths?

   (A) Humans hunted them to extinction.
   (B) The freezing temperatures of the Ice Age destroyed their food supply.
   (C) The cause of their extinction is not definitely known.
   (D) Competition with mastodons caused them to become extinct.

9. The word "cunning" in line 16 is closest in meaning to

   (A) clever
   (B) determined
   (C) efficient
   (D) cautious

10. Which of the following is NOT true about prehistoric humans at the time of the mammoths' extinction?

    (A) They were relatively few in number.
    (B) They knew how to use bows and arrows.
    (C) They were concentrated in a small area.
    (D) They were skilled hunters.

11. Which of the following types of elephants does the author discuss in the most detail in the passage?

    (A) the mastodon
    (B) the mammoth
    (C) the Indian elephant
    (D) the African elephant

QUESTIONS 12–23

Line   Just before and during World War I, a number of white musicians came to Chicago from New Orleans playing in an idiom they had learned from blacks in that city. Five of them formed what eventually became known as the Original Dixieland Band. They moved to New York in 1917 and won fame there. That year they recorded the first phonograph record identified as jazz.

5   The first important recording by black musicians was made in Chicago in 1923 by King Oliver's Creole Jazz Band, a group that featured some of the foremost jazz musicians of the time, including trumpet player Louis Armstrong. Armstrong's dynamic trumpet style became famous worldwide. Other band members had played in Fate Marable's band, which traveled up and down the Mississippi River entertaining passengers on riverboats.

10   The characteristics of this early type of jazz, known as Dixieland jazz, included a complex interweaving of melodic lines among the coronet or trumpet, clarinet, and trombone, and a steady chomp-chomp beat provided by the rhythm section, which included the piano, bass, and drums. Most bands used no written notations, preferring arrangements agreed on verbally.

     Improvisation was an indispensable element. Even bandleaders such as Duke Ellington, who
15 provided his musicians with written arrangements, permitted them plenty to freedom to improvise when playing solos.

     In the late 1920s, the most influential jazz artists in Chicago were members of small bands such as the Wolverines. In New York, the trend was toward larger groups. These groups played in revues, large dance halls, and theaters. Bands would become larger still during the next age of jazz, the Swing era.

12. What is the main topic of this passage?

(A) The early history of jazz.
(B) The music of World War I.
(C) The relationship of melody and rhythm in jazz.
(D) The New York recording industry in the 1920s.

13. The word "idiom" in line 2 is closest in meaning to

(A) slang
(B) tempo
(C) tune
(D) style

14. The musicians who made the earliest jazz recordings were originally from

(A) New Orleans
(B) Chicago
(C) New York
(D) Mississippi

15. When was the first important recording by black jazz musicians made?

(A) 1917
(B) 1923
(C) the late 1920s
(D) the early 1930s

16. According to the passage, Louis Armstrong was a member of which of the following?

(A) The Original Dixieland Band
(B) Fate Marable's riverboat band
(C) King Oliver's Creole Jazz Band
(D) The Wolverines

17. The word "steady" in line 11 is closest in meaning to

(A) constant
(B) basic
(C) urgent
(D) happy

18. According to the passage, which of the following instruments helped provide the beat for Dixieland jazz?

(A) the coronet
(B) the piano
(C) the trombone
(D) the clarinet

19. Duke Ellington is given as an example of a bandleader who

(A) could not read music
(B) did not value improvisation
(C) discouraged solo performances
(D) used written arrangements

20. Which of the following phrases would be LEAST likely to be applied to Dixieland jazz?

(A) relatively complex
(B) highly improvisational
(C) rhythmic and melodic
(D) rigidly planned

21. According to the passage, who were the Wolverines?

(A) a band that played in large dance halls
(B) a New York group
(C) a Swing band
(D) a small group

22. The author provides the most detailed description of early jazz music in the

(A) first paragraph
(B) second paragraph
(C) third paragraph
(D) fourth paragraph

23. The paragraph following this one most likely deals with

(A) the music of small bands
(B) the Swing era
(C) music that influenced Dixieland music
(D) other forms of music popular in the 1920s

QUESTIONS 24–32

Line A pioneering study by Donald Appleyard made the astounding discovery that a sudden increase in the volume of traffic through an area affects people in the way that a sudden increase in crime does. Appleyard observed this by finding three blocks of houses in San Francisco that looked much alike and had the same kind of middle-class and working-class residents, with approximately the same
5 ethnic mix. The difference was that only 2,000 cars a day ran down Octavia Street (LIGHT street, in Appleyard's terminology) while Gough Street (MEDIUM street) was used by 8,000 cars daily, and Franklin Street (HEAVY street) had around 16,000 cars a day. Franklin Street often had as many cars in an hour as Octavia Street had in a day.

Heavy traffic brought with it danger, noise, fumes, and soot, directly, and trash secondarily.
10 That is, the cars didn't bring in much trash, but when trash accumulated, residents seldom picked it up. The cars, Appleyard determined, reduced the amount of territory residents felt responsible for. Noise was a constant intrusion into their homes. Many Franklin Street residents covered their doors and windows and spent most of their time in the rear of their houses. Most families with children had already left.
15 Conditions on Octavia Street were much different. Residents picked up trash. They sat on their front steps and chatted with neighbors. They had three times as many friends and twice as many acquaintances as the people on Franklin.

On Gough Street, residents said that the old feeling of community was disappearing as traffic increased. People were becoming more and more preoccupied with their own lives. A number of
20 families had recently moved and more were considering. Those who were staying expressed deep regret at the destruction of their community.

24. The word "astounding" in line 1 is closest in meaning to

(A) startling
(B) disappointing
(C) dubious
(D) alternative

25. The three streets mentioned in this passage are different in that

(A) they are in different cities
(B) the residents are of different ethnic backgrounds
(C) they have varying amounts of traffic
(D) the income levels of the residents vary considerably

26. Approximately how many cars use Franklin Street daily?

(A) 2,000
(B) 8,000
(C) 16,000
(D) 20,000

27. All of the following are direct results of heavy traffic EXCEPT

(A) increased amounts of trash
(B) greater danger to residents
(C) more pollution
(D) more vibrations

28. The author's main purpose in the second paragraph is to

(A) discuss the problems of trash disposal
(B) point out the disadvantages of heavy traffic
(C) propose an alternate system of transportation
(D) suggest ways to cope with traffic problems

29. On which street is there the most social interaction?

(A) Octavia Street
(B) Gough Street
(C) Franklin Street
(D) There is no significant social interaction on any of the three streets.

30. The word "chatted" in line 16 is closest in meaning to

(A) joked
(B) talked
(C) argued
(D) walked

31. Which of the following is NOT a statement you would expect from a resident of Gough Street?

(A) People on this street are unhappy because the neighborhood is deteriorating.
(B) People on this street think mostly of themselves.
(C) People on this street have more and more space for which they feel responsible.
(D) A number of people are preparing to leave this street.

32. In what order does the author present detailed discussions of the three streets?

(A) LIGHT, MEDIUM, HEAVY
(B) HEAVY, MEDIUM, LIGHT
(C) HEAVY, LIGHT, MEDIUM
(D) LIGHT, HEAVY, MEDIUM

QUESTIONS 33–42

Line   Rachel Carson was born in 1907 in Springsdale, Pennsylvania. She studied biology at college and zoology at Johns Hopkins University, where she received her master's degree in 1933. In 1936, she was hired by the U.S. Fish and Wildlife Service, where she worked most of her life.

        Carson's first book, *Under the Sea Wind,* was published in 1941. It received excellent reviews,
5   but sales were poor until it was reissued in 1952. In that year she published *The Sea Around Us,* which provided a fascinating look beneath the ocean's surface, emphasizing human history as well as geology and marine biology. Her imagery and language had a poetic quality. Carson consulted no less than 1,000 printed sources. She had voluminous correspondence and frequent discussions with experts in the field. However, she always realized the limitations of her nontechnical readers.

10   In 1962, Carson published *Silent Spring,* a book that sparked considerable controversy. It proved how much harm was done by the uncontrolled, reckless use of insecticides. She detailed how they poison the food supply of animals, kill birds and fish, and contaminate human food. At the time, spokesmen for the chemical industry mounted personal attacks against Carson and issued propaganda to indicate that her findings were flawed. However, her work was vindicated by a 1963 report of the President's Science Advisory Committee.

33. The passage mainly discusses Rachel Carson's work

(A) as a researcher
(B) at college
(C) at the U.S. Fish and Wildlife Service
(D) as a writer

34. According to the passage, what did Carson primarily study at Johns Hopkins University?

(A) oceanography
(B) history
(C) literature
(D) zoology

35. When she published her first book, Carson was closest to the age of

(A) 26
(B) 29
(C) 34
(D) 45

36. It can be inferred from the passage that in 1952, Carson's book *Under the Sea Wind*

(A) was outdated
(B) became more popular than her other books
(C) was praised by critics
(D) sold many copies

37. Which of the following was NOT mentioned in the passage as a source of information for *The Sea Around Us*?

(A) printed matter
(B) talks with experts
(C) a research expedition
(D) letters from scientists

38. Which of the following words or phrases is LEAST accurate in describing *The Sea Around Us*?

(A) highly technical
(B) poetic
(C) fascinating
(D) well-researched

39. The word "reckless" in line 11 is closest in meaning to

(A) unnecessary
(B) limited
(C) continuous
(D) irresponsible

40. According to the passage, *Silent Spring* is primarily

(A) an attack on the use of chemical preservatives in food
(B) a discussion of the hazards insects pose to the food supply
(C) a warning about the dangers of misusing insecticides
(D) an illustration of the benefits of the chemical industry

41. The word "flawed" in line 14 is closest in meaning to

(A) faulty
(B) deceptive
(C) logical
(D) offensive

42. Why does the author of the passage mention the report of the President's Science Advisory Committee (lines 14–15)?

(A) To provide an example of government propaganda.
(B) To support Carson's ideas.
(C) To indicate a growing government concern with the environment.
(D) To validate the chemical industry's claims.

QUESTIONS 43–50

Line   What is meant by the term *economic resources*? In general, these are all the natural, man-made, and human resources that go into the production of goods and services. This obviously covers a lot of ground: factories and farms, tools and machines, transportation and communication facilities, all types of natural resources and labor. Economic resources can be broken down into two general categories:
5   property resources—land and capital—and human resources—labor and entrepreneurial skills.
           What do economists mean by *land*? Much more than the noneconomist. Land refers to all natural resources that are usable in the production process: arable land, forests, mineral and oil deposits, and so on. What about capital? Capital goods are all the man-made aids to producing, storing, transporting, and distributing goods and services. Capital goods differ from consumer goods
10   in that the latter satisfy wants directly, while the former do so indirectly by facilitating the production of consumer goods. It should be noted that *capital* as defined here does not refer to money. Money, as such, produces nothing.
           The term *labor* refers to the physical and mental talents of humans used to produce goods or services (with the exception of a certain set of human talents, entrepreneurial skills, which will be
15   considered separately because of their special significance).
           Thus the services of a factory worker or an office worker, a ballet dancer or an astronaut all fall under the general heading of labor.

43. What is the author's main purpose in writing this passage?

(A) To explain the concept of labor.
(B) To criticize certain uses of capital.
(C) To contrast capital goods and consumer goods.
(D) To define economic resources.

44. In lines 2–3, the author uses the expression "This obviously covers a lot of ground . . ." to indicate that

(A) the factories and farms discussed in the passage are very large
(B) economic resources will be discussed in great depth
(C) the topic of economic resources is a broad one
(D) land is an important concept in economics

45. When noneconomists use the term "land," its definition

    (A) is much more general than when economists use it
    (B) is much more restrictive than when economists use it
    (C) changes from place to place
    (D) includes all types of natural resources

46. The word "arable" in line 7 is closest in meaning to

    (A) dry
    (B) fertile
    (C) developed
    (D) open

47. The phrase "the latter" in line 10 refers to

    (A) economists
    (B) noneconomists
    (C) capital goods
    (D) consumer goods

48. Which of the following could be considered a capital good as defined in the passage?

    (A) a railroad
    (B) money
    (C) a coal mine
    (D) human skills

49. The word "heading" in line 17 is closest in meaning to

    (A) direction
    (B) practice
    (C) category
    (D) utility

50. The skills of all the following could be considered examples of labor, as defined in the passage, EXCEPT

    (A) artists and scientists
    (B) workers who produce services, not goods
    (C) office workers
    (D) entrepreneurs

THIS IS THE END OF SECTION 3, READING COMPREHENSION.
IF YOU FINISH BEFORE TIME IS CALLED, GO BACK AND CHECK YOUR WORK IN THIS SECTION ONLY.

Peterson's TOEFL CBT Success

Answer Sheet

Practice Test 2

Section 1: Listening Comprehension

1. Ⓐ Ⓑ Ⓒ Ⓓ   21. Ⓐ Ⓑ Ⓒ Ⓓ   41. Ⓐ Ⓑ Ⓒ Ⓓ
2. Ⓐ Ⓑ Ⓒ Ⓓ   22. Ⓐ Ⓑ Ⓒ Ⓓ   42. Ⓐ Ⓑ Ⓒ Ⓓ
3. Ⓐ Ⓑ Ⓒ Ⓓ   23. Ⓐ Ⓑ Ⓒ Ⓓ   43. Ⓐ Ⓑ Ⓒ Ⓓ
4. Ⓐ Ⓑ Ⓒ Ⓓ   24. Ⓐ Ⓑ Ⓒ Ⓓ   44. Ⓐ Ⓑ Ⓒ Ⓓ
5. Ⓐ Ⓑ Ⓒ Ⓓ   25. Ⓐ Ⓑ Ⓒ Ⓓ   45. Ⓐ Ⓑ Ⓒ Ⓓ
6. Ⓐ Ⓑ Ⓒ Ⓓ   26. Ⓐ Ⓑ Ⓒ Ⓓ   46. Ⓐ Ⓑ Ⓒ Ⓓ
7. Ⓐ Ⓑ Ⓒ Ⓓ   27. Ⓐ Ⓑ Ⓒ Ⓓ   47. Ⓐ Ⓑ Ⓒ Ⓓ
8. Ⓐ Ⓑ Ⓒ Ⓓ   28. Ⓐ Ⓑ Ⓒ Ⓓ   48. Ⓐ Ⓑ Ⓒ Ⓓ
9. Ⓐ Ⓑ Ⓒ Ⓓ   29. Ⓐ Ⓑ Ⓒ Ⓓ   49. Ⓐ Ⓑ Ⓒ Ⓓ
10. Ⓐ Ⓑ Ⓒ Ⓓ   30. Ⓐ Ⓑ Ⓒ Ⓓ   50. Ⓐ Ⓑ Ⓒ Ⓓ

11. Ⓐ Ⓑ Ⓒ Ⓓ   31. Ⓐ Ⓑ Ⓒ Ⓓ
12. Ⓐ Ⓑ Ⓒ Ⓓ   32. Ⓐ Ⓑ Ⓒ Ⓓ
13. Ⓐ Ⓑ Ⓒ Ⓓ   33. Ⓐ Ⓑ Ⓒ Ⓓ
14. Ⓐ Ⓑ Ⓒ Ⓓ   34. Ⓐ Ⓑ Ⓒ Ⓓ
15. Ⓐ Ⓑ Ⓒ Ⓓ   35. Ⓐ Ⓑ Ⓒ Ⓓ
16. Ⓐ Ⓑ Ⓒ Ⓓ   36. Ⓐ Ⓑ Ⓒ Ⓓ
17. Ⓐ Ⓑ Ⓒ Ⓓ   37. Ⓐ Ⓑ Ⓒ Ⓓ
18. Ⓐ Ⓑ Ⓒ Ⓓ   38. Ⓐ Ⓑ Ⓒ Ⓓ
19. Ⓐ Ⓑ Ⓒ Ⓓ   39. Ⓐ Ⓑ Ⓒ Ⓓ
20. Ⓐ Ⓑ Ⓒ Ⓓ   40. Ⓐ Ⓑ Ⓒ Ⓓ

Section 2: Structure and Written Expression

1. (A) (B) (C) (D)	21. (A) (B) (C) (D)	31. (A) (B) (C) (D)
2. (A) (B) (C) (D)	22. (A) (B) (C) (D)	32. (A) (B) (C) (D)
3. (A) (B) (C) (D)	23. (A) (B) (C) (D)	33. (A) (B) (C) (D)
4. (A) (B) (C) (D)	24. (A) (B) (C) (D)	34. (A) (B) (C) (D)
5. (A) (B) (C) (D)	25. (A) (B) (C) (D)	35. (A) (B) (C) (D)
6. (A) (B) (C) (D)	26. (A) (B) (C) (D)	36. (A) (B) (C) (D)
7. (A) (B) (C) (D)	27. (A) (B) (C) (D)	37. (A) (B) (C) (D)
8. (A) (B) (C) (D)	28. (A) (B) (C) (D)	38. (A) (B) (C) (D)
9. (A) (B) (C) (D)	29. (A) (B) (C) (D)	39. (A) (B) (C) (D)
10. (A) (B) (C) (D)	30. (A) (B) (C) (D)	40. (A) (B) (C) (D)

11. (A) (B) (C) (D)
12. (A) (B) (C) (D)
13. (A) (B) (C) (D)
14. (A) (B) (C) (D)
15. (A) (B) (C) (D)
16. (A) (B) (C) (D)
17. (A) (B) (C) (D)
18. (A) (B) (C) (D)
19. (A) (B) (C) (D)
20. (A) (B) (C) (D)

Section 3: Reading Comprehension

1. Ⓐ Ⓑ Ⓒ Ⓓ   21. Ⓐ Ⓑ Ⓒ Ⓓ   41. Ⓐ Ⓑ Ⓒ Ⓓ
2. Ⓐ Ⓑ Ⓒ Ⓓ   22. Ⓐ Ⓑ Ⓒ Ⓓ   42. Ⓐ Ⓑ Ⓒ Ⓓ
3. Ⓐ Ⓑ Ⓒ Ⓓ   23. Ⓐ Ⓑ Ⓒ Ⓓ   43. Ⓐ Ⓑ Ⓒ Ⓓ
4. Ⓐ Ⓑ Ⓒ Ⓓ   24. Ⓐ Ⓑ Ⓒ Ⓓ   44. Ⓐ Ⓑ Ⓒ Ⓓ
5. Ⓐ Ⓑ Ⓒ Ⓓ   25. Ⓐ Ⓑ Ⓒ Ⓓ   45. Ⓐ Ⓑ Ⓒ Ⓓ
6. Ⓐ Ⓑ Ⓒ Ⓓ   26. Ⓐ Ⓑ Ⓒ Ⓓ   46. Ⓐ Ⓑ Ⓒ Ⓓ
7. Ⓐ Ⓑ Ⓒ Ⓓ   27. Ⓐ Ⓑ Ⓒ Ⓓ   47. Ⓐ Ⓑ Ⓒ Ⓓ
8. Ⓐ Ⓑ Ⓒ Ⓓ   28. Ⓐ Ⓑ Ⓒ Ⓓ   48. Ⓐ Ⓑ Ⓒ Ⓓ
9. Ⓐ Ⓑ Ⓒ Ⓓ   29. Ⓐ Ⓑ Ⓒ Ⓓ   49. Ⓐ Ⓑ Ⓒ Ⓓ
10. Ⓐ Ⓑ Ⓒ Ⓓ   30. Ⓐ Ⓑ Ⓒ Ⓓ   50. Ⓐ Ⓑ Ⓒ Ⓓ

11. Ⓐ Ⓑ Ⓒ Ⓓ   31. Ⓐ Ⓑ Ⓒ Ⓓ
12. Ⓐ Ⓑ Ⓒ Ⓓ   32. Ⓐ Ⓑ Ⓒ Ⓓ
13. Ⓐ Ⓑ Ⓒ Ⓓ   33. Ⓐ Ⓑ Ⓒ Ⓓ
14. Ⓐ Ⓑ Ⓒ Ⓓ   34. Ⓐ Ⓑ Ⓒ Ⓓ
15. Ⓐ Ⓑ Ⓒ Ⓓ   35. Ⓐ Ⓑ Ⓒ Ⓓ
16. Ⓐ Ⓑ Ⓒ Ⓓ   36. Ⓐ Ⓑ Ⓒ Ⓓ
17. Ⓐ Ⓑ Ⓒ Ⓓ   37. Ⓐ Ⓑ Ⓒ Ⓓ
18. Ⓐ Ⓑ Ⓒ Ⓓ   38. Ⓐ Ⓑ Ⓒ Ⓓ
19. Ⓐ Ⓑ Ⓒ Ⓓ   39. Ⓐ Ⓑ Ⓒ Ⓓ
20. Ⓐ Ⓑ Ⓒ Ⓓ   40. Ⓐ Ⓑ Ⓒ Ⓓ

Practice Test 3

This section tests your ability to comprehend spoken English. It is divided into three parts, each with its own directions. You are *not* permitted to turn the page during the reading of the directions or to take notes at any time.

PART A

Directions: Each item in this part consists of a brief conversation involving two speakers. Following each conversation, a third voice will ask a question. You will hear the conversations and questions only once, and they will *not* be written out.

When you have heard each conversation and question, read the four answer choices and select the one—(A), (B), (C), or (D)—that best answers the question based on what is directly stated or on what can be inferred. Then fill in the space on your answer sheet (on page 459) that matches the letter of the answer that you have selected.

Here is an example.

You will hear:*

M1: Do you think I should leave this chair against the wall or put it somewhere else?

F1: Over by the window, I'd say.

M2: What does the woman think the man should do?

You will read:

(A) Open the window.
(B) Move the chair.
(C) Leave the room.
(D) Take a seat.

Sample Answer

 Ⓐ ● Ⓒ Ⓓ

From the conversation you find out that the woman thinks the man should put the chair over by the window. The best answer to the question, "What does the woman think the man should do?" is (B), "Move the chair." You should fill in (B) on your answer sheet.

---

* Note: M1 = first male voice   M2 = second male voice   F1 = first female voice   F2 = second female voice

1. (A) She broke the window herself.
   (B) She repaired the broken window.
   (C) She was able to get the window open.
   (D) She hurt herself on the broken glass.

2. (A) The golf tournament made it famous.
   (B) It's grown a lot lately.
   (C) It can't be found without a map.
   (D) Very few people there play golf.

3. (A) Where she got her information.
   (B) How the copy was made.
   (C) Who painted the picture.
   (D) Why the copy was made.

4. (A) Groceries.
   (B) A used car.
   (C) Gasoline.
   (D) Medicine.

5. (A) She read it again and again.
   (B) She covered it up.
   (C) She read every page of it.
   (D) She ripped its cover off.

6. (A) He can no longer play.
   (B) He's played every day for years.
   (C) His playing has improved.
   (D) He played quite well.

7. (A) He needs to get more camping equipment.
   (B) He is an experienced camper.
   (C) He is taking too much equipment.
   (D) He shouldn't go camping for such a long time.

8. (A) Try to get elected mayor.
   (B) Attend a class.
   (C) Interview the mayor.
   (D) Apply for a job.

9. (A) She was mistaken about Professor Leguin.
   (B) She just returned from San Francisco.
   (C) She doesn't know what the professor looks like.
   (D) She's an admirer of Professor Leguin.

10. (A) He's speaking a language they don't know.
    (B) He doesn't have a microphone.
    (C) He's speaking much too quickly.
    (D) He's using a defective microphone.

11. (A) It's near the elevator.
    (B) He doesn't know where it is.
    (C) It's on another floor.
    (D) The directory doesn't list it.

12. (A) She's only heard it a few times.
    (B) She doesn't get to listen to it very often.
    (C) She once liked it, but she's heard enough.
    (D) She enjoys it very much.

13. (A) It's no wonder that she had to work.
    (B) It wasn't busy because of the weather.
    (C) She was very busy at work.
    (D) The snow made her late for work.

14. (A) He doesn't have any money left either.
    (B) The club is looking for some new members.
    (C) He can lend the woman some money.
    (D) It doesn't cost much to join the club.

15. (A) He doesn't enjoy receptions.
    (B) He uses his computer a lot.
    (C) His computer isn't working.
    (D) He will definitely attend.

16. (A) Only one person in the group is older than he.
    (B) His group is almost the oldest.
    (C) He's the youngest person in the group.
    (D) He appears only in the second photograph.

17. (A) Pancakes are not his favorite dish.
    (B) His pancakes don't taste very good.
    (C) He never makes enough pancakes
    (D) He can't cook many dishes.

18. (A) She thinks Professor Bryant is unfair.
    (B) She doesn't know Professor Bryant.
    (C) She agrees with the man.
    (D) She doesn't understand the man's remark.

19. (A) In a few days.
    (B) Before they eat.
    (C) During lunch.
    (D) When lunch is over.

20. (A) The woman would enjoy the mountain scenery.
    (B) The weather has been hot this month.
    (C) The weather in the mountains is unusual.
    (D) The woman probably doesn't like cool weather.

21. (A) It has exceptionally good service.
    (B) It has excellent food.
    (C) The service there is disappointing.
    (D) Everything there is great.

22. (A) If his name sounds familiar.
    (B) If she's spoken to him on the phone.
    (C) If he's a musician.
    (D) If she likes his name.

23. (A) He thought other science courses would be harder.
    (B) It's a required class for all students.
    (C) He's studied geology before.
    (D) It was the only science course open to him.

24. (A) He's never been to the zoo.
    (B) He's seen only one bear.
    (C) He's never seen a bear in the wild.
    (D) There weren't any bears at that zoo.

25. (A) When she will answer the questions.
    (B) Where she drove.
    (C) What kind of car she has.
    (D) Why she asked so many questions.

26. (A) He thinks it will be better than the old one.
    (B) He's anxious for it to be completed.
    (C) He's worried that it's not long enough.
    (D) He feels that it shouldn't have been built.

27. (A) Where he's studying.
    (B) What subject he's studying.
    (C) How long he's been in Europe.
    (D) When he's returning.

28. (A) Charlotte wouldn't be attending graduate school.
    (B) Charlotte had gotten a scholarship.
    (C) Graduate school wouldn't start until September.
    (D) Scholarships were easy to get.

29. (A) He paid it today for the first time.
    (B) He pays it on the last day of the month.
    (C) He pays it after it's due.
    (D) He's planning to pay it tomorrow.

30. (A) The debate involved only a few issues.
    (B) Many people changed their plans.
    (C) A lot of people attended.
    (D) The debate lasted longer than expected.

PART B

Directions: This part of the test consists of extended conversations between two speakers. After each of these conversations, there are a number of questions. You will hear each conversation and question only once, and the questions are *not* written out.

When you have heard the questions, read the four answer choices and select the *one*—(A), (B), (C), or (D)—that best answers the question based on what is directly stated or on what can be inferred. Then fill in the space on your answer sheet corresponding to the letter of the answer that you have selected.

Don't forget: During actual exams, taking notes or writing in your test book is *not* permitted.

WAIT

Peterson's TOEFL CBT Success

31. (A) Because it was cheap.
    (B) Because it is in such good condition.
    (C) Because it is a collector's item.
    (D) Because he can resell it at a high price.

32. (A) In the 1930s.
    (B) In the 1940s.
    (C) In the 1950s.
    (D) In the 1960s.

33. (A) Replace its engine.
    (B) Enter it in some shows.
    (C) Take it on a long drive.
    (D) Resell it for more money.

34. (A) At a conference hall.
    (B) At an art gallery.
    (C) At an airport.
    (D) At a hotel.

35. (A) To attend a conference.
    (B) To see the planetarium.
    (C) To change planes.
    (D) To go sightseeing.

36. (A) She recently went there.
    (B) It's not a very good one.
    (C) There's one in her hometown.
    (D) It will be closed when she's free.

37. (A) On foot and by boat.
    (B) By car and on foot.
    (C) By air and by car.
    (D) By car and by bus.

PART C

Directions: This part of the test consists of several talks, each given by a single speaker. After each of these talks, there are a number of questions. You will hear each talk and question only once, and the questions are *not* written out.

When you have heard each question, read the four answer choices and select the *one*—(A), (B), (C), or (D)—that best answers the question based on what is directly stated or on what can be inferred. Then fill in the space on your answer sheet that matches the letter of the answer that you have selected.

Here is an example.

You will hear:*

M1: Students, this evening we'll have a chance to observe a phenomenon that we've discussed several times in class. Tonight there will be a lunar eclipse. As we've said, when an eclipse of the Moon occurs, the Earth passes between the Sun and the Moon. Therefore, the shadow of the Earth moves across the surface of the Moon and obscures it. Because you won't be looking at the Sun, it is not necessary to use the special lenses and filters that you need when observing a solar eclipse. You can observe a lunar eclipse with your unaided eye or with a telescope, and photograph it with an ordinary camera. So if the weather's not cloudy tonight, go out and take a look at this eclipse of the Moon. I'm sure you'll find it interesting.

Now here is a sample question.

You will hear:*

   In what course is this lecture probably being given?

You will read:

   (A) Philosophy
   (B) Meteorology
   (C) Astronomy
   (D) Photography

Sample Answer

The lecture concerns a lunar eclipse, a topic that would typically be discussed in an astronomy class. The choice that best answers the question, "In what course is this lecture probably being given?" is (C), "Astronomy." You should fill in (C) on your answer sheet.

Here is another sample question.

You will hear:*

   According to the speaker, which of the following occurs during a lunar eclipse?

You will read:

   (A) The Earth's shadow moves across the Moon.
   (B) Clouds block the view of the Moon.
   (C) The Moon moves between the Earth and the Sun.
   (D) The Sun can be observed without special equipment.

Sample Answer

From the lecture you learn that a lunar eclipse occurs when the Earth moves between the Sun and the Moon and the shadow of the Earth passes across the Moon. The choice that best answers the question, "According to the speaker, which of the following occurs during a lunar eclipse?" is (A), "The Earth's shadow moves across the Moon."

Don't forget: During actual exams, taking notes or writing in your test book is *not* permitted.

* Note: M1 = first male voice   M2 = second male voice   F1 = first female voice   F2 = second female voice

Peterson's TOEFL CBT Success

38. (A) Tourists.
(B) Professional dancers.
(C) Students.
(D) Traditional musicians.

39. (A) It will be different from the ones performed in Hawaii today.
(B) It will involve women wearing grass skirts.
(C) It will involve only male dancers.
(D) It was once performed for great Hawaiian leaders.

40. (A) They prohibited it.
(B) They sponsored it.
(C) They proposed some small changes in it.
(D) They exported it to other islands.

41. (A) Attend a live performance.
(B) Go on a tour.
(C) Perform a dance.
(D) Watch a video.

42. (A) To discuss a weather phenomenon.
(B) To explain how to drive during storms.
(C) To describe supercooled water.
(D) To warn gardeners of the danger of hail.

43. (A) Because of its size.
(B) Because of its color.
(C) Because of its layers.
(D) Because of its weight.

44. (A) As a drop of supercooled water.
(B) As a snowflake.
(C) As a particle of dust.
(D) As a ball of ice.

45. (A) In the spring.
(B) In the summer.
(C) In the fall.
(D) In the winter.

46. (A) New theories about the origin of language.
(B) How to teach grammar to children.
(C) Mistakes children sometimes make.
(D) The stages of children's language learning.

47. (A) "Coo, coo."
(B) "Da-da."
(C) "More milk!"
(D) "Na-na."

48. (A) Between four and eight months.
(B) Between one year and eighteen months.
(C) Between two and three years.
(D) Between three and four years.

49. (A) They are the same in all languages.
(B) They are often misinterpreted.
(C) They are learned by imitation.
(D) They are quite logical.

50. (A) They are too complicated.
(B) She doesn't have time to talk about them today.
(C) The class didn't have a chance to read about them.
(D) She does not agree with them.

THIS IS THE END OF SECTION 1, LISTENING COMPREHENSION.
STOP WORK ON SECTION 1.

End of Tape 4, Side B.

SECTION 2: STRUCTURE AND WRITTEN EXPRESSION
TIME—25 MINUTES

This section tests your ability to recognize grammar and usage suitable for standard written English. This section is divided into two parts, each with its own directions.

STRUCTURE

Directions: Items in this part are incomplete sentences. Following each of these sentences, there are four words or phrases. You should select the *one* word or phrase—(A), (B), (C), or (D)—that best completes the sentence. Then fill in the space on your answer sheet (on page 460) that matches the letter of the answer that you have selected.

Example I

Pepsin _____ an enzyme used in digestion

(A) that
(B) is
(C) of
(D) being

Sample Answer

(A) ● (C) (D)

This sentence should properly read, "Pepsin is an enzyme used in digestion." You should fill in (B) on your answer sheet.

Example II

_____ large natural lakes are found in the state of South Carolina.

(A) There are no
(B) Not the
(C) It is not
(D) No

Sample Answer

(A) (B) (C) ●

This sentence should properly read, "No large natural lakes are found in the state of South Carolina." You should fill in (D) on your answer sheet.

As soon as you understand the directions, begin work on this part.

Peterson's TOEFL CBT Success

1. Ellen Swallow Richards became the first woman to enter, graduate from, and _____ at the Massachusetts Institute of Technology.

   (A) teach
   (B) a teacher
   (C) who taught
   (D) to teach

2. Coins last approximately twenty times _____ paper bills.

   (A) longer
   (B) as long
   (C) long
   (D) longer than

3. It has been estimated that _____ species of animals.

   (A) more than a million
   (B) it is a million or more
   (C) there are over a million
   (D) are over a million of

4. Dr. Seuss, _____ was Theodor Seuss Geisel, wrote and illustrated delightfully humorous books for children.

   (A) his real name
   (B) who had as his real name
   (C) with his real name
   (D) whose real name

5. _____ American landscape architects was Hideo Sasaki.

   (A) The most famous one of
   (B) One of the most famous
   (C) Of the one most famous
   (D) The one most famous of

6. Most young geese leave their nests at an early age, and young snow geese are _____ exception.

   (A) not
   (B) no
   (C) none
   (D) never

7. Vancouver, British Columbia, has a temperate climate for a city situated _____ far north.

   (A) as
   (B) so
   (C) very
   (D) by

8. _____ in 1849, Manuel A. Alonso recorded the customs, language, and songs of the people of Puerto Rico in his poetry and prose.

   (A) Beginning
   (B) He began
   (C) Having begun
   (D) The beginning was

9. _____ the sails of a distant ship are visible before the body of the ship.

   (A) The curve of the Earth makes
   (B) The Earth, in that it curves, makes
   (C) Because the curve of the Earth,
   (D) Because of the curve of the Earth,

10. Printing ink is made _____ of a paste that is applied to the printing surface with rollers.

    (A) to form
    (B) the form
    (C) in the form
    (D) so that it forms

11. Although _____ cold climates, they can thrive in hot, dry climates as well.

    (A) sheep adapted well
    (B) well-adapted sheep
    (C) sheep, well adapted to
    (D) sheep are well adapted to

12. Rarely _____ seen far from water.

    (A) spotted turtles
    (B) spotted turtles are
    (C) are spotted turtles
    (D) have spotted turtles

13. _____ one of Laura Ingalls Wilder's many books about the American frontier are based on her own childhood experiences.

(A) Except
(B) All but
(C) Without
(D) Not only

14. One of the first industries to be affected by the Industrial Revolution _____.

(A) was the textile industry
(B) the textile industry
(C) in the textile industry
(D) the textile industry was

15. _____ the outer rings of a gyroscope are turned or twisted, the gyroscope itself continues to spin in exactly the same position.

(A) However
(B) Somehow
(C) Otherwise
(D) No matter

WRITTEN EXPRESSION

Directions: The items in this part have four underlined words or phrases, (A), (B), (C) and (D). You must identify the *one* underlined expression that must be changed for the sentence to be correct. Then find the number of the question on your answer sheet and fill in the space corresponding to the letter.

Example I

Lenses may to have either concave or convex shapes.
       A   B C   D

Sample Answer

● Ⓑ Ⓒ Ⓓ

This sentence should read, "Lenses may have either concave or convex shapes." You should therefore select answer (A).

Example II

A fresco is a painting applied directly to the damp plaster of a wall themselves.
A   B   C   D

Sample Answer

Ⓐ Ⓑ Ⓒ ●

This sentence should read, "A fresco is a painting applied directly to the damp plaster of a wall itself." You should therefore select answer (D).

As soon as you understand the directions, begin work on this section.

16. The rock formations in the Valley of Fire in Nevada <u>has</u> been <u>worn</u> into many <u>strange shapes</u> <u>by the</u>
                                                    A   B   C
<u>action</u> of wind and water.
  D

17. The <u>author</u> Susan Glaspell <u>won</u> a Pulitzer Prize in 1931 <u>for</u> <u>hers</u> play, *Alison's House*.
        A   B   C D

18. Haywood Broun was a <u>read widely</u> <u>newspaper</u> columnist <u>who wrote</u> <u>during</u> the 1920's and 1930's.
                                    A   B   C   D

19. <u>Researches</u> in <u>economics</u>, psychology, and <u>marketing</u> can <u>help</u> businesses.
        A   B   C   D

20. <u>Because of</u> their color and shape, seahorses blend <u>so well</u> with the seaweed <u>in which</u> they live that it
      A   B   C
is almost impossible to see <u>themselves</u>.
                              D

21. <u>Although</u> the social sciences <u>different</u> a great deal from <u>one another</u> they share a common <u>interest in</u>
      A   B   C   D
human relationships.

22. Herman Melville's <u>novel</u> *Moby Dick* describes the <u>dangers</u>, difficult, and often <u>violent</u> life <u>aboard</u> a
                              A   B   C   D
whaling ship.

23. Near <u>equator</u>, the slant of the Sun's rays is never <u>great enough</u> to cause temperatures <u>to fall</u> below
        A   B   C
the <u>freezing point</u>.
        D

24. Stephen Hopkins <u>was</u> a <u>cultural</u> and political <u>leadership</u> <u>in</u> colonial Rhode Island.
                    A   B   C   D

25. A mousebird's <u>tail</u> is <u>double</u> as <u>long</u> as <u>its</u> body.
               A   B   C   D

26. The Uinta Mountains of northeastern Utah are <u>the only</u> range of mountains in North America <u>that</u>
                                                  A
<u>runs</u> from east <u>and</u> west for its entire <u>length</u>.
  B   C   D

27. <u>The tools</u> used <u>most often</u> by <u>floral</u> designers are the <u>knives</u>, scissors, and glue gun.
      A   B   C   D

28. <u>Most</u> types of dolphins live <u>at less</u> twenty-five years, and <u>some</u> species may reach 50 years <u>of age</u>.
  A   B   C   D

29. Isle Royale National Park <u>in</u> Lake Superior <u>can</u> only <u>be reached</u> by <u>the</u> boat.
                        A   B   C   D

30. The main <u>divisions</u> of geologic <u>time</u>, <u>called</u> eras, are subdivided <u>in</u> periods.
              A   B   C   D

31. All <u>root</u> vegetables <u>grow</u> underground, <u>and</u> not all vegetables <u>that</u> grow underground are roots.
      A   B   C   D

32. The <u>process</u> of fermentation <u>takes place</u> <u>only</u> in the <u>absent</u> of oxygen.
      A   B   C   D

33. In about 1920, experimental psychologists have devoted more research to learning than to any other
    A   B   C   D
    topic.

34. Transfer taxes are imposed on the sell or exchange of stocks and bonds.
                        A   B   C   D

35. One of the greatest of mountains climbers, Carl Blaurock was the first to climb all of the mountains
                            A   B   C
    higher than 14,000 feet in the United States.
                       D

36. Biochemists have solved many of the mysteries about photosynthesis, the process which plants make
                   A   B   C
    food.
    D

37. Oceanic islands have been separated from the mainland for too long that they have evolved distinc-
                                          A   B   C
    tive animal populations.
                 D

38. Certain species of penicillin mold are used to ripe cheese.
    A   B   C   D

39. Many of the important products obtained from trees, one of the most important is wood pulp, which
    A   B   C
    is used in paper-making.
               D

40. Not longer are contributions to the advancement of industry made primarily by individuals.
    A   B   C   D

THIS IS THE END OF SECTION 2, STRUCTURE AND WRITTEN EXPRESSION.
IF YOU FINISH BEFORE TIME IS CALLED, CHECK YOUR WORK ON SECTION 2 ONLY.
DO NOT READ OR WORK ON ANY OTHER SECTION OF THE TEST.

SECTION 3: READING COMPREHENSION
TIME—55 MINUTES

This section of the test measures your ability to comprehend written materials.

Directions: This section contains several passages, each followed by a number of questions. Read the passages and, for each question, choose the *one* best answer—(A), (B), (C), or (D)—based on what is stated in or on what can be inferred from the passage. Then fill in the space on your answer sheet (on page 461) that matches the letter of the answer that you have selected.

Read the following passage:

> Like mammals, birds claim their own territories. A bird's territory may be small or large. Some birds claim only their nest and the area right around it, while others claim far larger territories that include their feeding areas. Gulls, penguins, and other waterfowl nest in huge colonies, but even in the biggest colonies, each male and his mate have small territories of their own immediately around their nests.
>
> Male birds defend their territory chiefly against other males of the same species. In some cases, a warning call or threatening pose may be all the defense needed, but in other cases, intruders may refuse to leave peacefully.

Example I

What is the main topic of this passage?

(A) Birds that live in colonies
(B) Birds' mating habits
(C) The behavior of birds
(D) Territoriality in birds

Sample Answer

The passage mainly concerns the territories of birds. You should fill in (D) on your answer sheet.

Example II

According to the passage, male birds defend their territory primarily against

(A) female birds
(B) birds of other species
(C) males of their own species
(D) mammals

Sample Answer

The passage states that "Male birds defend their territory chiefly against other males of the same species." You should fill in (C) on your answer sheet.

As soon as you understand the directions, begin work on this part.

QUESTIONS 1–11

Line To date, Canada has produced only one classic children's tale to rank with *Alice's Adventures in Wonderland* and the works of Mark Twain; this was Lucy Maud Montgomery's *Anne of Green Gables*. Lucy Maud Montgomery was born in Clinton, Prince Edward Island. Her mother died soon after her birth, and when her father went to Saskatchewan to assume a business position, she moved
5 in with her grandparents in Cavendish, Prince Edward Island. There she went to school and later qualified to be a teacher.

Montgomery wrote the *Anne* books while living in Cavendish and helping her grandmother at the post office. The first of the books, *Anne of Green Gables*, was published in 1908, and in the next three years she wrote two sequels. Like Montgomery, the heroine of the book is taken in by an
10 elderly couple who lives in the fictional town of Avonlea, and Montgomery incorporated many events from her life in Cavendish into the *Anne* books.

In 1911, Montgomery married Ewan MacDonald and the couple soon moved to Ontario, where she wrote many other books. However, it was her first efforts that secured her prominence, and the *Anne* books are still read all around the world. Her novels have helped create a warm picture of
15 Prince Edward Island's special character. Several movies, a television series, and a musical play have been based on her tales, and today visitors scour the Island for locations described in the book.

1. The main purpose of this passage is to

(A) introduce Montgomery and her *Anne* books
(B) contrast Canadian children's literature with that of other countries
(C) provide a brief introduction to Prince Edward Island
(D) show the similarities between Montgomery's life and that of her fictional character Anne.

2. The word "this" in line 2 refers to

(A) Canada
(B) the work of Mark Twain
(C) *Alice's Adventures in Wonderland*
(D) a Canadian children's classic

3. According to the passage, Montgomery was raised primarily

(A) in an orphanage
(B) by her grandparents
(C) by her mother
(D) by her father

4. Approximately when did Lucy Maud Montgomery write the two sequels to her book *Anne of Green Gables*?

(A) From 1874 to 1908
(B) From 1908 to 1911
(C) From 1911 to 1913
(D) From 1913 to 1918

5. The word "elderly" in line 10 is closest in meaning to

(A) kindly
(B) old
(C) friendly
(D) sly

6. In the *Anne* books, the main character lives in

(A) the town of Cavendish
(B) Saskatchewan
(C) the town of Avonlea
(D) Ontario

7. Which of the following can be concluded from the passage about the *Anne* books?

(A) They were at least partially autobiographical.
(B) They were influenced by the works of Mark Twain.
(C) They were not as successful as Montgomery's later works.
(D) They were not popular until after Montgomery had died.

8. The word "prominence" in line 13 is closest in meaning to

(A) reputation
(B) excellence
(C) effort
(D) permanence

9. Which of the following is closest in meaning to the word "character" in line 15?

(A) a person in a novel
(B) nature
(C) a written symbol
(D) location

10. All of the following have been based on the *Anne* books EXCEPT

(A) a television series
(B) movies
(C) a play
(D) a ballet

11. In line 16, the word "scour" could be replaced by which of the following without changing the meaning of the sentence?

(A) cleanse
(B) admire
(C) search
(D) request

QUESTIONS 12–23

Line Animals have an intuitive awareness of quantities. They know without analysis the difference between a number of objects and a smaller number. In his book *The Natural History of Selbourne*
(1786), the naturalist Gilbert White tells how he surreptitiously removed one egg a day from a
plover's nest, and how the mother laid another egg each day to make up for the missing one. He
5   noted that other species of birds ignore the absence of a single egg but abandon their nests if more
than one egg has been removed. It has also been noted by naturalists that a certain type of wasp
always provides five—never four, never six—caterpillars for each of their eggs so that their young
have something to eat when the eggs hatch. Research has also shown that both mice and pigeons
can be taught to distinguish between odd and even numbers of food pieces.
10   These and similar accounts have led some people to infer that creatures other than humans can
actually count. They also point to dogs that have been taught to respond to numerical questions with
the correct number of barks, or to horses that seem to solve arithmetic problems by stomping their
hooves the proper number of times.
        Animals respond to quantities only when they are connected to survival as a species—as in the
15   case of the eggs—or survival as individuals—as in the case of food. There is no transfer to other
situations or from concrete reality to the abstract notion of numbers. Animals can "count" only when
the objects are present and only when the numbers involved are small—not more than seven or
eight. In lab experiments, animals trained to "count" one kind of object were unable to count any
other type. The objects, not the numbers, are what interest them. Animals' admittedly remarkable
20   achievements simply do not amount to evidence of counting, nor do they reveal more than innate
instincts, refined by the genes of successive generations, or the results of clever, careful conditioning
by trainers.

12. What is the main idea of this passage?

(A) Careful training is required to teach animals to perform tricks involving numbers.
(B) Animals cannot "count" more than one kind of object.
(C) Of all animals, dogs and horses can count best.
(D) Although animals may be aware of quantities, they cannot actually count.

13. Why does the author refer to Gilbert Whites's book in line 2?

(A) To show how attitudes have changed since 1786.
(B) To contradict the idea that animals can count.
(C) To provide evidence that some birds are aware of quantities.
(D) To indicate that more research is needed in this field.

14. The word "surreptitiously" in line 3 is closest in meaning to

(A) quickly
(B) secretly
(C) occasionally
(D) stubbornly

15. The word "abandon" in line 5 is closest in meaning to

(A) vacate
(B) rebuild
(C) move
(D) guard

16. The word "odd," as used in line 9, refers to which of the following?

(A) unusual numbers
(B) numbers such as 1, 3, 5, and so on
(C) lucky numbers
(D) numbers such as 2, 4, 6, and so on

17. The author mentions that all of the following are aware of quantities in some way EXCEPT

(A) plovers
(B) mice
(C) caterpillars
(D) wasps

18. The word "accounts" in line 10 is closest in meaning to

(A) invoices
(B) reasons
(C) reports
(D) deceptions

19. According to information in the passage, which of the following is LEAST likely to occur as a result of animals' intuitive awareness of quantities?

(A) A pigeon is more attracted by a box containing two pieces of food than by a box containing one piece.
(B) When asked by its trainer how old it is, a monkey holds up five fingers.
(C) When one of its four kittens crawls away, a mother cat misses it and searches for the missing kitten.
(D) A lion follows one antelope instead of the herd of antelopes because it is easier to hunt a single prey.

20. How would the author probably characterize the people who are mentioned in line 10?

(A) As mistaken
(B) As demanding
(C) As clever
(D) As foolish

21. The word "admittedly" in line 19 is closest in meaning to

(A) improbably
(B) arguably
(C) apparently
(D) undeniably

22. In line 20, the word "they" refers to

(A) numbers
(B) animals
(C) achievements
(D) genes

23. Where in the passage does the author mention research that supports his own view of animals' inability to count?

(A) Lines 2–4
(B) Lines 8–9
(C) Lines 10–11
(D) Lines 18–19

QUESTIONS 24–33

Line   It would be hard to cite a development that has had more impact on American industry than the
Bessemer process of making steel. It made possible the production of low-cost steel and established
the foundation of the modern steel industry. In many ways it was responsible for the rapid industrialization of the United States that took place in the formative period of the late 1800s.

5   The first Bessemer plant in the United States was built in Wyandotte, Michigan, in 1864, near
the end of the Civil War. It was capable of producing only 2 tons of steel ingots at a time. The ingots
were rolled into rails—the first steel rails made in the United States. Acceptance of the process was
initially slow. By 1870, the annual output of Bessemer steel was a mere 42 thousand tons. Production
grew rapidly after about 1875, rising to 1.2 million tons in 1880, when it exceeded that of wrought
10   iron for the first time.

         The rise of the U.S. steel industry in the last quarter of the nineteenth century was brought
about largely by the demand for Bessemer steel rails for the nation's burgeoning rail network. Steel
rails were far more durable than those made of iron. Spurred by this demand, the U.S. steel industry
became the largest in the world in 1886, when it surpassed that of Great Britain.

15   The Bessemer process was the chief method of making steel until 1907, when it was overtaken
by the open-hearth process. By the 1950s, the Bessemer process accounted for less than 3 percent of
the total U.S. production.

24. With what topic is this passage mainly
concerned?

(A) The history of metal working
(B) A comparison of the U.S. and British
steel industries in the nineteenth
century
(C) The technical details of the Bessemer
process
(D) The effects of one method of making
steel

25. According to the passage, the Bessemer
process contributed to all of the following
EXCEPT

(A) the establishment of the modern steel
industry in the United States
(B) the manufacture of weapons during the
Civil War
(C) lowered costs for steel
(D) industrial development in the United
States during an important period

26. What can be inferred from the passage
about wrought iron?

(A) At one time, more of it was produced
than Bessemer steel.
(B) It is a by-product of the Bessemer
process.
(C) It was once primarily imported from
Great Britain.
(D) It later became a more important
product than Bessemer steel.

27. The word "burgeoning" in line 12 is closest
in meaning to

(A) overpowering
(B) planned
(C) expanding
(D) vital

28. According to the passage, why were
Bessemer steel rails used in place of iron
rails?

(A) They lasted longer.
(B) They did not have to be imported.
(C) They could be installed faster.
(D) They provided a smoother ride for
passengers.

29. The word "Spurred" in line 13 is closest in
meaning to which of the following?

(A) Driven
(B) Challenged
(C) Dominated
(D) Broken

30. According to the passage, in what year did
the steel industry of the United States begin
to produce more steel than that of Great
Britain?

(A) In 1864
(B) In 1875
(C) In 1880
(D) In 1886

31. What can be inferred about the steel industry in the United States during the 1950s?

(A) It had begun producing many new types of products.
(B) It was in a period of severe decline.
(C) It primarily involved methods of production other than the Bessemer product.
(D) It was becoming more and more important.

32. The paragraph following this one probably concerns

(A) innovations in the railroad industry
(B) the open-hearth method of making steel
(C) industrialization in the twentieth century
(D) new methods of making wrought iron

33. The author first begins to discuss the growth of the Bessemer process in

(A) lines 2–3
(B) lines 5–6
(C) lines 8–10
(D) lines 15–16

QUESTIONS 34–51

Line Nearly 515 blocks of San Francisco, including almost all of Nob Hill, were destroyed by the 1906 earthquake and fires. Many of San Francisco's "painted ladies"—its gaudy, nineteenth-century Victorian houses—were lost in the disaster. Today, some 14,000 surviving houses have been preserved, particularly in the Cow Hollow, Mission, Pacific Heights, and Alamo Square districts.

5 Distinguished by their design characteristics, three styles of San Franciscan Victorians can be found today. The Italianate, which flourished in the 1870s, is characterized by a flat roof, slim pillars flanking the front door, and bays with windows that slant inward. The ornamentation of these narrow row houses was patterned after features of the Roman Classical styles. The Stick style, which peaked in popularity during the 1880s, added ornate woodwork outlines to the doors and windows.

10 Other additions included the French cap, gables, and three-sided bays. Designs changed dramatically when the Queen Anne style became the rage in the 1890s. Turrets, towers, steep gabled roofs, and glass art windows distinguished Queen Anne houses from their predecessors.

In the period after the earthquake, the Victorians came to be regarded as impossibly old-fashioned, but beginning around 1960, owners began peeling off stucco, tearing off false fronts,

15 reapplying custom woodwork, and commissioning multi-hued paint jobs. Before long, many of these houses had been restored to their former splendor.

34. Which of the following is NOT one of the author's purposes in writing the passage?

(A) To talk about the restoration of Victorian houses in San Francisco in the 1960s.
(B) To discuss housing problems in San Francisco today.
(C) To briefly trace the history of Victorian houses in San Francisco.
(D) To categorize the three types of Victorian houses found in San Francisco.

35. The word "gaudy" in line 2 is closest in meaning to

(A) showy
(B) enormous
(C) antiquated
(D) simple

36. According to the passage, in what district of San Francisco are authentic Victorian houses LEAST likely to be found today?

(A) Cow Hollow
(B) Pacific Heights
(C) The Mission
(D) Nob Hill

37. According to the passage, which of the following styles of architecture was the last to become fashionable in San Francisco?

(A) Roman Classical
(B) Italianate
(C) Stick
(D) Queen Anne

38. As used in the second paragraph, the word "bays" refers to

(A) bodies of water
(B) colors
(C) architectural features
(D) trees

39. Which of the following is most likely to be seen only on a Queen Anne style house?

(A) a flat roof
(B) a tower
(C) a French cap
(D) gables

40. During which of the following periods were San Francisco's Victorian houses generally thought of as old-fashioned?

(A) from 1870 to 1890
(B) during the 1890s
(C) from 1907 to 1960
(D) during the 1960s

41. What can be inferred from the passage about Victorian houses after they had been restored?

(A) They were painted in many colors.
(B) They looked exactly like modern houses.
(C) They were covered with new fronts made of stucco.
(D) They were more attractive than the original houses.

QUESTIONS 42–50

Line   Sea otters dwell in the North Pacific. They are the largest of the mustelids, a group that also includes freshwater otters, weasels, and badgers. They are from 4 to 5 feet long and most weigh from 60 to 85 pounds. Large males may weigh 100 pounds or more.

Unlike most marine mammals, such as seals or dolphins, sea otters lack a layer of blubber, and
5   therefore have to eat up to 30 percent of their body weight a day in clams, crabs, fish, octopus, squids, and other delicacies to maintain body heat. Their voracious appetites do not create food shortages, though, because they are picky eaters, each animal preferring only a few food types. Thus no single type of food source is exhausted. Sea otters play an important environmental role by protecting forests of seaweed called kelp, which provide shelter and nutrients for many species.
10   Certain sea otters feast on invertebrates like sea urchins and abalones that destroy kelp.

Sea otters eat and sleep while floating on their backs, often on masses of kelp. They seldom come on shore. Sea otters keep warm by means of their luxuriant double-layered fur, the densest among animals. The soft outer fur forms a protective cover that keeps the fine underfur dry. One square inch of underfur contains up to 1 million hairs. Unfortunately, this essential feature almost led
15   to their extinction, as commercial hunters drastically reduced their numbers.

Under government protection, the sea otter population has recovered. While elated by the otters return, scientists are concerned about the California sea otter population growth of 5 percent a year, lagging behind the 18 percent a year rate among Alaska otters. Sea otters are extremely sensitive to pollution. In 1989, up to 5,000 sea otters perished when the Exxon Valdez spilled oil in Prince William Sound, Alaska.

42. According to the passage, what are mustelids?

   (A) A family of marine mammals that have blubber.
   (B) A type of sea otter.
   (C) A group of mammals that contains sea otters.
   (D) A kind of sea animal that includes clams, crabs, and many other creatures.

43. It can be inferred from that passage that, if a large male sea otter weighs 100 pounds, it must eat approximately how many pounds of food a day to maintain its body heat?

   (A) 5 pounds
   (B) 15 pounds
   (C) 30 pounds
   (D) 60 pounds

44. The author refers to sea otters as "picky eaters" (line 7) because

   (A) all sea otters eat many types of food
   (B) each sea otter eats only one type of food
   (C) all sea otters have voracious appetites
   (D) each sea otter eats only a few kinds of food

45. The word "exhausted" in line 8 is closest in meaning to

   (A) needed
   (B) used up
   (C) desired
   (D) tired out

46. According to the passage, which of the following best describes sea otters' relationship with kelp forests?

   (A) The kelp serves as food for the otters.
   (B) The otters protect the kelp by eating animals that destroy it.
   (C) The otters eliminate the kelp's source of nutrients.
   (D) The kelp is destroyed when the otters build shelters.

47. Which of the following could best replace the word "luxuriant" in line 12?

   (A) Expensive
   (B) Soft
   (C) Abundant
   (D) Attractive

48. According to the passage, the outer fur of sea otters

   (A) keeps the underfur from getting wet
   (B) seems finer than the underfur
   (C) is more desirable to hunters than the underfur
   (D) is not as soft as the underfur

49. The word "elated" in line 16 is closest in meaning to

   (A) disappointed
   (B) shocked
   (C) concerned
   (D) overjoyed

50. According to the passage, why are scientists concerned about the population of California sea otters?

   (A) It has been growing at too fast a rate.
   (B) Its growth rate has been steadily decreasing.
   (C) Its growth rate is not as fast as that of the Alaska sea otters.
   (D) It has been greatly reduced by oil spills and other forms of pollution.

THIS IS THE END OF SECTION 3, READING COMPREHENSION.
IF YOU FINISH BEFORE TIME IS CALLED, GO BACK AND CHECK YOUR WORK IN THIS SECTION ONLY.

Peterson's TOEFL CBT Success

Answer Sheet

Practice Test 3

Section 1: Listening Comprehension

1. (A) (B) (C) (D)
2. (A) (B) (C) (D)
3. (A) (B) (C) (D)
4. (A) (B) (C) (D)
5. (A) (B) (C) (D)
6. (A) (B) (C) (D)
7. (A) (B) (C) (D)
8. (A) (B) (C) (D)
9. (A) (B) (C) (D)
10. (A) (B) (C) (D)

11. (A) (B) (C) (D)
12. (A) (B) (C) (D)
13. (A) (B) (C) (D)
14. (A) (B) (C) (D)
15. (A) (B) (C) (D)
16. (A) (B) (C) (D)
17. (A) (B) (C) (D)
18. (A) (B) (C) (D)
19. (A) (B) (C) (D)
20. (A) (B) (C) (D)

21. (A) (B) (C) (D)
22. (A) (B) (C) (D)
23. (A) (B) (C) (D)
24. (A) (B) (C) (D)
25. (A) (B) (C) (D)
26. (A) (B) (C) (D)
27. (A) (B) (C) (D)
28. (A) (B) (C) (D)
29. (A) (B) (C) (D)
30. (A) (B) (C) (D)

31. (A) (B) (C) (D)
32. (A) (B) (C) (D)
33. (A) (B) (C) (D)
34. (A) (B) (C) (D)
35. (A) (B) (C) (D)
36. (A) (B) (C) (D)
37. (A) (B) (C) (D)
38. (A) (B) (C) (D)
39. (A) (B) (C) (D)
40. (A) (B) (C) (D)

41. (A) (B) (C) (D)
42. (A) (B) (C) (D)
43. (A) (B) (C) (D)
44. (A) (B) (C) (D)
45. (A) (B) (C) (D)
46. (A) (B) (C) (D)
47. (A) (B) (C) (D)
48. (A) (B) (C) (D)
49. (A) (B) (C) (D)
50. (A) (B) (C) (D)

Section 2: Structure and Written Expression

1. Ⓐ Ⓑ Ⓒ Ⓓ	21. Ⓐ Ⓑ Ⓒ Ⓓ	31. Ⓐ Ⓑ Ⓒ Ⓓ
2. Ⓐ Ⓑ Ⓒ Ⓓ	22. Ⓐ Ⓑ Ⓒ Ⓓ	32. Ⓐ Ⓑ Ⓒ Ⓓ
3. Ⓐ Ⓑ Ⓒ Ⓓ	23. Ⓐ Ⓑ Ⓒ Ⓓ	33. Ⓐ Ⓑ Ⓒ Ⓓ
4. Ⓐ Ⓑ Ⓒ Ⓓ	24. Ⓐ Ⓑ Ⓒ Ⓓ	34. Ⓐ Ⓑ Ⓒ Ⓓ
5. Ⓐ Ⓑ Ⓒ Ⓓ	25. Ⓐ Ⓑ Ⓒ Ⓓ	35. Ⓐ Ⓑ Ⓒ Ⓓ
6. Ⓐ Ⓑ Ⓒ Ⓓ	26. Ⓐ Ⓑ Ⓒ Ⓓ	36. Ⓐ Ⓑ Ⓒ Ⓓ
7. Ⓐ Ⓑ Ⓒ Ⓓ	27. Ⓐ Ⓑ Ⓒ Ⓓ	37. Ⓐ Ⓑ Ⓒ Ⓓ
8. Ⓐ Ⓑ Ⓒ Ⓓ	28. Ⓐ Ⓑ Ⓒ Ⓓ	38. Ⓐ Ⓑ Ⓒ Ⓓ
9. Ⓐ Ⓑ Ⓒ Ⓓ	29. Ⓐ Ⓑ Ⓒ Ⓓ	39. Ⓐ Ⓑ Ⓒ Ⓓ
10. Ⓐ Ⓑ Ⓒ Ⓓ	30. Ⓐ Ⓑ Ⓒ Ⓓ	40. Ⓐ Ⓑ Ⓒ Ⓓ

11. Ⓐ Ⓑ Ⓒ Ⓓ
12. Ⓐ Ⓑ Ⓒ Ⓓ
13. Ⓐ Ⓑ Ⓒ Ⓓ
14. Ⓐ Ⓑ Ⓒ Ⓓ
15. Ⓐ Ⓑ Ⓒ Ⓓ
16. Ⓐ Ⓑ Ⓒ Ⓓ
17. Ⓐ Ⓑ Ⓒ Ⓓ
18. Ⓐ Ⓑ Ⓒ Ⓓ
19. Ⓐ Ⓑ Ⓒ Ⓓ
20. Ⓐ Ⓑ Ⓒ Ⓓ

Section 3: Reading Comprehension

1. Ⓐ Ⓑ Ⓒ Ⓓ   21. Ⓐ Ⓑ Ⓒ Ⓓ   41. Ⓐ Ⓑ Ⓒ Ⓓ
2. Ⓐ Ⓑ Ⓒ Ⓓ   22. Ⓐ Ⓑ Ⓒ Ⓓ   42. Ⓐ Ⓑ Ⓒ Ⓓ
3. Ⓐ Ⓑ Ⓒ Ⓓ   23. Ⓐ Ⓑ Ⓒ Ⓓ   43. Ⓐ Ⓑ Ⓒ Ⓓ
4. Ⓐ Ⓑ Ⓒ Ⓓ   24. Ⓐ Ⓑ Ⓒ Ⓓ   44. Ⓐ Ⓑ Ⓒ Ⓓ
5. Ⓐ Ⓑ Ⓒ Ⓓ   25. Ⓐ Ⓑ Ⓒ Ⓓ   45. Ⓐ Ⓑ Ⓒ Ⓓ
6. Ⓐ Ⓑ Ⓒ Ⓓ   26. Ⓐ Ⓑ Ⓒ Ⓓ   46. Ⓐ Ⓑ Ⓒ Ⓓ
7. Ⓐ Ⓑ Ⓒ Ⓓ   27. Ⓐ Ⓑ Ⓒ Ⓓ   47. Ⓐ Ⓑ Ⓒ Ⓓ
8. Ⓐ Ⓑ Ⓒ Ⓓ   28. Ⓐ Ⓑ Ⓒ Ⓓ   48. Ⓐ Ⓑ Ⓒ Ⓓ
9. Ⓐ Ⓑ Ⓒ Ⓓ   29. Ⓐ Ⓑ Ⓒ Ⓓ   49. Ⓐ Ⓑ Ⓒ Ⓓ
10. Ⓐ Ⓑ Ⓒ Ⓓ   30. Ⓐ Ⓑ Ⓒ Ⓓ   50. Ⓐ Ⓑ Ⓒ Ⓓ

11. Ⓐ Ⓑ Ⓒ Ⓓ   31. Ⓐ Ⓑ Ⓒ Ⓓ
12. Ⓐ Ⓑ Ⓒ Ⓓ   32. Ⓐ Ⓑ Ⓒ Ⓓ
13. Ⓐ Ⓑ Ⓒ Ⓓ   33. Ⓐ Ⓑ Ⓒ Ⓓ
14. Ⓐ Ⓑ Ⓒ Ⓓ   34. Ⓐ Ⓑ Ⓒ Ⓓ
15. Ⓐ Ⓑ Ⓒ Ⓓ   35. Ⓐ Ⓑ Ⓒ Ⓓ
16. Ⓐ Ⓑ Ⓒ Ⓓ   36. Ⓐ Ⓑ Ⓒ Ⓓ
17. Ⓐ Ⓑ Ⓒ Ⓓ   37. Ⓐ Ⓑ Ⓒ Ⓓ
18. Ⓐ Ⓑ Ⓒ Ⓓ   38. Ⓐ Ⓑ Ⓒ Ⓓ
19. Ⓐ Ⓑ Ⓒ Ⓓ   39. Ⓐ Ⓑ Ⓒ Ⓓ
20. Ⓐ Ⓑ Ⓒ Ⓓ   40. Ⓐ Ⓑ Ⓒ Ⓓ

Practice Tests

TAPESCRIPTS AND ANSWER KEYS

Practice Test 1

SECTION 1: LISTENING COMPREHENSION

PART A

Answer Key

1. C	11. C	21. A	31. C	41. A
2. A	12. C	22. B	32. B	42. B
3. B	13. D	23. B	33. B	43. D
4. A	14. C	24. A	34. A	44. C
5. D	15. A	25. D	35. B	45. C
6. D	16. A	26. C	36. C	46. A
7. B	17. D	27. D	37. B	47. A
8. C	18. A	28. C	38. D	48. C
9. B	19. B	29. B	39. D	49. D
10. D	20. D	30. A	40. B	50. A

TAPESCRIPT

1. F1: Excuse me—do you know which apartment Sally Hill lives in?
   M1: Sally Hall? As far as I know, she doesn't live in this apartment complex at all.
   M2: What does the man imply about Sally Hill?

2. F2: Roger, may I use your phone? I think mine is out of order.
   M1: Feel free.
   M2: What does Roger tell the woman?

3. F1: Were you able to solve that math problem?
   M1: To tell you the truth, I found it simply impossible.
   M2: What does the man say about the math problem?

4. F1: Uh, oh. Your roommate's making dinner again. Your kitchen is going to look like a tornado hit it.
   M1: Maybe not. Last night he cooked dinner and left the kitchen spick-and-span.
   M2: What does the man say his roommate did?

5. F1: How did you learn so much about trees?
   M1: Mostly from my father—he studied forestry in college.
   M2: How did the man learn about trees?

6. (RING . . . RING . . . SOUND OF PHONE BEING PICKED UP)
   M1: Hello.
   F2: Hi, Tom, this is Brenda. Since you couldn't come to class today, I just thought I'd call to tell you what Professor Barclay told us. He said we're going to have to write a research paper.
   M1: Really? And how long do we have to finish it?
   M2: What does Tom ask Brenda?

7. M1: Julie certainly seems to like classical music.
    F2: She doesn't like just *any* classical music.
    M2: What does the woman imply about Julie?

8. F1: How did you do on Professor Dixon's history test?
    M1: Probably not too well. I skipped a couple of questions, and I didn't have time to go back to them.
    M2: What does the man say about the history test?

9. M1: I can't seem to get the lid off this glass jar.
    F2: Maybe you could heat it in some warm water.
    M2: What does the woman suggest?

10. M1: This desk must be an expensive antique.
    F2: It may look like that, but I got it for next to nothing.
    M2: What does the woman say about the desk?

11. M2: Traffic downtown was *terrible* today!
    F1: You don't have to tell *me*!
    M2: What does the woman imply?

12. F1: I wish my classes were over so I could get out and enjoy the sunshine.
    M1: Nice out there, isn't it?
    M2: What does the man mean?

13. M1: Gary's using that old tape player of yours.
    F2: He's welcome to it.
    M2: What does the woman mean?

14. F1: I'm going to make a run for it. You don't happen to have an umbrella I can borrow, do you?
    M1: No—but here's a newspaper.
    M2: What does the man imply the woman should do with the newspaper?

15. M1: I think Ed is the best choice for president of the student assembly.
    F2: So do I—now that Margaret's dropped out of the race.
    M2: What does the woman mean?

16. M1: Did you paint your apartment by yourself?
    F1: Actually, I got my brother to help—he owed me a favor.
    M2: What does the woman mean?

17. M1: I'd like to go swimming this afternoon, but it's such a long walk to the lake.
    F2: I know a shortcut. Let me show you on this map.
    M2: What does the woman offer to do for the man?

18. M1: I can't tell if this picture is straight or not.
    F2: I'll hold it while you stand back and take a look.
    M2: What are these people doing with the picture?

19. F1: I'm going to Stephanie's house. I have an assignment to complete, and I need to use her computer.
    M1: Why don't you buy one of your own? Think how much time you could save.
    M2: What does the man suggest the woman do?

20. F1: From what I saw, your volleyball team needs a little more practice.
    M1: Only if we want to win some games!
    M2: What does the man imply?

21. F2: Have you seen Shelly recently? The last time I spoke to her, she said she hadn't been feeling too well.

M1: Well, when I saw her this morning, she was the picture of health.

M2: What does the man say about Shelly?

22. F1: Everyone's getting a little impatient. Can't we call this meeting to order?

M1: Once Lou get's here, we can.

M2: What does the man mean?

23. M1: Mary Ann, are you going to buy those sunglasses you looked at?

F2: I wouldn't buy *that* pair even if I could afford them.

M2: What does Mary Ann say about the sunglasses?

24. F1: You can't expect to become a tennis pro after just a few lessons, Ken.

M1: I shouldn't have had such high hopes, I suppose.

M2: What did Ken probably expect?

25. F2: We only have a few more points to talk over.

M1: Good, because I need to wrap this up soon.

M2: What does the man want to do?

26. F2: Can I help you?

M1: I'd just like a couple of books of matches, please.

M2: What does the man mean?

27. M1: Should I take California Street or Oak Street to get downtown?

F1: What difference does it make? It's the same distance no matter how you go.

M2: What does the woman mean?

28. M2: Did you hear the announcement?

F1: Yes, and I could hardly believe my ears!

M2: What does the woman imply about the announcement?

29. M2: Brian, could you handle this suitcase too?

M1: How many hands do you think I have?

F2: What does Brian mean?

30. F1: I'm so glad I can go camping this weekend!

M1: Then you don't have to study for that physics test after all?

M2: What had the man originally thought about the woman?

PART B

Questions 31 to 34: Listen to the following conversation:

F1: Walter, why haven't you been coming to Professor Crosley's anthropology class?

M1: What do you mean? I've been there every morning!

F1: Every morning? But . . . oh, I get it—you must be in the professor's morning class in cultural anthropology. I'm in her afternoon class in social anthropology. So tell me, how do you like her class?

M1: Oh, it's very interesting. So far, we've been studying the art, the architecture, and the tools of different cultures. And this Saturday, our class is going down to the local museum. They're having an exhibit of the artifacts of the early inhabitants of this area.

F1: Your class has quite a different focus from mine. We're studying social relations in groups. For example, this week we've been talking about marriage customs and family life in a number of societies—including our own.

M1: So what's your opinion of Professor Crosley?

F1: Well, she asks her students to do a lot of work—we're going to have two tests and two research papers. But she's a fascinating lecturer. I've never taken an anthropology course before, but I'm glad I decided to take her course.

M1: Yeah, same for me. In fact, I never thought of anthropology as an interesting subject, but now I sure do.

31. What do the two speakers have in common?
32. When does the *woman's* class meet?
33. Which of the following topics would most likely be discussed in the *man's* class?
34. What had the man's opinion of anthropology been *before* this term?

Questions 35 to 38: Listen to the following phone conversation:

(*RING . . . RING . . . SOUND OF PHONE BEING PICKED UP*)

F1: Hello, this is WBCL Community Television studios. How may I help you?

M1: Hello. Uh, I'm calling because I saw an advertisement in the campus newspaper. It said there was a summer internship available for a student who wants to work on your local news program.

F1: Right. But you do realize that all of our interns are volunteers, right? It's an unpaid position.

M1: Oh, sure, I understand that. I just want to get some experience working for a television news program. You see, I'm thinking about a career in television news production after I get my degree.

F1: Oh? Are you majoring in telecommunications?

M1: No, in journalism, but I've taken some telecommunications courses.

F1: I see. Well, you'll need to talk to Ms. Wagner. She's in charge of the internship program. But first, you'll need to come here to fill out an application form. Can you drop by the studio later today?

35. Where does the woman work?
36. Why is the man applying for this position?
37. What is the man majoring in at the university?
38. What does the man need to do next in order to get the position?

PART C

Questions 39 to 42: Listen to the following lecture:

M2: How many of you were at the football game Saturday night? Did you notice the blimp circling the stadium? Today's blimps are much smaller descendants of the giant airships—sometimes called zeppelins—that were used in the early twentieth century. Like those zeppelins, blimps are lighter-than-air aircraft. But blimps differ from zeppelins in a number of ways. First, as I said, they are quite a bit smaller. The old airships were as long as football fields. And unlike zeppelins, blimps do not contain an internal metal frame. That's why blimps are sometimes called "nonrigid" airships. And blimps are a lot safer than the old zeppelins. That's because they use nonflammable helium in place of hydrogen to provide lift.

As you may know, the age of the airship ended when the famous German airship *Van Hindenburg* exploded disastrously at Lakehurst, New Jersey, in 1937. I say that airship travel ended then, but some engineers believe that large, rigid airships will fly again. These airships of the future could be equipped with jet engines and filled with helium. Although they wouldn't be as fast as modern airplanes, they would be much more fuel efficient.

39. What is the main topic of this talk?
40. Which of the following aircraft is classified as "nonrigid?"
41. What important event in the history of airships took place at Lakehurst, New Jersey, in 1937?
42. According to the talk, what advantage would the airships of the future have over jet airplanes?

Questions 43 to 46: Listen to the following talk:

F2: Twice a year, all the clocks in the United States are changed by one hour. In the spring, clocks are moved ahead an hour. This is called daylight savings time. In the fall, clocks are set back an hour to standard time. People remember how to change their clocks by remembering this saying: Spring forward, fall back. It seems Benjamin Franklin was the first person to propose the idea of daylight savings time, back in the 1790s. At the time, people thought he was joking. They couldn't believe he was serious. Many years later, during World War I, people realized what an innovative idea he'd had. In the spring and summer, the sun rises earlier. By moving the clock ahead, people can take advantage of the extra daylight and save energy. Energy is an important resource, of course, especially during wartime. The United States operated on daylight savings time during World War I and again during World War II. After that, some parts of the country observed daylight savings time and some didn't. Beginning and ending dates varied from place to place. This confusion ended in 1966, when the Congress passed the Uniform Time Act, standardizing the process and making daylight savings time a federal law. Since then, some lawmakers have proposed that the United States go to year-round daylight savings time.

43. What is the main topic of this talk?

44. According to the speaker, when are clocks in the United States set *back*?

45. According to the speaker, how would most people probably have characterized Benjamin Franklin's plan for daylight savings time when it was first proposed?

46. According to the speaker, what was the effect of the Uniform Time Act of 1966?

Questions 47 to 50: Listen to the following radio announcement:

M1: This week, the city will begin a new program of curbside recycling. If you take your recyclable materials out to the street, the city will haul them away in trucks to be recycled. At present, you can recycle newspapers, aluminum cans, and glass containers. The trucks will *not* pick up plastic bottles. However, if you want to recycle plastic bottles, you can take them to the city recycling center on Pine Street. If you live in the north or west side of town, trucks will pick up your recyclables on Monday. If you live in the east or south part of town, your recyclables will be picked up on Wednesday. If you live in the central section of town, your pickup day is Friday. For more details, see the map in today's newspaper. And remember, when it comes to newspaper, aluminum, and glass, don't throw it away—recycle it!

47. What is the main topic of this talk?

48. Which of the following must be brought to the city's facility on Pine Street to be recycled?

49. In which part of town are recyclables picked up on Friday?

50. To get more information, what does the speaker suggest?

End of Tape 3, Side B.

SECTION 2: STRUCTURE AND WRITTEN EXPRESSION

Answer Key

Structure

1.	C	4.	A	7.	B	10.	C	13.	C
2.	C	5.	C	8.	A	11.	B	14.	C
3.	C	6.	B	9.	A	12.	A	15.	D

Written Expression

16.	A	21.	B	26.	A	31.	C	36.	B
17.	C	22.	D	27.	D	32.	C	37.	B
18.	B	23.	C	28.	B	33.	C	38.	D
19.	C	24.	D	29.	A	34.	D	39.	C
20.	B	25.	A	30.	B	35.	C	40.	B

EXPLANATION: WRITTEN EXPRESSION ITEMS

16. In order to be parallel with the other adjectives in the series (*harder* and *more resistant*) the comparative form *lighter* must be used.

17. The correct superlative form is *largest*.

18. The adjective form *destructive* is required in place of the noun form.

19. The correct pattern is *both . . . and*.

20. The correct form of the infinitive (*to play*) is needed.

21. The correct word order is preposition + relative pronoun: *across which*.

22. Both the noun phrase (*these craftsmen*) and the pronoun refer to the same person, so the reflexive pronoun *themselves* should be used.

23. The singular form of the verb, *was*, should be used to agree with the singular subject *influence*.

24. The pronoun subject *they* is used unnecessarily and should be omitted.

25. The relative word *where* must be used to describe a place. (*When* is used to describe a time.)

26. With countable nouns such as *mammals*, the word *many* is used.

27. In order to agree with a plural noun (*sharks*), the possessive adjective *their* should be plural.

28. The correct word order is adjective + enough: *dense enough*.

29. The adjective form (*commercial*) is required.

30. *Such . . . that* is used with an adjective + noun. (*So . . . that* is used when an adjective appears alone.)

31. The noun form *ability* is required in place of the adjective form.

32. The correct verb is *make*.

33. In order to be parallel with the other items in the series (*physics* and *mathematics*), the name of the field must be used: *chemistry*.

34. The adjective *expert* should not be pluralized.

35. The correct word order is *almost exactly*.

36. The past tense form is required: *became*.

37. The word *lot* should not be pluralized.

38. The word *ago* is used unnecessarily.

39. The preposition *for* is used with the adjective *responsible*.

40. The noun form *collection* should be used in place of the gerund.

SECTION 3: READING COMPREHENSION

Answer Key

1. D	11. D	21. C	31. A	41. C
2. A	12. B	22. B	32. D	42. B
3. B	13. C	23. C	33. C	43. D
4. A	14. B	24. D	34. A	44. A
5. D	15. A	25. A	35. B	45. B
6. C	16. A	26. B	36. A	46. C
7. B	17. A	27. B	37. D	47. D
8. C	18. C	28. C	38. A	48. C
9. A	19. D	29. D	39. B	49. B
10. A	20. D	30. D	40. C	50. A

1. The primary purpose of this passage is to detail the stages of the Sun's life in the future.

2. The word "powered" is closest in meaning to "fueled."

3. The word "state" is closest in meaning to "condition" as it is used in the passage.

4. The Sun has existed in its present state for about 4 billion, 600 million years (lines 2–3). It is expected to become a red giant in about 5 billion years. Therefore, it is about halfway through its life as a yellow dwarf.

5. Line 5 states that "the core of the Sun will shrink and become hotter."

6. The second paragraph describes the process by which the Sun becomes a red giant star. The last sentence of that paragraph states: "Temperatures on the Earth will become too hot for life to exist."

7. Lines 10–11 indicate that the Sun will be a white dwarf "After it shrinks to about the size of the Earth." Line 3 indicates that the Sun today is thousands of times larger than the Earth. Therefore, the Sun will be thousands of times smaller than it is today.

8. According to the passage, the Sun is now a yellow dwarf star; it will then expand to a red giant star, shrink to a white dwarf star, and finally cool to a black dwarf.

9. The word "eject" has the same meaning as "throw off."

10. The reference is to the planet Earth.

11. The tone is scientifically objective. Although the passage describes the end of the Earth, that event is so far in the future that the author's tone is dispassionate.

12. Washington was one of the first persons to realize the importance of canals and headed the first company formed to build a canal, indicating that he was a pioneer in canal construction. Choice (C) is incorrect because the canal was never finished.

13. The word "possibility" is closest in meaning to "feasibility."

14. According to lines 7–9, the canal linked Albany on the Hudson River with Buffalo on Lake Erie.

15. The word "relatively" is closest in meaning to "comparatively."

16. The word "intermittent" is closest in meaning to "on-again-, off-again."

17. According to the passage, the governor of New York "persuaded the state to finance and build the Canal" (line 15).

18. The cost had been estimated at $5 million (line 13) but actually cost $2 million more (line 13), a total of $7 million.

19. The word "fees" is closest in meaning to the word "tolls."

20. According to lines 19-21, the canal "allowed New York to supplant (replace) Boston, Philadelphia, and other Eastern cities as the chief center of both domestic and foreign commerce." The other effects are mentioned in the fourth paragraph.

21. Line 24 indicates that the expansion of the canal would have been warranted "had it not been for the development of the railroads." (This means, "if the railroads had not been developed.") The railroads must have taken so much traffic away from the canal that the expansion was no longer needed.

22. The word "warranted" most nearly means "justified."

23. The passage begins to discuss the actual construction of the Erie Canal in line 11.

24. The passage mainly deals with the distress signals of trees. Choices (B) and (C) concern minor details. There is no information about (A).

25. The reference is to "trees" in line 2.

26. The word "dehydrated" has the same meaning as the word "parched."

27. The word "plight" means "condition."

28. The trees' signals are in the 50–500-kilohertz range; the unaided human ear can detect no more than 20 kilohertz (lines 6-7).

29. The word "broken" is closest in meaning to "fractured."

30. The signals are caused when the water column inside tubes in trees break, "a result of too little water" (line 10).

31. In the context of the passage, "pick up" means "perceive."

32. Choices (A) and (B) are mentioned in lines 14-15; (C) is mentioned throughout the passage; there is no mention of (D).

33. Lines 12-13 says, "Researchers are now running tests," implying that research is continuing.

34. The passage explains the difference between two concepts, analogy and homology, and gives examples of both.

35. Line 1 state, "The concepts . . . are probably easier to exemplify than define."

36. The word "rigid" is closest in meaning to "inflexible." This means that there are certain principles that cannot be altered.

37. Analogous organs are those that perform the same functions but are not derived from the same embryological structures. The structures given in (D) most likely demonstrate this relationship in that they both provide the same functions—locomotion and support—but are not otherwise related.

38. Homologous organs "are genetically related," according to line 9.

39. In the context of the passage, the term "structures" refers to different physical parts of animals: wings, limbs, fins, and so on.

40. The word "sense" is closest in meaning to "meaning."

41. The author begins to discuss homology in the sentence beginning "In contrast . . ." in line 6.

42. The purpose of the passage is primarily to describe Charlie Chaplin's movie *Modern Times*.

43. Line 2 states that Chaplin "was motivated to make the film by a reporter" during an interview.

44. The word "suddenly" is closest in meaning to the word "abruptly."

45. According to line 10, "scenes of factory interiors account for only about one third of the footage." Therefore, about two thirds of the film must have ben shot OUTSIDE the factory.

46. The phrase "losing his mind" means "going insane" (with the pressure of work).

47. The reference is to the phrase "another popular scene" in line 16.

48. Lines 16-17 state: "This (the scene) serves to illustrate people's utter helplessness in the face of machines that are meant to serve their basic needs."

49. The word "complete" is closest in meaning to that of "utter."

50. The film does NOT offer "a radical social message," and so would not be considered "revolutionary," (A). Line 9 states that "Chaplin prefers to entertain rather than lecture"; thus it is "entertaining," (B). Lines 12-13 mention that people who have seen the film cannot forget certain scenes, and so it is "memorable," (C). According to lines 8-9, the opening scene's "rather bitter note of criticism . . . is replaced by a gentler note of satire;" therefore, the author would consider the film "satirical," (D).

Practice Test 2

SECTION 1: LISTENING COMPREHENSION

PART A

Answer Key

1.	B	11.	C	21.	C	31.	A	41.	C
2.	D	12.	B	22.	A	32.	D	42.	C
3.	A	13.	C	23.	A	33.	A	43.	B
4.	A	14.	D	24.	B	34.	C	44.	C
5.	B	15.	C	25.	C	35.	B	45.	D
6.	A	16.	A	26.	B	36.	D	46.	D
7.	D	17.	D	27.	D	37.	A	47.	A
8.	A	18.	C	28.	B	38.	B	48.	C
9.	C	19.	C	29.	C	39.	A	49.	D
10.	B	20.	A	30.	D	40.	B	50.	C

TAPESCRIPT

1. **F1:** So are you still planning to fly to Orlando for your vacation?
   M1: Not the way airfares have been going up!
   F2: What does the man mean?

2. **M1:** I can't believe we have to buy eight books for Professor McKnight's class. That's going to cost a fortune.
   F1: But four of them are inexpensive paperbacks.
   F2: What does the woman tell the man?

3. **M1:** You still planning to play golf this afternoon?
   F1: I don't think so. It looks a lot like rain to me.
   F2: What does the woman mean?

4. **F1:** Can everyone in the class meet in the library on Friday?
   M1: Everyone but Lisa.
   F2: What does the man mean?

5. **M1:** I went for a hike in the woods and now my legs are all scratched up from the thorns.
   F1: Maybe next time you'll wear a pair of long pants when you go hiking.
   F2: What can be inferred about the man?

6. **F1:** So, Rob, what are you going to do with your free afternoon?
   M1: I thought I'd pay Michelle a visit.
   F2: What does Rob mean?

7. **F1:** There won't be enough chairs in the auditorium.
   M2: We could always rent more.
   F2: What does the man suggest?

8.   F1: What does that sign say?
      M2: Uh, I can't quite make it out either.
      F2: What does the man tell the woman?

9.   M1: It's getting harder and harder to find affordable housing near campus.
      F1: Isn't it, though!
      F2: What does the woman mean?

10. M1: I'm going to go now.
      F1: You'd better hurry. They're almost sold out of tickets for Saturday's game.
      F2: Where is the man probably going to go?

11. M1: We raised some money this week, but it was just a drop in the bucket.
      F1: Maybe we'll do better next week.
      F2: What is the problem?

12. M2: Tell me, what do you think of our waiter?
      F1: Kind of rude, isn't he?
      F2: What is the woman's opinion of the waiter?

13. F1: Tony spent the whole weekend fishing, and he didn't catch one single fish.
      M2: I'm not too surprised.
      F2: What does the man mean?

14. M1: I need a few more minutes to fill out this form.
      F1: Take your time.
      F2: What does the woman tell the man?

15. M2: Has Russell ever been to Seattle?
      F1: Once before, I believe.
      F2: What does the woman say about Russell?

16. F1: Is Lily still planning to study overseas?
      M1: No, her parents threw cold water on that plan.
      F2: What did Lily's parents do?

17. F2: David, do you think that the music was too loud?
      M2: Well, no—not if you wanted the people across town to hear it!
      F2: What does David imply about the music?

18. F1: This was *supposed* to be a quiet, relaxing weekend.
      M1: But it didn't quite turn out that way, did it?
      F2: What does the man imply about the weekend?

19. F1: The front door to the lab was unlocked on Saturday morning.
      M2: Really? That's strange.
      F2: What can be inferred from this conversation?

20. M1: This insurance policy has gotten so expensive, I can hardly afford it.
      F1: Yeah, but you can't really afford *not* to have it, can you?
      F2: What does the woman tell the man?

21. F1: Did Morgan pass the test?
      M2: Pass it? With flying colors!
      F2: What does the man say about Morgan?

22. M1: Oh, no, it's *still* out of order!
      F1: I guess we'll just have to walk up all those stairs again today.
      F2: What are these two people talking about?

23. M1: Did you take your raincoat to the cleaner's, Meg?
  F1: No, I had to go to class, so I got my sister to take it.
  F2: What happened to the raincoat?

24. M1: This schedule says we have to attend an orientation session before we can register.
  M2: That's just for new students.
  F2: What can be inferred about these two speakers?

25. F1: So, Doug, are you looking forward to helping your brother move this weekend?
  M1: Well, there *are* a couple of other ways I'd rather spend my weekend!
  F2: What does Doug mean?

26. F1: This coin you found is worth a lot. It's quite rare.
  M2: Oh, an expert, are you?
  F2: What does the man imply about the woman?

27. F2: That sure is a catchy song.
  F1: You're telling me. The melody's been running though my head all week.
  M2: What can be concluded about the song?

28. F1: You look great in this picture, Larry. Look how you're smiling!
  M1: So you *did* take that picture of me after all!
  F2: What had the man *originally* assumed?

29. F1: Hotel rooms along the beach must be very expensive.
  M2: Not now. During the off-season, they're dirt cheap.
  F2: What does the man say about the hotel rooms?

30. M1: Who was that woman you were talking to at the reception?
  F1: That was Carol Donovan. She was my sister's roommate in college.
  F2: How is the woman acquainted with Carol Donovan?

PART B

Questions 31 to 34: Listen to the following phone conversation:

(RING . . . RING . . . SOUND OF PHONE BEING PICKED UP)

  M2: Hello, *Campus Daily*, advertising department. This is Mark speaking.
  F2: Hi. I'm calling to place a couple of ads.
  M2: Sure. Under what classification?
  F2: Well, I wanted one in the "Roommate Wanted" section.
  M2: All right. And how would you like that to read?
  F2: OK, it should read, "Female roommate wanted for pleasant, sunny two-bedroom apartment on Elliewood Avenue, three blocks from campus. Share rent and utilities. Available September 1. Call between 5 and 9 p.m. and ask for Cecilia."
  M2: Fine, and what about your other ad?
  F2: That one I'd like under "Merchandise for Sale," and I'd like it to read "Matching blue and white sofa and easy chair, excellent condition, $350 or best offer. Call between 5 and 9 p.m. and ask for Cecilia." Did you get all that?
  M2: Uh-huh. You'll want your phone numbers on these, right?
  F2: Oh, sure. Thanks for reminding me—it's 555-6972.
  M2: And how long do you want these ads to run?
  F2: For a week, I suppose. How much would that be?
  M2: It's $5 a week per line. Each of your ads will take up three lines, so that's $15 per ad.
  31. Where does Mark work?
  32. Which of the following is Cecilia trying to find?
  33. Which of the following does Cecilia *initially* forget to tell Mark?
  34. What is the total amount that the two advertisements will cost for one week?

Questions 35 to 38: Listen to the following conversation:

M1: I'm sorry I'm late, Cindy.

F1: That's all right, Joe. My house isn't that easy to find. But you know, you wouldn't have gotten lost if you'd had a "smart" car.

M1: A smart car? What's that.

F1: I just read a magazine article about some new technology that can make a car smart. One device is a computerized map display and a synthesized voice. You just enter the address where you want to go, and the voice tells you how to get there, street by street.

M1: Hey, that's just like my brother. He never gets lost, and he's always telling me the best route. So what else will smart cars be able to do?

F1: Well, the article said that they'll be equipped with radar warning systems that will warn drivers if they're getting too close to other cars with an alarm signal, and they'll even put on the brakes if the drivers don't.

M1: Tell me, Cindy, will these cars be smart enough to fill themselves up with gas?

F1: Not that I know of. Why do you ask?

M1: Well, I'm not late because I got lost—I'm late because I ran out of gas on the way over here.

35. Where did Cindy get her information about "smart" cars?

36. According to Cindy, what is the purpose of the synthesized voice on "smart" cars?

37. What does Joe imply about his brother?

38. Why was Joe delayed on his way to Cindy's house?

PART C

Questions 39 to 42: Listen to a talk given at a ceremony:

M2: Good evening. I'd like to welcome the president of Colton College, the chancellors, the administrators, my fellow faculty members, and the students to the Academic Excellence Awards Night. Our first award, for Faculty Member of the Year, goes to Professor Patricia Callaghan. I'm particularly pleased that this year's winner is from my own department. Professor Callaghan has been at Colton College for a total of eight years now—two as a graduate student and six as a faculty member. She has consistently received top evaluations from the students as well as from her department head. Her papers on historical economics are well respected by all of her colleagues—including myself, if I may say so—and this year she received a government grant to continue her work of generating computer models of the economy. Please join me, ladies and gentlemen, in giving a round of applause to Professor Callaghan.

39. What is the purpose of this talk?

40. Who is the speaker?

41. What subject does Professor Callaghan probably teach?

42. How many years has Professor Callaghan been a teacher at Colton College?

Questions 43 to 46: Listen to the following announcement:

M1: Good morning, listeners. This is KUNI campus radio with the local news. Did you have any trouble getting around in traffic downtown this morning? Several streets are blocked off because of the bicycle races that are taking place today and for the next four days. Some races will be taking place downtown, some in Woodland Park on the north side of town, and some on campus. Long-distance road races will be held in the countryside nearby. Our own university is fielding a team to compete for prizes and glory, so come on out and cheer them on. And say, if you found yourself caught in traffic this morning, I suggest that you ride your own bike to class or to work tomorrow.

43. Who is the speaker?

44. What is the main topic of the talk?

45. According to the speaker, where will the long-distance road races be held?

46. What does the speaker suggest that his listeners do the next morning?

Questions 47 to 50: Listen to the following lecture about photorealistic art:

F1: Good morning, class. Today we'll continue our study of twentieth-century art movements with a discussion of photorealism, a style popular in the 1960's and 1970's. Painters who worked in this style realistically portrayed their subjects down to the smallest detail, and so their paintings resembled photographs in many respects. These painters usually chose subjects that were interesting only because they were so ordinary: a closed-down gas station, an old man waiting for a bus, a dilapidated billboard. Sculptors who worked in this style, such as Duane Hanson, created life-size sculptures of very ordinary people—construction workers, tourists, sales clerks, homeless people. His sculptures are so lifelike that sometimes visitors to a gallery or museum will try to engage them in a conversation. Now we're going to look at some slides of various works of photorealism. I'd like all of you to take notes while you're viewing the slides. And then tonight, I'd like you to write a short paper describing your reactions to these works.

47. Where was this talk probably given?
48. Which of the following would be the most likely subject of a photorealistic painting?
49. According to the speaker, why are the works of sculptor Duane Hanson so remarkable?
50. What will the audience for this talk do next?

End of Tape 4, Side A.

SECTION 2: STRUCTURE AND WRITTEN EXPRESSION

Answer Key

Structure

1. C	4. B	7. A	10. A	13. A
2. D	5. B	8. A	11. D	14. B
3. A	6. C	9. B	12. C	15. A

Written Expression

16. D	21. C	26. B	31. B	36. B
17. A	22. C	27. C	32. C	37. D
18. C	23. A	28. D	33. B	38. C
19. D	24. C	29. C	34. B	39. C
20. A	25. D	30. D	35. A	40. A

EXPLANATION: WRITTEN EXPRESSION ITEMS

16. The correct pattern is *either . . . or.*

17. The comparative *older* is needed in place of the superlative *oldest.*

18. The noun that names a field (*journalism*) is needed in place of the noun naming a person (*journalist*).

19. The correct word order is *college campuses.*

20. The definite article *the* should not be used before the name of a field such as *architecture.*

21. To be parallel with the other words in the series (*agriculture, finance,* and *accounting*), a noun that names a field should be used (*marketing*).

22. Before uncountable nouns, the word *amounts* should be used.

23. The correct expression is *so many . . . that.* (*Too* is used in phrases with infinitives: *too many to. . . .*)

24. The singular verb *is* must be used to agree with the singular subject *sum.*

25. The past participle *pulled* must be used to express a passive idea.

26. Before a series of three elements (*insulated, ventilated,* and *equipped*) the conjunction *both* cannot be used.

27. The plural pronoun *them* must be used to agree with the plural noun *bridges.*

28. To be parallel with the other nouns in the series (*hardness* and *brilliance*) another noun form (*transparency*) is needed.

29. The word *very* cannot be used to modify the word *relatively.*

30. The word *other* should be used in place of *another* before a plural noun (*types*).

31. This sentence incorrectly compares people and a sport (*running* and *race walkers*). For a logical comparison, the word *running* must be changed to *runners.*

32. The adjective *wild* should replace the adverb *wildly* because the phrase modifies a noun (*Magnolia Gardens*). The word *lovely* is used correctly in this sentence because it is an adjective ending in *-ly*, not an adverb.

Peterson's TOEFL CBT Success

33. The plural noun *instruments* is needed here.

34. The possessive form *his* should be used in place of the article *the*.

35. The past tense form of the verb (*won*) is needed.

36. The definite article *the* is required before the ordinal number *first*.

37. The preposition *in* has been omitted: *age in which*.

38. The noun *ease* is needed to be parallel with the noun *difficulty*.

39. The noun should be pluralized: *times*.

40. The noun *discovery* is required in place of the verb *discover*.

SECTION 3: READING COMPREHENSION

Answer Key

1. D	11. B	21. D	31. C	41. A
2. A	12. A	22. C	32. C	42. B
3. B	13. D	23. B	33. D	43. D
4. C	14. A	24. A	34. D	44. C
5. A	15. B	25. C	35. C	45. B
6. A	16. C	26. C	36. D	46. B
7. B	17. A	27. A	37. C	47. D
8. C	18. B	28. B	38. A	48. A
9. A	19. D	29. A	39. D	49. C
10. C	20. D	30. B	40. C	50. D

1. The passage generally deals with the time humans and mammoths coexisted in the New World, and the possible role humans played in the extinction of the mammoths. No specific details are offered about (A) or (B), and (C) is too general.

2. The word "tools" is closest in meaning to "implements."

3. The phrase refers to "humans."

4. Lines 8-9 mentions "the imperial mammoth of the South," meaning the southern section of North America.

5. Lines 9-10 state that "Here, as in the Old World, there is evidence that humans hunted these elephants," implying that humans had also hunted mammoths in Siberia.

6. The word "remains" can be defined as those parts of an animal's body that can be found after many years. In this case, they are mainly the bones of the mammoths.

7. The meaning of the word "apparently" is closest to that of "seemingly."

8. The author argues that choice (A) is unlikely. Choice (B) is not possible because the extinction of the mammoths came at the END of the Ice Age. There is no information about (D). Only (C) is a possible conclusion.

9. The word "cunning" means "clever."

10. Choice (A) is true; line 17 states that humans were "not very numerous." Choice (B) is true; line 3 states that humans had bows and arrows at the time that they crossed from Siberia, and that crossing took place before the extinction of the mammoths. Choice (D) is also true; line 16 states that humans were "cunning hunters." Only (C) is NOT true; lines 16-17 says that humans were ". . . still widely scattered."

11. The author provides the most detailed information about the mammoth.

12. The passage chiefly deals with the first decades of jazz, the Dixieland era.

13. As used in this sentence, the word "idiom" means a style of playing music.

14. According to the first paragraph, the earliest recordings were made by the Original Dixieland Band, who were among those White musicians who "came to Chicago from New Orleans."

15. According to the second paragraph, the first important recording made by black musicians was recorded by King Oliver's Creole Jazz Band in 1923.

16. Lines 5-7 state that King Oliver's Creole Jazz Band "featured some of the foremost jazz musicians of the time, including . . . Louis Armstrong."

17. The word "steady" is closest in meaning to "constant."

18. Lines 11-12 indicate that the beat was provided by the rhythm section, which included the piano.

19. According to lines 14-15, Duke Ellington "provided his musicians with written arrangements."

20. Line 14 states that "improvisation was an indispensable element," indicating that Dixieland was NOT rigidly planned. All of the other answer choices are referred to in the second paragraph.

21. Lines 17-18 refers to the Wolverines as an example of a small Chicago jazz band.

22. The author provides the most detailed description of early jazz in the third paragraph.

23. The last sentence of the passage indicates that the next era of jazz would be the Swing era, so it is logical that the next paragraph will continue with a discussion of this period.

24. The word "startling" is closest in meaning to "astounding."

25. All three streets are in San Francisco (line 3); the residents have the same approximate levels of income. (They are all middle class or working class, according to line 4.) They all have approximately the same ethnic mix as well (lines 4-5). The only difference is the amount of traffic.

26. Line 7 says that Franklin Street "had almost 16,000 cars a day."

27. According to lines 10-11, trash is a secondary effect of heavy traffic.

28. The author's main purpose in this paragraph is to discuss the negative impact heavy traffic has on Franklin Street.

29. The third paragraph deals with how Octavia Street residents interact; they have more friends and acquaintances on their block than do Franklin Street residents, and by implication, than do Gough Street residents as well.

30. The word "chatted" means "talked" (informally).

31. According to the passage, increased traffic REDUCES the amount of territory for which residents feel responsible (line 11). All the other statements would be consistent with information given about Gough Street residents in the fourth paragraph.

32. The author first presents a detailed discussions of Franklin Street (HEAVY), then Octavia Street (LIGHT), and finally Gough Street (MEDIUM).

33. The passage concentrates on the books written by Rachel Carson and on her career as a writer.

34. Line 2 states that Carson studied zoology at Johns Hopkins University.

35. Carson was born in 1907 (line 1) and published *Under the Sea Wind* in 1941 (line 4), so she must have been around 34 years of age at the time of publication.

36. According to lines 4-5, when *Under the Sea Wind* was first published "it received excellent reviews, but sales were poor until it was reissued in 1952."

37. There is no mention that Rachel Carson took part in a research expedition. The other sources are given in lines 7-9.

38. Carson "realized the limitations of her nontechnical readers" (line 9), implying that the book was not highly technical. It did have a poetic quality (line 7), and it was fascinating (interesting), according to line 6, and well-researched (lines 7-9).

39. The word "reckless" is closest in meaning to "irresponsible."

40. Line 9 state that the book *Silent Spring* "proved how much harm was done by the reckless use of insecticides."

41. The word "faulty" is closest in meaning to the word "flawed."

42. Carson's work "was vindicated" by the report (lines 14-15), implying that the report contradicted the chemical industry's claims and supported her ideas.

43. The passage deals with the two main divisions of economic resources: property resources and human resources. The other choices refer to minor details in the passage.

44. This expression is used figuratively in the passage to mean that economic resources is a broad topic.

45. According to line 6, economists "mean . . . much more than the noneconomist" by the term "land."

46. The word "arable" means "able to be cultivated"—and, therefore, "fertile."

47. The term "the latter" (which means the second concept mentioned before) refers to "consumer goods."

48. Capital goods include aids to transporting goods (lines 8-9), such as a railroad. Choice (B) is specifically mentioned as NOT being a type of capital (line 11). Choices (C) and (D) are examples of land, not of capital.

49. The word "heading" as used in this sentence means "category."

50. The third paragraph indicates that the term "labor" involves all types of human talents except entrepreneurial skills, which are considered a separate category.

Practice Test 3

SECTION 1: LISTENING COMPREHENSION

PART A

TAPESCRIPT

1. M1: Did Joan get someone to fix the broken window?
    F1: No, she did it herself.
    M2: What does the woman say about Joan?

2. M1: You're from Mayport? There's a big golf tournament held there every year, isn't there?
    F2: You're right. That golf tournament really put our little town on the map.
    M2: What does the woman say about the town of Mayport?

3. F2: This painting isn't an original—it's a copy.
    M1: How do you know that?
    M2: What does the man ask the woman?

4. F1: Do you know where the nearest pharmacy is?
    M1: There's one in the supermarket on Lexington Street, right next to that big used-car lot.
    M2: What does the woman probably want?

5. F2: Mandy, did you get a chance to read that magazine I gave you?
    F1: Cover to cover!
    M2: What does Mandy say about the magazine?

6. M1: Jack didn't sound bad at all.
    F1: Yeah, considering he hasn't played the guitar in years.
    M2: What do the speakers say about Jack?

7. M1: Do you think that I've packed too much equipment for my camping trip?
    F1: It should be just right, Max—if you plan to be gone for a couple of years!
    M2: What does the woman imply about Max?

8. F2: What should I take with me when I talk to the mayor?
   M1: I'd bring a pen and notebook and a small tape recorder. Oh, and a prepared list of questions, of course.
   M2: What is the woman probably planning to do?

9. M1: That couldn't have been Professor Leguin that you saw yesterday—he's been at a conference in San Francisco all week.
   F2: Well, it sure looked like him.
   M2: What can be inferred about the woman?

10. F1: There must be something wrong with that microphone the speaker is using. I can hardly understand a word he's saying.
    M1: Yeah, I can only catch a word or two myself.
    M2: Why are these people probably having trouble understanding the speaker?

11. F1: Do you know where Dr. Delany's office is?
    M1: There's a directory over by the elevators.
    M2: What does the man imply about Dr. Delany's office?

12. M1: Do you still like country music?
    F1: Can't get enough of it!
    M2: What does the woman say about country music?

13. M1: You weren't very busy at work today, I suppose.
    F2: *Not busy*! We were snowed under!
    M2: What does the woman mean?

14. F1: I've spent all my money for the month.
    M1: Join the club!
    M2: What does the man mean?

15. M1: Is Clark going to come to the reception with us?
    F2: If he can tear himself away from his computer for one evening, he might.
    M2: What does the woman imply about Clark?

16. M1: In this photograph, Gordon looks like the youngest person in your group.
    F1: Actually, he's the second oldest.
    M2: What is learned about Gordon from this conversation?

17. M1: Sam sure cooks good pancakes.
    F2: Yeah, but not much else.
    M2: What does the woman say about Sam?

18. M1: Professor Bryant always grades fairly.
    F1: I couldn't agree with you more.
    M2: What does the woman mean?

19. M1: We should discuss our presentation some time in the next few days.
    F2: Fine. How about over lunch today?
    M2: When does the woman want to talk about the presentation?

20. F1: I'd love to be up in the mountains where it's cool.
    M1: So you're not enjoying our weather this month?
    M2: What can be inferred from the man's remark?

21. M1: This is a great restaurant. You can get anything you want here.
    F2: Anything except good service.
    M2: What is the woman's opinion of the restaurant?

Peterson's TOEFL CBT Success

22. M1: Does the name John Casey ring a bell for you?
     F1: John Casey? I can't say that it does.
     M2: What does the man ask the woman about John Casey?

23. F1: I didn't know you were interested in geology.
     M1: Well, it's a requirement to take at least one science course, and geology seemed like the easiest one.
     M2: Why is the man taking the geology course?

24. F2: Have you ever seen a bear?
     M1: Only at the zoo.
     M2: What does the man mean?

25. F1: Connie asked you a lot of questions, didn't she?
     M1: Yes, she did, and I'd like to know what she was driving at.
     M2: What does the man wonder about Connie?

26. F2: Gary, do you know when the work on that new road will be done?
     M1: The sooner the better, as far as I'm concerned!
     M2: What does Gary say about the new road?

27. M1: My brother Charles is studying in Europe.
     F1: Really? Since when?
     M2: What does the woman want to know about the man's brother?

28. F2: Charlotte will be starting graduate school in September.
     M1: So she *did* get a scholarship.
     M2: What had the man *originally* assumed?

29. F2: Today is the first of the month. Isn't your rent due today?
     M1: Yes, but I always pay it on the day before it's due.
     M2: What does the man say about his rent?

30. F1: A lot of people were planning to attend the debate.
     M1: Not many were there, though.
     M2: What does the man mean?

PART B

Questions 31 to 33: Listen to the following conversation:

     F1: Don, I hear you bought a new car.
     M1: I *did* just buy a car, but it's not exactly a *new* one—it was made back in the 1950's. Here, take a look at this photo.
     F1: Wow, you're right—this car hasn't been new for a long time! Couldn't you afford a newer car?
     M1: Believe it or not, this car cost almost as much as a new one.
     F1: Really? How could that be?
     M1: Well, a lot of cars from the '40's, '50's, and '60's have become collectors' items and are worth a lot of money.
     F1: But this one doesn't seem to be in very good shape.
     M1: The engine is still in good condition. I plan to fix up the interior and to paint the car myself. Then it will be worth even more money.
     F1: So then you'll resell it?
     M1: No, I don't plan to resell it—but I might enter it in some classic auto shows. Maybe I'll win a prize.
     31. Why did Don buy an older car?
     32. When was Don's car made?
     33. What does Don plan to do with the car he bought?

Questions 34 to 37: Listen to the following conversation:

F1: You'll be in Room 207. Here's your key, and I hope you enjoy your stay with us, Ms. Cook.

F2: Thanks. Oh, by the way, I'd like to get some information from you. You see, the conference I'm attending will be over early Wednesday, and I don't fly out until Thursday. Do you have any recommendations for sightseeing?

F1: There's a great planetarium at our natural history museum. You might enjoy that.

F2: I don't know—I don't think I want to do that. The city I come from has a good planetarium.

F1: There are also some good art galleries downtown.

F2: I'm more interested in doing something outdoors.

F1: Oh, well there's a beautiful waterfall called Crystal Falls not far from here.

F2: That sounds like something I'd enjoy seeing. How do I get there?

F1: Do you have a car, or will you be taking a bus?

F2: I rented a car at the airport.

F1: Then just take Waterson Street west out of town and go about 5 miles. You'll see a sign that says Crystal Falls. It's a short walk from there.

F2: That sounds great. Thanks!

34. Where is this conversation taking place?

35. What does Ms. Cook imply that her main purpose was in coming to this town?

36. Why does Ms. Cook *not* want to go to the planetarium?

37. How will Ms. Cook probably get to the waterfall?

PART C

Questions 38 to 41: Listen to a part of a talk about a type of dance:

F1: Good afternoon. In today's class, we're going to continue our discussion of dance around the world with a look at the hula, a dance of the Hawaiian Islands, and we'll see a video of a traditional hula dance. Today, when we hear the word "hula," most of us think of women in grass skirts swaying to ukulele music while tourists take pictures. The traditional version, though, is quite different from the dance as it is performed today. The traditional hula was danced by both men and women who had been trained at special schools. It was accompanied by rhythmic chanting. The chants and the dances were originally performed to honor the gods, promote fertility, or praise great Hawaiian leaders. The traditional hula was banned by missionaries from New England around 1820, and the hula dance itself survived only in a radically different form. The performance you'll see on the screen this afternoon, though, is as much like the original dance as possible. Even the costumes the dancers are wearing are authentic. Now let's turn down the lights and watch.

38. Who is the audience for this lecture?

39. What can be inferred about the dance that the audience will see?

40. What effect did New England missionaries have on the traditional hula dance in around 1820?

41. What will the audience for this talk do next?

Questions 42 to 45: Listen to the following talk:

M1: Imagine you're driving down the highway one spring day and it begins to rain. You hear the sound of the rain on the car roof. Suddenly it sounds as if small stones are pounding on the car, and you see balls of ice bouncing on the road. You're in a hailstorm, and you'd better get your car under cover! Hailstones can damage vehicles as well as gardens and farmers' crops.

If you pick up a hailstone and cut it in half, you'll see it has layers, just like an onion. A hailstone begins its existence as a snowflake, high in the atmosphere. The snowflake comes in contact with what is called "supercooled water"—water that exists at temperatures below freezing, but is still in liquid form. This water forms a coating of ice around the snowflake, and it becomes a hailstone. As the hailstone falls, the layers of ice build up. Air currents may lift the hailstone back into the supercooled water many times, and more layers of ice form until the air currents can no longer hold it up. Then it falls to Earth.

Hailstorms occur most often in the spring. Some hailstones are as big as baseballs and may weigh over a pound.

42. What is the main purpose of this lecture?
43. Why does the speaker compare a hailstone to an onion?
44. According to the speaker, how does a hailstone begin its existence?
45. According to the speaker, when are hailstorms most common?

Questions 46 to 50: Listen to part of a lecture about child development:

F2: Now, in the last few minutes of class, I'd like to address a slightly different issue: the question of how children learn to talk. Learning to speak their own language is one of children's greatest accomplishments, yet it is a somewhat mysterious process. Children first begin to make language-like noises when they are between two and four months old. These noises generally begin with the letters *g* and *k* because these sounds—"goo" and "koo"—are the easiest sounds for infant mouths to make. Between four months and eight months, infants begin to babble meaningless syllables. Most common are those beginning with *p*, *b*, *d*, *m*, or *n* sounds, followed by a vowel sound. Parents sometimes misinterpret these as actual words, such as *mama* or *dada*. Between six months and a year, babies say their first true words. Vocabulary grows slowly at first, usually only a few words a month, but once a child has learned about fifty words—generally at around eighteen months—the pace picks up rapidly.

At first, children say single words, then they begin forming two-word combinations: "all gone," "more milk," "see doggie." Children's two-word combinations are so similar the world over that they read like translations of one another. Between the age of two and three, children can form complete sentences and have mastered the basics of grammar. Can you believe it? A 2½-year-old toddler is a grammatical genius, and all without studying a single rule! Typically, 4-year-olds know some 15,000 words and can form very sophisticated sentences. Even their mistakes are very logical: "I saw two mans" or "We goed to gramma's house."

So, how does this all happen? Well, there are several conflicting theories about language acquisition, but unfortunately, there just isn't time to discuss them today, so we'll take them up in Wednesday's class. In the meantime, please read Chapter Eight in your textbook. See you Wednesday.

46. What is the main topic of this talk?
47. Which of the following sounds would a two-month-old baby be most likely to produce?
48. At what age do most children begin to master the basics of grammar?
49. What does the speaker say about the grammatical mistakes that 4-year-olds make?
50. Why does the speaker not discuss the theories about how children acquire language?

End of Tape 4, Side B.

SECTION 2: STRUCTURE AND WRITTEN EXPRESSION

Answer Key

Structure

1. A	4. D	7. B	10. C	13. B
2. D	5. B	8. A	11. D	14. A
3. C	6. A	9. D	12. C	15. A

Written Expression

16. A	21. B	26. C	31. C	36. C
17. D	22. B	27. D	32. D	37. B
18. A	23. A	28. B	33. A	38. C
19. A	24. C	29. D	34. B	39. A
20. D	25. B	30. D	35. A	40. A

EXPLANATION: WRITTEN EXPRESSION ITEMS

16. The plural verb form *have* must be used to agree with the subject of the sentence, the plural noun *formations*.

17. The possessive adjective *her* should be used in place of the possessive pronoun *hers*.

18. The correct word order is adverb + participle: *widely read*.

19. *Research* is properly an uncountable noun, and should not be pluralized.

20. The personal pronoun *them* should be used instead of the reflexive pronoun *themselves*.

21. The verb *differ* should be used in place of the adjective *different*.

22. In order to be parallel with the other items in the series (*difficult* and *violent*), the adjective *dangerous* is needed in place of the plural noun *dangers*.

23. Before the word *equator*, the definite article *the* must be used.

24. The noun *leader* (a person who leads) should be used in place of the noun *leadership* (the quality that leaders have).

25. The word *twice* should be used in place of *double* in this sentence.

26. The phrase should correctly read *from east to west*.

27. To be parallel with the other items (*scissors* and *glue gun*), a singular noun (*knife*) should be used in place of the plural noun *knives*.

28. The phrase should correctly read *at least*.

29. The definite article *the* should not be used in the phrase *by boat*.

30. The preposition *into* should be used after the verb *subdivided*.

31. There is a contrast between the two clauses of this sentence, so the conjunction *but* should be used in place of *and*.

32. The noun *absence* is needed in place of the adjective *absent*.

33. The preposition *since* should be used in place of the preposition *in*. (This is clear because the verb—*have devoted*—is in the present perfect, not the past tense.)

Peterson's TOEFL CBT Success

34. The noun *sale* is needed in place of the verb form *sell*.

35. Only the second noun (*climbers*) of the compound noun (*mountain climbers*) should be pluralized.

36. The preposition *by* has been incorrectly omitted; the phrase should read *the process by which*.

37. The word *so* should be used in place of *too*.

38. The verb *ripen* should be used in place of the adjective *ripe*.

39. The correct word order for the opening phrase of the sentence is *of the many*.

40. This phrase should correctly read *no longer*.

SECTION 3: VOCABULARY AND READING COMPREHENSION

Answer Key

1. A	11. C	21. D	31. C	41. A
2. D	12. D	22. C	32. B	42. C
3. B	13. C	23. D	33. C	43. C
4. B	14. B	24. D	34. B	44. D
5. B	15. A	25. B	35. A	45. B
6. C	16. B	26. A	36. D	46. B
7. A	17. C	27. C	37. D	47. C
8. A	18. C	28. A	38. C	48. A
9. B	19. B	29. A	39. B	49. D
10. D	20. A	30. D	40. C	50. C

1. The passage provides an introduction to Lucy Maude Montgomery's life and works, especially her *Anne* books.

2. The reference is to *Anne of Green Gables*, which is a classic children's tale written by a Canadian author.

3. According to lines 4–5, Montgomery "moved in with her grandparents" after her mother died and her father moved to Saskatchewan.

4. Montgomery's first book was published in 1908 (line 8), and she wrote the two sequels "in the next three years."

5. The word "elderly" is closest in meaning to "old."

6. In lines 9–10, the author states that "the heroine of the book [Anne] is taken in by an elderly couple who lives in the fictional town of Avonlea."

7. According to lines 10–11, "Montgomery incorporated many events from her life in Cavendish into the *Anne* books."

8. The word "prominence" is closest in meaning to "reputation."

9. In the context of the passage, the word "character" means "nature."

10. There is no mention in the passage that a ballet was ever based on the *Anne* books. The other choices are mentioned in lines 15–16.

11. In the context of the passage, "scour" means "search."

12. Choices (A) and (B) are details; choice (C) implies that animals *can* count, an idea which is contradicted in the third paragraph.

13. The accounts from White's book indicate that certain animals *are* aware of quantities on an intuitional level.

14. The word "surreptitiously" is closest in meaning to the word "secretly."

15. As used in this passage, the word "abandon" means "vacate."

16. The word "odd" in this context refers to numbers that are not divisible by 2 (1, 3, 5, 7, and so on).

Peterson's TOEFL CBT Success

17. According to the first paragraph, caterpillars are used by wasps to supply food for their young. There is no mention that they are aware of quantities. The other choices are given in the paragraph as examples of creatures that *are* aware of quantities in some way.

18. The word "accounts" means "reports" or "stories" in the context of this passage.

19. According to the passage, "animals respond to quantities when they are connected to survival as a species . . . or survival as individuals." Choices (A) and (D) are connected to the pigeon's and the lion's survival as individuals (since these incidents involve food), and choice (C) is an incident involving the survival of a species (since it involves the cat's young). It can be inferred that choice (B) is the result of conditioning by a trainer rather than the result of the monkey's instinctive awareness of quantities.

20. Since these people believe that "creatures other than humans can actually count" (lines 10–11) and the author believes that none of the animal's achievements shows evidence of counting, the author must consider these people mistaken.

21. The word "admittedly" is closest in meaning to "undeniably."

22. The reference is to the remarkable achievements of animals.

23. The reference comes in the sentence beginning, "In lab experiments. . . ." The research mentioned in the first paragraph shows animals' ability to recognize quantities, not their inability to count.

24. The main topic of the passage is the impact of the Bessemer process. Choice (A) is too general; choices (B) and (C) are not directly discussed in the passage.

25. There is no mention that Bessemer steel was used in Civil War weapons; the other effects are cited in the first paragraph.

26. According to the passage, the production of Bessemer steel exceeded that of wrought iron in 1880 (lines 8–10), implying that wrought iron production was greater than Bessemer steel production before then.

27. The word "expanding" is closest in meaning to the word "burgeoning."

28. According to lines 12–13, "steel rails were far more durable (long-lasting) than those made of iron."

29. In the context of this passage, the word "driven" is closest in meaning to that of "spurred."

30. According to lines 13–14, "the U.S. steel industry became the largest in the world in 1886, when it surpassed that of Great Britain."

31. Because steel made by the Bessemer Process accounted for only 3 percent of the total U.S. production in the 1950s, steel production must have involved methods other than the Bessemer process.

32. Because the last paragraph deals with the declining importance of the Bessemer process and mentions that the open-hearth method supplanted it, it is logical to assume that the next paragraph discusses the open-hearth method.

33. The author first mentions the expansion of the Bessemer steel method in lines 8–10, in the sentence beginning "Production grew rapidly. . . ."

34. The author does not discuss San Francisco's current housing problems. Restoration is discussed in the third paragraph; the three styles are explained in the second paragraph; the entire passage provides a brief history of San Francisco's Victorian houses.

35. The word "gaudy" is closest in meaning to the word "showy."

36. The first paragraph indicates that almost all of Nob Hill was destroyed in 1906, and goes on to say that surviving Victorians can be found in Cow Hollow, Pacific Heights, and the Mission district.

37. Roman Classical is NOT one of the three styles of Victorian built in San Francisco; it is the style Italianate houses were influenced by, and so must have been an earlier style. Italianate styles were popular in the 1870s, Stick houses in the 1880s, and Queen Anne houses in the 1890s. Queen Anne houses were therefore the last to become fashionable.

38. In the context of the sentence, bays are features of Victorian houses. (They are a type of window.)

39. In lines 11–12, the author says that towers were among the features that "distinguished Queen Anne houses from their predecessors." The other choices are given as features of Italianate or Stick styles.

40. Victorian houses were considered "impossibly old-fashioned" in the period after the earthquake (which occurred in 1907) but interest in them was renewed during the 1960s, when many were restored.

41. According to lines 14–15, the owners of the houses commissioned "multi-hued (many-colored) paint jobs."

42. According to the first paragraph, sea otters, along with freshwater otters and other animals, are members of the group known as mustelids.

43. Lines 4–5 indicate that sea otters have to eat about 30 percent of their body weight a day. Thirty percent of 100 pounds is 30 pounds.

44. The term "picky eaters" (meaning creatures with selective appetites) is applied to sea otters because each animal prefers only a few food types (line 7).

45. In the context of this passage, the word "exhausted" means "used up."

46. Lines 8–9 indicate that sea otters protect kelp forests because they "feast on (eat) invertebrates such as sea urchins and abalones that destroy kelp."

47. The term "luxuriant" means "abundant."

48. According to line 13, "the soft outer fur forms a protective cover that keeps the fine underfur dry."

49. The word "elated" is closest in meaning to "overjoyed."

50. According to lines 17–18, scientists are worried because the California otter population rate of growth is only 5 percent a year, "lagging behind the 18 percent a year rate among Alaska otters."

Answer Keys and Tapescripts

Section 1

LISTENING COMPREHENSION

SAMPLE LISTENING COMPREHENSION TEST

Answer Key

1. C	11. C	21. A	31. A	41. D
2. B	12. D	22. D	32. C	42. C
3. B	13. A	23. A	33. C	43. B
4. A	14. B	24. D	34. A	44. B
5. A	15. A	25. D	35. D	45. B
6. C	16. D	26. A	36. B	46. A
7. B	17. C	27. C	37. D	47. A
8. D	18. A	28. B	38. D	48. A
9. B	19. D	29. C	39. D	49. C
10. C	20. B	30. B	40. A	50. D

TAPESCRIPTS

Part A

1. M1: I like your new bicycle, Helen.
   F1: Thanks, but it isn't new. I had my old one repainted.
   M2: What can be said about Helen's bicycle?

2. F2: Will that be cash, check, or charge?
   M1: I'm going to write a check, but I just realized I left my checkbook in my car. I'll be right back.
   M2: What will the man probably do next?

never be able to get through all these books on Professor Grey's reading list.

all of them are required.

tell Mark?

like about the novel?

for dinner.

the blue, I got a letter from him.

10.   F2: If you don't like this studio apartment, I can show you a one-bedroom unit up on the third floor.
      M1: All right. This one just doesn't have enough room for me.
      M2: How does the man feel about the studio apartment?

11.   M1: I think I deserved a higher grade in chemistry class. Does Professor Welch ever change the grades he gives?
      F1: Sure—about once a century!
      M2: What can be inferred about Professor Welch from this conversation?

12.   F1: I wonder how I did on Professor Porter's test.
      M1: Oh, she's already posted the grades on her office door.
      M2: What does the man say about Professor Porter?

13.   M1: I've invited some friends over to watch the game on television. I think I'll go out and get some drinks before they arrive here.
      F1: Shouldn't you get some snacks too?
      M2: What does the woman tell the man?

14.   M1: I'm going to drop my political science class. It meets too early in the morning for me.
      F2: Allen, is that really a good reason to drop the class?
      M2: What does the woman imply?

15.   F1: I can hardly hear anything from back here! Let's just go home.
      M1: Why don't we ask an usher if we can sit closer to the stage?
      M2: What does the man suggest?

16.   F1: William comes up with some weak excuse or another for just about every mistake he makes, doesn't he?
      F2: Wait till you hear his latest!
      M2: What do the speakers imply about William?

17.   M1: What a beautiful sunset! You should photograph it, Melissa.
      F1: If I had some film in my camera, I would.
      M2: What does Melissa mean?

18.   F2: We should be arriving at the airport in another 10 minutes.
      M1: Wait a second. This bus is going to the airport?
      M2: What can be inferred about the man?

19.   M1: I wonder when the board of regents will pick a new dean of students.
      F1: Who knows? They're not even scheduled to meet until next month.
      M2: What does the woman imply?

20.   M1: Are Randy and his friends still going to play cards this evening?
      F2: He's setting up the folding card table right now.
      M2: What does the woman say about Randy?

21.   M1: We should *never* have listened to Harvey.
      F1: If only we'd asked someone else for advice!
      M2: What do they mean?

22.   M1: All the people in the audience certainly seemed to enjoy the performance.
      F1: Well, *almost* all of them did.
      M2: What does the woman mean?

23.   M1: How was your room last night?
      M2: I slept like a baby. And the rates were quite reasonable.
      F2: What are these people probably discussing?

24.   F1: Professor White? A few of us in the back of the room didn't get a copy of your syllabus.
      M1: Hmmm . . . there are 23 names on my class list, so I only brought 23 copies of the syllabus.
      M2: What can be inferred from Professor White's remark?

25.   F2: We're not far from Mount Pleasant Street. There are some antique stores there that have some wonderful things, and they're fairly cheap.
      M1: They have some nice antiques, all right, but I sure wouldn't call them cheap.
      M2: What does the man mean?

26.   F1: Daniel said that San Diego is a great place to go to a conference.
      M1: He should know. He's been there often enough.
      M2: What does the man say about Daniel?

27. F2: Have you ever gone for a ride with Charlie?

    F1: I sure have. He seems to think he's a race-car driver, doesn't he?

    M2: What does the woman imply about Charlie?

28. F1: Try a bowl of this soup and see how you like it. It's a new brand.

    M1: Ummm . . . I'd say it stacks up pretty well against the other kinds.

    M2: What does the man mean?

29. F2: Peter is favored to win the tennis match Saturday.

    M1: Oh, then that match wasn't canceled after all?

    M2: What had the man *originally* assumed?

30. F2: Adam, do you remember the tools I lent you when you were building those bookshelves last month? I'd like to have them back.

    M1: Uh, well, I hate to tell you this . . . but I can't seem to lay my hands on them.

    M2: What does Adam imply?

Part B

Questions 31–33: Listen to the following conversation:

    M1: Good morning, Diana. What did you want to talk to me about?

    F1: Good morning, Professor Lane. I wanted to talk to you about changing my major. You see, I've decided that when I graduate in three years, I'd like to work in an art museum. I think I should change my major to art history.

    M1: You know, Diana, I think you should give this decision some more thought. You've done well in your year as a business major. Besides, all organizations need good managers, whether they're private companies or nonprofit foundations like museums.

    F1: I suppose that's true, but wouldn't I still have to know a lot about art?

    M1: Why not take a few elective courses in art history? And try working a few hours a week as a volunteer at the local art museum. See if you really like working there.

    31. What is the probable relationship between these two speakers?

    32. When does Diana hope to begin working at a museum?

    33. What does the man advise Diana to do?

Questions 34–37: Listen to a conversation between two students:

    M1: Gloria, hello! You're not looking too happy. What's the matter? Have you been studying too much?

    F2: Oh, hi. No, that's not it. The problem is that I was planning to go home over spring break, but my travel agent just told me all the airlines are fully booked that week.

    M1: Why not go by car?

    F2: It's too long a trip to take by myself, and gasoline is so expensive.

    M1: Have you checked the ride board? Maybe you can get a rider to go with you.

    F2: The ride board—what's that?

    M1: It's a bulletin board that has a map of the United States on it. The map is divided into different regions, and each region has a different number. Say you want to go to New England—that would be box number one. There are boxes for each number. You can put a white card or a blue card in one of the boxes.

    F2: What's the difference between a blue card and a white one?

    M1: Blue means you have a car and need riders to share the driving. White means that you're looking for a ride.

    F2: So I should go look at the white cards to see if anyone needs a ride to where I'm going, right?

    M1: Yeah, and fill out a blue card too.

    F2: So where is this ride board?

    M1: It's on the second floor of the Student Union building, right by the campus cinema.

    34. Why does Gloria look unhappy?

    35. According to the man, what do the numbers on the boxes at the ride board indicate?

    36. What does Gloria hope to obtain through the ride board?

    37. Where is the ride board?

Part C

Questions 38–42: Listen to a student telling his friends about an experience he had:

M1: I saw something rather unusual late last Sunday night. My roommate Ron and I were driving back here to the university from my parents' house. They live in a small town about 70 miles from here. We'd stopped so that I could drive—Ron was really tired—when all of a sudden, the whole sky was lit up. I thought I was seeing a UFO—a real flying saucer. Ron thought maybe it was an airliner going down, or a satellite coming out of orbit. A fireball shot across the sky. It looked almost like fireworks. Then the light disappeared behind the hills. It wasn't until the next morning when I was listening to the morning news on the radio that I found out what had happened. Apparently I'd seen a large meteorite. The light was caused by the heat of friction as the meteor traveled through the atmosphere. Most meteors burn up in the upper atmosphere, according to the announcer, but large ones can hit the ground. This one was unusual in that pieces of it were recovered. They landed in a parking lot about 20 miles from where we were.

My mother told me that when she was young, she read a story in a magazine about a meteorite that crashed through the roof of a house and hit a woman sleeping in her bedroom and broke her leg. Anyway, it was an incredible sight, and I'm glad I was lucky enough to see it.

38. What did the man initially believe he had seen?
39. Why had the man stopped the car?
40. How did the man learn what he had actually seen?
41. What happened to the meteor that the man had seen?
42. How did the man feel about what he had seen?

Questions 43–46: Listen to a talk given by a tour guide:

F2: Ladies and gentlemen, the bus will stop next at the Washington Monument, which honors the first president of the United States. The first stone of the monument was laid in 1848, but because of a variety of problems, work was delayed. So it was not until 1884 that the monument was completed. Imagine that—it took thirty-six years! And then it was another four years before it opened to the public. Now, if you like, you can go to the top of the Monument. On the way up, you'll have to take the elevator. You can take the elevator down, too, or you can walk—if you don't mind climbing down 898 steps. The monument is made of marble, except for a tiny aluminum tip. Incidentally, before the tip was put on the monument, it was displayed around the country. Some young people jumped over the tip so that later, they could truthfully claim that they'd jumped over the top of the Washington Monument. After visiting the Washington Monument, we'll be walking over to the Lincoln Memorial. Watch your step as you get off the bus, please.

43. Where is this talk probably being given?
44. How long did it take to build the Washington Monument?
45. According to the speaker, what must those people who go to the top of the Washington Monument do?
46. According to the speaker, what did some young people do when the tip of the monument was displayed?

Questions 47 to 50: Listen to the following lecture:

M2: Good day, class. Today we're going to continue our discussion of American music with a look at the songs of the frontier period. Nearly everyone who went west—the mountaineers, the miners, the river raftsmen, the railroad workers—had songs to accompany their work. And after work, the men and women of the frontier sang and danced to fiddle tunes or country dances. Some of these songs were new versions of old songs from Europe, while some were completely new. Some of the most popular of these songs were later used as theme songs for political campaigns.

Now, we're going to listen to a few of these songs performed much as they were almost two centuries ago. As you listen to the recordings, notice the difference between these lively songs and the slower, more genteel music of the Eastern choral societies that we listened to in our last class.

47. In what course was this lecture probably given?
48. What can be inferred about the songs of the frontier?
49. According to the speaker, how do these songs compare with the songs of Eastern choral societies?
50. What will the people who are listening to this lecture probably do next?

PART A, DIALOGS: EXERCISES AND MINI-TEST

EXERCISE 1

	Answer Key	
Set A	**Set B**	**Set C**
1. b	6. d	11. e
2. f	7. a	12. b
3. a	8. f	13. c
4. e	9. c	14. f
5. c	10. b	15. d

(There is no tapescript for Exercise 1.)

EXERCISE 2.1

	Answer Key	
1. B	6. B	11. B
2. B	7. B	12. A
3. A	8. B	13. B
4. A	9. B	14. B
5. A	10. A	15. B

TAPESCRIPT

1. M1: I've never had to wait so long just to pay for a few groceries!
   F1: I think you should get in another line.
   M2: What does the woman suggest the man do?

2. M1: How did your baby-sitting job go?
   F2: Oh, fine—the children spent most of the day going down the hill on their new sled.
   M2: What did the children do?

3. M1: Where should I put these letters for you?
   F1: Oh, just toss them in that file.
   M2: What does the woman tell the man to do with the letters?

4. F2: Did you get your suitcase packed?
   M1: Yeah—but now I can't close it!
   M2: What does the man mean?

5. F1: What kind of bread did Annie bake?
   F2: My favorite—whole wheat bread!
   M2: What is learned about Annie?

6. F1: Has Brenda finished writing her story for the radio news?
   M1: Oh, sure—she's just taping it now.
   M2: What does the man say about the story?

7. M1: Do you have Emily's address?
F1: She has a new one—let me see if I can find it for you.
M2: What does the woman mean?

8. F2: How's the coffee here, Dennis?
M1: It's a little bitter, to tell the truth.
M2: What does Dennis say about the coffee?

9. F1: I bought a ticket for the drawing. I hope I win.
M1: What's the prize, Ellen?
M2: What does the man ask Ellen?

10. M1: I wonder if this old bottle I found is worth any money. It's a beautiful color.
F2: Yes, but look—there's a chip in it.
M2: What does the woman say about the bottle?

11. F1: I saw Jerry is walking on crutches. Did he have an accident?
M1: His feet slipped in some oil and he twisted his knee.
M2: What happened to Jerry?

12. M2: This is a beautiful part of the state. What's it most famous for?
M1: Well, you'll see some remarkable racehorses here.
F2: Why is this area well known?

13. M1: So, did the committee finally reach a decision on that issue?
F2: Finally—after they fought about it all afternoon.
M2: How did the committee spend the afternoon?

14. F1: I've never seen you in that shirt before.
M1: I don't wear it very often—it's too tight in the collar.
M2: What is the problem with the shirt?

15. F1: Are you having a midterm exam in Professor Maguire's class?
F2: No, he assigned a paper instead.
M2: What did Professor Maguire do?

EXERCISE 2.2

Answer Key

1.	B	center	later
2.	C	appointment	appointed
3.	C	plants	cattle
4.	A	drain	train
5.	A	sister	missed her
6.	C	copy	cough drops
7.	B	hear	pain
8.	C	food	boots
9.	C	weakened	awakened
10.	B	texts	collect
11.	A	van	fine
12.	B	list	police

TAPESCRIPT

1. M1: Stephanie, did you ever phone your friend?
   F2: No, but I sent her a letter.
   M2: What did Stephanie do?

2. F1: I understand that Stuart is going to resign as vice president.
   M1: As a matter of fact, he's so disappointed that he wasn't elected president, he's quitting the club.
   M2: What does the man say about Stuart?

3. M1: So you're going to take that class in ecology. What will you be studying?
   F2: Well, according to the course catalog, it's the systematic study of life on this planet.
   M2: What does the woman say about the class she is going to take?

4. M1: Are you ready to go now, Janet?
   F1: As soon as the rain stops.
   M2: What does Janet tell the man?

5. M1: I heard Darlene was having a hard time with her physics homework.
   F2: Yes, but Sam has kindly offered to assist her.
   M2: What does the woman say about Sam?

6. F1: I need to get a quick bite before we go to the workshop.
   M1: There's a coffee shop here in the hotel.
   M2: What does the man suggest the woman do?

7. M1: How can I take notes if I don't have anything to write with?
   F2: You can probably borrow a pen from Gus—he always has one behind his ear.
   M2: What does the woman say about Gus?

8. M2: Was the flood bad in your part of town?
   F1: Bad! We practically needed boats to get home!
   M2: What does the woman imply?

9. F2: Terry wasn't in class Monday, I noticed.
   M1: Well, she came down with a cough this weekend, but she's feeling better now.
   M2: What does the man say about Terry?

10. M1: So, Jane, what are your duties as Professor Ramsey's assistant?
    F1: For one thing, I help him correct tests.
    M2: What does Jane help Professor Ramsey do?

11. M2: Ned's apartment is so hot this summer, I don't know how he can stand it.
    M1: It's a little better now that he got a fan.
    M2: What is learned about Ned?

12. F1: Bonnie, you did look over the lease before you signed it, didn't you?
    F2: Well, I tried to, but not even a lawyer could understand this lease.
    M2: What does Bonnie mean?

End of Tape 1, Side A.

EXERCISE 3.1

<table>
<tr><td colspan="8" align="center">**Answer Key**</td></tr>
<tr><td>1.</td><td>B</td><td>4.</td><td>A</td><td>7.</td><td>B</td><td>10.</td><td>A</td></tr>
<tr><td>2.</td><td>B</td><td>5.</td><td>B</td><td>8.</td><td>B</td><td>11.</td><td>B</td></tr>
<tr><td>3.</td><td>B</td><td>6.</td><td>A</td><td>9.</td><td>B</td><td>12.</td><td>B</td></tr>
</table>

TAPESCRIPT

1. M1: What did you get Suzie for her birthday?
F2: Didn't you read the invitation to her party? She said she didn't want anyone to bring any presents.

2. M2: I've got to go back to the library after dinner.
F1: I know you've got a lot of research to do, but don't *overdo* it. You're spending half your life in the library.

3. F2: I understand you had an accident this morning.
M2: Yes, I broke a windowpane.

4. F1: I can't find my coat.
M1: Well, I certainly don't know where it is.

5. F2: You'd better pay that parking ticket you got last week.
M2: Yeah, I would if I could find it.

6. M1: You need to fill out a change-of-address form.
M2: Oh—is this the right form for that?

7. M1: You went to the meeting last night?
M2: Yes, but I wish I hadn't. Was I ever bored!

8. M1: What kind of car are you looking for?
F1: I don't care, as long as it's dependable. I can't stand a car that breaks down all the time.

9. M2: Don't you just love Andrew's boat?
F2: It's terrific. And it's for sale, you know.

10. F1: So, what did I tell you? Wouldn't this be a great location to build a house?
M1: You're right, it's the perfect site. I wish I could afford to buy this lot.

11. F2: Did you get your garden planted?
M1: Well, I got a start—I planted a few rows of corn.

12. F1: Shh—talking isn't allowed in this part of the library.
M2: Oh, it's okay to talk in *this* part.

EXERCISE 3.2

Answer Key				
1. A	3. A	5. A	7. A	9. B
2. B	4. B	6. A	8. B	10. B

TAPESCRIPT

1. F1: Where have you been keeping yourself, Ben? I haven't seen you since January at least.
    M2: I've had this terrible cold, and I haven't gotten out much.

2. F2: What a kind person Glen is.
    M1: Isn't he, though!

3. M1: Will it be cold in the mountains?
    F1: I'd bring a light sweater if I were you—it may get a little chilly at night.

4. M2: Is this where the aeronautics exhibit is going to be?
    F2: No, it'll be in the north wing of the museum.

5. F1: Where did you get these statistics?
    M1: In the tables at the back of this book.

6. M1: I'm going to paint these old wooden chairs white. They'll look good as new.
    M2: You'd better take off that old coat of red first.

7. M1: How do you like your geology class?
    F2: It's an interesting subject—and tomorrow, we're going out into the field to look for fossils. That should be fun.

8. F1: Want to go see a movie?
    F2: I don't know—what's playing?

9. (RING . . . RING . . . SOUND OF PHONE BEING PICKED UP)
    F2: Good afternoon . . . Blue Dolphin Restaurant.
    M2: Yes, this is Mr. Adams. I'd like reservations for eight on Friday evening.
    F2: Fine, Mr. Adams. How many will there be in your party?

10. F2: When is your composition class?
    M1: Next period.

EXERCISE 3.3

				Answer Key						
1.	A	4.	A		7.	A		10.	A	
2.	B	5.	B		8.	A		11.	B	
3.	B	6.	A		9.	B		12.	A	

TAPESCRIPT

1. M1: I'm ready to hand in my research paper.
   F1: Better check your writing first, Scott.
   M2: What does the woman suggest Scott do?

2. F2: How did you do on the history exam?
   M1: Well, I passed anyway.
   M2: What are they discussing?

3. F2: Did you see the buffaloes in the wildlife park?
   M1: Yeah, and you know what? It was the first herd of buffaloes I'd ever seen.
   M2: What does the man mean?

4. M1: Which line do I get in if I've already preregistered?
   F2: Read the sign, why don't you?
   M2: What does the woman tell the man to do?

5. M1: I can't decide whether to buy one suit or two.
   F2: Just think about it for a second.
   M2: What does the woman suggest the man do?

6. M2: All right, Henry, you can just bring your suitcases upstairs now.
   M1: But I can't handle them all by myself.
   F2: What does Henry say about the suitcases?

7. F1: Your hair is soaked, John. What happened?
   M1: Oh, I was caught out in a sudden shower.
   M2: What does John mean?

8. F2: Patrick, what did your classmates think when you won the award?
   M1: Well, it certainly didn't hurt my standing with them.
   M2: What does Patrick mean?

9. F1: I hear your sister got a new job.
   M1: Yeah, she's now a loan officer at a bank.
   M2: What does the man say about his sister?

10. M1: Is that seminar you were always complaining about finally over?
   F2: Yeah, but you know, now that it's over, I miss going to it.
   M2: What does the woman mean?

11. M1: So where is this park where we're going to have the picnic?
   F1: It's on East Vine Street, across from the City Zoo.
   M2: What does the woman tell the man?

12. F2: Why don't you use that pay phone over there.
   M1: Okay, but, ummm . . . do you have any change?
   M2: What does the man ask the woman?

Exercise 4.1

Answer Key

1. A	was in trouble	7. B	a little sick
2. A	met unexpectedly	8. A	looks like
3. B	became friends	9. A	permanently
4. A	simple	10. B	Help
5. B	immediately	11. B	close to
6. A	nervous	12. B	didn't like

Tapescript

1. M1: So, Rita, you left work early yesterday?
    F1: Yeah, and did I ever get in hot water for that.
    M2: What does the woman mean?

2. F2: Where did you see Caroline?
    M1: I bumped into her at the coffee shop.
    M2: What does the man mean?

3. F2: Did you talk to Chuck at the party?
    M1: I sure did, and we hit it off right away.
    M2: What does the man mean?

4. M2: How was the test?
    F1: Piece of cake!
    M2: What does the woman mean?

5. F2: Robert, are you ready to leave?
    M1: At the drop of a hat!
    M2: What does Robert imply?

6. F2: Sit down, will you, and relax!
    M1: I'm sorry, I can't help it—I always pace when I'm on edge.
    M2: What does the man tell the woman?

7. F1: Julie wasn't at band practice today.
    M1: Oh, she's been under the weather lately.
    M2: What does the man imply about Julie.

8. F1: There's Albert and his grandfather.
    M1: Wow, Albert really takes after him, doesn't he?
    M2: What does the man say about Albert?

9. F1: Did you hear—Professor Holmes is going to quit teaching.
    M1: Not for good, I hope.
    M2: What does the man say about Professor Holmes?

10. M1: That box looks heavy, Paula.
    F2: It's heavy, all right. Could you please give me a hand with it?
    M2: What does Paula ask the man to do?

11. F1: You live near the park?
    M1: Just a stone's throw away.
    M2: What does the man mean?

12. M1: Have you heard Graham's proposal yet?
    F2: Yes, and I don't think much of it.
    M2: What does the woman say about Graham's proposal?

EXERCISE 4.2

	Answer Key	
Set A	**Set B**	**Set C**
1. A	9. A	17. B
2. B	10. B	18. A
3. A	11. A	19. B
4. A	12. B	20. A
5. A	13. B	21. B
6. B	14. B	22. B
7. B	15. A	23. A
8. B	16. B	24. A

TAPESCRIPT

Set A

1. F1: Did you know Max is planning to open his own business? He could make a lot of money.
   M1: Yeah, I suppose—if it ever gets off the ground.
   M2: What does the man mean?

2. M2: I've had these old tires on my car now for over five years. I wonder how much longer they'll last.
   F1: I wouldn't push my luck if I were you, Gary.
   M2: What does the woman imply?

3. F2: Well, that was a good program. Want to watch something else?
   M1: Not me—I'm ready to turn in.
   M2: What will the man do next?

4. F1: Alice, what did you think of that comedian's jokes.
   F2: Tell you the truth, a lot of them went over my head.
   M1: What does Alice mean?

5. F1: Let's go to the beach tomorrow.
   M1: If it clears up before then.
   M2: Under what circumstances will the man go to the beach?

6. F2: Your sister's name is Liz?
   F1: Well, everyone calls her that—it's short for Elizabeth.
   M2: What is learned from this conversation?

7. M1: So your roommate really likes that song?
   F1: You kidding? She listens to it for hours on end.
   M2: What does the woman say about her roommate and the song?

8. F2: I've heard some good things about that new restaurant on College Avenue. What did you think of it?
   M1: I'd call it run-of-the-mill.
   M2: What does the man say about the restaurant?

Set B

9. M1: You look hot and tired. How about some ice water?
   F1: Just what the doctor ordered!
   M2: What does the woman mean?

10. M1: You've been skiing a lot lately, Karen.
    F2: It really gets in the blood.
    M2: What does Karen mean?

11. M1: Just listen to the sound of the creek and the wind in the trees.
    F1: It's like music to my ears!
    M2: What does the woman mean?

12. M1: Norman thinks we don't study enough.
    F2: Look who's talking!
    M2: What does the woman imply?

13. F1: Have you ever gone sailing before?
    M1: No, but I've watched people sail, and it looks like a breeze.
    M2: What does the man mean?

14. M1: Whew, I'm tired. Chopping wood is hard work.
    F2: Want me to lend a hand?
    M2: What does the woman offer to do?

15. F1: I'm not sure if I can afford to take this trip with you and your friends. Gasoline alone will cost a fortune.
    M1: Not if we all chip in.
    M2: What does the man mean?

16. M1: Did you see that it was snowing early this morning?
    F1: Yeah, and I could hardly believe my eyes. Who ever saw snow here at this time of year!
    M2: What does the woman mean?

Set C

17. F2: So, I didn't even make an appointment. I just went right into the professor's office and told him why he should choose me as his teaching assistant.
    M1: Boy, that took a lot of nerve!
    M2: What does the man mean?

18. F1: We still need to paint the kitchen.
    M1: I know, but let's call it a day for now.
    M2: What does the man mean?

19. M1: You don't need to read from the script?
    F2: Oh, no—I've already learned my lines by heart.
    M2: What does the woman mean?

20. M1: So, Marina, your parents still don't think you should go to Hawaii this summer?
    F1: Oh, they'll come around, I think.
    M2: What does Marina think her parents will do?

21. F2: Was there someone on your basketball team last year named Rob Martin?
    M1: Rob Martin? Hmmm . . . the name doesn't ring a bell.
    M2: What does the man imply?

22. F1: I thought you were going to buy that shirt.
    M1: Well, I was planning to, but I didn't have enough money with me. I forgot to take tax into account.
    M2: What does the man mean?

23. F2: How's your research project coming, Arlene?
F1: Slowly but surely, it's getting done.
M2: What does Arlene mean?

24. M1: Were you sorry to see Molly leave?
F2: That goes without saying.
M2: What does the woman mean?

EXERCISE 4.3

1. M1: Want to go out for coffee?
F1: Maybe later. Right now, I'm going to go work out at the gym.
M2: What is the woman going to do next?

2. F2: The party is starting soon. Aren't you ready yet?
M1: I just have to decide on a tie. Do you think this red one goes with my shirt?
M2: What does the man want to know?

3. M1: Do you have notes from Professor Morrison's psychology class Friday? I missed class that day.
F2: Guess we're in the same boat!
M2: What does the woman imply?

4. M1: Is Ron still working as a cook?
F1: Not anymore. He decided he's not cut out for restaurant work.
M2: What can be concluded about Ron?

5. F2: Are you ready for the quiz in Professor Davenport's class today?
M1: A quiz? Today? Are you pulling my leg?
M2: What does the man mean?

6. F1: Brian, did you watch the launch of the space shuttle on television this morning?
M1: No, they had to put it off because of bad weather.
M2: What does Brian mean?

7. F1: You're sure Jennifer was at the lecture?
M1: Oh, she was definitely there. She really stood out in that bright red sweater of hers.
M2: What does the man say about Jennifer?

8. M1: Phil just got a speeding ticket.
F1: That serves him right!
M2: What does the woman say about Phil?

9. M1: I think I'll ask George to help.
F2: Save your breath!
M2: What does the woman imply about George?

10. F2: Do you like that real estate class you're taking, Roy?
M1: By and large, yes.
M2: What does Roy say about his class?

11.   F1: Let me guess—you bought Jill a watch for a graduation present.
      M1: You're not even warm.
      M2: What do we learn from this conversation?

12.   F2: I heard Dora was having some trouble at work.
      M1: Yes, but as usual, she'll come out of it smelling like a rose.
      M2: What does the man say about Dora?

13.   M1: Should I get Lucy some candy for her birthday?
      F1: Lucy doesn't care for sweets. Why don't you get her a basket of fruit?
      M2: What is learned about Lucy?

14.   F1: Are you going to take a trip during spring break?
      M1: With all the studying I have to do, that's out of the question.
      M2: What does the man mean?

15.   F2: So, Mick is going to go to medical school?
      M1: Yes, he's following in his father's footsteps.
      M2: What can be learned from this conversation?

16.   F1: I told Fred about the money I lost, but he didn't seem very sympathetic.
      M1: If it were *his* money that had been lost, he'd be singing another tune.
      M2: What does the man mean?

17.   F2: I've just heard Wally's going-away party has been canceled.
      M1: Oh no! Has anyone broken the news to Wally yet?
      M2: What does the man want to know?

18.   F1: Did you take a lot of photographs when you went to the Grand Canyon?
      M1: Yes, but not all of them turned out well.
      M2: What does the man mean?

19.   M1: I just heard Linda and Rob are going to open a photography studio. I think they'll do very well.
      F2: Well, with his talent as a photographer and hers for business, they're bound to be successful.
      M2: What is the woman's opinion of Linda and Rob?

20.   M1: Can we stay at your parents' cabin at the lake?
      F1: Sure, if you don't mind roughing it.
      M2: What does the woman mean?

End of Tape 1, Side B.

SECTION 1: LISTENING COMPREHENSION

EXERCISE 5

Answer Key

1.	C	5.	A	9.	B	13.	A	17.	A
2.	A	6.	C	10.	A	14.	C	18.	A
3.	C	7.	C	11.	B	15.	B	19.	B
4.	B	8.	B	12.	B	16.	B	20.	C

TAPESCRIPT

1. F2: I understand Larry won another dance contest.
   M1: It's hard to believe we're from the same family, isn't it?
   M2: What can be inferred about the man?

2. F1: Are you going to buy that suit?
   M1: Do I look like a millionaire?
   M2: What can be inferred from this conversation?

3. F1: Do you think I've made enough food for the party?
   M1: I'd say you've made just the right amount—if a couple of hundred people show up!
   M2: What does the man imply?

4. M2: Do you know where Dave is? I've gone over to his apartment several times, but he hasn't been there.
   M1: He's staying at his brother's house. Dave hates the smell of fresh paint.
   M2: What can be inferred from this conversation?

5. M1: Did you know Greg has changed his major?
   F2: Oh, no, how many times does that make?
   M2: What does the woman imply about Greg?

6. M1: Aren't Professor Sutton's lectures fascinating?
   F1: I can close my eyes when I'm listening to him, and I'm back in the Middle Ages.
   M2: What can be inferred from this conversation about Professor Sutton?

7. F2: Did you have to wait long to see the dentist yesterday?
   M1: It seemed like years!
   M2: What does the man imply?

8. F2: Do the experts agree with this plan?
   M1: That depends on which expert you ask.
   M2: What does the man imply about the experts and the plan?

9. F1: Did you know that Louis has a new boss?
   M1: Let's hope he gets along better with this one.
   M2: What does the man imply?

10. M1: Do you think the university will cancel classes tomorrow because of the snow?
    F1: Only if it keeps snowing all night.
    M2: What does the woman imply?

11. F2: You've joined the folk-dancing club? Since when are you interested in folk dancing?
    M1: Since I discovered it was a great way to meet people!
    M2: What does the man imply?

12. M1: Did you have a good seat for the concert?

    F1: A good seat! I practically needed a telescope just to see the stage!

    M2: What does the woman imply?

13. F1: Is it ever hot!

    M1: If you think *this* is hot, you should have been here last summer.

    M2: What does the man imply?

14. M1: Is the swimming pool on campus open to the public?

    F2: It is, but if you're not a student, you'll have to pay a fee to swim there.

    M2: What can be inferred from this conversation?

15. F1: Just look at those stars!

    M1: They certainly never look so clear and bright from the city.

    M2: What can be inferred about the speakers?

16. M1: There's a phone call for you Mike.

    M2: For me? But no one knows I'm at work today.

    F1: What does Mike imply?

17. F1: Are those Shelly's photographs hanging in the hall?

    M1: You know Shelly takes only black-and-white photos.

    M2: What can be inferred from the man's remark?

18. F1: Did you notice that bright blue scarf Fran was wearing.

    F2: Uh-huh. She should wear it more often.

    M2: What can be inferred from the conversation?

19. M1: Milly has a strong accent.

    F2: Nothing like her parents, though.

    M2: What can be inferred from this conversation?.

20. M1: That's a tough slope to ski.

    F2: Yeah, even Robert had trouble skiing down *that* slope.

    M2: What does the woman imply?

EXERCISE 6.1

Answer Key

1. A	4. A	7. A	10. B
2. A	5. B	8. B	11. A
3. B	6. B	9. A	12. A

TAPESCRIPT

1. M1: I don't care if it *is* raining—I'd rather go fishing than stay home.
   M2: I couldn't agree with you more!

2. F1: It sure is windy.
   M1: Is it ever!

3. M1: I didn't think Professor Hall's lecture was very informative.
   M2: I can't really agree with you on that.

4. F1: Anthony is quite a singer.
   M2: You bet he is!

5. M1: I think the service at that new cafe is pretty good.
   F2: I wish I could say the same.

6. M1: Certainly Mayor Curtis won't run for reelection now.
   F2: Don't be so sure about that.

7. M2: It's been a long, hard day.
   F1: Hasn't it, though!

8. F2: I think skydiving must be exciting.
   M2: You wouldn't catch *me* jumping out of an airplane!

9. M1: Good thing there was a fire extinguisher in the hallway.
   F1: I'll second that!

10. F2: There are some strange paintings in that gallery.
    F1: Strange? I wouldn't call them strange.

11. F1: I really like that sports car Michael bought.
    M1: Who wouldn't?

12. F2: We haven't heard from Harry for quite a while.
    M2: No, we certainly haven't.

EXERCISE 6.2

Answer Key

1. A	4. C	7. A	10. A
2. C	5. A	8. B	11. C
3. C	6. B	9. B	12. B

TAPESCRIPT

1. F1: I'd rather have a final exam than write a research paper.
   M1: Me, too. Research papers take a lot more time.
   M2: What does the man mean?

2. M1: This first chapter in the statistics textbook seems pretty simple, but I'm sure the other chapters are more difficult.
   F2: I think you're probably right about that.
   M2: How does the woman feel about the first chapter?

3. F1: The university should make it easier for students to register for classes.
   M1: I couldn't agree with you more.
   M2: How does the man feel about the woman's idea?

4. M1: Jack's story was certainly well written.
   F2: Wasn't it, though! And so full of interesting details.
   M2: What was the woman's opinion of Jack's story?

5. F1: What a perfect day to take a bike ride!
   M1: You can say that again!
   M2: What does the man mean?

6. M1: I can't understand why Arthur dropped his chemistry class. He was doing so well in it.
   F2: Well, me neither, but he must have a good reason.
   M2: What does the woman mean?

7. M1: Tom's plan is so impractical, it will never work.
   F1: That's not necessarily so.
   M2: What does the woman say about Tom's plan?

8. F2: That editorial in this morning's paper made me angry!
   M1: I felt the same way when I first read it, but the more I thought about it, the more I agreed with it.
   M2: What was the man's *initial* reaction to the editorial?

9. M1: The library is sure crowded this evening.
   F1: Is it ever! You can tell it's getting near final exam week.
   M2: What does the woman say about the library?

10. F2: Madelyn designed the costumes for the play. They're wonderful, don't you think?
    M1: Absolutely. Who wouldn't?
    M2: What does the man mean?

11. F1: That was an exciting movie, and what a happy ending.
    M1: Happy! You call that *happy*?
    M2: How does the man feel about the ending of the movie?

12. M1: Pamela thinks these new regulations are unfair, but I don't.
    F1: Oh, neither do I.
    M2: What does the woman mean?

Exercise 7.1

Tapescript

1. F1: May I help you?
   M1: Thanks, but I'm just looking around.

2. M2: Can you come to the recital this evening?
   F2: I'm supposed to be working on my research this evening, but you know, I think a break would be nice.

3. M1: That author we both like is going to be signing books at Appleton's Bookstore this afternoon.
   F1: I'm not busy this afternoon. Why don't we go?

4. F2: Mark, would you mind taking care of my tropical fish next week? I'm going to be out of town.
   M2: Oh, no, I wouldn't mind at all.

5. M1: I need to get more exercise.
   F2: You could always try bicycling. That's great exercise.

6. F1: Can I see the photographs you took on the field trip?
   M2: If you want to, why not?

7. M1: I can't seem to get my car started.
   M2: You know what *I'd* do, Ed?

8. M1: These math problems are hard.
   F2: Want me to give you a few hints?

9. M2: Cynthia, if you have a class, I could take your brother to the airport for you.
   F1: Could you? That would be great.

10. M1: Should I turn on the television?
    F2: Please don't.

11. F2: You could save a lot of time at the grocery by making up a list before you go.
    M1: It's worth a try, I guess.

12. M1: Bob, get me a cup of coffee, will you?
    M2: Who do you think I am, your waiter?

13. F1: I'm going to go out and get something to eat. Want to come?
    M1: I've got a better idea. Let's have a pizza delivered.

14. F2: My arm still hurts.
    M2: I'd get it X-rayed if I were you.

15. F2: You know, Paul, if you want your houseplants to grow, you should move them over by the window where they get more light.
    M2: Now why didn't I ever think of that?

16. F1: Have another sandwich, James.
    M1: Thanks—don't mind if I do.

EXERCISE 7.2

Answer Key

1. C	5. A	9. B	13. B
2. C	6. B	10. C	14. C
3. C	7. C	11. A	15. C
4. A	8. A	12. B	16. B

TAPESCRIPTS

1. F1: Do you mind if I smoke?
    M1: As a matter of fact, I do.
    M2: What does the man mean?

2. M1: My blue suit hasn't come back from the cleaners yet.
    F2: Well, there's always your gray one.
    M2: What does the woman say about the gray suit?

3. F1: You know, one of the best things about this cinema is the great popcorn they have here.
    M1: It *does* smell good. Let's go get some.
    M2: What does the man suggest they do?

4. M1: We need someone to plan the class trip.
    F1: How about Cathy?
    M2: What does the man say about Cathy?

5. F2: Shall I make some more coffee?
    M1: Not on my account.
    M2: What does the man mean?

6. M1: Should I open the window? It's getting a little warm in here.
    F1: Don't bother. I'll do it.
    M2: What does the woman mean?

7. M1: I don't know what to order for lunch. I'm tired of sandwiches.
    F2: What about some vegetable soup?
    M2: What does the woman mean?

8. M1: I'm going to clean my living room this afternoon.
    F2: Shouldn't you clean your kitchen too?
    M2: What does the woman suggest?

9. F1: Do you know where the registrar's office is?
    M1: It's across campus from here. Would you like me to show you on this map?
    M2: What does the man offer to do?

10. M1: Well, that's it for our chemistry homework. We should work on our math problems next.
    F1: What about taking a little break first?
    M2: What does the woman suggest they do?

11. F2: Do you think this toaster can be repaired?
    M1: If I were in your shoes, I'd just buy another one.
    M2: What does the man suggest that the woman do?

12. F2: Would you mind if I read your magazine?
    M1: No, go right ahead.
    M2: What does the woman ask the man?

13. M1: You know, I think I'm going to get a new computer desk. This one is too small for me to work at.
    F2: What about buying a computer instead? Yours is practically an antique!
    M2: What does the woman suggest the man do?

14. F1: Christopher, want to come to the library with Tim and me? We're going to study for our biology test tomorrow.
    M1: I think I'll pass on that. I spent the whole weekend going over my biology notes, and tonight I'm just going to relax.
    M2: What does Christopher tell the woman?

Peterson's TOEFL CBT Success

15. F2: Someone should answer these letters.
    M1: Don't look at me!
    M2: What does the man mean?

16. M1: I'm having some friends over for lunch today. Care to join us?
    F1: Can I take a rain check?
    M2: What does the woman mean?

EXERCISE 8

Answer Key

1.	C	5.	C	9.	B	13.	C	17.	A
2.	B	6.	A	10.	A	14.	B	18.	B
3.	B	7.	C	11.	A	15.	B	19.	B
4.	A	8.	C	12.	C	16.	A	20.	A

TAPESCRIPT

1. F1: I guess we'd better serve fish for dinner, because Ginny doesn't like chicken.
   M1: Actually, I'm sure she *does*.
   M2: What does the man say about Ginny?

2. F2: Mona is moving into a new apartment on Sunday.
   M1: So, she's finally found a place, has she?
   M2: What had the man assumed about Mona?

3. M1: I was told to go to the dean's office.
   F2: By whom?
   M2: What does the woman want to know?

4. F1: I told everyone that of course you weren't interested in running for class president.
   M1: But as a matter of fact, I *am*.
   M2: What does the man mean?

5. F2: Carol's typing the final draft of her paper.
   M1: Oh, so she finally finished the research for it?
   M2: What had the man assumed about Carol?

6. F1: Bert says he loves to ride horses.
   M1: Sure, but you don't see him on horseback very often, do you?
   M2: What does the man say about Bert?

7. F2: Your insurance agent called. He'd like you to call him back.
   M1: Did he say when?
   M2: What does the man want to know?

8. M1: Cliff is working part-time in the cafeteria.
   F1: Oh, he finally decided to get a job, then?
   M2: What had the woman assumed about Cliff?

9. M1: We spent the whole day hiking.
   F2: Oh? How far did you go?
   M2: What does the woman want to know?

10. F1: There are some nice clothes in this shop, and the prices are reasonable.
    M1: Reasonable! I wouldn't call them reasonable.
    M2: What does the man mean?

11. M1: There's going to be a meeting to discuss the proposed recreation center.
    F2: Oh? Where?
    M2: What does the woman ask the man?

12. M1: Joy is going to study overseas in a special program next year.
    F2: Oh, not until next year?
    M2: What had the woman assumed?

13. M1: I went to a party at Ben's house this weekend.
    F1: Did you have a good time?
    M2: What does the woman ask the man?

14. F1: Ted didn't do a good job on these problems. He'll have to do them all over.
    M1: Well, a few of them, anyway.
    M2: What does the man mean?

15. F2: I stopped at the grocery store on the way home from class.
    M1: Yeah? How come?
    M2: What does the man ask the woman?

16. F1: I think Robin only got the job because her brother works for that company.
    M1: Oh, but you're wrong. Her brother works in a completely different division.
    M2: What does the man mean?

17. M1: You know, I put new batteries in the flashlight, but it still doesn't work.
    F1: No kidding? I was sure it would.
    M2: What had the woman assumed?

18. F1: I plan to take Professor Brennon's seminar, but I have to get her permission first.
    M1: As a matter of fact, you don't.
    M2: What does the man mean?

19. M1: My friend Steve is traveling around in the Pacific Northwest.
    F2: Since when?
    M2: What does the woman want to know?

20. F1: Beverly, have you seen that new movie starring Calvin Pierce?
    F2: Oh, that's already out?
    M2: What had Beverly originally assumed?

EXERCISE 9

		Answer Key		
1. A	4. A	7. C	10. B	13. A
2. A	5. B	8. C	11. C	14. C
3. C	6. B	9. B	12. B	15. A

TAPESCRIPT

1. F2: I can't believe how icy the highway is.
   F1: Yeah, I've never seen it so bad. Maybe we should just stay at a motel and see if it's any better in the morning.
   M2: What are they talking about?

2. M1: Have you heard about that big outdoor jazz concert next month?
   F2: Heard about it! I already have tickets.
   M2: What is the woman going to do?

3. F1: Joe and Nancy and I were hoping to get a ride to the party with you.
   M1: With me? But I drive a little two-seater.
   M2: What is the problem?

4. F2: Looks like rain. Better look for your umbrella.
   M1: Yeah, I think it's definitely going to rain—that's why I'm not going out.
   M2: What is the man going to do?

5. M2: You mean it's *still* closed?
   M1: Yes, sir, the repairs won't be done for another two weeks. You'll have to take Highway 17 and cross downriver from here.
   M2: What are they talking about?

6. M2: OK, so I'll bring the portable stove and the food.
   M1: And I'll bring the tent and we'll each bring a sleeping bag. Hey, this is going to be fun!
   M2: What are the speakers probably planning to do?

7. F1: I like your new glasses, Brian.
   M1: I like these new frames, too, but my vision is blurry, and I've been having headaches. I've got to go back to Dr. Lamb and get some new lenses prescribed.
   M2: What does Brian intend to do?

8. F2: Do you think I'll need to put on two coats of this latex?
   M1: Will you be using brushes or a roller?
   M2: What are they discussing?

9. F1: Want to watch that documentary about Alaska?
   F2: Sure—what channel?
   M2: What are the speakers going to do?

10. F2: Ron, I need that art history book I leant you last month.
   M1: Umm, well, I'm going to have to replace it for you. See, Tuesday I was looking at it out in the yard, and forgot to bring it in with me—and you remember that rain we had Tuesday night?
   M2: What problem did Ron have with the book?

11. M2: Take a look at this model. It's incredibly fast.
   F1: Does it have much memory?
   M2: What are the speakers discussing?

12. F2: Shirley, are you going to go right on to business school when you finish your undergraduate studies?
   F1: Actually, I hope to get some practical experience with a big corporation first.
   M2: What will the woman probably do after she finishes her undergraduate program?

13. M1: I think we need a new deck. I haven't won a single hand.
   F1: Come on, it's your deal—I'll cut the cards.
   M2: What are these people doing?

14. F2: Dave, Phyllis is going to be upset with you if you don't send her a postcard while we're here.
   M1: Yeah, well, I'd send her one if I knew where to buy a stamp.
   M2: What is the problem?

15. M1: Let's go to that soup and salad restaurant, okay?
   F1: All right, we'll go there, but their soups are always much too salty for me.
   M2: What will the woman probably do?

EXERCISE 10

Answer Key

1. B	4. A	7. B	10. A	13. B
2. B	5. A	8. A	11. B	14. B
3. B	6. B	9. A	12. A	15. B

TAPESCRIPT

1. F1: Doug and Rose are such good friends.
   M1: Well—they *used* to be.
   M2: What does the man say?

2. M1: I'm going to rewire my house myself.
   F2: If I were you, Roger, I think I'd have a professional do it.
   M2: What does the woman tell Roger?

3. M1: I thought this was a classical music station.
   M2: It used to be, but now it's a 24-hour news station.
   F2: What does the man say about the radio station?

4. F1: Lynn, who did you get to change your oil?
   F2: Why would I get someone to do *that*?
   M2: What can be inferred from Lynn's remark?

5. F1: I'm having a hard time getting used to this early morning class.

M1: Yeah, me too.

M2: What does the man mean?

6. M2: Peggy, do you ever go roller-skating anymore?

F2: Sometimes, but not as much as I used to.

M2: What does Peggy mean?

7. F1: You got some egg on your tie.

M1: I know. I'll have to get it cleaned.

M2: What does the man mean?

8. F2: There's something different about your apartment, isn't there?

M1: That poster over my desk used to be over the sofa.

M2: What does the man mean?

9. M2: Will you be able to take a vacation in August?

F1: I don't know if my boss will let me. That's our busiest time of year.

M2: What does the woman mean?

10. F2: Greg, that was an interesting point you made in class.

M1: Thanks. But when the teacher made me explain what I meant, I didn't know exactly what to say.

M2: What did Greg's teacher do?

11. F1: Carter doesn't look the same at all these days.

F2: I'm not used to seeing him without glasses either.

M2: What do the speakers say about Carter?

12. F2: Nick, how do you like this hot, humid weather?

M1: Well, growing up in New Orleans, I'm pretty much used to it.

M2: What does Nick tell the woman?

13. F1: You look nice today, Sally.

M1: Thanks—our club is having our photo taken today for the yearbook.

M2: What does Sally mean?

14. M1: You finally bought a microwave oven, I see.

F2: Uh-huh, but I haven't gotten used to it yet.

M2: What does the woman mean?

15. M1: Jan, look behind you—there's a deer.

F2: Oh, isn't it beautiful. Do you think it will let us get a little closer to it?

M2: What does Jan ask the man?

End of Tape 2, Side A.

MINI-TEST 1: DIALOGS

Answer Key

1. D	7. C	13. A	19. B	25. C
2. A	8. D	14. D	20. D	26. A
3. A	9. B	15. A	21. C	27. D
4. C	10. D	16. C	22. B	28. B
5. A	11. C	17. C	23. C	29. D
6. B	12. B	18. A	24. A	30. D

TAPESCRIPT

1. M1: What do you think of Wanda?

F2: When I first met her, I didn't like her very much, but I really warmed up to her after awhile.

M1: What does the woman imply about Wanda?

2. F2: Now, if there are no more questions, let's move on to the next chapter.

M1: Excuse me, professor—could we go over that last point once more?

M2: What does the man want to do?

3. M2: Great weather we're having, huh?

F1: Yeah, but don't get too used to it. The weather report in the newspaper said that there's a big change in store.

M2: What does the woman mean?

4. F1: This is an interesting editorial—want to read it?

M2: I want to read the sports section and look over the classified ads first.

M2: What are these people doing?

5. M1: My sister is looking for a roommate. Do you know anyone who might want to move in with her?

F1: How about Grace?

M2: What do we learn from this conversation?

6. M1: I'm almost out of money again this month.

F2: Why don't you keep track of your expenses and payments? That might help you make ends meet.

M2: What does the woman think the man should do?

7. M1: Where do you think I should put this lamp, in my living room or in my bedroom?

F2: If I were you, I'd put it in the closet.

M2: What can be inferred from the woman's comment?

8. M1: We'd better leave right now.

F2: What's the rush, Mark?

M2: What does the woman want to know?

9. F1: Look over there. Is that Ernie in the red car?

M1: No, but it certainly looks like him.

M2: What does the man mean?

10. M1: It's freezing out there! I'm going to put on my scarf and gloves.

F2: Shouldn't you put on your hat too?

M2: What does the woman mean?

11. M1: Have you ever seen that old Humphrey Bogart movie *Casablanca*?

F1: Seen it! Only about a million times!

M2: What does the woman imply about the movie?

12. F1: I didn't think the team was well prepared for that game.

M1: To tell you the truth, neither did I.

M2: What does the man mean?

13. M2: Becky, are you going to be using that computer much longer? If so, I can go use one at the library.

F1: I'm almost finished.

M2: What can be inferred from this conversation?

14. F2: I didn't think John had ever been scuba diving before.

M1: Oh, sure. John's an old hand at scuba diving.

M2: What does the man say about John?

15. F2: Why are you walking that way, Richard? Did you hurt yourself when you went skiing?

M1: No, no—it's these shoes; they're not broken in yet.

M2: What problem is Richard having?

16. M1: Judy, I just wrote a new song. Want to hear it?

F1: Well, what are you waiting for?

M2: What does the woman mean?

17. M1: I didn't realize you were an art history major.

F2: I'm not. I'm taking a class in art history, but I'm studying to be a commercial artist.

M2: What are these people discussing?

18. M2: We should have a party.
    F1: You took the words right out of my mouth.
    M2: What does the woman mean?

19. M1: I'm going to drop by Sophie's apartment to give her the good news.
    F2: Why bother? She'll be at the meeting this afternoon.
    M2: What does the woman mean?

20. F2: Ted sure is outgoing.
    F1: Isn't he! It's hard to believe he used to be shy.
    M2: What do the speakers imply about Ted?

21. F1: Did you see that ring Laura bought?
    F2: Uh-huh—must have cost her a pretty penny.
    M2: What do the speakers mean?

22. F2: Bill, I thought you had so much work to do.
    M1: I'm just taking a little break.
    M2: What can be inferred from this conversation?

23. F1: Could you help me move this box upstairs?
    M1: Sure, I . . . say, what do you have in here? Your rock collection?
    M2: What can be inferred from the man's comment?

24. F1: What a great haircut, Sarah!
    F2: You think so? I think she took too much off.
    M2: What is Sarah's opinion?

25. F1: What room is Professor Clayburn speaking in tonight?
    M1: Professor Clayburn is speaking tonight?
    M2: What does the man imply by his remark?

26. M2: Can I look at that drawing for a second?
    F2: Be my guest.
    M2: What does the woman mean?

27. M1: Want me to turn up the heater?
    F2: Please don't—I'm burning up back here.
    M2: What does the woman mean?

28. M2: I thought I heard barking coming from Joe's room.
    M1: Barking! Doesn't Joe know there are regulations against keeping pets in the dorm?
    F2: What is learned from this conversation?

29. M1: I stopped by Doctor Norton's office at the Medical Center.
    F2: Really? What for?
    M2: What does the woman want to know?

30. F1: Did you know Angela had finished all her required courses? She'll be graduating in May.
    M1: Oh, so she doesn't have to repeat that chemistry course after all.
    M2: What had the man assumed about Angela?

PART B, EXTENDED CONVERSATIONS: EXERCISES AND MINI-TEST

EXERCISE 11

Answer Key		
Conversation 1	**Conversation 2**	**Conversation 3**
1. b	5. c	9. d
2. a	6. a	10. e
3. d	7. b	11. c
4. c	8. d	12. a
		13. b
B	A	D

(There is no tapescript for Exercise 11.)

EXERCISE 12

Answer Key			
1. B	5. A	9. A	13. C
2. C	6. C	10. C	14. A
3. A	7. B	11. C	15. C
4. A	8. C	12. B	16. B

TAPESCRIPT

Questions 1 and 2: Listen to a conversation between a teacher and a student:

M1: Professor Mueller, I've almost finished preparing my presentation for your class, but I'm not really satisfied with it. Could you give me some advice?

F2: I'll be happy to. What topic did you choose?

M1: It's about methods of predicting earthquakes, but so far, it's just a lot of facts and figures. How can I make it more interesting?

F2: Maybe you could use some computer graphics to help the class make sense of your statistics.

1. What will the main topic of this talk probably be?
2. For what class is the man probably preparing a presentation?

Questions 3 and 4: Listen to a conversation that takes place on a college campus:

F1: Hi there, Doctor Newman, do you remember me?

M2: Oh, sure. We met at the reception in the dean's office last week, didn't we?

F1: That's right. I'm Alice Hart. Are you on your way to a class?

M2: Yes, I am, but I'm not in any great hurry. How about you?

F1: Me, too. I've got a German class in a few minutes.

M2: Well, I'm going to a language class myself. You see, I teach signing.

F1: Signing?

M2: Right, signing. Signing is just a short way of saying American Sign Language. It's the language deaf people use to communicate.

3. Who are the people taking part in this conversation?
4. What will the rest of the conversation probably be about?

Questions 5 and 6: Listen to the following conversation:

F1: I'm in Professor Quinn's psychology class. She told us that she'd put some articles on reserve for her class.

F2: Yes, those would be at the reserve desk.

F1: Do I need a library card to look at those articles?

F2: No, just a student ID card. If you've never checked out any reserve materials, I can tell you what you need to do.

5. What will the main topic of this conversation probably be?

6. Where does this conversation probably take place?

Questions 7 to 9: Listen to a conversation that takes place at a hospital:

F1: Good afternoon, Dr. Marshall. I know you must be very busy, so I appreciate your taking some time to talk to me.

M2: That's all right. What can I do for you?

F1: Well, I'm interested in a career in hospital administration. My academic adviser suggested I speak to you. I was hoping you could give me some information about the field.

M2: I'd be glad to. Is there something in particular you wanted to know?

F1: I was wondering what type of educational background a hospital administrator needs. Is a degree in medicine required?

M2: No, not necessarily. Some hospital administrators are medical doctors, but many of us aren't. My own doctoral degree is in public administration.

7. Why does the woman want to talk to Dr. Marshall?

8. What is Dr. Marshall's occupation?

9. What is Dr. Marshall's attitude toward the woman?

Question 10: Listen to the following conversation:

M1: Come on, Dorothy, turn off that television and let's go. The softball game starts in twenty minutes.

F2: Just a second—I want to find out who won the race.

M1: What race—a marathon?

F2: Well, it's kind of a marathon, but for dogs and dog sledders. It's called the Iditarod. It's run every year in Alaska.

10. What will the main topic of this conversation probably be?

Questions 11 and 12: Listen to the following conversation:

M1: Well, I had a nice, relaxing vacation. How about you, Tina?

F2: I wouldn't exactly call it relaxing, but it was interesting.

M1: I remember you said you were either going to Europe or you were going to work at your parents' company.

F2: I changed my mind and didn't do either of those. I decided to volunteer for an archaeological project in New Mexico.

M1: That *does* sound interesting.

11. Who is Tina?

12. What will the two speakers probably discuss?

Questions 13 and 14: Listening to a telephone conversation:
(*RING . . . RING . . . SOUND OF PHONE BEING PICKED UP*)

F1: Good morning. Thanks for calling the Sales Office of Hillman and Johnson Publishers.

M2: Yes, hello. This is Dave Gruening. I'm the manager of Kennedy Bookstore at Southwestern State University. I'm calling to check on the availability of a textbook, *Case Studies in International Business,* for the spring semester.

F1: Let me just check that on my computer. (*sound of computer keystrokes*) Umm, let's see, is that the text by Sternberg?

M2: That's right. I'll need at least 120 copies sent to the bookstore at the latest by next Wednesday.

F1: I can't really promise they'll be there by next Wednesday—it may be the following week.

Peterson's TOEFL CBT Success

M2: But that class starts on Monday of the following week.
13. Who is the woman who answers the phone?
14. When does this conversation take place?

Questions 15 and 16: Listen to a conversation that takes place in a university office:

M1: Hi. How can I help you?
F2: I'm looking for an application form for the graduate school—can I pick one up here?
M1: No, this is the Financial Aid Office. Graduate Admissions is across campus from here. Do you know where Nicholson Hall is? It's in the office building next to that.
F2: Ummm, I'm not sure—I'm not very familiar with this campus.
15. Where does the man probably work?
16. What will the rest of the conversation probably deal with?

LISTENING EXERCISE 13.1

Answer Key					
1. C	4. C	7. A	10. A	13. C	16. C
2. B	5. A	8. B	11. C	14. C	17. B
3. C	6. A	9. A	12. C	15. B	

TAPESCRIPT

Questions 1 and 2: Listen to Portion 1 of Conversation A:

F1: I just read an article in a magazine that talked about different types of exercise. Guess what kind it recommended?
M1: Let's see—was it jogging?
F1: No, according to the article, jogging can cause leg and foot injuries for some people.
1. From what source did the woman get her information about exercising?
2. According to the woman, what is one of the disadvantages of jogging?

Questions 3 and 4: Listen to Portion 2 of Conversation A:

M1: Then what kind of exercise did the article suggest?
F1: Cross-country skiing. The article said cross-country skiing exercises almost all of the muscle-systems of the body, and that it's good for the heart and lungs.
M1: Cross-country skiing! I would never have guessed that. Tell me, how is cross-country skiing different from downhill skiing?
F1: Well, for one thing, you don't have to go to the mountains to go cross-country skiing. You can go anywhere there's snow.
3. What form of exercise did the article recommend?
4. What can be inferred about cross-country skiing from this conversation?

Questions 5 and 6: Listen to Portion 3 of Conversation A:

M1: But what if there isn't enough snow to go skiing?
F1: The article said that there are exercise machines that provide almost the same kind of exercise. The only problem is, they're fairly expensive.
M1: I see. So if you have one of these machines, you can get the best kind of exercise and not even get your ears cold!
5. What does the article suggest people do if there isn't enough snow for skiing?
6. What is one disadvantage of a cross-country skiing machine?

Questions 7 and 8: Listen to Portion 1 of Conversation B:

F2: You look exhausted this morning, Steve.

M1: I *am* pretty tired. I stayed up nearly all night getting ready for a midterm exam this morning.

F2: Have you gotten the results of the test yet?

M1: Yes, and unfortunately, my grade could have been much better. No matter how much time I spend studying, I never seem to do well on tests.

  7. Why is Steve tired?

  8. How does Steve feel about the grade he received on the test?

Questions 9 and 10: Listen to Portion 2 of Conversation B:

F2: You know, Steve, if I were you, I'd consider taking some of the seminars offered by the Study Skills Center.

M1: The Study Skills Center? Never heard of it.

F2: Well, it's run by a group of graduate students and professors who help undergraduate students improve their study techniques. See, last semester, I had to do a research paper for a sociology course, but I had no idea how to collect research materials until I took one of the seminars at the Center.

  9. Who are the Study Skills Center's seminars designed to help?

 10. How was the woman helped by the seminar that she took?

Questions 11 to 13: Refer to Portion 3 of Conversation B:

M1: What kind of seminars does the Center offer that could help me?

F2: They have one on test-taking skills. There's also a seminar that teaches you to manage your time efficiently. You should find *that* useful, I should think.

M1: You're probably right. Where is the Center?

F2: They hold most of their seminars in the library, but the main office is in Staunton Hall, right across the quadrangle from the Physics Tower.

M1: You know, I think I'll go over there right now.

F2: Why don't you wait until tomorrow? Right now, you should go home and catch up on your sleep.

 11. What is one type of seminar that the woman thinks Steve would find useful?

 12. Where is the Study Skills Center's main office?

 13. What does the woman suggest Steve do next?

Questions 14 and 15: Listen to Portion 1 of Conversation C:

F1: Hello, Roger. You're looking thoughtful today. What's on your mind?

M2: Well, Margie, you know the public television station is having an auction to raise money. They need to build a new transmitter tower so that viewers can get a clearer picture. I watch that channel a lot. I'd like to help out, but I don't really have anything to donate to the auction, and I can't afford to buy something new.

F1: Why not donate a service?

M2: What do you mean?

F1: Well, Roger, you're an experienced carpenter, right? Why don't you offer two hours of your carpentry work for free to whoever makes the highest bid?

 14. Why is the television station trying to raise money?

 15. What does the woman suggest that Roger do?

Questions 16 and 17: Refer to Portion 2 of Conversation C:

M2: That's a great idea! Thanks. And say, I know you watch some shows on that channel yourself. Why don't you donate a service too?

F1: You know, I'd like to help, but I have final exams coming up, so I'd better not make too many commitments. But I *will* come to the auction, and I'll bring my parents with me. I know they'd like to get some expert carpentry work done.

 16. What excuse does the woman make for not donating a service?

 17. What does the woman imply about her parents?

EXERCISE 13.2

Answer Key			
1. B	4. C	7. B	10. C
2. C	5. B	8. B	11. B
3. A	6. A	9. C	12. B

TAPESCRIPT

Questions 1-5: Listen to two students talk about a trip to California:

M1: So, Rebecca, what did *you* do for spring break?

F1: I went to southern California. I was in Los Angeles and San Diego. Oh, and I stopped in San Juan Capistrano. That's south of Los Angeles and north of San Diego. I happened to be there just about the time the swallows returned.

M1: Oh, I've heard about that—they always return on the same day, don't they?

F1: That's right, on March 19th. And they always fly away on the same day, October 23rd. In the meantime, they migrate over 7,000 miles to get to their winter homes.

M1: Seven thousand miles—imagine! And always coming back on the same day!

F1: Yes, except for one year, a long time ago—they were delayed for a day by a storm at sea.

M1: So, what's the town of San Juan Capistrano like?

F1: Oh, it's a pleasant little town. Once there was a famous mission church there.

M1: Once? What happened to it?

F1: It was destroyed by an earthquake almost two hundred years ago. But there *is* an old adobe church that survived. The swallows build their nests in the walls and towers of that church.

M1: You sure were lucky to be there on the one day of the year when the swallows return.

F1: Well, I wasn't there *exactly* on that day. I got to town a couple of days later—but I did see the parade celebrating the swallows' return.

M1: They have a parade? The people there must really like those swallows.

F1: Sure—they bring lots of tourists to town, and besides, the swallows eat insects—including mosquitoes!

1. Where is the town of San Juan Capistrano?
2. What can be inferred about the swallows mentioned in the conversation?
3. When do the swallows return to San Juan Capistrano?
4. How far do the swallows migrate?
5. Which of the following did Rebecca see?

Questions 6 to 8: Listen to a conversation that takes place on a college campus:

M1: I'm here for the campus tour.

F2: I'm sorry. We only offer a guided tour during the first week of classes.

M1: Oh, really? That's too bad. I was really hoping to get a good orientation. Last week, I spent nearly an hour trying to find a classroom in the Fine Arts Building.

F2: You know what you *can* do—you can take the self-guided tour. This pamphlet tells you exactly what to do, where to go, and what to look for, and it has a complete map of the campus.

M1: Sounds easy enough—where do I start?

F2: The first stop is right here, in the Student Center Building. Then you go next door to the Science Building—there's a great planetarium there, by the way—and from there you go to the University Recreation Center. After that, just follow the directions in the pamphlet and you can't go wrong.

6. When is the guided tour of the campus given?
7. What did the man have difficulty locating the week before?
8. Where does the self-guided tour start?

Questions 9 to 12: Listen to the following conversation:

M2: Hi, Helen. How did your driving test go? Did you get your driver's license yet?

F1: So far, I've just taken the written test. I did well enough on that, but I still have to take the road test.

M2: I remember when I took the road test a few years ago. The first time I took it, I failed.

F1: *You* failed! But you're such a good driver! What happened?

M2: Well, I took a left-hand turn from the right lane, and the examiner told me just to turn around and go back to the testing center. It was pretty embarrassing.

F1: My big problem is parallel parking. I just can't seem to get a car into those little spaces.

M2: If you like, we can go out in my car before you take the road test and practice parallel parking.

F1: That would be great. I've just *got* to get my license. I can't believe that I have a car that my parents gave me just sitting in my garage, and I can't even drive it.

9. What did Helen recently pass?
10. What problem did the man have when he took his road test several years before?
11. What does the man offer to do for Helen?
12. Why can't Helen use the car in her garage?

End of Tape 2, Side B.

MINI-TEST 2: EXTENDED CONVERSATIONS

Answer Key

| 1. A | 3. C | 5. D | 7. B |
| 2. C | 4. D | 6. A | 8. C |

TAPESCRIPT

Questions 1–4: Listen to a conversation at a university library:

M1: Hi, Martha. What are you doing here?

F2: Oh, I just came to look up some terms in the *Encyclopedia of Art* for my art history class. What about you, Stanley?

M1: I've got two papers due at the end of this term, and I've been getting an early start on them by collecting some references and writing down some statistics. I've spent most of the day here.

F2: Really? Well, you ought to be ready for a break then. Want to go get a snack or something?

M1: You know, that sounds great—let me just get my things together and . . . hey, where are my notes?

F2: What notes?

M1: The notes I spent all day working on. I don't see them.

F2: You mean, you lost your notebook?

M1: No, I don't use a notebook—I take notes on index cards.

F2: Well, just think about where you could have left them. Retrace your steps since you came in the library.

M1: Let's see—when I first arrived, I came here, to the reference room.

F2: Maybe they're somewhere in this room, then.

M1: No, I had them after that. I went to the stacks. . . .

F2: Stacks? What do you mean, the stacks?

M1: You know, the book stacks. That's what they call the main part of the library, where most of the books are shelved.

F2: Well, that's where you should look.

M1: No, because I took some more notes from journals in the periodicals room up on the third floor. I'll bet that's where they are.

F2: Well, you go look up there, and I'll check with one of the librarians behind the main desk, just in case someone turned them in.

M1: Okay, and thanks for helping me out. Just as soon as I find them, we'll go get a bite to eat.

1. Why did Martha come to the library?
2. What did Stanley lose?
3. According to Stanley, what does the term "stacks" refer to?
4. In what part of the library is this conversation taking place?

Questions 5–8: Listen to the following conversation:

M1: Guess what—I joined the Spelunking Society last month.

F1: Seriously? Aren't spelunkers people who go down into caves? I thought you were only interested in mountain climbing!

M1: I *do* like to climb, but you know, the two sports have a lot in common. I'll give you an example: The same technique for climbing down steep slopes is used in both sports. It's called *rappelling*. Of course, climbers use this technique to come down cliffs, while spelunkers use it to go down holes.

F1: What else does your society do?

M1: For one thing, we help preserve caves. Believe it or not, some people are so careless that they just leave their litter in caves. And some people even write on cave walls. So we pick up trash and clean away the graffiti.

F1: I don't think I'd like spelunking very much. Caves are wet and cold and dark, aren't they?

M1: I suppose they are, but they can also be beautiful. Tell you what, why don't you come along with me to the meeting tonight? They'll be showing slides that we took in a cave last weekend. You'll see some incredible rock formations and crystals. It might change the way you think about caves.

5. What is the main topic of this conversation?
6. According to the man, what is meant by the term *rappelling*?
7. What other activity does the Spelunking Society engage in besides exploring caves?
8. What does the man invite the woman to do?

This is the end of the Listening Program for Part B, Extended Conversations.

PART C, MINI-TALKS: EXERCISES AND MINI-TEST

EXERCISE 14

Answer Key

Talk 1	Talk 2	Talk 3
1. b	6. d	9. d
2. c	7. c	10. b
3. a	8. b	11. e
4. d		12. a
5. e		

(There is no tapescript for this exercise.)

LISTENING EXERCISE 15

Answer Key

1. B	5. B	9. B	13. C	17. A
2. A	6. A	10. C	14. A	18. A
3. C	7. A	11. A	15. B	19. A
4. B	8. C	12. C	16. B	20. C

TAPESCRIPT

Questions 1–2: Listen to the following talk:

F1: Hello there, ladies and gentlemen, and welcome to the Larabee Springs Wildlife Preserve. Today, you'll have the chance to see one of the largest herds of buffaloes in North America and many other types of wildlife. I hope all of you have your cameras with you.

1. Who is the speaker?
2. What will the talk probably be about?

Questions 3–4: Listen to a talk given at an athletic club:

M1: I'd like to take this opportunity to thank everyone for coming out to the Edgewood Athletic Club for our exhibition match. Before the match gets under way, I'd like to give you all a little background on how the sport of handball is played. Even though it's a game with a long tradition, some people aren't as familiar with the rules of this sport as they might be with, say, those of tennis.

3. What is the purpose of this talk?
4. When is this talk being given?

Questions 5–6: Listen to a talk given at a factory:

M1: Good morning. On behalf of our management team and our workers, I'd like to welcome all of you to our plant. You may have wondered, how do soft drinks get in those cans? How are the cans sealed? By the end of the tour, you'll know the answers. Now, please follow me out onto the factory floor.

5. Who is the audience for this talk?
6. What will the main topic for this talk probably be?

SECTION 1: LISTENING COMPREHENSION

Questions 7–8: Listen to the following talk:

F2: Since all of you have expressed interest in joining the university dance program, I probably don't have to say much about the physical and psychological rewards of being in a dance program such as this one. Instead, I want to concentrate on some of the drawbacks—the demands that will be put on your time and the sacrifices you'll be called on to make if you are chosen for the program.

7. What will the main topic of this talk probably be?
8. What is the speaker's probable occupation?

Questions 9–10: Listen to the following talk:

M2: As president of the State Historical Society, I'd like to call this meeting to order, and welcome all our members and guests. Tonight, I'm going to give you a short presentation on some famous shipwrecks, especially shipwrecks that took place in the waters off New England.

9. Who is the speaker?
10. What will this talk probably concern?

Questions 11–12: Listen to a lecture given in a university classroom:

F2: In the last few weeks, we have discussed how to organize your ideas, use your outline as a blueprint, and write the first draft of your essay. Today, we're going to consider another important process—the art of editing your paper.

11. In what course is this lecture probably being given?
12. What will the rest of this lecture probably deal with?

Questions 13–14: Listen to a talk given at a ski lodge:

M1: Good morning, and welcome to Winterstar Ski Area. We truly hope to make your introduction to skiing as safe and enjoyable as possible.

13. For whom is this talk probably intended?
14. What will this talk probably concern?

Questions 15–16: Listen to this talk given in a university classroom:

F2: I hope no one had any trouble finding the classroom this morning. In a few minutes, I'll be handing out the course syllabus. As you'll see, we'll be spending the first few days discussing the law of supply and demand.

15. What class does Professor Wills probably teach?
16. At what point in the semester is this talk being given?

Questions 17–18: Listen to the following talk:

M2: Good morning, everyone. This is Captain Jackson, and I'd like to welcome you aboard the whale-watch cruise on the *S. S. Bluefish*. In just a few minutes we'll be outside the harbor and we'll steer toward Travis Island. If we spot any whales today, you'll most likely see them off the starboard bow—that's the right-hand, forward side—as we approach the island. In the meantime, I'd like to take this opportunity to tell you a little about how these magnificent sea mammals live.

17. Where is this talk probably being given?
18. What will the rest of this talk probably be about?

Questions 19–20: Listen to a talk given by a campus police officer:

F2: Hello. I'm Officer Jane Kelly. Thanks to all of you for coming this evening. As you know, there have been a number of accidents recently involving bicyclists and pedestrians on campus. There have also been some incidents involving the theft of bicycles, and I know this is a special concern for all of you. I intend to address both these issues during the course of the meeting.

19. Who is the probable audience for this talk?
20. What is the speaker's main purpose in giving this talk?

LISTENING EXERCISE 16.1

Answer Key

Talk A	Talk B	Talk C
1. B	7. B	13. A
2. A	8. C	14. C
3. C	9. B	15. B
4. B	10. B	16. A
5. C	11. C	17. B
6. B	12. A	18. A
		19. C
		20. B
		21. B

TAPESCRIPT

Questions 1-2: Listen to Portion 1 of Talk A:

M1: I'd like to welcome all of you to what is, I think, the most unusual course offered by the biology department—the Ecology of Coral Reefs. This course is unique because of our research methods. We don't just collect data from the library. Instead, we go to a coral reef in the Virgin Islands to do field studies.

1. What does the speaker imply about the course?
2. How will students do research in this class?

Questions 3-4: Listen to Portion 2 of Talk A:

M1: To prepare you for this trip, we'll first do some formal classroom work in biology. We'll also be going to the university pool to practice scuba diving and to learn the basics of underwater photography. And we'll be talking about precautions you must take to avoid damaging the reef. A coral reef is a very fragile environment, as you'll see.

3. Which of the following will be studied in a formal classroom setting?
4. How does the speaker characterize tropical reefs?

Questions 5-6: Listen to Portion 3 of Talk A:

M1: Because of the nature of this course, it does require a certain financial commitment on your part. The department can only provide basic equipment for you. You have to pay for your own airfare to the Virgin Islands as well as for your food and lodging. There are a few limited scholarships available for those who might have financial problems. See me after class if you're interested in applying for one of these. Any questions?

5. What will the department provide the students in this class?
6. What does the speaker suggest for those who might have problems with the costs of this course?

Questions 7-8: Listen to Portion 1 of Talk B:

F1: The largest American land mammals are bears. Maybe because bears can stand up and walk on two legs, we humans have always found them fascinating. Another characteristic bears have in common with humans is their range of appetite. As a matter of fact, they'll eat almost anything: berries, roots, nuts, meat, fish—and of course, they're particularly fond of honey.

7. The speaker suggests that bears are interesting to humans for what reason?
8. What does the speaker imply about the eating habits of bears?

Questions 9–10: Listen to Portion 2 of Talk B:

F1: The largest bear is the giant kodiak of Alaska. When this giant stands up, it may reach a height of 10 feet, and it may weigh up to 1,500 pounds. Ten feet tall and weighing three-quarters of a ton—what a sight they must be! Outside of Alaska, the largest bear in the United States is the grizzly bear. There aren't many of these bears left in North America—probably only a few thousand. Most of those live in Yellowstone National Park in Wyoming.

9. How tall can kodiak bears be when they are standing?
10. Where do most grizzly bears live?

Questions 11–12: Listen to Portion 3 of Talk B:

F1: Now, the most common bear in the United States is the black bear, which you'll see in many parts of the country. These bears are smaller than grizzlies and may seem friendly, but watch out! Like all bears, they are unpredictable and can be dangerous.

11. What is the most common type of bear in the United States?
12. Which of the following can be inferred from the lecture about black bears?

Questions 13–14: Listen to Portion 1 of Talk C:

F2: The skies above Earth are turning into a junkyard, according to space scientists. Ever since the Soviet Union launched *Sputnik*, the first satellite way back in 1957, virtually every launch has contributed to the amount of debris in Earth orbit. Luckily, most of this junk burns up after it reenters the Earth's atmosphere, but some will be up there in orbit for years to come.

13. When did orbital debris first become a problem?
14. What happens to most pieces of orbital debris?

Questions 15–16: Listen to Portion 2 of Talk C:

F2: Today, there are about 8,000 bodies in orbit being monitored from Earth. Out of all those, only around three- to four-hundred are active and useful. There are also probably half a million pieces of debris too tiny to be monitored.

15. How many orbital bodies are being monitored today?
16. Why is it impossible to monitor most pieces of orbital debris?

Questions 17–18: Listen to Portion 3 of Talk C:

F2: Some orbital debris is as big as a bus, but most is in the form of tiny flecks of paint or pieces of metal. The debris also includes food wrappers, an astronaut's glove, the lens cap from a camera, broken tools, and bags of unwashed uniforms. The largest pieces—mostly empty booster rockets—are not necessarily the most dangerous because they can be detected and spacecraft can maneuver away from them. And the smallest particles generally cause only surface damage. However, a collision with a piece of metal only an eighth of an inch in diameter—say about the size of an aspirin—could puncture the hull of a spacecraft or space station and cause a catastrophic depressurization. That's because these particles are moving so incredibly fast!

17. Which of the following is probably most dangerous to astronauts on a spacecraft?
18. What makes particles in space so dangerous?

Questions 19–21: Listen to Portion 4 of Talk C:

F2: So what can be done about this problem? Well, two engineers recently proposed a novel solution to the problem of orbital junk, a device that consists of an array of water-spraying cones lined with plastic fibers to collect the debris and canisters to store it in. I brought a model of this device along with me so you could see what it looks like. Although this invention is still in its conceptual stage, two possible uses have been proposed. It could be launched as a free-flying satellite that actively seeks out debris or it could be launched into orbit with a spacecraft and serve as its shield.

19. What did the speaker bring with her?
20. What role do the cones play in the device described in this portion of the talk?
21. What can be inferred about the device described in this portion of the talk?

EXERCISE 16.2

Answer Key

1. B	5. B	9. C
2. C	6. A	10. B
3. B	7. C	11. C
4. A	8. A	12. C

TAPESCRIPT

Questions 1–5: Listen to a talk given on a university radio station:

F1: Hello, this is Dana Lockwood with the campus news at noon. Yesterday the Board of Regents voted to raise tuition here at Hambleton University for the third year in a row. As in the previous two years, there will also be increases in the student fees and the room and board charges at the dormitories. This five percent increase makes Hambleton the second most expensive school to attend in the state. Only Babcock University charges more. Penny Chang, co-executive of the Student Council, told us today that there should be some corresponding increase in student services, such as longer hours at the library, more contact time with faculty, and improved lab facilities. However, a spokesperson for the administration said that the additional money has already been earmarked to pay for the higher insurance premiums that the university is being charged and for the construction of a new dormitory.

1. For how many consecutive years has tuition at Hambleton University gone up?
2. Which of the following is NOT mentioned in the talk as going up?
3. What does the speaker say about Babcock University?
4. According to the speaker, who is Penny Chang?
5. What can be inferred from the remark made by the spokesperson for the administration?

Questions 6–9: Listen to a lecture given by a biologist:

F2: Wouldn't it be wonderful if a person who had lost a hand or a leg in an accident could simply grow another in its place? Humans can't do this, of course, nor can any other mammal. But there are creatures who can do this and more.

The champions at regeneration are starfish and some types of worms. If only a small piece of one of these creatures remains alive, it can regenerate an entire new body. Imagine that! Then there are animals such as salamanders or insects that can regenerate entire limbs. When these creatures grow a new limb, here's what happens: a regeneration "bud" forms at the surface of the wound. It is usually cone-shaped and contains the same kind of embryonic cells that were present at the birth of the creature. These develop into specialized cells as they grow, and a new organ is gradually formed.

Unfortunately, the more complex a creature, the less it is able to regenerate. Snakes can replace their skin when they shed it; birds replace lost feathers. Even humans have certain powers of regeneration. When our top layer of skin wears off, day by day, it is continually replaced. Our nails and hair are constantly being replenished. Even our second set of teeth represents a kind of regeneration. And we are able to repair damage such as bone fractures and injuries to the skin and muscles.

Some scientists are studying the process of regeneration in lower animals to try to learn more about it so that, someday, they will be able to apply the lessons they learn to humans. Although it's doubtful that humans will ever be able to do what salamanders or insects do, this research may in the future help doctors heal wounds more quickly.

6. Which of the following is best able to regenerate lost body tissues?
7. Which of the following would NOT be considered regeneration?
8. According to the speaker, what is in a regeneration bud?
9. According to the speaker, why are scientists studying the process of regeneration?

Questions 10–12: Listen to a lecture about Noah Webster:

M1: Today I'm going to talk a little about Noah Webster and the impact he had on American English. Webster was born in Connecticut in 1758 and graduated from Yale University in 1778. This was during the time of the American Revolution, and Webster joined George Washington's army to fight against the British. The end of the war brought independence, but political independence didn't satisfy Webster. He wanted the former colonies to be intellectually independent from Britain as well.

In 1783, Webster published a spelling book which would become known to generations of schoolchildren as the "blue-backed book" because of its blue cover. A couple of years later, he published his dictionary. It is for his dictionary that Webster is chiefly remembered today. The Webster's dictionary popular today is a direct descendant of that book published in the 1780's.

In his dictionary, Webster made many changes in the way English was used in the United States. He suggested new ways of pronouncing words and added words used only in the former colonies to the language. Most of the changes, though, involved spelling. Today, most people in the United States spell words differently from people in Britain because of Webster's original dictionary. Let me just give you a couple of examples—in Britain, words like *center* end in *re*. In the United States, these words end in *-er*. He also took the letter *u* from words like *color*. In the British spelling, that word ends with the letters *o-u-r*, but in the American spelling, it ends with *o-r*.

Still, Webster did not go as far in revising spelling as his friend Benjamin Franklin wanted him to. Franklin wanted to drop all silent letters from words. The word *wrong* would have been spelled *r-o-n-g*, and the word *love* would have been spelled *l-o-v*.

10. According to the speaker, when did Webster graduate from Yale University?
11. What is Noah Webster mainly remembered for today?
12. Which of the following is a spelling that Benjamin Franklin would have approved of?

End of Tape 3, Side A.

MINI-TEST 3: MINI-TALKS

Answer Key

1. D	5. D	9. C
2. C	6. C	10. A
3. B	7. A	11. A
4. D	8. C	12. C

TAPESCRIPT

Questions 1–3: Listen to the following radio talk:

F2: If you're too busy to brush your teeth after every meal, and you sometimes forget to use dental floss, you'll be glad to know that, in the near future, you may be able to have healthier teeth thanks to microphages.

What are microphages? They're tiny viruses that attack and destroy bacteria. Soon, they may be used to fight tooth decay if genetic engineers can develop a specialized type of phage to attack only those microbes that are harmful to the teeth.

These microphages could be used in toothpaste or mouthwash. Once in the mouth, they would consume bacteria that breed on the surface of teeth. The advantage of microphages is that they are absolutely harmless to humans. They attack only one specific bacterium and have no known side effects.

1. What is the main topic of this talk?
2. According to the speaker, which of the following can be said about microphages?
3. The use of microphages as described by the speaker depends on a development in which of the following fields?

Questions 4–8: Listen to a talk given at an orientation session:

F1: Hi, everyone. My name is Beth Sinclair, and I'm director of Campus Food Services. I'd like to join the previous speakers in welcoming you to Brooks College, and I want to give you some information on a very basic subject—staying well fed while you're getting your education.

Now most of you will be purchasing meal tickets soon if you haven't already. You should be aware that there are two plans available. Plan A, which is a little more expensive, allows you to have three meals a day, six days a week. With Plan B, you get two meals a day, your choice of breakfast and dinner or lunch and dinner. So, once again, Plan A is three meals a day, except on Sunday, and Plan B, two meals. On Sunday evenings, everyone's on their own, because all the dormitory cafeterias are closed. Food Services *does* operate some restaurants then, such as the Tiger's Lair over by the stadium or the Bengal Grill at the Student Center, but these restaurants don't take meal tickets. Of course, you can always eat at one of the restaurants near campus.

Now say you're living in Donahue Hall, and you have a friend over in Cooper Village. Can you eat with your friend? Sure, because a meal ticket is good at any cafeteria on campus. Just remember to bring your student ID card as well as your meal ticket. Oh, and what if you have a friend living off campus who wants to eat with you one night? That's fine too. One-time meal tickets are available at a very reasonable price. But remember, you may not sell or give your meal ticket to any other person.

Just one last note about the food in the dorms. Some people have the idea that all dorm food is bland and tastes the same. That may even have been true here at Brooks College until a few years ago. But these days we go out of our way to serve fresh, tasty, healthy food. We offer a great variety of dishes to choose from, including many international dishes, and you can always go back for seconds. So, we're looking forward to seeing you at mealtimes, and bring your appetite.

4. According to the speaker, how are Plan A and Plan B different?
5. Which of the following is closed on Sunday evenings?
6. Which of the following must a student bring to meals in addition to a meal ticket?
7. According to the speaker, which of the following is *not* permitted?
8. According to the speaker, how have the dormitory cafeterias changed in recent years?

Questions 9–12: Listen to a talk given at a zoo:

M1: Ladies and gentlemen, welcome to the City Zoological Gardens' newest exhibit, World of Darkness. Not too many years ago, zoo visitors were unable to observe the behavior of nocturnal animals because these creatures are active during the night and generally sleep during the day, when the zoo is open to visitors. But in the 1960's, zookeepers at the Bronx Zoo, in New York City, found a solution to this problem and developed the system that we now utilize in our exhibit. The animals' habitats are lit with white light at night. The animals think the white light is daylight, so of course, they go to sleep. During the day, their habitats are lit with red light. The animals can barely detect this light. But the red light enables visitors to observe these animals going about their normal nocturnal activities. So enjoy your visit to World of Darkness and enjoy observing these fascinating creatures of the night. And remember, next month is the grand opening of World Down Under, a new exhibit of Australian marsupials. Please join us for that event.

9. Who is the probable audience for this talk?
10. Which of the following does the speaker imply about nocturnal animals exhibited before the 1960's?
11. According to the speaker, why are red lights used to light nocturnal animals' habitats?
12. What will the audience for this talk probably do next?

Peterson's TOEFL CBT Success

ANSWER KEY

MINI-LESSONS FOR PART 1

MINI-LESSON 1.1

1.	about to	14.	by heart
2.	As a matter of fact	15.	bring . . . up
3.	bank on	16.	brought about
4.	broke in on	17.	by no means
5.	better off	18.	break the ice
6.	As a rule	19.	brush up on
7.	break down	20.	bit off more than . . . could chew
8.	all of a sudden	21.	at the drop of a hat
9.	bound to	22.	Beats me
10.	brought up	23.	a breeze
11.	by and large	24.	break up
12.	add up	25.	at ease
13.	be my guest		

MINI-LESSON 1.2

1.	called off	11.	clear up
2.	calm down	12.	cared for
3.	came across	13.	cost an arm and a leg
4.	count on	14.	care for
5.	come up with	15.	Cheer up
6.	checked into	16.	caught up with
	check out	17.	cut out for
7.	check . . . out from	18.	catch on
8.	call it a day	19.	come around to
9.	chip in	20.	calls on
10.	cut off	21.	clear up

MINI-LESSON 1.3

1.	figure out	10.	a far cry from
2.	drop off	11.	drop out of
3.	dreamed up	12.	died down
4.	feel like	13.	drop in on
5.	fallen behind	14.	day in and day out
6.	few and far between	15.	eyes . . . bigger than . . . stomach
7.	do . . . over	16.	Feel free
8.	fed up with	17.	drop . . . a line
9.	fell through		

MINI-LESSON 1.4

1. find out
2. fill out
3. fill in
4. filled . . . in on
5. for good
   for the time being
6. get rid of
7. give away
8. a fish out of water
9. get a kick out of
10. got on
11. get off the ground
12. get along with
13. fixed . . . up
14. gotten in touch with
15. get under way
16. gets in . . . blood
17. get off
18. filled in for

MINI-LESSON 1.5

1. grew up
2. handed out
3. handed in
4. heard of
5. hold on
6. go on with
7. Hold still
8. go easy on
9. go . . . with
10. had on
11. gave . . . hand
12. goes without saying
13. held up
14. heard from
    having the time of . . . life
15. give . . . a hand with
16. hold on to
17. hard to come by
18. hit the road
19. have a word with
20. went overboard

MINI-LESSON 1.6

1. keep an eye on
2. keeping up with
3. lay off
4. looking forward to
5. jump to conclusions
6. keep an eye out for
7. in the long run
8. left out
9. in no time
10. kill . . . time
11. let up
12. in the same boat
13. keep on
14. leave . . . alone
15. looked . . . for
16. looks after
17. in the dark
18. looking into
19. iron out
20. in hot water
21. learned the ropes
22. in favor of
23. know . . . like the back of . . . hand
24. keep track of
25. in store

Mini-Lesson 1.7

1.	looked over	16.	make up . . . mind
2.	on second thought	17.	look out for
3.	make . . . up	18.	on needles and pins
4.	out of order	19.	look . . . up
5.	looks up to	20.	make way for
6.	on hand	21.	next to nothing
7.	make sense of	22.	on the whole
8.	made a point of	23.	No harm done
	over and over	24.	out of . . . mind
9.	on the tip of . . . tongue	25.	mean to
10.	out of the question	26.	an old hand at
11.	out of	27.	mixed up
12.	music to . . . ears	28.	on . . . own
13.	on end	29.	Not at all
14.	odds and end	30.	over . . . head
15.	on the go		

Mini-Lesson 1.8

1.	put up with	11.	pick up
2.	picked up the tab for	12.	picked up
3.	point out		put . . . away
4.	play it by ear	13.	put off
5.	part with	14.	picked out
6.	picked . . . up	15.	pass . . . up
7.	put . . . on	16.	Pay attention
8.	put together	17.	pat . . . on the back
9.	a pretty penny	18.	passed . . . with flying colors
10.	push . . . luck	19.	put . . . aside
		20.	pulling . . . leg

Mini-Lesson 1.9

1.	saw . . . off	13.	show up
2.	see to	14.	run for office
3.	ran out of	15.	sleep on it
4.	right away	16.	showed . . . around
5.	shut down	17.	Save . . . breath
6.	sign up for	18.	rule . . . out
7.	So far, so good	19.	ran into
8.	ring a bell with	20.	slowly but surely
9.	spell . . . out for	21.	short for
10.	run of the mill	22.	snowed under
11.	singing another tune	23.	running a temperature
12.	rough it	24.	see eye to eye with . . . on

Mini-Lesson 1.10

1. stamp out
2. stay up
3. stay out
4. take after
5. taking apart
6. take a break
7. stand for
8. stuck with
9. takes a lot of nerve
10. Stick with
11. spick and span
12. stood out
13. Take it easy
14. stand for
15. straighten up
    stop by
16. take advantage of
17. stock up on
18. a stone's throw from
19. took a lot out of
20. stack up against

Mini-Lesson 1.11

1. try on
2. talked . . . into
3. tore up
4. tell . . . apart
5. take up
6. took part in
7. taking off
8. tear . . . away from
9. throw the book at
10. Take off
11. tried out
12. talked . . . out of
13. talk . . . over
14. throw away
15. think . . . over
16. took a shortcut
17. try out
    take the plunge
18. take . . . time off from

Mini-Lesson 1.12

1. turns into
2. Turn off
3. turn down
4. turn up
5. turn on
6. worn out
7. warm up
8. turned out
9. turn in
10. what the doctor ordered
11. without a hitch
12. work out
13. watch out for
14. Turn around
15. worked . . . out
16. wait on
17. turned . . . down
18. warm up
19. turned out
20. under the weather
21. walking on air

Peterson's TOEFL CBT Success

Section 2

SAMPLE STRUCTURE AND WRITTEN EXPRESSION TEST

Answer Key

Structure

1. C	4. D	7. D	10. C	13. D
2. A	5. B	8. A	11. A	14. C
3. C	6. B	9. C	12. B	15. C

Written Expression

16. B	21. C	26. A	31. D	36. B
17. A	22. B	27. D	32. A	37. C
18. C	23. C	28. C	33. A	38. C
19. B	24. D	29. D	34. C	39. A
20. C	25. C	30. A	35. B	40. B

EXPLANATION: WRITTEN EXPRESSION ITEMS

16. The plural verb *are* indicates that a plural subject, *thousands*, must be used.

17. The preposition *in* should replace the preposition *since*. (The preposition *since* is only used in sentences in which the verb is in the present perfect tense, not the simple past tense—*set*.)

18. The noun *variety* should be used in place of the adjective *various*.

19. The word *alike* is only used in the pattern *A and B are alike*. The correct pattern in this sentence is *A, like B*, ...

20. The subject of the sentence is *use*; *it* is an unnecessary repetition of the subject.

21. A plural pronoun (*their*) should be used to agree with the plural noun *cowboys*.

22. The relative pronoun *who* can only refer to a person, not to a thing. The relative pronoun *which* should be used instead.

23. An adverb (*potentially*), not an adjective (*potential*) is needed.

24. The subject of the clause (*one species*) is singular, so the singular verb *is* must be used.

25. *Almost* is the wrong word choice. The best word choice is *most* (or *almost all*).

26. *Despite* is only used before noun phrases. An adverb-clause marker (*although*) must be used with a clause.

27. A noun (*injury*), not a verb (*injure*) is required.

28. The preposition must precede the relative pronoun: *in which*.

29. After the verb *permit*, an infinitive (*to exist*) is used.

30. The correct pattern is *between A and B*.

31. In order to be parallel with the other words in the series (*logic* and *probability*), the name of the field (*engineering*) must be used.

32. The verb in this sentence should be passive; therefore, the past participle *known* (not the *-ing* form *knowing*) must be used.

33. Before a word beginning with a vowel sound (*honor*), the article *an* must be used.

34. The superlative form of a one-syllable adjective (*old*) is formed with the suffix *-est*: *oldest*.

35. The noun *belief* should be used in place of the verb *believe*.

36. The plural pronoun *those* should be used to refer to the plural noun phrase *public buildings*.

37. The correct pattern is *neither . . . nor*.

38. A past participle (*held*) is needed in place of the *-ing* form.

39. The correct pattern is *so* + adjective + *that* clause (*too* is used in the pattern *too* + adjective + infinitive).

40. A plural noun (*teeth*) is required.

PART A, STRUCTURE: EXERCISES AND MINI-TESTS

Note: Items marked with an asterisk (*) do not focus on the structures that are presented in that lesson.

Exercise 17

1. B	6. A	11. A	16. D	21. A
2. D	7. D	12. B	17. B	22. D*
3. A	8. C	13. A*	18. D	23. C
4. B	9. A*	14. D	19. C	24. C
5. A	10. B	15. A	20. C	25. D

Exercise 18

1. D	5. A	9. A	13. C
2. C*	6. B	10. C	14. C
3. B*	7. C	11. B	15. D
4. A	8. A*	12. D	16. A

Exercise 19

1. A	4. D	7. B*	10. C
2. B	5. A	8. D*	11. B
3. B	6. C	9. D	12. A

Exercise 20

1. B	4. A*	7. C	10. D
2. C	5. B	8. C	11. B
3. A	6. D	9. A	12. D

Exercise 21

1. C	4. D	7. C	10. A	13. D	16. A*
2. B	5. B	8. C	11. C	14. D	17. B
3. D	6. C*	9. D	12. B*	15. C	18. C

Exercise 22

1. D	4. D	7. A	10. C
2. B	5. B*	8. A	11. D
3. A	6. C	9. D	12. B*

Exercise 23

1. B*	4. B	7. D*	10. A
2. C	5. A	8. B	11. D
3. A	6. A	9. C	12. D

Mini-Test 4: Structure

1. D	4. A	7. C	10. A	13. C
2. C	5. B	8. D	11. A	14. C
3. D	6. D	9. B	12. D	15. A

Exercise 24

1. A	5. B	9. C	13. B	17. D
2. B	6. D	10. B	14. A	18. C
3. A	7. A	11. A	15. D	19. C
4. C	8. B	12. D	16. B	20. C

Exercise 25

1. B	4. A	7. B	10. C
2. D	5. C	8. B	11. A
3. C	6. A	9. C*	12. D

Exercise 26

1. D	4. C	7. D	10. B	13. A*
2. C	5. A	8. A	11. C	14. B
3. B*	6. B	9. B	12. C	15. A

Exercise 27

1. C	4. A	7. D	10. C	13. C
2. C	5. B	8. D	11. A	14. B
3. A	6. A	9. C	12. C*	15. D

Exercise 28

1. A	4. D	7. A	10. C
2. D	5. C	8. B	11. B
3. B	6. C	9. A	12. D

Exercise 29

1. B	4. A	7. C	10. B
2. A	5. B	8. D	11. D
3. B	6. C	9. C	12. A

Exercise 30

1. B	4. C*	7. A	10. C
2. D	5. A	8. A	11. B
3. B	6. C	9. D*	12. B

Exercise 31

1. A	3. B	5. A	7. B	9. D	11. A	13. A
2. D	4. A	6. C	8. C	10. D	12. B	14. B

Mini-Test 5: Structure

1. C	4. D	7. C	10. A	13. A
2. A	5. C	8. B	11. A	14. A
3. D	6. B	9. C	12. B	15. C

PART B, WRITTEN EXPRESSION: EXERCISES AND MINI-TESTS

Note: Items marked with an asterisk (*) do not focus on the structures that are presented in that lesson.

Exercise 32.1

1. differ	difference	different	differently
2. invent	invention		inventively
3.	competition (*or* competitiveness)	competitive	competitively
4.	fertility (*or* fertilization *or* fertilizer)	fertile	fertilely
5. deepen	depth	deep	
6. decide		decisive	decisively
7.	beauty (*or* beautification)	beautiful	beautifully
8.	prohibition	prohibitive	prohibitively
9.	origin	original	originally
10. emphasize	emphasis		emphatically
11. inconvenience	inconvenience	inconvenient	inconveniently
12. glorify (*or* glory)		glorious	gloriously
13.	mystery (*or* mystification)	mysterious	mysteriously
14. equalize (or equal)	equality	equal	
15. generalize	generality (*or* generalization)		generally
16. simplify	simplicity	simple	
17. familiarize	familiarity (*or* familiarization)		familiarly
18. purify	purity		purely
19.	freedom	free	freely
20.	restriction	restrictive	restrictively

Exercise 32.2

1. music	musician	musical
2. surgery		surgical
3. poetry	poet	
4. architecture		architectural
5.	administrator	administrative
6. finance	financier	
7. photography		photographic
8.	theoretician (*or* theorist)	theoretical
9. athletics	athlete	
10.	editor	editorial
11. philosophy		philosophical
12. crime		criminal
13. politics	politician	
14. law		legal
15.	humorist	humorous

Exercise 32.3

1. greatly
2. annually

3. Regular
4. simple
5. beautiful

6. simultaneously
7. generally
   simple
8. painstakingly
9. permanently
10. widely

11. close
12. easy

13. incredible
14. automatically
15. formal

16. profound
17. commercially
18. persuasively
19. masterful deeply
20. distinct

Exercise 32.4

1. fictional (N/Adj)
2. industry (N/Adj)
   products (V/N)
3. fragrant (N/Adj)
4. mathematical (N/Adj)
   equal (Adj/N)
5. evidence (N/Adj)
   illegal (Adj/Adv)
6. severity (Adv/N)
7. development (G/N)
8. transport (N/V)
9. differ (V/Adj)
   originate (V/N)
10. magician (N/PN)
11. depth (Adj/N)
12. distinction (N/Adj)
    perfectly (Adj/Adv)
13. collection (N/G)
14. present (Adj/N)
    open (Adj/Adv)

15. choices (V/N)
    approved (V/N)
16. scholarly (PN/Adj)
    immigration (PN/N)
17. food (V/N)
    rainy (N or V/Adj)
18. symbolize (Adj/V)
    occupation (N/Adj)
19. relieve (V/N)
20. respiration (V/N)
    chemical (N/Adj)
21. member (PN/N)
    interpreter (V/PN)
22. outer (Adv/Adj)
    constantly (Adj/Adv)
23. tropical (N/Adj)
    ability (N/Adj)
24. lose (N/V)
    rapidly (N/Adv)
25. ripen (Adj/N)

Exercise 32.5

1. B intellectual
2. A destructive
3. C importance
4. C analyzes
5. A dances

6. A strength
7. D weight
8. D* purposes
9. D ranching
10. B well

11. B measurement
12. C literature
13. D* exposed to
14. B reaction
15. C sharpness

16. C life
17. D health
18. D neighborhoods
19. D successful
20. C collection

21. D* and
22. D luck
23. A absence
24. C politicians
25. D harden

Exercise 33.1

1. made	3. made	5. did	7. made	9. do
2. done	4. do	6. make	8. make	10. make

Exercise 33.2

1. alike	3. Like	5. like	7. as	9. as
2. like	4. as	6. like	8. like	10. alike

Exercise 33.3

1. so	3. So	5. too	7. such a	9. too
2. too	4. such a	6. as	8. so	10. such

Exercise 33.4

1. another	3. other	5. another	7. other	9. another
2. other	4. another	6. other	8. another	10. other

Exercise 33.5

1. Although	4. Because of	7. Although	10. Although
2. Because	5. When	8. because	11. during
3. In spite of	6. Despite	9. because of	12. because

Exercise 33.6

1. Many	3. much	5. number . . . amount	7. amounts	9. Many
2. little	4. few	6. little	8. many	10. little

Exercise 33.7

1. before	6. earliest	11. doubled	16. No
2. twice	7. round	12. live	17. Almost
3. afterward	8. somewhat	13. percent	18. tell
4. Most	9. tell	14. old	19. nearly
5. age	10. near	15. after	20. ever

Exercise 33.8

1. C no longer	5. C little	9. C doing
2. C as much	6. B never	10. D like
3. D nearly	7. B many	11. D other
4. C old	8. D* symbol	12. A number
(or of age)		

13. C* is
14. A earliest
15. A during
16. C a live

Exercise 34.1

1. was	4. was	7. are	10. are	13. are
2. is	5. moves	8. was	11. is	14. was
3. are	6. are	9. makes	12. varies	15. goes

Exercise 34.2

1. X shipped	6. X does	11. X contain
2. X was built	7. X are played	12. X ran
3. C	8. X was	13. X were chosen
4. X worn	9. X came	14. X have used
5. X has been growing	10. C	15. X were produced
(or has grown)		

Exercise 34.3

1. A study	6. D spun	11. B described
2. D lived	7. D eat	12. A shaken
3. D do	8. C is suited	13. D built
4. B requires	9. A took	14. A* emphasis
5. C have	10. D was	15. B dipped

Exercise 35.1

1. C	7. X grinding
2. X industrial	8. X religion
3. C	9. X heat
4. X warm	10. X a critic
5. X stories	11. X is inexpensive
6. C	12. X control floods

Exercise 35.2

1. D and on mountain	6. C more specialized	11. C mineral
2. B adjust	7. D economic	12. D* have
3. D* other	8. B package	13. C economics
4. A historic	9. C loyal	14. A* front teeth
5. A designer	10. D a game	15. C hearing

Exercise 36.1

1. X its	6. X their	11. X their
2. X them	7. X it	12. X its
3. X it	8. X who	13. X which
4. C	9. C	14. X their
5. X that	10. X those	15. X that
(or which)		

Exercise 36.2

1. C	3. C	5. X our	7. X they	9. X its
2. X them	4. X that	6. X themselves	8. X whose	10. X themselves
	(or which)			

Exercise 36.3

1. X *it*	4. X *he*	7. X *them*	10. C
2. X *which*	5. C	8. C	11. X *which*
3. X *that*	6. X *they*	9. X *she*	12. X *it*

Exercise 36.4

1. D their	6. D themselves	11. A who
2. C are	7. A resemble	12. D itself
3. B them	8. D those	13. A this
4. B uses	9. D their	14. C themselves
5. A* unusual	10. B its	15. A* illustrated

Exercise 37

1. D mammals	6. B percent	11. D editorial
2. C human	7. A All colleges	12. C appliances
3. B automobile	8. C thousands	13. D feet
4. A year	9. C 60-mile	14. C* grown
5. B sources	10. C men	15. A pioneer

16. C* be made
17. B* most
18. D women
19. B trillion
20. D sunlight

Mini-Test 6: Written Expression

1. C	6. C	11. A	16. C	21. D
2. A	7. C	12. C	17. D	22. B
3. C	8. A	13. D	18. C	23. C
4. D	9. D	14. B	19. C	24. D
5. C	10. C	15. A	20. B	25. A

EXPLANATION

1. The adjective *different* is required.

2. Before a clause, an adverb-clause marker such as *although* is required.

3. For parallelism, the noun *color* must be used.

4. The noun *beliefs* must be used in place of the verb *believes*.

5. The past participle *played* must be used after *has* (or *have*) to form the present perfect tense.

6. The plural form *designers* is required.

7. The verb *made* (meaning "to manufacture") is needed.

8. The word *like* is required in this pattern.

9. The correct pronoun is *them*. (The animals can't carry themselves!)

10. For parallelism, the adjective *safe* is needed.

11. The adjective *pure* is required.

12. The word *amounts* is used to refer to uncountable nouns like *food*.

13. Only the second noun of a compound noun is pluralized: *railroad workers*.

14. *Such a* is used with an adjective + noun + *that* clause.

15. The adjective *light* is required.

16. The pronoun *she* is an unnecessary repetition of the subject.

17. To be parallel with the two other adjectives (*biological* and *psychological*), the adjective *medical* must be used.

18. A passive verb phrase is needed: *were given*.

19. The object form of the pronoun *them* must be used.

20. For parallelism, a noun phrase is needed: *a composer of*.

21. The adjective *spicy* must be used.

22. The pronoun must be plural to agree with its referent: *themselves*.

23. A singular verb (*is*) is required to agree with the subject *knowledge*.

24. *Furniture* is an uncountable noun and cannot be pluralized.

25. *Soonest* is the wrong word choice; the correct word is *earliest*.

Exercise 38.1

1. to control	6. to catch	11. to snap
2. to move	7. bend	12. to rupture
3. producing	8. bringing	13. to describe
4. to have	9. to communicate	14. to be awarded
5. to grow	10. miss	15. achieving

Exercise 38.2

1. known	4. twisting	7. named	10. regarded
2. written	5. working	8. appearing	11. cracked
3. astonishing	6. filled	9. deposited	12. stimulating

Exercise 38.3

1. C packaging	6. D to catch	11. D* 40 miles
2. C to cut	7. B obtained	12. A crushed
3. B classifying	8. A Bathing	13. C for playing
4. A mixed	9. D sparkle	14. D smoking
5. D or	10. B painting	15. C leading

Exercise 39.1

1. in on of	9. In for from to
2. For against within of	10. In at to on
3. of for since into	11. In on of of at
4. At of of along between	12. to of by in of in
5. of in of on in	13. In of by of in through
6. at on to on	14. on of to on
7. of in by with on	15. in for of in since
8. off of for of	

Exercise 39.2

1. X	*According polls*	to	11. X	*related the*	to
2. X	*thanks improved*	to	12. X	*expert the*	on
3. C			13. C		
4. X	*of*		14. X	*by*	
5. X	*on*		15. X	*points away*	
6. X	*regardless the*	of	16. X	*in*	from
7. C			17. X	*of*	
8. X	*of*		18. X	*side the*	of
9. X	*attached bones*	to	19. X	*familiar people*	with
10. X	*to*		20. C		

Exercise 39.3

1. A which	6. A from	11. A For
2. B deals with	7. A in	12. A thousands of eggs
3. A Many	8. C belongs to	13. A Nowadays
4. C on its	9. D native to	14. D* to reach
5. D life	10. B in	15. A Since

Exercise 40.1

1. one the water fresh
2. The mineral the most fertilizers
3. The a electrical
4. Humor American the earliest the present
5. The ozone an umbrella most the Sun's
6. the early a Cherokee the a North
7. The Goddard New the the United the seventeenth
8. Popcorn the corn
9. the most research a well-written
10. the American the the twentieth the
11. The nineteenth refracting his
12. The Hawaiian the most Earth

Exercise 40.2

1. A Most	6. A the only	11. C her career
2. C their	7. A a third	12. A the first
3. D attention	8. D their customers	13. C a heated
4. A an underwater	9. B is an imaginary	14. A the highest
5. D the young	10. B the most common	15. D* and

16. B an accurate
17. B history
18. A At the beginning
19. B* opened
20. D a height

Exercise 41

1. X the easiest	7. C	13. X best-known
2. X stronger and larger	8. X most destructive	14. X finest
3. C	9. X least	15. C
4. X lower	10. X worse	16. X larger
5. C	11. C	17. C
6. X heavier	12. X more bitter	18. C
	(*or* bitterer)	

Exercise 42.1

1. X chief source
2. X brightly colored
3. C
4. X long before
5. X at which
6. C
7. X miles longer
8. X natural habitats
9. X they are
10. X dense enough
11. X any other
12. X almost entirely
13. C
14. X formal training
15. X children's books

Exercise 42.2

1. C major barrier
2. D large enough
3. D greatly reduced
4. C in which
5. D it is
6. B it possible
7. C each second
8. D* of radiation
9. A slow-moving
10. A such as
11. C light is
12. B highly original
13. B only one
14. D feet long
15. C is surrounded
16. B workers' satisfaction
17. D trading center
18. C about how
19. D* loneliness
20. A the sky is

Exercise 43

1. X either
2. C
3. X but also
4. X nor
5. X or
6. X and
7. X both
8. C
9. X but
10. X and
11. C
12. X not only
13. X frogs
14. X neither
15. C

Mini-Test 7: Written Expression

1. C
2. A
3. A
4. D
5. B
6. D
7. C
8. B
9. C
10. A
11. B
12. B
13. C
14. B
15. B
16. A
17. A
18. C
19. D
20. C
21. B
22. B
23. A
24. C
25. B

1. The wrong preposition is used; the phrase should correctly read *at one time*.

2. When a noun phrase includes an ordinal number (*third*), a definite article (*the third*) must be used.

3. The correct pattern is *neither . . . nor*.

4. After a preposition, a gerund form (*photographing*) is needed.

5. An infinitive (*to transport*) is needed to show purpose.

6. The correct superlative form is *highest*.

7. In a *wh-* clause that is not a direct question, the correct word order is subject-verb: *they are*.

8. The conjunction *but* is used before the word *rather* to show contrast.

9. The preposition *in* is used before months.

10. The correct form of the infinitive is *to walk*.

11. The preposition *of* is used in the phrase *instead of*.

12. The article *an* must be used before words that begin with a vowel sound.

13. The correct word order is *almost all*.

14. The past participle *written* is required.

15. The verb *result* is used with the preposition *in*. (The noun *result* is followed by the preposition *of*.)

16. A comparative form (*much rarer*) must be used.

17. An indefinite article is needed before the noun: *a picture*.

18. A preposition is needed after the adjective: *suitable for*.

19. The correct word order is *human psychology*.

20. A full infinitive (*to teach*) is required in place of the simple form.

21. *Enough* must follow adjectives: *safe enough*.

22. After the verb *allow*, the infinitive *to approach* is needed.

23. The definite article is used before *most* when it is part of a superlative adjective phrase: *the most*.

24. The correct pattern is *whether . . . or*.

25. An indefinite article is required: *a banana*.

MINI-LESSONS FOR SECTION 2

Mini-Lesson 2.1

1. in (or with)	6. with	11. of	16. with
2. to	7. of	12. to (or for)	17. to
3. on	8. from	13. of	18. on
4. to	9. for	14. of	19. for
5. of	10. to	15. for	20. to

Mini-Lesson 2.2

1. to	6. to	11. to	16. of
2. to	7. at (or by)	12. of	17. for
3. of	8. of	13. to	18. to
4. for	9. to	14. with	
5. for	10. for	15. to	

Mini-Lesson 2.3

1. in of in of	6. to	11. of	16. to
2. of for	7. of	12. to	17. for
3. in of	8. for	13. to	18. of
4. on	9. in	14. of	19. on
5. with	10. of	15. on of	20. of

Mini-Lesson 2.4

1. to	7. on	13. with	19. in
2. with	8. in	14. on	20. for
3. with	9. with	15. to	21. in
4. on	10. on	16. on	22. to
5. on	11. in	17. to	
6. of	12. with	18. for	

Mini-Lesson 2.5

1. of	5. to	9. to
2. In of	6. in of	10. of
3. with	7. On of of	11. by of
4. to	8. of	12. to

Mini-Lesson 2.6

1. in	5. in at in	9. on	13. in on
2. in	6. on in	10. in on on	14. in
3. in in	7. in	11. in in	
4. in at	8. in	12. at on	

Mini-Lesson 2.7

1. on in	6. on	11. in in	16. in
2. at	7. at in	12. at	17. at
3. at in	8. On	13. in in	18. in
4. in	9. in	14. in	19. on
5. at	10. in	15. In	20. In on in

Mini-Lesson 2.8

1. with	3. for	5. without with	7. by	9. with
2. by	4. by	6. by	8. by	10. on

Section 3

SAMPLE VOCABULARY AND READING COMPREHENSION TEST

Answer Key

1. B	11. C	21. D	31. D	41. C
2. B	12. D	22. C	32. A	42. B
3. D	13. D	23. A	33. B	43. A
4. A	14. A	24. A	34. A	44. B
5. C	15. A	25. C	35. C	45. D
6. D	16. D	26. B	36. B	46. C
7. B	17. D	27. A	37. D	47. C
8. C	18. B	28. D	38. A	48. A
9. A	19. A	29. C	39. B	49. D
10. A	20. B	30. D	40. B	50. C

EXPLANATION

1. The passage discusses the plentiful supply of wood in the colonies and the advantages and disadvantages this involved.

2. *Strikingly* means *dramatically*.

3. Lines 4–5 state, "The first colonists did not, as many people imagine, find an entire continent covered by a climax forest."

4. *Abounded* means *present in large numbers*.

5. Lines 7–8 state that "by the end of the colonial era, the price of wood had risen slightly in eastern cities."

6. Lines 10–11 indicate that, in the colonies, "buildings were made of wood to a degree unknown in Britain." Therefore, many British houses must have been made of materials other than wood.

7. According to lines 11–12, wood was the source of industrial compounds, and charcoal is given as an example. Charcoal, according to lines 12–13, is a component of gunpowder.

8. In the context of the passage, the word "conferred" means "provided." (However, in other contexts, "conferred" may mean "consulted.")

9. The phrase *follow suit* means *do the same*.

10. Lines 20–21 state that "the former colonies lagged behind Britain . . . because their supply of wood led them to cling to charcoal iron."

11. In the context of the passage, *cling to* means *continue to use*.

12. The author begins to discuss the disadvantages brought on by an abundance of wood in the colonies in line 14.

13. The passage deals with the entire Peale family; (A) and (C) are too narrow, and (B) is too general.

14. The passage indicates that the portrait was "so realistic" that Washington mistook the painted figures for real ones.

15. The word *settings* is closest in meaning to *environments*.

16. The author defines the term *mastodon* in lines 10–11 as "a huge, extinct elephant." The other terms are undefined.

17. There is no information about when the museum was founded. All of the other questions are answered in the second paragraph: Charles Wilson Peale found and prepared the animal exhibits; the museum was located in Philadelphia; its most popular exhibit, a mastodon's skeleton, was found on a farm in New York.

18. In the context of the passage, the word *unearthed* means *dug up, removed from the ground.*

19. As used in this context, *rage* means the current style or *fashion.*

20. Charles Wilson Peale painted over a dozen portraits of Washington (line 3); Rembrandt Peale also painted at least one (lines 15–16).

21. Sarah Miriam Peale is the daughter of Charles Wilson Peale's brother James Peale (lines 18–19); Titian and Raphaelle are identified as Charles' sons in lines 3–4, Rubens in line 17.

22. The author praises the art and work of Charles Wilson Peale and other members of the family; that, together with the absence of any critical comments, makes *admiring* the best choice.

23. The main theme of this passage is the idea of transforming Mars; choice (A) best summarizes this idea.

24. The word *stark* means *harsh, severe.*

25. The word *there* refers to Mars.

26. The passage states that, "daytime temperatures may reach above freezing," but there is no mention that temperatures ever become dangerously hot. The other characteristics are given in the first passage.

27. According to the passage, "The air there is 95 percent carbon dioxide" (line 3).

28. According to the passage, building up the atmosphere "could create a 'greenhouse effect' that would stop heat from radiating back into space." The author points out in lines 4–6 that the fact that heat radiates back into space makes Mars so cold.

29. The word *suitable* is closest in meaning to *appropriate.*

30. According to scientist Christopher McKay, the project could be started "in four or five decades"—forty or fifty years (lines 17–18).

31. *Terra-forming* refers to the process of "transforming Mars into a more Earth-like planet" (lines 10–11).

32. The phrase *more profound* means *deeper.*

33. The passage indicates that the possibility of transforming Mars comes from an "understanding of how Earth's ecology supports life" (line 20).

34. The word *staggering* means *astonishing.*

35. The first paragraph indicates that age is "another" factor in susceptibility to colds; therefore, it is logical that a previous paragraph must deal with some other factor.

36. *Specific facts* is closest in meaning to the word *particulars.*

37. Lines 2–3 state that the study "revealed particulars that seem to hold true for the general population."

38. Line 3 indicates that "Infants are the most cold-ridden group" and that infant boys have more colds than infant girls (line 3).

39. No matter what age they are, parents of young children show an increase in cold infections; it is reasonable to assume that these parents are infected by their children.

40. The reference is to people in their twenties.

41. This paragraph deals with the influence of economics on incidence of colds.

42. The word *cramped* means *small and crowded.*

43. This is a neutral, objective scientific report.

44. The passage generally discusses an experiment in which plant roots are grown in isolation—in other words, without the tops of the plants.

45. The reference is to the roots of plants.

46. According to the passage (line 6–7), ATP is a "high-energy compound . . . which drives the biochemical reactions."

47. The word *intact* means *whole.*

48. The phrase *comes in handy* means *is useful.*

49. The fact that roots provide organic nitrogen compounds is useful for "the growth of buds in the early spring when leaves are not yet functioning" (lines 12–13).

50. The passage discusses an experiment involving plant roots and the significance of that experiment.

Section 3

EXERCISES AND MINI-TESTS

Exercise 44.1

1.	(A) S	3.	(A) C	5.	(A) G	7.	(A) G	9.	(A) X
	(B) C		(B) I		(B) C		(B) C		(B) I
	(C) X		(C) S		(C) S		(C) X		(C) C
2.	(A) G	4.	(A) X	6.	(A) X	8.	(A) C	10.	(A) X
	(B) S		(B) C		(B) I		(B) X		(B) S
	(C) C		(C) I		(C) C		(C) I		(C) C

Exercise 44.2

1.	A	5.	C	9.	A	13.	C
2.	B	6.	C	10.	D	14.	B
3.	D	7.	B	11.	D	15.	A
4.	A	8.	D	12.	A	16.	D

Exercise 44.3

1.	C	4.	B	7.	A	10.	A	13.	A
2.	A	5.	A	8.	A	11.	B	14.	C
3.	D	6.	C	9.	C	12.	A	15.	D

Exercise 45.1

1. lines 1–2	9. line 3	17. line 3
2. lines 2–4	10. lines 5–6	18. lines 6–7
3. lines 5–6	11. line 8	19. lines 9–10
4. lines 8–9	12. lines 10–12	20. lines 11–13
5. line 12	13. lines 15–16	21. lines 16–18
6. lines 12–13	14. line 1	22. lines 20–21
7. line 14	15. line 2	23. line 20
8. line 1	16. line 2	

Exercise 45.2

1.	B	9.	B	17.	A	25.	A
2.	B	10.	C	18.	B	26.	C
3.	B	11.	A	19.	D	27.	D
4.	A	12.	B	20.	D	28.	A
5.	C	13.	A	21.	A	29.	B
6.	A	14.	C	22.	D	30.	C
7.	B	15.	C	23.	B	31.	C
8.	C	16.	C	24.	B	32.	D

Exercise 46.1

1.	B	5.	B	9.	A	13.	B
2.	C	6.	A	10.	C	14.	A
3.	C	7.	A	11.	C	15.	C
4.	B	8.	C	12.	A	16.	C

Exercise 46.2

1.	X	5.	I	9.	X	13.	I	17.	X
2.	I	6.	X	10.	I	14.	X	18.	X
3.	X	7.	I	11.	X	15.	I	19.	I
4.	I	8.	I	12.	X	16.	I	20.	X

Exercise 46.3

1.	D	5.	B	9.	B	13.	B	17.	C
2.	D	6.	B	10.	B	14.	C	18.	A
3.	D	7.	A	11.	A	15.	B	19.	C
4.	C	8.	C	12.	D	16.	A	20.	D

Exercise 47.1

1.	C	4.	C	7.	B	10.	A	13.	B
2.	B	5.	A	8.	C	11.	B	14.	C
3.	A	6.	B	9.	A	12.	A	15.	A

Exercise 47.2

1.	A	8.	B	15.	C	22.	C	29.	A	36. A
2.	C	9.	B	16.	D	23.	B	30.	B	37. C
3.	C	10.	A	17.	B	24.	B	31.	D	38. B
4.	D	11.	A	18.	D	25.	A	32.	B	39. A
5.	B	12.	C	19.	A	26.	B	33.	D	40. D
6.	D	13.	D	20.	A	27.	D	34.	C	41. D
7.	C	14.	A	21.	D	28.	A	35.	A	42. C

Exercise 48.1

1.	B	5.	B	9.	B	13.	D	17. A
2.	C	6.	B	10.	C	14.	A	18. B
3.	C	7.	A	11.	A	15.	A	19. A
4.	A	8.	B	12.	B	16.	A	20. B

Exercise 48.2

1.	D	5.	C	9.	C	13.	D	17.	C	21. C
2.	B	6.	B	10.	A	14.	B	18.	D	22. A
3.	D	7.	B	11.	A	15.	B	19.	A	23. D
4.	C	8.	C	12.	A	16.	A	20.	B	24. A
										25. C
										26. C

Mini-Test 8: Reading

1.	C	11.	C	21.	B	31.	B	41.	D
2.	A	12.	A	22.	B	32.	A	42.	D
3.	C	13.	D	23.	C	33.	A	43.	B
4.	B	14.	B	24.	B	34.	A	44.	D
5.	D	15.	A	25.	A	35.	A	45.	A
6.	C	16.	B	26.	D	36.	D	46.	C
7.	B	17.	C	27.	C	37.	B	47.	A
8.	A	18.	D	28.	C	38.	B	48.	C
9.	A	19.	B	29.	B	39.	A	49.	B
10.	C	20.	D	30.	A	40.	B	50.	A

EXPLANATION

1. The passage generally concerns the advantages of biological agents and the disadvantages of chemical agents.

2. The word *marring* means *spoiling, ruining.*

3. The word *clog* is closest in meaning to the word *obstruct.*

4. The author defines "weeds" as "any plants that thrive where they are unwanted" (line 2). No definitions are offered for the other terms.

5. Line 6 says "herbicides . . . are sometimes necessary."

6. Choice (A) is given in lines 13-14, which says that the use of biological agents "leave[s] crops and other plants untouched" while chemical agents "kill virtually all the plants they come in contact with." Choice (B) is also given; chemical agents "harm workers who apply them" (line 8) while biological agents "are harmless to humans" (line 12); Choice (D) is given in lines 16-17; "biological agents can be administered only once" while chemical agents "must be used several times per growing season."

7. The word *hence* means *consequently* or *therefore.*

8. The word *innate* means *natural* or *in-born.*

9. According to the passage, the living organisms used to kill weeds are "primarily insects and micro-organisms."

10. The reference is to *plants.*

11. In this context, *applications* means treatments with biological agents.

12. The problem is the need to control weeds; the possible solutions are the use of chemical or biological agents.

13. The author refers to the fact that the plot is "tightly choreographed," that Bernstein's score is "brilliant," and that Stephen Sondheim revealed "a remarkable talent." All of these positive factors, and the absence of negative ones, add up to a favorable attitude.

14. Lines 1-2 say the play "is set in the early 1950s."

15. Since the Jets and Sharks were rival gangs and were based on the Montagues and Capulets, it is reasonable to assume that the latter groups were also rivals.

16. The word *feuding* means *hostile, antagonistic.*

17. The word *ultimately* means *eventually.*

18. Lines 7-8 state: "Stephen Sondheim . . . revealed a remarkable talent for writing lyrics."

19. A "score" is the written form of a piece of music.

20. Lines 10-11 indicate that, after it first opened, the play ran for 734 performances.

21. The summary sentence (beginning "The plot . . .") runs from lines 5-7.

22. There were 8,000 people at the 1900 New York auto show, according to line 1. By coincidence, this was the same number of cars as there were in the United States in 1900 (lines 1-3).

23. *By happenstance* means *by chance, coincidentally.*

24. According to the passage, only around 4,000 cars were assembled in the United States in 1900, and only a quarter of those were gasoline powered (lines 6-7). One quarter of 4,000 is 1,000.

25. Lines 8-9 state that "the show's audience favored electric cars."

Peterson's TOEFL CBT Success

26. The word *fumes* means *gases, vapors.*

27. The word *launched* means *initiated, began.*

28. According to the passage, "The Duryea Motor Works . . . offered an additive designed to mask the smell of the naphtha that it burned."

29. Line 13 indicates that the highest-priced cars sold for $1500 in 1900.

30. The word *cumbersome* is closest in meaning to *clumsy.*

31. Lines 15-16 indicate that the Gasmobile, Franklin, and Orient steered with tillers; the Duryea probably used a steering wheel.

32. Lines 17-18 state that "the black tie (i.e., very formal) audience viewed the display . . . as a social outing."

33. According to the passage, auto shows were about to become "sales extravaganzas."

34. The passage deals with an interpretation of an experiment involving children's art.

35. The passage says that the children drew both "front views" (line 4) and "rear views" (line 5).

36. The reference is to the children.

37. The word *markedly* means *noticeably.*

38. There is nothing in the article particularly useful to commercial artists.

39. The word *odd* means *unusual.*

40. In the context of this passage, *scale* means *proportion.*

41. Lines 7-8 indicate that the head size "is a form of planning and not an indication of a poor sense of scale." There is no information in the passage to support any of the other choices.

42. Choice (A) is not correct; the author is not critical of O'Keefe's style. Choice (B) is too specific. There is no comparison of abstract art and landscape art, so (C) is not correct. Choice (D) is the best statement of the author's purpose.

43. Lines 1-2 state that O'Keefe "studied art in Chicago and New York."

44. The expression refers to 1918.

45. The word *frequented* is closest in meaning to *visited.*

46. The word *intuitively* means *instinctively.*

47. Line 10 indicate that "her style changed dramatically . . . during a visit to New Mexico." The reference to the "Southwestern sun" tells you that New Mexico is in the Southwest.

48. The word *blanched* means *whitened, bleached.*

49. According to the passage, she "most often painted desert landscapes" after a trip to New Mexico in 1929."

50. Lines 15-17 state that she became "the dean of Southwestern painters and one of the best known of American artists." There is no information to support the other choices.

ANSWER KEY
MINI-LESSONS FOR PART 3

Mini-Lesson 3.1

1. A	4. A	7. A	10. C	13. B
2. C	5. B	8. B	11. A	14. B
3. A	6. B	9. C	12. A	15. C

Mini-Lesson 3.2

1. C	3. A	5. B	7. A	9. C	11. B
2. C	4. C	6. B	8. B	10. A	12. C

Mini-Lesson 3.3

1. C	3. B	5. B	7. A	9. A	11. A
2. A	4. B	6. C	8. C	10. B	12. C

Mini-Lesson 3.4

1. C	3. A	5. C	7. A	9. B
2. C	4. B	6. B	8. C	10. B

Mini-Lesson 3.5

1. A	4. A	7. A	10. A
2. A	5. B	8. B	11. C
3. B	6. C	9. C	12. B

Mini-Lesson 3.6

1. B	4. B	7. C	10. C
2. B	5. A	8. C	11. C
3. C	6. C	9. A	12. B

Mini-Lesson 3.7

1. C	4. A	7. A	10. A
2. B	5. A	8. B	11. C
3. B	6. C	9. C	12. A

Mini-Lesson 3.8

1. C	5. C	9. C	13. A
2. C	6. A	10. B	14. C
3. A	7. B	11. A	15. C
4. C	8. C	12. B	16. A

Mini-Lesson 3.9

1. A	4. A	7. A	10. A
2. C	5. B	8. B	11. B
3. C	6. B	9. C	12. A

Mini-Lesson 3.10

1. B	4. B	7. B	10. A
2. B	5. C	8. C	11. B
3. A	6. B	9. C	12. C
			13. B
			14. C

Mini-Lesson 3.11

1. C	4. A	7. C	10. A	13. B
2. B	5. B	8. C	11. A	14. C
3. B	6. C	9. B	12. A	15. B

Mini-Lesson 3.12

1. A	4. C	7. A	10. C	13. A
2. C	5. C	8. C	11. A	14. C
3. A	6. B	9. A	12. C	15. B

Mini-Lesson 3.13

1. A	4. B	7. C	10. A
2. A	5. B	8. C	11. B
3. C	6. B	9. B	12. A

Mini-Lesson 3.14

1. B	5. C	9. B	13. A
2. B	6. B	10. B	14. B
3. C	7. C	11. B	15. C
4. B	8. C	12. A	16. B

Mini-Lesson 3.15

1. C	4. C	7. B	10. B
2. A	5. C	8. C	11. A
3. C	6. A	9. B	12. A

Mini-Lesson 3.16

1. C	4. A	7. A	10. A
2. B	5. A	8. B	11. B
3. A	6. C	9. C	12. A

Mini-Lesson 3.17

1. C	3. C	5. C	7. C	9. A
2. B	4. A	6. A	8. B	10. C

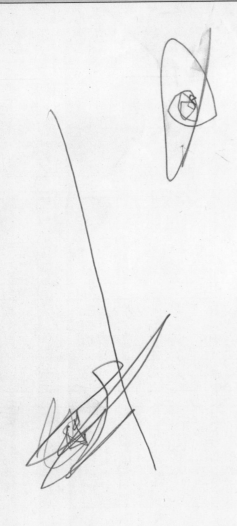

Peterson's TOEFL CBT Success